THE WRITINGS OF

Irenæus

Edited by
THE REV. ALEXANDER ROBERTS, DD
JAMES DONALDSON, LLD

Chronologically arranged, with
brief notes and prefaces by
A. CLEVELAND COXE, DD

the apocryphile press
BERKELEY, CA
www.apocryphile.org

apocryphile press
BERKELEY, CA

Apocryphile Press
1700 Shattuck Ave #81
Berkeley, CA 94709
www.apocryphile.org

First published in Edinburgh in 1867. First American edition, 1885. Apocryphile Press edition, 2007.

Printed in the United States of America
ISBN 1-933993-47-2

INTRODUCTORY NOTE

TO

IRENÆUS AGAINST HERESIES

[A.D. 120–202.] THIS history introduces us to the Church in her Western outposts. We reach the banks of the Rhone, where for nearly a century Christian missions have flourished. Between Marseilles and Smyrna there seems to have been a brisk trade, and Polycarp had sent Pothinus into Celtic Gaul at an early date as its evangelist. He had fixed his see at Lyons, when Irenæus joined him as a presbyter, having been his fellow-pupil under Polycarp. There, under the "good Aurelius," as he is miscalled (A.D. 177), arose the terrible persecution which made "the martyrs of Lyons and Vienne" so memorable. It was during this persecution that Irenæus was sent to Rome with letters of remonstrance against the rising pestilence of heresy; and he was probably the author of the account of the sufferings of the martyrs which is appended to their testimony.[1] But he had the mortification of finding the Montanist heresy patronized by Eleutherus the Bishop of Rome; and there he met an old friend from the school of Polycarp, who had embraced the Valentinian heresy. We cannot doubt that to this visit we owe the life-long struggle of Irenæus against the heresies that now came in, like locusts, to devour the harvests of the Gospel. But let it be noted here, that, so far from being "the mother and mistress" of even the Western Churches, Rome herself is a mission of the Greeks;[2] Southern Gaul is evangelized from Asia Minor, and Lyons checks the heretical tendencies of the Bishop at Rome. Ante-Nicene Christianity, and indeed the Church herself, appears in Greek costume which lasts through the synodical period; and Latin Christianity, when it begins to appear, is African, and not Roman. It is strange that those who have recorded this great historical fact have so little perceived its bearings upon Roman pretensions in the Middle Ages and modern times.

Returning to Lyons, our author found that the venerable Pothinus had closed his holy career by a martyr's death; and naturally Irenæus became his successor. When the emissaries of heresy followed him, and began to disseminate their licentious practices and foolish doctrines by the aid of "silly women," the great work of his life began. He condescended to study these diseases of the human mind like a wise physician; and, sickening as was the process of classifying and describing them, he made this also his laborious task, that he might enable others to withstand and to overcome them. The works he has left us are monuments of his fidelity to Christ, and to the charges of St. Paul, St. Peter, and St. Jude, whose solemn warnings now proved to be prophecies. No marvel that the great apostle, "night and day with tears," had forewarned the churches of "the grievous wolves" which were to make havoc of the fold.

If it shocks the young student of the virgin years of Christianity to find such a state of things, let him reflect that it was all foretold by Christ himself, and demonstrates the malice and power of the adversary. "An enemy hath done this," said the Master. The spirit that was then work-

---

[1] Eusebius, book v. to the twenty-seventh chapter, should be read as an introduction to this author.

[2] Milman, *Hist. Latin Christianity*, b. i. pp. 27, 28, and the notes.

ing "in the children of disobedience," now manifested itself. The awful visions of the Apocalypse began to be realized. It was now evident in what sense "the Prince of peace" had pronounced His mission, "not peace, but a sword." In short, it became a conspicuous fact, that the Church here on earth is "militant;" while, at the same time, there was seen to be a profound philosophy in the apostolic comment,[1] "There must be also heresies among you, that they which are approved may be made manifest." In the divine economy of Providence it was permitted that every form of heresy which was ever to infest the Church should now exhibit its essential principle, and attract the censures of the faithful. Thus testimony to primitive truth was secured and recorded: the language of catholic orthodoxy was developed and defined, and landmarks of faith were set up for perpetual memorial to all generations. It is a striking example of this divine economy, that the see of Rome was allowed to exhibit its fallibility very conspicuously at this time, and not only to receive the rebukes of Irenæus, but to accept them as wholesome and necessary; so that the heresy of Eleutherus, and the spirit of Diotrephes in Victor, have enabled reformers ever since, and even in the darkest days of pontifical despotism, to testify against the manifold errors patronized by Rome. Hilary and other Gallicans have been strengthened by the example of Irenæus, and by his faithful words of reproof and exhortation, to resist Rome, even down to our own times.

That the intolerable absurdities of Gnosticism should have gained so many disiciples, and proved itself an adversary to be grappled with and not despised, throws light on the condition of the human mind under heathenism, even when it professed "knowledge" and "philosophy." The task of Irenæus was twofold: (1) to render it impossible for any one to confound Gnosticism with Christianity, and (2) to make it impossible for such a monstrous system to survive, or ever to rise again. His task was a nauseous one; but never was the spirit enjoined by Scripture more patiently exhibited, nor with more entire success.[2] If Julian had found Gnosticism just made to his hand, and powerful enough to suit his purposes, the whole history of his attempt to revive Paganism would have been widely different. Irenæus demonstrated its essential unity with the old mythology, and with heathen systems of philosophy. If the fog and malaria that rose with the Day-star, and obscured it, were speedily dispersed, our author is largely to be identified with the radiance which flowed from the Sun of righteousness, and with the breath of the Spirit that banished them for ever.

The Episcopate of Irenæus was distinguished by labours, "in season and out of season," for the evangelization of Southern Gaul; and he seems to have sent missionaries into other regions of what we now call France. In spite of Paganism and heresy, he rendered Lyons a Christian city; and Marcus seems to have retreated before his terrible castigation, taking himself off to regions beyond the Pyrenees.[3] But the pacific name he bears, was rendered yet more illustrious by his interposition to compose the Easter Controversy, then threatening to impair, if not to destroy, the unity of the Church. The beautiful *concordat* between East and West, in which Polycarp and Anicetus had left the question, was now disturbed by Victor, Bishop of Rome, whose turbulent spirit would not accept the compromise of his predecessor. Irenæus remonstrates with him in a catholic spirit, and overrules his impetuous temper. At the Council of Nice, the rule for the observance of Easter was finally settled by the whole Church; and the forbearing example of Irenæus, no doubt contributed greatly to this happy result. The blessed peacemaker survived this great triumph, for a short time only, closing his life, like a true shepherd, with thousands of his flock, in the massacre (A.D. 202) stimulated by the wolfish Emperor Severus.

The INTRODUCTORY NOTICE of the learned translators[4] is as follows:—

---

[1] 1 Cor. xi. 19. [2] 2 Tim. ii. 24, 25, 26.
[3] On the authority of St. Jerome. See Guettee, *De l'église de France*, vol. 1. p. 27.
[4] The first two books of Irenæus *Against Heresies* have been translated by Dr. Roberts. The groundwork of the translation of the third book, and that portion of the fourth book which is continued in this volume, has been furnished by the Rev. W. H. Rambaut. An attempt has been made, in rendering this important author into English, to adhere as closely as possible to the original. It would have been far easier to give a loose and flowing translation of the obscure and involved sentences of Irenæus; but the object has been studiously kept in view, to place the English reader, as much as possible, in the position of one who has immediate access to the Greek or Latin text.

THE work of Irenæus *Against Heresies* is one of the most precious remains of early Christian antiquity. It is devoted, on the one hand, to an account and refutation of those multiform Gnostic heresies which prevailed in the latter half of the second century; and, on the other hand, to an exposition and defence of the Catholic faith.

In the prosecution of this plan, the author divides his work into five books. The first of these contains a minute description of the tenets of the various heretical sects, with occasional brief remarks in illustration of their absurdity, and in confirmation of the truth to which they were opposed. In his second book, Irenæus proceeds to a more complete demolition of those heresies which he has already explained, and argues at great length against them, on grounds principally of reason. The three remaining books set forth more directly the true doctrines of revelation, as being in utter antagonism to the views held by the Gnostic teachers. In the course of this argument, many passages of Scripture are quoted and commented on; many interesting statements are made, bearing on the rule of faith; and much important light is shed on the doctrines held, as well as the practices observed, by the Church of the second century.

It may be made matter of regret, that so large a portion of the work of Irenæus is given to an exposition of the manifold Gnostic speculations. Nothing more absurd than these has probably ever been imagined by rational beings. Some ingenious and learned men have indeed endeavoured to reconcile the wild theories of these heretics with the principles of reason; but, as Bishop Kaye remarks (*Eccl. Hist. of the Second and Third Centuries*, p. 524), "a more arduous or unpromising undertaking cannot well be conceived." The fundamental object of the Gnostic speculations was doubtless to solve the two grand problems of all religious philosophy, viz., How to account for the existence of evil; and, How to reconcile the finite with the infinite. But these ancient theorists were not more successful in grappling with such questions than have been their successors in modern times. And by giving loose reins to their imagination, they built up the most incongruous and ridiculous systems; while, by deserting the guidance of Scripture they were betrayed into the most pernicious and extravagant errors.

Accordingly, the patience of the reader is sorely tried, in following our author through those mazes of absurdity which he treads, in explaining and refuting these Gnostic speculations. This is especially felt in the perusal of the first two books, which, as has been said, are principally devoted to an exposition and subversion of the various heretical systems. But the vagaries of the human mind, however melancholy in themselves, are never altogether destitute of instruction. And in dealing with those set before us in this work, we have not only the satisfaction of becoming acquainted with the currents of thought prevalent in these early times, but we obtain much valuable information regarding the primitive Church, which, had it not been for these heretical schemes, might never have reached our day.

Not a little of what is contained in the following pages will seem almost unintelligible to the English reader. And it is scarcely more comprehensible to those who have pondered long on the original. We have inserted brief notes of explanation where these seemed specially necessary. But we have not thought it worth while to devote a great deal of space to the elucidation of those obscure Gnostic views which, in so many varying forms, are set forth in this work. For the same reason, we give here no account of the origin, history, and successive phases of Gnosticism. Those who wish to know the views of the learned on these points, may consult the writings of Neander, Baur, and others, among the Germans, or the lectures of Dr. Burton in English; while a succinct description of the whole matter will be found in the " Preliminary Observations on the Gnostic System," prefixed to Harvey's edition of Irenæus.

The great work of Irenæus, now for the first time translated into English, is unfortunately no longer extant in the original. It has come down to us only in an ancient Latin version, with the exception of the greater part of the first book, which has been preserved in the original Greek, through means of copious quotations made by Hippolytus and Epiphanius. The text, both Latin and Greek, is often most uncertain.   Only three MSS. of the work *Against Heresies* are at present known to exist.   Others, however, were used in the earliest printed editions put forth by Erasmus. And as these codices were more ancient than any now available, it is greatly to be regretted that they have disappeared or perished.   One of our difficulties throughout, has been to fix the readings we should adopt, especially in the first book.   Varieties of reading, actual or conjectural, have been noted only when some point of special importance seemed to be involved.

After the text has been settled, according to the best judgment which can be formed, the work of translation remains ; and that is, in this case, a matter of no small difficulty.   Irenæus, even in the original Greek, is often a very obscure writer.   At times he expresses himself with remarkable clearness and terseness ; but, upon the whole, his style is very involved and prolix.   And the Latin version adds to these difficulties of the original, by being itself of the most barbarous character. In fact, it is often necessary to make a conjectural re-translation of it into Greek, in order to obtain some inkling of what the author wrote.   Dodwell supposes this Latin version to have been made about the end of the fourth century ; but as Tertullian seems to have used it, we must rather place it in the beginning of the third.   Its author is unknown, but he was certainly little qualified for his task.   We have endeavoured to give as close and accurate a translation of the work as possible, but there are not a few passages in which a guess can only be made as to the probable meaning.

Irenæus had manifestly taken great pains to make himself acquainted with the various heretical systems which he describes.   His mode of exposing and refuting these is generally very effective. It is plain that he possessed a good share of learning, and that he had a firm grasp of the doctrines of Scripture.   Not unfrequently he indulges in a kind of sarcastic humour, while inveighing against the folly and impiety of the heretics.   But at times he gives expression to very strange opinions.   He is, for example, quite peculiar in imagining that our Lord lived to be an *old* man, and that His public ministry embraced at least *ten* years.   But though, on these and some other points, the judgment of Irenæus is clearly at fault, his work contains a vast deal of sound and valuable exposition of Scripture, in opposition to the fanciful systems of interpretation which prevailed in his day.

We possess only very scanty accounts of the personal history of Irenæus.   It has been generally supposed that he was a native of Smyrna, or some neighbouring city, in Asia Minor.   Harvey, however, thinks that he was probably born in Syria, and removed in boyhood to Smyrna.   He himself tells us (iii. 3, 4) that he was in early youth acquainted with Polycarp, the illustrious bishop of that city.   A sort of clue is thus furnished as to the date of his birth.   Dodwell supposes that he was born so early as A.D. 97, but this is clearly a mistake ; and the general date assigned to his birth is somewhere between A.D. 120 and A.D. 140.

It is certain that Irenæus was bishop of Lyons, in France, during the latter quarter of the second century.   The exact period or circumstances of his ordination cannot be determined. Eusebius states (*Hist. Eccl.*, v. 4) that he was, while yet a presbyter, sent with a letter, from certain members of the Church of Lyons awaiting martyrdom, to Eleutherus, bishop of Rome ; and that (v. 5) he succeeded Pothinus as bishop of Lyons, probably about A.D. 177.   His great work *Against Heresies* was, we learn, written during the episcopate of Eleutherus, that is, between A.D. 182 and A.D. 188, for Victor succeeded to the bishopric of Rome in A.D. 189.   This new bishop of Rome took very harsh measures for enforcing uniformity throughout the Church as to the observance of the paschal solemnities.   On account of the severity thus evinced, Irenæus addressed to him a letter (only a fragment of which remains), warning him that if he persisted in the course on which he had entered, the effect would be to rend the Catholic Church in pieces.   This letter had the desired result ; and the question was more temperately debated, until finally settled by the Council of Nice.

The full title of the principal work of Irenæus, as given by Eusebius (*Hist. Eccl.*, v. 7), and indicated frequently by the author himself, was *A Refutation and Subversion of Knowledge falsely so called*, but it is generally referred to under the shorter title, *Against Heresies*. Several other smaller treatises are ascribed to Irenæus ; viz., *An Epistle to Florinus*, of which a small fragment has been preserved by Eusebius ; a treatise *On the Valentinian Ogdoad;* a work called forth by the paschal controversy, entitled *On Schism*, and another *On Science;* all of which that remain will be found in our next volume of his writings. Irenæus is supposed to have died about A.D. 202 ; but there is probably no real ground for the statement of Jerome, repeated by subsequent writers, that he suffered martyrdom, since neither Tertullian nor Eusebius, nor other early authorities, make any mention of such a fact.

As has been already stated, the first printed copy of our author was given to the world by Erasmus. This was in the year 1526. Between that date and 1571, a number of reprints were produced in both folio and octavo. All these contained merely the ancient barbarous Latin version, and were deficient towards the end by five entire chapters. These latter were supplied by the edition of Feuardent, Professor of Divinity at Paris, which was published in 1575, and went through six subsequent editions. Previously to this, however, another had been set forth by Gallasius, a minister of Geneva, which contained the first portions of the Greek text from Epiphanius. Then, in 1702, came the edition of Grabe, a learned Prussian, who had settled in England. It was published at Oxford, and contained considerable additions to the Greek text, with fragments. Ten years after this there appeared the important Paris edition by the Benedictine monk Massuet. This was reprinted at Venice in the year 1724, in two thin folio volumes, and again at Paris in a large octavo, by the Abbé Migne, in 1857. A German edition was published by Stieren in 1853.

In the year 1857 there was also brought out a Cambridge edition, by the Rev. Wigan Harvey, in two octavo volumes. The two principal features of this edition are : the additions which have been made to the Greek text from the recently discovered *Philosophoumena* of Hippolytus ; and the further addition of thirty-two fragments of a Syriac version of the Greek text of Irenæus, culled from the Nitrian collection of Syriac MSS. in the British Museum. These fragments are of considerable interest, and in some instances rectify the readings of the barbarous Latin version, where, without such aid, it would have been unintelligible. The edition of Harvey will be found constantly referred to in the notes appended to our translation.

IRENÆUS AGAINST HERESIES

BOOK I

PREFACE.

1. INASMUCH[1] as certain men have set the truth aside, and bring in lying words and vain genealogies, which, as the apostle says,[2] "minister questions rather than godly edifying which is in faith," and by means of their craftily-constructed plausibilities draw away the minds of the inexperienced and take them captive, [I have felt constrained, my dear friend, to compose the following treatise in order to expose and counteract their machinations.] These men falsify the oracles of God, and prove themselves evil interpreters of the good word of revelation. They also overthrow the faith of many, by drawing them away, under a pretence of [superior] knowledge, from Him who founded and adorned the universe; as if, forsooth, they had something more excellent and sublime to reveal, than that God who created the heaven and the earth, and all things that are therein. By means of specious and plausible words, they cunningly allure the simple-minded to inquire into their system; but they nevertheless clumsily destroy them, while they initiate them into their blasphemous and impious opinions respecting the Demiurge;[3] and these simple ones are unable, even in such a matter, to distinguish falsehood from truth.

2. Error, indeed, is never set forth in its naked deformity, lest, being thus exposed, it should at once be detected. But it is craftily decked out in an attractive dress, so as, by its outward form, to make it appear to the inexperienced (ridiculous as the expression may seem) more true than the truth itself. One[4] far superior to me has well said, in reference to this point, "A clever imitation in glass casts contempt, as it were, on that precious jewel the emerald (which is most highly esteemed by some), unless it come under the eye of one able to test and expose the counterfeit. Or, again, what inexperienced person can with ease detect the presence of brass when it has been mixed up with silver?" Lest, therefore, through my neglect, some should be carried off, even as sheep are by wolves, while they perceive not the true character of these men,—because they outwardly are covered with sheep's clothing (against whom the Lord has enjoined[5] us to be on our guard), and because their language resembles ours, while their sentiments are very different,—I have deemed it my duty (after reading some of the *Commentaries*, as they call them, of the disciples of Valentinus, and after making myself acquainted with their tenets through personal intercourse with some of them) to unfold to thee, my friend, these portentous and profound mysteries, which do not fall within the range of every intellect, because all have not sufficiently purged[6] their brains. I do this, in order that thou, obtaining an acquaintance with these things, mayest in turn explain them to all those with whom thou art connected, and exhort them to avoid such an abyss of madness and of blasphemy against Christ. I intend, then, to the best of my ability, with brevity and clearness to set forth the opinions of those who are now

---

[1] The Greek original of the work of Irenæus is from time to time recovered through the numerous quotations made from it by subsequent writers, especially by the author's pupil Hippolytus, and by Epiphanius. The latter preserves (*Hær.*, xxxi. secs. 9-32) the preface of Irenæus, and most of the first book. An important difference of reading occurs between the Latin and Greek in the very first word. The translator manifestly read ἐπεί, *quatenus*, while in Epiphanius we find ἐπί, *against*. The former is probably correct, and has been followed in our version. We have also supplied a clause, in order to avoid the extreme length of the sentence in the original, which runs on without any apodosis to the words ἀναγκαῖον ἡγησάμην, "I have judged it necessary."

[2] 1 Tim. i. 4. The Latin has here *genealogias infinitas*, "endless genealogies," as in *textus receptus* of New Testament.

[3] As will be seen by and by, this fancied being was, in the Valentinian system, the creator of the material universe, but far inferior to the supreme ruler Bythus.

[4] There are frequent references in Irenæus to some venerable men who had preceded him in the Church. It is supposed that Pothinus, whom he succeeded at Lyons, is generally meant; but the reference may sometimes be to Polycarp, with whom in early life he had been acquainted.

[5] Comp. Matt. vii. 15.

[6] The original is ἐγκέφαλον ἐξεπτύκασιν, which the Latin translator renders simply, "have not sufficient brains." He probably followed a somewhat different reading. Various emendations have been proposed, but the author may be understood by the ordinary text to be referring ironically to the boasted subtlety and sublimity of the Gnostics.

promulgating heresy. I refer especially to the disciples of Ptolemæus, whose school may be described as a bud from that of Valentinus. I shall also endeavour, according to my moderate ability, to furnish the means of overthrowing them, by showing how absurd and inconsistent with the truth are their statements. Not that I am practised either in composition or eloquence ; but my feeling of affection prompts me to make known to thee and all thy companions those doctrines which have been kept in concealment until now, but which are at last, through the goodness of God, brought to light. " For there is nothing hidden which shall not be revealed, nor secret that shall not be made known." [1]

3. Thou wilt not expect from me, who am resident among the Keltæ,[2] and am accustomed for the most part to use a barbarous dialect, any display of rhetoric, which I have never learned, or any excellence of composition, which I have never practised, or any beauty and persuasiveness of style, to which I make no pretensions. But thou wilt accept in a kindly spirit what I in a like spirit write to thee simply, truthfully, and in my own homely way ; whilst thou thyself (as being more capable than I am) wilt expand those ideas of which I send thee, as it were, only the seminal principles ; and in the comprehensiveness of thy understanding, wilt develop to their full extent the points on which I briefly touch, so as to set with power before thy companions those things which I have uttered in weakness. In fine, as I (to gratify thy long-cherished desire for information regarding the tenets of these persons) have spared no pains, not only to make these doctrines known to thee, but also to furnish the means of showing their falsity ; so shalt thou, according to the grace given to thee by the Lord, prove an earnest and efficient minister to others, that men may no longer be drawn away by the plausible system of these heretics, which I now proceed to describe.[3]

CHAP. I. — ABSURD IDEAS OF THE DISCIPLES OF VALENTINUS AS TO THE ORIGIN, NAME, ORDER, AND CONJUGAL PRODUCTIONS OF THEIR FANCIED ÆONS, WITH THE PASSAGES OF SCRIPTURE WHICH THEY ADAPT TO THEIR OPINIONS.

1. THEY maintain, then, that in the invisible and ineffable heights above there exists a certain perfect, pre-existent Æon,[4] whom they call Proarche, Propator, and Bythus, and describe as being invisible and incomprehensible. Eternal and unbegotten, he remained throughout innumerable cycles of ages in profound serenity and quiescence. There existed along with him Ennœa, whom they also call Charis and Sige.[5] At last this Bythus determined to send forth from himself the beginning of all things, and deposited this production (which he had resolved to bring forth) in his contemporary Sige, even as seed is deposited in the womb. She then, having received this seed, and becoming pregnant, gave birth to Nous, who was both similar and equal to him who had produced him, and was alone capable of comprehending his father's greatness. This Nous they call also Monogenes, and Father, and the Beginning of all Things. Along with him was also produced Aletheia ; and these four constituted the first and first-begotten Pythagorean Tetrad, which they also denominate the root of all things. For there are first Bythus and Sige, and then Nous and Aletheia. And Monogenes, perceiving for what purpose he had been produced, also himself sent forth Logos and Zoe, being the father of all those who were to come after him, and the beginning and fashioning of the entire Pleroma. By the conjunction of Logos and Zoe were brought forth Anthropos and Ecclesia ; and thus was formed the first-begotten Ogdoad, the root and substance of all things, called among them by four names, viz., Bythus, and Nous, and Logos, and Anthropos. For each of these is masculo-feminine, as follows : Propator was united by a conjunction with his Ennœa ; then Monogenes, that is Nous, with Aletheia ; Logos with Zoe, and Anthropos with Ecclesia.

2. These Æons having been produced for the glory of the Father, and wishing, by their own efforts, to effect this object, sent forth emanations by means of conjunction. Logos and Zoe, after producing Anthropos and Ecclesia, sent forth other ten Æons, whose names are the following : Bythius and Mixis, Ageratos and Henosis, Autophyes and Hedone, Acinetos and Syncrasis, Monogenes and Macaria.[6] These are

---

[1] Matt. x. 26.

[2] As Cæsar informs us (*Comm.*, i. 1), Gaul was divided into three parts, one of which was called Celtic Gaul, lying between the Seine and the Garonne. Of this division Lyons is the principal city.

[3] [The reader will find a logical and easy introduction to the crabbed details which follow, by turning to chap. xxiii., and reading through succeeding chapters down to chap. xxix.]

[4] This term Æon (Αἰών) seems to have been formed from the words ἀεὶ ὤν, *ever-existing.* "We may take αἰών, therefore," says Harvey (*Irenæus*, cxix.), " in the Valentinian acceptation of the word, to mean an emanation from the divine substance, subsisting co-ordinately and co-eternally with the Deity, the Pleroma still remaining one."

[5] Sige, however, was no true consort of Bythus, who included in himself the idea of male and female, and was the one cause of all things: comp. Hippolytus, *Philosop.*, vi. 29. There seems to have been considerable disagreement among these heretics as to the completion of the mystical number thirty. Valentinus himself appears to have considered Bythus as a monad, and Sige as a mere nonentity. The two latest Æons, Christ and the Holy Spirit, would then complete the number thirty. But other Gnostic teachers included both Bythus and Sige in that mystical number.

[6] It may be well to give here the English equivalents of the names of these Æons and their authors. They are as follows : Bythus, *Profundity* ; Proarche, *First-Beginning* ; Propator, *First-Father* ; Ennœa, *Idea* ; Charis, *Grace* ; Sige, *Silence* ; Nous, *Intelligence* ; Aletheia, *Truth* ; Logos, *Word* ; Zoe, *Life* ; Anthropos, *Man* ; Ecclesia, *Church* ; Bythius, *Deep* ; Mixis, *Mingling* ; Ageratos, *Undecaying* ; Henosis, *Union* ; Autophyes, *Self-existent* ; Hedone, *Pleasure* ; Acinetos, *Immoveable* ; Syncrasis, *Blending* ; Monogenes, *Only-Begotten* ; Macaria, *Happiness* ; Paracletus, *Advocate* ; Pistis, *Faith* ; Patricos, *Ancestral* ; Elpis, *Hope* ; Metricos, *Metrical* ; Agape, *Love* ; Ainos, *Praise* ; Synesis, *Understanding* ; Ecclesiasticus, *Ecclesiastical* ; Macariotes, *Felicity* ; Theletos, *Desiderated* ; Sophia, *Wisdom.*

the ten Æons whom they declare to have been produced by Logos and Zoe. They then add that Anthropos himself, along with Ecclesia, produced twelve Æons, to whom they give the following names : Paracletus and Pistis, Patricos and Elpis, Metricos and Agape, Ainos and Synesis, Ecclesiasticus and Macariotes, Theletos and Sophia.

3. Such are the thirty Æons in the erroneous system of these men ; and they are described as being wrapped up, so to speak, in silence, and known to none [except these professing teachers]. Moreover, they declare that this invisible and spiritual Pleroma of theirs is tripartite, being divided into an Ogdoad, a Decad, and a Duodecad. And for this reason they affirm it was that the " Saviour "— for they do not please to call Him "Lord "— did no work in public during the space of thirty years,[1] thus setting forth the mystery of these Æons. They maintain also, that these thirty Æons are most plainly indicated in the parable[2] of the labourers sent into the vineyard. For some are sent about the first hour, others about the third hour, others about the sixth hour, others about the ninth hour, and others about the eleventh hour. Now, if we add up the numbers of the hours here mentioned, the sum total will be thirty : for one, three, six, nine, and eleven, when added together, form thirty. And by the hours, they hold that the Æons were pointed out ; while they maintain that these are great, and wonderful, and hitherto unspeakable mysteries which it is their special function to develop ; and so they proceed when they find anything in the multitude[3] of things contained in the Scriptures which they can adopt and accommodate to their baseless speculations.

CHAP. II. — THE PROPATOR WAS KNOWN TO MONOGENES ALONE. AMBITION, DISTURBANCE, AND DANGER INTO WHICH SOPHIA FELL ; HER SHAPELESS OFFSPRING : SHE IS RESTORED BY HOROS. THE PRODUCTION OF CHRIST AND OF THE HOLY SPIRIT, IN ORDER TO THE COMPLETION OF THE ÆONS. MANNER OF THE PRODUCTION OF JESUS.

1. They proceed to tell us that the Propator of their scheme was known only to Monogenes, who sprang from him ; in other words, only to Nous, while to all the others he was invisible and incomprehensible. And, according to them, Nous alone took pleasure in contemplating the Father, and exulting in considering his immeasurable greatness ; while he also meditated how he might communicate to the rest of the Æons the greatness of the Father, revealing to them how vast and mighty he was, and how he was without beginning, — beyond comprehension, and altogether incapable of being seen. But, in accordance with the will of the Father, Sige restrained him, because it was his design to lead them all to an acquaintance with the aforesaid Propator, and to create within them a desire of investigating his nature. In like manner, the rest of the Æons also, in a kind of quiet way, had a wish to behold the Author of their being, and to contemplate that First Cause which had no beginning.

2. But there rushed forth in advance of the rest that Æon who was much the latest of them, and was the youngest of the Duodecad which sprang from Anthropos and Ecclesia, namely Sophia, and suffered passion apart from the embrace of her consort Theletos. This passion, indeed, first arose among those who were connected with Nous and Aletheia, but passed as by contagion to this degenerate Æon, who acted under a pretence of love, but was in reality influenced by temerity, because she had not, like Nous, enjoyed communion with the perfect Father. This passion, they say, consisted in a desire to search into the nature of the Father ; for she wished, according to them, to comprehend his greatness. When she could not attain her end, inasmuch as she aimed at an impossibility, and thus became involved in an extreme agony of mind, while both on account of the vast profundity as well as the unsearchable nature of the Father, and on account of the love she bore him, she was ever stretching herself forward, there was danger lest she should at last have been absorbed by his sweetness, and resolved into his absolute essence, unless she had met with that Power which supports all things, and preserves them outside of the unspeakable greatness. This power they term Horos ; by whom, they say, she was restrained and supported ; and that then, having with difficulty been brought back to herself, she was convinced that the Father is incomprehensible, and so laid aside her original design, along with that passion which had arisen within her from the overwhelming influence of her admiration.

3. But others of them fabulously describe the passion and restoration of Sophia as follows : They say that she, having engaged in an impossible and impracticable attempt, brought forth an amorphous substance, such as her female nature enabled her to produce.[4] When she looked upon it, her first feeling was one of grief, on account of the imperfection of its generation, and then of fear lest this should end[5] her own existence. Next she lost, as it were, all com-

---

[1] Luke iii. 23.
[2] Matt. xx. 1-16.
[3] Some omit ἐν πλήθει, while others render the words " a definite number," thus : " And if there is anything else in Scripture which is referred to by a definite number."

[4] Alluding to the Gnostic notion that, in generation, the male gives form, the female substance. Sophia, therefore, being a female Æon, gave to her enthymesis substance alone, without form. Comp. Hippol., *Philosop.*, vi. 30.
[5] Some render this obscure clause, " lest it should never attain perfection," but the above seems preferable. See Hippol., vi. 31, where the fear referred to is extended to the whole Pleroma.

mand of herself, and was in the greatest perplexity while endeavouring to discover the cause of all this, and in what way she might conceal what had happened. Being greatly harassed by these passions, she at last changed her mind, and endeavoured to return anew to the Father. When, however, she in some measure made the attempt, strength failed her, and she became a suppliant of the Father. The other Æons, Nous in particular, presented their supplications along with her. And hence they declare material substance[1] had its beginning from ignorance and grief, and fear and bewilderment.

4. The Father afterwards produces, in his own image, by means of Monogenes, the above-mentioned Horos, without conjunction,[2] masculo-feminine. For they maintain that sometimes the Father acts in conjunction with Sige, but that at other times he shows himself independent both of male and female. They term this Horos both Stauros and Lytrotes, and Carpistes, and Horothetes, and Metagoges.[3] And by this Horos they declare that Sophia was purified and established, while she was also restored to her proper conjunction. For her enthymesis (or inborn idea) having been taken away from her, along with its supervening passion, she herself certainly remained within the Pleroma; but her enthymesis, with its passion, was separated from her by Horos, fenced[4] off, and expelled from that circle. This enthymesis was, no doubt, a spiritual substance, possessing some of the natural tendencies of an Æon, but at the same time shapeless and without form, because it had received nothing.[5] And on this account they say that it was an imbecile and feminine production.[6]

5. After this substance had been placed outside of the Pleroma of the Æons, and its mother restored to her proper conjunction, they tell us that Monogenes, acting in accordance with the prudent forethought of the Father, gave origin to another conjugal pair, namely Christ and the Holy Spirit (lest any of the Æons should fall into a calamity similar to that of Sophia), for the purpose of fortifying and strengthening the Pleroma, and who at the same time completed the number of the Æons. Christ then instructed them as to the nature of their conjunction, and taught them that those who possessed a comprehension of the Unbegotten were sufficient for themselves.[7] He also announced among them what related to the knowledge of the Father, — namely, that he cannot be understood or comprehended, nor so much as seen or heard, except in so far as he is known by Monogenes only. And the reason why the rest of the Æons possess perpetual existence is found in that part of the Father's nature which is incomprehensible; but the reason of their origin and formation was situated in that which may be comprehended regarding him, that is, in the Son.[8] Christ, then, who had just been produced, effected these things among them.

6. But the Holy Spirit[9] taught them to give thanks on being all rendered equal among themselves, and led them to a state of true repose. Thus, then, they tell us that the Æons were constituted equal to each other in form and sentiment, so that all became as Nous, and Logos, and Anthropos, and Christus. The female Æons, too, became all as Aletheia, and Zoe, and Spiritus, and Ecclesia. Everything, then, being thus established, and brought into a state of perfect rest, they next tell us that these beings sang praises with great joy to the Propator, who himself shared in the abounding exaltation. Then, out of gratitude for the great benefit which had been conferred on them, the whole Pleroma of the Æons, with one design and desire, and with the concurrence of Christ and the Holy Spirit, their Father also setting the seal of His approval on their conduct, brought together whatever each one had in himself of the greatest beauty and preciousness; and uniting all these contributions so as skilfully to blend the whole, they produced, to the honour and glory of Bythus, a being of most perfect beauty, the very star of the Pleroma, and the perfect fruit [of it], namely Jesus. Him they also speak of under the name of Saviour, and Christ, and patronymically, Logos, and Everything, because He was formed from the contributions of all. And then we are told that, by way of honour, angels of the same nature as Himself were simultaneously produced, to act as His body-guard.

---

[1] "The reader will observe the parallel; as the enthymesis of Bythus produced intelligent substance, so the enthymesis of Sophia resulted in the formation of material substance." — HARVEY.

[2] Some propose reading these words in the dative rather than the accusative, and thus to make them refer to the *image of the Father*.

[3] The meaning of these terms is as follows: Stauros means primarily *a stake*, and then *a cross*; Lytrotes is *a Redeemer*; Carpistes, according to Grabe, means *an Emancipator*, according to Neander *a Reaper*; Horothetes is *one that fixes boundaries*; and Metagoges is explained by Neander as being *one that brings back*, from the supposed function of Horos, to bring back all that sought to wander from the special grade of being assigned them.

[4] The common text has ἀποστερηθῆναι, *was deprived*; but Billius proposes to read ἀποσταυρωθῆναι, in conformity with the ancient Latin version, "crucifixam."

[5] That is, had not shared in any male influence, but was a purely female production.

[6] Literally, "fruit." Harvey remarks on this expression, "that what we understand by *emanations*, the Gnostic described as spiritual *fructification*; and as the seed of a tree is in itself, even in the embryo state, so these various Æons, as existing always in the divine nature, were co-eternal with it."

[7] This is an exceedingly obscure and difficult passage. Harvey's rendering is: "For, say they, Christ taught them the nature of their copulæ, (namely,) that being cognisant of their (limited) perception of the Unbegotten they needed no higher knowledge, and that He enounced," etc. The words seem scarcely capable of yielding this sense: we have followed the interpretation of Billius.

[8] Both the text and meaning are here very doubtful. Some think that the import of the sentence is, that the knowledge that the Father is incomprehensible secured the continued safety of the Æons, while the same knowledge conferred upon Monogenes his origin and form.

[9] The Greek text inserts ἐν, *one*, before "Holy Spirit."

CHAP. III. — TEXTS OF HOLY SCRIPTURE USED BY THESE HERETICS TO SUPPORT THEIR OPINIONS.

1. Such, then, is the account they give of what took place within the Pleroma; such the calamities that flowed from the passion which seized upon the Æon who has been named, and who was within a little of perishing by being absorbed in the universal substance, through her inquisitive searching after the Father; such the consolidation [1] [of that Æon] from her condition of agony by Horos, and Stauros, and Lytrotes, and Carpistes, and Horothetes, and Metagoges.[2] Such also is the account of the generation of the later Æons, namely of the first Christ and of the Holy Spirit, both of whom were produced by the Father after the repentance [3] [of Sophia], and of the second [4] Christ (whom they also style Saviour), who owed his being to the joint contributions [of the Æons]. They tell us, however, that this knowledge has not been openly divulged, because all are not capable of receiving it, but has been mystically revealed by the Saviour through means of parables to those qualified for understanding it. This has been done as follows. The thirty Æons are indicated (as we have already remarked) by the thirty years during which they say the Saviour performed no public act, and by the parable of the labourers in the vineyard. Paul also, they affirm, very clearly and frequently names these Æons, and even goes so far as to preserve their order, when he says, "To all the generations of the Æons of the Æon."[5] Nay, we ourselves, when at the giving [6] of thanks we pronounce the words, "To Æons of Æons" (for ever and ever), do set forth these Æons. And, in fine, wherever the words Æon or Æons occur, they at once refer them to these beings.

2. The production, again, of the Duodecad of the Æons, is indicated by the fact that the Lord was *twelve* [7] years of age when He disputed with the teachers of the law, and by the election of the apostles, for of these there were twelve.[8] The other eighteen Æons are made manifest in this way: that the Lord, [according to them,]

conversed with His disciples for eighteen months [9] after His resurrection from the dead. They also affirm that these eighteen Æons are strikingly indicated by the first two letters of His name ['Ιησοῦς], namely *Iota* [10] and *Eta*. And, in like manner, they assert that the ten Æons are pointed out by the letter *Iota*, which begins His name; while, for the same reason, they tell us the Saviour said, "One *Iota*, or one tittle, shall by no means pass away until all be fulfilled."[11]

3. They further maintain that the passion which took place in the case of the twelfth Æon is pointed at by the apostasy of Judas, who was the twelfth apostle, and also by the fact that Christ suffered in the twelfth month. For their opinion is, that He continued to preach for one year only after His baptism. The same thing is also most clearly indicated by the case of the woman who suffered from an issue of blood. For after she had been thus afflicted during twelve years, she was healed by the advent of the Saviour, when she had touched the border of His garment; and on this account the Saviour said, "Who touched me?"[12] — teaching his disciples the mystery which had occurred among the Æons, and the healing of that Æon who had been involved in suffering. For she who had been afflicted twelve years represented that power whose essence, as they narrate, was stretching itself forth, and flowing into immensity; and unless she had touched the garment of the Son,[13] that is, Aletheia of the first Tetrad, who is denoted by the hem spoken of, she would have been dissolved into the general essence [14] [of which she participated]. She stopped short, however, and ceased any longer to suffer. For the power that went forth from the Son (and this power they term Horos) healed her, and separated the passion from her.

4. They moreover affirm that the Saviour [15] is shown to be derived from all the Æons, and to be in Himself *everything* by the following passage: "Every male that openeth the womb."[16] For He, being everything, opened the womb [17] of the enthymesis of the suffering Æon, when

---

[1] The reading is here very doubtful. We have followed the text of Grabe (approved by Harvey), ἐξ ἀγῶνος σύμπηξις.

[2] These are all names of the same person: see above, ii. 4. Hence some have proposed the reading ἐξαιώνιος instead of ἐξ ἀγῶνος, alluding to the *sixfold* appellation of the Æon Horos.

[3] Billius renders, "from the repentance of the Father," but the above seems preferable.

[4] Harvey remarks, "Even in their Christology the Valentinians must have their part and counterpart."

[5] Or, "to all the generations of the ages of the age." See Eph. iii. 21. The apostle, of course, simply uses these words as a strong expression to denote "for ever."

[6] Literally, "at the thanksgiving," or "eucharist." Massuet, the Benedictine editor, refers this to the Lord's Supper, and hence concludes that some of the ancient liturgies still extant must even then have been in use. Harvey and others, however, deny that there is any necessity for supposing the Holy Eucharist to be referred to; the ancient Latin version translates in the plural, "in gratiarum actionibus."

[7] Luke ii. 42.

[8] Luke vi. 13.

[9] This opinion is in positive contradiction to the *forty days* mentioned by St. Luke (Acts i. 3). But the Valentinians seem to have followed a spurious writing of their own called "The Gospel of Truth." See iii. 11, 8.

[10] The numeral value of *Iota* in Greek is ten, and of *Eta*, eight.

[11] Matt. v. 18.

[12] Mark v. 31.

[13] The Latin reads "filii," which we have followed. Reference is made in this word to Nous, who was, as we have already seen, also called *Son*, and who interested himself in the recovery of Sophia. Aletheia was his consort, and was typified by the hem of the Saviour's garment.

[14] Her individuality (μορφή) would have been lost, while her substance (οὐσία) would have survived in the common essence of the Æons.

[15] That is, the "second Christ" referred to above, sec. 1. [It is much to be wished that this *second* were always distinguished by the untranslated name *Soter*.]

[16] Ex. xiii. 2; Luke ii. 23.

[17] Not as being born of it, but as fecundating it, and so producing a manifold offspring. See below.

it had been expelled from the Pleroma. This they also style the second Ogdoad, of which we shall speak presently. And they state that it was clearly on this account that Paul said, "And He Himself is all things;"[1] and again, "All things are to Him, and of Him are all things;"[2] and further, "In Him dwelleth all the fulness of the Godhead;"[3] and yet again, "All things are gathered together by God in Christ."[4] Thus do they interpret these and any like passages to be found in Scripture.

5. They show, further, that that Horos of theirs, whom they call by a variety of names, has two faculties, — the one of supporting, and the other of separating; and in so far as he supports and sustains, he is Stauros, while in so far as he divides and separates, he is Horos. They then represent the Saviour as having indicated this twofold faculty: first, the sustaining power, when He said, "Whosoever doth not bear his cross (Stauros), and follow after me, cannot be my disciple;"[5] and again, "Taking up the cross, follow me;"[6] but the separating power when He said, "I came not to send peace, but a sword."[7] They also maintain that John indicated the same thing when he said, "The fan is in His hand, and He will thoroughly purge the floor, and will gather the wheat into His garner; but the chaff He will burn with fire unquenchable."[8] By this declaration He set forth the faculty of Horos. For that fan they explain to be the cross (Stauros), which consumes, no doubt, all material[9] objects, as fire does chaff, but it purifies all them that are saved, as a fan does wheat. Moreover, they affirm that the Apostle Paul himself made mention of this cross in the following words: "The doctrine of the cross is to them that perish foolishness, but to us who are saved it is the power of God."[10] And again: "God forbid that I should glory in anything[11] save in the cross of Christ, by whom the world is crucified to me, and I unto the world."

6. Such, then, is the account which they all give of their Pleroma, and of the formation[12] of the universe, striving, as they do, to adapt the good words of revelation to their own wicked inventions. And it is not only from the writings of the evangelists and the apostles that they endeavour to derive proofs for their opinions by means of perverse interpretations and deceitful expositions: they deal in the same way with the law and the prophets, which contain many parables and allegories that can frequently be drawn into various senses, according to the kind of exegesis to which they are subjected. And others[13] of them, with great craftiness, adapted such parts of Scripture to their own figments, lead away captive from the truth those who do not retain a stedfast faith in one God, the Father Almighty, and in one Lord Jesus Christ, the Son of God.

CHAP. IV. — ACCOUNT GIVEN BY THE HERETICS OF THE FORMATION OF ACHAMOTH; ORIGIN OF THE VISIBLE WORLD FROM HER DISTURBANCES.

1. The following are the transactions which they narrate as having occurred outside of the Pleroma: The enthymesis of that Sophia who dwells above, which they also term Achamoth,[14] being removed from the Pleroma, together with her passion, they relate to have, as a matter of course, become violently excited in those places of darkness and vacuity [to which she had been banished]. For she was excluded from light[15] and the Pleroma, and was without form or figure, like an untimely birth, because she had received nothing[16] [from a male parent]. But the Christ dwelling on high took pity upon her; and having extended himself through and beyond Stauros,[17] he imparted a figure to her, but merely as respected substance, and not so as to convey intelligence.[18] Having effected this, he withdrew his influence, and returned, leaving Achamoth to herself, in order that she, becoming sensible of her suffering as being severed from the Pleroma, might be influenced by the desire of better things, while she possessed in the meantime a kind of odour of immortality left in her by Christ and the Holy Spirit. Wherefore also she is called by two names — Sophia after her father (for Sophia is spoken of as being her father), and Holy Spirit from that Spirit who is along with Christ. Having then obtained a form, along with intelligence, and being immediately deserted by that Logos who had been invisibly present with her — that is, by Christ — she strained herself to discover that light which had forsaken her, but could not

---

[1] Col. iii. 11.
[2] Rom. xi. 36.
[3] Col. ii. 9.
[4] Eph. i. 10.
[5] Luke xiv. 27. It will be observed that the quotations of Scripture made by Irenæus often vary somewhat from the received text. This may be due to various reasons — his quoting from memory; his giving the texts in the form in which they were quoted by the heretics; or, as Harvey conjectures, from his having been more familiar with a Syriac version of the New Testament than with the Greek original.
[6] Matt. x. 21.
[7] Matt. x. 34.
[8] Luke iii. 17.
[9] Hence Stauros was called by the agricultural name Carpistes, as separating what was gross and material from the spiritual and heavenly.
[10] 1 Cor. i. 18.
[11] Gal. vi. 14. The words ἐν μηδενί do not occur in the Greek text.
[12] Billius renders, "of their opinion."

[13] The punctuation and rendering are here slightly doubtful.
[14] This term, though Tertullian declares himself to have been ignorant of its derivation, was evidently formed from the Hebrew word חָכְמָה — chockmah, wisdom.
[15] The reader will observe that light and fulness are the exact correlatives of the darkness and vacuity which have just been mentioned.
[16] As above stated (ii. 3), the Gnostics held that form and figure were due to the male, substance to the female parent.
[17] The Valentinian Stauros was the boundary fence of the Pleroma beyond which Christ extended himself to assist the enthymesis of Sophia.
[18] The peculiar gnosis which Nous received from his father, and communicated to the other Æons.

effect her purpose, inasmuch as she was prevented by Horos. And as Horos thus obstructed her further progress, he exclaimed, IAO,[1] whence, they say, this name *Iao* derived its origin. And when she could not pass by Horos on account of that passion in which she had been involved, and because she alone had been left without, she then resigned herself to every sort of that manifold and varied state of passion to which she was subject ; and thus she suffered grief on the one hand because she had not obtained the object of her desire, and fear on the other hand, lest life itself should fail her, as light had already done, while, in addition, she was in the greatest perplexity. All these feelings were associated with ignorance. And this ignorance of hers was not, like that of her mother, the first Sophia, an Æon, due to degeneracy by means of passion, but to an [innate] opposition [of nature to knowledge].[2] Moreover, another kind of passion fell upon her (Achamoth), namely, that of desiring to return to him who gave her life.

2. This collection [of passions] they declare was the substance of the matter from which this world was formed. For from [her desire of] returning [to him who gave her life], every soul belonging to this world, and that of the Demiurge[3] himself, derived its origin. All other things owed their beginning to her terror and sorrow. For from her tears all that is of a liquid nature was formed ; from her smile all that is lucent ; and from her grief and perplexity all the corporeal elements of the world. For at one time, as they affirm, she would weep and lament on account of being left alone in the midst of darkness and vacuity ; while, at another time, reflecting on the light which had forsaken her, she would be filled with joy, and laugh ; then, again, she would be struck with terror ; or, at other times, would sink into consternation and bewilderment.

3. Now what follows from all this? No light tragedy comes out of it, as the fancy of every man among them pompously explains, one in one way, and another in another, from what kind of passion and from what element being derived its origin. They have good reason, as seems to me, why they should not feel inclined to teach these things to all in public, but only to such as are able to pay a high price for an acquaintance with such profound mysteries. For these doctrines are not at all similar to those of which our Lord said, " Freely ye have received, freely give."[4] They are, on the contrary, abstruse, and portentous, and profound mysteries, to be

got at only with great labour by such as are in love with falsehood. For who would not expend all that he possessed, if only he might learn in return, that from the tears of the enthymesis of the Æon involved in passion, seas, and fountains, and rivers, and every liquid substance derived its origin ; that light burst forth from her smile ; and that from her perplexity and consternation the corporeal elements of the world had their formation?

4. I feel somewhat inclined myself to contribute a few hints towards the development of their system. For when I perceive that waters are in part fresh, such as fountains, rivers, showers, and so on, and in part salt, such as those in the sea, I reflect with myself that all such waters cannot be derived from her tears, inasmuch as these are of a saline quality only. It is clear, therefore, that the waters which are salt are alone those which are derived from her tears. But it is probable that she, in her intense agony and perplexity, was covered with perspiration. And hence, following out their notion, we may conceive that fountains and rivers, and all the fresh water in the world, are due to this source. For it is difficult, since we know that all tears are of the same quality, to believe that waters both salt and fresh proceeded from them. The more plausible supposition is, that some are from her tears, and some from her perspiration. And since there are also in the world certain waters which are hot and acrid in their nature, thou must be left to guess their origin, how and whence. Such are some of the results of their hypothesis.

5. They go on to state that, when the mother Achamoth had passed through all sorts of passion, and had with difficulty escaped from them, she turned herself to supplicate the light which had forsaken her, that is, Christ. He, however, having returned to the Pleroma, and being probably unwilling again to descend from it, sent forth to her the Paraclete, that is, the Saviour.[5] This being was endowed with all power by the Father, who placed everything under his authority, the Æons[6] doing so likewise, so that " by him were all things, visible and invisible, created, thrones, divinities, dominions."[7] He then was sent to her along with his contemporary angels. And they related that Achamoth, filled with reverence, at first veiled herself through modesty, but that by and by, when she had looked upon him with all his endowments, and had acquired strength from his appearance, she ran forward to meet him. He then imparted to her form as respected intelligence, and brought healing to her passions, separating them from her, but not

---

[1] Probably corresponding to the Hebrew יהוה, *Jehovah.*
[2] This sentence is very elliptical in the original, but the sense is as given above. Sophia fell from *Gnosis* by degradation; Achamoth never possessed this knowledge, her nature being from the first opposed to it.
[3] " The Demiurge derived from Enthymesis an animal, and not a spiritual nature." — HARVEY.
[4] Matt. x. 8.

[5] " Jesus, or Soter, was also called the Paraclete in the sense of Advocate, or one acting as the representative of others." — HARVEY.
[6] Both the Father and the other Æons constituting Soter an impersonation of the entire Pleroma.
[7] Col. i. 16.

so as to drive them out of thought altogether. For it was not possible that they should be annihilated as in the former case,[1] because they had already taken root and acquired strength [so as to possess an indestructible existence]. All that he could do was to separate them and set them apart, and then commingle and condense them, so as to transmute them from incorporeal passion into unorganized matter.[2] He then by this process conferred upon them a fitness and a nature to become concretions and corporeal structures, in order that two substances should be formed, — the one evil, resulting from the passions, and the other subject indeed to suffering, but originating from her conversion. And on this account (i.e., on account of this hypostatizing of ideal matter) they say tnat the Saviour virtually[3] created the world. But when Achamoth was freed from her passion, she gazed with rapture on the dazzling vision of the angels that were with him ; and in her ecstasy, conceiving by them, they tell us that she brought forth new beings, partly after her own image, and partly a spiritual progeny after the image of the Saviour's attendants.

CHAP. V. — FORMATION OF THE DEMIURGE ; DESCRIPTION OF HIM. HE IS THE CREATOR OF EVERYTHING OUTSIDE OF THE PLEROMA.

1. These three kinds of existence, then, having, according to them, been now formed, — one from the passion, which was matter ; a second from the conversion, which was animal ; and the third, that which she (Achamoth) herself brought forth, which was spiritual, — she next addressed herself to the task of giving these form. But she could not succeed in doing this as respected the spiritual existence, because it was of the same nature with herself. She therefore applied herself to give form to the animal substance which had proceeded from her own conversion, and to bring forth to light the instructions of the Saviour.[4] And they say she first formed out of animal substance him who is Father and King of all things, both of these which are of the same nature with himself, that is, animal substances, which they also call right-handed, and those which sprang from the passion, and from matter, which they call left-handed. For they affirm that he formed all the things which came into existence after him, being secretly impelled thereto by his mother. From this circumstance they

style him Metropator,[5] Apator, Demiurge, and Father, saying that he is Father of the substances on the right hand, that is, of the animal, but Demiurge of those on the left, that is, of the material, while he is at the same time the king of all. For they say that this Enthymesis, desirous of making all things to the honour of the Æons, formed images of them, or rather that the Saviour[6] did so through her instrumentality. And she, in the image[7] of the invisible Father, kept herself concealed from the Demiurge. But he was in the image of the only-begotten Son, and the angels and archangels created by him were in the image of the rest of the Æons.

2. They affirm, therefore, that he was constituted the Father and God of everything outside of the Pleroma, being the creator of all animal and material substances. For he it was that discriminated these two kinds of existence hitherto confused, and made corporeal from incorporeal substances, fashioned things heavenly and earthly, and became the Framer (Demiurge) of things material and animal, of those on the right and those on the left, of the light and of the heavy, and of those tending upwards as well as of those tending downwards. He created also seven heavens, above which they say that he, the Demiurge, exists. And on this account they term him Hebdomas, and his mother Achamoth Ogdoads, preserving the number of the first-begotten and primary Ogdoad as the Pleroma. They affirm, moreover, that these seven heavens are intelligent, and speak of them as being angels, while they refer to the Demiurge himself as being an angel bearing a likeness to God ; and in the same strain, they declare that Paradise, situated above the third heaven, is a fourth angel possessed of power, from whom Adam derived certain qualities while he conversed with him.

3. They go on to say that the Demiurge imagined that he created all these things of himself, while he in reality made them in conjunction with the productive power of Achamoth. He formed the heavens, yet was ignorant of the heavens ; he fashioned man, yet knew not man ; he brought to light the earth, yet had no acquaintance with the earth ; and, in like manner, they declare that he was ignorant of the forms of all that he made, and knew not even of the existence of his own mother, but imagined that he himself was all things. They further affirm

---

[1] That is, as in the case of her mother Sophia, who is sometimes called " the Sophia above," Achamoth being " the Sophia below," or " the second Sophia."

[2] Thus Harvey renders ἀσώματον ὕλην : so Baur, *Chr. Gnos.*, as quoted by Stieren. Billius proposes to read ἐνσώματον, *corporeal*.

[3] Though not actually, for that was the work of the Demiurge. See next chapter.

[4] " In order that," says Grabe, " this formation might not be merely *according to essence*, but also *according to knowledge*, as the formation of the mother Achamoth was characterized above."

[5] Metropator, as proceeding only from his mother Achamoth: Apator, as having no male progenitor.

[6] Harvey remarks, " The Valentinian Saviour being an aggregation of all the æonic perfections, the images of them were reproduced by the spiritual conception of Achamoth beholding the glory of Σωτήρ. The reader will not fail to observe that every successive development is the reflex of a more divine antecedent."

[7] The relation indicated seems to be as follows: Achamoth, after being formed " according to knowledge," was outside of the Pleroma as the image of Propator, the Demiurge was as Nous, and the mundane angels which he formed corresponded to the other Æons of the Pleroma.

that his mother originated this opinion in his mind, because she desired to bring him forth possessed of such a character that he should be the head and source of his own essence, and the absolute ruler over every kind of operation [that was afterwards attempted]. This mother they also call Ogdoad, Sophia, Terra, Jerusalem, Holy Spirit, and, with a masculine reference, Lord.[1] Her place of habitation is an intermediate one, above the Demiurge indeed, but below and outside of the Pleroma, even to the end.[2]

4. As, then, they represent all material substance to be formed from three passions, viz., fear, grief, and perplexity, the account they give is as follows : Animal substances originated from fear and from conversion ; the Demiurge they also describe as owing his origin to conversion ; but the existence of all the other animal substances they ascribe to fear, such as the souls of irrational animals, and of wild beasts, and men. And on this account, he (the Demiurge), being incapable of recognising any spiritual essences, imagined himself to be God alone, and declared through the prophets, " I am God, and besides me there is none else." [3] They further teach that the spirits of wickedness derived their origin from grief. Hence the devil, whom they also call Cosmocrator (the ruler of the world), and the demons, and the angels, and every wicked spiritual being that exists, found the source of their existence. They represent the Demiurge as being the son of that mother of theirs (Achamoth), and Cosmocrator as the creature of the Demiurge. Cosmocrator has knowledge of what is above himself, because he is a *spirit* of wickedness ; but the Demiurge is ignorant of such things, inasmuch as he is merely *animal*. Their mother dwells in that place which is above the heavens, that is, in the intermediate abode ; the Demiurge in the heavenly place, that is, in the hebdomad ; but the Cosmocrator in this our world. The corporeal elements of the world, again, sprang, as we before remarked, from bewilderment and perplexity, as from a more ignoble source. Thus the earth arose from her state of stupor ; water from the agitation caused by her fear ; air from the consolidation of her grief ; while fire, producing death and corruption, was inherent in all these elements, even as they teach that ignorance also lay concealed in these three passions.

5. Having thus formed the world, he (the Demiurge) also created the earthy [part of] man, not taking him from this dry earth, but from an invisible substance consisting of fusible and fluid matter, and then afterwards, as they define the process, breathed into him the animal part of his nature. It was this latter which was created after his image and likeness. The material part, indeed, was very near to God, so far as the image went, but not of the same substance with him. The animal, on the other hand, was so in respect to likeness ; and hence his substance was called the spirit of life, because it took its rise from a spiritual outflowing. After all this, he was, they say, enveloped all round with a covering of skin ; and by this they mean the outward sensitive flesh.

6. But they further affirm that the Demiurge himself was ignorant of that offspring of his mother Achamoth, which she brought forth as a consequence of her contemplation of those angels who waited on the Saviour, and which was, like herself, of a spiritual nature. She took advantage of this ignorance to deposit it (her production) in him without his knowledge, in order that, being by his instrumentality infused into that animal soul proceeding from himself, and being thus carried as in a womb in this material body, while it gradually increased in strength, might in course of time become fitted for the reception of perfect rationality.[4] Thus it came to pass, then, according to them, that, without any knowledge on the part of the Demiurge, the man formed by his inspiration was at the same time, through an unspeakable providence, rendered a spiritual man by the simultaneous inspiration received from Sophia. For, as he was ignorant of his mother, so neither did he recognise her offspring. This [offspring] they also declare to be the Ecclesia, an emblem of the Ecclesia which is above. This, then, is the kind of man whom they conceive of : he has his animal soul from the Demiurge, his body from the earth, his fleshy part from matter, and his spiritual man from the mother Achamoth.

CHAP. VI. — THE THREEFOLD KIND OF MAN FEIGNED BY THESE HERETICS : GOOD WORKS NEEDLESS FOR THEM, THOUGH NECESSARY TO OTHERS : THEIR ABANDONED MORALS.

1. There being thus three kinds of substances, they declare of all that is material (which they also describe as being " on the left hand ") that it must of necessity perish, inasmuch as it is incapable of receiving any *afflatus* of incorruption. As to every animal existence (which they also denominate " on the right hand "), they hold that, inasmuch as it is a mean between the spiritual and the material, it passes to the side to

---

[1] " Achamoth by these names must be understood to have an intermediate position between the divine prototypal idea and creation: she was the reflex of the one, and therefore *masculo-feminine ;* she was the pattern to be realized in the latter, and therefore was named *Earth and Jerusalem.*" — HARVEY.

[2] But after the consummation here referred to, Achamoth regained the Pleroma: see below, chap. vii. 1.

[3] Isa. xlv. 5, 6, xlvi. 9.

[4] An account is here given of the infusion of a spiritual principle into mankind. The Demiurge himself could give no more than the animal soul; but, unwittingly to himself, he was made the instrument of conveying that spiritual essence from Achamoth, which had grown up within her from the contemplation of those angels who accompanied the Saviour.

which inclination draws it. Spiritual substance, again, they describe as having been sent forth for this end, that, being here united with that which is animal, it might assume shape, the two elements being simultaneously subjected to the same discipline. And this they declare to be "the salt" [1] and "the light of the world." For the animal substance had need of training by means of the outward senses; and on this account they affirm that the world was created, as well as that the Saviour came to the animal substance (which was possessed of free-will), that He might secure for it salvation. For they affirm that He received the first-fruits of those whom He was to save [as follows], from Achamoth that which was spiritual, while He was invested by the Demiurge with the animal Christ, but was begirt [2] by a [special] dispensation with a body endowed with an animal nature, yet constructed with unspeakable skill, so that it might be visible and tangible, and capable of enduring suffering. At the same time, they deny that He assumed anything material [into His nature], since indeed matter is incapable of salvation. They further hold that the consummation of all things will take place when all that is spiritual has been formed and perfected by Gnosis (knowledge); and by this they mean spiritual men who have attained to the perfect knowledge of God, and been initiated into these mysteries by Achamoth. And they represent themselves to be these persons.

2. Animal men, again, are instructed in animal things; such men, namely, as are established by their works, and by a mere faith, while they have not perfect knowledge. We of the Church, they say, are these persons.[3] Wherefore also they maintain that good works are necessary to us, for that otherwise it is impossible we should be saved. But as to themselves, they hold that they shall be entirely and undoubtedly saved, not by means of conduct, but because they are spiritual by nature.[4] For, just as it is impossible that material substance should partake of salvation (since, indeed, they maintain that it is incapable of receiving it), so again it is impossible that spiritual substance (by which they mean themselves) should ever come under the power of corruption, whatever the sort of actions in which they indulged. For even as gold, when submersed in filth, loses not on that account its beauty, but retains its own native qualities, the filth having no power to injure the gold, so they affirm that they cannot in any measure suffer hurt, or lose their spiritual substance, whatever the material actions in which they may be involved.

3. Wherefore also it comes to pass, that the "most perfect" among them addict themselves without fear to all those kinds of forbidden deeds of which the Scriptures assure us that "they who do such things shall not inherit the kingdom of God." [5] For instance, they make no scruple about eating meats offered in sacrifice to idols, imagining that they can in this way contract no defilement. Then, again, at every heathen festival celebrated in honour of the idols, these men are the first to assemble; and to such a pitch do they go, that some of them do not even keep away from that bloody spectacle hateful both to God and men, in which gladiators either fight with wild beasts, or singly encounter one another. Others of them yield themselves up to the lusts of the flesh with the utmost greediness, maintaining that carnal things should be allowed to the carnal nature, while spiritual things are provided for the spiritual. Some of them, moreover, are in the habit of defiling those women to whom they have taught the above doctrine, as has frequently been confessed by those women who have been led astray by certain of them, on their returning to the Church of God, and acknowledging this along with the rest of their errors. Others of them, too, openly and without a blush, having become passionately attached to certain women, seduce them away from their husbands, and contract marriages of their own with them. Others of them, again, who pretend at first to live in all modesty with them as with sisters, have in course of time been revealed in their true colours, when the sister has been found with child by her [pretended] brother.

4. And committing many other abominations and impieties, they run us down (who from the fear of God guard against sinning even in thought or word) as utterly contemptible and ignorant persons, while they highly exalt themselves, and claim to be perfect, and the elect seed. For they declare that we simply receive grace for use, wherefore also it will again be taken away from us; but that they themselves have grace as their own special possession, which has descended from above by means of an unspeakable and indescribable conjunction; and on this account more will be given them.[6] They maintain, therefore, that in every way it is always necessary for them to practise the mystery of conjunction. And that they may persuade the thoughtless to believe this, they are in the habit of using these very words, "Whosoever being in this world does not so love a woman as to

---

[1] Matt. v. 13, 14.
[2] "The doctrine of Valentinus, therefore," says Harvey, "as regards the human nature of Christ, was essentially Docetic. His body was *animal*, but not *material*, and only visible and tangible as having been formed κατ' οἰκονομίαν and κατεσκευασμένον ἀῤῥήτῳ τέχνῃ"
[3] [That is, *carnal*; men of the carnal mind, *psychic* instead of *pneumatic*. Rom. viii. 6.]
[4] On account of what they had received from Achamoth.
[5] Gal. v. 21.
[6] Comp. Luke xix. 26.

obtain possession of her, is not of the truth, nor shall attain to the truth. But whosoever being *of* [1] this world has intercourse with woman, shall not attain to the truth, because he has so acted under the power of concupiscence." On this account, they tell us that it is necessary for us whom they call *animal* men, and describe as being *of* the world, to practise continence and good works, that by this means we may attain at length to the intermediate habitation, but that to them who are called "the spiritual and perfect" such a course of conduct is not at all necessary. For it is not conduct of any kind which leads into the Pleroma, but the seed sent forth thence in a feeble, immature state, and here brought to perfection.

CHAP. VII. — THE MOTHER ACHAMOTH, WHEN ALL HER SEED ARE PERFECTED, SHALL PASS INTO THE PLEROMA, ACCOMPANIED BY THOSE MEN WHO ARE SPIRITUAL; THE DEMIURGE, WITH ANIMAL MEN, SHALL PASS INTO THE INTERMEDIATE HABITATION; BUT ALL MATERIAL MEN SHALL GO INTO CORRUPTION. THEIR BLASPHEMOUS OPINIONS AGAINST THE TRUE INCARNATION OF CHRIST BY THE VIRGIN MARY. THEIR VIEWS AS TO THE PROPHECIES. STUPID IGNORANCE OF THE DEMIURGE.

1. When all the seed shall have come to perfection, they state that then their mother Achamoth shall pass from the intermediate place, and enter in within the Pleroma, and shall receive as her spouse the Saviour, who sprang from all the Æons, that thus a conjunction may be formed between the Saviour and Sophia, that is, Achamoth. These, then, are the bridegroom and bride, while the nuptial chamber is the full extent of the Pleroma. The spiritual seed, again, being divested of their animal souls,[2] and becoming intelligent spirits, shall in an irresistible and invisible manner enter in within the Pleroma, and be bestowed as brides on those angels who wait upon the Saviour. The Demiurge himself will pass into the place of his mother Sophia;[3] that is, the intermediate habitation. In this intermediate place, also, shall the souls of the righteous repose; but nothing of an animal nature shall find admittance to the Pleroma. When these things have taken place as described, then shall that fire which lies hidden in the world blaze forth and burn; and while destroying all matter, shall also be extinguished along with it, and have no further existence. They affirm that the Demiurge was acquainted with none of these things before the advent of the Saviour.

2. There are also some who maintain that he also produced Christ as his own proper son, but of an animal nature, and that mention was[4] made of him by the prophets. This Christ passed through Mary[5] just as water flows through a tube; and there descended upon him in the form of a dove at the time of his baptism, that Saviour who belonged to the Pleroma, and was formed by the combined efforts of all its inhabitants. In him there existed also that spiritual seed which proceeded from Achamoth. They hold, accordingly, that our Lord, while preserving the type of the first-begotten and primary tetrad, was compounded of these four substances, — of that which is spiritual, in so far as He was from Achamoth; of that which is animal, as being from the Demiurge by a special dispensation, inasmuch as He was formed [corporeally] with unspeakable skill; and of the Saviour, as respects that dove which descended upon Him. He also continued free from all suffering, since indeed it was not possible that He should suffer who was at once incomprehensible and invisible. And for this reason the Spirit of Christ, who had been placed within Him, was taken away when He was brought before Pilate. They maintain, further, that not even the seed which He had received from the mother [Achamoth] was subject to suffering; for it, too, was impassible, as being spiritual, and invisible even to the Demiurge himself. It follows, then, according to them, that the animal Christ, and that which had been formed mysteriously by a special dispensation, underwent suffering, that the mother might exhibit through him a type of the Christ above, namely, of him who extended himself through Stauros,[6] and imparted to Achamoth shape, so far as substance was concerned. For they declare that all these transactions were counterparts of what took place above.

3. They maintain, moreover, that those souls which possess the seed of Achamoth are superior to the rest, and are more dearly loved by the Demiurge than others, while he knows not the true cause thereof, but imagines that they are what they are through his favour towards them. Wherefore, also, they say he distributed them to prophets, priests, and kings; and they declare that many things were spoken[7] by this seed through the prophets, inasmuch as it was endowed with a transcendently lofty nature. The

---

[1] Comp. John xvii. 16. The Valentinians, while *in the world*, claimed to be not *of the world*, as animal men were.

[2] Their spiritual substance was received from Achamoth; their animal souls were created by the Demiurge. These are now separated; the spirit enters the Pleroma, while the soul remains in heaven.

[3] Viz., Achamoth.

[4] A Syriac fragment here reads, "He spake by the prophets through him."

[5] "Thus," says Harvey, "we may trace back to the Gnostic period the Apollinarian error, closely allied to the Docetic, that the body of Christ was not derived from the blessed Virgin, but that it was of heavenly substance, and was only brought forth into the world through her instrumentality."

[6] By thus extending himself through Stauros, who bounded the Pleroma, the Christ above became the type of the Christ below, who was extended upon the cross.

[7] Billius, following the old Latin version, reads, "They interpret many things, spoken by the prophets, of this seed."

mother also, they say, spake much about things above, and that both through him and through the souls which were formed by him. Then, again, they divide the prophecies [into different classes], maintaining that one portion was uttered by the mother, a second by her seed, and a third by the Demiurge. In like manner, they hold that Jesus uttered some things under the influence of the Saviour, others under that of the mother, and others still under that of the Demiurge, as we shall show further on in our work.

4. The Demiurge, while ignorant of those things which were higher than himself, was indeed excited by the announcements made [through the prophets], but treated them with contempt, attributing them sometimes to one cause and sometimes to another; either to the prophetic spirit (which itself possesses the power of self-excitement), or to [mere unassisted] man, or that it was simply a crafty device of the lower [and baser order of men].[1] He remained thus ignorant until the appearing of the Lord. But they relate that when the Saviour came, the Demiurge learned all things from Him, and gladly with all his power joined himself to Him. They maintain that he is the centurion mentioned in the Gospel, who addressed the Saviour in these words: "For I also am one having soldiers and servants under my authority; and whatsoever I command they do."[2] They further hold that he will continue administering the affairs of the world as long as that is fitting and needful, and specially that he may exercise a care over the Church; while at the same time he is influenced by the knowledge of the reward prepared for him, namely, that he may attain to the habitation of his mother.

5. They conceive, then, of three kinds of men, spiritual, material, and animal, represented by Cain, Abel, and Seth. These three natures are no longer found in one person,[3] but constitute various kinds [of men]. The material goes, as a matter of course, into corruption. The animal, if it make choice of the better part, finds repose in the intermediate place; but if the worse, it too shall pass into destruction. But they assert that the spiritual principles which have been sown by Achamoth, being disciplined and nourished here from that time until now in righteous souls (because when given forth by her they were yet but weak), at last attaining to perfection, shall be given as brides to the angels of the Saviour, while their animal souls of necessity rest for ever with the Demiurge in the intermediate place. And again subdividing the animal souls themselves, they say that some are by nature good, and others by nature evil. The good are those who become capable of receiving the [spiritual] seed; the evil by nature are those who are never able to receive that seed.

CHAP. VIII. — HOW THE VALENTINIANS PERVERT THE SCRIPTURES TO SUPPORT THEIR OWN IMPIOUS OPINIONS.

1. Such, then, is their system, which neither the prophets announced, nor the Lord taught, nor the apostles delivered, but of which they boast that beyond all others they have a perfect knowledge. They gather their views from other sources than the Scriptures;[4] and, to use a common proverb, they strive to weave ropes of sand, while they endeavour to adapt with an air of probability to their own peculiar assertions the parables of the Lord, the sayings of the prophets, and the words of the apostles, in order that their scheme may not seem altogether without support. In doing so, however, they disregard the order and the connection of the Scriptures, and so far as in them lies, dismember and destroy the truth. By transferring passages, and dressing them up anew, and making one thing out of another, they succeed in deluding many through their wicked art in adapting the oracles of the Lord to their opinions. Their manner of acting is just as if one, when a beautiful image of a king has been constructed by some skilful artist out of precious jewels, should then take this likeness of the man all to pieces, should re-arrange the gems, and so fit them together as to make them into the form of a dog or of a fox, and even that but poorly executed; and should then maintain and declare that this was the beautiful image of the king which the skilful artist constructed, pointing to the jewels which had been admirably fitted together by the first artist to form the image of the king, but have been with bad effect transferred by the latter one to the shape of a dog, and by thus exhibiting the jewels, should deceive the ignorant who had no conception what a king's form was like, and persuade them that that miserable likeness of the fox was, in fact, the beautiful image of the king. In like manner do these persons patch together old wives' fables, and then endeavour, by violently drawing away from their proper connection, words, expressions, and parables whenever found, to adapt the oracles of God to their baseless fictions. We have already stated how far they proceed in this way with respect to the interior of the Pleroma.

2. Then, again, as to those things outside of their Pleroma, the following are some specimens of what they attempt to accommodate out of the Scriptures to their opinions. They affirm that

---

[1] Such appears to be the meaning of this sentence, but the original is very obscure. The writer seems to refer to the spiritual, the animal, and the material classes of men, and to imply that the Demiurge supposed some prophecies to be due to one of these classes, and some to the others.

[2] Matt. viii. 9; Luke vii. 8.

[3] As was the case at first, in Adam.

[4] Literally, "reading from things unwritten."

the Lord came in the last times of the world to endure suffering, for this end, that He might indicate the passion which occurred to the last of the Æons, and might by His own end announce the cessation of that disturbance which had risen among the Æons. They maintain, further, that that girl of twelve years old, the daughter of the ruler of the synagogue,[1] to whom the Lord approached and raised her from the dead, was a type of Achamoth, to whom their Christ, by extending himself, imparted shape, and whom he led anew to the perception of that light which had forsaken her. And that the Saviour appeared to her when she lay outside of the Pleroma as a kind of abortion, they affirm Paul to have declared in his Epistle to the Corinthians [in these words], "And last of all, He appeared to me also, as to one born out of due time."[2] Again, the coming of the Saviour with His attendants to Achamoth is declared in like manner by him in the same Epistle, when he says, "A woman ought to have a veil upon her head, because of the angels."[3] Now, that Achamoth, when the Saviour came to her, drew a veil over herself through modesty, Moses rendered manifest when he put a veil upon his face. Then, also, they say that the passions which she endured were indicated by the Lord upon the cross. Thus, when He said, "My God, my God, why hast Thou forsaken Me?"[4] He simply showed that Sophia was deserted by the light, and was restrained by Horos from making any advance forward. Her anguish, again, was indicated when He said, "My soul is exceeding sorrowful, even unto death;"[5] her fear by the words, "Father, if it be possible, let this cup pass from Me;"[6] and her perplexity, too, when He said, "And what I shall say, I know not."[7]

3. And they teach that He pointed out the three kinds of men as follows: the *material*, when He said to him that asked Him, "Shall I follow Thee?"[8] "The Son of man hath not where to lay His head;"—the *animal*, when He said to him that declared, "I will follow Thee, but suffer me first to bid them farewell that are in my house," "No man, putting his hand to the plough, and looking back, is fit for the kingdom of heaven"[9] (for this man they declare to be of the intermediate class, even as they do that other who, though he professed to

have wrought a large amount of righteousness, yet refused to follow Him, and was so overcome by [the love of] riches, as never to reach perfection) — this one it pleases them to place in the animal class; — the *spiritual*, again, when He said, "Let the dead bury their dead, but go thou and preach the kingdom of God,"[10] and when He said to Zaccheus the publican, "Make haste, and come down, for to-day I must abide in thine house"[11] — for these they declared to have belonged to the spiritual class. Also the parable of the leaven which the woman is described as having hid in three measures of meal, they declare to make manifest the three classes. For, according to their teaching, the woman represented Sophia; the three measures of meal, the three kinds of men — spiritual, animal, and material; while the leaven denoted the Saviour Himself. Paul, too, very plainly set forth the material, animal, and spiritual, saying in one place, "As is the earthy, such are they also that are earthy;"[12] and in another place, "But the animal man receiveth not the things of the Spirit;"[13] and again: "He that is spiritual judgeth all things."[14] And this, "The animal man receiveth not the things of the Spirit," they affirm to have been spoken concerning the Demiurge, who, as being animal, knew neither his mother who was spiritual, nor her seed, nor the Æons in the Pleroma. And that the Saviour received first-fruits of those whom He was to save, Paul declared when he said, "And if the first-fruits be holy, the lump is also holy,"[15] teaching that the expression "first-fruits" denoted that which is spiritual, but that "the lump" meant us, that is, the animal Church, the lump of which they say He assumed, and blended it with Himself, inasmuch as He is "the leaven."

4. Moreover, that Achamoth wandered beyond the Pleroma, and received form from Christ, and was sought after by the Saviour, they declare that He indicated when He said, that He had come after that sheep which was gone astray.[16] For they explain the wandering sheep to mean their mother, by whom they represent the Church as having been sown. The wandering itself denotes her stay outside of the Pleroma in a state of varied passion, from which they maintain that matter derived its origin. The woman, again, who sweeps the house and finds the piece of money, they declare to denote the Sophia above, who, having lost her enthymesis, afterwards recovered it, on all things

---

[1] Luke viii. 41.
[2] 1 Cor. xv. 8.
[3] 1 Cor. xi. 10. Irenæus here reads κάλυμμα, *veil*, instead of ἐξουσίαν, *power*, as in the received text. [An interesting fact, as it betokens an old gloss, which may have slipped into the text of some ancient MSS.]
[4] Matt. xxvii. 46.
[5] Matt. xxvi. 38.
[6] Matt. xxvi. 39.
[7] John xii. 27. The Valentinians seem, for their own purposes, to have added οὐκ οἶδα to this text.
[8] Luke ix. 57, 58.
[9] Luke ix. 61, 62.

[10] Luke ix. 60.
[11] Luke xix. 5.
[12] 1 Cor. xv. 48.
[13] 1 Cor. ii. 14.
[14] 1 Cor. ii. 15.
[15] Rom. xi. 16.
[16] Luke xv. 4, 8.

being purified by the advent of the Saviour. Wherefore this substance also, according to them, was reinstated in Pleroma. They say, too, that Simeon, "who took Christ into his arms, and gave thanks to God, and said, Lord, now lettest Thou Thy servant depart in peace, according to Thy word,"[1] was a type of the Demiurge, who, on the arrival of the Saviour, learned his own change of place, and gave thanks to Bythus. They also assert that by Anna, who is spoken of in the gospel[2] as a prophetess, and who, after living seven years with her husband, passed all the rest of her life in widowhood until she saw the Saviour, and recognised Him, and spoke of Him to all, was most plainly indicated Achamoth, who, having for a little while looked upon the Saviour with His associates, and dwelling all the rest of the time in the intermediate place, waited for Him till He should come again, and restore her to her proper consort. Her name, too, was indicated by the Saviour, when He said, "Yet wisdom is justified by her children."[3] This, too, was done by Paul in these words, "But we speak wisdom among them that are perfect."[4] They declare also that Paul has referred to the conjunctions within the Pleroma, showing them forth by means of one; for, when writing of the conjugal union in this life, he expressed himself thus: "This is a great mystery, but I speak concerning Christ and the Church."[5]

5. Further, they teach that John, the disciple of the Lord, indicated the first Ogdoad, expressing themselves in these words: John, the disciple of the Lord, wishing to set forth the origin of all things, so as to explain how the Father produced the whole, lays down a certain principle,— that, namely, which was first-begotten by God, which Being he has termed both the only-begotten Son and God, in whom the Father, after a seminal manner, brought forth all things. By him the Word was produced, and in him the whole substance of the Æons, to which the Word himself afterwards imparted form. Since, therefore, he treats of the first origin of things, he rightly proceeds in his teaching from the beginning, that is, from God and the Word. And he expresses himself thus: "In the beginning was the Word, and the Word was with God, and the Word was God; the same was in the beginning with God."[6] Having first of all distinguished these three — God, the Beginning, and the Word — he again unites them, that he may exhibit the production of each of them, that is, of the Son and of the Word, and may at the same time show their union with one another, and with the Father. For "the beginning" is in the Father, and of the Father, while "the Word" is in the beginning, and of the beginning. Very properly, then, did he say, "In the beginning was the Word," for He was in the Son; "and the Word was with God," for He was the beginning; "and the Word was God," of course, for that which is begotten of God is God. "The same was in the beginning with God"— this clause discloses the order of production. "All things were made by Him, and without Him was nothing made;"[7] for the Word was the author of form and beginning to all the Æons that came into existence after Him. But "what was made in Him," says John, "is life."[8] Here again he indicated conjunction; for all things, he said, were made by Him, but in Him was life. This, then, which is in Him, is more closely connected with Him than those things which were simply made by Him, for it exists along with Him, and is developed by Him. When, again, he adds, "And the life was the light of men," while thus mentioning Anthropos, he indicated also Ecclesia by that one expression, in order that, by using only one name, he might disclose their fellowship with one another, in virtue of their conjunction. For Anthropos and Ecclesia spring from Logos and Zoe. Moreover, he styled life (Zoe) the light of men, because they are enlightened by her, that is, formed and made manifest. This also Paul declares in these words: "For whatsoever doth make manifest is light."[9] Since, therefore, Zoe manifested and begat both Anthropos and Ecclesia, she is termed their light. Thus, then, did John by these words reveal both other things and the second Tetrad, Logos and Zoe, Anthropos and Ecclesia. And still further, he also indicated the first Tetrad. For, in discoursing of the Saviour, and declaring that all things beyond the Pleroma received form from Him, he says that He is the fruit of the entire Pleroma. For he styles Him a "light which shineth in darkness, and which was not comprehended"[10] by it, inasmuch as, when He imparted form to all those things which had their origin from passion, He was not known by it.[11] He also styles Him Son, and Aletheia, and Zoe, and the "Word made flesh, whose glory," he says, "we beheld; and His glory was as that of the Only-begotten (given to Him by the Father), full of grace and truth."[12] (But what John really does

---

[1] Luke ii. 28.
[2] Luke ii. 36.
[3] Luke vii. 35.
[4] 1 Cor. ii. 6.
[5] Eph. v. 32.
[6] John i. 1, 2.
[7] John i. 3.
[8] John i. 3, 4. The punctuation here followed is different from that commonly adopted, but is found in many of the Fathers, and in some of the most ancient MSS.
[9] Eph. v. 13.
[10] John i. 5.
[11] ὑπ' αὐτῆς, occurring twice, is rendered both times in the old Latin version, "ab eis." The reference is to σκοτία, *darkness*, i.e., all those not belonging to the spiritual seed.
[12] Comp. John i. 14.

say is this : " And the Word was made flesh, and dwelt among us ; and we beheld His glory, the glory as of the only-begotten of the Father, full of grace and truth." [1]) Thus, then, does he [according to them] distinctly set forth the first Tetrad, when he speaks of the Father, and Charis, and Monogenes, and Aletheia. In this way, too, does John tell of the first Ogdoad, and that which is the mother of all the Æons. For he mentions the Father, and Charis, and Monogenes, and Aletheia, and Logos, and Zoe, and Anthropos, and Ecclesia. Such are the views of Ptolemæus. [2]

CHAP. IX. — REFUTATION OF THE IMPIOUS INTERPRETATIONS OF THESE HERETICS.

1. You see, my friend, the method which these men employ to deceive themselves, while they abuse the Scriptures by endeavouring to support their own system out of them. For this reason, I have brought forward their modes of expressing themselves, that thus thou mightest understand the deceitfulness of their procedure, and the wickedness of their error. For, in the first place, if it had been John's intention to set forth that Ogdoad above, he would surely have preserved the order of its production, and would doubtless have placed the primary Tetrad first, as being, according to them, most venerable, and would then have annexed the second, that, by the sequence of the names, the order of the Ogdoad might be exhibited, and not after so long an interval, as if forgetful for the moment ; and then again calling the matter to mind, he, last of all, made mention of the primary Tetrad. In the next place, if he had meant to indicate their conjunctions, he certainly would not have omitted the name of Ecclesia ; while, with respect to the other conjunctions, he either would have been satisfied with the mention of the male [Æons] (since the others [like Ecclesia] might be understood), so as to preserve a uniformity throughout ; or if he enumerated the conjunctions of the rest, he would also have announced the spouse of Anthropos, and would not have left us to find out her name by divination.

2. The fallacy, then, of this exposition is manifest. For when John, proclaiming one God, the Almighty, and one Jesus Christ, the Only-begotten, by whom all things were made, declares that this was the Son of God, this the Only-begotten, this the Former of all things, this the true Light who enlighteneth every man, this the Creator of the world, this He that came to His own, this He that became flesh and dwelt among us, — these men, by a plausible kind of

exposition, perverting these statements, maintain that there was another Monogenes, according to production, whom they also style Arche. They also maintain that there was another Saviour, and another Logos, the son of Monogenes, and another Christ produced for the re-establishment of the Pleroma. Thus it is that, wresting from the truth every one of the expressions which have been cited, and taking a bad advantage of the names, they have transferred them to their own system ; so that, according to them, in all these terms John makes no mention of the Lord Jesus Christ. For if he has named the Father, and Charis, and Monogenes, and Aletheia, and Logos, and Zoe, and Anthropos, and Ecclesia, according to their hypothesis, he has, by thus speaking, referred to the primary Ogdoad, in which there was as yet no Jesus, and no Christ, the teacher of John. But that the apostle did not speak concerning their conjunctions, but concerning our Lord Jesus Christ, whom he also acknowledges as the Word of God, he himself has made evident. For, summing up his statements respecting the Word previously mentioned by him, he further declares, " And the Word was made flesh, and dwelt among us." But, according to their hypothesis, the Word did not become flesh at all, inasmuch as He never went outside of the Pleroma, but that Saviour [became flesh] who was formed by a special dispensation [out of all the Æons], and was of later date than the Word.

3. Learn then, ye foolish men, that Jesus who suffered for us, and who dwelt among us, is Himself the Word of God. For if any other of the Æons had become flesh for our salvation, it would have been probable that the apostle spoke of another. But if the Word of the Father who descended is the same also that ascended, He, namely, the Only-begotten Son of the only God, who, according to the good pleasure of the Father, became flesh for the sake of men, the apostle certainly does not speak regarding any other, or concerning any Ogdoad, but respecting our Lord Jesus Christ. For, according to them, the Word did not originally become flesh. For they maintain that the Saviour assumed an animal body, formed in accordance with a special dispensation by an unspeakable providence, so as to become visible and palpable. But *flesh* is that which was of old formed for Adam by God out of the dust, and it is this that John has declared the Word of God became. Thus is their primary and first-begotten Ogdoad brought to nought. For, since Logos, and Monogenes, and Zoe, and Phōs, and Soter, and Christus, and the Son of God, and He who became incarnate for us, have been proved to be one and the same, the Ogdoad which they have built up at once falls to pieces. And when this is destroyed,

---

[1] This is parenthetically inserted by the author, to show the misquotation of Scripture by these heretics.
[2] These words are wanting in the Greek, but are inserted in the old Latin version.

their whole system sinks into ruin, — a system which they falsely dream into existence, and thus inflict injury on the Scriptures, while they build up their own hypothesis.

4. Then, again, collecting a set of expressions and names scattered here and there [in Scripture], they twist them, as we have already said, from a natural to a non-natural sense. In so doing, they act like those who bring forward any kind of hypothesis they fancy, and then endeavour to support[1] them out of the poems of Homer, so that the ignorant imagine that Homer actually composed the verses bearing upon that hypothesis, which has, in fact, been but newly constructed; and many others are led so far by the regularly-formed sequence of the verses, as to doubt whether Homer may not have composed them. Of this kind[2] is the following passage, where one, describing Hercules as having been sent by Eurystheus to the dog in the infernal regions, does so by means of these Homeric verses, — for there can be no objection to our citing these by way of illustration, since the same sort of attempt appears in both : —

"Thus saying, there sent forth from his house deeply groaning." — *Od.*, x. 76.
"The hero Hercules conversant with mighty deeds." — *Od.*, xxi. 26.
Eurystheus, the son of Sthenelus, descended from Perseus." — *Il.*, xix. 123.
"That he might bring from Erebus the dog of gloomy Pluto." — *Il.*, viii. 368.
"And he advanced like a mountain-bred lion confident of strength." — *Od.*, vi. 130.
"Rapidly through the city, while all his friends followed." — *Il.*, xxiv. 327.
"Both maidens, and youths, and much-enduring old men." — *Od.*, xi. 38.
"Mourning for him bitterly as one going forward to death." — *Il.*, xxiv. 328.
"But Mercury and the blue-eyed Minerva conducted him." — *Od.*, xi. 626.
"For she knew the mind of her brother, how it laboured with grief." — *Il.*, ii. 409.

Now, what simple-minded man, I ask, would not be led away by such verses as these to think that Homer actually framed them so with reference to the subject indicated? But he who is acquainted with the Homeric writings will recognise the verses indeed, but not the subject to which they are applied, as knowing that some of them were spoken of Ulysses, others of Hercules himself, others still of Priam, and others again of Menelaus and Agamemnon. But if he takes them and restores each of them to its proper position, he at once destroys the narrative in question. In like manner he also who retains

unchangeable[3] in his heart the rule of the truth which he received by means of baptism, will doubtless recognise the names, the expressions, and the parables taken from the Scriptures, but will by no means acknowledge the blasphemous use which these men make of them. For, though he will acknowledge the gems, he will certainly not receive the fox instead of the likeness of the king. But when he has restored every one of the expressions quoted to its proper position, and has fitted it to the body of the truth, he will lay bare, and prove to be without any foundation, the figment of these heretics.

5. But since what may prove a finishing-stroke[4] to this exhibition is wanting, so that any one, on following out their farce to the end, may then at once append an argument which shall overthrow it, we have judged it well to point out, first of all, in what respects the very fathers of this fable differ among themselves, as if they were inspired by different spirits of error. For this very fact forms an *a priori* proof that the truth proclaimed by the Church is immoveable,[5] and that the theories of these men are but a tissue of falsehoods.

CHAP. X. — UNITY OF THE FAITH OF THE CHURCH THROUGHOUT THE WHOLE WORLD.

1. The Church, though dispersed throughout the whole world, even to the ends of the earth, has received from the apostles and their disciples this faith : [She believes] in one God, the Father Almighty, Maker of heaven, and earth, and the sea, and all things that are in them ; and in one Christ Jesus, the Son of God, who became incarnate for our salvation ; and in the Holy Spirit, who proclaimed through the prophets the dispensations[6] of God, and the advents, and the birth from a virgin, and the passion, and the resurrection from the dead, and the ascension into heaven in the flesh of the beloved Christ Jesus, our Lord, and His [future] manifestation from heaven in the glory of the Father "to gather all things in one,"[7] and to raise up anew all flesh of the whole human race, in order that to Christ Jesus, our Lord, and God, and Saviour, and King, according to the will of the invisible Father, "every knee should bow, of things in heaven, and things in earth, and things under the earth, and that every tongue should confess"[8] to Him, and that He should execute just judgment towards all ; that He may send "spiritual wickednesses,"[9] and

---

[1] It is difficult to give an exact rendering of μελετᾶν in this passage: the old Lat. version translates it by *meditari*, which Massuet proposes to render " skilfully to fit."
[2] Tertullian refers (*Præscrip. Hær.*) to those Homeric centos of which a specimen follows. We have given each line as it stands in the original: the text followed by Irenæus differs slightly from the received text.

[3] Literally," immoveable in himself," the word ἀκλινῆ being used with an apparent reference to the original meaning of κανόνα, *a builder's rule.*
[4] The meaning of the word ἀπολύτρωσις here is not easily determined; but it is probably a scenic term equivalent to ἀπόλυσις, and may be rendered as above.
[5] [The Creed, in the sublime simplicity of its fundamental articles, is established; that is, by the impossibility of framing anything to take their place.]
[6] " Of God " is added from the old Latin.
[7] Eph. i. 10.
[8] Phil. ii. 10, 11.
[9] Eph. vi. 12.

the angels who transgressed and became apostates, together with the ungodly, and unrighteous, and wicked, and profane among men, into everlasting fire; but may, in the exercise of His grace, confer immortality on the righteous, and holy, and those who have kept His commandments, and have persevered in His love, some from the beginning [of their Christian course], and others from [the date of] their repentance, and may surround them with everlasting glory.

2. As I have already observed, the Church, having received this preaching and this faith, although scattered throughout the whole world, yet, as if occupying but one house, carefully preserves it. She also believes these points [of doctrine] just as if she had but one soul, and one and the same heart, and she proclaims them, and teaches them, and hands them down, with perfect harmony, as if she possessed only one mouth. For, although the languages of the world are dissimilar, yet the import of the tradition is one and the same. For the Churches which have been planted in Germany do not believe or hand down anything different, nor do those in Spain, nor those in Gaul, nor those in the East, nor those in Egypt, nor those in Libya, nor those which have been established in the central regions [1] of the world. But as the sun, that creature of God, is one and the same throughout the whole world, so also the preaching of the truth shineth everywhere, and enlightens all men that are willing to come to a knowledge of the truth. Nor will any one of the rulers in the Churches, however highly gifted he may be in point of eloquence, teach doctrines different from these (for no one is greater than the Master); nor, on the other hand, will he who is deficient in power of expression inflict injury on the tradition. For the faith being ever one and the same, neither does one who is able at great length to discourse regarding it, make any addition to it, nor does one, who can say but little, diminish it.

3. It does not follow because men are endowed with greater and less degrees of intelligence, that they should therefore change the subject-matter [of the faith] itself, and should conceive of some other God besides Him who is the Framer, Maker, and Preserver of this universe, (as if He were not sufficient [2] for them), or of another Christ, or another Only-begotten. But the fact referred to simply implies this, that one may [more accurately than another] bring out the meaning of those things which have been spoken in parables, and accommodate them to the general scheme of the faith; and explain [with

special clearness] the operation and dispensation of God connected with human salvation; and show that God manifested longsuffering in regard to the apostasy of the angels who transgressed, as also with respect to the disobedience of men; and set forth why it is that one and the same God has made some things temporal and some eternal, some heavenly and others earthly; and understand for what reason God, though invisible, manifested Himself to the prophets not under one form, but differently to different individuals; and show why it was that more covenants than one were given to mankind; and teach what was the special character of each of these covenants; and search out for what reason "God [3] hath concluded every man [4] in unbelief, that He may have mercy upon all;" and gratefully [5] describe on what account the Word of God became flesh and suffered; and relate why the advent of the Son of God took place in these last times, that is, in the end, rather than in the beginning [of the world]; and unfold what is contained in the Scriptures concerning the end [itself], and things to come; and not be silent as to how it is that God has made the Gentiles, whose salvation was despaired of, fellow-heirs, and of the same body, and partakers with the saints; and discourse how it is that "this mortal body shall put on immortality, and this corruptible shall put on incorruption;" [6] and proclaim in what sense [God] says, "That is a people who was not a people; and she is beloved who was not beloved;" [7] and in what sense He says that "more are the children of her that was desolate, than of her who possessed a husband." [8] For in reference to these points, and others of a like nature, the apostle exclaims: "Oh! the depth of the riches both of the wisdom and knowledge of God; how unsearchable are His judgments, and His ways past finding out!" [9] But [the superior skill spoken of] is not found in this, that any one should, beyond the Creator and Framer [of the world], conceive of the Enthymesis of an erring Æon, their mother and his, and should thus proceed to such a pitch of blasphemy; nor does it consist in this, that he should again falsely imagine, as being above this [fancied being], a Pleroma at one time supposed to contain thirty, and at another time an innumerable tribe of Æons, as these teachers who are destitute of truly divine wisdom maintain; while the Catholic Church pos-

---

1 Probably referring to the Churches in Palestine.

2 The text here is ἀρκουμένους τούτους, which is manifestly corrupt. Various emendations have been proposed: we prefer reading ἀρκούμενος τούτοις, and have translated accordingly.

3 Rom. xi. 32.

4 Irenæus here reads πάντα instead of πάντας, as in Text. Rec. of New Testament.

5 εὐχαριστεῖν — this word has been deemed corrupt, as it certainly appears out of keeping with the other verbs; but it may be rendered as above.

6 1 Cor. xv. 54.

7 Hos. ii. 23; Rom. ix. 25.

8 Isa. liv. 1; Gal. iv. 27.

9 Rom. xi. 33.

sesses one and the same faith throughout the whole world, as we have already said.

CHAP. XI. — THE OPINIONS OF VALENTINUS, WITH THOSE OF HIS DISCIPLES AND OTHERS.

1. Let us now look at the inconsistent opinions of those heretics (for there are some two or three of them), how they do not agree in treating the same points, but alike, in things and names, set forth opinions mutually discordant. The first[1] of them, Valentinus, who adapted the principles of the heresy called "Gnostic" to the peculiar character of his own school, taught as follows: He maintained that there is a certain Dyad (twofold being), who is inexpressible by any name, of whom one part should be called Arrhetus (unspeakable), and the other Sige (silence). But of this Dyad a second was produced, one part of whom he names Pater, and the other Aletheia. From this Tetrad, again, arose Logos and Zoe, Anthropos and Ecclesia. These constitute the primary Ogdoad. He next states that from Logos and Zoe ten powers were produced, as we have before mentioned. But from Anthropos and Ecclesia proceeded twelve, one of which separating from the rest, and falling from its original condition, produced the rest[2] of the universe. He also supposed two beings of the name of Horos, the one of whom has his place between Bythus and the rest of the Pleroma, and divides the created Æons from the uncreated Father, while the other separates their mother from the Pleroma. Christ also was not produced from the Æons within the Pleroma, but was brought forth by the mother who had been excluded from it, in virtue of her remembrance of better things, but not without a kind of shadow. He, indeed, as being masculine, having severed the shadow from himself, returned to the Pleroma; but his mother being left with the shadow, and deprived of her spiritual substance, brought forth another son, namely, the Demiurge, whom he also styles the supreme ruler of all those things which are subject to him. He also asserts that, along with the Demiurge, there was produced a left-hand power, in which particular he agrees with those falsely called Gnostics, of whom to we have yet to speak. Sometimes, again, he maintains that Jesus was produced from him who was separated from their mother, and united to the rest, that is, from Theletus, sometimes as springing from him who returned into the Pleroma, that is, from Christ; and at other times still as derived from Anthropos and Ecclesia. And he declares that the Holy Spirit was produced by

Aletheia[3] for the inspection and fructification of the Æons, by entering invisibly into them, and that, in this way, the Æons brought forth the plants of truth.

2. Secundus again affirms that the primary Ogdoad consists of a right hand and a left hand Tetrad, and teaches that the one of these is called light, and the other darkness. But he maintains that the power which separated from the rest, and fell away, did not proceed directly from the thirty Æons, but from their fruits.

3. There is another,[4] who is a renowned teacher among them, and who, struggling to reach something more sublime, and to attain to a kind of higher knowledge, has explained the primary Tetrad as follows: There is [he says] a certain Proarche who existed before all things, surpassing all thought, speech, and nomenclature, whom I call Monotes (unity). Together with this Monotes there exists a power, which again I term Henotes (oneness). This Henotes and Monotes, being one, produced, yet not so as to bring forth [apart from themselves, as an emanation] the beginning of all things, an intelligent, unbegotten, and invisible being, which beginning language terms " Monad." With this Monad there co-exists a power of the same essence, which again I term Hen (One). These powers then — Monotes, and Henotes, and Monas, and Hen — produced the remaining company of the Æons.

4. Iu, Iu! Pheu, Pheu! — for well may we utter these tragic exclamations at such a pitch of audacity in the coining of names as he has displayed without a blush, in devising a nomenclature for his system of falsehood. For when he declares: There is a certain Proarche before all things, surpassing all thought, whom I call Monotes; and again, with this Monotes there co-exists a power which I also call Henotes, — it is most manifest that he confesses the things which have been said to be his own invention, and that he himself has given names to his scheme of things, which had never been previously suggested by any other. It is manifest also, that he himself is the one who has had sufficient audacity to coin these names; so that, unless *he* had appeared in the world, the truth would still have been destitute of a name. But, in that case, nothing hinders any other, in dealing with the same subject, to affix names after such a fashion as the following: There[5] is a certain Proarche, royal, surpassing all thought, a power existing before every other substance, and extended into space in every direction. But along with it there exists a power which I term a *Gourd;* and along

---

[1] That is, the first of the two or three here referred to, not the first of the Gnostic teachers, as some have imagined. [The Gnosticism of one age may be essentially the same in spirit as the *Agnosticism* of another.]

[2] Viz., all outside of the Pleroma.

[3] Corrected from *Ecclesia* in the text.

[4] Some have supposed that the name of this teacher was *Epiphanes*, and that the old Latin mistakenly translates this by *clarus;* others think that Colorbasus is the teacher in question.

[5] The Greek text is wanting till the end of this section.

with this Gourd there exists a power which again I term *Utter-Emptiness*. This Gourd and Emptiness, since they are one, produced (and yet did not simply produce, so as to be apart from themselves) a fruit, everywhere visible, eatable, and delicious, which fruit-language calls a *Cucumber*. Along with this Cucumber exists a power of the same essence, which again I call a *Melon*. These powers, the Gourd, Utter-Emptiness, the Cucumber, and the Melon, brought forth the remaining multitude of the delirious melons of Valentinus.[1] For if it is fitting that that language which is used respecting the universe be transformed to the primary Tetrad, and if any one may assign names at his pleasure, who shall prevent us from adopting these names, as being much more credible [than the others], as well as in general use, and understood by all?

5. Others still, however, have called their primary and first-begotten Ogdoad by the following names: first, Proarche; then Anennoetos; thirdly, Arrhetos; and fourthly, Aoratos. Then, from the first, Proarche, there was produced, in the first and fifth place, Arche; from Anennoetos, in the second and sixth place, Acataleptos; from Arrhetos, in the third and seventh place, Anonomastos; and from Aoratos, in the fourth and eighth place, Agennetos. This is the Pleroma of the first Ogdoad. They maintain that these powers were anterior to Bythus and Sige, that they may appear more perfect than the perfect, and more knowing than the very Gnostics! To these persons one may justly exclaim: "O ye trifling sophists!" since, even respecting Bythus himself, there are among them many and discordant opinions. For some declare him to be without a consort, and neither male nor female, and, in fact, nothing at all; while others affirm him to be masculo-feminine, assigning to him the nature of a hermaphrodite; others, again, allot Sige to him as a spouse, that thus may be formed the first conjunction.

CHAP. XII. — THE DOCTRINES OF THE FOLLOWERS OF PTOLEMY AND COLORBASUS.

1. But the followers of Ptolemy say[2] that he [Bythos] has two consorts, which they also name *Diatheses* (affections), viz., Ennœa and Thelesis. For, as they affirm, he first conceived the thought of producing something, and then willed to that effect. Wherefore, again, these two affections, or powers, Ennœa and Thelesis, having intercourse, as it were, between themselves, the production of Monogenes and Aletheia took place according to conjunction. These two came forth

as types and images of the two affections of the Father, — visible representations of those that were invisible, — Nous (i.e., Monogenes) of Thelesis, and Aletheia of Ennœa, and accordingly the image resulting from Thelesis was masculine,[3] while that from Ennœa was feminine. Thus Thelesis (will) became, as it were, a faculty of Ennœa (thought). For Ennœa continually yearned after offspring; but she could not of herself bring forth that which she desired. But when the power of Thelesis (the faculty of will) came upon her, then she brought forth that on which she had brooded.

2. These fancied beings[4] (like the Jove of Homer, who is represented[5] as passing an anxious sleepless night in devising plans for honouring Achilles and destroying numbers of the Greeks) will not appear to you, my dear friend, to be possessed of greater knowledge than He who is the God of the universe. He, as soon as He thinks, also performs what He has willed; and as soon as He wills, also thinks that which He has willed; then thinking when He wills, and then willing when He thinks, since He is all thought, [all will, all mind, all light,][6] all eye, all ear, the one entire fountain of all good things.

3. Those of them, however, who are deemed more skilful than the persons who have just been mentioned, say that the first Ogdoad was not produced gradually, so that one Æon was sent forth by another, but that all[7] the Æons were brought into existence at once by Propator and his Ennœa. He (Colorbasus) affirms this as confidently as if he had assisted at their birth. Accordingly, he and his followers maintain that Anthropos and Ecclesia were not produced,[8] as others hold, from Logos and Zoe; but, on the contrary, Logos and Zoe from Anthropos and Ecclesia. But they express this in another form, as follows: When the Propator conceived the thought of producing something, he received the name of *Father*. But because what he did produce was *true*, it was named Aletheia. Again, when he wished to reveal himself, this was termed Anthropos. Finally, when he produced those whom he had previously thought of, these were named Ecclesia. Anthropos, by speaking, formed Logos: this is the first-born son. But Zoe followed upon Logos; and thus the first Ogdoad was completed.

4. They have much contention also among themselves respecting the Saviour. For some

---

[1] [1 Kings xviii. 27. "It came to pass that Elijah mocked them," etc. This *reductio ad absurdum* of our author is singularly applicable to certain forms of what is called "Modern Thought."]
[2] We here follow the Greek as preserved by Hippolytus (*Philosoph.*, vi. 38). The text followed by Epiphanius (*Hær.*, xxxiii. 1) does not so well agree with the Latin.

[3] The text is here hopelessly corrupt; but the general meaning seems to be that given above.
[4] This sentence exists only in the Latin version, and we can give only a free translation.
[5] *Iliad*, ii. 1, etc.
[6] These words are found in *Epiphanius*, but omitted in the old Latin version. The Latin gives "sense" instead of "light."
[7] The text is here very uncertain. Some propose to read *six* Æons instead of *all*.
[8] Here again the text is corrupt and obscure. We have followed what seems the most probable emendation.

maintain that he was formed out of all; wherefore also he was called Eudocetos, because the whole Pleroma was *well pleased* through him to glorify the Father. But others assert that he was produced from those ten Æons alone who sprung from Logos and Zoe, and that on this account he was called Logos and Zoe, thus preserving the ancestral names.[1] Others, again, affirm that he had his being from those twelve Æons who were the offspring of Anthropos and Ecclesia; and on this account he acknowledges himself the Son of man, as being a descendant of Anthropos. Others still, assert that he was produced by Christ and the Holy Spirit, who were brought forth for the security of the Pleroma; and that on this account he was called Christ, thus preserving the appellation of the Father, by whom he was produced. And there are yet others among them who declare that the Propator of the whole, Proarche, and Proanennoetos is called Anthropos; and that this is the great and abstruse mystery, namely, that the Power which is above all others, and contains all in his embrace, is termed Anthropos; hence does the Saviour style himself the "Son of man."

CHAP. XIII. — THE DECEITFUL ARTS AND NEFARIOUS PRACTICES OF MARCUS.

1. But[2] there is another among these heretics, Marcus by name, who boasts himself as having improved upon his master. He is a perfect adept in magical impostures, and by this means drawing away a great number of men, and not a few women, he has induced them to join themselves to him, as to one who is possessed of the greatest knowledge and perfection, and who has received the highest power from the invisible and ineffable regions above. Thus it appears as if he really were the precursor of Antichrist. For, joining the buffooneries of Anaxilaus[3] to the craftiness of the *magi*, as they are called, he is regarded by his senseless and cracked-brain followers as working miracles by these means.

2. Pretending[4] to consecrate cups mixed with wine, and protracting to great length the word of invocation, he contrives to give them a purple and reddish colour, so that Charis,[5] who is one of those that are superior to all things, should be thought to drop her own blood into that cup through means of his invocation, and that thus those who

are present should be led to rejoice to taste of that cup, in order that, by so doing, the Charis, who is set forth by this magician, may also flow into them. Again, handing mixed cups to the women, he bids them consecrate these in his presence. When this has been done, he himself produces another cup of much larger size than that which the deluded woman has consecrated, and pouring from the smaller one consecrated by the woman into that which has been brought forward by himself, he at the same time pronounces these words: "May that Charis who is before all things, and who transcends all knowledge and speech, fill thine inner man, and multiply in thee her own knowledge, by sowing the grain of mustard seed in thee as in good soil." Repeating certain other like words, and thus goading on the wretched woman [to madness], he then appears a worker of wonders when the large cup is seen to have been filled out of the small one, so as even to overflow by what has been obtained from it. By accomplishing several other similar things, he has completely deceived many, and drawn them away after him.

3. It appears probable enough that this man possesses a demon as his familiar spirit, by means of whom he seems able to prophesy,[6] and also enables as many as he counts worthy to be partakers of his Charis themselves to prophesy. He devotes himself especially to women, and those such as are well-bred, and elegantly attired, and of great wealth, whom he frequently seeks to draw after him, by addressing them in such seductive words as these: "I am eager to make thee a partaker of my Charis, since the Father of all doth continually behold thy angel before His face. Now the place of thy angel is among us:[7] it behoves us to become one. Receive first from me and by me [the gift of] Charis. Adorn thyself as a bride who is expecting her bridegroom, that thou mayest be what I am, and I what thou art. Establish the germ of light in thy nuptial chamber. Receive from me a spouse, and become receptive of him, while thou art received by him. Behold Charis has descended upon thee; open thy mouth and prophesy." On the woman replying, "I have never at any time prophesied, nor do I know how to prophesy;" then engaging, for the second time, in certain invocations, so as to astound his deluded victim, he says to her, "Open thy mouth, speak whatsoever occurs to thee, and thou shalt prophesy." She then, vainly puffed up and elated by these words, and greatly excited in soul by the expectation that it is herself who is to prophesy, her heart beating violently [from emotion], reaches the requisite pitch of audacity, and idly as well as impudently utters some nonsense as it happens to occur to her, such as might be ex-

---

[1] Harvey justly remarks, that "one cause of perplexity in unravelling the Valentinian scheme is the recurrence of similar names at different points of the system, e.g., the Enthymesis of Sophia was called Sophia and Spiritus; and Pater, Arche, Monogenes, Christus, Anthropos, Ecclesia, were all of them terms of a double denomination."

[2] The Greek text of this section is preserved both by Epiphanius (*Hær.*, xxxiv. 1) and by Hippolytus (*Philosoph.*, vi. 39, 40). Their citations are somewhat discordant, and we therefore follow the old Latin version.

[3] Pliny, *Hist. Nat.*, xxxv. 15, etc.

[4] Epiphanius now gives the Greek text *verbatim*, to which, therefore, we return.

[5] Probably referring to Sige, the consort of Bythus.

[6] [Comp. Acts xvi. 16.]

[7] Literally, "the place of thy mightiness is in us."

pected from one heated by an empty spirit. (Referring to this, one superior to me has observed, that the soul is both audacious and impudent when heated with empty air.) Henceforth she reckons herself a prophetess, and expresses her thanks to Marcus for having imparted to her of his own Charis. She then makes the effort to reward him, not only by the gift of her possessions (in which way he has collected a very large fortune), but also by yielding up to him her person, desiring in every way to be united to him, that she may become altogether one with him.

4. But already some of the most faithful women, possessed of the fear of God, and not being deceived (whom, nevertheless, he did his best to seduce like the rest by bidding them prophesy), abhorring and execrating him, have withdrawn from such a vile company of revellers. This they have done, as being well aware that the gift of prophecy is not conferred on men by Marcus, the magician, but that only ᴛhose to whom God sends His grace from above possess the divinely-bestowed power of prophesying; and then they speak where and when God pleases, and not when Marcus orders them to do so. For that which commands is greater and of higher authority than that which is commanded, inasmuch as the former rules, while the latter is in a state of subjection. If, then, Marcus, or any one else, does command, — as these are accustomed continually at their feasts to play at drawing lots, and [in accordance with the lot] to command one another to prophesy, giving forth as oracles what is in harmony with their own desires, — it will follow that he who commands is greater and of higher authority than the prophetic spirit, though he is but a man, which is impossible. But such spirits as are commanded by these men, and speak when they desire it, are earthly and weak, audacious and impudent, sent forth by Satan for the seduction and perdition of those who do not hold fast that well-compacted faith which they received at first through the Church.

5. Moreover, that this Marcus compounds philters and love-potions, in order to insult the persons of some of these women, if not of all, those of them who have returned to the Church of God — a thing which frequently occurs — have acknowledged, confessing, too, that they have been defiled by him, and that they were filled with a burning passion towards him. A sad example of this occurred in the case of a certain Asiatic, one of our deacons, who had received him (Marcus) into his house. His wife, a woman of remarkable beauty, fell a victim both in mind and body to this magician, and, for a long time, travelled about with him. At last, when, with no small difficulty, the brethren had con-

verted her, she spent her whole time in the exercise of public confession,[1] weeping over and lamenting the defilement which she had received from this magician.

6. Some of his disciples, too, addicting themselves[2] to the same practices, have deceived many silly women, and defiled them. They proclaim themselves as being "perfect," so that no one can be compared to them with respect to the immensity of their knowledge, nor even were you to mention Paul or Peter, or any other of the apostles. They assert that they themselves know more than all others, and that they alone have imbibed the greatness of the knowledge of that power which is unspeakable. They also maintain that they have attained to a height above all power, and that therefore they are free in every respect to act as they please, having no one to fear in anything. For they affirm, that because of the "Redemption"[3] it has come to pass that they can neither be apprehended, nor even seen by the judge. But even if he should happen to lay hold upon them, then they might simply repeat these words, while standing in his presence along with the "Redemption:" "O thou, who sittest beside God,[4] and the mystical, eternal Sige, thou through whom the angels (mightiness), who continually behold the face of the Father, having thee as their guide and introducer, do derive their forms[5] from above, which she in the greatness of her daring inspiring with mind on account of the goodness of the Propator, produced us as their images, having her mind then intent upon the things above, as in a dream, — behold, the judge is at hand, and the crier orders me to make my defence. But do thou, as being acquainted with the affairs of both, present the cause of both of us to the judge, inasmuch as it is in reality but one cause."[6] Now, as soon as the Mother hears these words, she puts the Homeric[7] helmet of Pluto upon them, so that they may invisibly escape the judge. And then she immediately catches them up, conducts them into the bridal chamber, and hands them over to their consorts.

---

[1] [Note this manner of primitive "confession;" and see Bingham, *Antiquities*, book xv. cap. 8.]

[2] We here follow the rendering of Billius, "in iisdem studiis versantes." Others adhere to the received text, and translate περιπολί-ζοντες "going about idly."

[3] Grabe is of opinion that reference is made in this term to an imprecatory formula in use among the Marcosians, analogous to the form of thanksgiving employed night and morning by the Jews for their redemption from Egypt. Harvey refers the word to the *second* baptism practised among these and other heretics, by which it was supposed they were removed from the cognizance of the Demiurge, who is styled the "judge" in the close of the above sentence.

[4] That is, Sophia, of whom Achamoth, afterwards referred to, was the emanation.

[5] The angels accompanying Soter were the consorts of spiritual Gnostics, to whom they were restored after death.

[6] The syntax in this long sentence is very confused, but the meaning is tolerably plain. The gist of it is, that these Gnostics, as being the spiritual seed, claimed a consubstantiality with Achamoth, and consequently escaped from the material Demiurge, and attained at last to the Pleroma.

[7] Rendering the wearer invisible. See *Il.*, v. 844.

7. Such are the words and deeds by which, in our own district of the Rhone, they have deluded many women, who have their consciences seared as with a hot iron.[1] Some of them, indeed, make a public confession of their sins; but others of them are ashamed to do this, and in a tacit kind of way, despairing of [attaining to] the life of God, have, some of them, apostatized altogether; while others hesitate between the two courses, and incur that which is implied in the proverb, "neither without nor within;" possessing this as the fruit from the seed of the children of knowledge.

CHAP. XIV. — THE VARIOUS HYPOTHESES OF MARCUS AND OTHERS. THEORIES RESPECTING LETTERS AND SYLLABLES.

1. This Marcus[2] then, declaring that he alone was the matrix and receptacle of the Sige of Colorbasus, inasmuch as he was only-begotten, has brought to the birth in some such way as follows that which was committed to him of the defective Enthymesis. He declares that the infinitely exalted Tetrad descended upon him from the invisible and indescribable places in the form of a woman (for the world could not have borne it coming in its male form), and expounded to him alone its own nature, and the origin of all things, which it had never before revealed to any one either of gods or men. This was done in the following terms: When first the unoriginated, inconceivable Father, who is without material substance,[3] and is neither male nor female, willed to bring forth that which is ineffable to Him, and to endow with form that which is invisible, He opened His mouth, and sent forth the Word similar to Himself, who, standing near, showed Him what He Himself was, inasmuch as He had been manifested in the form of that which was invisible. Moreover, the pronunciation of His name took place as follows: — He spake the first word of it, which was the beginning[4] [of all the rest], and that utterance consisted of four letters. He added the second, and this also consisted of four letters. Next He uttered the third, and this again embraced ten letters. Finally, He pronounced the fourth, which was composed of twelve letters. Thus took place the enunciation of the whole name, consisting of thirty letters, and four distinct utterances. Each of these elements has its own peculiar letters, and character, and pronunciation, and forms, and images, and there is not one of them that perceives the shape of that [utterance] of which it is an element. Neither does any one know[5] itself, nor is it acquainted with the pronunciation of its neighbour, but each one imagines that by its own utterance it does in fact name the whole. For while every one of them is a part of the whole, it imagines its own sound to be the whole name, and does not leave off sounding until, by its own utterance, it has reached the last letter of each of the elements. This teacher declares that the restitution of all things will take place, when all these, mixing into one letter, shall utter one and the same sound. He imagines that the emblem of this utterance is found in Amen, which we pronounce in concert.[6] The diverse sounds (he adds) are those which give form to that Æon who is without material substance and unbegotten, and these, again, are the forms which the Lord has called angels, who continually behold the face of the Father.[7]

2. Those names of the elements which may be told, and are common, he has called Æons, and words, and roots, and seeds, and fulnesses, and fruits. He asserts that each of these, and all that is peculiar to every one of them, is to be understood as contained in the name Ecclesia. Of these elements, the last letter of the last one uttered its voice, and this sound[8] going forth generated its own elements after the image of the [other] elements, by which he affirms, that both the things here below were arranged into the order they occupy, and those that preceded them were called into existence. He also maintains that the letter itself, the sound of which followed that sound below, was received up again by the syllable to which it belonged, in order to the completion of the whole, but that the sound remained below as if cast outside. But the element itself from which the letter with its special pronunciation descended to that below, he affirms to consist of thirty letters, while each of these letters, again, contains other letters in itself, by means of which the name of the letter is expressed. And thus, again, others are named by other letters, and others still by others, so that the multitude of letters swells out into infinitude. You may more clearly understand what I mean by the following example: — The word *Delta* con-

---

[1] 2 Tim. iii. 6.

[2] This sentence has completely baffled all the critics. [Its banter, or mock gravity, has not been self-evident.] We cannot enter upon the wide field of discussion which it has opened up, but would simply state that Irenæus here seems to us, as often, to be playing upon the terms which were in common use among these heretics. Marcus probably received his system from Colorbasus, and is here declared, by the use of that jargon which Irenæus means to ridicule while so employing it, to have proceeded to develop it in the way described.

[3] Such appears to be the meaning of ἀνούσιος in this passage. The meaning of οὐσία fluctuated for a time in the early Church, and was sometimes used to denote *material substance*, instead of its usual significance of *being*.

[4] The old Latin preserves ἀρχή untranslated, implying that this was the first word which the Father spoke. Some modern editors adopt this view, while others hold the meaning simply to be, as given above, that that first sound which the Father uttered was the origin of all the rest.

[5] The letters are here confounded with the Æons, which they represented.

[6] [1 Cor. xiv. 16.]

[7] Matt. xviii. 10.

[8] By this Achamoth is denoted, who was said to give rise to the material elements, after the image of the Divine.

tains five letters, viz., D, E, L, T, A : these letters, again, are written by other letters,[1] and others still by others. If, then, the entire composition of the word Delta [when thus analyzed] runs out into infinitude, letters continually generating other letters, and following one another in constant succession, how much vaster than that [one] word is the [entire] ocean of letters ! And if even one letter be thus infinite, just consider the immensity of the letters in the entire name; out of which the Sige of Marcus has taught us the Propator is composed. For which reason the Father, knowing the incomprehensibleness of His own nature, assigned to the elements, which He also terms Æons, [the power] of each one uttering its own enunciation, because no one of them was capable by itself of uttering the whole.

3. Moreover, the Tetrad, explaining these things to him more fully, said : — I wish to show thee Aletheia (Truth) herself; for I have brought her down from the dwellings above, that thou mayest see her without a veil, and understand her beauty — that thou mayest also hear her speaking, and admire her wisdom. Behold, then, her head on high, *Alpha* and *Omega ;* her neck, *Beta* and *Psi ;* her shoulders with her hands, *Gamma* and *Chi ;* her breast, *Delta* and *Phi ;* her diaphragm, *Epsilon* and *Upsilon ;* her back, *Zeta* and *Tau ;* her belly, *Eta* and *Sigma ;* her thighs, *Theta* and *Rho ;* her knees, *Iota* and *Pi ;* her legs, *Kappa* and *Omicron ;·* her ancles, *Lambda* and *Xi ;* her feet, *Mu* and *Nu.* Such is the body of Truth, according to this magician, such the figure of the element, such the character of the letter. And he calls this element Anthropos (Man), and says that is the fountain of all speech, and the beginning of all sound, and the expression of all that is unspeakable, and the mouth of the silent Sige. This indeed is the body of Truth. But do thou, elevating the thoughts of thy mind on high, listen from the mouth of Truth to the self-begotten Word, who is also the dispenser of the bounty of the Father.

4. When she (the Tetrad) had spoken these things, Aletheia looked at him, opened her mouth, and uttered a word. That word was a name, and the name was this one which we do know and speak of, viz., Christ Jesus. When she had uttered this name, she at once relapsed into silence. And as Marcus waited in the expectation that she would say something more, the Tetrad again came forward and said, " Thou hast reckoned as contemptible that word which thou hast heard from the mouth of Aletheia. This which thou knowest and seemest to possess, is not an ancient name. For thou possessest the sound of

it merely, whilst thou art ignorant of its power. For Jesus ('Ιησοῦς) is a name arithmetically[2] symbolical, consisting of six letters, and is known by all those that belong to the called. But that which is among the Æons of the Pleroma consists of many parts, and is of another form and shape, and is known by those [angels] who are joined in affinity with Him, and whose figures (mightinesses) are always present with Him.

5. Know, then, that the four-and-twenty letters which you possess are symbolical emanations of the three powers that contain the entire number of the elements above. For you are to reckon thus — that the nine mute[3] letters are [the images] of Pater and Aletheia, because they are without voice, that is, of such a nature as cannot be uttered or pronounced. But the semi-vowels[4] represent Logos and Zoe, because they are, as it were, midway between the consonants and the vowels, partaking[5] of the nature of both. The vowels, again, are representative of Anthropos and Ecclesia, inasmuch as a voice proceeding from Anthropos gave being to them all ; for the sound of the voice imparted to them form. Thus, then, Logos and Zoe possess eight [of these letters] ; Anthropos and Ecclesia seven ; and Pater and Aletheia nine. But since the number allotted to each was unequal, He who existed in the Father came down, having been specially sent by Him from whom He was separated, for the rectification of what had taken place, that the unity of the Pleromas, being endowed with equality, might develop in all that one power which flows from all. Thus that division which had only seven letters, received the power of eight,[6] and the three sets were rendered alike in point of number, all becoming Ogdoads ; which three, when brought together, constitute the number four-and-twenty. The three elements, too (which he declares to exist in conjunction with three powers,[7] and thus form the six from which have flowed the twenty-four letters), being quadrupled by the word of the ineffable Tetrad, give rise to the same number with them ; and these elements he maintains to belong to Him who cannot be named. These, again, were endowed by the three powers with a resemblance to Him who is invisible. And he says that those letters which we call double[8] are the images of

---

[1] That is, their names are spelt by other letters.

[2] The old Latin version renders ἐπίσημον, *insigne, illustrious,* but there seems to be a reference to the Valentinian notion of the mystic number of 888 formed (10+8+200+70+400+200) by the numerical value of the letters in the word 'Ιησοῦς.

[3] The mutes are π, κ, τ, β, γ, δ, φ, χ, θ.

[4] The semi-vowels are λ, μ, ν, ρ, σ, ζ, ξ, ψ.

[5] It seems scarcely possible to give a more definite rendering of this clause: it may be literally translated thus: " And because they receive the outflow of those above, but the turning back again of those below."

[6] The ninth letter being taken from the mutes and added to the semi-vowels, an equal division of the twenty-four was thus secured.

[7] Viz., Pater, Athropos, and Logos.

[8] Viz., ζ, ξ, ψ = δς, κς, πς.

the images of these elements; and if these be added to the four-and-twenty letters, by the force of analogy they form the number thirty.

6. He asserts that the fruit of this arrangement and analogy has been manifested in the likeness of an image, namely, Him who, after six days, ascended[1] into the mountain along with three others, and then became one of six (the sixth),[2] in which character He descended, and was contained in the Hebdomad, since He was the illustrious Ogdoad,[3] and contained in Himself the entire number of the elements, which the descent of the dove (who is Alpha and Omega) made clearly manifest, when He came to be baptized; for the number of the dove is eight hundred and one.[4] And for this reason did Moses declare that man was formed on the sixth day; and then, again, according to arrangement, it was on the sixth day, which is the preparation, that the last man appeared, for the regeneration of the first. Of this arrangement, both the beginning and the end were formed at that sixth hour, at which He was nailed to the tree. For that perfect being Nous, knowing that the number six had the power both of formation and regeneration, declared to the children of light, that regeneration which has been wrought out by Him who appeared as the *Episemon* in regard to that number. Whence also he declares it is that the double letters[5] contain the Episemon number; for this Episemon, when joined to the twenty-four elements, completed the name of thirty letters.

7. He employed as his instrument, as the Sige of Marcus declares, the power of seven letters,[6] in order that the fruit of the independent will [of Achamoth] might be revealed. "Consider this present *Episemon*," she says — "Him who was formed after the [original] *Episemon*, as being, as it were, divided or cut into two parts, and remaining outside; who, by His own power and wisdom, through means of that which had been produced by Himself, gave life to this world, consisting of seven powers,[7] after the likeness of the power of the Hebdomad, and so formed it, that it is the soul of everything visible. And He indeed uses this work Himself as if it had been formed by His own free will; but the rest, as being images of what cannot be [fully] imitated, are subservient to the Enthymesis of the mother. And the first heaven indeed pronounces *Alpha*, the next to this *Epsilon*, the third *Eta*, the fourth, which is also in the midst of the seven, utters the sound of *Iota*, the fifth *Omicron*, the sixth *Upsilon*, the seventh, which is also the fourth from the middle, utters the elegant *Omega*," — as the Sige of Marcus, talking a deal of nonsense, but uttering no word of truth, confidently asserts. "And these powers," she adds, "being all simultaneously clasped in each other's embrace, do sound out the glory of Him by whom they were produced; and the glory of that sound is transmitted upwards to the Propator." She asserts, moreover, that "the sound of this uttering of praise, having been wafted to the earth, has become the Framer and the Parent of those things which are on the earth."

8. He instances, in proof of this, the case of infants who have just been born, the cry of whom, as soon as they have issued from the womb, is in accordance with the sound of every one of these elements. As, then, he says, the seven powers glorify the Word, so also does the complaining soul of infants.[8] For this reason, too, David said: "Out of the mouth of babes and sucklings Thou hast perfected praise;"[9] and again: "The heavens declare the glory of God."[10] Hence also it comes to pass, that when the soul is involved in difficulties and distresses, for its own relief it calls out, "Oh" (Ω), in honour of the letter in question,[11] so that its cognate soul above may recognise [its distress], and send down to it relief.

9. Thus it is, that in regard to the whole name,[12] which consists of thirty letters, and Bythus, who receives his increase from the letters of this [name], and, moreover, the body of Aletheia, which is composed of twelve members, each of which consists of two letters, and the voice which she uttered without having spoken at all, and in regard to the analysis of that name which cannot be expressed in words, and the soul of the world and of man, according as they possess that arrangement, which is after the image [of things above], he has uttered his nonsensical opinions. It remains that I relate how the Tetrad showed him from the names a power equal in number; so that nothing, my friend, which I have received as spoken by him, may remain unknown to thee; and thus thy request, often proposed to me, may be fulfilled.

---

[1] Matt. xvii. 7; Mark ix. 2.
[2] Moses and Elias being added to the company.
[3] Referring to the word Χρειστός, according to Harvey, who remarks, that " generally the Ogdoad was the receptacle of the spiritual seed."
[4] The Saviour, as Alpha and Omega, was symbolized by the dove, the sum of the Greek numerals, π, ε, ρ, ι, σ, τ, ε, ρ, α (περιστερά, *dove*), being, like that of A and Ω, 801.
[5] That is, the letters ζ, ξ, ψ all contain ς, whose value is *six*, and which was called ἐπίσημον by the Greeks.
[6] Referring to *Aletheia*, which, in Greek, contains seven letters.
[7] By these seven powers are meant the seven heavens (also called angels), formed by the Demiurge.

[8] We here follow the text of Hippolytus: the ordinary text and the old Latin read, " So does the soul of infants, weeping and mourning over Marcus, deify him."
[9] Ps. viii. 2.
[10] Ps. xix. 1.
[11] The text is here altogether uncertain: we have given the probable meaning.
[12] That is, the name of Soter, the perfect result of the whole Pleroma.

CHAP. XV. — SIGE RELATES TO MARCUS THE GEN-
ERATION OF THE TWENTY-FOUR ELEMENTS AND
OF JESUS. EXPOSURE OF THESE ABSURDITIES.

1. The all-wise Sige then announced the production of the four-and-twenty elements to him
as follows: — Along with Monotes there coexisted Henotes, from which sprang two productions, as we have remarked above, Monas and
Hen, which, added to the other two, make four,
for twice two are four. And again, two and four,
when added together, exhibit the number six.
And further, these six being quadrupled, give
rise to the twenty-four forms. And the names
of the first Tetrad, which are understood to be
most holy, and not capable of being expressed
in words, are known by the Son alone, while the
father also knows what they are. The other
names which are to be uttered with respect, and
faith, and reverence, are, according to him, Arrhetos and Sige, Pater and Aletheia. Now the
entire number of this Tetrad amounts to four-and-
twenty letters; for the name Arrhetos contains
in itself seven letters, Seige [1] five, Pater five, and
Aletheia seven. If all these be added together
— twice five, and twice seven — they complete
the number twenty-four. In like manner, also,
the second Tetrad, Logos and Zoe, Anthropos
and Ecclesia, reveal the same number of elements. Moreover, that name of the Saviour
which may be pronounced, viz., Jesus ['Ιησοῦς],
consists of six letters, but His unutterable name
comprises four-and-twenty letters. The name
Christ the Son [2] (υἱὸς Χρειστός) comprises
twelve letters, but that which is unpronounceable
in Christ contains thirty letters. And for this
reason he declares that He is *Alpha* and *Omega*,
that he may indicate the dove, inasmuch as that
bird has this number [in its name].

2. But Jesus, he affirms, has the following
unspeakable origin. From the mother of all
things, that is, the first Tetrad, there came forth
the second Tetrad, after the manner of a daughter; and thus an Ogdoad was formed, from
which, again, a Decad proceeded: thus was produced a Decad and an Ogdoad. The Decad,
then, being joined with the Ogdoad, and multiplying it ten times, gave rise to the number
eighty; and, again, multiplying eighty ten times,
produced the number *eight hundred.* Thus,
then, the whole number of the letters proceeding
from the Ogdoad [multiplied] into the Decad,
is eight hundred and eighty-eight. [3] This is the
name of Jesus; for this name, if you reckon up
the numerical value of the letters, amounts to
eight hundred and eighty-eight. Thus, then,

you have a clear statement of their opinion as to
the origin of the supercelestial Jesus. Wherefore, also, the alphabet of the Greeks contains
eight Monads, eight Decads, and eight Heca-
tads[4], which present the number eight hundred
and eighty-eight, that is, *Jesus*, who is formed of
all numbers; and on this account He is called
Alpha and *Omega*, indicating His origin from
all. And, again, they put the matter thus: If
the first Tetrad be added up according to the
progression of number, the number ten appears.
For one, and two, and three, and four, when
added together, form ten; and this, as they will
have it, is Jesus. Moreover, Chreistus, he says,
being a word of eight letters, indicates the first
Ogdoad, and this, when multiplied by ten, gives
birth to Jesus (888). And Christ the Son, he
says, is also spoken of, that is, the Duodecad.
For the name Son, (υἱός) contains four letters,
and Christ (Chreistus) eight, which, being combined, point out the greatness of the Duodecad.
But, he alleges, before the *Episemon* of this
name appeared, that is Jesus the Son, mankind
were involved in great ignorance and error.
But when this name of six letters was manifested
(the person bearing it clothing Himself in flesh,
that He might come under the apprehension of
man's senses, and having in Himself these six
and twenty-four letters), then, becoming acquainted with Him, they ceased from their ignorance, and passed from death unto life, this name
serving as their guide to the Father of truth.[5]
For the Father of all had resolved to put an end
to ignorance, and to destroy death. But this
abolishing of ignorance was just the knowledge
of Him. And therefore that man (Anthropos)
was chosen according to His will, having been
formed after the image of the [corresponding]
power above.

3. As to the Æons, they proceeded from the
Tetrad, and in that Tetrad were Anthropos and
Ecclesia, Logos and Zoe. The powers, then, he
declares, who emanated from these, generated
that Jesus who appeared upon the earth. The
angel Gabriel took the place of Logos, the Holy
Spirit that of Zoe, the Power of the Highest that
of Anthropos, while the Virgin pointed out the
place of Ecclesia. And thus, by a special dispensation, there was generated by Him, through
Mary, that man, whom, as He passed through
the womb, the Father of all chose to [obtain]
the knowledge of Himself by means of the Word.
And on His coming to the water [of baptism],
there descended on Him, in the form of a dove,

---

[1] Manifestly to be so spelt here, as in the sequel *Chreistus*, for
Christus.
[2] The text is here altogether uncertain, and the meaning obscure.
[3] The reading is exceedingly doubtful: some prefer the number
eighty-eight.

[4] There were, as Harvey here observes, three extraneous characters introduced into the Greek alphabet for the sake of numeration —
the three *episema* for 6, 90, and 900 respectively. The true alphabet,
then, as employed to denote number, included eight units, eight tens,
and eight hundreds.
[5] Or, according to the Greek text, "being as the way to the
Father;" comp. John xiv. 6.

that Being who had formerly ascended on high, and completed the twelfth number, in whom there existed the seed of those who were produced contemporaneously with Himself, and who descended and ascended along with Him. Moreover, he maintains that that power which descended was the seed of the Father, which had in itself both the Father and the Son, as well as that power of Sige which is known by means of them, but cannot be expressed in language, and also all the Æons. And this was that Spirit who spoke by the mouth of Jesus, and who confessed that He was the son of Man as well as revealed the Father, and who, having descended into Jesus, was made one with Him. And he says that the Saviour formed by special dispensation did indeed destroy death, but that Christ made known the Father.[1] He maintains, therefore, that Jesus is the name of that man formed by a special dispensation, and that He was formed after the likeness and form of that [heavenly] Anthropos, who was about to descend upon Him. After He had received that Æon, He possessed Anthropos himself, and Logos himself, and Pater, and Arrhetus, and Sige, and Aletheia, and Ecclesia, and Zoe.

4. Such ravings, we may now well say, go beyond *Iu, Iu, Pheu, Pheu,* and every kind of tragic exclamation or utterance of misery.[2] For who would not detest one who is the wretched contriver of such audacious falsehoods, when he perceives the truth turned by Marcus into a mere image, and that punctured all over with the letters of the alphabet? The Greeks confess that they first received sixteen letters from Cadmus, and that but recently, as compared with the beginning, [the vast antiquity of which is implied] in the common proverb: "Yesterday and before;"[3] and afterwards, in the course of time, they themselves invented at one period the aspirates, and at another the double letters, while, last of all, they say Palamedes added the long letters to the former. Was it so, then, that until these things took place among the Greeks, truth had no existence? For, according to thee, Marcus, the body of truth is posterior to Cadmus and those who preceded him — posterior also to those who added the rest of the letters — posterior even to thyself! For thou alone hast formed that which is called by thee the truth into an [outward, visible] image.

5. But who will tolerate thy nonsensical Sige, who names Him that cannot be named, and expounds the nature of Him that is unspeakable, and searches out Him that is unsearchable, and declares that He whom thou maintainest to be

destitute of body and form, opened His mouth and sent forth the Word, as if He were included among organized beings; and that His Word, while like to His Author, and bearing the image of the invisible, nevertheless consisted of thirty elements and four syllables? It will follow, then, according to thy theory, that the Father of all, in accordance with the likeness of the Word, consists of thirty elements and four syllables! Or, again, who will tolerate thee in thy juggling with forms and numbers, — at one time thirty, at another twenty-four, and at another, again, only six, — whilst thou shuttest up [in these] the Word of God, the Founder, and Framer, and Maker of all things; and then, again, cutting Him up piecemeal into four syllables and thirty elements; and bringing down the Lord of all who founded the heavens to the number eight hundred and eighty-eight, so that He should be similar to the alphabet; and subdividing the Father, who cannot be contained, but contains all things, into a Tetrad, and an Ogdoad, and a Decad, and a Duodecad; and by such multiplications, setting forth the unspeakable and inconceivable nature of the Father, as thou thyself declarest it to be? And showing thyself a very Dædalus for evil invention, and the wicked architect of the supreme power, thou dost construct a nature and substance for Him whom thou callest incorporeal and immaterial, out of a multitude of letters, generated the one by the other. And that power whom thou affirmest to be indivisible, thou dost nevertheless divide into consonants, and vowels, and semivowels; and, falsely ascribing those letters which are mute to the Father of all things, and to His Ennœa (thought), thou hast driven on all that place confidence in thee to the highest point of blasphemy, and to the grossest impiety.[4]

6. With good reason, therefore, and very fittingly, in reference to thy rash attempt, has that divine elder[5] and preacher of the truth burst forth in verse against thee as follows: —

"Marcus, thou former of idols, inspector of portents,
Skill'd in consulting the stars, and deep in the black arts of magic,
Ever by tricks such as these confirming the doctrines of error,
Furnishing signs unto those involved by thee in deception,
Wonders of power that is utterly severed from God and apostate,
Which Satan, thy true father, enables thee still to accomplish,
By means of Azazel, that fallen and yet mighty angel,—
Thus making thee the precursor of his own impious actions."

Such are the words of the saintly elder. And I shall endeavour to state the remainder of their mystical system, which runs out to great length, in brief compass, and to bring to the light what

---

[1] The text is here uncertain: we follow that suggested by Grabe.
[2] [Comp. cap. xi. 4, *supra.*]
[3] Comp. Gen. xxxi. 2. — We here follow the punctuation of Scaliger, now generally accepted by the editors, though entirely different from the old Latin.

[4] [Mosheim thinks this Marcus was a lunatic.]
[5] [Some think Pothinus.]

has for a long time been concealed. For in this way such things will become easily susceptible of exposure by all.

CHAP. XVI. — ABSURD INTERPRETATIONS OF THE MARCOSIANS.

1. Blending in one the production of their own Æons, and the straying and recovery of the sheep [spoken of in the Gospel [1]], these persons endeavour to set forth things in a more mystical style, while they refer everything to numbers, maintaining that the universe has been formed out of a Monad and a Dyad. And then, reckoning from unity on to four, they thus generate the Decad. For when one, two, three, and four are added together, they give rise to the number of the ten Æons. And, again, the Dyad advancing from itself [by twos] up to six — two, and four, and six — brings out the Duodecad. Once more, if we reckon in the same way up to ten, the number thirty appears, in which are found eight, and ten, and twelve. They therefore term the Duodecad — because it contains the Episemon,[2] and because the Episemon [so to speak] waits upon it — the passion. And for this reason, because an error occurred in connection with the twelfth number,[3] the sheep frisked off, and went astray; for they assert that a defection took place from the Duodecad. In the same way they oracularly declare, that one power having departed also from the Duodecad, has perished; and this was represented by the woman who lost the drachma,[4] and, lighting a lamp, again found it. Thus, therefore, the numbers that were left, viz., nine, as respects the pieces of money, and eleven in regard to the sheep,[5] when multiplied together, give birth to the number ninety-nine, for nine times eleven are ninety-nine. Wherefore also they maintain the word " Amen " contains this number.

2. I will not, however, weary thee by recounting their other interpretations, that you may perceive the results everywhere. They maintain, for instance, that the letter *Eta* (η) along with the *Episemon* (ς) constitutes an Ogdoad, inasmuch as it occupies the eighth place from the first letter. Then, again, without the *Episemon*, reckoning the number of the letters, and adding them up till we come to *Eta*, they bring out the Triacontad. For if one begins at *Alpha* and ends with *Eta*, omitting the *Episemon*, and adds together the value of the letters in succession, he will find their number altogether to amount to thirty. For up to *Epsilon* (ε) fifteen are formed ;

then adding seven to that number, the sum of twenty-two is reached. Next, *Eta* being added to these, since its value is eight, the most wonderful Triacontad is completed. And hence they give forth that the Ogdoad is the mother of the thirty Æons. Since, therefore, the number thirty is composed of three powers [the Ogdoad, Decad, and Duodecad], when multiplied by three, it produces ninety, for three times thirty are ninety. Likewise this Triad, when multiplied by itself, gives rise to nine. Thus the Ogdoad generates, by these means, ninety-nine. And since the twelfth Æon, by her defection, left eleven in the heights above, they maintain that therefore the position of the letters is a true co-ordinate of the method of their calculation [6] (for Lambda is the eleventh in order among the letters, and represents the number thirty), and also forms a representation of the arrangement of affairs above, since, on from Alpha, omitting *Episemon*, the number of the letters up to Lambda, when added together according to the successive value of the letters, and including *Lambda* itself, forms the sum of ninety-nine ; but that this *Lambda*, being the eleventh in order, descended to seek after one equal to itself, so as to complete the number of twelve letters, and when it found such a one, the number was completed, is manifest from the very configuration of the letter ; for *Lambda* being engaged, as it were, in the quest of one similar to itself, and finding such an one, and clasping it to itself, thus filled up the place of the twelfth, the letter *Mu* (M) being composed of two *Lambdas* (ΛΛ). Wherefore also they, by means of their " knowledge," avoid the place of ninety-nine, that is, the defection — a type of the left hand,[7] — but endeavour to secure *one* more, which, when added to the ninety and nine, has the effect of changing their reckoning to the right hand.

3. I well know, my dear friend, that when thou hast read through all this, thou wilt indulge in a hearty laugh over this their inflated wise folly ! But those men are really worthy of being mourned over, who promulgate such a kind of religion, and who so frigidly and perversely pull to pieces the greatness of the truly unspeakable power, and the dispensations of God in themselves so striking, by means of Alpha and Beta, and through the aid of numbers. But as many as separate from the Church, and give heed to such old wives' fables as these, are truly self-condemned ; and these men Paul commands us, " after a first and second admonition, to avoid." [8]

---

[1] Luke xv. 4.
[2] All the editors, Grabe, Massuet, Stieren, and Harvey, differ as to the text and interpretation of this sentence. We have given what seems the simplest rendering of the text as it stands.
[3] Referring to the last of the twelve Æons.
[4] Luke xv. 8.
[5] Meaning the Æon who left the Duodecad, when eleven remained, and not referring to the lost sheep of the parable.

[6] Harvey gives the above paraphrase of the very obscure original; others propose to read λ′ instead of λόγου.
[7] Massuet explains this and the following reference, by remarking that the ancients used the fingers of the hand in counting: by the left hand they indicated all the numbers below a hundred, but by the right hand all above that sum. — Comp. Juvenal, *Sat.*, x. 249.
[8] Tit. iii. 10.

And John, the disciple of the Lord, has intensified their condemnation, when he desires us not even to address to them the salutation of " good-speed ; " for, says he, " He that bids them be of good-speed is a partaker with their evil deeds ; " [1] and that with reason, " for there is no good-speed to the ungodly," [2] saith the LORD. Impious indeed, beyond all impiety, are these men, who assert that the Maker of heaven and earth, the only God Almighty, besides whom there is no God, was produced by means of a defect, which itself sprang from another defect, so that, according to them, He was the product of the third defect.[3] Such an opinion we should detest and execrate, while we ought everywhere to flee far apart from those that hold it ; and in proportion as they vehemently maintain and rejoice in their fictitious doctrines, so much the more should we be convinced that they are under the influence of the wicked spirits of the Ogdoad, — just as those persons who fall into a fit of frenzy, the more they laugh, and imagine themselves to be well, and do all things as if they were in good health [both of body and mind], yea, some things better than those who really are so, are only thus shown to be the more seriously diseased. In like manner do these men, the more they seem to excel others in wisdom, and waste their strength by drawing the bow too tightly,[4] the greater fools do they show themselves. For when the unclean spirit of folly has gone forth, and when afterwards he finds them not waiting upon God, but occupied with mere worldly questions, then, " taking seven other spirits more wicked than himself," [5] and inflating the minds of these men with the notion of their being able to conceive of something beyond God, and having fitly prepared them for the reception of deceit, he implants within them the Ogdoad of the foolish spirits of wickedness.

CHAP. XVII. — THE THEORY OF THE MARCOSIANS, THAT CREATED THINGS WERE MADE AFTER THE IMAGE OF THINGS INVISIBLE.

1. I wish also to explain to thee their theory as to the way in which the creation itself was formed through the mother by the Demiurge (as it were without his knowledge), after the image of things invisible. They maintain, then, that first of all the four elements, fire, water, earth, and air, were produced after the image of the primary Tetrad above, and that then, if we add their operations, viz., heat, cold, dryness, and humidity, an exact likeness of the Ogdoad

is presented. They next reckon up ten powers in the following manner : — There are seven globular bodies, which they also call heavens ; then that globular body which contains these, which also they name the eighth heaven ; and, in addition to these, the sun and moon. These, being ten in number, they declare to be types of the invisible Decad, which proceeded from Logos and Zoe. As to the Duodecad, it is indicated by the zodiacal circle, as it is called ; for they affirm that the twelve signs do most manifestly shadow forth the Duodecad, the daughter of Anthropos and Ecclesia. And since the highest heaven, bearing upon the very sphere [of the seventh heaven], has been linked with the most rapid precession of the whole system, as a check, and balancing that system with its own gravity, so that it completes the cycle from sign to sign in thirty years, — they say that this is an image of Horus, encircling their thirty-named mother.[6] And then, again, as the moon travels through her allotted space of heaven in thirty days, they hold, that by these days she expresses the number of the thirty Æons. The sun also, who runs through his orbit in twelve months, and then returns to the same point in the circle, makes the Duodecad manifest by these twelve months ; and the days, as being measured by twelve hours, are a type of the invisible Duodecad. Moreover, they declare that the hour, which is the twelfth part of the day, is composed [7] of thirty parts, in order to set forth the image of the Triacontad. Also the circumference of the zodiacal circle itself contains three hundred and sixty degrees (for each of its signs comprises thirty) ; and thus also they affirm, that by means of this circle an image is preserved of that connection which exists between the twelve and the thirty. Still further, asserting that the earth is divided into twelve zones, and that in each zone it receives power from the heavens, according to the perpendicular [position of the sun above it], bringing forth productions corresponding to that power which sends down its influence upon it, they maintain that this is a most evident type of the Duodecad and its offspring.

2. In addition to these things, they declare that the Demiurge, desiring to imitate the infinitude, and eternity, and immensity, and freedom from all measurement by time of the Ogdoad above, but, as he was the fruit of defect, being unable to express its permanence and eternity, had recourse to the expedient of spreading out its eternity into times, and seasons, and vast numbers of years, imagining, that by the multitude of such times he might imitate its immen-

---

[1] 2 John 10, 11.
[2] Isa. xlviii. 22.
[3] The Demiurge being the fruit of the abortive conversion of the abortive passion of Achamoth, who, again, was the abortive issue of Sophia.
[4] i.e., by aiming at what transcends their ability, they fall into absurdity, as a bow is broken by bending it too far.
[5] Matt. xii. 43.

[6] Such is the translation which Harvey, following the text preserved by Hippolytus, gives of the above intricate and obscure sentence.
[7] Literally, "is adorned with."

sity. They declare further, that the truth having escaped him, he followed that which was false, and that, for this reason, when the times are fulfilled, his work shall perish.

CHAP. XVIII. — PASSAGES FROM MOSES, WHICH THE HERETICS PERVERT TO THE SUPPORT OF THEIR HYPOTHESIS.

1. And while they affirm such things as these concerning the creation, every one of them generates something new, day by day, according to his ability; for no one is deemed "perfect," who does not develop among them some mighty fictions. It is thus necessary, first, to indicate what things they metamorphose [to their own use] out of the prophetical writings, and next, to refute them. Moses, then, they declare, by his mode of beginning the account of the creation, has at the commencement pointed out the mother of all things when he says, " In the beginning God created the heaven and the earth ;" [1] for, as they maintain, by naming these four, — God, beginning, heaven, and earth, — he set forth their Tetrad. Indicating also its invisible and hidden nature, he said, " Now the earth was invisible and unformed." [2] They will have it, moreover, that he spoke of the second Tetrad, the offspring of the first, in this way — by naming an abyss and darkness, in which were also water, and the Spirit moving upon the water. Then, proceeding to mention the Decad, he names light, day, night, the firmament, the evening, the morning, dry land, sea, plants, and, in the tenth place, trees. Thus, by means of these ten names, he indicated the ten Æons. The power of the Duodecad, again, was shadowed forth by him thus : — He names the sun, moon, stars, seasons, years, whales, fishes, reptiles, birds, quadrupeds, wild beasts, and after all these, in the twelfth place, man. Thus they teach that the Triacontad was spoken of through Moses by the Spirit. Moreover, man also, being formed after the image of the power above, had in himself that ability which flows from the one source. This ability was seated in the region of the brain, from which four faculties proceed, after the image of the Tetrad above, and these are called : the first, *sight*, the second, *hearing*, the third, *smell*, and the fourth,[3] *taste*. And they say that the Ogdoad is indicated by man in this way : that he possesses two ears, the like number of eyes, also two nostrils, and a twofold taste, namely, of bitter and sweet. Moreover, they teach that the whole man contains the entire image of the Triacontad as follows : In his hands, by means of his fingers, he bears the

Decad ; and in his whole body the Duodecad, inasmuch as his body is divided into twelve members ; for they portion that out, as the body of Truth is divided by them — a point of which we have already spoken.[4] But the Ogdoad, as being unspeakable and invisible, is understood as hidden in the viscera.

2. Again, they assert that the sun, the great light-giver, was formed on the fourth day, with a reference to the number of the Tetrad. So also, according to them, the courts [5] of the tabernacle constructed by Moses, being composed of fine linen, and blue, and purple, and scarlet, pointed to the same image. Moreover, they maintain that the long robe of the priest falling over his feet, as being adorned with four rows of precious stones,[6] indicates the Tetrad ; and if there are any other things in the Scriptures which can possibly be dragged into the number *four*, they declare that these had their being with a view to the Tetrad. The Ogdoad, again, was shown as follows : — They affirm that man was formed on the eighth day, for sometimes they will have him to have been made on the sixth day, and sometimes on the eighth, unless, perchance, they mean that his earthly part was formed on the sixth day, but his fleshly part on the eighth, for these two things are distinguished by them. Some of them also hold that one man was formed after the image and likeness of God, masculo-feminine, and that this was the spiritual man ; and that another man was formed out of the earth.

3. Further, they declare that the arrangement made with respect to the ark in the Deluge, by means of which eight persons were saved,[7] most clearly indicates the Ogdoad which brings salvation. David also shows forth the same, as holding the eighth place in point of age among his brethren.[8] Moreover, that circumcision which took place on the eighth day,[9] represented the circumcision of the Ogdoad above. In a word, whatever they find in the Scriptures capable of being referred to the number *eight*, they declare to fulfil the mystery of the Ogdoad. With respect, again, to the Decad, they maintain that it is indicated by those ten nations which God promised to Abraham for a possession.[10] The arrangement also made by Sarah when, after ten years, she gave [11] her handmaid Hagar to him, that by her he might have a son, showed the same thing. Moreover, the servant of Abraham who was sent to Rebekah, and presented her at the well with ten bracelets of gold, and her

---

[1] Gen. i. 1.
[2] Gen. i. 2.
[3] One of the senses was thus capriciously cancelled by these heretics.

[4] See above, chap. xiv. 2.
[5] Or, rather, perhaps " curtains." Ex. xxvi. 1.
[6] Ex. xxviii. 17.
[7] Gen. vi. 18; 1 Pet. iii. 20.
[8] 1 Sam. xvi. 10.
[9] Gen. xvii. 12.
[10] Gen. xv. 19.
[11] Gen. xvi. 2.

brethren who detained her for ten days ;[1] Jeroboam also, who received the ten sceptres[2] (tribes), and the ten courts[3] of the tabernacle, and the columns of ten cubits[4] [high], and the ten sons of Jacob who were at first sent into Egypt to buy corn,[5] and the ten apostles to whom the Lord appeared after His resurrection, — Thomas[6] being absent, — represented, according to them, the invisible Decad.

4. As to the Duodecad, in connection with which the mystery of the passion of the defect occurred, from which passion they maintain that all things visible were framed, they assert that is to be found strikingly and manifestly everywhere [in Scripture]. For they declare that the twelve sons of Jacob,[7] from whom also sprung twelve tribes, — the breastplate of the high priest, which bore twelve precious stones and twelve little bells,[8] — the twelve stones which were placed by Moses at the foot of the mountain,[9] — the same number which was placed by Joshua in the river,[10] and again, on the other side, the bearers of the ark of the covenant,[11] — those stones which were set up by Elijah when the heifer was offered as a burnt-offering ;[12] the number, too, of the apostles ; and, in fine, every event which embraces in it the number *twelve*, — set forth their Duodecad. And then the union of all these, which is called the Triacontad, they strenuously endeavour to demonstrate by the ark of Noah, the height of which was thirty cubits ;[13] by the case of Samuel, who assigned Saul the chief place among thirty guests ;[14] by David, when for thirty days he concealed himself in the field ;[15] by those who entered along with him into the cave ; also by the fact that the length (height) of the holy tabernacle was thirty cubits ;[16] and if they meet with any other like numbers, they still apply these to their Triacontad.

CHAP. XIX. — PASSAGES OF SCRIPTURE BY WHICH THEY ATTEMPT TO PROVE THAT THE SUPREME FATHER WAS UNKNOWN BEFORE THE COMING OF CHRIST.

1. I judge it necessary to add to these details also what, by garbling passages of Scripture, they try to persuade us concerning their Propa-

tor, who was unknown to all before the coming of Christ. Their object in this is to show that our Lord announced another Father than the Maker of this universe, whom, as we said before, they impiously declare to have been the fruit of a defect. For instance, when the prophet Isaiah says, " But Israel hath not known Me, and My people have not understood Me,"[17] they pervert his words to mean ignorance of the invisible Bythus. And that which is spoken by Hosea, " There is no truth in them, nor the knowledge of God,"[18] they strive to give the same reference. And, " There is none that understandeth, or that seeketh after God : they have all gone out of the way, they are together become unprofitable,"[19] they maintain to be said concerning ignorance of Bythus. Also that which is spoken by Moses, " No man shall see God and live,"[20] has, as they would persuade us, the same reference.

2. For they falsely hold, that the Creator was seen by the prophets. But this passage, " No man shall see God and live," they would interpret as spoken of His greatness unseen and unknown by all ; and indeed that these words, " No man shall see God," are spoken concerning the invisible Father, the Maker of the universe, is evident to us all ; but that they are not used concerning that Bythus whom they conjure into existence, but concerning the Creator (and He is the invisible God), shall be shown as we proceed. They maintain that Daniel also set forth the same thing when he begged of the angels explanations of the parables, as being himself ignorant of them. But the angel, hiding from him the great mystery of Bythus, said unto him, " Go thy way quickly, Daniel, for these sayings are closed up until those who have understanding do understand them, and those who are white be made white."[21] Moreover, they vaunt themselves as being the *white* and the men of *good understanding.*

CHAP. XX. — THE APOCRYPHAL AND SPURIOUS SCRIPTURES OF THE MARCOSIANS, WITH PASSAGES OF THE GOSPELS WHICH THEY PERVERT.

1. Besides the above [misrepresentations], they adduce an unspeakable number of apocryphal and spurious writings, which they themselves have forged, to bewilder the minds of foolish men, and of such as are ignorant of the Scriptures of truth. Among other things, they bring forward that false and wicked story[22] which

---

[1] Gen. xxiv. 22, 25.
[2] 1 Kings xi. 31.
[3] Ex. xxvi. 1, xxxvi. 8.
[4] Ex. xxxvi. 21.
[5] Gen. xlii. 3.
[6] John xx. 24.
[7] Gen. xxxv. 22, xlix. 28.
[8] Ex. xxviii. 2. — There is no mention of the *number* of the bells in Scripture.
[9] Ex. xxiv. 4.
[10] Josh. iv. 3.
[11] Josh. iii. 12.
[12] 1 Kings xviii. 31.
[13] Gen. vi. 15.
[14] 1 Sam. ix. 22.
[15] 1 Sam. xx. 5.
[16] Ex. xxvi. 8. *Numbers* appear to have been often capriciously introduced by these heretics to give a colour of support to their own theories.

[17] Isa. i. 3.
[18] Hos. iv. 1.
[19] Rom. iii. 11 ; Ps. xiv. 3.
[20] Ex. xxxiii. 20.
[21] Dan. xii. 9, 10. The words in the above quotation not occurring in the Hebrew text of the passage, seem to have been interpolated by these heretics.
[22] [From the *Protevangel of Thomas.* Compare the curious work of Dominic Deodati, *De Christo Græce loquente*, p. 95. London, 1843.]

relates that our Lord, when He was a boy learning His letters, on the teacher saying to Him, as is usual, "Pronounce Alpha," replied [as He was bid], "Alpha." But when, again, the teacher bade Him say, "Beta," the Lord replied, "Do thou first tell me what Alpha is, and then I will tell thee what Beta is." This they expound as meaning that He alone knew the Unknown, which He revealed under its type Alpha.

2. Some passages, also, which occur in the Gospels, receive from them a colouring of the same kind, such as the answer which He gave His mother when He was twelve years of age : "Wist ye not that I must be about My Father's business?"[1] Thus, they say, He announced to them the Father of whom they were ignorant. On this account, also, He sent forth the disciples to the twelve tribes, that they might proclaim to them the unknown God. And to the person who said to Him, "Good Master,"[2] He confessed that God who is truly good, saying, "Why callest thou Me good : there is One who is good, the Father in the heavens;"[3] and they assert that in this passage the Æons receive the name of heavens. Moreover, by His not replying to those who said to Him, "By what power doest Thou this?"[4] but by a question on His own side, put them to utter confusion; by His thus not replying, according to their interpretation, He showed the unutterable nature of the Father. Moreover, when He said, "I have often desired to hear one of these words, and I had no one who could utter it,"[5] they maintain, that by this expression "one" He set forth the one true God whom they knew not. Further, when, as He drew nigh to Jerusalem, He wept over it and said, "If thou hadst known, even thou, in this thy day, the things that belong unto thy peace, but they are hidden from thee,"[6] by this word "hidden" He showed the abstruse nature of Bythus. And again, when He said, "Come unto Me all ye that labour and are heavy laden, and I will give you rest, and learn of Me,"[7] He announced the Father of truth. For what they knew not, these men say that He promised to teach them.

3. But they adduce the following passage as the highest testimony,[8] and, as it were, the very crown of their system : — "I thank Thee, O Father, Lord of heaven and earth, because Thou hast hid these things from the wise and prudent, and hast revealed them to babes. Even so, my Father ; for so it seemed good in Thy sight.

All things have been delivered to Me by My Father ; and no one knoweth the Father but the Son, or the Son but the Father, and he to whom the Son will reveal Him."[9] In these words they affirm that He clearly showed that the Father of truth, conjured into existence by them, was known to no one before His advent. And they desire to construe the passage as if teaching that the Maker and Framer [of the world] was always known by all, while the Lord spoke these words concerning the Father unknown to all, whom they now proclaim.

CHAP. XXI. — THE VIEWS OF REDEMPTION ENTERTAINED BY THESE HERETICS.

1. It happens that their tradition respecting *redemption*[10] is invisible and incomprehensible, as being the mother of things which are incomprehensible and invisible ; and on this account, since it is fluctuating, it is impossible simply and all at once to make known its nature, for every one of them hands it down just as his own inclination prompts. Thus there are as many schemes of "redemption" as there are teachers of these mystical opinions. And when we come to refute them, we shall show in its fitting-place, that this class of men have been instigated by Satan to a denial of that baptism which is regeneration to God, and thus to a renunciation of the whole [Christian] faith.

2. They maintain that those who have attained to perfect knowledge must of necessity be regenerated into that power which is above all. For it is otherwise impossible to find admittance within the Pleroma, since this [regeneration] it is which leads them down into the depths of Bythus. For the baptism instituted by the visible Jesus was for the remission of sins, but the redemption brought in by that Christ who descended upon Him, was for perfection ; and they allege that the former is animal, but the latter spiritual. And the baptism of John was proclaimed with a view to repentance, but the redemption by Jesus[11] was brought in for the sake of perfection. And to this He refers when He says, "And I have another baptism to be baptized with, and I hasten eagerly towards it."[12] Moreover, they affirm that the Lord added this redemption to the sons of Zebedee, when their mother asked that they might sit, the one on His right hand, and the other on His left, in His kingdom, saying, "Can ye be baptized with the baptism which I shall be baptized with?"[13] Paul, too, they declare, has often set forth, in express terms, the redemption which is in Christ

---

1 Luke ii. 49.
2 Mark x. 17.
3 Luke xviii. 18.
4 Matt. xxi. 23.
5 Taken from some apocryphal writing.
6 Luke xix. 42, loosely quoted.
7 Matt. xi. 28.
8 The translator evidently read τῶν for τήν, in which case the rendering will be "proof of those most high," but the Greek text seems preferable.

9 Matt. xi. 25–27.
10 Comp. chap. xiii. 6.
11 The Latin reads "Christ."
12 Luke xii. 50. The text was probably thus corrupted by the heretics.
13 Mark x. 38.

Jesus ; and this was the same which is handed down by them in so varied and discordant forms.

3. For some of them prepare a nuptial couch, and perform a sort of mystic rite (pronouncing certain expressions) with those who are being initiated, and affirm that it is a spiritual marriage which is celebrated by them, after the likeness of the conjunctions above. Others, again, lead them to a place where water is, and baptize them, with the utterance of these words, " Into the name of the unknown Father of the universe — into truth, the mother of all things — into Him who descended on Jesus — into union, and redemption, and communion with the powers." Others still repeat certain Hebrew words, in order the more thoroughly to bewilder those who are being initiated, as follows : " Basema, Chamosse, Baœnaora, Mistadia, Ruada, Kousta, Babaphor, Kalachthei." [1] The interpretation of these terms runs thus : " I invoke that which is above every power of the Father, which is called light, and good Spirit, and life, because Thou hast reigned in the body." Others, again, set forth the redemption thus : The name which is hidden from every deity, and dominion, and truth, which Jesus of Nazareth was clothed with in the lives [2] of the light of Christ — of Christ, who lives by the Holy Ghost, for the angelic redemption. The name of restitution stands thus : Messia, Uphareg, Namempsœman, Chaldœaur, Mosomedœa, Acphranœ, Psaua, Jesus Nazaria.[3] The interpretation of these words is as follows : " I do not divide the Spirit of Christ, neither the heart nor the supercelestial power which is merciful ; may I enjoy Thy name, O Saviour of truth ! " Such are words of the initiators ; but he who is initiated, replies, " I am established, and I am redeemed ; I redeem my soul from this age (world), and from all things connected with it in the name of Iao, who redeemed his own soul into redemption in Christ who liveth." Then the bystanders add these words, " Peace be to all on whom this name rests." After this they anoint the initiated person with balsam ; for they assert that this unguent is a type of that sweet odour which is above all things.

4. But there are some of them who assert that it is superfluous to bring persons to the water, but mixing oil and water together, they place this mixture on the heads of those who are to be initiated, with the use of some such expressions as we have already mentioned. And this they maintain to be the redemption. They, too, are accustomed to anoint with balsam. Others, however, reject all these practices, and maintain that the mystery of the unspeakable and invisible power ought not to be performed by visible and corruptible creatures, nor should that of those [beings] who are inconceivable, and incorporeal, and beyond the reach of sense, [be performed] by such as are the objects of sense, and possessed of a body. These hold that the knowledge of the unspeakable Greatness is itself perfect redemption. For since both defect and passion flowed from ignorance, the whole substance of what was thus formed is destroyed by knowledge ; and therefore knowledge is the redemption of the inner man. This, however, is not of a corporeal nature, for the body is corruptible ; nor is it animal, since the animal soul is the fruit of a defect, and is, as it were, the abode of the spirit. The redemption must therefore be of a spiritual nature ; for they affirm that the inner and spiritual man is redeemed by means of knowledge, and that they, having acquired the knowledge of all things, stand thenceforth in need of nothing else. This, then, is the true redemption.

5. Others still there are who continue to redeem persons even up to the moment of death, by placing on their heads oil and water, or the pre-mentioned ointment with water, using at the same time the above-named invocations, that the persons referred to may become incapable of being seized or seen by the principalities and powers, and that their inner man may ascend on high in an invisible manner, as if their body were left among created things in this world, while their soul is sent forward to the Demiurge. And they instruct them, on their reaching the principalities and powers, to make use of these words : " I am a son from the Father — the Father who had a pre-existence, and a son in Him who is pre-existent. I have come to behold all things, both those which belong to myself and others, although, strictly speaking, they do not belong to others, but to Achamoth, who is female in nature, and made these things for herself. For I derive being from Him who is pre-existent, and I come again to my own place whence I went forth." And they affirm that, by saying these things, he escapes from the powers. He then advances to the companions of the Demiurge, and thus addresses them : — " I am a vessel more precious than the female who formed you. If your mother is ignorant of her own descent, I know myself, and am aware whence I am, and I call upon the incorruptible Sophia, who is in the Father, and is the mother of your mother, who has no father, nor any male consort ; but a female springing from a female formed you, while ignorant of her own mother, and imagining that she alone existed ; but I call upon her mother." And they declare, that when the companions of the Demiurge hear these words, they are greatly agitated, and upbraid their origin and the race of their mother. But he goes into his own place, having

---

[1] We have given these words as they stand in the Greek text: a very different list, but equally unmeaning, is found in the Latin.
[2] The Latin reads *zonis*, " zones," instead of " lives," as in the Greek.
[3] Here, again, are many variations.

thrown [off] his chain, that is, his animal nature. These, then, are the particulars which have reached us respecting "redemption."[1] But since they differ so widely among themselves both as respects doctrine and tradition, and since those of them who are recognised as being most modern make it their effort daily to invent some new opinion, and to bring out what no one ever before thought of, it is a difficult matter to describe all their opinions.

CHAP. XXII. — DEVIATIONS OF HERETICS FROM THE TRUTH.

1. The rule[2] of truth which we hold, is, that there is one God Almighty, who made all things by His Word, and fashioned and formed, out of that which had no existence, all things which exist. Thus saith the Scripture, to that effect: "By the Word of the Lord were the heavens established, and all the might of them, by the spirit of His mouth."[3] And again, "All things were made by Him, and without Him was nothing made."[4] There is no exception or deduction stated; but the Father made all things by Him, whether visible or invisible, objects of sense or of intelligence, temporal, on account of a certain character given them, or eternal; and these eternal[5] things He did not make by angels, or by any powers separated from His Ennœa. For God needs none of all these things, but is He who, by His Word and Spirit, makes, and disposes, and governs all things, and commands all things into existence, — He who formed the world (for the world is of all), — He who fashioned man, — He [who][6] is the God of Abraham, and the God of Isaac, and the God of Jacob, above whom there is no other God, nor initial principle, nor power, nor pleroma, — He is the Father of our Lord Jesus Christ, as we shall prove. Holding, therefore, this rule, we shall easily show, notwithstanding the great variety and multitude of their opinions, that these men have deviated from the truth; for almost all the different sects of heretics admit that there is one God; but then, by their pernicious doctrines, they change [this truth into error], even as the Gentiles do through idolatry, — thus proving themselves ungrateful to Him that created them. Moreover, they despise the workmanship of God, speaking against their own salvation, becoming

their own bitterest accusers, and being false witnesses [against themselves]. Yet, reluctant as they may be, these men shall one day rise again in the flesh, to confess the power of Him who raises them from the dead; but they shall not be numbered among the righteous on account of their unbelief.

2. Since, therefore, it is a complex and multiform task to detect and convict all the heretics, and since our design is to reply to them all according to their special characters, we have judged it necessary, first of all, to give an account of their source and root, in order that, by getting a knowledge of their most exalted Bythus, thou mayest understand the nature of the tree which has produced such fruits.

CHAP. XXIII. — DOCTRINES AND PRACTICES OF SIMON MAGUS AND MENANDER.

1. Simon the Samaritan was that magician of whom Luke, the disciple and follower of the apostles, says, "But there was a certain man, Simon by name, who beforetime used magical arts in that city, and led astray the people of Samaria, declaring that he himself was some great one, to whom they all gave heed, from the least to the greatest, saying, This is the power of God, which is called great. And to him they had regard, because that of long time he had driven them mad by his sorceries."[7] This Simon, then — who feigned faith, supposing that the apostles themselves performed their cures by the art of magic, and not by the power of God; and with respect to their filling with the Holy Ghost, through the imposition of hands, those that believed in God through Him who was preached by them, namely, Christ Jesus — suspecting that even this was done through a kind of greater knowledge of magic, and offering money to the apostles, thought he, too, might receive this power of bestowing the Holy Spirit on whomsoever he would, — was addressed in these words by Peter: "Thy money perish with thee, because thou hast thought that the gift of God can be purchased with money: thou hast neither part nor lot in this matter, for thy heart is not right in the sight of God; for I perceive that thou art in the gall of bitterness, and in the bond of iniquity."[8] He, then, not putting faith in God a whit the more, set himself eagerly to contend against the apostles, in order that he himself might seem to be a wonderful being, and applied himself with still greater zeal to the study of the whole magic art, that he might the better bewilder and overpower multitudes of men. Such was his procedure in the reign of Claudius Cæsar, by whom also he is said to have been honoured with a statue, on account of his

---

[1] The Greek text, which has hitherto been preserved almost entire, ends at this point. With only brief extracts from the original, now and then, we are henceforth exclusively dependent on the old Latin version, with some Syriac and Armenian fragments recently discovered.
[2] The Latin here begins with the words "cum teneamus," and the apodosis is found afterwards at "facile arguimus." But we have broken up the one long sentence into several.
[3] Ps. xxxiii. 6.
[4] John i. 3.
[5] The text is here uncertain and obscure: eternal things seem to be referred to, not as regarded *substance*, but the *forms* assigned them.
[6] This word would perhaps be better cancelled.
[7] Acts viii. 9–11.
[8] Acts viii. 20, 21, 23.

magical power.[1] This man, then, was glorified by many as if he were a god; and he taught that it was himself who appeared among the Jews as the Son, but descended in Samaria as the Father, while he came to other nations in the character of the Holy Spirit. He represented himself, in a word, as being the loftiest of all powers, that is, the Being who is the Father over all, and he allowed himself to be called by whatsoever title men were pleased to address him.

2. Now this Simon of Samaria, from whom all sorts of heresies derive their origin, formed his sect out of the following materials: — Having redeemed from slavery at Tyre, a city of Phœnicia, a certain woman named Helena, he was in the habit of carrying her about with him, declaring that this woman was the first conception of his mind, the mother of all, by whom, in the beginning, he conceived in his mind [the thought] of forming angels and archangels. For this Ennœa leaping forth from him, and comprehending the will of her father, descended to the lower regions [of space], and generated angels and powers, by whom also he declared this world was formed. But after she had produced them, she was detained by them through motives of jealousy, because they were unwilling to be looked upon as the progeny of any other being. As to himself, they had no knowledge of him whatever; but his Ennœa was detained by those powers and angels who had been produced by her. She suffered all kinds of contumely from them, so that she could not return upwards to her father, but was even shut up in a human body, and for ages passed in succession from one female body to another, as from vessel to vessel. She was, for example, in that Helen on whose account the Trojan war was undertaken; for whose sake also Stesichorus[2] was struck blind, because he had cursed her in his verses, but afterwards, repenting and writing what are called *palinodes*, in which he sang her praise, he was restored to sight. Thus she, passing from body to body, and suffering insults in every one of them, at last became a common prostitute; and she it was that was meant by the lost sheep.[3]

3. For this purpose, then, he had come that he might win her first, and free her from slavery, while he conferred salvation upon men, by making himself known to them. For since the angels ruled the world ill because each one of them coveted the principal power for himself, he had come to amend matters, and had descended, transfigured and assimilated to powers and prin-

cipalities and angels, so that he might appear among men to be a man, while yet he was not a man; and that thus he was thought to have suffered in Judæa, when he had not suffered. Moreover, the prophets uttered their predictions under the inspiration of those angels who formed the world; for which reason those who place their trust in him and Helena no longer regarded them, but, as being free, live as they please; for men are saved through his grace, and not on account of their own righteous actions. For such deeds are not righteous in the nature of things, but by mere accident, just as those angels who made the world, have thought fit to constitute them, seeking, by means of such precepts, to bring men into bondage. On this account, he pledged himself that the world should be dissolved, and that those who are his should be freed from the rule of them who made the world.

4. Thus, then, the mystic priests belonging to this sect both lead profligate lives and practise magical arts, each one to the extent of his ability. They use exorcisms and incantations. Love-potions, too, and charms, as well as those beings who are called "Paredri" (familiars) and "Oniropompi" (dream-senders), and whatever other curious arts can be had recourse to, are eagerly pressed into their service. They also have an image of Simon fashioned after the likeness of Jupiter, and another of Helena in the shape of Minerva; and these they worship. In fine, they have a name derived from Simon, the author of these most impious doctrines, being called Simonians; and from them "knowledge, falsely so called,"[4] received its beginning, as one may learn even from their own assertions.

5. The successor of this man was Menander, also a Samaritan by birth, and he, too, was a perfect adept in the practice of magic. He affirms that the primary Power continues unknown to all, but that he himself is the person who has been sent forth from the presence of the invisible beings as a saviour, for the deliverance of men. The world was made by angels, whom, like Simon, he maintains to have been produced by Ennœa. He gives, too, as he affirms, by means of that magic which he teaches, knowledge to this effect, that one may overcome those very angels that made the world; for his disciples obtain the *resurrection* by being baptized into him, and can die no more, but remain in the possession of immortal youth.

CHAP. XXIV. — DOCTRINES OF SATURNINUS AND BASILIDES.

1. Arising among these men, Saturninus (who was of that Antioch which is near Daphne) and Basilides laid hold of some favourable opportunities, and promulgated different systems of

---

[1] Comp. Just. Mart., *Apol.*, i. 26. It is generally supposed that Simon Magus was thus confounded with the Sabine god, Semo Sancus; but see our note, *loc. cit.* [And mine at end of the First Apology. Consult *Orelli's Inscriptions* there noted.]
[2] A lyric poet of Sicily, said to have been dealt with, as stated above, by Castor and Pollux.
[3] Matt. xviii. 12.

[4] 1 Tim. vi. 20.

doctrine — the one in Syria, the other at Alexandria. Saturninus, like Menander, set forth one father unknown to all, who made angels, archangels, powers, and potentates. The world, again, and all things therein, were made by a certain company of seven angels. Man, too, was the workmanship of angels, a shining image bursting forth below from the presence of the supreme power; and when they could not, he says, keep hold of this, because it immediately darted upwards again, they exhorted each other, saying, "Let us make man after our image and likeness." [1] He was accordingly formed, yet was unable to stand erect, through the inability of the angels to convey to him that power, but wriggled [on the ground] like a worm. Then the power above taking pity upon him, since he was made after his likeness, sent forth a spark of life, which gave man an erect posture, compacted his joints, and made him live. He declares, therefore, that this spark of life, after the death of a man, returns to those things which are of the same nature with itself, and the rest of the body is decomposed into its original elements.

2. He has also laid it down as a truth, that the Saviour was without birth, without body, and without figure, but was, by supposition, a visible man; and he maintained that the God of the Jews was one of the angels; and, on this account, because all the powers wished to annihilate his father, Christ came to destroy the God of the Jews, but to save such as believe in him; that is, those who possess the spark of his life. This heretic was the first to affirm that two kinds of men were formed by the angels, — the one wicked, and the other good. And since the demons assist the most wicked, the Saviour came for the destruction of evil men and of the demons, but for the salvation of the good. They declare also, that marriage and generation are from Satan.[2] Many of those, too, who belong to his school, abstain from animal food, and draw away multitudes by a feigned temperance of this kind. They hold, moreover, that some of the prophecies were uttered by those angels who made the world, and some by Satan; whom Saturninus represents as being himself an angel, the enemy of the creators of the world, but especially of the God of the Jews.

3. Basilides again, that he may appear to have discovered something more sublime and plausible, gives an immense development to his doctrines. He sets forth that Nous was first born of the unborn father, that from him, again, was born Logos, from Logos Phronesis, from Phronesis Sophia and Dynamis, and from Dynamis and Sophia the powers, and principalities, and angels, whom he also calls the *first;* and that

by them the first heaven was made. Then other powers, being formed by emanation from these, created another heaven similar to the first; and in like manner, when others, again, had been formed by emanation from them, corresponding exactly to those above them, these, too, framed another third heaven; and then from this third, in downward order, there was a fourth succession of descendants; and so on, after the same fashion, they declare that more and more principalities and angels were formed, and three hundred and sixty-five heavens.[3] Wherefore the year contains the same number of days in conformity with the number of the heavens.

4. Those angels who occupy the lowest heaven, that, namely, which is visible to us, formed all the things which are in the world, and made allotments among themselves of the earth and of those nations which are upon it. The chief of them is he who is thought to be the God of the Jews; and inasmuch as he desired to render the other nations subject to his own people, that is, the Jews, all the other princes resisted and opposed him. Wherefore all other nations were at enmity with his nation. But the father without birth and without name, perceiving that they would be destroyed, sent his own first-begotten Nous (he it is who is called Christ) to bestow deliverance on them that believe in him, from the power of those who made the world. He appeared, then, on earth as a man, to the nations of these powers, and wrought miracles. Wherefore he did not himself suffer death, but Simon, a certain man of Cyrene, being compelled, bore the cross in his stead; so that this latter being transfigured by him, that he might be thought to be Jesus, was crucified, through ignorance and error, while Jesus himself received the form of Simon, and, standing by, laughed at them. For since he was an incorporeal power, and the Nous (mind) of the unborn father, he transfigured himself as he pleased, and thus ascended to him who had sent him, deriding them, inasmuch as he could not be laid hold of, and was invisible to all. Those, then, who know these things have been freed from the principalities who formed the world; so that it is not incumbent on us to confess him who was crucified, but him who came in the form of a man, and was thought to be crucified, and was called Jesus, and was sent by the father, that by this dispensation he might destroy the works of the makers of the world. If any one, therefore, he declares, confesses the crucified, that man is still a slave, and under the power of those who formed our bodies; but he who denies him has been freed from these beings, and is acquainted with the dispensation of the unborn father.

---

[1] Gen. i. 26.
[2] [1. Tim. iv. 3.]

[3] The ordinary text reads, "three hundred and seventy-five," but it should manifestly be corrected as above.

5. Salvation belongs to the soul alone, for the body is by nature subject to corruption. He declares, too, that the prophecies were derived from those powers who were the makers of the world, but the law was specially given by their chief, who led the people out of the land of Egypt. He attaches no importance to [the question regarding] meats offered in sacrifice to idols, thinks them of no consequence, and makes use of them without any hesitation; he holds also the use of other things, and the practice of every kind of lust, a matter of perfect indifference. These men, moreover, practise magic, and use images, incantations, invocations, and every other kind of curious art. Coining also certain names as if they were those of the angels, they proclaim some of these as belonging to the first, and others to the second heaven; and then they strive to set forth the names, principles, angels, and powers of the three hundred and sixty-five imagined heavens. They also affirm that the barbarous name in which the Saviour ascended and descended, is Caulacau.[1]

6. He, then, who has learned [these things], and known all the angels and their causes, is rendered invisible and incomprehensible to the angels and all the powers, even as Caulacau also was. And as the son was unknown to all, so must they also be known by no one; but while they know all, and pass through all, they themselves remain invisible and unknown to all; for, "Do thou," they say, "know all, but let nobody know thee." For this reason, persons of such a persuasion are also ready to recant [their opinions], yea, rather, it is impossible that they should suffer on account of a mere name, since they are like to all. The multitude, however, cannot understand these matters, but only one out of a thousand, or two out of ten thousand. They declare that they are no longer Jews, and that they are not yet Christians; and that it is not at all fitting to speak openly of their mysteries, but right to keep them secret by preserving silence.

7. They make out the local position of the three hundred and sixty-five heavens in the same way as do mathematicians. For, accepting the theorems of these latter, they have transferred them to their own type of doctrine. They hold that their chief is *Abraxas;*[2] and, on this account, that word contains in itself the numbers amounting to three hundred and sixty-five.

CHAP. XXV. — DOCTRINES OF CARPOCRATES.

1. Carpocrates, again, and his followers maintain that the world and the things which are therein were created by angels greatly inferior to the unbegotten Father. They also hold that Jesus was the son of Joseph, and was just like other men, with the exception that he differed from them in this respect, that inasmuch as his soul was stedfast and pure, he perfectly remembered those things which he had witnessed[3] within the sphere of the unbegotten God. On this account, a power descended upon him from the Father, that by means of it he might escape from the creators of the world; and they say that it, after passing through them all, and remaining in all points free, ascended again to him, and to the powers,[4] which in the same way embraced like things to itself. They further declare, that the soul of Jesus, although educated in the practices of the Jews, regarded these with contempt, and that for this reason he was endowed with faculties, by means of which he destroyed those passions which dwelt in men as a punishment [for their sins].

2. The soul, therefore, which is like that of Christ can despise those rulers who were the creators of the world, and, in like manner, receives power for accomplishing the same results. This idea has raised them to such a pitch of pride, that some of them declare themselves similar to Jesus; while others, still more mighty, maintain that they are superior to his disciples, such as Peter and Paul, and the rest of the apostles, whom they consider to be in no respect inferior to Jesus. For their souls, descending from the same sphere as his, and therefore despising in like manner the creators of the world, are deemed worthy of the same power, and again depart to the same place. But if any one shall have despised the things in this world more than he did, he thus proves himself superior to him.

3. They practise also magical arts and incantations; philters, also, and love-potions; and have recourse to familiar spirits, dream-sending demons, and other abominations, declaring that they possess power to rule over, even now, the princes and formers of this world; and not only them, but also all things that are in it. These men, even as the Gentiles, have been sent forth by Satan[5] to bring dishonour upon the Church, so that, in one way or another, men hearing the things which they speak, and imagining that we all are such as they, may turn away their ears from the preaching of the truth; or, again, seeing the things they practise, may speak evil of

---

[1] This sentence is wholly unintelligible as it stands in the Latin version. Critics differ greatly as to its meaning; Harvey tries to bring out of it something like the translation given above. [This name is manufactured from a curious abuse of (קַו לָקָו) Isaiah xxviii. 10-13, which is variously understood. See (Epiphanius ed. *Oehler*, vol. i.) *Philastr.*, p. 38.]

[2] So written in Latin, but in Greek 'Αβρασάξ, the numerical value of the letters in which is three hundred and sixty-five. [See *Aug.* (ed. *Migne*), vol. viii. p. 26.] It is doubtful to whom or what this word refers; probably to the heavens.

[3] [I note again this "Americanism."]

[4] Such seems to be the meaning of the Latin, but the original text is conjectural.

[5] [See cap. xxvii. 3.]

us all, who have in fact no fellowship with them, either in doctrine or in morals, or in our daily conduct. But they lead a licentious life,[1] and, to conceal their impious doctrines, they abuse the name [of Christ], as a means of hiding their wickedness; so that "their condemnation is just,"[2] when they receive from God a recompense suited to their works.

4. So unbridled is their madness, that they declare they have in their power all things which are irreligious and impious, and are at liberty to practise them; for they maintain that things are evil or good, simply in virtue of human opinion.[3] They deem it necessary, therefore, that by means of transmigration from body to body, souls should have experience of every kind of life as well as every kind of action (unless, indeed, by a single incarnation, one may be able to prevent any need for others, by once for all, and with equal completeness, doing all those things which we dare not either speak or hear of, nay, which we must not even conceive in our thoughts, nor think credible, if any such thing is mooted among those persons who are our fellow-citizens), in order that, as their writings express it, their souls, having made trial of every kind of life, may, at their departure, not be wanting in any particular. It is necessary[4] to insist upon this, lest, on account of some one thing being still wanting to their deliverance, they should be compelled once more to become incarnate. They affirm that for this reason Jesus spoke the following parable: — "Whilst thou art with thine adversary in the way, give all diligence, that thou mayest be delivered from him, lest he give thee up to the judge, and the judge surrender thee to the officer, and he cast thee into prison. Verily, I say unto thee, thou shalt not go out thence until thou pay the very last farthing."[5] They also declare the "adversary" is one of those angels who are in the world, whom they call the Devil, maintaining that he was formed for this purpose, that he might lead those souls which have perished from the world to the Supreme Ruler. They describe him also as being chief among the makers of the world, and maintain that he delivers such souls [as have been mentioned] to another angel, who ministers to him, that he may shut them up in other bodies; for they declare that the body is "the prison." Again, they interpret these expressions, "Thou shalt not go out thence until thou pay the very last farthing," as meaning that no one can escape from the power of those angels

who made the world, but that he must pass from body to body, until he has experience of every kind of action which can be practised in this world, and when nothing is longer wanting to him, then his liberated soul should soar upwards to that God who is above the angels, the makers of the world. In this way also all souls are saved, whether their own which, guarding against all delay, participate in all sorts of actions during one incarnation, or those, again, who, by passing from body to body, are set free, on fulfilling and accomplishing what is requisite in every form of life into which they are sent, so that at length they shall no longer be [shut up] in the body.

5. And thus, if ungodly, unlawful, and forbidden actions are committed among them, I can no longer find ground for believing them to be such.[6] And in their writings we read as follows, the interpretation which they give [of their views], declaring that Jesus spoke in a mystery to His disciples and apostles privately, and that they requested and obtained permission to hand down the things thus taught them, to others who should be worthy and believing. We are saved, indeed, by means of faith and love; but all other things, while in their nature indifferent, are reckoned by the opinion of men — some good and some evil, there being nothing really evil by nature.

6. Others of them employ outward marks, branding their disciples inside the lobe of the right ear. From among these also arose Marcellina, who came to Rome under [the episcopate of] Anicetus, and, holding these doctrines, she led multitudes astray. They style themselves Gnostics. They also possess images, some of them painted, and others formed from different kinds of material; while they maintain that a likeness of Christ was made by Pilate at that time when Jesus lived among them.[7] They crown these images, and set them up along with the images of the philosophers of the world; that is to say, with the images of Pythagoras, and Plato, and Aristotle, and the rest. They have also other modes of honouring these images, after the same manner of the Gentiles.

CHAP. XXVI. — DOCTRINES OF CERINTHUS, THE EBIONITES, AND NICOLAITANES.

1. Cerinthus, again, a man who was educated[8] in the wisdom of the Egyptians, taught that the world was not made by the primary God, but by a certain Power far separated from him, and at a distance from that Principality who is su-

---

[1] The text is here defective, but the above meaning seems to be indicated by Epiphanius.
[2] Rom. iii. 8.
[3] [Isaiah v. 20. Horne Tooke derives our word *Truth* from what any one *troweth*.]
[4] The text here has greatly puzzled the editors. We follow the simple emendation proposed by Harvey.
[5] Matt. v. 25, 26; Luke xii. 58.

[6] The meaning is here very doubtful, but Tertullian understood the words as above. If sinning were a *necessity*, then it could no longer be regarded as evil.
[7] [This censure of images as a Gnostic peculiarity, and as a heathenish corruption, should be noted.]
[8] We here follow the text as preserved by Hippolytus. The Latin has, "a certain man in Asia."

preme over the universe, and ignorant of him who is above all. He represented Jesus as having not been born of a virgin, but as being the son of Joseph and Mary according to the ordinary course of human generation, while he nevertheless was more righteous, prudent, and wise than other men. Moreover, after his baptism, Christ descended upon him in the form of a dove from the Supreme Ruler, and that then he proclaimed the unknown Father, and performed miracles. Bnt at last Christ departed from Jesus, and that then Jesus suffered and rose again, while Christ remained impassible, inasmuch as he was a spiritual being.

2. Those who are called Ebionites agree that the world was made by God ; but their opinions with respect to the Lord are similar to those of Cerinthus and Carpocrates. They use the Gospel according to Matthew only, and repudiate the Apostle Paul, maintaining that he was an apostate from the law. As to the prophetical writings, they endeavour to expound them in a somewhat singular manner : they practise circumcision, persevere in the observance of those customs which are enjoined by the law, and are so Judaic in their style of life, that they even adore Jerusalem as if it were the house of God.

3. The Nicolaitanes are the followers of that Nicolas who was one of the seven first ordained to the diaconate by the apostles.[1] They lead lives of unrestrained indulgence. The character of these men is very plainly pointed out in the Apocalypse of John, [when they are represented] as teaching that it is a matter of indifference to practise adultery, and to eat things sacrificed to idols. Wherefore the Word has also spoken of them thus : " But this thou hast, that thou hatest the deeds of the Nicolaitanes, which I also hate."[2]

CHAP. XXVII. — DOCTRINES OF CERDO AND MARCION.

1. Cerdo was one who took his system from the followers of Simon, and came to live at Rome in the time of Hyginus, who held the ninth place in the episcopal succession from the apostles downwards. He taught that the God proclaimed by the law and the prophets was not the Father of our Lord Jesus Christ. For the former was known, but the latter unknown ; while the one also was righteous, but the other benevolent.

2. Marcion of Pontus succeeded him, and developed his doctrine. In so doing, he advanced the most daring blasphemy against Him who is proclaimed as God by the law and the prophets, declaring Him to be the author of evils, to take delight in war, to be infirm of pur-

pose, and even to be contrary to Himself. But Jesus being derived from that father who is above the God that made the world, and coming into Judæa in the times of Pontius Pilate the governor, who was the procurator of Tiberius Cæsar, was manifested in the form of a man to those who were in Judæa, abolishing the prophets and the law, and all the works of that God who made the world, whom also he calls Cosmocrator. Besides this, he mutilates the Gospel which is according to Luke, removing all that is written respecting the generation of the Lord, and setting aside a great deal of the teaching of the Lord, in which the Lord is recorded as most clearly confessing that the Maker of this universe is His Father. He likewise persuaded his disciples that he himself was more worthy of credit than are those apostles who have handed down the Gospel to us, furnishing them not with the Gospel, but merely a fragment of it. In like manner, too, he dismembered the Epistles of Paul, removing all that is said by the apostle respecting that God who made the world, to the effect that He is the Father of our Lord Jesus Christ, and also those passages from the prophetical writings which the apostle quotes, in order to teach us that they announced beforehand the coming of the Lord.

3. Salvation will be the attainment only of those souls which had learned his doctrine ; while the body, as having been taken from the earth, is incapable of sharing in salvation. In addition to his blasphemy against God Himself, he advanced this also, truly speaking as with the mouth of the devil, and saying all things in direct opposition to the truth, — that Cain, and those like him, and the Sodomites, and the Egyptians, and others like them, and, in fine, all the nations who walked in all sorts of abomination, were saved by the Lord, on His descending into Hades, and on their running unto Him, and that they welcomed Him into their kingdom. But the serpent[3] which was in Marcion declared that Abel, and Enoch, and Noah, and those other righteous men who sprang[4] from the patriarch Abraham, with all the prophets, and those who were pleasing to God, did not partake in salvation. For since these men, he says, knew that their God was constantly tempting them, so now they suspected that He was tempting them, and did not run to Jesus, or believe His announcement : and for this reason he declared that their souls remained in Hades.

4. But since this man is the only one who has dared openly to mutilate the Scriptures, and unblushingly above all others to inveigh against God, I purpose specially to refute him, convict-

---

[1] [This is disputed by other primitive authorities.]
[2] Rev. ii. 6.

[3] [Comp. cap. xxv. 3.]
[4] We here follow the amended version proposed by the Benedictine editor.

ing him out of his own writings; and, with the help of God, I shall overthrow him out of those [1] discourses of the Lord and the apostles, which are of authority with him, and of which he makes use. At present, however, I have simply been led to mention him, that thou mightest know that all those who in any way corrupt the truth, and injuriously affect the preaching of the Church, are the disciples and successors of Simon Magus of Samaria. Although they do not confess the name of their master, in order all the more to seduce others, yet they do teach his doctrines. They set forth, indeed, the name of Christ Jesus as a sort of lure, but in various ways they introduce the impieties of Simon; and thus they destroy multitudes, wickedly disseminating their own doctrines by the use of a good name, and, through means of its sweetness and beauty, extending to their hearers the bitter and malignant poison of the serpent, the great author of apostasy.[2]

CHAP. XXVIII. — DOCTRINES OF TATIAN, THE ENCRATITES, AND OTHERS.

1. Many offshoots of numerous heresies have already been formed from those heretics we have described. This arises from the fact that numbers of them — indeed, we may say all — desire themselves to be teachers, and to break off from the particular heresy in which they have been involved. Forming one set of doctrines out of a totally different system of opinions, and then again others from others, they insist upon teaching something new, declaring themselves the inventors of any sort of opinion which they may have been able to call into existence. To give an example: Springing from Saturninus and Marcion, those who are called Encratites (self-controlled) preached against marriage, thus setting aside the original creation of God, and indirectly blaming Him who made the male and female for the propagation of the human race. Some of those reckoned among them have also introduced abstinence from animal food, thus proving themselves ungrateful to God, who formed all things. They deny, too, the salvation of him who was first created. It is but lately, however, that this opinion has been invented among them. A certain man named Tatian first introduced the blasphemy. He was a hearer of Justin's, and as long as he continued with him he expressed no such views; but after his martyrdom he separated from the Church, and, excited and puffed up by the thought of being a teacher, as if he were superior to others, he composed his own peculiar type of doctrine. He invented a system of certain invisible Æons, like the followers of Valen-

tinus; while, like Marcion and Saturninus, he declared that marriage was nothing else than corruption and fornication.[3] But his denial of Adam's salvation was an opinion due entirely to himself.

2. Others, again, following upon Basilides and Carpocrates, have introduced promiscuous intercourse and a plurality of wives, and are indifferent about eating meats sacrificed to idols, maintaining that God does not greatly regard such matters. But why continue? For it is an impracticable attempt to mention all those who, in one way or another, have fallen away from the truth.

CHAP. XXIX. — DOCTRINES OF VARIOUS OTHER GNOSTIC SECTS, AND ESPECIALLY OF THE BARBELIOTES OR BORBORIANS.

1. Besides those, however, among these heretics who are Simonians, and of whom we have already spoken, a multitude of Gnostics have sprung up, and have been manifested like mushrooms growing out of the ground. I now proceed to describe the principal opinions held by them. Some of them, then, set forth a certain Æon who never grows old, and exists in a virgin spirit: him they style Barbelos.[4] They declare that somewhere or other there exists a certain father who cannot be named, and that he was desirous to reveal himself to this Barbelos. Then this Ennœa went forward, stood before his face, and demanded from him Prognosis (prescience). But when Prognosis had, [as was requested,] come forth, these two asked for Aphtharsia (incorruption), which also came forth, and after that Zoe Aionios (eternal life). Barbelos, glorying in these, and contemplating their greatness, and in conception [5] [thus formed], rejoicing in this greatness, generated light similar to it. They declare that this was the beginning both of light and of the generation of all things; and that the Father, beholding this light, anointed it with his own benignity, that it might be rendered perfect. Moreover, they maintain that this was Christ, who again, according to them, requested that Nous should be given him as an assistant; and Nous came forth accordingly. Besides these, the Father sent forth Logos. The conjunctions of Ennœa and Logos, and of Aphtharsia and Christ, will thus be formed; while Zoe Aionios was united to Thelema, and Nous to Prognosis. These, then, magnified the great light and Barbelos.

2. They also affirm that Autogenes was afterwards sent forth from Ennœa and Logos, to be

---

[1] A promise never fulfilled: comp. book iii. 12, and Euseb., *Hist. Eccl.*, v. 8.
[2] [Rev. xii. 9.

[3] [The whole casuistical system of the Trent divines, *De Matrimonio*, proceeds on this principle: marriage is licensed evil.]
[4] Harvey supposes this name to be derived from two Syriac words, meaning "God in a Tetrad." Matter again derives it from two Hebrew words, denoting "Daughter of the Lord."
[5] Both the text and meaning are here altogether doubtful.

a representation of the great light, and that he was greatly honoured, all things being rendered subject unto him. Along with him was sent forth Aletheia, and a conjunction was formed between Autogenes and Aletheia. But they declare that from the Light, which is Christ, and from Aphtharsia, four luminaries were sent forth to surround Autogenes; and again from Thelema and Zoe Aionios four other emissions took place, to wait upon these four luminaries; and these they name Charis (grace), Thelesis (will), Synesis (understanding), and Phronesis (prudence). Of these, Charis is connected with the great and first luminary: him they represent as Soter (Saviour), and style Armogenes.[1] Thelesis, again, is united to the second luminary, whom they also name Raguel; Synesis to the third, whom they call David; and Phronesis to the fourth, whom they name Eleleth.

3. All these, then, being thus settled, Autogenes moreover produces a perfect and true man, whom they also call Adamas, inasmuch as neither has he himself ever been conquered, nor have those from whom he sprang; he also was, along with the first light, severed from Armogenes. Moreover, perfect knowledge was sent forth by Autogenes along with man, and was united to him; hence he attained to the knowledge of him that is above all. Invincible power was also conferred on him by the virgin spirit; and all things then rested in him, to sing praises to the great Æon. Hence also they declare were manifested the mother, the father, the son; while from Anthropos and Gnosis that Tree was produced which they also style Gnosis itself.

4. Next they maintain, that from the first angel, who stands by the side of Monogenes, the Holy Spirit has been sent forth, whom they also term Sophia and Prunicus.[2] He then, perceiving that all the others had consorts, while he himself was destitute of one, searched after a being to whom he might be united; and not finding one, he exerted and extended himself to the uttermost, and looked down into the lower regions, in the expectation of there finding a consort; and still not meeting with one, he leaped forth [from his place] in a state of great impatience, [which had come upon him] because he had made his attempt without the good-will of his father. Afterwards, under the influence of simplicity and kindness, he produced a work in which were to be found ignorance and audacity. This work of his they declare to be Protarchontes, the former of this [lower] creation. But they relate that a mighty power carried him away from his mother, and that he settled far away

from her in the lower regions, and formed the firmament of heaven, in which also they affirm that he dwells. And in his ignorance he formed those powers which are inferior to himself — angels, and firmaments, and all things earthly. They affirm that he, being united to Authadia (audacity), produced Kakia (wickedness), Zelos (emulation), Phthonos (envy), Erinnys (fury), and Epithymia (lust). When these were generated, the mother Sophia deeply grieved, fled away, departed into the upper regions, and became the last of the Ogdoad, reckoning it downwards. On her thus departing, he imagined he was the only being in existence; and on this account declared, "I am a jealous God, and besides me there is no one."[3] Such are the falsehoods which these people invent.

CHAP. XXX. — DOCTRINES OF THE OPHITES AND SETHIANS.

1. Others, again, portentously declare that there exists, in the power of Bythus, a certain primary light, blessed, incorruptible, and infinite: this is the Father of all, and is styled the first man. They also maintain that his Ennœa, going forth from him, produced a son, and that this is the son of man — the second man. Below these, again, is the Holy Spirit, and under this superior spirit the elements were separated from each other, viz., water, darkness, the abyss, chaos, above which they declare the Spirit was borne, calling him the first woman. Afterwards, they maintain, the first man, with his son, delighting over the beauty of the Spirit — that is, of the woman — and shedding light upon her, begat by her an incorruptible light, the third male, whom they call Christ, — the son of the first and second man, and of the Holy Spirit, the first woman.

2. The father and son thus both had intercourse with the woman (whom they also call the mother of the living). When, however,[4] she could not bear nor receive into herself the greatness of the lights, they declare that she was filled to repletion, and became ebullient on the left side; and that thus their only son Christ, as belonging to the right side, and ever tending to what was higher, was immediately caught up with his mother to form an incorruptible Æon. This constitutes the true and holy Church, which has become the appellation, the meeting together, and the union of the father of all, of the first man, of the son, of the second man, of Christ their son, and of the woman who has been mentioned.

3. They teach, however, that the power which proceeded from the woman by ebullition, being besprinkled with light, fell downward from the place occupied by its progenitors, yet possessing

---

[1] Harvey refers to the cabbalistic books in explanation of this and the following names, but their meanings are very uncertain.
[2] Various explanations of this word have been proposed, but its signification remains altogether doubtful.

[3] Ex. xx. 5; Isa. xlv. 5, 6.
[4] The punctuation is here difficult and doubtful.

by its own will that besprinkling of light; and it they call Sinistra, Prunicus, and Sophia, as well as masculo-feminine. This being, in its simplicity, descended into the waters while they were yet in a state of immobility, and imparted motion to them also, wantonly acting upon them even to their lowest depths, and assumed from them a body. For they affirm that all things rushed towards and clung to that sprinkling of light, and begirt it all round. Unless it had possessed that, it would perhaps have been totally absorbed in, and overwhelmed by, material substance. Being therefore bound down by a body which was composed of matter, and greatly burdened by it, this power regretted the course it had followed, and made an attempt to escape from the waters and ascend to its mother: it could not effect this, however, on account of the weight of the body lying over and around it. But feeling very ill at ease, it endeavoured at least to conceal that light which came from above, fearing lest it too might be injured by the inferior elements, as had happened to itself. And when it had received power from that besprinkling of light which it possessed, it sprang back again, and was borne aloft; and being on high, it extended itself, covered [a portion of space], and formed this visible heaven out of its body; yet remained under the heaven which it made, as still possessing the form of a watery body. But when it had conceived a desire for the light above, and had received power by all things, it laid down this body, and was freed from it. This body which they speak of that power as having thrown off, they call a female from a female.

4. They declare, moreover, that her son had also himself a certain breath of incorruption left him by his mother, and that through means of it he works; and becoming powerful. he himself, as they affirm, also sent forth from the waters a son without a mother; for they do not allow him either to have known a mother. His son, again, after the example of his father, sent forth another son. This third one, too, generated a fourth; the fourth also generated a son: they maintain that again a son was generated by the fifth; and the sixth, too, generated a seventh. Thus was the Hebdomad, according to them, completed, the mother possessing the eighth place; and as in the case of their generations, so also in regard to dignities and powers, they precede each other in turn.

5. They have also given names to [the several persons] in their system of falsehood, such as the following: he who was the first descendant of the mother is called Ialdabaoth;[1] he,

again, descended from him, is named Iao; he, from this one, is called Sabaoth; the fourth is named Adoneus; the fifth, Eloeus; the sixth, Oreus; and the seventh and last of all, Astanphæus. Moreover, they represent these heavens, potentates, powers, angels, and creators, as sitting in their proper order in heaven, according to their generation, and as invisibly ruling over things celestial and terrestrial. The first of them, namely Ialdabaoth, holds his mother in contempt, inasmuch as he produced sons and grandsons without the permission of any one, yea, even angels, archangels, powers, potentates, and dominions. After these things had been done, his sons turned to strive and quarrel with him about the supreme power, — conduct which deeply grieved Ialdabaoth, and drove him to despair. In these circumstances, he cast his eyes upon the subjacent dregs of matter, and fixed his desire upon it, to which they declare his son owes his origin. This son is Nous himself, twisted into the form of a serpent;[2] and hence were derived the spirit, the soul, and all mundane things: from this too were generated all oblivion, wickedness, emulation, envy, and death. They declare that the father imparted[3] still greater crookedness to this serpent-like and contorted Nous of theirs, when he was with their father in heaven and Paradise.

6. On this account, Ialdabaoth, becoming uplifted in spirit, boasted himself over all those things that were below him, and exclaimed, " I am father, and God, and above me there is no one." But his mother, hearing him speak thus, cried out against him, " Do not lie, Ialdabaoth: for the father of all, the first Anthropos (man), is above thee; and so is Anthropos the son of Anthropos." Then, as all were disturbed by this new voice, and by the unexpected proclamation, and as they were inquiring whence the noise proceeded, in order to lead them away and attract them to himself, they affirm that Ialdabaoth exclaimed, " Come, let us make man after our image."[4] The six powers, on hearing this, and their mother furnishing them with the idea of a man (in order that by means of him she might empty them of their original power), jointly formed a man of immense size, both in regard to breadth and length. But as he could merely writhe along the ground, they carried him to their father; Sophia so labouring in this matter, that she might empty him (Ialdabaoth) of the light with which he had been sprinkled, so that he might no longer, though still powerful, be able to lift up himself against the powers above. They declare, then, that by breathing

---

[1] The probable meaning of this and the following names is thus given by Harvey: Ialdabaoth, *Lord God of the Fathers;* Iao, *Jehovah;* Oreus, *Light;* Astanphæus, *Crown:* Sabaoth, of course, means *Hosts;* Adoneus, *Lord;* and Eloeus, *God.* All the names are derived from the cabbalistic theology of the Jews.

[2] Hence their name of Ophites, from ὄφις, *a serpent.*
[3] The Latin has *evertisse,* implying that thus Nous was more degraded.
[4] Gen. i. 26.

into man the spirit of life, he was secretly emptied of his power ; that hence man became a possessor of nous (intelligence) and enthymesis (thought) ; and they affirm that these are the faculties which partake in salvation. He [they further assert] at once gave thanks to the first Anthropos (man), forsaking those who had created him.

7. But Ialdabaoth, feeling envious at this, was pleased to form the design of again emptying man by means of woman, and produced a woman from his own enthymesis, whom that Prunicus [above mentioned] laying hold of, imperceptibly emptied her of power. But the others coming and admiring her beauty, named her Eve, and falling in love with her, begat sons by her, whom they also declare to be the angels. But their mother (Sophia) cunningly devised a scheme to seduce Eve and Adam, by means of the serpent, to transgress the command of Ialdabaoth. Eve listened to this as if it had proceeded from a son of God, and yielded an easy belief. She also persuaded Adam to eat of the tree regarding which God had said that they should not eat of it. They then declare that, on their thus eating, they attained to the knowledge of that power which is above all, and departed from those who had created them.[1] When Prunicus perceived that the powers were thus baffled by their own creature, she greatly rejoiced, and again cried out, that since the father was incorruptible, he (Ialdabaoth) who formerly called himself the father was a liar ; and that, while Anthropos and the first woman (the Spirit) existed previously, this one (Eve) sinned by committing adultery.

8. Ialdabaoth, however, through that oblivion in which he was involved, and not paying any regard to these things, cast Adam and Eve out of Paradise, because they had transgressed his commandment. For he had a desire to beget sons by Eve, but did not accomplish his wish, because his mother opposed him in every point, and secretly emptied Adam and Eve of the light with which they had been sprinkled, in order that that spirit which proceeded from the supreme power might participate neither in the curse nor opprobrium [caused by transgression]. They also teach that, thus being emptied of the divine substance, they were cursed by him, and cast down from heaven to this world.[2] But the serpent also, who was acting against the father, was cast down by him into this lower world ; he reduced, however, under his power the angels here, and begat six sons, he himself forming the seventh person, after the example of that Hebdomad which surrounds the father. They further declare that these are the seven mundane demons, who always oppose and resist the human

race, because it was on their account that their father was cast down to this lower world.

9. Adam and Eve previously had light, and clear, and as it were spiritual bodies, such as they were at their creation ; but when they came to this world, these changed into bodies more opaque, and gross, and sluggish. Their soul also was feeble and languid, inasmuch as they had received from their creator a merely mundane inspiration. This continued until Prunicus, moved with compassion towards them, restored to them the sweet savour of the besprinkling of light, by means of which they came to a remembrance of themselves, and knew that they were naked, as well as that the body was a material substance, and thus recognised that they bore death about with them. They thereupon became patient, knowing that only for a time they would be enveloped in the body. They also found out food, through the guidance of Sophia ; and when they were satisfied, they had carnal knowledge of each other, and begat Cain, whom the serpent, that had been cast down along with his sons, immediately laid hold of and destroyed by filling him with mundane oblivion, and urging into folly and audacity, so that, by slaying his brother Abel, he was the first to bring to light envy and death. After these, they affirm that, by the forethought of Prunicus, Seth was begotten, and then Norea,[3] from whom they represent all the rest of mankind as being descended. They were urged on to all kinds of wickedness by the inferior Hebdomad, and to apostasy, idolatry, and a general contempt for everything by the superior holy Hebdomad,[4] since the mother was always secretly opposed to them, and carefully preserved what was peculiarly her own, that is, the besprinkling of light. They maintain, moreover, that the holy Hebdomad is the seven stars which they call planets ; and they affirm that the serpent cast down has two names, Michael and Samael.

10. Ialdabaoth, again, being incensed with men, because they did not worship or honour him as father and God, sent forth a deluge upon them, that he might at once destroy them all. But Sophia opposed him in this point also, and Noah and his family were saved in the ark by means of the besprinkling of that light which proceeded from her, and through it the world was again filled with mankind. Ialdabaoth himself chose a certain man named Abraham from among these, and made a covenant with him, to the effect that, if his seed continued to serve him, he would give to them the earth for an inheritance. Afterwards, by means of Moses, he

---

[1] That is, from Ialdabaoth, etc. [*Philastr.* (*ut supra*), Oehler, i. p. 38.]
[2] There is constant reference in this section to rabbinical conceits and follies.

[3] A name probably derived from the Hebrew נַעֲרָה, *girl*, but of the person referred to we know nothing.
[4] We here follow the emendation of Grabe: the defection of Prunicus is intended.

brought forth Abraham's descendants from Egypt, and gave them the law, and made them the Jews. Among that people he chose seven days,[1] which they also call the holy Hebdomad. Each of these receives his own herald for the purpose of glorifying and proclaiming God ; so that, when the rest hear these praises, they too may serve those who are announced as gods by the prophets.

11. Moreover, they distribute the prophets in the following manner : Moses, and Joshua the son of Nun, and Amos, and Habakkuk, belonged to Ialdabaoth ; Samuel, and Nathan, and Jonah, and Micah, to Iao ; Elijah, Joel, and Zechariah, to Sabaoth ; Isaiah, Ezekiel, Jeremiah, and Daniel, to Adonai ; Tobias and Haggai to Eloi ; Michaiah and Nahum to Oreus ; Esdras and Zephaniah to Astanphæus. Each one of these, then, glorifies his own father and God, and they maintain that Sophia · herself has also spoken many things through them regarding the first Anthropos (man),[2] and concerning that Christ who is above, thus admonishing and reminding men of the incorruptible light, the first Anthropos, and of the descent of Christ. The [other] powers being terrified by these things, and marvelling at the novelty of those things which were announced by the prophets, Prunicus brought it about by means of Ialdabaoth (who knew not what he did), that emissions of two men took place, the one from the barren Elizabeth, and the other from the Virgin Mary.

12. And since she herself had no rest either in heaven or on earth, she invoked her mother to assist her in her distress. Upon this, her mother, the first woman, was moved with compassion towards her daughter, on her repentance, and begged from the first man that Christ should be sent to her assistance, who, being sent forth, descended to his sister, and to the besprinkling of light. When he recognised her (that is, the Sophia below), her brother descended to her, and announced his advent through means of John, and prepared the baptism of repentance, and adopted Jesus beforehand, in order that on Christ descending he might find a pure vessel, and that by the son of that Ialdabaoth the woman might be announced by Christ. They further declare that he descended through the seven heavens, having assumed the likeness of their sons, and gradually emptied them of their power. For they maintain that the whole besprinkling of light rushed to him, and that Christ, descending to this world, first clothed his sister Sophia [with it], and that then both exulted in the mutual

refreshment they felt in each other's society : this scene they describe as relating to bridegroom and bride. But Jesus, inasmuch as he was begotten of the Virgin through the agency of God, was wiser, purer, and more righteous than all other men : Christ united to Sophia descended into him, and thus Jesus Christ was produced.

13. They affirm that many of his disciples were not aware of the descent of Christ into him ; but that, when Christ did descend on Jesus, he then began to work miracles, and heal, and announce the unknown Father, and openly to confess himself the son of the first man. The powers and the father of Jesus were angry at these proceedings, and laboured to destroy him ; and when he was being led away for this purpose, they say that Christ himself, along with Sophia, departed from him into the state of an incorruptible Æon, while Jesus was crucified. Christ, however, was not forgetful of his Jesus, but sent down a certain energy into him from above, which raised him up again in the body, which they call both animal and spiritual ; for he sent the mundane parts back again into the world. When his disciples saw that he had risen, they did not recognise him — no, not even Jesus himself, by whom he rose again from the dead. And they assert that this very great error prevailed among his disciples, that they imagined he had risen in a mundane body, not knowing that "flesh[3] and blood do not attain to the kingdom of God."

14. They strove to establish the descent and ascent of Christ, by the fact that neither before his baptism, nor after his resurrection from the dead, do his disciples state that he did any mighty works, not being aware that Jesus was united to Christ, and the incorruptible Æon to the Hebdomad ; and they declare his mundane body to be of the same nature as that of animals. But after his resurrection he tarried [on earth] eighteen months ; and knowledge descending into him from above, he taught what was clear. He instructed a few of his disciples, whom he knew to be capable of understanding so great mysteries, in these things, and was then received up into heaven, Christ sitting down at the right hand of his father Ialdabaoth, that he may receive to himself the souls of those who have known them,[4] after they have laid aside their mundane flesh, thus enriching himself without the knowledge or perception of his father ; so that, in proportion as Jesus enriches himself with holy souls, to such an extent does his father suffer loss and is diminished, being emptied of his own power by these souls. For he will not now possess holy souls to send them down again into

<hr/>

[1] The Latin here is "ex quibus," and the meaning is exceedingly obscure. Harvey thinks it is the representative ἐξ ὧν (χρόνων) in the Greek, but we prefer to refer it to "Judæos," as above. The next sentence seems unintelligible: but, according to Harvey, "each deified day of the week had his ministering prophets."
[2] The common text inserts "et incorruptibili Æone," but this seems better rejected as a glossarial interpolation.

[3] 1 Cor. xv. 50. The Latin text reads "apprehendunt," which can scarcely be the translation of κληρονομῆσαι in the Greek text of the New Testament.
[4] That is, Christ and Jesus.

the world, except those only which are of his substance, that is, those into which he has breathed. But the consummation [of all things] will take place, when the whole besprinkling of the spirit of light is gathered together, and is carried off to form an incorruptible Æon.

15. Such are the opinions which prevail among these persons, by whom, like the Lernæan hydra, a many-headed beast has been generated from the school of Valentinus. For some of them assert that Sophia herself became the serpent; on which account she was hostile to the creator of Adam, and implanted knowledge in men, for which reason the serpent was called wiser than all others. Moreover, by the position of our intestines, through which the food is conveyed, and by the fact that they possess such a figure, our internal configuration [1] in the form of a serpent reveals our hidden generatrix.

CHAP. XXXI. — DOCTRINES OF THE CAINITES.

1. Others again declare that Cain derived his being from the Power above, and acknowledge that Esau, Korah, the Sodomites, and all such persons, are related to themselves. On this account, they add, they have been assailed by the Creator, yet no one of them has suffered injury. For Sophia was in the habit of carrying off that which belonged to her from them to herself. They declare that Judas the traitor was thoroughly acquainted with these things, and that he alone, knowing the truth as no others did, accomplished the mystery of the betrayal; by him all things, both earthly and heavenly, were thus thrown into confusion. They produce a fictitious history of this kind, which they style the Gospel of Judas.

2. I have also made a collection of their writings in which they advocate the abolition of the doings of Hystera.[2] Moreover, they call this Hystera the creator of heaven and earth. They also hold, like Carpocrates, that men cannot be saved until they have gone through all kinds of experience. An angel, they maintain, attends them in every one of their sinful and abominable actions, and urges them to venture on audacity and incur pollution. Whatever may be the nature [3] of the action, they declare that they do it in the name of the angel, saying, "O thou angel, I use thy work; O thou power, I accomplish thy operation!" And they maintain that this is "perfect knowledge," without shrinking to rush into such actions as it is not lawful even to name.

3. It was necessary clearly to prove, that, as their very opinions and regulations exhibit them,

those who are of the school of Valentinus derive their origin from such mothers, fathers, and ancestors, and also to bring forward their doctrines, with the hope that perchance some of them, exercising repentance and returning to the only Creator, and God the Former of the universe, may obtain salvation, and that others may not henceforth be drawn away by their wicked, although plausible, persuasions, imagining that they will obtain from them the knowledge of some greater and more sublime mysteries. But let them rather, learning to good effect from us the wicked tenets of these men, look with contempt upon their doctrines, while at the same time they pity those who, still cleaving to these miserable and baseless fables, have reached such a pitch of arrogance as to reckon themselves superior to all others on account of such knowledge, or, as it should rather be called, ignorance. They have now been fully exposed; and simply to exhibit their sentiments, is to obtain a victory over them.

4. Wherefore I have laboured to bring forward, and make clearly manifest, the utterly ill-conditioned carcase of this miserable little fox.[4] For there will not now be need of many words to overturn their system of doctrine, when it has been made manifest to all. It is as when, on a beast hiding itself in a wood, and by rushing forth from it is in the habit of destroying multitudes, one who beats round the wood and thoroughly explores it, so as to compel the animal to break cover, does not strive to capture it, seeing that it is truly a ferocious beast; but those present can then watch and avoid its assaults, and can cast darts at it from all sides, and wound it, and finally slay that destructive brute. So, in our case, since we have brought their hidden mysteries, which they keep in silence among themselves, to the light, it will not now be necessary to use many words in destroying their system of opinions. For it is now in thy power, and in the power of all thy associates, to familiarize yourselves with what has been said, to overthrow their wicked and undigested doctrines, and to set forth doctrines agreeable to the truth. Since then the case is so, I shall, according to promise, and as my ability serves, labour to overthrow them, by refuting them all in the following book. Even to give an account of them is a tedious affair, as thou seest.[5] But I shall furnish means for overthrowing them, by meeting all their opinions in the order in which they have been described, that I may not only expose the wild beast to view, but may inflict wounds upon it from every side.

---

[1] The text of this sentence is hopelessly corrupt, but the meaning is as given above.
[2] According to Harvey, Hystera corresponds to the "passions" of Achamoth. [Note the "Americanism," *advocate* used as a verb.]
[3] The text is here imperfect, and the translation only conjectural.

[4] [Cant. ii. 15; St. Luke xiii. 32.]
[5] [Let the reader bear in mind that the Greek of this original and very precious author exists only in fragments. We are reading the translation of a translation; the Latin very rude, and the subject itself full of difficulties. It may yet be discovered that some of the faults of the work are not chargeable to Irenæus.]

IRENÆUS AGAINST HERESIES

BOOK II

PREFACE.

1. In the first book, which immediately precedes this, exposing " knowledge falsely so called," [1] I showed thee, my very dear friend, that the whole system devised, in many and opposite ways, by those who are of the school of Valentinus, was false and baseless. I also set forth the tenets of their predecessors, proving that they not only differed among themselves, but had long previously swerved from the truth itself. I further explained, with all diligence, the doctrine as well as practice of Marcus the magician, since he, too, belongs to these persons ; and I carefully noticed [2] the passages which they garble from the Scriptures, with the view of adapting them to their own fictions. Moreover, I minutely narrated the manner in which, by means of numbers, and by the twenty-four letters of the alphabet, they boldly endeavour to establish [what they regard as] truth. I have also related how they think and teach that creation at large was formed after the image of their invisible Pleroma, and what they hold respecting the Demiurge, declaring at the same time the doctrine of Simon Magus of Samaria, their progenitor, and of all those who succeeded him. I mentioned, too, the multitude of those Gnostics who are sprung from him, and noticed [2] the points of difference between them, their several doctrines, and the order of their succession, while I set forth all those heresies which have been originated by them. I showed, moreover, that all these heretics, taking their rise from Simon, have introduced impious and irreligious doctrines into this life ; and I explained the nature of their "redemption," and their method of initiating those who are rendered "perfect," along with their invocations and their mysteries. I proved also that there is one God, the Creator, and that He is not the fruit of any defect, nor is there anything either above Him, or after Him.

2. In the present book, I shall establish those points which fit in with my design, so far as time permits, and overthrow, by means of lengthened treatment under distinct heads, their whole system ; for which reason, since it is an exposure and subversion of their opinions, I have so entitled the composition of this work. For it is fitting, by a plain revelation and overthrow of their conjunctions, to put an end to these hidden alliances,[3] and to Bythus himself, and thus to obtain a demonstration that he never existed at any previous time, nor now has any existence.

CHAP. I. — THERE IS BUT ONE GOD : THE IMPOSSIBILITY OF ITS BEING OTHERWISE.

1. It is proper, then, that I should begin with the first and most important head, that is, God the Creator, who made the heaven and the earth, and all things that are therein (whom these men blasphemously style the fruit of a defect), and to demonstrate that there is nothing either above Him or after Him ; nor that, influenced by any one, but of His own free will, He created all things, since He is the only God, the only Lord, the only Creator, the only Father, alone containing all things, and Himself commanding all things into existence.

2. For how can there be any other Fulness, or Principle, or Power, or God, above Him, since it is matter of necessity that God, the Pleroma (Fulness) of all these, should contain all things in His immensity, and should be contained by no one ? But if there is anything beyond Him, He is not then the Pleroma of all, nor does He contain all. For that which they declare to be beyond Him will be wanting to the Pleroma, or, [in other words,] to that God who is above all things. But that which is wanting, and falls in any way short, is not the

---

[1] 1 Tim. vi. 20.
[2] [Note this " Americanism."]

[3] This passage is very obscure: we have supplied " et," which, as Harvey conjectures, may have dropped out of the text.

Pleroma of all things. In such a case, He would have both beginning, middle, and end, with respect to those who are beyond Him. And if He has an end in regard to those things which are below, He has also a beginning with respect to those things which are above. In like manner, there is an absolute necessity that He should experience the very same thing at all other points, and should be held in, bounded, and enclosed by those existences that are outside of Him. For that being who is the end downwards, necessarily circumscribes and surrounds him who finds his end in it. And thus, according to them, the Father of all (that is, He whom they call Proön and Proarche), with their Pleroma, and the good God of Marcion, is established and enclosed in some other, and is surrounded from without by another mighty Being, who must of necessity be greater, inasmuch as that which contains is greater than that which is contained. But then that which is greater is also stronger, and in a greater degree Lord; and that which is greater, and stronger, and in a greater degree Lord — must be God.

3. Now, since there exists, according to them, also something else which they declare to be outside of the Pleroma, into which they further hold there descended· that higher power who went astray, it is in every way necessary that the Pleroma either contains that which is beyond, yet is contained (for otherwise, it will not be beyond the Pleroma; for if there is anything beyond the Pleroma, there will be a Pleroma within this very Pleroma which they declare to be outside of the Pleroma, and the Pleroma will be contained by that which is beyond : and with the Pleroma is understood also the first God) ; or, again, they must be an infinite distance separated from each other — the Pleroma [I mean], and that which is beyond it. But if they maintain this, there will then be a third kind of existence, which separates by immensity the Pleroma and that which is beyond it. This third kind of existence will therefore bound and contain both the others, and will be greater both than the Pleroma, and than that which is beyond it, inasmuch as it contains both in its bosom. In this way, talk might go on for ever concerning those things which are contained, and those which contain. For if this third existence has its beginning above, and its end beneath, there is an absolute necessity that it be also bounded on the sides, either beginning or ceasing at certain other points, [where new existences begin.] These, again, and others which are above and below, will have their beginnings at certain other points, and so on *ad infinitum ;* so that their thoughts would never rest in one God, but, in consequence of seeking after more than exists,

would wander away to that which has no existence, and depart from the true God.

4. These remarks are, in like manner, applicable against the followers of Marcion. For his two gods will also be contained and circumscribed by an immense interval which separates them from one another. But then there is a necessity to suppose a multitude of gods separated by an immense distance from each other on every side, beginning with one another, and ending in one another. Thus, by that very process of reasoning on which they depend for teaching that there is a certain Pleroma or God above the Creator of heaven and earth, any one who chooses to employ it may maintain that there is another Pleroma above the Pleroma, above that again another, and above Bythus another ocean of Deity, while in like manner the same successions hold with respect to the sides ; and thus, their doctrine flowing out into immensity, there will always be a necessity to conceive of other Pleromata, and other Bythi, so as never at any time to stop, but always to continue seeking for others besides those already mentioned. Moreover, it will be uncertain whether these which we conceive of are below, or are, in fact, themselves the things which are above ; and, in like manner, [it will be doubtful] respecting those things which are said by them to be above, whether they are really above or below ; and thus our opinions will have no fixed conclusion or certainty, but will of necessity wander forth after worlds without limits, and gods that cannot be numbered.

5. These things, then, being so, each deity will be contented with his own possessions, and will not be moved with any curiosity respecting the affairs of others ; otherwise he would be unjust, and rapacious, and would cease to be what God is. Each creation, too, will glorify its own maker, and will be contented with him, not knowing any other ; otherwise it would most justly be deemed an apostate by all the others, and would receive a richly-deserved punishment. For it must be either that there is one Being who contains all things, and formed in His own territory all those things which have been created, according to His own will ; or, again, that there are numerous unlimited creators and gods, who begin from each other, and end in each other on every side ; and it will then be necessary to allow that all the rest are contained from without by some one who is greater, and that they are each of them shut up within their own territory, and remain in it. No one of them all, therefore, is God. For there will be [much] wanting to every one of them, possessing [as he will do] only a very small part when compared with all the rest. The name of the Omnipotent will thus be brought to an end, and such an opinion will of necessity fall into impiety.

CHAP. II. — THE WORLD WAS NOT FORMED BY ANGELS, OR BY ANY OTHER BEING, CONTRARY TO THE WILL OF THE MOST HIGH GOD, BUT WAS MADE BY THE FATHER THROUGH THE WORD.[1]

1. Those, moreover, who say that the world was formed by angels, or by any other maker of it, contrary to the will of Him who is the Supreme Father, err first of all in this very point, that they maintain that angels formed such and so mighty a creation, contrary to the will of the Most High God. This would imply that angels were more powerful than God; or if not so, that He was either careless, or inferior, or paid no regard to those things which took place among His own possessions, whether they turned out ill or well, so that He might drive away and prevent the one, while He praised and rejoiced over the other. But if one would not ascribe such conduct even to a man of any ability, how much less to God!

2. Next let them tell us whether these things have been formed within the limits which are contained by Him, and in His proper territory, or in regions belonging to others, and lying beyond Him? But if they say [that these things were done] beyond Him, then all the absurdities already mentioned will face them, and the Supreme God will be enclosed by that which is beyond Him, in which also it will be necessary that He should find His end. If, on the other hand, [these things were done] within His own proper territory, it will be very idle to say that the world was thus formed within His proper territory against His will by angels who are themselves under His power, or by any other being, as if either He Himself did not behold all things which take place among His own possessions, or[2] was not aware of the things to be done by angels.

3. If, however, [the things referred to were done] not against His will, but with His concurrence and knowledge, as some [of these men] think, the angels, or the Former of the world [whoever that may have been], will no longer be the causes of that formation, but the will of God. For if He is the Former of the world, He too made the angels, or at least was the cause of their creation; and *He* will be regarded as having made the world who prepared the causes of its formation. Although they maintain that the angels were made by a long succession downwards, or that the Former of the world [sprang] from the Supreme Father, as Basilides asserts; nevertheless that which is the cause of those things which have been made will still be traced to Him who was the Author of such a succession. [The case stands] just as regards success in war,

which is ascribed to the king who prepared those things which are the cause of victory; and, in like manner, the creation of any state, or of any work, is referred to him who prepared materials for the accomplishment of those results which were afterwards brought about. Wherefore, we do not say that it was the axe which cut the wood, or the saw which divided it; but one would very properly say that the *man* cut and divided it who formed the axe and the saw for this purpose, and [who also formed] at a much earlier date all the tools by which the axe and the saw themselves were formed. With justice, therefore, according to an analogous process of reasoning, the Father of all will be declared the Former of this world, and not the angels, nor any other [so-called] former of the world, other than He who was its Author, and had formerly[3] been the cause of the preparation for a creation of this kind.

4. This manner of speech may perhaps be plausible or persuasive to those who know not God, and who liken Him to needy human beings, and to those who cannot immediately and without assistance form anything, but require many instrumentalities to produce what they intend. But it will not be regarded as at all probable by those who know that God stands in need of nothing, and that He created and made all things by His Word, while He neither required angels to assist Him in the production of those things which are made, nor any power greatly inferior to Himself, and ignorant of the Father, nor of any defect or ignorance, in order that he who should know Him might become man.[4] But He Himself in Himself, after a fashion which we can neither describe nor conceive, predestinating all things, formed them as He pleased, bestowing harmony on all things, and assigning them their own place, and the beginning of their creation. In this way He conferred on spiritual things a spiritual and invisible nature, on supercelestial things a celestial, on angels an angelical, on animals an animal, on beings that swim a nature suited to the water, and on those that live on the land one fitted for the land — on all, in short, a nature suitable to the character of the life assigned them — while He formed all things that were made by His Word that never wearies.

5. For this is a peculiarity of the pre-eminence of God, not to stand in need of other instruments for the creation of those things which are summoned into existence. His own Word is both suitable and sufficient for the formation of all things, even as John, the disciple of the Lord,

---

[1] [This noble chapter is a sort of homily on Hebrews i.]
[2] The common text has "ut:" we prefer to read "aut" with Erasmus and others.

[3] Vossius and others read "primus" instead of "prius," but on defective MS. authority.
[4] Harvey here observes: "Grabe misses the meaning by applying to the redeemed that which the author says of the Redeemer;" but it may be doubted if this is really the case. Perhaps Massuet's rendering of the clause, "that that man might be formed who should know Him," is, after all, preferable to that given above.

declares regarding Him : "All things were made by Him, and without Him was nothing made." [1] Now, among the "all things" our world must be embraced. It too, therefore, was made by His Word, as Scripture tells us in the book of Genesis that He made all things connected with our world by His Word. David also expresses the same truth [when he says], " For He spake, and they were made ; He commanded, and they were created." [2] Whom, therefore, shall we believe as to the creation of the world — these heretics who have been mentioned that prate so foolishly and inconsistently on the subject, or the disciples of the Lord, and Moses, who was both a faithful servant of God and a prophet? He at first narrated the formation of the world in these words : "In the beginning God created the heaven and the earth," [3] and all other things in succession ; but neither gods nor angels [had any share in the work].

Now, that this God is the Father of our Lord Jesus Christ, Paul the apostle also has declared, [saying,] "There is one God, the Father, who is above all, and through all things, and in us all." [4] I have indeed proved already that there is only one God ; but I shall further demonstrate this from the apostles themselves, and from the discourses of the Lord. For what sort of conduct would it be, were we to forsake the utterances of the prophets, of the Lord, and of the apostles, that we might give heed to these persons, who speak not a word of sense?

CHAP. III. — THE BYTHUS AND PLEROMA OF THE VALENTINIANS, AS WELL AS THE GOD OF MARCION, SHOWN TO BE ABSURD ; THE WORLD WAS ACTUALLY CREATED BY THE SAME BEING WHO HAD CONCEIVED THE IDEA OF IT, AND WAS NOT THE FRUIT OF DEFECT OR IGNORANCE.

1. The Bythus, therefore, whom they conceive of with his Pleroma, and the God of Marcion, are inconsistent. If indeed, as they affirm, he has something subjacent and beyond himself, which they style vacuity and shadow, this vacuum is then proved to be greater than their Pleroma. But it is inconsistent even to make this statement, that while he contains all things within himself, the creation was formed by some other. For it is absolutely necessary that they acknowledge a certain void and chaotic kind of existence (below the spiritual Pleroma) in which this universe was formed, and that the Propator purposely left this chaos as it was, either [5] knowing beforehand what things were to happen in it, or

being ignorant of them. If he was really ignorant, then God will not be prescient of all things. But they will not even [in that case] be able to assign a reason on what account He thus left this place void during so long a period of time. If, again, He is prescient, and contemplated mentally that creation which was about to have a being in that place, then He Himself created it who also formed it beforehand [ideally] in Himself.

2. Let them cease, therefore, to affirm that the world was made by any other ; for as soon as God formed a conception in His mind, that was also done which He had thus mentally conceived. For it was not possible that one Being should mentally form the conception, and another actually produce the things which had been conceived by Him in His mind. But God, according to these heretics, mentally conceived either an eternal world or a temporal one, *both* of which suppositions cannot be true. Yet if He had mentally conceived of it as eternal, spiritual, [6] and visible, it would also have been formed such. But if it was formed such as it really is, then *He* made it such who had mentally conceived of it as such ; or He willed it to exist in the ideality [7] of the Father, according to the conception of His mind, such as it now is, compound, mutable, and transient. Since, then, it is just such as the Father had [ideally] formed in counsel with Himself, it must be worthy of the Father. But to affirm that what was mentally conceived and pre-created by the Father of all, just as it has been actually formed, is the fruit of defect, and the production of ignorance, is to be guilty of great blasphemy. For, according to them, the Father of all will thus be [regarded as] generating in His breast, according to His own mental conception, the emanations of defect and the fruits of ignorance, since the things which He had conceived in His mind have actually been produced.

CHAP. IV. — THE ABSURDITY OF THE SUPPOSED VACUUM AND DEFECT OF THE HERETICS IS DEMONSTRATED.

1. The cause, then, of such a dispensation on the part of God, is to be inquired after ; but the formation of the world is not to be ascribed to any other. And all things are to be spoken of as having been so prepared by God beforehand, that they should be made as they have been

---

[1] John i. 3.
[2] Ps. xxxiii. 9, cxlviii. 5.
[3] Gen. i. 1.
[4] Eph. iv. 6, differing somewhat from Text. Rec. of New Testament.
[5] In the barbarous Latin version we here find *utrum* . . . *an* as the translation of ἤ . . . ἤ, instead of *aut* . . . *aut*.

[6] We have translated the text as it here stands in the MSS. Grabe omits *spiritalem et ;* Massuet proposes to read *et invisibilem,* and Stieren *invisibilem.*
[7] *In præsentia:* Grabe proposes *in præscientia,* but without MS. authority. "The reader," says Harvey, " will observe that there are three suppositions advanced by the author: that the world, as some heretics asserted, was eternal; that it was created in time, with no previous idea of it in the divine mind; or that it existed as a portion of the divine counsels from all eternity, though with no temporal subsistence until the time of its creation, — and of this the author now speaks." The whole passage is most obscurely expressed.

made; but shadow and vacuity are not to be conjured into existence. But whence, let me ask, came this vacuity [of which they speak]? If it was indeed produced by Him who, according to them, is the Father and Author of all things, then it is both equal in honour and related to the rest of the Æons, perchance even more ancient than they are. Moreover, if it proceeded from the same source [as they did], it must be similar in nature to Him who produced it, as well as to those along with whom it was produced. There will therefore be an absolute necessity, both that the Bythus of whom they speak, along with Sige, be similar in nature to a vacuum, that is, that He really is a vacuum; and that the rest of the Æons, since they are the brothers of vacuity, should also be devoid [1] of substance. If, on the other hand, it has not been thus produced, it must have sprung from and been generated by itself, and in that case it will be equal in point of age to that Bythus who is, according to them, the Father of all; and thus vacuity will be of the same nature and of the same honour with Him who is, according to them, the universal Father. For it must of necessity have been either produced by some one, or generated by itself, and sprung from itself. But if, in truth, vacuity was produced, then its producer Valentinus is also a vacuum, as are likewise his followers. If, again, it was not produced, but was generated by itself, then that which is really a vacuum is similar to, and the brother of, and of the same honour with, that Father who has been proclaimed by Valentinus; while it is more ancient, and dating its existence from a period greatly anterior, and more exalted in honour than the remaining Æons of Ptolemy himself, and Heracleon, and all the rest [2] who hold the same opinions.

2. But if, driven to despair in regard to these points, they confess that the Father of all contains all things, and that there is nothing whatever outside of the Pleroma (for it is an absolute necessity that, [if there be anything outside of it,] it should be bounded and circumscribed by something greater than itself), and that they speak of what is *without* and what *within* in reference to knowledge and ignorance, and not with respect to local distance; but that, in the Pleroma, or in those things which are contained by the Father, the whole creation which we know to have been formed, having been made by the Demiurge, or by the angels, is contained by the unspeakable greatness, as the centre is in a circle, or as a spot is in a garment, — then, in the first place, what sort of a being must that

Bythus be, who allows a stain to have place in His own bosom, and permits another one to create or produce within His territory, contrary to His own will? Such a mode of acting would truly entail [the charge of] degeneracy upon the entire Pleroma, since it might from the first have cut off that defect, and those emanations which derived their origin from it,[3] and not have agreed to permit the formation of creation either in ignorance, or passion, or in defect. For he who can afterwards rectify a defect, and does, as it were, wash away a stain,[4] could at a much earlier date have taken care that no such stain should, even at first, be found among his possessions. Or if at the first he allowed that the things which were made [should be as they are], since they could not, in fact, be formed otherwise, then it follows that they must always continue in the same condition. For how is it possible, that those things which cannot at the first obtain rectification, should subsequently receive it? Or how can men say that they are called to perfection, when those very beings who are the causes from which men derive their origin — either the Demiurge himself, or the angels — are declared to exist in defect? And if, as is maintained, [the Supreme Being,] inasmuch as He is benignant, did at last take pity upon men, and bestow on them perfection, He ought at first to have pitied those who were the creators of man, and to have conferred on them perfection. In this way, men too would verily have shared in His compassion, being formed perfect by those that were perfect. For if He pitied the *work* of these beings, He ought long before to have pitied *themselves*, and not to have allowed them to fall into such awful blindness.

3. Their talk also about shadow and vacuity, in which they maintain that the creation with which we are concerned was formed, will be brought to nothing, if the things referred to were created within the territory which is contained by the Father. For if they hold that the light of their Father is such that it fills all things which are inside of Him, and illuminates them all, how can any vacuum or shadow possibly exist within that territory which is contained by the Pleroma, and by the light of the Father? For, in that case, it behoves them to point out some place within the Propator, or within the Pleroma, which is not illuminated, nor kept possession of by any one, and in which either the angels or the Demiurge formed whatever they pleased. Nor will it be a small amount of space in which such and so great a creation can be

---

[1] Literally, "should also possess a vacant substance."
[2] The text has "reliquis omnibus," which would refer to the Æons; but we follow the emendation proposed by Massuet, "reliquorum omnium," as the reference manifestly is to other heretics.

[3] "*Ab eo:*" some refer "eo" to the Demiurge, but it is not unusual for the Latin translator to follow the Greek gender, although different from that of the Latin word which he has himself employed. We may therefore here refer "eo" to "labem," which is the translation of the neuter noun ὑστέρημα.
[4] *Labem* is here repeated, probably by mistake.

conceived of as having been formed. There will therefore be an absolute necessity that, within the Pleroma, or within the Father of whom they speak, they should conceive [1] of some place, void, formless, and full of darkness, in which those things were formed which have been formed. By such a supposition, however, the light of their Father would incur a reproach, as if He could not illuminate and fill those things which are within Himself. Thus, then, when they maintain that these things were the fruit of defect and the work of error, they do moreover introduce defect and error within the Pleroma, and into the bosom of the Father.

CHAP. V. — THIS WORLD WAS NOT FORMED BY ANY OTHER BEINGS WITHIN THE TERRITORY WHICH IS CONTAINED BY THE FATHER.

1. The remarks, therefore, which I made a little while ago [2] are suitable in answer to those who assert that this world was formed outside of the Pleroma, or under a "good God;" and such persons, with the Father they speak of, will be quite cut off from that which is outside the Pleroma, in which, at the same time, it is necessary that they should finally rest.[3] In answer to those, again, who maintain that this world was formed by certain other beings within that territory which is contained by the Father, all those points which have now [4] been noticed will present themselves [as exhibiting their] absurdities and incoherencies; and they will be compelled either to acknowledge all those things which are within the Father, lucid, full, and energetic, or to accuse the light of the Father as if He could not illuminate all things; or, as a portion of their Pleroma [is so described], the whole of it must be confessed to be void, chaotic, and full of darkness. And they accuse all other created things as if these were merely temporal, or [at the best], if eternal,[5] yet material. But [6] these (the Æons) ought to be regarded as beyond the reach of such accusations, since they are within the Pleroma, or the charges in question will equally fall against the entire Pleroma; and thus the Christ of whom they speak is dis-

covered to be the author of ignorance. For, according to their statements, when He had given a form so far as substance was concerned to the Mother they conceive of, He cast her outside of the Pleroma; that is, He cut her off from knowledge. He, therefore, who separated her from knowledge, did in reality produce ignorance in her. How then could the very same person bestow the gift of knowledge on the rest of the Æons, those who were anterior to Him [in production], and yet be the author of ignorance to His Mother? For He placed her beyond the pale of knowledge, when He cast her outside of the Pleroma.

2. Moreover, if they explain being within and without the Pleroma as implying knowledge and ignorance respectively, as certain of them do (since he who has knowledge is within that which knows), then they must of necessity grant that the Saviour Himself (whom they designate All Things) was in a state of ignorance. For they maintain that, on His coming forth outside of the Pleroma, He imparted form to their Mother [Achamoth]. If, then, they assert that whatever is outside [the Pleroma] is ignorant of all things, and if the Saviour went forth to impart form to their Mother, then He was situated beyond the pale of the knowledge of all things; that is, He was in ignorance. How then could He communicate knowledge to her, when He Himself was beyond the pale of knowledge? For we, too, they declare to be outside the Pleroma, inasmuch as we are outside of the knowledge which they possess. And once more.: If the Saviour really went forth beyond the Pleroma to seek after the sheep which was lost, but the Pleroma is [co-extensive with] knowledge, then He placed Himself beyond the pale of knowledge, that is, in ignorance. For it is necessary either that they grant that what is outside the Pleroma is so in a local sense, in which case all the remarks formerly made will rise up against them; or if they speak of that which is within in regard to knowledge, and of that which is without in respect to ignorance, then their Saviour, and Christ long before Him, must have been formed in ignorance, inasmuch as they went forth beyond the Pleroma, that is, beyond the pale of knowledge, in order to impart form to their Mother.

3. These arguments may, in like manner, be adapted to meet the case of all those who, in any way, maintain that the world was formed either by angels or by any other one than the true God. For the charges which they bring against the Demiurge, and those things which were made material and temporal, will in truth fall back on the Father; if indeed the [7] very things which

---

[1] The Latin is *fieri eos:* Massuet conjectures that the Greek had been ποιεῖσθαι αὐτούς, and that the translator rendered ποιεῖσθαι as a passive instead of a middle verb, *fieri* for *facere*.

[2] See above, chap. i.

[3] The Latin text here is, "et concluderentur tales cum patre suo ab eo qui est extra Pleroma, in quo etiam et desinere eos necesse est." None of the editors notice the difficulty or obscurity of the clause, but it appears to us absolutely untranslateable. We have rendered it as if the reading were "ab eo quod," though, if the strict grammatical construction be followed, the translation must be, "from *Him* who." But then to what does "in quo," which follows, refer? It may be ascribed either to the immediate antecedent *Pleroma*, or to *Him* who is described as being beyond it.

[4] Chap. ii., iii., iv.

[5] This is an extremely difficult passage. We follow the reading *æternochoica* adopted by Massuet, but Harvey reads *æterna choica*, and renders, "They charge all other substance (i.e., spiritual) with the imperfections of the material creation, as though Æon substance were equally ephemeral and choic."

[6] The common reading is "aut;" we adopt Harvey's conjectural emendation of "at."

[7] The above clause is very obscure; Massuet reads it interrogatively.

were formed in the bosom of the Pleroma began by and by in fact to be dissolved, in accordance with the permission and good-will of the Father. The [immediate] Creator, then, is not the [real] Author of this work, thinking, as He did, that He formed it very good, but *He* who allows and approves of the productions of defect, and the works of error having a place among his own possessions, and that temporal things should be mixed up with eternal, corruptible with incorruptible, and those which partake of error with those which belong to truth. If, however, these things were formed without the permission or approbation of the Father of all, then that Being must be more powerful, stronger, and more kingly, who made these things within a territory which properly belongs to Him (the Father), and did so without His permission. If again, as some say, their Father permitted these things without approving of them, then He gave the permission on account of some necessity, being either able to prevent [such procedure], or not able. But if indeed He could not [hinder it], then He is weak and powerless ; while, if He could, He is a seducer, a hypocrite, and a slave of necessity, inasmuch as He does not consent [to such a course], and yet allows it as if He did consent. And allowing error to arise at the first, and to go on increasing, He endeavours in later times to destroy it, when already many have miserably perished on account of the [original] defect.

4. It is not seemly, however, to say of Him who is God over all, since He is free and independent, that He was a slave to necessity, or that anything takes place with His permission, yet against His desire ; otherwise they will make necessity greater and more kingly than God, since that which has the most power is superior [1] to all [others]. And He ought at the very beginning to have cut off the causes of [the fancied] necessity, and not to have allowed Himself to be shut up to yielding to that necessity, by permitting anything besides that which became Him. For it would have been much better, more consistent, and more God-like, to cut off at the beginning the principle of this kind of necessity, than afterwards, as if moved by repentance, to endeavour to extirpate the results of necessity when they had reached such a development. And if the Father of all be a slave to necessity, and must yield to fate, while He unwillingly tolerates the things which are done, but is at the same time powerless to do anything in opposition to necessity and fate (like the Homeric Jupiter, who says of necessity, " I have willingly given thee, yet with unwilling mind "), then, according to this reasoning, the Bythus of whom they speak will be found to be the slave of necessity and fate.

CHAP. VI. — THE ANGELS AND THE CREATOR OF THE WORLD COULD NOT HAVE BEEN IGNORANT OF THE SUPREME GOD.

1. How, again, could either the angels, or the Creator of the world, have been ignorant of the Supreme God, seeing they were His property, and His creatures, and were contained by Him ? He might indeed have been invisible to them on account of His superiority, but He could by no means have been unknown to them on account of His providence. For though it is true, as they declare, that they were very far separated from Him through their inferiority [of nature], yet, as His dominion extended over all of them, it behoved them to know their Ruler, and to be aware of this in particular, that He who created them is Lord of all. For since His invisible essence is mighty, it confers on all a profound mental intuition and perception of His most powerful, yea, omnipotent greatness. Wherefore, although " no one knows the Father, except the Son, nor the Son except the Father, and those to whom the Son will reveal Him," [2] yet all [beings] do know this one fact at least, because reason, implanted in their minds, moves them, and reveals to them [the truth] that there is one God, the Lord of all.

2. And on this account all things have been [by general consent] placed under the sway of Him who is styled the Most High, and the Almighty. By calling upon Him, even before the coming of our Lord, men were saved both from most wicked spirits, and from all kinds of demons, and from every sort of apostate power. This was the case, not as if earthly spirits or demons had seen Him, but because they knew of the existence of Him who is God over all, at whose invocation they trembled, as there does tremble every creature, and principality, and power, and every being endowed with energy under His government. By way of parallel, shall not those who live under the empire of the Romans, although they have never seen the emperor, but are far separated from him both by land and sea, know very well, as they experience his rule, who it is that possesses the principal power in the state ? How then could it be, that those angels who were superior to us [in nature], or even He whom they call the Creator of the world, did not know the Almighty, when even dumb animals tremble and yield at the invocation of His name ? And as, although they have not seen Him, yet all things are subject to the name of our Lord,[3] so must they also be to His who made and established all things by His word, since it was no other than He who formed the world. And for this reason do the Jews even now put demons to flight by means

---

1 The text has " antiquius," literally " more ancient," but it may here be rendered as above.

2 Matt. xi. 27.
3 Massuet refers this to the Roman emperor.

of this very adjuration, inasmuch as all beings fear the invocation of Him who created them.

3. If, then, they shrink from affirming that the angels are more irrational than the dumb animals, they will find that it behoved these, although they had not seen Him who is God over all, to know His power and sovereignty. For it will appear truly ridiculous, if they maintain that they themselves indeed, who dwell upon the earth, know Him who is God over all whom they have never seen, but will not allow Him who, according to their opinion, formed them and the whole world, although He dwells in the heights and above the heavens, to know those things with which they themselves, though they dwell below, are acquainted. [This is the case], unless perchance they maintain that Bythus lives in Tartarus below the earth, and that on this account they have attained to a knowledge of Him before those angels who have their abode on high. Thus do they rush into such an abyss of madness as to pronounce the Creator of the world void of understanding. They are truly deserving of pity, since with such utter folly they affirm that He (the Creator of the world) neither knew His Mother, nor her seed, nor the Pleroma of the Æons, nor the Propator, nor what the things were which He made ; but that these are images of those things which are within the Pleroma, the Saviour having secretly laboured that they should be so formed [by the unconscious Demiurge], in honour of those things which are above.

CHAP. VII. — CREATED THINGS ARE NOT THE IMAGES OF THOSE ÆONS WHO ARE WITHIN THE PLEROMA.

1. While the Demiurge was thus ignorant of all things, they tell us that the Saviour conferred honour upon the Pleroma by the creation [which he summoned into existence] through means of his Mother, inasmuch as he produced similitudes and images of those things which are above. But I have already shown that it was impossible that anything should exist *beyond* the Pleroma (in which external region they tell us that images were made of those things which are within the Pleroma), or that this world was formed by any other one than the Supreme God. But if it is a pleasant thing to overthrow them on every side, and to prove them vendors of falsehood ; let us say, in opposition to them, that if these things were made by the Saviour to the honour of those which are above, after their likeness, then it behoved them always to endure, that those things which have been honoured should perpetually continue in honour. But if they do in fact pass away, what is the use of this very brief period of honour, — an honour which at one time had no existence, and which shall again come to nothing ? In that case I shall prove that the Saviour

is rather an aspirant after vainglory, than [1] one who honours those things which are above. For what honour can those things which are temporal confer on such as are eternal and endure for ever? or those which pass away on such as remain? or those which are corruptible on such as are incorruptible? — since, even among men who are themselves mortal, there is no value attached to that honour which speedily passes away, but to that which endures as long as it possibly can. But those things which, as soon as they are made, come to an end, may justly be said rather to have been formed for the contempt of such as are thought to be honoured by them ; and that that which is eternal is contumeliously treated when its image is corrupted and dissolved. But what if their Mother had not wept, and laughed, and been involved in despair? The Saviour would not then have possessed any means of honouring the Fulness, inasmuch as her last state of confusion [2] did not have substance of its own by which it might honour the Propator.

2. Alas for the honour of vainglory which at once passes away, and no longer appears ! There will be some [3] Æon, in whose case such honour will not be thought at all to have had an existence, and then the things which are above will be unhonoured ; or it will be necessary to produce once more another Mother weeping, and in despair, in order to the honour of the Pleroma. What a dissimilar, and at the same time blasphemous image ! Do you tell me that an image of the Only-begotten was produced by the former [4] of the world, whom [5] again ye wish to be considered the Nous (mind) of the Father of all, and [yet maintain] that this image was ignorant of itself, ignorant of creation, — ignorant, too, of the Mother, — ignorant of everything that exists, and of those things which were made by it ; and are you not ashamed while, in opposition to yourselves, you ascribe ignorance even to the Only-begotten Himself ? For if these things [below] were made by the Saviour after the similitude of those which are above, while He (the Demiurge) who was made after such similitude was in so great ignorance, it necessarily follows that around Him, and in accordance with Him, after whose likeness he that is thus ignorant was formed, ignorance of the kind in question spiritually exists.

---

[1] Harvey supposes that the translator here read ἤ *quam* instead of ἤ *quâ* (gloria) ; but Grabe, Massuet, and Stieren prefer to delete *erit.*

[2] Reference is here made to the supposed wretched state of Achamoth as lying in the region of shadow, vacuity, and, in fact, non-existence, until compassionated by the Christ above, who gave her form as respected *substance.*

[3] We have literally translated the above very obscure sentence. According to Massuet, the sense is: " There will some time be, or perhaps even now there is, some Æon utterly destitute of such honour, inasmuch as those things which the Saviour, for the sake of honouring it, had formed after its image, have been destroyed; and then those things which are above will remain without honour," etc.

[4] The Saviour is here referred to, as having formed all things through means of Achamoth and the Demiurge.

[5] Massuet deletes *quem*, and reads *nûn* as a genitive.

For it is not possible, since both were produced spiritually, and neither fashioned nor composed, that in some the likeness was preserved, while in others the likeness of the image was spoiled, that image which was here produced that it might be according to the image of that production which is above. But if it is not similar, the charge will then attach to the Saviour, who produced a dissimilar image, — of being, so to speak, an incompetent workman. For it is out of their power to affirm that the Saviour had not the faculty of production, since they style Him *All Things.* If, then, the image is dissimilar, he is a poor workman, and the blame lies, according to their hypothesis, with the Saviour. If, on the other hand, it is similar, then the same ignorance will be found to exist in the Nous (mind) of their Propator, that is, in the Only-begotten. The Nous of the Father, in that case, was ignorant of Himself; ignorant, too, of the Father; ignorant, moreover, of those very things which were formed by Him. But if *He* has knowledge, it necessarily follows also that he who was formed after his likeness by the Saviour should know the things which are like; and thus, according to their own principles, their monstrous blasphemy is overthrown.

3. Apart from this, however, how can those things which belong to creation, various, manifold, and innumerable as they are, be the images of those thirty Æons which are within the Pleroma, whose names, as these men fix them, I have set forth in the book which precedes this? And not only will they be unable to adapt the [vast] variety of creation at large to the [comparative] smallness of their Pleroma, but they cannot do this even with respect to any one part of it, whether [that possessed by] celestial or terrestrial beings, or those that live in the waters. For they themselves testify that their Pleroma consists of thirty Æons; but any one will undertake to show that, in a single department of those [created beings] which have been mentioned, they reckon that there are not thirty, but many thousands of species. How then can those things, which constitute such a multiform creation, which are opposed in nature to each other, and disagree among themselves, and destroy the one the other, be the images and likenesses of the thirty Æons of the Pleroma, if indeed, as they declare, these being possessed of one nature, are of equal and similar properties, and exhibit no differences [among themselves]? For it was incumbent, if these things are images of those Æons, — inasmuch as they declare that some men are wicked by nature, and some, on the other hand, naturally good, — to point out such differences also among their Æons, and to maintain that some of them were produced naturally good, while some were naturally evil, so that the

supposition of the likeness of those things might harmonize with the Æons. Moreover, since there are in the world some creatures that are gentle, and others that are fierce, some that are innocuous, while others are hurtful and destroy the rest; some have their abode on the earth, others in the water, others in the air, and others in the heaven; in like manner, they are bound to show that the Æons possess such properties, if indeed the one are the images of the others. And besides; "the eternal fire which the Father has prepared for the devil and his angels,"[2] — they ought to show of which of those Æons that are above it is the image; for it, too, is reckoned part of the creation.

4. If, however, they say that these things are the images of the Enthymesis of that Æon who fell into passion, then, first of all, they will act impiously against their Mother, by declaring her to be the first cause of evil and corruptible images. And then, again, how can those things which are manifold, and dissimilar, and contrary in their nature, be the images of one and the same Being? And if they say that the angels of the Pleroma are numerous, and that those things which are many are the images of these — not in this way either will the account they give be satisfactory. For, in the first place, they are then bound to point out differences among the angels of the Pleroma, which are mutually opposed to each other, even as the images existing below are of a contrary nature among themselves. And then, again, since there are many, yea, innumerable angels who surround the Creator, as all the prophets acknowledge, — [saying, for instance,] "Ten thousand times ten thousand stood beside Him, and many thousands of thousands ministered unto Him,"[2] — then, according[3] to them, the angels of the Pleroma will have as images the angels of the Creator, and the entire creation remains in the image of the Pleroma, but so that the thirty Æons no longer correspond to the manifold variety of the creation.

5. Still further, if these things [below] were made after the similitude of those [above], after the likeness of which again will those then be made? For if the Creator of the world did not form these things directly from His own[4] conception, but, like an architect of no ability, or a boy receiving his first lesson, copied them from archetypes furnished by others, then whence did their Bythus obtain the forms of that creation which He at first produced? It clearly follows

---

[1] Matt. xxv. 41.
[2] Dan. vii. 10, agreeing neither with the Greek nor Hebrew text.
[3] This clause is exceedingly obscure. Harvey remarks upon it as follows: " The reasoning of Irenæus seems to be this: According to the Gnostic theory, the Æons and angels of the Pleroma were homogeneous. They were also the archetypes of things created. But things created are heterogeneous: therefore either these Æons are heterogeneous, which is contrary to theory; or things created are homogeneous, which is contrary to fact."
[4] Literally, " from Himself."

that He must have received the model from some other one who is above Him, and that one, in turn, from another. And none the less [for these suppositions], the talk about images, as about gods, will extend to infinity, if we do not at once fix our mind on one Artificer, and on one God, who of Himself formed those things which have been created. Or is it really the case that, in regard to mere men, one will allow that they have of themselves invented what is useful for the purposes of life, but will not grant to that God who formed the world, that of Himself He created the forms of those things which have been made, and imparted to it its orderly arrangement?

6. But, again, how can these things [below] be images of those [above], since they are really contrary to them, and can in no respect have sympathy with them? For those things which are contrary to each other may indeed be destructive of those to which they are contrary, but can by no means be their images — as, for instance, water and fire; or, again, light and darkness, and other such things, can never be the images of one another. In like manner, neither can those things which are corruptible and earthly, and of a compound nature, and transitory, be the images of those which, according to these men, are spiritual; unless these very things themselves be allowed to be compound, limited in space, and of a definite shape, and thus no longer spiritual, and diffused, and spreading into vast extent, and incomprehensible. For they must of necessity be possessed of a definite figure, and confined within certain limits, that they may be true images: and then it is decided that they are not spiritual. If, however, these men maintain that they are spiritual, and diffused, and incomprehensible, how can those things which are possessed of figure, and confined within certain limits, be the images of such as are destitute of figure and incomprehensible?

7. If, again, they affirm that neither according to configuration nor formation, but according to number and the order of production, those things [above] are the images [of these below], then, in the first place, these things [below] ought not to be spoken of as images and likenesses of those Æons that are above. For how can the things which have neither the fashion nor shape of those [above] be their images? And, in the next place, they would adapt both the numbers and productions of the Æons above, so as to render them identical with and similar to thoseth at belong to the creation [below]. But now, since they refer to only thirty Æons, and declare that the vast multitude of things which are embraced within the creation [below] are images of those that are but thirty, we may justly condemn them as utterly destitute of sense.

CHAP. VIII. — CREATED THINGS ARE NOT A SHADOW OF THE PLEROMA.

1. If, again, they declare that these things [below] are a shadow of those [above], as some of them are bold enough to maintain, so that in this respect they are images, then it will be necessary for them to allow that those things which are above are possessed of bodies. For those bodies which are above do cast a shadow, but spiritual substances do not, since they can in no degree darken others. If, however, we also grant them this point (though it is, in fact, an impossibility), that there is a shadow belonging to those essences which are spiritual and lucent, into which they declare their Mother descended; yet, since those things [which are above] are eternal, and that shadow which is cast by them endures for ever, [it follows that] these things [below] are also not transitory, but endure along with those which cast their shadow over them. If, on the other hand, these things [below] are transitory, it is a necessary consequence that those [above] also, of which these are the shadow, pass away; while, if they endure, their shadow likewise endures.

2. If, however, they maintain that the shadow spoken of does not exist as being produced by the shade of [those above], but simply in this respect, that [the things below] are far separated from those [above], they will then charge the light of their Father with weakness and insufficiency, as if it cannot extend so far as these things, but fails to fill that which is empty, and to dispel the shadow, and that when no one is offering any hindrance. For, according to them, the light of their Father will be changed into darkness and buried in obscurity, and will come to an end in those places which are characterized by emptiness, since it cannot penetrate and fill all things. Let them then no longer declare that their Bythus is the fulness of all things, if indeed he has neither filled nor illuminated that which is vacuum and shadow; or, on the other hand, let them cease talking of vacuum and shadow, if the light of their Father does in truth fill all things.

3. Beyond the primary Father, then — that is, the God who is over all — there can neither be any Pleroma into which they declare the Enthymesis of that Æon who suffered passion, descended (so that the Pleroma itself, or the primary God, should not be limited and circumscribed by that which is beyond, and should, in fact, be contained by it); nor can vacuum or shadow have any existence, since the Father exists beforehand, so that His light cannot fail, and find end in a vacuum. It is, moreover, irrational and impious to conceive of a place in which He who is, according to them, Propator, and Proarche, and Father of all, and of this

Pleroma, ceases and has an end. Nor, again, is it allowable, for the reasons [1] already stated, to allege that some other being formed so vast a creation in the bosom of the Father, either with or without His consent. For it is equally impious and infatuated to affirm that so great a creation was [2] formed by angels, or by some particular production ignorant of the true God in that territory which is His own. Nor is it possible that those things which are earthly and material could have been formed within their Pleroma, since that is wholly spiritual. And further, it is not even possible that those things which belong to a multiform creation, and have been formed with mutually opposite qualities, [could have been created] after the image of the things above, since these (i.e., the Æons) are said to be few, and of a like formation, and homogeneous. Their talk, too, about the shadow of *kenoma* — that is, of a vacuum — has in all points turned out false. Their figment, then, [in what way soever viewed,] has been proved groundless,[3] and their doctrines untenable. Empty, too, are those who listen to them, and are verily descending into the abyss of perdition.

CHAP. IX. — THERE IS BUT ONE CREATOR OF THE WORLD, GOD THE FATHER : THIS THE CONSTANT BELIEF OF THE CHURCH.

1. That God is the Creator of the world is accepted even by those very persons who in many ways speak against Him, and yet acknowledge Him, styling Him the Creator, and an angel, not to mention that all the Scriptures call out [to the same effect], and the Lord teaches us of this Father[4] who is in heaven, and no other, as I shall show in the sequel of this work. For the present, however, that proof which is derived from those who allege doctrines opposite to ours, is of itself sufficient, — all men, in fact, consenting to this truth : the ancients on their part preserving with special care, from the tradition of the first-formed man, this persuasion, while they celebrate the praises of one God, the Maker of heaven and earth ; others, again, after them, being reminded of this fact by the prophets of God, while the very heathen learned it from creation itself. For even creation reveals Him who formed it, and the very work made suggests Him who made it, and the world manifests Him who ordered it. The Universal Church, moreover, through the whole world, has received this tradition from the apostles.

2. This God, then, being acknowledged, as I have said, and receiving testimony from all to the fact of His existence, that Father whom they conjure into existence is beyond doubt untenable, and has no witnesses [to his existence]. Simon Magus was the first who said that he himself was God over all, and that the world was formed by his angels. Then those who succeeded him, as I have shown in the first book,[5] by their several opinions, still further depraved [his teaching] through their impious and irreligious doctrines against the Creator. These [heretics now referred to],[6] being the disciples of those mentioned, render such as assent to them worse than the heathen. For the former "serve the creature rather than the Creator," [7] and "those which are not gods," [8] notwithstanding that they ascribe the first place in Deity to that God who was the Maker of this universe. But the latter maintain that He, [i.e., the Creator of this world,] is the fruit of a defect, and describe Him as being of an animal nature, and as not knowing that Power which is above Him, while He also exclaims, "I am God, and besides Me there is no other God." [9] Affirming that He lies, they are themselves liars, attributing all sorts of wickedness to Him ; and conceiving of one who is not above this Being as really having an existence, they are thus convicted by their own views of blasphemy against that God who really exists, while they conjure into existence a god who has no existence, to their own condemnation. And thus those who declare themselves " perfect," and as being possessed of the knowledge of all things, are found to be worse than the heathen, and to entertain more blasphemous opinions even against their own Creator.

CHAP. X. — PERVERSE INTERPRETATIONS OF SCRIPTURE BY THE HERETICS : GOD CREATED ALL THINGS OUT OF NOTHING, AND NOT FROM PRE-EXISTENT MATTER.

1. It is therefore in the highest degree irrational, that we should take no account of Him who is truly God, and who receives testimony from all, while we inquire whether there is above Him that [other being] who really has no existence, and has never been proclaimed by any one. For that nothing has been clearly spoken regarding Him, they themselves furnish testimony ; for since they, with wretched success, transfer to that being who has been conceived of by them, those parables [of Scripture] which, whatever the form in which they have been spoken, are sought after [for this purpose], it is manifest that they now generate another [god], who was

---

[1] See above, chap. ii. and v.
[2] The text has *fabricásse*, for which, says Massuet, should be read *fabricatam esse;* or *fabricásse* itself must be taken in a passive signification. It is possible, however, to translate, as Harvey indicates, " that He (Bythus) formed so great a creation by angels," etc., though this seems harsh and unsuitable.
[3] Literally, *empty:* there is a play on the words *vacuum* and *vacui* (which immediately follows), as there had been in the original Greek.
[4] Comp. e.g., Matt. v. 16, v. 45, vi. 9, etc.

[5] See chap. xxiii. etc.
[6] Viz., the Valentinians.
[7] Rom. i. 25.
[8] Gal. iv. 8.
[9] Isa. xlvi. 9.

never previously sought after. For by the fact that they thus endeavour to explain ambiguous passages of Scripture (ambiguous, however, not as if referring to another god, but as regards the dispensations of [the true] God), they have constructed another god, weaving, as I said before, ropes of sand, and affixing a more important to a less important question. For no question can be solved by means of another which itself awaits solution; nor, in the opinion of those possessed of sense, can an ambiguity be explained by means of another ambiguity, or enigmas by means of another greater enigma, but things of such character receive their solution from those which are manifest, and consistent, and clear.

2. But these [heretics], while striving to explain passages of Scripture and parables, bring forward another more important, and indeed impious question, to this effect, "Whether there be really another god above that God who was the Creator of the world?" They are not in the way of solving the questions [which they propose]; for how could they find means of doing so? But they append an important question to one of less consequence, and thus insert [in their speculations] a difficulty incapable of solution. For in order that they may [1] know "knowledge" itself (yet not learning this fact, that the Lord, when thirty years old, came to the baptism of truth), they do impiously despise that God who was the Creator, and who sent Him for the salvation of men. And that they may be deemed capable of informing us whence is the substance of matter, while they believe not that God, according to His pleasure, in the exercise of His own will and power, formed all things (so that those things which now are should have an existence) out of what did not previously exist, they have collected [a multitute of] vain discourses. They thus truly reveal their infidelity; they do not believe in that which really exists, and they have fallen away into [the belief of] that which has, in fact, no existence.

3. For, when they tell us that all moist substance proceeded from the tears of Achamoth, all lucid substance from her smile, all solid substance from her sadness, all mobile substance from her terror, and that thus they have sublime knowledge on account of which they are superior to others, — how can these things fail to be regarded as worthy of contempt, and truly ridiculous? They do not believe that God (being powerful, and rich in all resources) created matter itself, inasmuch as they know not how much a spiritual and divine essence can accomplish. But they do believe that their Mother, whom they style a female from a female, produced from her passions aforesaid the so vast material substance of creation. They inquire, too, whence the substance of creation was supplied to the Creator; but they do not inquire whence [were supplied] to their Mother (whom they call the Enthymesis and impulse of the Æon that went astray) so great an amount of tears, or perspiration, or sadness, or that which produced the remainder of matter.

4. For, to attribute the substance of created things to the power and will of Him who is God of all, is worthy both of credit and acceptance. It is also agreeable [to reason], and there may be well said regarding such a belief, that "the things which are impossible with men are possible with God."[2] While men, indeed, cannot make anything out of nothing, but only out of matter already existing, yet God is in this point preeminently superior to men, that He Himself called into being the substance of His creation, when previously it had no existence. But the assertion that matter was produced from the Enthymesis of an Æon going astray, and that the Æon [referred to] was far separated from her Enthymesis, and that, again, her passion and feeling, apart from herself, became matter — is incredible, infatuated, impossible, and untenable.

CHAP. XI. — THE HERETICS, FROM THEIR DISBELIEF OF THE TRUTH, HAVE FALLEN INTO AN ABYSS OF ERROR: REASONS FOR INVESTIGATING THEIR SYSTEMS.

1. They do not believe that He, who is God above all, formed by His Word, in His own territory, as He Himself pleased, the various and diversified [works of creation which exist], inasmuch as He is the former of all things, like a wise architect, and a most powerful monarch. But they believe that angels, or some power separate from God, and who was ignorant of Him, formed this universe. By this course, therefore, not yielding credit to the truth, but wallowing in falsehood, they have lost the bread of true life, and have fallen into vacuity [3] and an abyss of shadow. They are like the dog of Æsop, which dropped the bread, and made an attempt at seizing its shadow, thus losing the [real] food. It is easy to prove from the very words of the Lord, that He acknowledges one Father and Creator of the world, and Fashioner of man, who was proclaimed by the law and the prophets, while He knows no other, and that this One is really God over all; and that He teaches that that adoption of sons pertaining to the Father, which is eternal life, takes place through Himself, conferring it [as He does] on all the righteous.

---

[1] This clause is unintelligible in the Latin text: by a conjectural restoration of the Greek we have given the above translation.

[2] Luke xviii. 27.
[3] Playing upon the doctrines of the heretics with respect to *vacuity* and *shade*.

2. But since these men delight in attacking us, and in their true character of cavillers assail us with points which really tell not at all against us, bringing forward in opposition to us a multitude of parables and [captious] questions, I have thought it well, on the other side, first of all to put to them the following inquiries concerning their own doctrines, to exhibit their improbability, and to put an end to their audacity. After this has been done, [I intend] to bring forward the discourses of the Lord, so that they may not only be rendered destitute of the means of attacking us, but that, since they will be unable reasonably to reply to those questions which are put, they may see that their plan of argument is destroyed; so that, either returning to the truth, and humbling themselves, and ceasing from their multifarious phantasies, they may propitiate God for those· blasphemies they have uttered against Him, and obtain salvation; or that, if they still persevere in that system of vainglory which has taken possession of their minds, they may at least find it necessary to change their kind of argument against us.

CHAP. XII. — THE TRIACONTAD OF THE HERETICS ERRS BOTH BY DEFECT AND EXCESS: SOPHIA COULD NEVER HAVE PRODUCED ANYTHING APART FROM HER CONSORT; LOGOS AND SIGE COULD NOT HAVE BEEN CONTEMPORARIES.

1. We may [1] remark, in the first place, regarding their Triacontad, that the whole of it marvellously falls to ruin on both sides, that is, both as respects defect and excess. They say that to indicate it the Lord came to be baptized at the age of thirty years. But this assertion really amounts to a manifest subversion of their entire argument. As to defect, this happens as follows: first of all, because they reckon the Propator among the other Æons. For the Father of all ought not to be counted with other productions; He who was not produced with that which was produced; He who was unbegotten with that which was born; He whom no one comprehends with that which is comprehended by Him, and who is on this account [Himself] incomprehensible; and He who is without figure with that which has a definite shape. For inasmuch as He is superior to the rest, He ought not to be numbered with them, and that so that He who is impassible and not in error should be reckoned with an Æon subject to passion, and actually in error. For I have shown in the book which immediately precedes this, that, beginning with Bythus, they reckon up the Tricontad to Sophia, whom they describe as the erring Æon; and I have also there set forth the names of their [Æons]; but if He be not reckoned,

there are no longer, on their own showing, thirty productions of Æons, but these then become only twenty-nine.

2. Next, with respect to the first production Ennœa, whom they also term Sige, from whom again they describe Nous and Aletheia as having been sent forth, they err in both particulars. For it is impossible that the thought (Ennœa) of any one, or his silence (Sige), should be understood apart from himself; and that, being sent forth beyond him, it should possess a special figure of its own. But if they assert that the (Ennœa) was not sent forth beyond Him, but continued one with the Propator, why then do they reckon her with the other Æons — with those who were not one [with the Father], and are on this account ignorant of His greatness? If, however, she was so united (let us take this also into consideration), there is then an absolute necessity, that from this united and inseparable conjunction, which constitutes but one being, there [2] should proceed an unseparated and united production, so that it should not be dissimilar to Him who sent it forth. But if this be so, then just as Bythus and Sige, so also Nous and Aletheia will form one and the same being, ever cleaving mutually together. And inasmuch as the one cannot be conceived of without the other, just as water cannot [be conceived of] without [the thought of] moisture, or fire without [the thought of] heat, or a stone without [the thought] of hardness (for these things are mutually bound together, and the one cannot be separated from the other, but always co-exists with it), so it behoves Bythus to be united in the same way with Ennœa, and Nous with Aletheia. Logos and Zoe again, as being sent forth by those that are thus united, ought themselves to be united, and to constitute only one being. But, according to such a process of reasoning, Homo and Ecclesia too, and indeed all the remaining conjunctions of the Æons produced, ought to be united, and always to co-exist, the one with the other. For there is a necessity in their opinion, that a female Æon should exist side by side with a male one, inasmuch as she is, so to speak, [the forthputting of] his affection.

3. These things being so, and such opinions being proclaimed by them, they again venture, without a blush, to teach that the younger Æon of the Duodecad, whom they also style Sophia, did, apart from union with her consort, whom they call Theletus, endure passion, and separately, without any assistance from him, gave birth to a production which they name "a female from a female." They thus rush into such utter frenzy, as to form two most clearly opposite opinions respecting the same point. For if

---

[1] The text vacillates between "dicemus" and "dicamus."

[2] This sentence is confused in the Latin text, but the meaning is evidently that given above.

Bythus is ever one with Sige, Nous with Aletheia, Logos with Zoe, and so on, as respects the rest, how could Sophia, without union with her consort, either suffer or generate anything? And if, again, she did really suffer passion apart from him, it necessarily follows that the other conjunctions also admit of disjunction and separation among themselves, — a thing which I have already shown to be impossible. It is also impossible, therefore, that Sophia suffered passion apart from Theletus; and thus, again, their whole system of argument is overthrown. For they have yet[1] again derived the whole of remaining [material substance], like the composition of a tragedy, from that passion which they affirm she experienced apart from union with her consort.

4. If, however, they impudently maintain, in order to preserve from ruin their vain imaginations, that the rest of the conjunctions also were disjoined and separated from one another on account of this latest conjunction, then [I reply that], in the first place, they rest upon a thing which is impossible. For how can they separate the Propator from his Ennœa, or Nous from Aletheia, or Logos from Zoe, and so on with the rest? And how can they themselves maintain that they tend again to unity, and are, in fact, all at one, if indeed these very conjunctions, which are within the Pleroma, do not preserve unity, but are separate from one another; and that to such a degree, that they both endure passion and perform the work of generation without union one with another, just as hens do apart from intercourse with cocks.

5. Then, again, their first and first-begotten Ogdoad will be overthrown as follows: They must admit that Bythus and Sige, Nous and Aletheia, Logos and Zoe, Anthropos and Ecclesia, do individually dwell in the same Pleroma. But it is impossible that Sige (silence) can exist in the presence of Logos (speech), or again, that Logos can manifest himself in the presence of Sige. For these are mutually destructive of each other, even as light and darkness can by no possibility exist in the same place: for if light prevails, there cannot be darkness; and if darkness, there cannot be light, since, where light appears, darkness is put to flight. In like manner, where Sige is, there cannot be Logos; and where Logos is, there certainly cannot be Sige. But if they say that Logos simply exists within[2] (unexpressed), Sige also will exist within, and will not the less be destroyed by the Logos within. But that he really is not merely conceived of in the mind, the very order of the production of their (Æons) shows.

6. Let them not then declare that the first and principal Ogdoad consists of Logos and Sige, but let them [as a matter of necessity] exclude either Sige or Logos; and then their first and principal Ogdoad is at an end. For if they describe the conjunctions [of the Æons] as united, then their whole argument falls to pieces. Since, if they were united, how could Sophia have generated a defect without union with her consort? If, on the other hand, they maintain that, as in production, each of the Æons possesses his own peculiar substance, then how can Sige and Logos manifest themselves in the same place? So far, then, with respect to defect.

7. But again, their Triacontad is overthrown as to excess by the following considerations. They represent Horos (whom they call by a variety of names which I have mentioned in the preceding book) as having been produced by Monogenes just like the other Æons. Some of them maintain that this Horos was produced by Monogenes, while others affirm that he was sent forth by the Propator himself in His own image. They affirm further, that a production was formed by Monogenes — Christ and the Holy Spirit; and they do not reckon these in the number of the Pleroma, nor the Saviour either, whom they also declare to be *Totum*[3] (all things). Now, it is evident even to a blind man, that not merely thirty productions, as they maintain, were sent forth, but four more along with these thirty. For they reckon the Propator himself in the Pleroma, and those too, who in succession were produced by one another. Why is it, then, that those [other beings] are not reckoned as existing with these in the same Pleroma, since they were produced in the same manner? For what just reason can they assign for not reckoning along with the other Æons, either Christ, whom they describe as having, according to the Father's will, been produced by Monogenes, or the Holy Spirit, or Horos, whom they also call Soter[4] (Saviour), and not even the Saviour Himself, who came to impart assistance and form to their Mother? Whether is this as if these latter were weaker than the former, and therefore unworthy of the name of Æons, or of being numbered among them, or as if they were superior and more excellent? But how could they be weaker, since they were produced for the establishment and rectification of the others? And then, again, they cannot possibly be superior to the first and principal Tetrad, by which they were also produced; for it, too, is reckoned in the number above men-

---

[1] It is difficult to see the meaning of "iterum" here. Harvey begins a new paragraph with this sentence.

[2] ἐνδιάθετος — simply *conceived* in the mind — used in opposition to προφορικός, *expressed.*

[3] Harvey remarks that "the author perhaps wrote Ορον (*Horos*), which was read by the translator" Ὅλον (*totum*).

[4] Since *Soter* does not occur among the various appellations of Horos mentioned by Irenæus (i. 11, 4), Grabe proposes to read *Stauros*, and Massuet *Lytrotes;* but Harvey conceives that the difficulty is explained by the fact that Horos was a *power* of Soter (i. 3, 3).

tioned. These latter beings, then, ought also to have been numbered in the Pleroma of the Æons, or that should be deprived of the honour of those Æons which bear this appellation (the Tetrad).

8. Since, therefore, their Triacontad is thus brought to nought, as I have shown, both with respect to defect and excess (for in dealing with such a number, either excess or defect [to any extent] will render the number untenable, and how much more so great variations?), it follows that what they maintain respecting their Ogdoad and Duodecad is a mere fable which cannot stand. Their whole system, moreover, falls to the ground, when their very foundation is destroyed and dissolved into Bythus,[1] that is, into what has no existence. Let them, then, henceforth seek to set forth some other reasons why the Lord came to be baptized at the age of thirty years, and [explain in some other way] the Duodecad of the apostles; and [the fact stated regarding] her who suffered from an issue of blood; and all the other points respecting which they so madly labour in vain.

CHAP. XIII. — THE FIRST ORDER OF PRODUCTION MAINTAINED BY THE HERETICS IS ALTOGETHER INDEFENSIBLE.

1. I now proceed to show, as follows, that the first order of production, as conceived of by them, must be rejected. For they maintain that Nous and Aletheia were produced from Bythus and his Ennœa, which is proved to be a contradiction. For Nous is that which is itself chief, and highest, and, as it were, the principle and source of all understanding. Ennœa, again, which arises from him, is any sort of emotion concerning any subject. It cannot be, therefore, that Nous was produced by Bythus and Ennœa; it would be more like the truth for them to maintain that Ennœa was produced as the daughter of the Propator and this Nous. For Ennœa is not the daughter of Nous, as they assert, but Nous becomes the father of Ennœa. For how can Nous have been produced by the Propator, when he holds the chief and primary place of that hidden and invisible affection which is within Him? By this affection sense is produced, and Ennœa, and Enthymesis, and other things which are simply synonyms for Nous himself. As I have said already, they are merely certain definite exercises in thought of that very power concerning some particular subject. We understand the [several] terms according to their[2] length

and breadth of meaning, not according to any [fundamental] change [of signification]; and the [various exercises of thought] are limited by [the same sphere of] knowledge, and are expressed together by [the same] term, the [very same] sense remaining within, and creating, and administering, and freely governing even by its own power, and as it pleases, the things which have been previously mentioned.

2. For the first exercise of that [power] respecting anything, is styled Ennœa; but when it continues, and gathers strength, and takes possession of the whole soul, it is called Enthymesis. This Enthymesis, again, when it exercises itself a long time on the same point, and has, as it were, been proved, is named Sensation. And this Sensation, when it is much developed, becomes Counsel. The increase, again, and greatly developed exercise of this Counsel becomes the Examination of thought (Judgment); and this remaining in the mind is most properly termed Logos (reason), from which the spoken Logos (word) proceeds.[3] But all the [exercises of thought] which have been mentioned are [fundamentally] one and the same, receiving their origin from Nous, and obtaining [different] appellation according to their increase. Just as the human body, which is at one time young, then in the prime of life, and then old, has received [different] appellations according to its increase and continuance, but not according to any change of substance, or on account of any [real] loss of body, so is it with those [mental exercises]. For, when one [mentally] contemplates anything, he also thinks of it; and when he thinks of it, he has also knowledge regarding it; and when he knows it, he also considers it; and when he considers it, he also mentally handles it; and when he mentally handles it, he also speaks of it. But, as I have already said, it is Nous who governs all these [mental processes], while He is himself invisible, and utters speech of himself by means of those processes which have been mentioned, as it were by rays [proceeding from Him], but He himself is not sent forth by any other.

3. These things may properly be said to hold good in men, since they are compound by nature, and consist of a body and a soul. But those who affirm that Ennœa was sent forth from God, and Nous from Ennœa, and then, in succession, Logos from these, are, in the first place, to be blamed as having improperly used these productions; and, in the next place, as describing the affections, and passions, and mental tendencies of men, while they [thus prove them-

---

[1] Irenæus here, after his custom, plays upon the word *Bythus* (profundity), which, in the phraseology of the Valentinians, was a name of the Propator, but is in this passage used to denote *an unfathomable abyss.*

[2] This sentence appears to us, after long study, totally untranslateable. The general meaning seems to be, that whatever name is given to mental acts, whether they are called *Ennœa, Enthymesis,* or by whatever other appellation, they are all but exercises of the same fundamental power, styled *Nous.* Compare the following section.

[3] "The following," says Harvey, "may be considered to be consecutive steps in the evolution of λόγος as a psychological entity. Ennœa, *conception;* Enthymesis, *intention;* Sensation, *thought;* Consilium, *reasoning;* Cogitationis Examinatio, *judgment;* in Mente Perseverans, Λόγος ἐνδιάθετος; Emissibile Verbum, Λόγος προφοικός."

selves] ignorant of God. By their manner of speaking, they ascribe those things which apply to men to the Father of all, whom they also declare to be unknown to all; and they deny that He himself made the world, to guard against attributing want of power[1] to Him; while, at the same time, they endow Him with human affections and passions. But if they had known the Scriptures, and been taught by the truth, they would have known, beyond doubt, that God is not as men are; and that His thoughts are not like the thoughts of men.[2] For the Father of all is at a vast distance from those affections and passions which operate among men. He is a simple, uncompounded Being, without diverse members,[3] and altogether like, and equal to Himself, since He is wholly understanding, and wholly spirit, and wholly thought, and wholly intelligence, and wholly reason, and wholly hearing, and wholly seeing, and wholly light, and the whole source of all that is good — even as the religious and pious are wont to speak concerning God.

4. He is, however, above [all] these properties, and therefore indescribable. For He may well and properly be called an Understanding which comprehends all things, but He is not [on that account] like the understanding of men; and He may most properly be termed Light, but He is nothing like that light with which we are acquainted. And so, in all other particulars, the Father of all is in no degree similar to human weakness. He is spoken of in these terms according to the love [we bear Him]; but in point of greatness, our thoughts regarding Him transcend these expressions. If then, even in the case of human beings, understanding itself does not arise from emission, nor is that intelligence which produces other things separated from the living man, while its motions and affections come into manifestation, much more will the mind of God, who is all understanding, never by any means be separated from Himself; nor can anything[4] [in His case] be produced as if by a different Being.

5. For if He produced intelligence, then He who did thus produce intelligence must be understood, in accordance with their views, as a compound and corporeal Being; so that God, who sent forth [the intelligence referred to], is separate from it, and the intelligence which was sent forth separate [from Him]. But if they affirm that intelligence was sent forth from intelligence, they then cut asunder the intelligence of God, and divide it into parts. And whither has it gone? Whence was it sent forth? For whatever is sent forth from any place, passes of necessity into some other. But what existence was there more ancient than the intelligence of God, into which they maintain it was sent forth? And what a vast region that must have been which was capable of receiving and containing the intelligence of God! If, however, they affirm [that this emission took place] just as a ray proceeds from the sun, then, as the subjacent air which receives the ray must have had an existence prior to it, so [by such reasoning] they will indicate that there was something in existence, into which the intelligence of God was sent forth, capable of containing it, and more ancient than itself. Following upon this, we must hold that, as we see .the sun, which is less than all things, sending forth rays from himself to a great distance, so likewise we say that the Propator sent forth a ray beyond, and to a great distance from, Himself. But what can be conceived of beyond, or at a distance from, God, into which He sent forth this ray?

6. If, again, they affirm that that [intelligence] was not sent forth beyond the Father, but within the Father Himself, then, in the first place, it becomes superfluous to say that it was sent forth at all. For how could it have been sent forth if it continued within the Father? For an emission is the manifestation of that which is emitted, beyond him who emits it. In the next place, this [intelligence] being sent forth, both that Logos who springs from Him will still be within the Father, as will also be the future emissions proceeding from Logos. These, then, cannot in such a case be ignorant of the Father, since they are within Him; nor, being all equally surrounded by the Father, can any one know Him less [than another] according to the descending order of their emission. And all of them must also in an equal measure continue impassible, since they exist in the bosom of their Father, and none of them can ever sink into a state of degeneracy or degradation. For with the Father there is no degeneracy, unless perchance as in a great circle a smaller is contained, and within this one again a smaller; or unless they affirm of the Father, that, after the manner of a sphere or a square, He contains within Himself on all sides the likeness of a sphere, or. the production of the rest of the Æons in the form of a square, each one of these being surrounded by that one who is above him in greatness, and surrounding in turn that one who is after him in smallness; and that on this account, the smallest and the last of all, having its place in the centre, and thus being far separated from the Father, was really ignorant of the Propator. But if they maintain any such hypothesis, they must shut up their Bythus with .

---

[1] That is, lest He should be thought destitute of power, as having been unable to prevent evil from having a place in creation.
[2] Isa. lv. 8.
[3] The Latin expression is "similimembrius," which some regard as the translation of ὁμοιόκωλος, and others of ὁμοιομερής; but in either case the meaning will be as given above.
[4] That is, His Nous, Ennœa, etc., can have no independent existence. The text fluctuates between "emittitur" and "emittetur."

in a definite form and space, while He both surrounds others, and is surrounded by them ; for they must of necessity acknowledge that there is something outside of Him which surrounds Him. And none the less will the talk concerning those that contain, and those that are contained, flow on into infinitude ; and all [the Æons] will most clearly appear to be bodies enclosed [by one another].

7. Further, they must also confess either that He is mere vacuity, or that the entire universe is within Him ; and in that case all will in like degree partake of the Father. Just as, if one forms circles in water, or round or square figures, all these will equally partake of water ; just as those, again, which are framed in the air, must necessarily partake of air, and those which [are formed] in light, of light ; so must those also who are within Him all equally partake of the Father, ignorance having no place among them. Where, then, is this partaking of the Father who fills [all things] ? If, indeed, He has filled [all things], there will be no ignorance among them. On this ground, then, their work of [supposed] degeneracy is brought to nothing, and the production of matter with the formation of the rest of the world ; which things they maintain to have derived their substance from passion and ignorance. If, on the other hand, they acknowledge that He is vacuity, then they fall into the greatest blasphemy ; they deny His spiritual nature. For how can He be a spiritual being, who cannot fill even those things which are within Him ?

8. Now, these remarks which have been made concerning the emission of intelligence are in like manner applicable in opposition to those who belong to the school of Basilides, as well as in opposition to the rest of the Gnostics, from whom these also (the Valentinians) have adopted the ideas about emissions, and were refuted in the first book. But I have now plainly shown that the first production of Nous, that is, of the intelligence they speak of, is an untenable and impossible opinion. And let us see how the matter stands with respect to the rest [of the Æons]. For they maintain that Logos and Zoe were sent forth by him (i.e., Nous) as fashioners of this Pleroma ; while they conceive of an emission of Logos, that is, the Word after the analogy of human feelings, and rashly form conjectures respecting God, as if they had discovered something wonderful in their assertion that Logos was produced by Nous. All indeed have a clear perception that this may be logically affirmed with respect to men.[1] But in Him who is God over all, since He is all Nous, and all Logos, as I have said before, and has in Himself nothing more ancient or late than another, and nothing

at variance with another, but continues altogether equal, and similar, and homogeneous, there is no longer ground for conceiving of such production in the order which has been mentioned. Just as he does not err who declares that God is all vision, and all hearing (for in what manner He sees, in that also He hears ; and in what manner He hears, in that also He sees), so also he who affirms that He is all intelligence, and all word, and that, in whatever respect He is intelligence, in that also He is word, and that this Nous is His Logos, will still indeed have only an inadequate conception of the Father of all, but will entertain far more becoming [thoughts regarding Him] than do those who transfer the generation of the word to which men gave utterance to the eternal Word of God, assigning a beginning and course of production [to Him], even as they do to their own word. And in what respect will the Word of God — yea, rather God Himself, since He is the Word — differ from the word of men, if He follows the same order and process of generation?

9. They have fallen into error, too, respecting Zoe, by maintaining that she was produced in the sixth place, when it behoved her to take precedence of all [the rest], since God is life, and incorruption, and truth. And these and such like attributes have not been produced according to a gradual scale of descent, but they are names of those perfections which always exist in God, so far as it is possible and proper for men to hear and to speak of God. For with the name of God the following words will harmonize : intelligence, word, life, incorruption, truth, wisdom, goodness, and such like. And neither can any one maintain that intelligence is more ancient than life, for intelligence itself is life ; nor that life is later than intelligence, so that He who is the intellect of all, that is God, should at one time have been destitute of life. But if they affirm that life was indeed [previously] in the Father, but was produced in the sixth place in order that the Word might live, surely it ought long before, [according to such reasoning,] to have been sent forth, in the fourth place, that Nous might have life ; and still further, even before Him, [it should have been] with Bythus, that their Bythus might live. For to reckon Sige, indeed, along with their Propator, and to assign her to Him as His consort, while they do not join Zoe to the number, — is not this to surpass all other madness?

10. Again, as to the second production which proceeds from these [Æons who have been mentioned], — that, namely, of Homo and Ecclesia, — their very fathers, falsely styled Gnostics, strive among themselves, each one seeking to make good his own opinions, and thus convicting themselves of being wicked thieves.

---

[1] That is, in human beings no doubt, *thought* (Nous) precedes *speech* (Logos).

They maintain that it is more suitable to [the theory of] production — as being, in fact, truth-like — that the Word was produced by man, and not man by the Word; and that man existed prior to the Word, and that this is really He who is God over all. And thus it is, as I have previously remarked, that heaping together with a kind of plausibility all human feelings, and mental exercises, and formation of intentions, and utterances of words, they have lied with no plausibility at all against God. For while they ascribe the things which happen to men, and whatsoever they recognise themselves as experiencing, to the divine reason, they seem to those who are ignorant of God to make statements suitable enough. And by these human passions, drawing away their intelligence, while they describe the origin and production of the Word of God in the fifth place, they assert that thus they teach wonderful mysteries, unspeakable and sublime, known to no one but themselves. It was, [they affirm,] concerning these that the Lord said, "Seek, and ye shall find,"[1] that is, that they should inquire how Nous and Aletheia proceeded from Bythus and Sige; whether Logos and Zoe again derive their origin from these; and then, whether Anthropos and Ecclesia proceed from Logos and Zoe.

CHAP. XIV. — VALENTINUS AND HIS FOLLOWERS DERIVED THE PRINCIPLES OF THEIR SYSTEM FROM THE HEATHEN; THE NAMES ONLY ARE CHANGED.

1. Much more like the truth, and more pleasing, is the account which Antiphanes,[2] one of the ancient comic poets, gives in his *Theogony* as to the origin of all things. For he speaks of Chaos as being produced from Night and Silence; relates that then Love[3] sprang from Chaos and Night; from this again, Light; and that from this, in his opinion, were derived all the rest of the first generation of the gods. After these he next introduces a second generation of gods, and the creation of the world; then he narrates the formation of mankind by the second order of the gods. These men (the heretics), adopting this fable as their own, have ranged their opinions round it, as if by a sort of natural process, changing only the names of the things referred to, and setting forth the very same beginning of the generation of all things, and their production. In place of Night and Silence they substitute Bythus and Sige; instead of Chaos, they put Nous; and for Love (by whom, says the comic poet, all other things were

set in order) they have brought forward the Word; while for the primary and greatest gods they have formed the Æons; and in place of the secondary gods, they tell us of that creation by their mother which is outside of the Pleroma, calling it the second Ogdoad. They proclaim to us, like the writer referred to, that from this (Ogdoad) came the creation of the world and the formation of man, maintaining that they alone are acquainted with these ineffable and unknown mysteries. Those things which are everywhere acted in the theatres by comedians with the clearest voices they transfer to their own system, teaching them undoubtedly through means of the same arguments, and merely changing the names.

2. And not only are they convicted of bringing forward, as if their own [original ideas], those things which are to be found among the comic poets, but they also bring together the things which have been said by all those who were ignorant of God, and who are termed philosophers; and sewing together, as it were, a motley garment out of a heap of miserable rags, they have, by their subtle manner of expression, furnished themselves with a cloak which is really not their own. They do, it is true, introduce a new kind of doctrine, inasmuch as by a new sort of art it has been substituted [for the old]. Yet it is in reality both old and useless, since these very opinions have been sewed together out of ancient dogmas redolent of ignorance and irreligion. For instance, Thales[4] of Miletus affirmed that water was the generative and initial principle of all things. Now it is just the same thing whether we say *water* or *Bythus*. The poet Homer,[5] again, held the opinion that Oceanus, along with mother Tethys, was the origin of the gods: this idea these men have transferred to Bythus and Sige. Anaximander laid it down that infinitude is the first principle of all things, having seminally in itself the generation of them all, and from this he declares the immense worlds [which exist] were formed: this, too, they have dressed up anew, and referred to Bythus and their Æons. Anaxagoras, again, who has also been surnamed "Atheist," gave it as his opinion that animals were formed from seeds falling down from heaven upon earth. This thought, too, these men have transferred to "the seed" of their Mother, which they maintain to be themselves; thus acknowledging at once, in the judgment of such as are possessed of sense, that they themselves are the offspring of the irreligious Anaxagoras.

3. Again, adopting the [ideas of] shade and vacuity from Democritus and Epicurus, they

---

[1] Matt. vii. 7.
[2] Nothing is known of this writer. Several of the same name are mentioned by the ancients, but to none of them is a work named *Theogonia* ascribed. He is supposed to be the same poet as is cited by Athenæus, but that writer quotes from a work styled Ἀφροδίτης γοναι.
[3] The Latin is "Cupidinem;" and Harvey here refers to Aristotle, who "quotes the authority of Hesiod and Parmenides as saying that Love is the eternal intellect, reducing Chaos into order."

[4] Compare, on the opinions of the philosophers referred to in this chapter, Hippolytus, *Philosoph.*, book i.
[5] *Iliad*, xiv. 201; vii. 99.

have fitted these to their own views, following upon those [teachers] who had already talked a great deal about a vacuum and atoms, the one of which they called *that which is,* and the other *that which is not.* In like manner, these men call those things which are within the Pleroma real existences, just as those philosophers did the atoms ; while they maintain that those which are without the Pleroma have no true existence, even as those did respecting the vacuum. They have thus banished themselves in this world (since they are here outside of the Pleroma) into a place which has no existence. Again, when they maintain that these things [below] are images of those which have a true existence [above], they again most manifestly rehearse the doctrine of Democritus and Plato. For Democritus was the first who maintained that numerous and diverse figures were stamped, as it were, with the forms [of things above], and descended from universal space into this world. But Plato, for his part, speaks of matter, and exemplar,[1] and God. These men, following those distinctions, have styled what he calls ideas, and exemplar, the *images* of those things which are above ; while, through a mere change of name, they boast themselves as being discoverers and contrivers of this kind of imaginary fiction.

4. This opinion, too, that they hold the Creator formed the world out of previously existing matter, both Anaxagoras, Empedocles, and Plato expressed before them ; as, forsooth, we learn they also do under the inspiration of their Mother. Then again, as to the opinion that everything of necessity passes away to those things out of which they maintain it was also formed, and that God is the slave of this necessity, so that He cannot impart immortality to what is mortal, or bestow incorruption on what is corruptible, but every one passes into a substance similar in nature to itself, both those who are named Stoics from the portico (στοὰ), and indeed all that are ignorant of God, poets and historians alike, make the same affirmation.[2] Those [heretics] who hold the same [system of] infidelity have ascribed, no doubt, their own proper region to spiritual beings, — that, namely, which is within the Pleroma, but to animal beings the intermediate space, while to corporeal they assign that which is material. And they assert that God Himself can do no otherwise, but that every one of the [different kinds of substance] mentioned passes

away to those things which are of the same nature [with itself].

5. Moreover, as to their saying that the Saviour was formed out of all the Æons, by every one of them depositing, so to speak, in Him his own special flower, they bring forward nothing new that may not be found in the Pandora of Hesiod. For what he says respecting her, these men insinuate concerning the Saviour, bringing Him before us as Pandoros (All-gifted), as if each of the Æons had bestowed on Him what He possessed in the greatest perfection. Again, their opinion as to the indifference of [eating of] meats and other actions, and as to their thinking that, from the nobility of their nature, they can in no degree at all contract pollution, whatever they eat or perform, they have derived it from the Cynics, since they do in fact belong to the same society as do these [philosophers]. They also strive to transfer to [the treatment of matters of] faith that hairsplitting and subtle mode of handling questions which is, in fact, a copying of Aristotle.

6. Again, as to the desire they exhibit to refer this whole universe to numbers, they have learned it from the Pythagoreans. For these were the first who set forth numbers as the initial principle of all things, and [described] that initial principle of theirs as being both equal and unequal, out of which [two properties] they conceived that both things sensible[3] and immaterial derived their origin. And [they held] that one set of first principles[4] gave rise to the matter [of things], and another to their form. They affirm that from these first principles all things have been made, just as a statue is of its metal and its special form. Now, the heretics have adapted this to the things which are outside of the Pleroma. The [Pythagoreans] maintained that the[5] principle of intellect is proportionate to the energy wherewith mind, as a recipient of the comprehensible, pursues its inquiries, until, worn out, it is resolved at length in the Indivisible and One. They further affirm that Hen—that is, One— is the first principle of all things, and the substance of all that has been formed. From this again proceeded the Dyad, the Tetrad, the Pentad, and the manifold generation of the others. These things the heretics repeat, word for word, with a reference to their Pleroma and Bythus.

---

[1] The Latin has here *exemplum,* corresponding doubtless to παράδειγμα, and referring to those ἰδέαι of all things which Plato supposed to have existed for ever in the divine mind.

[2] [Our author's demonstration of the essential harmony of Gnosticism with the old mythologies, and the philosophies of the heathen, explains the hold it seems to have gained among nominal converts to Christianity, and also the necessity for a painstaking refutation of what seem to us mere absurdities. The great merit of Irenæus is thus illustrated: he gave the death-blow to heathenism in extirpating heresy.]

[3] The Latin text reads "sensibilia et insensata;" but these words, as Harvey observes, must be the translation of αἰσθητὰ καὶ ἀναίσθητα, — " the former referring to material objects of sense, the latter to the immaterial world of intellect."

[4] This clause is very obscure, and we are not sure if the above rendering brings out the real meaning of the author. Harvey takes a different view of it, and supposes the original Greek to have been, καὶ ἄλλας μὲν τῆς ὑποστάσεως ἀρχὰς εἶναι ἄλλας δὲ τῆς αἰσθήσεως καὶ τῆς οὐσίας. He then remarks: " The reader will observe that the word ὑπόστασις here means *intellectual substance,* οὐσία *material;* as in V. c. ult.* The meaning therefore of the sentence will be, *And they affirmed that the first principles of intellectual substance and of sensible and material existence were diverse,* viz., unity was the exponent of the first, duality of the second."

[5] All the editors confess the above sentence hopelessly obscure. We have given Harvey's conjectural translation.

From the same source, too, they strive to bring into vogue those conjunctions which proceed from unity. Marcus boasts of such views as if they were his own, and as if he were seen to have discovered something more novel than others, while he simply sets forth the Tetrad of Pythagoras as the originating principle and mother of all things.

7. But I will merely say, in opposition to these men — Did all those who have been mentioned, with whom you have been proved to coincide in expression, know, or not know, the truth? If they knew it, then the descent of the Saviour into this world was superfluous. For why [in that case] did He descend? Was it that He might bring that truth which was [already] known to the knowledge of those who knew it? If, on the other hand, these men did *not* know it, then how is it that, while you express yourselves in the same terms as do those who knew not the truth, ye boast that yourselves alone possess that knowledge which is above all things, although they who are ignorant of God [likewise] possess it? Thus, then, by a complete perversion [1] of language, they style ignorance of the truth knowledge : and Paul well says [of them, that [they make use of] "novelties of words of false knowledge." [2] For that knowledge of theirs is truly found to be false. If, however, taking an impudent course with respect to these points, they declare that men indeed did not know the truth, but that their Mother,[3] the seed of the Father, proclaimed the mysteries of truth through such men, even as also through the prophets, while the Demiurge was ignorant [of the proceeding], then I answer, in the first place, that the things which were predicted were not of such a nature as to be intelligible to no one ; for the men themselves knew what they were saying, as did also their disciples, and those again succeeded these. And, in the next place, if either the Mother or her seed knew and proclaimed those things which were of the truth (and the Father [4] is truth), then on their theory the Saviour spake falsely when He said, "No one knoweth the Father but the Son," [5] unless indeed they maintain that their seed or Mother is *No-one*.

8. Thus far, then, by means of [ascribing to their Æons] human feelings, and by the fact that they largely coincide in their language with many of those who are ignorant of God, they have been seen plausibly drawing a certain number away [from the truth]. They lead them on by the use of those [expressions] with which they have been familiar, to that sort of discourse which treats of all things, setting forth the production of the Word of God, and of Zoe, and of Nous, and bringing into the world, as it were, the [successive] emanations of the Deity. The views, again, which they propound, without either plausibility or parade, are simply lies from beginning to end. Just as those who, in order to lure and capture any kind of animals, place their accustomed food before them, gradually drawing them on by means of the familiar aliment, until at length they seize it, but, when they have taken them captive, they subject them to the bitterest of bondage, and drag them along with violence whithersoever they please ; so also do these men gradually and gently persuading [others], by means of their plausible speeches, to accept of the emission which has been mentioned, then bring forward things which are not consistent, and forms of the remaining emissions which are not such as might have been expected. They declare, for instance, that [ten] [6] Æons were sent forth by Logos and Zoe, while from Anthropos and Ecclesia there proceeded twelve, although they have neither proof, nor testimony, nor probability, nor anything whatever of such a nature [to support these assertions] ; and with equal folly and audacity do they wish it to be believed that from Logos and Zoe, being Æons, were sent forth Bythus and Mixis, Ageratos and Henosis, Autophyes and Hedone, Acinetos and Syncrasis, Monogenes and Macaria. Moreover, [as they affirm,] there were sent forth, in a similar way, from Anthropos and Ecclesia, being Æons, Paracletus and Pistis, Patricos and Elpis, Metricos and Agape, Ainos and Synesis, Ecclesiasticus and Macariotes, Theletos and Sophia.

9. The passions and error of this Sophia, and how she ran the risk of perishing through her investigation [of the nature] of the Father, as they relate, and what took place outside of the Pleroma, and from what sort of a defect they teach that the Maker of the world was produced, I have set forth in the preceding book, describing in it, with all diligence, the opinions of these heretics. [I have also detailed their views] respecting Christ, whom they describe as having been produced subsequently to all these, and also regarding Soter, who, [according to them,] derived his being from those Æons who were formed within the Pleroma.[7] But I have of necessity mentioned their names at present, that from these the absurdity of their falsehood may be made manifest, and also the confused nature of the nomenclature they have devised. For

---

[1] Literally, "antiphrasis."
[2] 1 Tim. vi. 20. The text is, "Vocum novitates falsæ agnitionis," καινοφωνίας having apparently been read in the Greek instead of κενοφωνίας as in Text. Rec.
[3] Grabe and others insert " vel " between these words.
[4] It seems necessary to regard these words as parenthetical, though the point is overlooked by all the editors.
[5] Matt. xi. 27.

[6] "Decem" is of doubtful authority.
[7] The text has "qui in labe facti sunt;" but, according to Harvey, "the sense requires πληρώματι instead of ἐκτρώματι in the original."

they themselves detract from [the dignity of] their Æons by a multitude of names of this sort. They give out names plausible and credible to the heathen, [as being similar] to those who are called their twelve gods,[1] and even these they will have to be images of their twelve Æons. But the images [so called] can produce names [of their own] much more seemly, and more powerful through their etymology to indicate divinity [than are those of their fancied prototypes].

CHAP. XV. — NO ACCOUNT CAN BE GIVEN OF THESE PRODUCTIONS.

1. But let us return to the fore-mentioned question as to the production [of the Æons]. And, in the first place, let them tell us the reason of the production of the Æons being of such a kind that they do not come in contact with any of those things which belong to creation. For they maintain that those things [above] were not made on account of creation, but creation on account of them; and that the former are not images of the latter, but the latter of the former. As, therefore, they render a reason for the images, by saying that the month has thirty days on account of the thirty Æons, and the day twelve hours, and the year twelve months, on account of the twelve Æons which are within the Pleroma, with other such nonsense of the same kind, let them now tell us also the reason for that production of the Æons, why it was of such a nature, for what reason the first and first-begotten *Ogdoad* was sent forth, and not a Pentad, or a Triad, or a Septenad, or any one of those which are defined by a different number? Moreover, how did it come to pass, that from Logos and Zoe were sent forth ten Æons, and neither more nor less; while again from Anthropos and Ecclesia proceeded twelve, although these might have been either more or less numerous?

2. And then, again, with reference to the entire Pleroma, what reason is there that it should be divided into these three — an Ogdoad, a Decad, and a Duodecad — and not into some other number different from these? Moreover, with respect to the division itself, why has it been made into *three* parts, and not into four, or five, or six, or into some other number among those which have no connection with such numbers[2] as belong to creation? For they describe those [Æons above] as being more ancient than these [created things below], and it behoves them to possess their principle [of being] in themselves, one which existed before creation, and

not after the pattern of creation, all exactly agreeing as to the point.[3]

3. The account which *we* give of creation is one harmonious with that regular order [of things prevailing in the world], for this scheme of ours is adapted to the[4] things which have [actually] been made; but it is a matter of necessity that they, being unable to assign any reason belonging to the things themselves, with regard to those beings that existed before [creation], and were perfected by themselves, should fall into the greatest perplexity. For, as to the points on which they interrogate us as knowing nothing of creation, they themselves, when questioned in turn respecting the Pleroma, either make mention of mere human feelings, or have recourse to that sort of speech which bears only upon that harmony observable in creation, improperly giving us replies concerning things which are secondary, and not concerning those which, as they maintain, are primary. For we do not question them concerning that harmony which belongs to creation, nor concerning human feelings; but because they must acknowledge, as to their octiform, deciform, and duodeciform Pleroma (the image of which they declare creation to be), that their Father formed it of that figure vainly and thoughtlessly, and must ascribe to Him deformity, if He made anything without a reason. Or, again, if they declare that the Pleroma was so produced in accordance with the foresight of the Father, for the sake of creation, as if He had thus symmetrically arranged its very essence, then it follows that the Pleroma can no longer be regarded as having been formed on its own account, but for the sake of that [creation] which was to be its image as possessing its likeness (just as the clay model is not moulded for its own sake, but for the sake of the statue in brass, or gold, or silver about to be formed), then creation will have greater honour than the Pleroma, if, for its sake, those things [above] were produced.

CHAP. XVI. — THE CREATOR OF THE WORLD EITHER PRODUCED OF HIMSELF THE IMAGES OF THINGS TO BE MADE, OR THE PLEROMA WAS FORMED AFTER THE IMAGE OF SOME PREVIOUS SYSTEM; AND SO ON AD INFINITUM.

1. But if they will not yield assent to any one of these conclusions, since in that case they would be proved by us as incapable of rendering any reason for such a production of their Pleroma, they will of necessity be shut up to this — that they confess that, above the Pleroma, there was some other system more spiritual and more powerful, after the image of which their Pleroma was

---

[1] Viz., the "Dii majorum gentium" of the Gentiles.
[2] Referring to numbers like 4, 5, 6, which do not correspond to any important fact in creation, as 7 e.g., does to the number of the planets.

[3] The Latin text is here scarcely intelligible, and is variously pointed by the editors.
[4] Harvey explains "his" as here denoting "in his," but we are at a loss to know how he would translate the passage. It is in the highest degree obscure.

formed. For if the Demiurge did not of himself construct that figure of creation which exists, but made it after the form of those things which are above, then from whom did their Bythus — who, to be sure, brought it about that the Pleroma should be possessed of a configuration of this kind — receive the figure of those things which existed before Himself? For it must needs be, either that the intention [of creating] dwelt in that god who made the world, so that of his own power, and from himself, he obtained the model of its formation; or, if any departure is made from this being, then there will arise a necessity for constantly asking whence there came to that one who is above him the configuration of those things which have been made; what, too, was the number of the productions; and what the substance of the model itself? If, however, it was in the power of Bythus to impart of himself such a configuration to the Pleroma, then why may it not have been in the power of the Demiurge to form of himself such a world as exists? And then, again, if creation be an image of those things [above], why should we not affirm that those are, in turn, images of others above them, and those above these again, of others, and thus go on supposing innumerable images of images?

2. This difficulty presented itself to Basilides after he had utterly missed the truth, and was conceiving that, by an infinite succession of those beings that were formed from one another, he might escape such perplexity. When he had proclaimed that three hundred and sixty-five heavens were formed through succession and similitude by one another, and that a manifest proof [of the existence] of these was found in the number of the days of the year, as I stated before; and that above these there was a power which they also style Unnameable, and its dispensation — he did not even in this way escape such perplexity. For, when asked whence came the image of its configuration to that heaven which is above all, and from which he wishes the rest to be regarded as having been formed by means of succession, he will say, from that dispensation which belongs to the Unnameable. He must then say, either that the Unspeakable formed it of himself, or he will find it necessary to acknowledge that there is some other power above this being, from whom his unnameable One derived such vast numbers of configurations as do, according to him, exist.

3. How much safer and more accurate a course is it, then, to confess at once that which is true: that this God, the Creator, who formed the world, is the only God, and that there is no other God besides Him — He Himself receiving from Himself the model and figure of those things which have been made — than that, after wearying ourselves with such an impious and circuitous de-

scription, we should be compelled, at some point or another, to fix the mind on some One, and to confess that from Him proceeded the configuration of things created.

4. As to the accusation brought against us by the followers of Valentinus, when they declare that we continue in that Hebdomad which is below, as if we could not lift our minds on high, nor understand those things which are above, because we do not accept their monstrous assertions: this very charge do the followers of Basilides bring in turn against them, inasmuch as they (the Valentinians) keep circling about those things which are below, [going] as far as the first and second Ogdoad, and because they unskilfully imagine that, immediately after the thirty Æons, they have discovered Him who is above all things Father, not following out in thought their investigations to that Pleroma which is above the three hundred and sixty-five heavens, which [1] is above forty-five Ogdoads. And any one, again, might bring against them the same charge, by imagining four thousand three hundred and eighty heavens, or Æons, since the days of the year contain that number of hours. If, again, some one adds also the nights, thus doubling the hours which have been mentioned, imagining that [in this way] he has discovered a great multitude of Ogdoads, and a kind of innumerable company [2] of Æons, and thus, in opposition to Him who is above all things Father, conceiving himself more perfect than all [others], he will bring the same charge against all, inasmuch as they are not capable of rising to the conception of such a multitude of heavens or Æons as he has announced, but are either so deficient as to remain among those things which are below, or continue in the intermediate space.

CHAP. XVII. — INQUIRY INTO THE PRODUCTION OF THE ÆONS : WHATEVER ITS SUPPOSED NATURE, IT IS IN EVERY RESPECT INCONSISTENT ; AND ON THE HYPOTHESIS OF THE HERETICS, EVEN NOUS AND THE FATHER HIMSELF WOULD BE STAINED WITH IGNORANCE.

1. That system, then, which has respect to their Pleroma, and especially that part of it which refers to the primary Ogdoad being thus burdened with so great contradictions and perplexities, let me now go on to examine the remainder of their scheme. [In doing so] on account of their madness, I shall be making inquiry respecting things which have no real existence ; yet it is necessary to do this, since the treatment of this subject has been entrusted to me, and since I desire all men

---

[1] The text is here doubtful: Harvey proposes to read " qui " instead of " quæ," but we prefer " quod " with Grabe. The meaning is, that three hundred and sixty-five is more than forty-five Ogdoads (45 × 8 = 360).

[2] " Operositatem," corresponding to πραγματείαν, lit. *manufacture*.

to come to the knowledge of the truth, as well as because thou thyself hast asked to receive from me full and complete means for overturning [the views of] these men.

2. I ask, then, in what manner were the rest of the Æons produced? Was it so as to be united with Him who produced them, even as the solar rays are with the sun; or was it actually[1] and separately, so that each of them possessed an independent existence and his own special form, just as has a man from another man, and one herd of cattle from another? Or was it after the manner of germination, as branches from a tree? And were they of the same substance with those who produced them, or did they derive their substance from some other [kind of] substance? Also, were they produced at the same time, so as to be contemporaries; or after a certain order, so that some of them were older, and others younger? And, again, are they uncompounded and uniform, and altogether equal and similar among themselves, as spirit and light are produced; or are they compounded and different, unlike [to each other] in their members?

3. If each of them was produced, after the manner of men, actually and according to its own generation, then either those thus generated by the Father will be of the same substance with Him, and similar to their Author; or if[2] they appear dissimilar, then it must of necessity be acknowledged that they are [formed of some different substance. Now, if the beings generated by the Father be similar to their Author, then those who have been produced must remain for ever impassible, even as is He who produced them; but if, on the other hand, they are of a different substance, which is capable of passion, then whence came this dissimilar substance to find a place within the incorruptible Pleroma? Further, too, according to this principle, each one of them must be understood as being completely separated from every other, even as men are not mixed with nor united the one to the other, but each having a distinct shape of his own, and a definite sphere of action, while each one of them, too, is formed of a particular size, — qualities characteristic of a body, and not of a spirit. Let them therefore no longer speak of the Pleroma as being *spiritual*, or of themselves as "spiritual," if indeed their Æons sit feasting with the Father, just as if they were men, and He Himself is of such a configuration as those reveal Him to be who were produced by Him.

4. If, again, the Æons were derived from Logos, Logos from Nous, and Nous from Bythus, just as lights are kindled from a light — as, for example, torches are from a torch — then they may no doubt differ in generation and size from one another; but since they are of the same substance with the Author of their production, they must either all remain for ever impassible, or their Father Himself must participate in passion. For the torch which has been kindled subsequently cannot be possessed of a different kind of light from that which preceded it. Wherefore also their lights, when blended in one, return to the original identity, since that one light is then formed which has existed even from the beginning. But we cannot speak, with respect to light itself, of some part being more recent in its origin, and another being more ancient (for the whole is but one light); nor can we so speak even in regard to those torches which have received the light (for these are all contemporary as respects their material substance, for the substance of torches is one and the same), but simply as to [the time of] its being kindled, since one was lighted a little while ago, and another has just now been kindled.

5. The defect, therefore, of that passion which has regard to ignorance, will either attach alike to their whole Pleroma, since [all its members] are of the same substance; and the Propator will share in this defect of ignorance — that is, will be ignorant of Himself; or, on the other hand, all those lights which are within the Pleroma will alike remain for ever impassible. Whence, then, comes the passion of the youngest Æon, if the light of the Father is that from which all other lights have been formed, and which is by nature impassible? And how can one Æon be spoken of as either younger or older among themselves, since there is but one light in the entire Pleroma? And if any one calls them stars, they will all nevertheless appear to participate in the same nature. For if "one star differs from another star in glory,"[3] but not in qualities, nor substance, nor in the fact of being passible or impassible; so all these, since they are alike derived from the light of the Father, must either be naturally impassible and immutable, or they must all, in common with the light of the Father, be passible, and are capable of the varying phases of corruption.

6. The same conclusion will follow, although they affirm that the production of Æons sprang from Logos, as branches from a tree, since Logos has his generation from their Father. For all [the Æons] are formed of the same substance with the Father, differing from one another only in size, and not in nature, and filling up the greatness of the Father, even as the fingers com-

---

[1] *Efficabiliter* in the Latin text is thought to correspond to ἐνεργῶς in the original Greek.
[2] *Si* is inserted by most of the editors; and although Harvey argues for its omission, we agree with Massuet in deeming it indispensable.

[3] 1 Cor. xv. 41.

plete the hand. If therefore He exists in passion and ignorance, so must also those Æons who have been generated by Him. But if it is impious to ascribe ignorance and passion to the Father of all, how can they describe an Æon produced by Him as being passible; and while they ascribe the same impiety to the very wisdom (Sophia) of God, how can they still call themselves religious men?

7. If, again, they declare that their Æons were sent forth just as rays are from the sun, then, since all are of the same substance and sprung from the same source, all must either be capable of passion along with Him who produced them, or all will remain impassible for ever. For they can no longer maintain that, of beings so produced, some are impassible and others passible. If, then, they declare all impassible, they do themselves destroy their own argument. For how could the youngest Æon have suffered passion if all were impassible? If, on the other hand, they declare that all partook of this passion, as indeed some of them venture to maintain, then, inasmuch as it originated with Logos,[1] but flowed onwards to Sophia, they will thus be convicted of tracing back the passion to Logos, who is the[2] Nous of this Propator, and so acknowledging the Nous of the Propator and the Father Himself to have experienced passion. For the Father of all is not to be regarded as a kind of compound Being, who can be separated from his Nous (mind), as I have already shown; but Nous is the Father, and the Father Nous. It necessarily follows, therefore, both that he who springs from Him as Logos, or rather that Nous himself, since he is Logos, must be perfect and impassible, and that those productions which proceed from him, seeing that they are of the same substance with himself, should be perfect and impassible, and should ever remain similar to him who produced them.

8. It cannot therefore longer be held, as these men teach, that Logos, as occupying the third place in generation, was ignorant of the Father. Such a thing might indeed perhaps be deemed probable in the case of the generation of human beings, inasmuch as these frequently know nothing of their parents; but it is altogether impossible in the case of the Logos of the Father. For if, existing in the Father, he knows Him in whom he exists — that is, is not ignorant of himself — then those productions which issue from him being his powers (faculties), and always present with him, will not be ignorant of him who emitted them, any more than rays [may be supposed to be] of the sun. It is impossible,

therefore, that the Sophia (wisdom) of God, she who is within the Pleroma, inasmuch as she has been produced in such a manner, should have fallen under the influence of passion, and conceived such ignorance. But it *is* possible that that Sophia (wisdom) who pertains to [the scheme] of Valentinus, inasmuch as she is a production of the devil, should fall into every kind of passion, and exhibit the profoundest ignorance. For when they themselves bear testimony concerning their mother, to the effect that she was the offspring of an erring Æon, we need no longer search for a reason why the sons of such a mother should be ever swimming in the depths of ignorance.

9. I am not aware that, besides these productions [which have been mentioned], they are able to speak of any other; indeed, they have not been known to me (although I have had very frequent discussions with them concerning forms of this kind) as ever setting forth any other peculiar kind of being as produced [in the manner under consideration]. This only they maintain, that each one of these *was so produced* as to know merely that one who produced him, while he was ignorant of the one who immediately preceded. But they do not in this matter go forward [in their account] with any kind of demonstration as to the manner in which these were produced, or how such a thing could take place among spiritual beings. For, in whatsoever way they may choose to go forward, they will feel themselves bound (while, as regards the truth, they depart[3] entirely from right reason) to proceed so far as to maintain that their Word, who springs from the Nous of the Propator, — to maintain, I say, that he was produced in a state of degeneracy. For [they hold] that perfect Nous, previously begotten by the perfect Bythus, was not capable of rendering that production which issued from him perfect, but [could only bring it forth] utterly blind to the knowledge and greatness of the Father. They also maintain that the Saviour exhibited an emblem of this mystery in the case of that man who was blind from his birth,[4] since the Æon was in this manner produced by Monogenes blind, that is, in ignorance, thus falsely ascribing ignorance and blindness to the Word of God, who, according to their own theory, holds the second [place of] production from the Propator. Admirable sophists, and explorers of the sublimities of the unknown Father, and rehearsers of those super-celestial mysteries "which the angels desire to look into!"[5] — that they may learn that from the Nous of that Father who is above all, the Word was produced *blind*, that is, ignorant of the Father who produced him!

---

[1] Comp. i. 2, 2.
[2] It seems needless to insert an "et" before this word, as Harvey suggests, or, as an alternative, to strike out the first "Nun Propatoris."

[3] Some read "cæcutientes" instead of "circumeuntes," as above.
[4] John ix. 1, etc.
[5] 1 Pet. i. 12.

10. But, ye miserable sophists, how could the Nous of the Father, or rather the very Father Himself, since He is Nous and perfect in all things, have produced his own Logos as an imperfect and blind Æon, when He was able also to produce along with him the knowledge of the Father? As ye affirm that Christ was generated [1] after the rest, and yet declare that he was produced perfect, much more then should Logos, who is anterior to him in age, be produced by the same Nous, unquestionably perfect, and not blind; nor could he, again, have produced Æons still blinder than himself, until at last your Sophia, always utterly blinded, gave birth to so vast a body of evils. And your Father is the cause of all this mischief; for ye declare the magnitude and power of your Father to be the causes of ignorance, assimilating Him to Bythus, and assigning this as a name to Him who is the unnameable Father. But if ignorance is an evil, and ye declare all evils to have derived their strength from it, while ye maintain that the greatness and power of the Father is the cause of this ignorance, ye do thus set Him forth as the author of [all] evils. For ye state as the cause of evil this fact, that [no one] could contemplate His greatness. But if it was really impossible for the Father to make Himself known from the beginning to those [beings] that were formed by Him, He must in that case be held free from blame, inasmuch as He *could not* remove the ignorance of those who came after Him. But if, at a subsequent period, when He so willed it, He *could* take away that ignorance which had increased with the successive productions as they followed each other, and thus become deeply seated in the Æons, much more, had He so willed it might He formerly have prevented that ignorance, which as yet was not, from coming into existence.

11. Since therefore, as soon as He so pleased, He did become known not only to the Æons, but also to these men who lived in these latter times; but, as He did not so please to be known from the beginning, He remained unknown — the cause of ignorance is, according to you, the will of the Father. For if He foreknew that these things would in future happen in such a manner, why then did He not guard against the ignorance of these beings before it had obtained a place among them, rather than afterwards, as if under the influence of repentance, deal with it through the production of Christ? For the knowledge which through Christ He conveyed to all, He might long before have imparted through Logos, who was also the first-begotten

of Monogenes. Or if, knowing them beforehand, He willed that these things should happen [as they have done], then the works of ignorance must endure for ever, and never pass away. For the things which have been made in accordance with the will of your Propator must continue along with the will of Him who willed them; or if they pass away, the will of Him also who decreed that they should have a being will pass away along with them. And why did the Æons find rest and attain perfect knowledge through learning [at last] that the Father is altogether [2] incomprehensible? They might surely have possessed this knowledge before they became involved in passion; for the greatness of the Father did not suffer diminution from the beginning, so that these might [3] know that He was altogether incomprehensible. For if, on account of His infinite greatness, He remained unknown, He ought also on account of His infinite love. to have preserved those impassible who were produced by Him, since nothing hindered, and expediency rather required, that they should have known from the beginning that the Father was altogether incomprehensible.

CHAP. XVIII. — SOPHIA WAS NEVER REALLY IN IGNORANCE OR PASSION; HER ENTHYMESIS COULD NOT HAVE BEEN SEPARATED FROM HERSELF, OR EXHIBITED SPECIAL TENDENCIES OF ITS OWN.

1. How can it be regarded as otherwise than absurd, that they also affirm this Sophia (wisdom) to have been involved in ignorance, and degeneracy, and passion? For these things are alien and contrary to wisdom, nor can they ever be qualities belonging to it. For wherever there is a want of foresight, and an ignorance of the course of utility, there wisdom does not exist. Let them therefore no longer call this suffering Æon, Sophia, but let them give up either her name or her sufferings. And let them, moreover, not call their entire Pleroma spiritual, if this Æon had a place within it when she was involved in such a tumult of passion. For even a vigorous soul, not to say a spiritual substance, would not pass through any such experience.

2. And, again, how could the Enthymesis, going forth [from her] along with the passion, have become a separate existence? For Enthymesis (thought) is understood in connection with some person, and can never have an isolated existence by itself. For a bad Enthymesis is destroyed and absorbed by a good one, even as a state of disease is by health. What, then, was the sort of Enthymesis which preceded that of passion? [It was this]: to investigate the [nature of] the Father, and to consider His

---

1 " Postgenitum quidem reliquis," the representative, according to Grabe, of ἀπόγονον μὲν λοιποῖς in the Greek. Harvey remarks that τῶν λοιπῶν would have been better, and proposes to read " progenitum " in the Latin; but we do not see any necessity for change.

2 " Incapabilis et incomprehensibilis," corresponding to ἀχώρητος καὶ ἀκατάληπτος in the Greek.
3 Literally, " to these knowing," " his scientibus."

greatness. But what did she afterwards become persuaded of, and so was restored to health? [This, viz.], that the Father is incomprehensible, and that He is past finding out. It was not, then, a proper feeling that she wished to know the Father, and on this account she became passible ; but when she became persuaded that He is unsearchable, she was restored to health. And even Nous himself, who was inquiring into the [nature of] the Father, ceased, according to them, to continue his researches, on learning that the Father is incomprehensible.

3. How then could the Enthymesis separately conceive passions, which themselves also were her affections? For affection is necessarily connected with an individual : it cannot come into being or exist apart by itself. This opinion [of theirs], however, is not only untenable, but also opposed to that which was spoken by our Lord : "Seek, and ye shall find."[1] For the Lord renders His disciples perfect by their seeking after and finding the Father ; but that Christ of theirs, who is above, has rendered them perfect, by the fact that He has commanded the Æons not to seek after the Father, persuading them that, though they should labour hard, they would not find Him. And they[2] declare that they themselves are perfect, by the fact that they maintain they have found their Bythus ; while the Æons [have been made perfect] through means of this, that *He* is unsearchable who was inquired after by them.

4. Since, therefore, the Enthymesis herself could not exist separately, apart from the Æon, [it is obvious that] they bring forward still greater falsehood concerning her passion, when they further proceed to divide and separate it from her, while they declare that it was the substance of matter. As if God were not light, and as if no Word existed who could convict them, and overthrow their wickedness. For it is certainly true, that whatsoever the Æon thought, that she also suffered ; and what she suffered, that she also thought. And her Enthymesis was, according to them, nothing else than the passion of one thinking how she might comprehend the incomprehensible. And thus Enthymesis (thought) was the passion ; for she was thinking of things impossible. How then could affection and passion be separated and set apart from the Enthymesis, so as to become the substance of so vast a material creation, when Enthymesis herself was the passion, and the passion Enthymesis? Neither, therefore, can Enthymesis apart from the Æon, nor the affections apart from Enthymesis, separately possess substance ; and thus once more their system breaks down and is destroyed.

5. But how did it come to pass that the Æon

was both dissolved [into her component parts], and became subject to passion? She was undoubtedly of the same substance as the Pleroma ; but the entire Pleroma was of the Father. Now, any substance, when brought in contact with what is of a similar nature, will not be dissolved into nothing, nor will be in danger of perishing, but will rather continue and increase, such as fire in fire, spirit in spirit, and water in water ; but those which are of a contrary nature to each other do, [when they meet,] suffer and are changed and destroyed. And, in like manner, if there had been a production of light, it would not suffer passion, or incur any danger in light like itself, but would rather glow with the greater brightness, and increase, as the day does from [the increasing brilliance of] the sun ; for they maintain that Bythus [himself] was the image of their father[3] (Sophia). Whatever animals are alien [in habits] and strange to each other, or are mutually opposed in nature, fall into danger [on meeting together], and are destroyed ; whereas, on the other hand, those who are accustomed to each other, and of a harmonious disposition, suffer no peril from being together in the same place, but rather secure both safety and life by such a fact. If, therefore, this Æon was produced by the Pleroma of the same substance as the whole of it, she could never have undergone change, since she was consorting with beings similar to and familiar with herself, a spiritual essence among those that were spiritual. For fear, terror, passion, dissolution, and such like, may perhaps occur through the struggle of contraries among such beings as we are, who are possessed of bodies ; but among spiritual beings, and those that have the light diffused among them, no such calamities can possibly happen. But these men appear to me to have endowed their Æon with the [same sort of] passion as belongs to that character in the comic poet Menander,[4] who was himself deeply in love, but an object of hatred [to his beloved]. For those who have invented such opinions have rather had an idea and mental conception of some unhappy lover among men, than of a spiritual and divine substance.

6. Moreover, to meditate how to search into [the nature of] the perfect Father, and to have a desire to exist within Him, and to have a comprehension of His [greatness], could not entail the stain of ignorance or passion, and that upon a spiritual Æon ; but would rather [give rise to] perfection, and impassibility, and truth. For they do not say that even they, though they be but men, by meditating on Him who was before

[1] Matt. vii. 7.
[2] It seems necessary to read " se quidem " instead of " si quidem," as in the mss.

[3] Although Sophia was a feminine Æon, she was regarded as being the father of Enthymesis, who again was the *mother* of the Valentinians.
[4] Stieren refers for this allusion to Meineke's edition of the *Reliquiæ Menan. et Philem.*, p. 116.

them, — and while now, as it were, comprehending the perfect, and being placed within the knowledge of Him, — are thus involved in a passion of perplexity, but rather attain to the knowledge and apprehension of truth. For they affirm that the Saviour said, " Seek, and ye shall find," to His disciples with this view, that they should seek after Him who, by means of imagination, has been conceived of by them as being above the Maker of all — the ineffable Bythus; and they desire themselves to be regarded as " the perfect," because they have sought and found the perfect One, while they are still on earth. Yet they declare that that Æon who was within the Pleroma, a wholly spiritual being, by seeking after the Propator, and endeavouring to find a place within His greatness, and desiring to have a comprehension of the truth of the Father, fell down into. [the endurance of] passion, and such a passion that, unless she had met with that Power who upholds all things, she would have been dissolved into the general substance [of the Æons], and thus come to an end of her [personal] existence.

7. Absurd is such presumption, and truly an opinion of men totally destitute of the truth. For, that this Æon is superior to themselves, and of greater antiquity, they themselves acknowledge, according to their own system, when they affirm that they are the fruit of the Enthymesis of that Æon who suffered passion, so that this Æon is the father of their mother, that is, their own grandfather. And to them, the later grandchildren, the search after the Father brings, as they maintain, truth, and perfection, and establishment, and deliverance from unstable matter, and reconciliation to the Father; but on their grandfather this same search entailed ignorance, and passion, and terror, and perplexity, from which [disturbances] they also declare that the substance of matter was formed. To say, therefore, that the search after and investigation of the perfect Father, and the desire for communion and union with Him, were things quite beneficial to them, but to an Æon, from whom also they derive their origin, these things were the cause of dissolution and destruction, how can such assertions be otherwise viewed than as totally inconsistent, foolish, and irrational? Those, too, who listen to these teachers, truly blind themselves, while they possess blind guides, justly [are left to] fall along with them into the gulf of ignorance which lies below them.

CHAP. XIX. — ABSURDITIES OF THE HERETICS AS TO THEIR OWN ORIGIN : THEIR OPINIONS RESPECTING THE DEMIURGE SHOWN TO BE EQUALLY UNTENABLE AND RIDICULOUS.

1. But what sort of talk also is this concerning their seed — that it was conceived by the mother according to the configuration of those angels who wait upon the Saviour, — shapeless, without form, and imperfect; and that it was deposited in the Demiurge without his knowledge, in order that through his instrumentality it might attain to perfection and form in that soul which he had, [so to speak,] filled with seed? This is to affirm, in the first place, that those angels who wait upon their Saviour are imperfect, and without figure or form; if indeed that which was conceived according to their appearance was generated any such kind of being [as has been described].

2. Then, in the next place, as to their saying that the Creator was ignorant of that deposit of seed which took place into him, and again, of that impartation of seed which was made by him to man, their words are futile and vain, and are in no way susceptible of proof. For how could he have been ignorant of it, if that seed had possessed any substance and peculiar properties? If, on the other hand, it was without substance and without quality, and so was really nothing, then, as a matter of course, he was ignorant of it. For those things which have a certain motion of their own, and quality, either of heat, or swiftness, or sweetness, or which differ from others in brilliance, do not escape the notice even of men, since they mingle in the sphere of human action : far less can they [be hidden from] God, the Maker of this universe. With reason, however, [is it said, that] their seed was not known to Him, since it is without any quality of general utility, and without the substance requisite for any action, and is, in fact, a pure nonentity. It really seems to me, that, with a view to such opinions, the Lord expressed Himself thus : " For every idle word that men speak, they shall give account on the day of judgment." [1] For all teachers of a like character to these, who fill men's ears with idle talk, shall, when they stand at the throne of judgment, render an account for those things which they have vainly imagined and falsely uttered against the Lord, proceeding, as they have done, to such a height of audacity as to declare of themselves that, on account of the substance of their seed, they are acquainted with the spiritual Pleroma, because that man who dwells within reveals to them the true Father; for the animal nature required [2] to be disciplined by means of the senses. But [they hold that] the Demiurge, while receiving into himself the whole of this seed, through its being deposited in him by the Mother, still remained utterly ignorant of all things, and had no understanding of anything connected with the Pleroma.

---

[1] Matt. xii. 36. [The serious spirit of this remark lends force to it as exposition.]
[2] Comp. i. 6, 1.

3. And that they are the truly "spiritual," inasmuch as a certain particle of the Father of the universe has been deposited in their souls, since, according to their assertions, they have souls formed of the same substance as the Demiurge himself, yet that he, although he received from the Mother, once for all, the whole [of the divine] seed, and possessed it in himself, still remained of an animal nature, and had not the slightest understanding of those things which are above, which things they boast that they themselves understand, while they are still on earth; — does not this crown all possible absurdity? For to imagine that the very same seed conveyed knowledge and perfection to the souls of these men, while it only gave rise to ignorance in the God who made them, is an opinion that can be held only by those utterly frantic, and totally destitute of common sense.

4. Further, it is also a most absurd and groundless thing for them to say that the seed was, by being thus deposited, reduced to form and increased, and so was prepared for all the reception of perfect rationality. For there will be in it an admixture of matter — that substance which they hold to have been derived from ignorance and defect; [and this will prove itself] more apt and useful than was the light of their Father, if indeed, when born, according to the contemplation of that [light], it was without form or figure, but derived from this [matter], form, and appearance, and increase, and perfection. For if that light which proceeds from the Pleroma was the cause to a spiritual being that it possessed neither form, nor appearance, nor its own special magnitude, while its descent to this world added all these things to it, and brought it to perfection, then a sojourn here (which they also term darkness) would seem much more efficacious and useful than was the light of their Father. But how can it be regarded as other than ridiculous, to affirm that their mother ran the risk of being almost extinguished in matter, and was almost on the point of being destroyed by it, had she not then with difficulty stretched herself outwards, and leaped, [as it were,] out of herself, receiving assistance from the Father; but that her seed increased in this same matter, and received a form, and was made fit for the reception of perfect rationality; and this, too, while "bubbling up" among substances dissimilar and unfamiliar to itself, according to their own declaration that the earthly is opposed to the spiritual, and the spiritual to the earthly? How, then, could "a little particle," [1] as they say, increase, and receive shape, and reach perfection, in the midst of substances contrary to and unfamiliar to itself?

5. But further, and in addition to what has been said, the question occurs, Did their mother, when she beheld the angels, bring forth the seed all at once, or only one by one [in succession]? If she brought forth the whole simultaneously and at once, that which was thus produced cannot now be of an infantile character: its descent, therefore, into those men who now exist must be superfluous. [2] But if one by one, then she did not form her conception according to the figure of those angels whom she beheld; for, contemplating them all together, and once for all, so as to conceive by them, she ought to have brought forth once for all the offspring of those from whose forms she had once for all conceived.

6. Why was it, too, that, beholding the angels along with the Saviour, she did indeed conceive *their* images, but not that of the *Saviour*, who is far more beautiful than they? Did He not please her; and did she not, on that account, conceive after His likeness? [3] How was it, too, that the Demiurge, whom they can call an animal being, having, as they maintain, his own special magnitude and figure, was produced perfect as respects his substance; while that which is spiritual, which also ought to be more effective than that which is animal, was sent forth imperfect, and he required to descend into a soul, that in it he might obtain form, and thus becoming perfect, might be rendered fit for the reception of perfect reason? If, then, he obtains form in mere earthly and animal men, he can no longer be said to be after the likeness of angels whom they call lights, but [after the likeness] of those men who are here below. For he will not possess in that case the likeness and appearance of angels, but of those souls in whom also he receives shape; just as water when poured into a vessel takes the form of that vessel, and if on any occasion it happens to congeal in it, it will acquire the form of the vessel in which it has thus been frozen, since souls themselves possess the figure [4] of the body [in which they dwell]; for they themselves have been adapted to the vessel [in which they exist], as I have said before. If, then, that seed [referred to] is here solidified and formed into a definite shape, it will possess the figure of a man, and not the form of the angels. How is it possible, therefore, that that seed should be after images of the angels, seeing it has obtained a form after the likeness of men? Why, again, since it was of a spiritual nature, had it any need of descending into flesh? For what is carnal stands in need of that which is spiritual, if indeed

---

[2] That is, there could be no need for its descending into them that it might increase, receive form, and thus be prepared for the reception of perfect reason.

[3] Or, " on beholding Him."

[4] As Massuet here remarks, we may infer from this passage that Irenæus believed souls to be corporeal, as being possessed of a definite form, — an opinion entertained by not a few of the ancients. [And, before we censure them, let us reflect whether their perceptions of " the carnal mind " as differing from the spirit of a man, may not account for it. I Thess. v. 23.]

it is to be saved, that in it it may be sanctified and cleared from all impurity, and that what is mortal may be swallowed up by immortality;[1] but that which is spiritual has no need whatever of those things which are here below. For it is not we who benefit it, but it that improves us.

7. Still more manifestly is that talk of theirs concerning their seed proved to be false, and that in a way which must be evident to every one, by the fact that they declare those souls which have received seed from the Mother to be superior to all others; wherefore also they have been honoured by the Demiurge, and constituted princes, and kings, and priests. For if this were true, the high priest Caiaphas, and Annas, and the rest of the chief priests, and doctors of the law, and rulers of the people, would have been the first to believe in the Lord, agreeing as they did with respect[2] to that relationship; and even before them should have been Herod the king. But since neither he, nor the chief priests, nor the rulers, nor the eminent of the people, turned to Him [in faith], but, on the contrary, those who sat begging by the highway, the deaf, and the blind, while He was rejected and despised by others, according to what Paul declares, "For ye see your calling, brethen, that there are not many wise men among you, not many noble, not many mighty; but those things of the world which were despised hath God chosen."[3] Such souls, therefore, were not superior to others on account of the seed deposited in them, nor on this account were they honoured by the Demiurge.

8. As to the point, then, that their system is weak and untenable as well as utterly chimerical, enough has been said. For it is not needful, to use a common proverb, that one should drink up the ocean who wishes to learn that its water is salt. But, just as in the case of a statue which is made of clay, but coloured on the outside that it may be thought to be of gold, while it really is of clay, any one who takes out of it a small particle, and thus laying it open reveals the clay, will set free those who seek the truth from a false opinion; in the same way have I (by exposing not a small part only, but the several heads of their system which are of the greatest importance) shown to as many as do not wish wittingly to be led astray, what is wicked, deceitful, seductive, and pernicious, connected with the school of the Valentinians, and all those other

heretics who promulgate[4] wicked opinions respecting the Demiurge, that is, the Fashioner and Former of this universe, and who is in fact the only true God—exhibiting, [as I have done,] how easily their views are overthrown.

9. For who that has any intelligence, and possesses only a small proportion of truth, can tolerate them, when they affirm that there is another god above the Creator; and that there is another Monogenes as well as another Word of God, whom also they describe as having been produced in [a state of] degeneracy; and another Christ, whom they assert to have been formed, along with the Holy Spirit, later than the rest of the Æons; and another Saviour, who, they say, did not proceed from the Father of all, but was a kind of joint production of those Æons who were formed in [a state of] degeneracy, and that He was produced of necessity on account of this very degeneracy? It is thus their opinion that, unless the Æons had been in a state of ignorance and degeneracy, neither Christ, nor the Holy Spirit, nor Horos, nor the Saviour, nor the angels, nor their Mother, nor her seed, nor the rest of the fabric of the world, would have been produced at all; but the universe would have been a desert, and destitute of the many good things which exist in it. They are therefore not only chargeable with impiety against the Creator, declaring Him the fruit of a defect, but also against Christ and the Holy Spirit, affirming that they were produced on account of that defect; and, in like manner, that the Saviour [was produced] subsequently to [the existence of] that defect. And who will tolerate the remainder of their vain talk, which they cunningly endeavour to accommodate to the parables, and have in this way plunged both themselves, and those who give credit to them, in the profoundest depths of impiety?

CHAP. XX. — FUTILITY OF THE ARGUMENTS ADDUCED TO DEMONSTRATE THE SUFFERINGS OF THE TWELFTH ÆON, FROM THE PARABLES, THE TREACHERY OF JUDAS, AND THE PASSION OF OUR SAVIOUR.

1. That they improperly and illogically apply both the parables and the actions of the Lord to their falsely-devised system, I prove as follows: They endeavour, for instance, to demonstrate that passion which, they say, happened in the case of the twelfth Æon, from this fact, that the passion of the Saviour was brought about by the twelfth apostle, and happened in the twelfth month. For they hold that He preached [only] for one year after His baptism. They maintain also that the same thing was clearly set forth in the case of her who suffered from the issue of blood. For the woman suffered during twelve years, and

---

[1] Comp. 1 Cor. xv. 44; 2 Cor. v. 4. [As a Catholic I cannot accept everything contained in the *Biblical Psychology* of Dr. Delitzsch, but may I entreat the reader who has not studied it to do so before dismissing the ideas of Irenæus on such topics. A translation has been provided for English readers, by the Messrs. T. & T. Clark of Edinburgh, 1867.]

[2] The meaning apparently is, that by the high position which all these in common occupied, they proved themselves, on the principles of the heretics, to belong to the favoured "seed," and should therefore have eagerly have welcomed the Lord. Or the meaning may be, "hurrying together to that relationship," that is, to the relationship secured by faith in Christ.

[3] 1 Cor. i. 26, 28, somewhat loosely quoted.

[4] "Male tractant;" literally, *handle badly.*

through touching the hem of the Saviour's garment she was made whole by that power which went forth from the Saviour, and which, they affirm, had a previous existence. For that Power who suffered was stretching herself outwards and flowing into immensity, so that she was in danger of being dissolved into the general substance [of the Æons] ; but then, touching the primary Tetrad, which is typified by the hem of the garment, she was arrested, and ceased from her passion.

2. Then, again, as to their assertion that the passion of the twelfth Æon was proved through the conduct of Judas, how is it possible that Judas can be compared [with this Æon] as being an emblem of her — he who was expelled from the number of the twelve,[1] and never restored to his place? For that Æon, whose type they declare Judas to be, after being separated from her Enthymesis, was restored or recalled [to her former position] ; but Judas was deprived [of his office], and cast out, while Matthias was ordained in his place, according to what is written, "And his bishopric let another take."[2] They ought therefore to maintain that the twelfth Æon was cast out of the Pleroma, and that another was produced, or sent forth to fill her place ; if, that is to say, she is pointed at in Judas. Moreover, they tell us that it was the Æon herself who suffered, but Judas was the betrayer, [and not the sufferer.] Even they themselves acknowledge that it was the suffering Christ, and not Judas, who came to [the endurance of] passion. How, then, could Judas, the betrayer of Him who had to suffer for our salvation, be the type and image of that Æon who suffered?

3. But, in truth, the passion of Christ was neither similar to the passion of the Æon, nor did it take place in similar circumstances. For the Æon underwent a passion of dissolution and destruction, so that she who suffered was in danger also of being destroyed. But the Lord, our Christ, underwent a valid, and not a merely[3] accidental passion ; not only was He Himself not in danger of being destroyed, but He also established fallen man[4] by His own strength, and recalled him to incorruption. The Æon, again, underwent passion while she was seeking after the Father, and was not able to find Him ; but the Lord suffered that He might bring those who have wandered from the Father, back to knowledge and to His fellowship. The search into the greatness of the Father became to her a passion leading to destruction ; but the Lord,

having suffered, and bestowing the knowledge of the Father, conferred on us salvation. Her passion, as they declare, gave origin to a female offspring, weak, infirm, unformed, and ineffective ; but His passion gave rise to strength and power. For the Lord, through means of suffering, "ascending into the lofty place, led captivity captive, gave gifts to men,"[5] and conferred on those that believe in Him the power "to tread upon serpents and scorpions, and on all the power of the enemy,"[6] that is, of the leader of apostasy. Our Lord also by His passion destroyed death, and dispersed error, and put an end to corruption, and destroyed ignorance, while He manifested life and revealed truth, and bestowed the gift of incorruption. But their Æon, when she had suffered, established[7] ignorance, and brought forth a substance without shape, out of which all material works have been produced — death, corruption, error, and such like.

4. Judas, then, the twelfth in order of the disciples, was not a type of the suffering Æon, nor, again, was the passion of the Lord ; for these two things have been shown to be in every respect mutually dissimilar and inharmonious. This is the case not only as respects the points which I have already mentioned, but with regard to the very number. For that Judas the traitor is the twelfth in order, is agreed upon by all, there being twelve apostles mentioned by name in the Gospel. But this Æon is not the *twelfth*, but the *thirtieth*; for, according to the views under consideration, there were not twelve Æons only produced by the will of the Father, nor was she sent forth the twelfth in order : they reckon her, [on the contrary,] as having been produced in the thirtieth place. How, then, can Judas, the twelfth in order, be the type and image of that Æon who occupies the thirtieth place?

5. But if they say that Judas in perishing was the image of her Enthymesis, neither in this way will the image bear any analogy to that truth which [by hypothesis] corresponds to it. For the Enthymesis having been separated fromt he Æon, and itself afterwards receiving a shape from Christ,[8] then being made a partaker of intelligence by the Saviour, and having formed all things which are outside of the Pleroma, after the image of those which are within the Pleroma, is said at last to have been received by them into the Pleroma, and, according to [the principle of] conjunction, to have been united to that Saviour who was formed out of all. But Judas having been once for all cast away, never returns

---

[1] Or, "from the twelfth number" — the twelfth position among the apostles.
[2] Acts i. 20, from Ps. cix. 8.
[3] The text is here uncertain. Most editions read "et quæ non cederet," but Harvey prefers "quæ non accederet" (for "accideret"), and remarks that the corresponding Greek would be καὶ οὐ τυχὸν, which we have translated as above.
[4] "Corruptum hominem."

[5] Ps. lxviii. 18; Eph. iv. 8.
[6] Luke x. 19; [Mark xvi. 17, 18.]
[7] Though the reading "substituit" is found in all the MSS. and editions, it has been deemed corrupt, and "sustinuit" has been proposed instead of it. Harvey supposes it the equivalent of ὑπεστηυ·, and then somewhat strangely adds "for ἀπέστησε." There seems to us no difficulty in the word, and consequently no necessity for change.
[8] Compare, in illustration of this sentence, book i. 4, 1, and i. 4, 5.

into the number of the disciples; otherwise a different person would not have been chosen to fill his place. Besides, the Lord also declared regarding him, "Woe to the man by whom the Son of man shall be betrayed;"[1] and, "It were better for him if he had never been born;"[2] and he was called the "son of perdition"[3] by Him. If, however, they say that Judas was a type of the Enthymesis, not as separated from the Æon, but of the passion entwined with her, neither in this way can the number twelve be regarded as a [fitting] type of the number three. For in the one case Judas was cast away, and Matthias was ordained instead of him; but in the other case, the Æon is said to have been in danger of dissolution and destruction, and [there are also] her Enthymesis and passion: for they markedly distinguish Enthymesis from the passion; and they represent the Æon as being restored, and Enthymesis as acquiring form, but the passion, when separated from these, as becoming matter. Since, therefore, there are thus these three, the Æon, her Enthymesis, and her passion, Judas and Matthias, being only two, cannot be the types of them.

CHAP. XXI.—THE TWELVE APOSTLES WERE NOT A TYPE OF THE ÆONS.

1. If, again, they maintain that the twelve apostles were a type only of that group of twelve Æons which Anthropos in conjunction with Ecclesia produced, then let them produce ten other apostles as a type of those ten remaining Æons, who, as they declare, were produced by Logos and Zoe. For it is unreasonable to suppose that the junior, and for that reason inferior Æons, were set forth by the Saviour through the election of the apostles, while their seniors, and on this account their superiors, were not thus foreshown; since the Saviour (if, that is to say, He chose the apostles with this view, that by means of them He might show forth the Æons who are in the Pleroma) might have chosen other ten apostles also, and likewise other eight before these, that thus He might set forth the original and primary Ogdoad. He could not,[4] in regard to the second [Duo] Decad, show forth [any emblem of it] through the number of the apostles being [already] constituted a type. For [He made choice of no such other number of disciples; but] after the twelve apostles, our Lord is found to have sent seventy others before Him.[5] Now *seventy* cannot possibly be the type either of an Ogdoad,

a Decad, or a Triacontad. What is the reason, then, that the inferior Æons are, as I have said, represented by means of the apostles; but the superior, from whom, too, the former derived their being, are not prefigured at all? But if[6] the twelve apostles were chosen with this object, that the number of the twelve Æons might be indicated by means of them, then the seventy also ought to have been chosen to be the type of seventy Æons; and in that case, they must affirm that the Æons are no longer thirty, but eighty-two in number. For He who made choice of the apostles, that they might be a type of those Æons existing in the Pleroma, would never have constituted them types of some and not of others; but by means of the apostles He would have tried to preserve an image and to exhibit a type of those Æons that exist in the Pleroma.

2. Moreover, we must not keep silence respecting Paul, but demand from them after the type of what Æon that apostle has been handed down to us, unless perchance [they affirm that he is a representative] of the Saviour compounded of them [all], who derived his being from the collected gifts of the whole, and whom they term *All Things*, as having been formed out of them all. Respecting this being the poet Hesiod has strikingly expressed himself, styling him Pandora — that is, "The gift of all" — for this reason, that the best gift in the possession of all was centred in him. In describing these gifts the following account is given: Hermes (so[7] he is called in the Greek language), Αἰμυλίους[8] τε λόγους καὶ ἐπίκλοπον ἦθος αὐτοὺς Κάτθετο (or to express this in the English[9] language), "implanted words of fraud and deceit in their minds, and thievish habits," for the purpose of leading foolish men astray, that such should believe their falsehoods. For their Mother — that is, Leto[10] — secretly stirred them up (whence also she is called Leto,[11] according to the meaning of the Greek word, because she *secretly* stirred up men), without the knowledge of the Demiurge, to give forth profound and unspeakable mysteries to itching ears.[12] And not only did their Mother bring it about that this mystery should be declared by Hesiod; but very skilfully also by means of the lyric poet Pindar, when he describes to the Demiurge[13] the

---

[1] Matt. xxvi. 24.
[2] Mark xiv. 21.
[3] John xvii. 12.
[4] This passage is hopelessly corrupt. The editors have twisted it in every direction, but with no satisfactory result. Our version is quite as far from being certainly trustworthy as any other that has been proposed, but it seems something like the meaning of the words as they stand. Both the text and punctuation of the Latin are in utter confusion.
[5] Luke x. 1.

[6] "Si" is wanting in the MSS. and early editions, and Harvey pleads for its exclusion, but the sense becomes clearer through inserting it.
[7] This clause is, of course, an interpolation by the Latin translator.
[8] The words are loosely quoted *memoriter*, as is the custom with Irenæus. See Hesiod, *Works and Days*, i. 77, etc.
[9] *Latin*, of course, in the text.
[10] There is here a play upon the words Λητώ and ληθεῖν, the former being supposed to be derived from the latter, so as to denote *secrecy*.
[11] This clause is probably an interpolation by the translator.
[12] 2 Tim. iv. 3.
[13] "Cœlet Demiurgo," such is the reading in all the MSS. and editions. Harvey, however, proposes to read "celet Demiurgum;" but the change which he suggests, besides being without authority, does not clear away the obscurity which hangs upon the sentence.

case of Pelops, whose flesh was cut in pieces by the Father, and then collected and brought together, and compacted anew by all the gods,[1] did she in this way indicate Pandora; and these men having their consciences seared[*2] by her, declaring, as they maintain, the very same things, are [proved] of the same family and spirit as the others.

CHAP. XXII. — THE THIRTY ÆONS ARE NOT TYPIFIED BY THE FACT THAT CHRIST WAS BAPTIZED IN HIS THIRTIETH YEAR: HE DID NOT SUFFER IN THE TWELFTH MONTH AFTER HIS BAPTISM, BUT WAS MORE THAN FIFTY YEARS OLD WHEN HE DIED.

1. I have shown that the number *thirty* fails them in every respect; too few Æons, as they represent them, being at one time found within the Pleroma, and then again too many [to correspond with that number]. There are not, therefore, thirty Æons, nor did the Saviour come to be baptized when He was thirty years old, for this reason, that He might show forth the thirty silent[3] Æons of their system, otherwise they must first of all separate and eject [the Saviour] Himself from the Pleroma of all. Moreover, they affirm that He suffered in the twelfth month, so that He continued to preach for one year after His baptism; and they endeavour to establish this point out of the prophet (for it is written, "To proclaim the acceptable year of the Lord, and the day of retribution"[4]), being truly blind, inasmuch as they affirm they have found out the mysteries of Bythus, yet not understanding that which is called by Isaiah the acceptable year of the Lord, nor the day of retribution. For the prophet neither speaks concerning a day which includes the space of twelve hours, nor of a year the length of which is twelve months. For even they themselves acknowledge that the prophets have very often expressed themselves in parables and allegories, and [are] not [to be understood] according to the mere sound of the words.

2. That, then, was called the day of retribution on which the Lord will render to every one according to his works — that is, the judgment. The acceptable year of the Lord, again, is this present time, in which those who believe Him are called by Him, and become acceptable to God — that is, the whole time from His advent onwards to the consummation [of all things], during which He acquires to Himself as fruits [of the scheme of mercy] those who are saved.

For, according to the phraseology of the prophet, the day of retribution follows the [acceptable] year; and the prophet will be proved guilty of falsehood if the Lord preached only for a year, and if he speaks of it. For where is the day of retribution? For the year has passed, and the day of retribution has not yet come; but He still "makes His sun to rise upon the good and upon the evil, and sends rain upon the just and unjust."[5] And the righteous suffer persecution, are afflicted, and are slain, while sinners are possessed of abundance, and "drink with the sound of the harp and psaltery, but do not regard the works of the Lord."[6] But, according to the language [used by the prophet], they ought to be combined, and the day of retribution to follow the [acceptable] year. For the words are, "to proclaim the acceptable year of the Lord, and the day of retribution." This present time, therefore, in which men are called and saved by the Lord, is properly understood to be denoted by "the acceptable year of the Lord;" and there follows on this "the day of retribution," that is, the judgment. And the time thus referred to is not called "a year" only, but is also named "a day" both by the prophet and by Paul, of whom the apostle, calling to mind the Scripture, says in the Epistle addressed to the Romans, "As it is written, for thy sake we are killed all the day long, we are counted as sheep for the slaughter."[7] But here the expression "all the day long" is put for all this time during which we suffer persecution, and are killed as sheep. As then this *day* does not signify one which consists of twelve hours, but the whole time during which believers in Christ suffer and are put to death for His sake, so also the *year* there mentioned does not denote one which consists of twelve months, but the whole time of faith during which men hear and believe the preaching of the Gospel, and those become acceptable to God who unite themselves to Him.

3. But it is greatly to be wondered at, how it has come to pass that, while affirming that they have found out the mysteries of God, they have not examined the Gospels to ascertain how often after His baptism the Lord went up, at the time of the passover, to Jerusalem, in accordance with what was the practice of the Jews from every land, and every year, that they should assemble at this period in Jerusalem, and there celebrate the feast of the passover. First of all, after He had made the water wine at Cana of Galilee, He went up to the festival day of the passover, on which occasion it is written, "For many believed in Him, when they saw the signs which He did,"[8]

---

[1] Comp. Pindar, *Olymp.*, i. 38, etc.
[2] "Compuncti," supposed to correspond to κεκαυτηριασμένοι: see 1 Tim. iv. 2. The whole passage is difficult and obscure.
[3] Harvey wishes, without any authority, to substitute "tacitus" for "tacitos," but there is no necessity for alteration. Irenæus is here playing upon the word, according to a practice in which he delights, and quietly scoffs at the *Sige* (Silence) of the heretics by styling those Æons *silent* who were derived from her.
[4] Isa. lxi. 2.

[5] Matt. v. 45.
[6] Isa. v. 12.
[7] Rom. viii. 36.
[8] John ii. 23.

as John the disciple of the Lord records. Then, again, withdrawing Himself [from Judæa], He is found in Samaria; on which occasion, too, He conversed with the Samaritan woman, and while at a distance, cured the son of the centurion by a word, saying, "Go thy way, thy son liveth."[1] Afterwards He went up, the second time, to observe the festival day of the passover[2] in Jerusalem; on which occasion He cured the paralytic man, who had lain beside the pool thirty-eight years, bidding him rise, take up his couch, and depart. Again, withdrawing from thence to the other side of the sea of Tiberias,[3] He there, seeing a great crowd had followed Him, fed all that multitude with five loaves of bread, and twelve baskets of fragments remained over and above. Then, when He had raised Lazarus from the dead, and plots were formed against Him by the Pharisees, He withdrew to a city called Ephraim; and from that place, as it is written, "He came to Bethany six days before the passover,"[4] and going up from Bethany to Jerusalem, He there ate the passover, and suffered on the day following. Now, that these three occasions of the passover are not included within one year, every person whatever must acknowledge. And that the special month in which the passover was celebrated, and in which also the Lord suffered, was not the twelfth, but the first, those men who boast that they know all things, if they know not this, may learn it from Moses. Their explanation, therefore, both of the year and of the twelfth month has been proved false, and they ought to reject either their explanation or the Gospel; otherwise [this unanswerable question forces itself upon them], How is it possible that the Lord preached for one year only?

4. Being thirty years old when He came to be baptized, and then possessing the full age of a Master,[5] He came to Jerusalem, so that He might be properly acknowledged[6] by all as a Master. For He did not seem one thing while He was another, as those affirm who describe Him as being man only in appearance; but what He was, that He also appeared to be. Being a Master, therefore, He also possessed the age of a Master, not despising or evading any condition

of humanity, nor setting aside in Himself that law which He had[7] appointed for the human race, but sanctifying every age, by that period corresponding to it which belonged to Himself. For He came to save all through means of Himself—all, I say, who through Him are born again to God[8]—infants,[9] and children, and boys, and youths, and old men. He therefore passed through every age, becoming an infant for infants, thus sanctifying infants; a child for children, thus sanctifying those who are of this age, being at the same time made to them an example of piety, righteousness, and submission; a youth for youths, becoming an example to youths, and thus sanctifying them for the Lord. So likewise He was an old man for old men, that He might be a perfect Master for all, not merely as respects the setting forth of the truth, but also as regards age, sanctifying at the same time the aged also, and becoming an example to them likewise. Then, at last, He came on to death itself, that He might be "the first-born from the dead, that in all things He might have the pre-eminence,"[10] the Prince of life,[11] existing before all, and going before all.[12]

5. They, however, that they may establish their false opinion regarding that which is written, "to proclaim the acceptable year of the Lord," maintain that He preached for one year only, and then suffered in the twelfth month. [In speaking thus], they are forgetful to their own disadvantage, destroying His whole work, and robbing Him of that age which is both more necessary and more honourable than any other; that more advanced age, I mean, during which also as a teacher He excelled all others. For how could He have had disciples, if He did not teach? And how could He have taught, unless He had reached the age of a Master? For when He came to be baptized, He had not yet completed His thirtieth year, but was beginning to be about thirty years of age (for thus Luke, who has mentioned His years, has expressed it: "Now Jesus was, as it were, beginning to be thirty years old,"[13] when He came to receive baptism); and, [according to these men,] He preached only one year reckoning from His baptism. On completing His thirtieth year He suffered, being in fact still a young man, and who had by no means attained to advanced age. Now, that the first

1 John iv. 50.
2 John v. 1, etc. It is well known that, to fix what is meant by the ἑορτή, referred to in this passage of St. John, is one of the most difficult points in New Testament criticism. Some modern scholars think that the feast of Purim is intended by the Evangelist: but, upon the whole, the current of opinion that has always prevailed in the Church has been in favour of the statement here made by Irenæus. Christ would therefore be present at four passovers after His baptism: (1) John ii. 13; (2) John v. 1; (3) John vi. 4; (4) John xiii. 1.
3 John vi. 1, etc.
4 John xi. 54, xii. 1.
5 Or, "teacher," magistri.
6 Harvey strangely remarks here, that "the reading audiret, followed by Massuet, makes no sense." He gives audiretur in his text, but proposes to read ordiretur. The passage may, however, be translated as above, without departing from the Benedictine reading audiret.

7 "Neque solvens suam legem in se humani generis." Massuet would expunge "suam;" but, as Harvey well observes, "it has a peculiar significance, nor abrogating his own law."
8 "Renascuntur in Deum." The reference in these words is doubtless to baptism, as clearly appears from comparing book iii. 17, 1.
9 It has been remarked by Wall and others, that we have here the statement of a valuable fact as to the baptism of infants in the primitive Church.
10 Col. i. 18.
11 Acts iii. 15.
12 [That our Lord was prematurely old may be inferred from the text which Irenæus regards as proof that he literally lived to be old. St. John viii. 56, 57; comp. Is. liii. 2.]
13 Luke iii. 23.

stage of early life embraces thirty years,[1] and that this extends onwards to the fortieth year, every one will admit; but from the fortieth and fiftieth year a man begins to decline towards old age, which our Lord possessed while He still fulfilled the office of a Teacher, even as the Gospel and all the elders testify; those who were conversant in Asia with John, the disciple of the Lord, [affirming] that John conveyed to them that information.[2] And he remained among them up to the times of Trajan.[3] Some of them, moreover, saw not only John, but the other apostles also, and heard the very same account from them, and bear testimony as to the [validity of] the statement. Whom then should we rather believe? Whether such men as these, or Ptolemæus, who never saw the apostles, and who never even in his dreams attained to the slightest trace of an apostle?

6. But, besides this, those very Jews who then disputed with the Lord Jesus Christ have most clearly indicated the same thing. For when the Lord said to them, "Your father Abraham rejoiced to see My day; and he saw it, and was glad," they answered Him, "Thou art not yet fifty years old, and hast Thou seen Abraham?"[4] Now, such language is fittingly applied to one who has already passed the age of forty, without having as yet reached his fiftieth year, yet is not far from this latter period. But to one who is only thirty years old it would unquestionably be said, "Thou art not yet forty years old." For those who wished to convict Him of falsehood would certainly not extend the number of His years far beyond the age which they saw He had attained; but they mentioned a period near His real age, whether they had truly ascertained this out of the entry in the public register, or simply made a conjecture from what they observed that He was above forty years old, and that He certainly was not one of only thirty years of age. For it is altogether unreasonable to suppose that they were mistaken by twenty years, when they wished to prove Him younger than the times of Abraham. For what they saw, that they also expressed; and He whom they beheld was not

a mere phantasm, but an actual being[5] of flesh and blood. He did not then want much of being fifty years old;[6] and, in accordance with that fact, they said to Him, "Thou art not yet fifty years old, and hast Thou seen Abraham?" He did not therefore preach only for one year, nor did He suffer in the twelfth month of the year. For the period included between the thirtieth and the fiftieth year can never be regarded as *one* year, unless indeed, among their Æons, there be so long years assigned to those who sit in their ranks with Bythus in the Pleroma; of which beings Homer the poet, too, has spoken, doubtless being inspired by the Mother of their [system of] error: —

Οἱ δὲ θεοὶ πὰρ Ζηνὶ καθήμενοι ἠγορόωντο
Χρυσέῳ ἐν δαπέδῳ:[7]

which we may thus render into English:[8] —

"The gods sat round, while Jove presided o'er,
And converse held upon the golden floor."

CHAP. XXIII. — THE WOMAN WHO SUFFERED FROM AN ISSUE OF BLOOD WAS NO TYPE OF THE SUFFERING ÆON.

1. Moreover, their ignorance comes out in a clear light with respect to the case of that woman who, suffering from an issue of blood, touched the hem of the Lord's garment, and so was made whole; for they maintain that through her was shown forth that twelfth power who suffered passion, and flowed out towards immensity, that is, the twelfth Æon. [This ignorance of theirs appears] first, because, as I have shown, according to their own system, that was not the twelfth Æon. But even granting them this point [in the meantime], there being twelve Æons, eleven of these are said to have continued impassible, while the twelfth suffered passion; but the woman, on the other hand, being healed in the twelfth year, it is manifest that she had continued to suffer during eleven years, and was healed in the twelfth. If indeed they were to say that eleven Æons were involved in passion, but the twelfth one was healed, it would then be a plausible thing to say that the woman was a type of these. But since she suffered during eleven years, and [all that time] obtained no cure, but was healed in the twelfth year, in what way can she be a type of the twelfth of the Æons, eleven of whom, [according to hypothesis,] did not suffer at all, but the twelfth alone participated in suffering? For a type and emblem is, no doubt, sometimes diverse from the truth [signified] as to matter and substance; but it ought, as to the general form and features, to maintain

---

[1] The Latin text of this clause is, "Quia autem triginta annorum ætas prima indolis est juvenis" — words which it seems almost impossible to translate. Grabe regarded "indolis" as being in the nominative, while Massuet contends it is in the genitive case; and so regarding it, we might translate, " Now that the age of thirty is the first age of the mind of youth," etc. But Harvey re-translates the clause into Greek as follows: Ὅτι δὲ ἡ τῶν τριάκοντα ἐτῶν ἡλικία ἡ πρώτη τῆς διαθέσεώς ἐστι νέας — words which we have endeavoured to render as above. The meaning clearly is, that the age of thirty marked the transition point from youth to maturity.

[2] With respect to this extraordinary assertion of Irenæus, Harvey remarks: " The reader may here perceive the unsatisfactory character of tradition, where a mere fact is concerned. From reasonings founded upon the evangelical history, as well as from a preponderance of external testimony, it is most certain that our Lord's ministry extended but little over three years; yet here Irenæus states that it included more than ten years, and appeals to a tradition derived, as he says, from those who had conversed with an apostle.

[3] Trajan's reign commenced A.D. 98, and St. John is said to have lived to the age of a hundred years.

[4] John viii. 56, 57.

[5] Sed veritas " — literally, " the truth."

[6] [This statement is simply astounding, and might seem a providential illustration of the worthlessness of *mere* tradition unsustained by the written Word. No mere tradition could be more creditably authorized than this.]

[7] *Iliad*, iv. 1.

[8] *Latin*, of course, in the text.

a likeness [to what is typified], and in this way to shadow forth by means of things present those which are yet to come.

2. And not only in the case of this woman have the years of her infirmity (which they affirm to fit in with their figment) been mentioned, but, lo ! another woman was also healed, after suffering in like manner for eighteen years ; concerning whom the Lord said, "And ought not this daughter of Abraham, whom Satan has bound during eighteen years, to be set free on the Sabbath-day?"[1] If, then, the former was a type of the twelfth Æon that suffered, the latter should also be a type of the eighteenth Æon in suffering. But they cannot maintain this ; otherwise their primary and original Ogdoad will be included in the number of Æons who suffered together. Moreover, there was also a certain other person[2] healed by the Lord, after he had suffered for eight-and-thirty years : they ought therefore to affirm that the Æon who occupies the thirty-eighth place suffered. For if they assert that the things which were done by the Lord were types of what took place in the Pleroma, the type ought to be preserved throughout. But they can neither adapt to their fictitious system the case of her who was cured after eighteen years, nor of him who was cured after thirty-eight years. Now, it is in every way absurd and inconsistent to declare that the Saviour preserved the type in certain cases, while He did not do so in others. The type of the woman, therefore, [with the issue of blood] is shown to have no analogy to their system of Æons.[3]

CHAP. XXIV. — FOLLY OF THE ARGUMENTS DERIVED BY THE HERETICS FROM NUMBERS, LETTERS, AND SYLLABLES.

1. This very thing, too, still further demonstrates their opinion false, and their fictitious system untenable, that they endeavour to bring forward proofs of it, sometimes through means of numbers and the syllables of names, sometimes also through the letter of syllables, and yet again through those numbers which are, according to the practice followed by the Greeks, contained in [different] letters ; — [this, I say,] demonstrates in the clearest manner their overthrow or confusion,[4] as well as the untenable and perverse character of their [professed] knowledge. For, transferring the name *Jesus*, which belongs to another language, to the numeration of the Greeks, they sometimes call it "Episemon,"[5] as having six letters, and at other

times "the Plenitude of the Ogdoads," as containing the number eight hundred and eighty-eight. But His [corresponding] Greek name, which is "Soter," that is, *Saviour*, because it does not fit in with their system, either with respect to numerical value or as regards its letters, they pass over in silence. Yet surely, if they regard the names of the Lord, as, in accordance with the preconceived purpose of the Father, by means of their numerical value and letters, indicating number in the Pleroma, *Soter*, as being a Greek name, ought by means of its letters and the numbers [expressed by these], in virtue of its being Greek, to show forth the mystery of the Pleroma. But the case is not so, because it is a word of five letters, and its numerical value is one thousand four hundred and eight.[6] But these things do not in any way correspond with their Pleroma : the account, therefore, which they give of transactions in the Pleroma cannot be true.

2. Moreover, *Jesus*, which is a word belonging to the proper tongue of the Hebrews, contains, as the learned among them declare, two letters and a half,[7] and signifies that Lord who contains heaven and earth ;[8] for *Jesus* in the ancient Hebrew language means "heaven," while again "earth" is expressed by the words *sura usser*.[9] The word, therefore, which contains heaven and earth is just *Jesus*. Their explanation, then, of the *Episemon* is false, and their numerical calculation is also manifestly overthrown. For, in their own language, *Soter* is a Greek word of five letters ; but, on the other hand, in the Hebrew tongue, *Jesus* contains only two letters and a half. The total which they reckon up, viz., eight hundred and eighty-eight, therefore falls to the ground. And throughout, the Hebrew letters do not correspond in number with the Greek, although these especially, as being the more ancient and unchanging, ought to uphold the reckoning connected with the names. For these ancient, original, and generally called *sacred* letters[10] of the Hebrews are ten in number (but they are written by means of fifteen[11]), the last letter

[1] Luke xiii. 16.
[2] John v. 5.
[3] The text of this sentence is very uncertain. We follow Massuet's reading, "negotio Æonum," in preference to that suggested by Harvey.
[4] "Sive confusionem" is very probably a marginal gloss which has found its way into the text. The whole clause is difficult and obscure.
[5] Comp. i. 14, 4.

[6] Thus: Σωτήρ (σ = 200, ω = 800, τ = 300, η = 8, ρ = 100) = 1408.
[7] Being written thus, יש׳, and the small ׳ being apparently regarded as only half a letter. Harvey proposes a different solution which seems less probable.
[8] This is one of the most obscure passages in the whole work of Irenæus, and the editors have succeeded in throwing very little light upon it. We may merely state that יש׳ seems to be regarded as containing in itself the initials of the three words יהוה, *Jehovah;* שמים, *heaven;* and וארץ, *and earth.*
[9] Nothing can be made of these words: they have probably been corrupted by ignorant transcribers, and are now wholly unintelligible.
[10] "Literæ sacerdotales," — another enigma which no man can solve. Massuet supposes the reference to be to the archaic Hebrew characters, still used by the *priests* after the square Chaldaic letters had been generally adopted. Harvey thinks that *sacerdotales* represents the Greek λειτουργικά, "meaning letters as popularly used in common computation."
[11] The editors have again long notes on this most obscure passage. Massuet expunges "quæque," and gives a lengthened explanation of the clause, to which we can only refer the curious reader.

being joined to the first. And thus they write some of these letters according to their natural sequence, just as we do, but others in a reverse direction, from the right hand towards the left, thus tracing the letters backwards. The name *Christ*, too, ought to be capable of being reckoned up in harmony with the Æons of their Pleroma, inasmuch as, according to their statements, He was produced for the establishment and rectification of their Pleroma. The Father, too, in the same way, ought, both by means of letters and numerical value, to contain the number of those Æons who were produced by Him; Bythus, in like manner, and not less Monogenes; but pre-eminently the name which is above all others, by which God is called, and which in the Hebrew tongue is expressed by *Baruch*,[1] [a word] which also contains two and a half letters. From this fact, therefore, that the more important names, both in the Hebrew and Greek languages, do not conform to their system, either as respects the number of letters or the reckoning brought out of them, the forced character of their calculations respecting the rest becomes clearly manifest.

3. For, choosing out of the law whatever things agree with the number adopted in their system, they thus violently strive to obtain proofs of its validity. But if it was really the purpose of their Mother, or the Saviour, to set forth, by means of the Demiurge, types of those things which are in the Pleroma, they should have taken care that the types were found in things more exactly correspondent and more holy; and, above all, in the case of the Ark of the Covenant, on account of which the whole tabernacle of witness was formed. Now it was constructed thus: its length[2] was two cubits and a half, its breadth one cubit and a half, its height one cubit and a half; but such a number of cubits in no respect corresponds with their system, yet by it the type ought to have been, beyond everything else, clearly set forth. The mercy-seat[3] also does in like manner not at all harmonize with their expositions. Moreover, the table of shew-bread[4] was two cubits in length, while its height was a cubit and a half. These stood before the holy of holies, and yet in them not a single number is of such an amount as contains an indication of the Tetrad, or the Ogdoad, or of the rest of their Pleroma. What of the candlestick,[5] too, which had seven[6] branches and seven lamps? while, if these had

been made according to the type, it ought to have had eight branches and a like number of lamps, after the type of the primary Ogdoad, which shines pre-eminently among the Æons, and illuminates the whole Pleroma. They have carefully enumerated the curtains[7] as being ten, declaring these a type of the ten Æons; but they have forgotten to count the coverings of skin, which were eleven[8] in number. Nor, again, have they measured the size of these very curtains, each curtain[9] being eight-and-twenty cubits in length. And they set forth the length of the pillars as being ten cubits, with a reference to the Decad of Æons. "But the breadth of each pillar was a cubit and a half;"[10] and this they do not explain, any more than they do the entire number of the pillars or of their bars, because that does not suit the argument. But what of the anointing oil,[11] which sanctified the whole tabernacle? Perhaps it escaped the notice of the Saviour, or, while their Mother was sleeping, the Demiurge of himself gave instructions as to its weight; and on this account it is out of harmony with their Pleroma, consisting,[12] as it did, of five hundred shekels of myrrh, five hundred of cassia, two hundred and fifty of cinnamon, two hundred and fifty of calamus, and oil in addition, so that it was composed of five ingredients. The incense[13] also, in like manner, [was compounded] of stacte, onycha, galbanum, mint, and frankincense, all which do in no respect, either as to their mixture or weight, harmonize with their argument. It is therefore unreasonable and altogether absurd [to maintain] that the types were not preserved in the sublime and more imposing enactments of the law; but in other points, when any number coincides with their assertions, to affirm that it was a type of the things in the Pleroma; while [the truth is, that] every number occurs with the utmost variety in the Scriptures, so that, should any one desire it, he might form not only an Ogdoad, and a Decad, and a Duodecad, but any sort of number from the Scriptures, and then maintain that this was a type of the system of error devised by himself.

4. But that this point is true, that that number which is called *five*, which agrees in no respect with their argument, and does not harmonize with their system, nor is suitable for a typical manifestation of the things in the Pleroma, [yet has a wide prevalence,[14]] will be proved as follows from the Scriptures. Soter is a name of

---

1 בָּרוּךְ, Baruch, *blessed*, one of the commonest titles of the Almighty. The final ך seems to be reckoned only a half-letter, as being different in form from what it is when accompanied by a vowel at the beginning or in the middle of a word.
2 Ex. xxv. 10.
3 Ex. xxv. 17.
4 Ex. xxv. 23.
5 Ex. xxv. 31, etc.
6 Only *six* branches are mentioned in Ex. xxv. 32.

7 Ex. xxvi. 1.
8 Ex. xxvi. 7.
9 Ex. xxvi. 2.
10 Ex. xxvi. 16.
11 Ex. xxvi. 26.
12 Ex. xxx. 23, etc.
13 Ex. xxx. 34.
14 Some such supplement as this seems requisite, but the syntax in the Latin text is very confused.

five letters; Pater, too, contains five letters; Agape (love), too, consists of five letters; and our Lord, after [1] blessing the five loaves, fed with them five thousand men. Five virgins [2] were called wise by the Lord; and, in like manner, five were styled foolish. Again, five men are said to have been with the Lord when He obtained testimony [3] from the Father, — namely, Peter, and James, and John, and Moses, and Elias. The Lord also, as the fifth person, entered into the apartment of the dead maiden, and raised her up again; for, says [the Scripture], "He suffered no man to go in, save Peter and James, [4] and the father and mother of the maiden." [5] The rich man in hell [6] declared that he had five brothers, to whom he desired that one rising from the dead should go. The pool from which the Lord commanded the paralytic man to go into his house, had five porches. The very form of the cross, too, has five extremities, [7] two in length, two in breadth, and one in the middle, on which [last] the person rests who is fixed by the nails. Each of our hands has five fingers; we have also five senses; our internal organs may also be reckoned as five, viz., the heart, the liver, the lungs, the spleen, and the kidneys. Moreover, even the whole person may be divided into this number [of parts], — the head, the breast, the belly, the thighs, and the feet. The human race passes through five ages: first infancy, then boyhood, then youth, then maturity, [8] and then old age. Moses delivered the law to the people in five books. Each table which he received from God contained five [9] commandments. The veil covering [10] the holy of holies had five pillars. The altar of burnt-offering also was five cubits in breadth. [11] Five priests were chosen in the wilderness, — namely, Aaron, [12] Nadab, Abiud, Eleazar, Ithamar. The ephod and the breastplate, and other sacerdotal vestments, were formed out of five [13] materials; for they combined in themselves gold, and blue, and purple, and scarlet, and fine linen. And there were five [14] kings of the Amorites, whom Joshua the son of Nun shut up in a cave, and directed the people to trample upon their heads. Any one, in fact, might collect many thousand other things of the same kind, both with respect to this number and any other he chose to fix upon, either from the Scriptures, or from the works of nature lying under his observation. [15] But although such is the case, we do not therefore affirm that there are five Æons above the Demiurge; nor do we consecrate the Pentad, as if it were some divine thing; nor do we strive to establish things that are untenable, nor ravings [such as they indulge in], by means of that vain kind of labour; nor do we perversely force a creation well adapted by God [for the ends intended to be served], to change itself into types of things which have no real existence; nor do we seek to bring forward impious and abominable doctrines, the detection and overthrow of which are easy to all possessed of intelligence.

5. For who can concede to them that the year has three hundred and sixty-five days only, in order that there may be twelve months of thirty days each, after the type of the twelve Æons, when the type is in fact altogether out of harmony [with the antitype]? For, in the one case, each of the Æons is a thirtieth part of the entire Pleroma, while in the other they declare that a month is the twelfth part of a year. If, indeed, the year were divided into thirty parts, and the month into twelve, then a fitting type might be regarded as having been found for their fictitious system. But, on the contrary, as the case really stands, their Pleroma is divided into thirty parts, and a portion of it into twelve; while again the whole year is divided into twelve parts, and a certain portion of it into thirty. The Saviour therefore acted unwisely in constituting the month a type of the entire Pleroma, but the year a type only of that Duodecad which exists in the Pleroma; for it was more fitting to divide the year into thirty parts, even as the whole Pleroma is divided, but the month into twelve, just as the Æons are in their Pleroma. Moreover, they divide the entire Pleroma into three portions, — namely, into an Ogdoad, a Decad, and a Duodecad. But our year is divided into four parts, — namely, spring, summer, autumn, and winter. And again, not even do the months, which they maintain to be a type of the Triacontad, consist precisely of thirty days, but some have more and some less, inasmuch as five days remain to them as an overplus. [16] The day, too, does not always consist precisely of twelve hours, but rises from nine [17] to fifteen, and then falls again from fifteen to nine. It cannot therefore be held that months of thirty days each were so formed for the sake of [typifying]

---

[1] Matt. xiv. 19, 21; Mark vi. 41, 44; Luke ix. 13, 14; John vi. 9, 10, 11.
[2] Matt. xxv. 2, etc.
[3] Matt. xvii. 1.
[4] St. John is here strangely overlooked.
[5] Luke viii. 51.
[6] Luke xvi. 28.
[7] "Fines et summitates;" comp. Justin Mart., *Dial. c. Tryph.*, 91.
[8] "Juvenis," *one in the prime of life.*
[9] It has been usual in the Christian Church to reckon four commandments in the first table, and six in the second; but the above was the ancient Jewish division. See Joseph., *Antiq.*, iii. 6.
[10] Ex. xxvi. 37.
[11] Ex. xxvii. 1; "altitudo" in the text must be exchanged for "latitudo."
[12] Ex. xxviii. 1.
[13] Ex. xxviii. 5.
[14] Josh. x. 17.

[15] [Note the manly contempt with which our author dismisses a class of similitudes, which seem, even in our day, to have great attractions for some minds not otherwise narrow.]
[16] 365 (the days of the year) = 12 × 30 + 5.
[17] These hours of daylight, at the winter and summer solstice respectively, correspond to the latitude of Lyons, 45° 45′ N., where Irenæus resided.

the Æons; for, in that case, they would have consisted precisely of thirty days: nor, again, the days of these months, that by means of twelve hours they might symbolize the twelve Æons; for, in that case, they would always have consisted precisely of twelve hours.

6. But further, as to their calling material substances "on the left hand," and maintaining that those things which are thus on the left hand of necessity fall into corruption, while they also affirm that the Saviour came to the lost sheep, in order to transfer it to the right hand, that is, to the ninety and nine sheep which were in safety, and perished not, but continued within the fold, yet were of the left hand,[1] it follows that they must acknowledge that the enjoyment[2] of rest did not imply salvation. And that which has not in like manner the same number, they will be compelled to acknowledge as belonging to the left hand, that is, to corruption. This Greek word *Agape* (love), then, according to the letters of the Greeks, by means of which reckoning is carried on among them, having a numerical value of *ninety-three*,[3] is in like manner assigned to the place of rest on the left hand. Aletheia (truth), too, having in like manner, according to the principle indicated above, a numerical value of sixty-four,[4] exists among material substances. And thus, in fine, they will be compelled to acknowledge that all those sacred names which do not reach a numerical value of one hundred, but only contain the numbers summed by the left hand, are corruptible and material.

CHAP. XXV. — GOD IS NOT TO BE SOUGHT AFTER BY MEANS OF LETTERS, SYLLABLES, AND NUMBERS; NECESSITY OF HUMILITY IN SUCH INVESTIGATIONS.

1. If any one, however, say in reply to these things, What then? Is it a meaningless and accidental thing, that the positions of names, and the election of the apostles, and the working of the Lord, and the arrangement of created things, are what they are?—we answer them: Certainly not; but with great wisdom and diligence, all things have clearly been made by God, fitted and prepared [for their special purposes]; and His word formed both things ancient and those belonging to the latest times; and men ought not to connect those things with the

number *thirty*,[5] but to harmonize them with what actually exists, or with right reason. Nor should they seek to prosecute inquiries respecting God by means of numbers, syllables, and letters. For this is an uncertain mode of proceeding, on account of their varied and diverse systems, and because every sort of hypothesis may at the present day be, in like manner, devised[6] by any one; so that[7] they can derive arguments against the truth from these very theories, inasmuch as they may be turned in many different directions. But, on the contrary, they ought to adapt the numbers themselves, and those things which have been formed, to the true theory lying before them. For system[8] does not spring out of numbers, but numbers from a system; nor does God derive His being from things made, but things made from God. For all things originate from one and the same God.

2. But since created things are various and numerous, they are indeed well fitted and adapted to the whole creation; yet, when viewed individually, are mutually opposite and inharmonious, just as the sound of the lyre, which consists of many and opposite notes, gives rise to one unbroken melody, through means of the interval which separates each one from the others. The lover of truth therefore ought not to be deceived by the interval between each note, nor should he imagine that one was due to one artist and author, and another to another, nor that one person fitted the treble, another the bass, and yet another the tenor strings; but he should hold that one and the same person [formed the whole], so as to prove the judgment, goodness, and skill exhibited in the whole work and [specimen of] wisdom. Those, too, who listen to the melody, ought to praise and extol the artist, to admire the tension of some notes, to attend to the softness of others, to catch the sound of others between both these extremes, and to consider the special character of others, so as to inquire at what each one aims, and what is the cause of their variety, never failing to apply our rule, neither giving up the [one[9]] artist, nor casting off faith in the one God who formed all things, nor blaspheming our Creator.

3. If, however, any one do not discover the cause of all those things which become objects of investigation, let him reflect that man is infinitely inferior to God; that he has received grace only in part, and is not yet equal or similar to his Maker; and, moreover, that he cannot have experience or form a conception of all things

---

[1] "Alluding," says Harvey, "to a custom among the ancients, of summing the numbers below 100 by various positions of the left hand and its fingers; 100 and upwards being reckoned by corresponding gestures of the right hand. The ninety and nine sheep, therefore, that remained quietly in the fold were summed upon the left hand, and Gnostics professed that they were typical of the true spiritual seed; but Scripture always places the workers of iniquity on the left hand, and in the Gnostic theory the evil principle of matter was sinistral, therefore," etc., as above.

[2] "Levamen," corresponding probably to the Greek ἀνάπαυσιν.

[3] Ἀγάπη (α = 1, γ = 3, a = 1, π = 80, η = 8) = 93.

[4] Ἀλήθεια (α = 1, λ = 30, η = 8, θ = 9, ε = 5, ι = 10, α = 1) = 64.

[5] Some read xx., but xxx. is probably correct.

[6] Harvey proposes "commentitum" instead of "commentatum," but the alteration seems unnecessary.

[7] The syntax is in confusion, and the meaning obscure.

[8] "Regula."

[9] "Errantes ab artifice." The whole sentence is most obscure.

like God ; but in the same proportion as he who was formed but to-day, and received the beginning of his creation, is inferior to Him who is uncreated, and who is always the same, in that proportion is he, as respects knowledge and the faculty of investigating the causes of all things, inferior to Him who made him. For thou, O man, art not an uncreated being, nor didst thou always co-exist [1] with God, as did His own Word ; but now, through His pre-eminent goodness, receiving the beginning of thy creation, thou dost gradually learn from the Word the dispensations of God who made thee.

4. Preserve therefore the proper order of thy knowledge, and do not, as being ignorant of things really good, seek to rise above God Himself, for He cannot be surpassed ; nor do thou seek after any one above the Creator, for thou wilt not discover such. For thy Former cannot be contained within limits ; nor, although thou shouldst measure all this [universe], and pass through all His creation, and consider it in all its depth, and height, and length, wouldst thou be able to conceive of any other above the Father Himself. For thou wilt not be able to think Him fully out, but, indulging in trains of reflection opposed to thy nature, thou wilt prove thyself foolish ; and if thou persevere in such a course, thou wilt fall into utter madness, whilst thou deemest thyself loftier and greater than thy Creator, and imaginest that thou canst penetrate beyond His dominions.

CHAP. XXVI. — " KNOWLEDGE PUFFETH UP, BUT LOVE EDIFIETH."

1. It is therefore better and more profitable to belong to the simple and unlettered class, and by means of love to attain to nearness to God, than, by imagining ourselves learned and skilful, to be found [among those who are] blasphemous against their own God, inasmuch as they conjure up another God as the Father. And for this reason Paul exclaimed, " Knowledge puffeth up, but love edifieth : " [2] not that he meant to inveigh against a true knowledge of God, for in that case he would have accused himself ; but, because he knew that some, puffed up by the pretence of knowledge, fall away from the love of God, and imagine that they themselves are perfect, for this reason that they set forth an imperfect Creator, with the view of putting an end to the pride which they feel on account of knowledge of this kind, he says, " Knowledge puffeth up, but love edifieth." Now there can be no greater conceit than this, that any one should imagine he is better and more perfect than He who made and fashioned him, and im-

parted to him the breath of life, and commanded this very thing into existence. It is therefore better, as I have said, that one should have no knowledge whatever of any one reason why a single thing in creation has been made, but should believe in God, and continue in His love, than [3] that, puffed up through knowledge of this kind, he should fall away from that love which is the life of man ; and that he should search after no other knowledge except [the knowledge of] Jesus Christ the Son of God, who was crucified for us, than that by subtle questions and hairsplitting expressions he should fall into impiety. [4]

2. For how would it be, if any one, gradually elated by attempts of the kind referred to, should, because the Lord said that " even the hairs of your head are all numbered," [5] set about inquiring into the number of hairs on each one's head, and endeavour to search out the reason on account of which one man has so many, and another so many, since all have not an equal number, but many thousands upon thousands are to be found with still varying numbers, on this account that some have larger and others smaller heads, some have bushy heads of hair, others thin, and others scarcely any hair at all, — and then those who imagine that they have discovered the number of the hairs, should endeavour to apply that for the commendation of their own sect which they have conceived ? Or again, if any one should, because of this expression which occurs in the Gospel, " Are not two sparrows sold for a farthing? and not one of them falls to the ground without the will of your Father," [6] take occasion to reckon up the number of sparrows caught daily, whether over all the world or in some particular district, and to make inquiry as to the reason of so many having been captured yesterday, so many the day before, and so many again on this day, and should then join on the number of sparrows to his [particular] hypothesis, would he not in that case mislead himself altogether, and drive into absolute insanity those that agreed with him, since men are always eager in such matters to be thought to have discovered something more extraordinary than their masters ? [7]

3. But if any one should ask us whether every number of all the things which have been made, and which are made, is known to God, and whether every one of these [numbers] has, according to His providence, received that special amount which it contains ; and on our agreeing

---

[1] Alluding to the imaginary Æon *Anthropos*, who existed from eternity.
[2] 1 Cor. viii. 1.

[3] " Aut; " ἢ having been thus mistakenly rendered instead of " quam."
[4] [This seems anticipatory of the dialectics of scholasticism, and of its immense influence in Western Christendom, after St. Bernard's feeble adhesion to the Biblical system of the ancients.]
[5] Matt. x. 30.
[6] Matt. x. 29.
[7] [Illustrated by the history of modern thought in Germany. See the meritorious work of Professor Kahnis, on *German Protestantism*," (translated). Edinburgh, T. & T. Clark, 1856.]

that such is the case, and acknowledging that not one of the things which have been, or are, or shall be made, escapes the knowledge of God, but that through His providence every one of them has obtained its nature, and rank, and number, and special quantity, and that nothing whatever either has been or is produced in vain or accidentally, but with exceeding suitability [to the purpose intended], and in the exercise of transcendent knowledge, and that it was an admirable and truly divine intellect [1] which could both distinguish and bring forth the proper causes of such a system : if, [I say,] any one, on obtaining our adherence and consent to this, should proceed to reckon up the sand and pebbles of the earth, yea also the waves of the sea and the stars of heaven, and should endeavour to think out the causes of the number which he imagines himself to have discovered, would not his labour be in vain, and would not such a man be justly declared mad, and destitute of reason, by all possessed of common sense? And the more he occupied himself beyond others in questions of this kind, and the more he imagines himself to find out beyond others, styling them unskilful, ignorant, and animal beings, because they do not enter into his so useless labour, the more is he [in reality] insane, foolish, struck as it were with a thunderbolt, since indeed he does in no one point own himself inferior to God ; but, by the knowledge which he imagines himself to have discovered, he changes God Himself, and exalts his own opinion above the greatness of the Creator.

CHAP. XXVII. — PROPER MODE OF INTERPRETING PARABLES AND OBSCURE PASSAGES OF SCRIPTURE.

1. A sound mind, and one which does not expose its possessor to danger, and is devoted to piety and the love of truth, will eagerly meditate upon those things which God has placed within the power of mankind, and has subjected to our knowledge, and will make advancement in [acquaintance with] them, rendering the knowledge of them easy to him by means of daily study. These things are such as fall [plainly] under our observation, and are clearly and unambiguously in express terms set forth in the Sacred Scriptures. And therefore the parables ought not to be adapted to ambiguous expressions. For, if this be not done, both he who explains them will do so without danger, and the parables will receive a like interpretation from all, and the body [2] of truth remains entire, with a harmonious adaptation of its members, and without any collision [of its several parts]. But to apply expressions which are not clear or evident to

interpretations of the parables, such as every one discovers for himself as inclination leads him, [is absurd.[3]] For in this way no one will possess the rule of truth ; but in accordance with the number of persons who explain the parables will be found the various systems of truth, in mutual opposition to each other, and setting forth antagonistic doctrines, like the questions current among the Gentile philosophers.

2. According to this course of procedure, therefore, man would always be inquiring but never finding, because he has rejected the very method of discovery. And when the Bridegroom [4] comes, he who has his lamp untrimmed, and not burning with the brightness of a steady light, is classed among those who obscure the interpretations of the parables, forsaking Him who by His plain announcements freely imparts gifts to all who come to Him, and is excluded from His marriage-chamber. Since, therefore, the entire Scriptures, the prophets, and the Gospels, can be clearly, unambiguously, and harmoniously understood by all, although all do not believe them ; and [5] since they proclaim that one only God, to the exclusion of all others, formed all things by His word, whether visible or invisible, heavenly or earthly, in the water or under the earth, as I have shown [6] from the very words of Scripture ; and since the very system of creation to which we belong testifies, by what falls under our notice, that one Being made and governs it, — those persons will seem truly foolish who blind their eyes to such a clear demonstration, and will not behold the light of the announcement [made to them] ; but they put fetters upon themselves, and every one of them imagines, by means of their obscure interpretations of the parables, that he has found out a God of his own. For that there is nothing whatever openly, expressly, and without controversy said in any part of Scripture respecting the Father conceived of by those who hold a contrary opinion, they themselves testify, when they maintain that the Saviour privately taught these same things not to all, but to certain only of His disciples who could comprehend them, and who understood what was intended by Him through means of arguments, enigmas, and parables. They come, [in fine,] to this, that they maintain there is one Being who is proclaimed as God, and another as Father, He who is set forth as such through means of parables and enigmas.

---

[1] "Rationem."
[2] We read "veritatis corpus" for "a veritate corpus" in the text.

[3] Some such expression of disapproval must evidently be supplied, though wanting in the Latin text.
[4] Matt. xxv. 5, etc.
[5] The text is here elliptical, and we have supplied what seems necessary to complete the sense.
[6] It is doubtful whether "demonstravimus" or "demonstrabimus" be the proper reading: if the former, the reference will be to book i. 22, or ii. 2; if the latter, to book iii. 8.

3. But since parables admit of many interpretations, what lover of truth will not acknowledge, that for them to assert God is to be searched out from these, while they desert what is certain, indubitable, and true, is the part of men who eagerly throw themselves into danger, and act as if destitute of reason? And is not such a course of conduct not to build one's house upon a rock [1] which is firm, strong, and placed in an open position, but upon the shifting sand? Hence the overthrow of such a building is a matter of ease.

CHAP. XXVIII. — PERFECT KNOWLEDGE CANNOT BE ATTAINED IN THE PRESENT LIFE : MANY QUESTIONS MUST BE SUBMISSIVELY LEFT IN THE HANDS OF GOD.

1. Having therefore the truth itself as our rule, and the testimony concerning God set clearly before us, we ought not, by running after numerous and diverse answers to questions, to cast away the firm and true knowledge of God. But it is much more suitable that we, directing our inquiries after this fashion, should exercise ourselves in the investigation of the mystery and administration of the living God, and should increase in the love of Him who has done, and still does, so great things for us ; but never should fall from the belief by which it is most clearly proclaimed that this Being alone is truly God and Father, who both formed this world, fashioned man, and bestowed the faculty of increase on His own creation, and called him upwards from lesser things to those greater ones which are in His own presence, just as He brings an infant which has been conceived in the womb into the light of the sun, and lays up wheat in the barn after He has given it full strength on the stalk. But it is one and the same Creator who both fashioned the womb and created the sun ; and one and the same Lord who both reared the stalk of corn, increased and multiplied the wheat, and prepared the barn.

2. If, however, we cannot discover explanations of all those things in Scripture which are made the subject of investigation, yet let us not on that account seek after any other God besides Him who really exists. For this is the very greatest impiety. We should leave things of that nature to God who created us, being most properly assured that the Scriptures are indeed perfect, since they were spoken by the Word of God and His Spirit ; but we, inasmuch as we are inferior to, and later in existence than, the Word of God and His Spirit, are on that very account [2] destitute of the knowledge of His mysteries. And there is no cause for wonder if this is the case with us as respects things spiritual and heavenly, and such as require to be made known to us by revelation, since many even of

those things which lie at our very feet (I mean such as belong to this world, which we handle, and see, and are in close contact with) transcend our knowledge, so that even these we must leave to God. For it is fitting that He should excel all [in knowledge]. For how stands the case, for instance, if we endeavour to explain the cause of the rising of the Nile? We may say a great deal, plausible or otherwise, on the subject ; but what is true, sure, and incontrovertible regarding it, belongs only to God. Then, again, the dwelling-place of birds — of those, I mean, which come to us in spring, but fly away again on the approach of autumn — though it is a matter connected with this world, escapes our knowledge. What explanation, again, can we give of the flow and ebb of the ocean, although every one admits there must be a certain cause [for these phenomena]? Or what can we say as to the nature of those things which lie beyond it? [3] What, moreover, can we say as to the formation of rain, lightning, thunder, gatherings of clouds, vapours, the bursting forth of winds, and such like things ; or tell as to the storehouses of snow, hail, and other like things? [What do we know respecting] the conditions requisite for the preparation of clouds, or what is the real nature of the vapours in the sky? What as to the reason why the moon waxes and wanes, or what as to the cause of the difference of nature among various waters, metals, stones, and such like things? On all these points we may indeed say a great deal while we search into their causes, but God alone who made them can declare the truth regarding them.

3. If, therefore, even with respect to creation, there are some things [the knowledge of] which belongs only to God, and others which come within the range of our own knowledge, what ground is there for complaint, if, in regard to those things which we investigate in the Scriptures (which are throughout spiritual), we are able by the grace of God to explain some of them, while we must leave others in the hands of God, and that not only in the present world, but also in that which is to come, so that God should for ever teach, and man should for ever learn the things taught him by God? As the apostle has said on this point, that, when other things have been done away, then these three, " faith, hope, and charity, shall endure." [4] For faith, which has respect to our Master, endures [5] unchangeably,

[1] Matt. vii. 25.
[2] Or, " to that degree."

[3] Comp. Clem. Rom., Ep. to Cor., c. xx. ; and August., De. Civit Dei, xvi. 9.
[4] 1 Cor. xiii. 13.
[5] " Permanet firma," — no doubt corresponding to the μένει of the apostle, 1 Cor. xiii. 13. Harvey here remarks, that " the author seems to misapprehend the apostle's meaning. . . . There will be no longer room for hope, when the substance of things hoped for shall have become a matter of fruition; neither will there be any room for faith, when the soul shall be admitted to see God as He is." But the best modern interpreters take the same view of the passage as Irenæus. They regard the νυνὶ δὲ of St. Paul as not being temporal, but logical, and conclude therefore the meaning to be, that faith and hope, as well as love, will, in a sense, endure for ever. Comp., e.g , Alford, in loc.

assuring us that there is but one true God, and that we should truly love Him for ever, seeing that He alone is our Father ; while we hope ever to be receiving more and more from God, and to learn from Him, because He is good, and possesses boundless riches, a kingdom without end, and instruction that can never be exhausted. If, therefore, accòrding to the rule which I have stated, we leave some questions in the hands of God, we shall both preserve our faith uninjured, and shall continue without danger ; and all Scripture, which has been given to us by God, shall be found by us perfectly consistent ; and the parables shall harmonize with those passages which are perfectly plain ; and those statements the meaning of which is clear, shall serve to explain the parables ; and through the many diversified utterances [of Scripture] there shall be heard [1] one harmonious melody in us, praising in hymns that God who created all things. If, for instance, any one asks, "What was God doing before He made the world?" we reply that the answer to such a question lies with God Himself. For that this world was formed perfect [2] by God, receiving a beginning in time, the Scriptures teach us ; but no Scripture reveals to us what God was employed about before this event. The answer therefore to that question remains with God, and it is not proper [3] for us to aim at bringing forward foolish, rash, and blasphemous suppositions [in reply to it] ; so, as by one's imagining that he has discovered the origin of matter, he should in reality set aside God Himself who made all things.

4. For consider, all ye who invent such opinions, since the Father Himself is alone called God, who has a real existence, but whom ye style the Demiurge ; since, moreover, the Scriptures acknowledge Him alone as God ; and yet again, since the Lord confesses Him alone as His own Father, and knows no other, as I shall show from His very words, — when ye style this very Being the fruit of defect, and the offspring of ignorance, and describe Him as being ignorant of those things which are above Him, with the various other allegations which you make regarding Him, — consider the terrible blasphemy [ye are thus guilty of] against Him who truly is God. Ye seem to affirm gravely and honestly enough that ye believe in God ; but then, as ye are utterly unable to reveal any other God, ye declare this very Being in whom ye profess to believe, the fruit of defect and the offspring of ignorance. Now this blindness and foolish talk-

ing flow to you from the fact that ye reserve nothing for God, but ye wish to proclaim the nativity and production both of God Himself, of His Ennœa, of His Logos, and Life, and Christ ; and ye form the idea of these from no other than a mere human experience ; nòt understanding, as I said before, that it is possible, in the case of man, who is a compound being, to speak in this way of the mind of man and the thought of man ; and to say that thought (ennœa) springs from mind (sensus), intention (enthymesis) again from thought, and word (logos) from intention (but which logos? [4] for there is among the Greeks one logos which is the principle that thinks, and another which is the instrument by means of which thought is expressed) ; and [to say] that a man sometimes is at rest and silent, while at other times he speaks and is active. But since God is [5] all mind, all reason, all active spirit, all light, and always exists one and the same, as it is both beneficial for us to think of God, and as we learn regarding Him from the Scriptures, such feelings and divisions [of operation] cannot fittingly be ascribed to Him. For our tongue, as being carnal, is not sufficient to minister to the rapidity of the human mind, inasmuch as that is of a spiritual nature, for which reason our word is restrained [6] within us, and is not at once expressed as it has been conceived by the mind, but is uttered by successive efforts, just as the tongue is able to serve it.

5. But God being all Mind, and all Logos, both speaks exactly what He thinks, and thinks exactly what He speaks. For His thought is Logos, and Logos is Mind, and Mind comprehending all things is the Father Himself. He, therefore, who speaks of the mind of God, and ascribes to it a special origin of its own, declares Him a compound Being, as if God were one thing, and the original Mind another. So, again, with respect to Logos, when one attributes to him the third [7] place of production from the Father ; on which supposition he is ignorant of His greatness ; and thus Logos has been far separated from God. As for the prophet, he declares respecting Him, "Who shall describe His generation?" [8] But ye pretend to set forth His generation from the Father, and ye transfer the production of the word of men which takes place by means of a tongue to the Word of God, and thus are righteously exposed by your own

---

[1] The Latin text is here untranslateable. Grabe proposes to read, " *una consonans melodia in nobis sentietur ; *" while Stieren and others prefer to exchange αἰσθήσεται for ἀσθήσεται.
[2] "Apotelesticos." This word, says Harvey, " may also refer to the vital energy of nature, whereby its effects are for ever reproduced in unceasing succession." Comp. Hippol., *Philos.*, vii. 24.
[3] We here follow Grabe, who understands *decet.* Harvey less simply explains the very obscure Latin text.

[4] The Greek term λόγος, as is well known, denotes both *ratio* (reason) and *sermo* (speech). Some deem the above parenthesis an interpolation.
[5] Comp. i. 12, 2.
[6] "Suffugatur : " some read " suffocatur : " and Harvey proposes " suffragatur," as the representative of the Greek ψηφίζεται. The meaning in any case is, that while ideas are instantaneously formed in the human mind, they can be expressed through means of words only fractionally, and by successive utterances.
[7] Thus: *Bythus, Nous, Logos.*
[8] Isa. liii. 8.

selves as knowing neither things human nor divine.

6. But, beyond reason inflated [with your own wisdom], ye presumptuously maintain that ye are acquainted with the unspeakable mysteries of God; while even the Lord, the very Son of God, allowed that the Father alone knows the very day and hour of judgment, when He plainly declares, "But of that day and that hour knoweth no man, neither the Son, but the Father only."[1] If, then, the Son was not ashamed to ascribe the knowledge of that day to the Father only, but declared what was true regarding the matter, neither let us be ashamed to reserve for God those greater questions which may occur to us. For no man is superior to his master.[2] If any one, therefore, says to us, "How then was the Son produced by the Father?" we reply to him, that no man understands that production, or generation, or calling, or revelation, or by whatever name one may describe His generation, which is in fact altogether indescribable. Neither Valentinus, nor Marcion, nor Saturninus, nor Basilides, nor angels, nor archangels, nor principalities, nor powers [possess this knowledge], but the Father only who begat, and the Son who was begotten. Since therefore His generation is unspeakable, those who strive to set forth generations and productions cannot be in their right mind, inasmuch as they undertake to describe things which are indescribable. For that a word is uttered at the bidding of thought and mind, all men indeed well understand. Those, therefore, who have excogitated [the theory of] emissions have not discovered anything great, or revealed any abstruse mystery, when they have simply transferred what all understand to the only-begotten Word of God; and while they style Him unspeakable and unnameable, they nevertheless set forth the production and formation of His first generation, as if they themselves had assisted at His birth, thus assimilating Him to the word of mankind formed by emissions.

7. But we shall not be wrong if we affirm the same thing also concerning the substance of matter, that God produced it. For we have learned from the Scriptures that God holds the supremacy over all things. But whence or in what way He produced it, neither has Scripture anywhere declared; nor does it become us to conjecture, so as, in accordance with our own opinions, to form endless conjectures concerning God, but we should leave such knowledge in the hands of God Himself. In like manner, also, we must leave the cause why, while all things were made by God, certain of His creatures

sinned and revolted from a state of submission to God, and others, indeed the great majority, persevered, and do still persevere, in [willing] subjection to Him who formed them, and also of what nature those are who sinned, and of what nature those who persevere, — [we must, I say, leave the cause of these things] to God and His Word, to whom alone He said, "Sit at my right hand, until I make Thine enemies Thy footstool."[3] But as for us, we still dwell upon the earth, and have not yet sat down upon His throne. For although the Spirit of the Saviour that is in Him "searcheth all things, even the deep things of God,"[4] yet as to us "there are diversities of gifts, differences of administrations, and diversities of operations;"[5] and we, while upon the earth, as Paul also declares, "know in part, and prophesy in part."[6] Since, therefore, we know but in part, we ought to leave all sorts of [difficult] questions in the hands of Him who in some measure, [and that only,] bestows grace on us. That eternal fire, [for instance,] is prepared for sinners, both the Lord has plainly declared, and the rest of the Scriptures demonstrate. And that God foreknew that this would happen, the Scriptures do in like manner demonstrate, since He prepared eternal fire from the beginning for those who were [afterwards] to transgress [His commandments]; but the cause itself of the nature of such transgressors neither has any Scripture informed us, nor has an apostle told us, nor has the Lord taught us. It becomes us, therefore, to leave the knowledge of this matter to God, even as the Lord does of the day and hour [of judgment], and not to rush to such an extreme of danger, that we will leave nothing in the hands of God, even though we have received only a measure of grace [from Him in this world]. But when we investigate points which are above us, and with respect to which we cannot reach satisfaction, [it is absurd[7]] that we should display such an extreme of presumption as to lay open God, and things which are not yet discovered,[8] as if already we had found out, by the vain talk about emissions, God Himself, the Creator of all things, and to assert that He derived His substance from apostasy and ignorance, so as to frame an impious hypothesis in opposition to God.

8. Moreover, they possess no proof of their system, which has but recently been invented by them, sometimes resting upon certain numbers, sometimes on syllables, and sometimes, again, on names; and there are occasions, too, when

---

[1] Mark xiii. 32. The words, "neither the angels which are in heaven," are here omitted, probably because, as usual, the writer quotes from memory.
[2] Comp. Matt. x. 24; Luke xi. 40.

[3] Ps. cx. 1.
[4] 1 Cor. ii. 10.
[5] 1 Cor. xii. 4, 5, 6.
[6] 1 Cor. xiii. 9.
[7] Massuet proposes to insert these words, and some such supplement seems clearly necessary to complete the sense. But the sentence still remains confused and doubtful.
[8] [Gen. xl. 8; Deut. xxix. 29; Ps. cxxxi.]

by means of those letters which are contained in letters, by parables not properly interpreted, or by certain [baseless] conjectures, they strive to establish that fabulous account which they have devised. For if any one should inquire the reason why the Father, who has fellowship with the Son in all things, has been declared by the Lord alone to know the hour and the day [of judgment], he will find at present no more suitable, or becoming, or safe reason than this (since, indeed, the Lord is the only true Master), that we may learn through Him that the Father is above all things. For "the Father," says He, "is greater than I."[1] The Father, therefore, has been declared by our Lord to excel with respect to knowledge; for this reason, that we, too, as long as we are connected with the scheme of things in this world, should leave perfect knowledge, and such questions [as have been mentioned], to God, and should not by any chance, while we seek to investigate the sublime nature of the Father, fall into the danger of starting the question whether there is another God above God.[2]

9. But if any lover of strife contradict what I have said, and also what the apostle affirms, that "we know in part, and prophesy in part,"[3] and imagine that he has acquired not a partial, but a universal, knowledge of all that exists, — being such an one as Valentinus, or Ptolemæus, or Basilides, or any other of those who maintain that they have searched out the deep[4] things of God, — let him not (arraying himself in vainglory) boast that he has acquired greater knowledge than others with respect to those things which are invisible, or cannot be placed under our observation; but let him, by making diligent inquiry, and obtaining information from the Father, tell us the reasons (which we know not) of those things which are in this world, — as, for instance, the number of hairs on his own head, and the sparrows which are captured day by day, and such other points with which we are not previously acquainted, — so that we may credit him also with respect to more important points. But if those who are *perfect* do not yet understand the very things in their hands, and at their feet, and before their eyes, and on the earth, and especially the rule followed with respect to the hairs of their head, how can we believe them regarding things spiritual, and super-celestial,[5] and those which, with a vain confidence, they assert to be above God? So much, then, I have said concerning numbers, and names, and syl-

lables, and questions respecting such things as are above our comprehension, and concerning their improper expositions of the parables: [I add no more on these points,] since thou thyself mayest enlarge upon them.

CHAP. XXIX. — REFUTATION OF THE VIEWS OF THE HERETICS AS TO THE FUTURE DESTINY OF THE SOUL AND BODY.

1. Let us return, however, to the remaining points of their system. For when they declare[6] that, at the consummation of all things, their mother shall re-enter the Pleroma, and receive the Saviour as her consort; that they themselves, as being spiritual, when they have got rid of their animal souls, and become intellectual spirits, will be the consorts of the spiritual angels; but that the Demiurge, since they call him animal, will pass into the place of the Mother; that the souls of the righteous shall psychically repose in the intermediate place; — when they declare that like will be gathered to like, spiritual things to spiritual, while material things continue among those that are material, they do in fact contradict themselves, inasmuch as they no longer maintain that souls pass, on account of their nature, into the intermediate place to those substances which are similar to themselves, but [that they do so] on account of the deeds done [in the body], since they affirm that those of the righteous do pass [into that abode], but those of the impious continue in the fire. For if it is on account of their nature that all souls attain to the place of enjoyment,[7] and all belong to the intermediate place simply because they are souls, as being thus of the same nature with it, then it follows that faith is altogether superfluous, as was also the descent[8] of the Saviour [to this world]. If, on the other hand, it is on account of their righteousness [that they attain to such a place of rest], then it is no longer because they are *souls* but because they are *righteous*. But if souls would have[9] perished unless they had been righteous, then righteousness must have power to save the bodies also [which these souls inhabited]; for why should it not save them, since they, too, participated in righteousness? For if nature and substance are the means of salvation, then all souls shall be saved; but if righteousness and faith, why should these not save those bodies which, equally with the souls, will enter[10] into

---

[1] John xiv. 28.
[2] [On the great matter of the περιχώρησις, the subordination of the Son, etc., Bull has explored Patristic doctrine, and may well be consulted here. *Defens. Fid. Nicænæ,* sect. iv.; see also vol. v. 363.]
[3] 1. Cor. xiii. 9.
[4] "Altitudines," literally, *heights.*
[5] [Wisdom, ix. 13, 17. A passage of marvellous beauty.]

[6] Comp. i. 7, 1.
[7] "Refrigerium," *place of refreshment.*
[8] Billius, with great apparent reason, proposes to read "descensio" for the unintelligible "discessio" of the Latin text.
[9] Grabe and Massuet read, "Si autem animæ perire inciperent, nisi justæ fuissent," for "Si autem animæ quæ perituræ essent inciperent nisi justæ fuissent," — words which defy all translation.
[10] The text is here uncertain and confused; but, as Harvey remarks, "the argument is this, That if souls are saved *qua* intellectual substance, then all are saved alike; but if by reason of any moral qualities, then the bodies that have executed the moral purposes of the soul, must also be considered to be heirs of salvation."

immortality? For righteousness will appear, in matters of this kind, either impotent or unjust, if indeed it saves some substances through participating in it, but not others.

2. For it is manifest that those acts which are deemed righteous are performed in bodies. Either, therefore, all souls will of necessity pass into the intermediate place, and there will never be a judgment; or bodies, too, which have participated in righteousness, will attain to the place of enjoyment, along with the souls which have in like manner participated, if indeed righteousness is powerful enough to bring thither those substances which have participated in it. And then the doctrine concerning the resurrection of bodies which we believe, will emerge true and certain [from their system]; since, [as we hold,] God, when He resuscitates our mortal bodies which preserved righteousness, will render them incorruptible and immortal. For God is superior to nature, and has in Himself the disposition [to show kindness], because He is good; and the ability to do so, because He is mighty; and the faculty of fully carrying out His purpose, because He is rich and perfect.

3. But these men are in all points inconsistent with themselves, when they decide that all souls do not enter into the intermediate place, but those of the righteous only. For they maintain that, according to nature and substance, three sorts [of being] were produced by the Mother: the first, which proceeded from perplexity, and weariness, and fear — that is material substance; the second from impetuosity[1] — that is animal substance; but that which she brought forth after the vision of those angels who wait upon Christ, is spiritual substance. If, then, that substance[2] which she brought forth will by all means enter into the Pleroma because it is spiritual, while that which is material will remain below because it is material, and shall be totally consumed by the fire which burns within it, why should not the whole animal substance go into the intermediate place, into which also they send the Demiurge? But what is it which shall enter within their Pleroma? For they maintain that souls shall continue in the intermediate place, while bodies, because they possess material substance, when they have been resolved into matter, shall be consumed by that fire which exists in it; but their body being thus destroyed, and their soul remaining in the intermediate place, no part of man will any longer be left to enter in within the Pleroma. For the intellect of man — his mind, thought, mental intention, and such like — is nothing else than his soul; but the

emotions and operations of the soul itself have no substance apart from the soul. What part of them, then, will still remain to enter into the Pleroma? For they themselves, in as far as they are souls, remain in the intermediate place; while, in as far as they are body, they will be consumed with the rest of matter.

CHAP. XXX. — ABSURDITY OF THEIR STYLING THEMSELVES SPIRITUAL, WHILE THE DEMIURGE IS DECLARED TO BE ANIMAL.

1. Such being the state of the case, these infatuated men declare that they rise above the Creator (Demiurge); and, inasmuch as they proclaim themselves superior to that God who made and adorned the heavens, and the earth, and all things that are in them, and maintain that they themselves are spiritual, while they are in fact shamefully carnal on account of their so great impiety, — affirming that He, who has made His angels[3] spirits, and is clothed with light as with a garment, and holds the circle[4] of the earth, as it were, in His hand, in whose sight its inhabitants are counted as grasshoppers, and who is the Creator and Lord of all spiritual substance, is of an animal nature, — they do beyond doubt and verily betray their own madness; and, as if truly struck with thunder, even more than those giants who are spoken of in [heathen] fables, they lift up their opinions against God, inflated by a vain presumption and unstable glory, — men for whose purgation all the hellebore[5] on earth would not suffice, so that they should get rid of their intense folly.

2. The superior person is to be proved by his deeds. In what way, then, can they show themselves superior to the Creator (that I too, through the necessity of the argument in hand, may come down to the level of their impiety, instituting a comparison between God and foolish men, and, by descending to their argument, may often refute them by their own doctrines; but in thus acting may God be merciful to me, for I venture on these statements, not with the view of comparing Him to them, but of convicting and overthrowing their insane opinions) — they, for whom many foolish persons entertain so great an admiration, as if, forsooth, they could learn from them something more precious than the truth itself! That expression of Scripture, "Seek, and ye shall find,"[6] they interpret as spoken with this view, that they should discover themselves to be above the Creator, styling themselves greater and better than God, and calling themselves spiritual, but the Creator animal; and [affirming] that for this reason they rise upwards above God, for that

1 "De impetu:" it is generally supposed that these words correspond to ἐκ τῆς ἐπιστροφῆς (comp. i. 5, 1), but Harvey thinks ἐξ ὁρμῆς preferable (i. 4, 1).
2 The syntax of this sentence is in utter confusion, but the meaning is doubtless that given above.

3 Ps. civ. 2, 4.
4 Isa. xl. 12, 22.
5 Irenæus was evidently familiar with Horace; comp. Ars Poet., 300.
6 Matt. vii. 7.

they enter in within the Pleroma, while He remains in the intermediate place. Let them, then, prove themselves by their deeds superior to the Creator; for the superior person ought to be proved not by what is said, but by what has a real existence.

3. What work, then, will they point to as having been accomplished through themselves by the Saviour, or by their Mother, either greater, or more glorious, or more adorned with wisdom, than those which have been produced by Him who was the disposer of all around us? What heavens have they established? what earth have they founded? what stars have they called into existence? or what lights of heaven have they caused to shine? within what circles, moreover, have they confined them? or, what rains, or frosts, or snows, each suited to the season, and to every special climate, have they brought upon the earth? And again, in opposition to these, what heat or dryness have they set over against them? or, what rivers have they made to flow? what fountains have they brought forth? with what flowers and trees have they adorned this sublunary world? or, what multitude of animals have they formed, some rational, and others irrational, but all adorned with beauty? And who can enumerate one by one all the remaining objects which have been constituted by the power of God, and are governed by His wisdom? or who can search out the greatness of that God who made them? And what can be told of those existences which are above heaven, and which do not pass away, such as Angels, Archangels, Thrones, Dominions, and Powers innumerable? Against what one of these works, then, do they set themselves in opposition? What have they similar to show, as having been made through themselves, or by themselves, since even they too are the workmanship and creatures of this [Creator]? For whether the Saviour or their Mother (to use their own expressions, proving them false by means of the very terms they themselves employ) used this Being, as they maintain, to make an image of those things which are within the Pleroma, and of all those beings which she saw waiting upon the Saviour, she used him (the Demiurge) as being [in a sense] superior to herself, and better fitted to accomplish her purpose through his instrumentality; for she would by no means form the images of such important beings through means of an inferior, but by a superior, agent.

4. For, [be it observed,] they themselves, according to their own declarations, were then existing, as a spiritual conception, in consequence of the contemplation of those beings who were arranged as satellites around Pandora. And they indeed continued useless, the Mother accomplishing nothing through their instrumental-ity,[1] — an idle conception, owing their being to the Saviour, and fit for nothing, for not a thing appears to have been done by them. But the God who, according to them, was produced, while, as they argue, inferior to themselves (for they maintain that he is of an animal nature), was nevertheless the active agent in all things, efficient, and fit for the work to be done, so that by him the images of all things were made; and not only were these things which are seen formed by him, but also all things invisible, Angels, Archangels, Dominations, Powers, and Virtues, — [by him, I say,] as being the superior, and capable of ministering to her desire. But it seems that the Mother made nothing whatever through their instrumentality, as indeed they themselves acknowledge; so that one may justly reckon them as having been an abortion produced by the painful travail of their Mother. For no accoucheurs performed their office upon her, and therefore they were cast forth as an abortion, useful for nothing, and formed to accomplish no work of the Mother. And yet they describe themselves as being superior to Him by whom so vast and admirable works have been accomplished and arranged, although by their own reasoning they are found to be so wretchedly inferior!

5. It is as if there were two iron tools, or instruments, the one of which was continually in the workman's hands and in constant use, and by the use of which he made whatever he pleased, and displayed his art and skill, but the other of which remained idle and useless, never being called into operation, the workman never appearing to make anything by it, and making no use of it in any of his labours; and then one should maintain that this useless, and idle, and unemployed tool was superior in nature and value to that which the artisan employed in his work, and by means of which he acquired his reputation. Such a man, if any such were found, would justly be regarded as imbecile, and not in his right mind. And so should those be judged of who speak of themselves as being spiritual and superior, and of the Creator as possessed of an animal nature, and maintain that for this reason they will ascend on high, and penetrate within the Pleroma to their own husbands (for, according to their own statements, they are themselves feminine), but that God [the Creator] is of an inferior nature, and therefore remains in the intermediate place, while all the time they bring forward no proofs of these assertions: for the better man is shown by his works, and all works have been accomplished by the Creator; but they, having nothing worthy of reason to point to as having been produced by themselves, are

---

[1] The punctuation is here doubtful. With Massuet and Stieren we expunge " vel " from the text.

labouring under the greatest and most incurable madness.

6. If, however, they labour to maintain that, while all material things, such as the heaven, and the whole world which exists below it, were indeed formed by the Demiurge, yet all things of a more spiritual nature than these, — those, namely, which are above the heavens, such as Principalities, Powers, Angels, Archangels, Dominations, Virtues, — were produced by a spiritual process of birth (which they declare themselves to be), then, in the first place, we prove from the authoritative Scriptures [1] that all the things which have been mentioned, visible and invisible, have been made by one God. For these men are not more to be depended on than the Scriptures; nor ought we to give up the declarations of the Lord, Moses, and the rest of the prophets, who have proclaimed the truth, and give credit to them, who do indeed utter nothing of a sensible nature, but rave about untenable opinions. And, in the next place, if those things which are above the heavens were really made through their instrumentality, then let them inform us what is the nature of things invisible, recount the number of the Angels, and the ranks of the Archangels, reveal the mysteries of the Thrones, and teach us the differences between the Dominations, Principalities, Powers, and Virtues. But they can say nothing respecting them; therefore these beings were not made by them. If, on the other hand, these were made by the Creator, as was really the case, and are of a spiritual and holy character, then it follows that He who produced spiritual beings is not Himself of an animal nature, and thus their fearful system of blasphemy is overthrown.

7. For that there are spiritual creatures in the heavens, all the Scriptures loudly proclaim; and Paul expressly testifies that there are spiritual things when he declares that he was caught up into the third heaven,[2] and again, that he was carried away to paradise, and heard unspeakable words which it is not lawful for a man to utter. But what did that profit him, either his entrance into paradise or his assumption into the third heaven, since all these things are still but under the power of the Demiurge, if, as some venture to maintain, he had already begun [3] to be a spectator and a hearer of those mysteries which are affirmed to be above the Demiurge? For if it is true that he was becoming acquainted with that order of things which is above the Demiurge, he would by no means have remained in the regions of the Demiurge, and that so as not even thoroughly to explore even these (for, according to

their manner of speaking, there still lay before him four heavens,[4] if he were to approach the Demiurge, and thus behold the whole seven lying beneath him); but he might have been admitted, perhaps, into the intermediate place, that is, into the presence of the Mother, that he might receive instruction from her as to the things within the Pleroma. For that inner man which was in him, and spoke in him, as they say, though invisible, could have attained not only to the third heaven, but even as far as the presence of their Mother. For if they maintain that they themselves, that is, their [inner] man, at once ascends above the Demiurge, and departs to the Mother, much more must this have occurred to the [inner] man of the apostle; for the Demiurge would not have hindered him, being, as they assert, himself already subject to the Saviour. But if he had tried to hinder him, the effort would have gone for nothing. For it is not possible that he should prove stronger than the providence of the Father, and that when the inner man is said to be invisible even to the Demiurge. But since he (Paul) has described that assumption of himself up to the third heaven as something great and pre-eminent, it cannot be that these men ascend above the seventh heaven, for they are certainly not superior to the apostle. If they do maintain that they are more excellent than he, let them prove themselves so by their works, for they have never pretended to anything like [what he describes as occurring to himself]. And for this reason he added, "Whether in the body, or whether out of the body, God knoweth," [5] that the body might neither be thought to be a partaker in that vision,[6] as if it could have participated in those things which it had seen and heard; nor, again, that any one should say that he was not carried higher on account of the weight of the body; but it is therefore thus far permitted even without the body to behold spiritual mysteries which are the operations of God, who made the heavens and the earth, and formed man, and placed him in paradise, so that those should be spectators of them who, like the apostle, have reached a high degree of perfection in the love of God.

8. This Being, therefore, also made spiritual things, of which, as far as to the third heaven, the apostle was made a spectator, and heard un-

---

[1] Or, "the Scriptures of the Lord;" but the words "dominicis scripturis" probably here represent the Greek κυρίων γραφῶν, and are to be rendered as above.
[2] 2 Cor. xii. 2, 3, 4.
[3] "Inciperet fieri;" perhaps for "futurus esset," was to be.

[4] "Quartum cœlum;" there still being, according to their theory of seven heavens, a *fourth* beyond that to which St. Paul had penetrated.
[5] 2 Cor. xii. 3, defectively quoted.
[6] This is an exceedingly obscure and difficult sentence. Grabe and some of the later editors read, "uti neque *non* corpus," thus making Irenæus affirm that the body *did* participate in the vision. But Massuet contends strenuously that this is contrary to the author's purpose, as wishing to maintain, against a possible exception of the Valentinians, that Paul then witnessed *spiritual* realities, and by omitting this "non" before "corpus," makes Irenæus deny that the body was a partaker in the vision. The point can only be doubtfully decided, but Massuet's ingenious note inclines us to his side of the question.

speakable words which it is not possible for a man to utter, inasmuch as they are spiritual ; and He Himself bestows[1] [gifts] on the worthy as inclination prompts Him, for paradise is His ; and He is truly the Spirit of God, and not an animal Demiurge, otherwise He should never have created spiritual things. But if He really is of an animal nature, then let them inform us by whom spiritual things were made. They have no proof which they can give that this was done by means of the travail of their Mother, which they declare themselves to be. For, not to speak of spiritual things, these men cannot create even a fly, or a gnat, or any other small and insignificant animal, without observing that law by which from the beginning animals have been and are naturally produced by God — through the deposition of seed in those that are of the same species. Nor was anything formed by the Mother alone ; [for] they say that this Demiurge was produced by her, and that *he* was the Lord (the author) of all creation. And they maintain that he who is the Creator and Lord of all that has been made is of an animal nature, while they assert that they themselves are spiritual, — they who are neither the authors nor lords of any one work, not only of those things which are extraneous to them, but not even of their own bodies ! Moreover, these men, who call themselves spiritual, and superior to the Creator, do often suffer much bodily pain, sorely against their will.

9. Justly, therefore, do we convict them of having departed far and wide from the truth. For if the Saviour formed the things which have been made, by means of him (the Demiurge), he is proved in that case not to be inferior but superior to them, since he is found to have been the former even of themselves ; for they, too, have a place among created things. How, then, can it be argued that these men indeed are spiritual, but that he by whom they were created is of an animal nature? Or, again, if (which is indeed the only true supposition, as I have shown by numerous arguments of the very clearest nature) He (the Creator) made all things freely, and by His own power, and arranged and finished them, and His will is the substance[2] of all things, then He is discovered to be the one only God who created all things, who alone is Omnipotent, and who is the only Father founding and forming all things, visible and invisible, such as may be perceived by our senses and such as cannot, heavenly and earthly, " by the word of His power ; "[3] and He has fitted and arranged all things by His wisdom, while He contains all things, but He Himself can be contained by no one :

He is the Former, He the Builder, He the Discoverer, He the Creator, He the Lord of all; and there is no one besides Him, or above Him, neither has He any mother, as they falsely ascribe to Him ; nor is there a second God, as Marcion has imagined ; nor is there a Pleroma of thirty Æons, which has been shown a vain supposition ; nor is there any such being as Bythus or Proarche ; nor are there a series of heavens ; nor is there a virginal light,[4] nor an unnameable Æon, nor, in fact, any one of those things which are madly dreamt of by these, and by all the heretics. But there is one only God, the Creator — He who is above every Principality, and Power, and Dominion, and Virtue : He is Father, He is God, He the Founder, He the Maker, He the Creator, who made those things by Himself, that is, through His Word and His Wisdom — heaven and earth, and the seas, and all things that are in them : He is just ; He is good ; He it is who formed man, who planted paradise, who made the world, who gave rise to the flood, who saved Noah ; He is the God of Abraham, and the God of Isaac, and the God of Jacob, the God of the living : He it is whom the law proclaims, whom the prophets preach, whom Christ reveals, whom the apostles make known[5] to us, and in whom the Church believes. He is the Father of our Lord Jesus Christ : through His Word, who is His Son, through Him He is revealed and manifested to all to whom He *is* revealed ; for those [only] know Him to whom the Son has revealed Him. But the Son, eternally co-existing with the Father, from of old, yea, from the beginning, always reveals the Father to Angels, Archangels, Powers, Virtues, and all to whom He wills that God should be revealed.

CHAP. XXXI. — RECAPITULATION AND APPLICATION OF THE FOREGOING ARGUMENTS.

1. Those, then, who are of the school of Valentinus being overthrown, the whole multitude of heretics are, in fact, also subverted. For all the arguments I have advanced against their Pleroma, and with respect to those things which are beyond it, showing how the Father of all is shut up and circumscribed by that which is beyond Him (if, indeed, there be anything beyond Him), and how there is an absolute necessity [on their theory] to conceive of many Fathers, and many Pleromas, and many creations of worlds, beginning with one set and ending with another, as existing on every side ; and that all [the beings referred to] continue in their own domains, and do not curiously intermeddle with others, since, indeed, no common interest nor any fellowship exists between them ; and that there is no other

---

[1] " Præstat dignis : " here a very ambiguous expression.
[2] That is, as Massuet notes, all things derive not only their *existence,* but their *qualities,* from His will. Harvey proposes to read *causa* instead of *substantia,* but the change seems needless.
[3] Heb. i. 3.

[4] That is, *Barbelos:* comp. i. 29, 1.
[5] " Tradunt;" literally, *hand down.*

God of all, but that that name belongs only to the Almighty; — [all these arguments, I say,] will in like manner apply against those who are of the school of Marcion, and Simon, and Menander, or whatever others there may be who, like them, cut off that creation with which we are connected from the Father. The arguments, again, which I have employed against those who maintain that the Father of all no doubt contains all things, but that the creation to which we belong was not formed by Him, but by a certain other power, or by angels having no knowledge of the Propator, who is surrounded as a centre by the immense extent of the universe, just as a stain is by the [surrounding] cloak; when I showed that it is not a probable supposition that any other being than the Father of all formed that creation to which we belong, — these same arguments will apply against the followers of Saturninus, Basilides, Carpocrates, and the rest of the Gnostics, who express similar opinions. Those statements, again, which have been made with respect to the emanations, and the Æons, and the [supposed state of] degeneracy, and the inconstant character of their Mother, equally overthrow Basilides, and all who are falsely styled Gnostics, who do, in fact, just repeat the same views under different names, but do, to a greater extent than the former,[1] transfer those things which lie outside[2] of the truth to the system of their own doctrine. And the remarks I have made respecting numbers will also apply against all those who misappropriate things belonging to the truth for the support of a system of this kind. And all that has been said respecting the Creator (Demiurge) to show that he alone is God and Father of all, and whatever remarks may yet be made in the following books, I apply against the heretics at large. The more moderate and reasonable among them thou wilt convert and convince, so as to lead them no longer to blaspheme their Creator, and Maker, and Sustainer, and Lord, nor to ascribe His origin to defect and ignorance; but the fierce, and terrible, and irrational [among them] thou wilt drive far from thee, that you may no longer have to endure their idle loquaciousness.

2. Moreover, those also will be thus confuted who belong to Simon and Carpocrates, and if there be any others who are said to perform miracles — who do not perform what they do either through the power of God, or in connection with the truth, nor for the well-being of men, but for the sake of destroying and misleading mankind, by means of magical deceptions, and with universal deceit, thus entailing greater harm than good on those who believe them, with respect to the point on which they lead them astray. For they can neither confer sight on the blind, nor hearing on the deaf, nor chase away all sorts of demons — [none, indeed,] except those that are sent into others by themselves, if they can even do so much as this. Nor can they cure the weak, or the lame, or the paralytic, or those who are distressed in any other part of the body, as has often been done in regard to bodily infirmity. Nor can they furnish effective remedies for those external accidents which may occur. And so far are they from being able to raise the dead, as the Lord raised them, and the apostles did by means of prayer, and as has been frequently done in the brotherhood on account of some necessity — the entire Church in that particular locality entreating [the boon] with much fasting and prayer, the spirit of the dead man has returned, and he has been bestowed in answer to the prayers of the saints — that they do not even believe this can be possibly be done, [and hold] that the resurrection from the dead[3] is simply an acquaintance with that truth which they proclaim.

3. Since, therefore, there exist among them error and misleading influences, and magical illusions are impiously wrought in the sight of men; but in the Church, sympathy, and compassion, and stedfastness, and truth, for the aid and encouragement of mankind, are not only displayed[4] without fee or reward, but we ourselves lay out for the benefit of others our own means; and inasmuch as those who are cured very frequently do not possess the things which they require, they receive them from us; — [since such is the case,] these men are in this way undoubtedly proved to be utter aliens from the divine nature, the beneficence of God, and all spiritual excellence. But they are altogether full of deceit of every kind, apostate inspiration, demoniacal working, and the phantasms of idolatry, and are in reality the predecessors of that dragon[5] who, by means of a deception of the same kind, will with his tail cause a third part of the stars to fall from their place, and will cast them down to the earth. It behoves us to flee from them as we would from him; and the greater the display with which they are said to perform [their marvels], the more carefully should we watch them, as having been endowed with a greater spirit of wickedness. If any one will consider the prophecy referred to, and the daily practices of these men, he will find that

---

[1] *Qui,* though here found in all the MSS., seems to have been rightly expunged by the editors.
[2] The reference probably is to opinions and theories of the heathen.

[3] Comp. 2 Tim. ii. 17, 18. [On the sub-apostolic age and this subject of miracles, Newman, in spite of his sophistical argumentation, may well be consulted for his references, etc. *Translation of the Abbé Fleury,* p. xi. Oxford, 1842.]
[4] "Perficiatur:" it is difficult here to give a fitting translation of this word. Some prefer to read "impertiatur."
[5] Rev. xii. 14.

their manner of acting is one and the same with the demons.

CHAP. XXXII. — FURTHER EXPOSURE OF THE WICKED AND BLASPHEMOUS DOCTRINES OF THE HERETICS.

1. Moreover, this impious opinion of theirs with respect to actions — namely, that it is incumbent on them to have experience of all kinds of deeds, even the most abominable — is refuted by the teaching of the Lord, with whom not only is the adulterer rejected, but also the man who desires to commit adultery; [1] and not only is the actual murderer held guilty of having killed another to his own damnation, but the man also who is angry with his brother without a cause : who commanded [His disciples] not only not to hate men, but also to love their enemies ; and enjoined them not only not to swear falsely, but not even to swear at all ; and not only not to speak evil of their neighbours, but not even to style any one " Raca " and " fool ; " [declaring] that otherwise they were in danger of hell-fire ; and not only not to strike, but even, when themselves struck, to present the other cheek [to those that maltreated them] ; and not only not to refuse to give up the property of others, but even if their own were taken away, not to demand it back again from those that took it ; and not only not to injure their neighbours, nor to do them any evil, but also, when themselves wickedly dealt with, to be long-suffering, and to show kindness towards those [that injured them], and to pray for them, that by means of repentance they might be saved — so that we should in no respect imitate the arrogance, lust, and pride of others. Since, therefore, He whom these men boast of as their Master, and of whom they affirm that He had a soul greatly better and more highly toned than others, did indeed, with much earnestness, command certain things to be done as being good and excellent, and certain things to be abstained from not only in their actual perpetration, but even in the thoughts which lead to their performance, as being wicked, pernicious, and abominable, — how then can they escape being put to confusion, when they affirm that such a Master was more highly toned [in spirit] and better than others, and yet manifestly give instruction of a kind utterly opposed to His teaching? And, again, if there were really no such thing as good and evil, but certain things were deemed righteous, and certain others unrighteous, in human opinion only, He never would have expressed Himself thus in His teaching : " The righteous shall shine forth as the sun in the kingdom of their Father ; " [2] but He shall send the unrighteous, and those who do not the works of righteousness, " into everlasting fire, where their worm shall not die, and the fire shall not be quenched." [3]

2. When they further maintain that it is incumbent on them to have experience of every kind [4] of work and conduct, so that, if it be possible, accomplishing all during one manifestation in this life, they may [at once] pass over to the state of perfection, they are, by no chance, found striving to do those things which wait upon virtue, and are laborious, glorious, and skilful, [5] which also are approved universally as being good. For if it be necessary to go through every work and every kind of operation, they ought, in the first place, to learn all the arts : all of them, [I say,] whether referring to theory or practice, whether they be acquired by self-denial, or are mastered through means of labour, exercise, and perseverance ; as, for example, every kind of music, arithmetic, geometry, astronomy, and all such as are occupied with intellectual pursuits : then, again, the whole study of medicine, and the knowledge of plants, so as to become acquainted with those which are prepared for the health of man ; the art of painting and sculpture, brass and marble work, and the kindred arts : moreover, [they have to study] every kind of country labour, the veterinary art, pastoral occupations, the various kinds of skilled labour, which are said to pervade the whole circle of [human] exertion ; those, again, connected with a maritime life, gymnastic exercises, hunting, military and kingly pursuits, and as many others as may exist, of which, with the utmost labour, they could not learn the tenth, or even the thousandth part, in the whole course of their lives. The fact indeed is, that they endeavour to learn none of these, although they maintain that it is incumbent on them to have experience of every kind of work ; but, turning aside to voluptuousness, and lust, and abominable actions, they stand self-condemned when they are tried by their own doctrine. For, since they are destitute of all those [virtues] which have been mentioned, they will [of necessity] pass into the destruction of fire. These men, while they boast of Jesus as being their Master, do in fact emulate the philosophy of Epicurus and the indifference of the Cynics, [calling Jesus their Master,] who not only turned His disciples away from evil deeds, but even from [wicked] words and thoughts, as I have already shown.

3. Again, while they assert that they possess souls from the same sphere as Jesus, and that they are like to Him, sometimes even maintaining that they are superior ; while [they affirm that they were] produced, like Him, for the

---

[1] Matt. v. 21, etc.
[2] Matt. xiii. 43.

[3] Matt. xxv. 41 ; Mark ix. 44.
[4] Comp. i. 25, 4.
[5] " Artificialia."

performance of works tending to the benefit and establishment of mankind, they are found doing nothing of the same or a like kind [with His actions], nor what can in any respect be brought into comparison with them. And if they have in truth accomplished anything [remarkable] by means of magic, they strive [in this way] deceitfully to lead foolish people astray, since they confer no real benefit or blessing on those over whom they declare that they exert] supernatural] power; but, bringing forward mere boys [1] [as the subjects on whom they practise], and deceiving their sight, while they exhibit phantasms that instantly cease, and do not endure even a moment of time,[2] they are proved to be like, not Jesus our Lord, but Simon the magician. It is certain,[3] too, from the fact that the Lord rose from the dead on the third day, and manifested Himself to His disciples, and was in their sight received up into heaven, that, inasmuch as these men die, and do not rise again, nor manifest themselves to any, they are proved as possessing souls in no respect similar to that of Jesus.

4. If, however, they maintain that the Lord, too, performed such works simply in appearance, we shall refer them to the prophetical writings, and prove from these both that all things were thus[4] predicted regarding Him, and did take place undoubtedly, and that He is the only Son of God. Wherefore, also, those who are in truth His disciples, receiving grace from Him, do in His name perform [miracles], so as to promote the welfare of other men, according to the gift which each one has received from Him. For some do certainly and truly drive out devils, so that those who have thus been cleansed from evil spirits frequently both believe [in Christ], and join themselves to the Church. Others have foreknowledge of things to come: they see visions, and utter prophetic expressions. Others still, heal the sick by laying their hands upon them, and they are made whole. Yea, moreover, as I have said, the dead even have been raised up, and remained[5] among us for many years. And what shall I more say? It is not possible to name the number of the gifts which the Church, [scattered] throughout the whole world, has received from God, in the name of Jesus Christ, who was crucified under Pontius Pilate, and which she exerts day by day for the benefit of the Gentiles, neither practising deception upon any, nor taking any reward[6] from them [on account of such miraculous interpositions]. For as she has received freely[7] from God, freely also does she minister [to others].

5. Nor does she perform anything by means of angelic invocations,[8] or by incantations, or by any other wicked curious art; but, directing her prayers to the Lord, who made all things, in a pure, sincere, and straightforward spirit, and calling upon the name of our Lord Jesus Christ, she has been accustomed to work[9] miracles for the advantage of mankind, and not to lead them into error. If, therefore, the name of our Lord Jesus Christ even now confers benefits [upon men], and cures thoroughly and effectively all who anywhere believe on Him, but not that of Simon, or Menander, or Carpocrates, or of any other man whatever, it is manifest that, when He was made man, He held fellowship with His own creation, and[10] did all things truly through the power of God, according to the will of the Father of all, as the prophets had foretold. But what these things were, shall be described in dealing with the proofs to be found in the prophetical writings.

CHAP. XXXIII. — ABSURDITY OF THE DOCTRINE OF THE TRANSMIGRATION OF SOULS.

1. We may subvert their doctrine as to transmigration from body to body by this fact, that souls remember nothing whatever of the events which took place in their previous states of existence. For if they were sent forth with this object, that they should have experience of every kind of action, they must of necessity retain a remembrance of those things which have been previously accomplished, that they might fill up those in which they were still deficient, and not by always hovering, without intermission, round the same pursuits, spend their labour wretchedly in vain (for the mere union of a body [with a soul] could not altogether extinguish the memory and contemplation of those things which had formerly been experienced[11]), and especially as they came [into the world] for this very purpose. For as, when the body is asleep and at rest, whatever things the soul sees by herself, and does in a vision, recollecting

---

[1] "Pureos investes," boys that have not yet reached the age of puberty.
[2] The text has "stillicidio temporis," literally "a *drop* of time (σταγμῇ χρόνου); but the original text was perhaps στιγμῇ χρόνου, "a *moment* of time." With either reading the meaning is the same.
[3] Some have deemed the words "firmum esse" an interpolation.
[4] That is, as being done *in reality*, and not in appearance.
[5] Harvey here notes : "The reader will not fail to remark this highly interesting testimony, that the divine χαρίσματα bestowed upon the infant Church were not wholly extinct in the days of Irenæus. Possibly the venerable Father is speaking from his own personal recollection of some who had been raised from the dead, and had continued for a time living witnesses of the efficacy of Christian faith." [See cap. xxxi., *supra*.]

[6] Comp. Acts viii. 9, 18.
[7] Matt. x. 8.
[8] Grabe contends that these words imply that no invocations of angels, good or bad, were practised in the primitive Church. Massuet, on the other hand, maintains that the words of Irenæus are plainly to be restricted to evil spirits, and have no bearing on the general question of angelic invocation.
[9] We follow the common reading, "perfecit;" but one MS. has "perficit," *works*, which suits the context better.
[10] We insert "et," in accordance with Grabe's suggestion.
[11] Harvey thinks that this parenthesis has fallen out of its proper place, and would insert it immediately after the opening period of the chapter.

many of these, she also communicates them to the body; and as it happens that, when one awakes, perhaps after a long time, he relates what he saw in a dream, so also would he undoubtedly remember those things which he did before he came into this particular body. For if that which is seen only for a very brief space of time, or has been conceived of simply in a phantasm, and by the soul alone, through means of a dream, is remembered after she has mingled again with the body, and been dispersed through all the members, much more would she remember those things in connection with which she stayed during so long a time, even throughout the whole period of a bypast life.

2. With reference to these objections, Plato, that ancient Athenian, who also was the first [1] to introduce this opinion, when he could not set them aside, invented the [notion of] a cup of oblivion, imagining that in this way he would escape this sort of difficulty. He attempted no kind of proof [of his supposition], but simply replied dogmatically [to the objection in question], that when souls enter into this life, they are caused to drink of oblivion by that demon who watches their entrance [into the world], before they effect an entrance into the bodies [assigned them]. It escaped him, that [by speaking thus] he fell into another greater perplexity. For if the cup of oblivion, after it has been drunk, can obliterate the memory of all the deeds that have been done, how, O Plato, dost thou obtain the knowledge of this fact (since thy soul is now in the body), that, before it entered into the body, it was made to drink by the demon a drug which caused oblivion? For if thou hast a remembrance of the demon, and the cup, and the entrance [into life], thou oughtest also to be acquainted with other things; but if, on the other hand, thou art ignorant of them, then there is no truth in the story of the demon, nor in the cup of oblivion prepared with art.

3. In opposition, again, to those who affirm that the body itself is the drug of oblivion, this observation may be made: How, then, does it come to pass, that whatsoever the soul sees by her own instrumentality, both in dreams and by reflection or earnest mental exertion, while the body is passive, she remembers, and reports to her neighbours? But, again, if the body itself were [the cause of] oblivion, then the soul, as existing in the body, could not remember even those things which were perceived long ago either by means of the eyes or the ears; but, as soon as the eye was turned from the things looked at, the memory of them also would undoubtedly be destroyed. For the soul, as existing in the very [cause of] oblivion, could have no knowledge of anything else than that only which it saw at the present moment. How, too, could it become acquainted with divine things, and retain a remembrance of them while existing in the body, since, as they maintain, the body itself is [the cause of] oblivion? But the prophets also, when they were upon the earth, remembered likewise, on their returning to their ordinary state of mind,[2] whatever things they spiritually saw or heard in visions of heavenly objects, and related them to others. The body, therefore, does not cause the soul to forget those things which have been spiritually witnessed; but the soul teaches the body, and shares with it the spiritual vision which it has enjoyed.

4. For the body is not possessed of greater power than the soul, since indeed the former is inspired, and vivified, and increased, and held together by the latter; but the soul possesses[3] and rules over the body. It is doubtless retarded in its velocity, just in the exact proportion in which the body shares in its motion; but it never loses the knowledge which properly belongs to it. For the body may be compared to an instrument; but the soul is possessed of the reason of an artist. As, therefore, the artist finds the idea of a work to spring up rapidly in his mind, but can only carry it out slowly by means of an instrument, owing to the want of perfect pliability in the matter acted upon, and thus the rapidity of his mental operation, being blended with the slow action of the instrument, gives rise to a moderate kind of movement [towards the end contemplated]; so also the soul, by being mixed up with the body belonging to it, is in a certain measure impeded, its rapidity being blended with the body's slowness. Yet it does not lose altogether its own peculiar powers; but while, as it were, sharing life with the body, it does not itself cease to live. Thus, too, while communicating other things to the body, it neither loses the knowledge of them, nor the memory of those things which have been witnessed.

5. If, therefore, the soul remembers nothing[4] of what took place in a former state of existence, but has a perception of those things which are here, it follows that she never existed in other bodies, nor did things of which she has no knowledge, nor [once] knew things which she cannot [now mentally] contemplate. But, as each one of us receives his body through the skilful

---

[1] It is a mistake of Irenæus to say that the doctrine of metempsychosis originated with Plato: it was first publicly taught by Pythagoras, who learned it from the Egyptians. Comp. Clem. Alex., *Strom.*, i. 15: Herodot., ii. 123.

[2] "In hominem conversi," literally, "returning into man."
[3] "Possidet." Massuet supposes this word to represent κυριεύει, "rules over," and Stieren κρατύνει, *governs*; while Harvey thinks the whole clause corresponds to κρατεῖ καὶ κυριεύει τοῦ σώματος, which we have rendered as above.
[4] Literally, *none of things past.*

working of God, so does he also possess his soul. For God is not so poor or destitute in resources, that He cannot confer its own proper soul on each individual body, even as He gives it also its special character. And therefore, when the number [fixed upon] is completed, [that number] which He had predetermined in His own counsel, all those who have been enrolled for life [eternal] shall rise again, having their own bodies, and having also their own souls, and their own spirits, in which they had pleased God. Those, on the other hand, who are worthy of punishment, shall go away into it, they too having their own souls, and their own bodies, in which they stood apart from the grace of God. Both classes shall then cease from any longer begetting and being begotten, from marrying and being given in marriage ; so that the number of mankind, corresponding to the fore-ordination of God, being completed, may fully realize the scheme formed by the Father.[1]

CHAP. XXXIV. — SOULS CAN BE RECOGNISED IN THE SEPARATE STATE, AND ARE IMMORTAL ALTHOUGH THEY ONCE HAD A BEGINNING.

1. The Lord has taught with very great fulness, that souls not only continue to exist, not by passing from body to body, but that they preserve the same form[2] [in their separate state] as the body had to which they were adapted, and that they remember the deeds which they did in this state of existence, and from which they have now ceased, — in that narrative which is recorded respecting the rich man and that Lazarus who found repose in the bosom of Abraham. In this account He states[3] that Dives knew Lazarus after death, and Abraham in like manner, and that each one of these persons continued in his own proper position, and that [Dives] requested Lazarus to be sent to relieve him — [Lazarus], on whom he did not [formerly] bestow even the crumbs [which fell] from his table. [He tells us] also of the answer given by Abraham, who was acquainted not only with what respected himself, but Dives also, and who enjoined those who did not wish to come into that place of torment to believe Moses and the prophets, and to receive[4] the preaching of Him who was[5] to rise again from the dead. By these things, then, it is plainly declared that souls continue to exist, that they do not pass from body to body, that they possess the form of a man, so that they may be recognised, and retain the memory of things in this world ; moreover, that the gift of prophecy was possessed by Abraham, and that each class [of souls] receives a habitation such as it has deserved, even before the judgment.

2. But if any persons at this point maintain that those souls, which only began a little while ago to exist, cannot endure for any length of time ; but that they must, on the one hand, either be unborn, in order that they may be immortal, or if they have had a beginning in the way of generation, that they should die with the body itself — let them learn that God alone, who is Lord of all, is without beginning and without end, being truly and for ever the same, and always remaining the same unchangeable Being. But all things which proceed from Him, whatsoever have been made, and are made, do indeed receive their own beginning of generation, and on this account are inferior to Him who formed them, inasmuch as they are not unbegotten. Nevertheless they endure, and extend their existence into a long series of ages in accordance with the will of God their Creator ; so that He grants them that they should be thus formed at the beginning, and that they should so exist afterwards.

3. For as the heaven which is above us, the firmament, the sun, the moon, the rest of the stars, and all their grandeur, although they had no previous existence, were called into being, and continue throughout a long course of time according to the will of God, so also any one who thinks thus respecting souls and spirits, and, in fact, respecting all created things, will not by any means go far astray, inasmuch as all things that have been made had a beginning when they were formed, but endure as long as God wills that they should have an existence and continuance. The prophetic Spirit bears testimony to these opinions, when He declares, " For He spake, and they were made ; He commanded, and they were created : He hath established them for ever, yea, for ever and ever." [6] And again, He thus speaks respecting the salvation of man : " He asked life of Thee, and Thou gavest him length of days for ever and ever ; "[7] indicating that it is the Father of all who imparts continuance for ever and ever on those who are saved. For life does not arise from us, nor from our own nature ; but it is bestowed according to the grace of God. And therefore he who shall preserve the life bestowed upon him, and give thanks to Him who imparted it, shall receive also length of days for ever and ever. But he who shall reject it, and prove himself ungrateful to his Maker, inasmuch as he has been created, and has not recognised Him who

---

[1] The Latin text is here very confused, but the Greek original of the greater part of this section has happily been preserved. [This Father here anticipates in outline many ideas which St. Augustine afterwards corrected and elaborated.]

[2] Grabe refers to Tertullian, *De Anima*, ch. vii., as making a similiar statement. Massuet, on the other hand, denies that Irenæus here expresses an opinion like that of Tertullian in the passage referred to, and thinks that the special form (*character*) mentioned is to be understood as simply denoting individual *spiritual* properties. But his remarks are not satisfactory.

[3] Luke xvi. 19, etc.

[4] With Massuet and Stieren, we here supply *esse*.

[5] Some read *resurgeret*, and others *resurrexerit ;* we deem the former reading preferable.

[6] Ps. cxlviii. 5, 6.

[7] Ps. xxi. 4.

bestowed [the gift upon him], deprives himself of [the privilege of] continuance for ever and ever.[1] And, for this reason, the Lord declared to those who showed themselves ungrateful towards Him : " If ye have not been faithful in that which is little, who will give you that which is great?"[2] indicating that those who, in this brief temporal life, have shown themselves ungrateful to Him who bestowed it, shall justly not receive from Him length of days for ever and ever.

4. But as the animal body is certainly not itself the soul, yet has fellowship with the soul as long as God pleases; so the soul herself is not life,[3] but partakes in that life bestowed upon her by God. Wherefore also the prophetic word declares of the first-formed man, " He became a living soul,"[4] teaching us that by the participation of life the soul became alive ; so that the soul, and the life which it possesses, must be understood as being separate existences. When God therefore bestows life and perpetual duration, it comes to pass that even souls which did not previously exist should henceforth endure [for ever], since God has both willed that they should exist, and should continue in existence. For the will of God ought to govern and rule in all things, while all other things give way to Him, are in subjection, and devoted to His service. Thus far, then, let me speak concerning the creation and the continued duration of the soul.

CHAP. XXXV. — REFUTATION OF BASILIDES, AND OF THE OPINION THAT THE PROPHETS UTTERED THEIR PREDICTIONS UNDER THE INSPIRATION OF DIFFERENT GODS.

1. Moreover, in addition to what has been said, Basilides himself will, according to his own principles, find it necessary to maintain not only that there are three hundred and sixty-five heavens made in succession by one another, but that an immense and innumerable multitude of heavens have always been in the process of being made, and are being made, and will continue to be made, so that the formation of heavens of this kind can never cease. For if from the efflux[5] of the first heaven the second was made after its likeness, and the third after the likeness of the second, and so on with all the remaining subsequent ones, then it follows, as a matter of necessity, that from the efflux of our heaven, which he indeed terms the last, another be formed like to it, and from that again a third ; and thus there can never cease, either the process of efflux from

those heavens which have been already made, or the manufacture of [new] heavens, but the operation must go on ad infinitum, and give rise to a number of heavens which will be altogether indefinite.

2. The remainder of those who are falsely termed Gnostics, and who maintain that the prophets uttered their prophecies under the inspiration of different gods, will be easily overthrown by this fact, that all the prophets proclaimed one God and Lord, and that the very Maker of heaven and earth, and of all things which are therein ; while they moreover announced the advent of His Son, as I shall demonstrate from the Scriptures themselves, in the books which follow.

3. If, however, any object that, in the Hebrew language, diverse expressions [to represent God] occur in the Scriptures, such as Sabaoth, Eloë, Adonai, and all other such terms, striving to prove from these that there are different powers and gods, let them learn that all expressions of this kind are but announcements and appellations of one and the same Being. For the term Eloë in the Jewish language denotes God, while Elöeim[6] and Elöeuth in the Hebrew language signify " that which contains all." As to the appellation Adonai, sometimes it denotes what is nameable[7] and admirable; but at other times, when the letter Daleth in it is doubled, and the word receives an initial[8] guttural sound — thus Addonai — [it signifies], " One who bounds and separates the land from the water," so that the water should not subsequently[9] submerge the land. In like manner also, Sabaoth,[10] when it is spelled by a Greek Omega in the last syllable [Sabaöth], denotes " a voluntary agent; " but when it is spelled with a Greek Omicron — as, for instance, Sabaŏth — it expresses " the first heaven." In the same way, too, the word Jaŏth,[11] when the last syllable is made long and aspirated,

---

[1] As Massuet observes, this statement is to be understood in harmony with the repeated assertion of Irenæus that the wicked will exist in misery for ever. It refers not to annihilation, but to deprivation of happiness.
[2] Luke xvi. 11, quoted loosely from memory. Grabe, however, thinks they are cited from the apocryphal Gospel according to the Egyptians.
[3] Comp. Justin Martyr, Dial. c. Tryph., ch. vi.
[4] Gen. ii. 7.
[5] Ex defluxu, corresponding to ἐξ ἀπορροίας in the Greek.

[6] Eloæ here occurs in the Latin text, but Harvey supposes that the Greek had been Ἐλωείμ. He also remarks that Eloeuth (אֱלָהוּת) is the rabbinical abstract term, Godhead.
[7] All that can be remarked on this is, that the Jews substituted the term Adonai (אֲדֹנָי) for the name Jehovah, as often as the latter occurred in the sacred text. The former might therefore be styled nameable.
[8] The Latin text is, " aliquando autem duplicata litera delta cum aspiratione," and Harvey supposes that the doubling of the Daleth would give " to the scarcely articulate א a more decidedly guttural character; " but the sense is extremely doubtful.
[9] Instead of " nec posteaquam insurgere," Feuardent and Massuet read " ne possit insurgere," and include the clause in the definition of Addonai.
[10] The author is here utterly mistaken, and, notwithstanding Harvey's earnest claim for him of a knowledge of Hebrew, seems clearly to betray his ignorance of that language. The term Sabaoth is never written with an Omicron, either in the LXX. or by the Greek Fathers, but always with an Omega (Σαβαώθ). Although Harvey remarks in his preface, that " it is hoped the Hebrew attainments of Irenæus will no longer be denied," there appears enough, in the etymologies and explanations of Hebrew terms given in this chapter by the venerable Father, to prevent such a conclusion; and Massuet's observation on the passage seems not improbable, when he says, " Sciolus quispiam Irenæo nostro, in Hebraicis haud satis perito, hic fucum ecisse videtur."
[11] Probably corresponding to the Hebrew term Jehovah (יְהֹוָה).

denotes "*a predetermined measure;*" but when it is written shortly by the Greek letter Omicron, namely *Jaöth*, it signifies "*one who puts evils to flight.*" All the other expressions likewise bring out [1] the title of one and the same Being; as, for example (in English [2]), *The Lord of Powers, The Father of all, God Almighty, The Most High, The Creator, The Maker*, and such like. These are not the names and titles of a succession of different beings, but of one and the same, by means of which the one God and Father is revealed, He who contains all things, and grants to all the boon of existence.

4. Now, that the preaching of the apostles, the authoritative teaching of the Lord, the announcements of the prophets, the dictated utterances of the apostles,[3] and the ministration of the law — all of which praise one and the same Being, the God and Father of all, and not many diverse beings, nor one deriving his substance from different gods or powers, but [declare] that all things [were formed] by one and the same Father (who nevertheless adapts [His works] to the natures and tendencies of the materials dealt with), things visible and invisible, and, in short, all things that have been made [were created] neither by angels, nor by any other power, but by God alone, the Father — are all in harmony with our statements, has, I think, been sufficiently proved, while by these weighty arguments it has been shown that there is but one God, the Maker of all things. But that I may not be thought to avoid that series of proofs which may be derived from the Scriptures of the Lord (since, indeed, these Scriptures do much more evidently and clearly proclaim this very point), I shall, for the benefit of those at least who do not bring a depraved mind to bear upon them, devote a special book to the Scriptures referred to, which shall fairly follow them out [and explain them], and I shall plainly set forth from these divine Scriptures proofs to [satisfy] all the lovers of truth.[4]

---

[1] Literally, "belong to one and the same name."
[2] "Secundum *Latinitatem*" in the text.
[3] The words are "apostolorum dictatio," probably referring to the *letters* of the apostles, as distinguished from their *preaching* already mentioned.

[4] This last sentence is very confused and ambiguous, and the editors throw but little light upon it. We have endeavoured to translate it according to the ordinary text and punctuation, but strongly suspect interpolation and corruption. If we might venture to strike out "has Scripturas," and connect "his tamen" with "prædicantibus," a better sense would be yielded, as follows: "But that I may not be thought to avoid that series of proofs which may be derived from the Scriptures of the Lord (since, indeed, these Scriptures do much more evidently and clearly set forth this very point, to those at least who do not bring a depraved mind to their consideration), I shall devote the particular book which follows to them, and shall," etc.

IRENÆUS AGAINST HERESIES

BOOK III.

THOU hast indeed enjoined upon me, my very dear friend, that I should bring to light the Valentinian doctrines, concealed, as their votaries imagine ; that I should exhibit their diversity, and compose a treatise in refutation of them. I therefore have undertaken — showing that they spring from Simon, the father of all heretics — to exhibit both their doctrines and successions, and to set forth arguments against them all. Wherefore, since the conviction of these men and their exposure is in many points but one work, I have sent unto thee [certain] books, of which the first comprises the opinions of all these men, and exhibits their customs, and the character of their behaviour. In the second, again, their perverse teachings are cast down and overthrown, and, such as they really are, laid bare and open to view. But in this, the third book, I shall adduce proofs from the Scriptures, so that I may come behind in nothing of what thou hast enjoined ; yea, that over and above what thou didst reckon upon, thou mayest receive from me the means of combating and vanquishing those who, in whatever manner, are propagating falsehood. For the love of God, being rich and ungrudging, confers upon the suppliant more than he can ask from it. Call to mind, then, the things which I have stated in the two preceding books, and, taking these in connection with them, thou shalt have from me a very copious refutation of all the heretics ; and faithfully and strenuously shalt thou resist them in defence of the only true and life-giving faith, which the Church has received from the apostles and imparted to her sons. For the Lord of all gave to His apostles the power of the Gospel, through whom also we have known the truth, that is, the doctrine of the Son of God ; to whom also did the Lord declare : " He that heareth you, heareth Me ; and he that despiseth you, despiseth Me, and Him that sent Me." [1]

CHAP. I.—THE APOSTLES DID NOT COMMENCE TO PREACH THE GOSPEL, OR TO PLACE ANYTHING ON RECORD, UNTIL THEY WERE ENDOWED WITH THE GIFTS AND POWER OF THE HOLY SPIRIT. THEY PREACHED ONE GOD ALONE, MAKER OF HEAVEN AND EARTH.

1. WE have learned from none others the plan of our salvation, than from those through whom the Gospel has come down to us, which they did at one time proclaim in public, and, at a later period, by the will of God, handed down to us in the Scriptures, to be the ground and pillar of our faith.[2] For it is unlawful to assert that they preached before they possessed " perfect knowledge," as some do even venture to say, boasting themselves as improvers of the apostles. For, after our Lord rose from the dead, [the apostles] were invested with power from on high when the Holy Spirit came down [upon them], were filled from all [His gifts], and had perfect knowledge : they departed to the ends of the earth, preaching the glad tidings of the good things [sent] from God to us, and proclaiming the peace of heaven to men, who indeed do all equally and individually possess the Gospel of God. Matthew also issued a written Gospel among the Hebrews [3] in their own dialect, while Peter and Paul were preaching at Rome, and laying the foundations of the Church. After their departure, Mark, the disciple and interpreter of Peter, did also hand down to us in writing what had been preached by Peter. Luke also, the companion of Paul, recorded in a book the Gospel preached by him. Afterwards, John, the disciple of the Lord, who also had leaned upon His breast, did himself publish a Gospel during his residence at Ephesus in Asia.

2. These have all declared to us that there is one God, Creator of heaven and earth, announced

---

[2] See 1 Tim. iii. 15, where these terms are used in reference to the Church.
[3] On this and similar statements in the Fathers, the reader may consult Dr. Roberts's *Discussions on the Gospels*, in which they are fully criticised, and the Greek original of St. Matthew's Gospel maintained.

---

[1] Luke x. 16.

by the law and the prophets; and one Christ, the Son of God. If any one do not agree to these truths, he despises the companions of the Lord; nay more, he despises Christ Himself the Lord; yea, he despises the Father also, and stands self-condemned, resisting and opposing his own salvation, as is the case with all heretics.

CHAP. II. — THE HERETICS FOLLOW NEITHER SCRIPTURE NOR TRADITION.

1. When, however, they are confuted from the Scriptures, they turn round and accuse these same Scriptures, as if they were not correct, nor of authority, and [assert] that they are ambiguous, and that the truth cannot be extracted from them by those who are ignorant of tradition. For [they allege] that the truth was not delivered by means of written documents, but vivâ voce: wherefore also Paul declared, "But we speak wisdom among those that are perfect, but not the wisdom of this world." [1] And this wisdom each one of them alleges to be the fiction of his own inventing, forsooth; so that, according to their idea, the truth properly resides at one time in Valentinus, at another in Marcion, at another in Cerinthus, then afterwards in Basilides, or has even been indifferently in any other opponent,[2] who could speak nothing pertaining to salvation. For every one of these men, being altogether of a perverse disposition, depraving the system of truth, is not ashamed to preach himself.

2. But, again, when we refer them to that tradition which originates from the apostles, [and] which is preserved by means of the successions of presbyters in the Churches, they object to tradition, saying that they themselves are wiser not merely than the presbyters, but even than the apostles, because they have discovered the unadulterated truth. For [they maintain] that the apostles intermingled the things of the law with the words of the Saviour; and that not the apostles alone, but even the Lord Himself, spoke as at one time from the Demiurge, at another from the intermediate place, and yet again from the Pleroma, but that they themselves, indubitably, unsulliedly, and purely, have knowledge of the hidden mystery: this is, indeed, to blaspheme their Creator after a most impudent manner! It comes to this, therefore, that these men do now consent neither to Scripture nor to tradition.

3. Such are the adversaries with whom we have to deal, my very dear friend, endeavouring like slippery serpents to escape at all points. Wherefore they must be opposed at all points, if perchance, by cutting off their retreat, we may succeed in turning them back to the truth. For, though it is not an easy thing for a soul under the in-

fluence of error to repent, yet, on the other hand, it is not altogether impossible to escape from error when the truth is brought alongside it.

CHAP. III. — A REFUTATION OF THE HERETICS, FROM THE FACT THAT, IN THE VARIOUS CHURCHES, A PERPETUAL SUCCESSION OF BISHOPS WAS KEPT UP.

1. It is within the power of all, therefore, in every Church, who may wish to see the truth, to contemplate clearly the tradition of the apostles manifested throughout the whole world; and we are in a position to reckon up those who were by the apostles instituted bishops in the Churches, and [to demonstrate] the succession of these men to our own times; those who neither taught nor knew of anything like what these [heretics] rave about. For if the apostles had known hidden mysteries, which they were in the habit of imparting to "the perfect" apart and privily from the rest, they would have delivered them especially to those to whom they were also committing the Churches themselves. For they were desirous that these men should be very perfect and blameless in all things, whom also they were leaving behind as their successors, delivering up their own place of government to these men; which men, if· they discharged their functions honestly, would be a great boon [to the Church], but if they should fall away, the direst calamity.

2. Since, however, it would be very tedious, in such a volume as this, to reckon up the successions of all the Churches, we do put to confusion all those who, in whatever manner, whether by an evil self-pleasing, by vainglory, or by blindness and perverse opinion, assemble in unauthorized meetings; [we do this, I say,] by indicating that tradition derived from the apostles, of the very great, the very ancient, and universally known Church founded and organized at Rome by the two most glorious apostles, Peter and Paul; as also [by pointing out] the faith preached to men, which comes down to our time by means of the successions of the bishops. For it is a matter of necessity that every Church should agree with this Church, on account of its pre-eminent authority,[3] that is, the faithful every-

---

[1] 1 Cor. ii. 6.
[2] This is Harvey's rendering of the old Latin, in illo qui contra disputat.

[3] The Latin text of this difficult but important clause is, "Ad hanc enim ecclesiam propter potiorem principalitatem necesse est omnem convenire ecclesiam." Both the text and meaning have here given rise to much discussion. It is impossible to say with certainty of what words in the Greek original "potiorem principalitatem" may be the translation. We are far from sure that the rendering given above is correct, but we have been unable to think of anything better. [A most extraordinary confession. It would be hard to find a worse; but take the following from a candid Roman Catholic, which is better and more literal: "For to this Church, on account of more potent principality, it is necessary that every Church (that is, those who are on every side faithful) resort; in which Church ever, by those who are on every side, has been preserved that tradition which is from the apostles." (Berington and Kirk, vol. i. p. 252.) Here it is obvious that the faith was kept at Rome, by those who resort there from all quarters. She was a mirror of the Catholic World, owing her orthodoxy to them; not the Sun, dispensing her own light to others, but the glass bringing their rays into a focus. See note at end of book iii.] A discussion of the subject may be seen in chap. xii. of Dr. Wordsworth's St. Hippolytus and the Church of Rome.

where, inasmuch as the apostolical tradition has been preserved continuously by those [faithful men] who exist everywhere.

3. The blessed apostles, then, having founded and built up the Church, committed into the hands of Linus the office of the episcopate. Of this Linus, Paul makes mention in the Epistles to Timothy. To him succeeded Anacletus; and after him, in the third place from the apostles, Clement was allotted the bishopric. This man, as he had seen the blessed apostles, and had been conversant with them, might be said to have the preaching of the apostles still echoing [in his ears], and their traditions before his eyes. Nor was he alone [in this], for there were many still remaining who had received instructions from the apostles. In the time of this Clement, no small dissension having occurred among the brethren at Corinth, the Church in Rome despatched a most powerful letter to the Corinthians, exhorting them to peace, renewing their faith, and declaring the tradition which it had lately received from the apostles, proclaiming the one God, omnipotent, the Maker of heaven and earth, the Creator of man, who brought on the deluge, and called Abraham, who led the people from the land of Egypt, spake with Moses, set forth the law, sent the prophets, and who has prepared fire for the devil and his angels. From this document, whosoever chooses to do so, may learn that He, the Father of our Lord Jesus Christ, was preached by the Churches, and may also understand the apostolical tradition of the Church, since this Epistle is of older date than these men who are now propagating falsehood, and who conjure into existence another god beyond the Creator and the Maker of all existing things. To this Clement there succeeded Evaristus. Alexander followed Evaristus; then, sixth from the apostles, Sixtus was appointed; after him, Telephorus, who was gloriously martyred; then Hyginus; after him, Pius; then after him, Anicetus. Soter having succeeded Anicetus, Eleutherius does now, in the twelfth place from the apostles, hold the inheritance of the episcopate. In this order, and by this succession, the ecclesiastical tradition from the apostles, and the preaching of the truth, have come down to us. And this is most abundant proof that there is one and the same vivifying faith, which has been preserved in the Church from the apostles until now, and handed down in truth.

4. But Polycarp also was not only instructed by apostles, and conversed with many who had seen Christ, but was also, by apostles in Asia, appointed bishop of the Church in Smyrna, whom I also saw in my early youth, for he tarried [on earth] a very long time, and, when a very old man, gloriously and most nobly suffering martyrdom,[1] departed this life, having always taught the things which he had learned from the apostles, and which the Church has handed down, and which alone are true. To these things all the Asiatic Churches testify, as do also those men who have succeeded Polycarp down to the present time, — a man who was of much greater weight, and a more stedfast witness of truth, than Valentinus, and Marcion, and the rest of the heretics. He it was who, coming to Rome in the time of Anicetus caused many to turn away from the aforesaid heretics to the Church of God, proclaiming that he had received this one and sole truth from the apostles, — that, namely, which is handed down by the Church.[2] There are also those who heard from him that John, the disciple of the Lord, going to bathe at Ephesus, and perceiving Cerinthus within, rushed out of the bath-house without bathing, exclaiming, "Let us fly, lest even the bath-house fall down, because Cerinthus, the enemy of the truth, is within." And Polycarp himself replied to Marcion, who met him on one occasion, and said, "Dost thou know me?" "I do know thee, the first-born of Satan." Such was the horror which the apostles and their disciples had against holding even verbal communication with any corrupters of the truth; as Paul also says, "A man that is an heretic, after the first and second admonition, reject; knowing that he that is such is subverted, and sinneth, being condemned of himself."[3] There is also a very powerful[4] Epistle of Polycarp written to the Philippians, from which those who choose to do so, and are anxious about their salvation, can learn the character of his faith, and the preaching of the truth. Then, again, the Church in Ephesus, founded by Paul, and having John remaining among them permanently until the times of Trajan, is a true witness of the tradition of the apostles.

CHAP. IV. — THE TRUTH IS TO BE FOUND NOWHERE ELSE BUT IN THE CATHOLIC CHURCH, THE SOLE DEPOSITORY OF APOSTOLICAL DOCTRINE. HERESIES ARE OF RECENT FORMATION, AND CANNOT TRACE THEIR ORIGIN UP TO THE APOSTLES.

1. Since therefore we have such proofs, it is not necessary to seek the truth among others which it is easy to obtain from the Church; since the apostles, like a rich man [depositing his money] in a bank, lodged in her hands most copiously all things pertaining to the truth: so that every man, whosoever will, can draw from her the

---

[1] Polycarp suffered about the year 167, in the reign of Marcus Aurelius. His great age of eighty-six years implies that he was contemporary with St. John for nearly twenty years.
[2] So the Greek. The Latin reads: "which he also handed down to the Church."
[3] Tit. iii. 10.
[4] ἱκανωτάτη. Harvey translates this all-sufficient, and thus paraphrases: But his Epistle is all-sufficient, to teach those that are desirous to learn.

water of life.[1] For she is the entrance to life; all others are thieves and robbers. On this account are we bound to avoid *them*, but to make choice of the things pertaining to the Church with the utmost diligence, and to lay hold of the tradition of the truth. For how stands the case? Suppose there arise a dispute relative to some important question[2] among us, should we not have recourse to the most ancient Churches with which the apostles held constant intercourse, and learn from them what is certain and clear in regard to the present question? For how should it be if the apostles themselves had not left us writings? Would it not be necessary, [in that case,] to follow the course of the tradition which they handed down to those to whom they did commit the Churches?

2. To which course many nations of those barbarians who believe in Christ do assent, having salvation written in their hearts by the Spirit, without paper or ink, and, carefully preserving the ancient tradition,[3] believing in one God, the Creator of heaven and earth, and all things therein, by means of Christ Jesus, the Son of God; who, because of His surpassing love towards His creation, condescended to be born of the virgin, He Himself uniting man through Himself to God, and having suffered under Pontius Pilate, and rising again, and having been received up in splendour, shall come in glory, the Saviour of those who are saved, and the Judge of those who are judged, and sending into eternal fire those who transform the truth, and despise His Father and His advent. Those who, in the absence of written documents,[4] have believed this faith, are barbarians, so far as regards our language; but as regards doctrine, manner, and tenor of life, they are, because of faith, very wise indeed; and they do please God, ordering their conversation in all righteousness, chastity, and wisdom. If any one were to preach to these men the inventions of the heretics, speaking to them in their own language, they would at once stop their ears, and flee as far off as possible, not enduring even to listen to the blasphemous address. Thus, by means of that ancient tradition of the apostles, they do not suffer their mind to conceive anything of the [doctrines suggested by the] portentous language of these teachers, among whom neither Church nor doctrine has ever been established.

3. For, prior to Valentinus, those who follow Valentinus had no existence; nor did those from Marcion exist before Marcion; nor, in short, had

any of those malignant-minded people, whom I have above enumerated, any being previous to the initiators and inventors of their perversity. For Valentinus came to Rome in the time of Hyginus, flourished under Pius, and remained until Anicetus. Cerdon, too, Marcion's predecessor, himself arrived in the time of Hyginus, who was the ninth bishop.[5] Coming frequently into the Church, and making public confession, he thus remained, one time teaching in secret, and then again making public confession; but at last, having been denounced for corrupt teaching, he was excommunicated[6] from the assembly of the brethren. Marcion, then, succeeding him, flourished under Anicetus, who held the tenth place of the episcopate. But the rest, who are called Gnostics, take rise from Menander, Simon's disciple, as I have shown; and each one of them appeared to be both the father and the high priest of that doctrine into which he has been initiated. But all these (the Marcosians) broke out into their apostasy much later, even during the intermediate period of the Church.

CHAP. V. — CHRIST AND HIS APOSTLES, WITHOUT ANY FRAUD, DECEPTION, OR HYPOCRISY, PREACHED THAT ONE GOD, THE FATHER, WAS THE FOUNDER OF ALL THINGS. THEY DID NOT ACCOMMODATE THEIR DOCTRINE TO THE PREPOSSESSIONS OF THEIR HEARERS.

1. Since, therefore, the tradition from the apostles does thus exist in the Church, and is permanent among us, let us revert to the Scriptural proof furnished by those apostles who did also write the Gospel, in which they recorded the doctrine regarding God, pointing out that our Lord Jesus Christ is the truth,[7] and that no lie is in Him. As also David says, prophesying His birth from a virgin, and the resurrection from the dead, "Truth has sprung out of the earth."[8] The apostles, likewise, being disciples of the truth, are above all falsehood; for a lie has no fellowship with the truth, just as darkness has none with light, but the presence of the one shuts out that of the other. Our Lord, therefore, being the truth, did not speak lies; and whom He knew to have taken origin from a defect, He never would have acknowledged as God, even the God of all, the Supreme King, too, and His own Father, an imperfect being as a perfect one, an animal one as a spiritual, Him who was without the Pleroma as Him who was within it.

---

[1] Rev. xxii. 17.
[2] Latin, "modica quæstione."
[3] [The uneducated barbarians must receive the Gospel on testimony. Irenæus puts *apostolic* traditions, genuine and uncorrupt, in this relation to the primary authority of the written word. 2 Thess. ii. 15, iii. 6.]
[4] Literally, "without letters;" equivalent to, "without paper and ink," a few lines previously.

[5] The old Latin translation says the *eighth bishop;* but there is no discrepancy. Eusebius, who has preserved the Greek of this passage, probably counted the apostles as the *first step* in the episcopal succession. As Irenæus tells us in the preceding chapter, Linus is to be counted as the first bishop.
[6] It is thought that this does not mean excommunication properly so called, but a species of *self-excommunication*, i.e., anticipating the sentence of the Church, by quitting it altogether. See Valesius's note in his edition of Eusebius.
[7] John xiv. 6.
[8] Ps. lxxxv. 11.

Neither did His disciples make mention of any other God, or term any other Lord, except Him, who was truly the God and Lord of all, as these most vain sophists affirm that the apostles did with hypocrisy frame their doctrine according to the capacity of their hearers, and gave answers after the opinions of their questioners, — fabling blind things for the blind, according to their blindness; for the dull according to their dulness; for those in error according to their error. And to those who imagined that the Demiurge alone was God, they preached him; but to those who are capable of comprehending the unnameable Father, they did declare the unspeakable mystery through parables and enigmas: so that the Lord and the apostles exercised the office of teacher not to further the cause of truth, but even in hypocrisy, and as each individual was able to receive it!

2. Such [a line of conduct] belongs not to those who heal, or who give life: it is rather that of those bringing on diseases, and increasing ignorance; and much more true than these men shall the law be found, which pronounces every one accursed who sends the blind man astray in the way. For the apostles, who were commissioned to find out the wanderers, and to be for sight to those who saw not, and medicine to the weak, certainly did not address them in accordance with their opinion at the time, but according to revealed truth. For no persons of any kind would act properly, if they should advise blind men, just about to fall over a precipice, to continue their most dangerous path, as if it were the right one, and as if they might go on in safety. Or what medical man, anxious to heal a sick person, would prescribe in accordance with the patient's whims, and not according to the requisite medicine? But that the Lord came as the physician of the sick, He does Himself declare, saying, "They that are whole need not a physician, but they that are sick; I came not to call the righteous, but sinners to repentance."[1] How then shall the sick be strengthened, or how shall sinners come to repentance? Is it by persevering in the very same courses? or, on the contrary, is it by undergoing a great change and reversal of their former mode of living, by which they have brought upon themselves no slight amount of sickness, and many sins? But ignorance, the mother of all these, is driven out by knowledge. Wherefore the Lord used to impart knowledge to His disciples, by which also it was His practice to heal those who were suffering, and to keep back sinners from sin. He therefore did not address them in accordance with their pristine notions, nor did He reply to them in harmony with the opinion of His questioners,

but according to the doctrine leading to salvation, without hypocrisy or respect of person.

3. This is also made clear from the words of the Lord, who did truly reveal the Son of God to those of the circumcision — Him who had been foretold as Christ by the prophets; that is, He set Himself forth, who had restored liberty to men, and bestowed on them the inheritance of incorruption. And again, the apostles taught the Gentiles that they should leave vain stocks and stones, which they imagined to be gods, and worship the true God, who had created and made all the human family, and, by means of His creation, did nourish, increase, strengthen, and preserve them in being; and that they might look for His Son Jesus Christ, who redeemed us from apostasy with His own blood, so that we should also be a sanctified people, — who shall also descend from heaven in His Father's power, and pass judgment upon all, and who shall freely give the good things of God to those who shall have kept His commandments. He, appearing in these last times, the chief cornerstone, has gathered into one, and united those that were far off and those that were near;[2] that is, the circumcision and the uncircumcision, enlarging Japhet, and placing him in the dwelling of Shem.[3]

CHAP. VI. — THE HOLY GHOST, THROUGHOUT THE OLD TESTAMENT SCRIPTURES, MADE MENTION OF NO OTHER GOD OR LORD, SAVE HIM WHO IS THE TRUE GOD.

1. Therefore neither would the Lord, nor the Holy Spirit, nor the apostles, have ever named as God, definitely and absolutely, him who was not God, unless he were truly God; nor would they have named any one in his own person Lord, except God the Father ruling over all, and His Son who has received dominion from His Father over all creation, as this passage has it: "The Lord said unto my Lord, Sit Thou at my right hand, until I make Thine enemies Thy footstool."[4] Here the [Scripture] represents to us the Father addressing the Son; He who gave Him the inheritance of the heathen, and subjected to Him all His enemies. Since, therefore, the Father is truly Lord, and the Son truly Lord, the Holy Spirit has fitly designated them by the title of Lord. And again, referring to the destruction of the Sodomites, the Scripture says, "Then the LORD rained upon Sodom and upon Gomorrah fire and brimstone from the LORD out of heaven."[5] For it here points out that the Son, who had also been talking with Abraham, had received power to judge the Sodomites

---

[1] Luke v. 31, 32.

[2] Eph. ii. 17.
[3] Gen. ix. 27.
[4] Ps. cx. 1.
[5] Gen. xix. 24.

for their wickedness. And this [text following] does declare the same truth: "Thy throne, O God, is for ever and ever; the sceptre of Thy kingdom is a right sceptre. Thou hast loved righteousness, and hated iniquity: therefore God, Thy God, hath anointed Thee."[1] For the Spirit designates both [of them] by the name of God — both Him who is anointed as Son, and Him who does anoint, that is, the Father. And again: "God stood in the congregation of the gods, He judges among the gods."[2] He [here] refers to the Father and the Son, and those who have received the adoption; but these are the Church. For she is the synagogue of God, which God — that is, the Son Himself — has gathered by Himself. Of whom He again speaks: "The God of gods, the Lord hath spoken, and hath called the earth."[3] Who is meant by God? He of whom He has said, "God shall come openly, our God, and shall not keep silence;"[4] that is, the Son, who came manifested to men, who said, "I have openly appeared to those who seek Me not."[5] But of what gods [does he speak]? [Of those] to whom He says, "I have said, Ye are gods, and all sons of the Most High."[6] To those, no doubt, who have received the grace of the "adoption, by which we cry, Abba Father."[7]

2. Wherefore, as I have already stated, no other is named as God, or is called Lord, except Him who is God and Lord of all, who also said to Moses, "I AM THAT I AM. And thus shalt thou say to the children of Israel: He who is, hath sent me unto you;"[8] and His Son Jesus Christ our Lord, who makes those that believe in His name the sons of God. And again, when the Son speaks to Moses, He says, "I am come down to deliver this people."[9] For it is He who descended and ascended for the salvation of men. Therefore God has been declared through the Son, who is in the Father, and has the Father in Himself — He who is, the Father bearing witness to the Son, and the Son announcing the Father. — As also Esaias says, "I too am witness," he declares, "saith the Lord God, and the Son whom I have chosen, that ye may know, and believe, and understand that I AM."[10]

3. When, however, the Scripture terms them [gods] which are no gods, it does not, as I have already remarked, declare them as gods in every sense, but with a certain addition and signification, by which they are shown to be no gods at all. As with David: "The gods of the heathen are idols of demons;"[11] and, "Ye shall not follow other gods."[12] For in that he says "the gods of the heathen" — but the heathen are ignorant of the true God — and calls them "other gods," he bars their claim [to be looked upon] as gods at all. But as to what they are in their own person, he speaks concerning them; "for they are," he says, "the idols of demons." And Esaias: "Let them be confounded, all who blaspheme God, and carve useless things;[13] even I am witness, saith God."[14] He removes them from [the category of] gods, but he makes use of the word alone, for this [purpose], that we may know of whom he speaks. Jeremiah also says the same: "The gods that have not made the heavens and earth, let them perish from the earth which is under the heaven."[15] For, from the fact of his having subjoined their destruction, he shows them to be no gods at all. Elias, too, when all Israel was assembled at Mount Carmel, wishing to turn them from idolatry, says to them, "How long halt ye between two opinions?[16] If the Lord be God,[17] follow Him."[18] And again, at the burnt-offering, he thus addresses the idolatrous priests: "Ye shall call upon the name of your gods, and I will call on the name of the Lord my God; and the Lord that will hearken by fire,[19] He is God." Now, from the fact of the prophet having said these words, he proves that these gods which were reputed so among those men, are no gods at all. He directed them to that God upon whom he believed, and who was truly God; whom invoking, he exclaimed, "Lord God of Abraham, God of Isaac, and God of Jacob, hear me to-day, and let all this people know that Thou art the God of Israel."[20]

4. Wherefore I do also call upon thee, Lord God of Abraham, and God of Isaac, and God of Jacob and Israel, who art the Father of our Lord Jesus Christ, the God who, through the abundance of Thy mercy, hast had a favour towards us, that we should know Thee, who hast made heaven and earth, who rulest over all, who art the only and the true God, above whom there is none other God; grant, by our Lord Jesus Christ, the governing power of the Holy Spirit; give to every reader of this book to know Thee, that Thou art God alone, to be strengthened in Thee, and to avoid every heretical, and godless, and impious doctrine.

---

[11] Ps. xcvi. 5.
[12] Ps. lxxxi. 9.
[13] These words are an interpolation: it is supposed they have been carelessly repeated from the preceding quotation of Isaiah.
[14] Isa. xliv. 9.
[15] Jer. x. 11.
[16] Literally, "In both houghs," *in ambabus suffraginibus.*
[17] The old Latin translation has, "Si *unus* est Dominus Deus"— *If the Lord God is one;* which is supposed by the critics to have occurred through carelessness of the translator.
[18] 1 Kings xviii. 21, etc.
[19] The Latin version has, "that answereth to-day" (*hodie*), — an evident error for *igne.*
[20] 1 Kings xviii. 36.

---

[1] Ps. xlv. 6.
[2] Ps. lxxxii. 1.
[3] Ps. l. 1.
[4] Ps. l. 3.
[5] Isa. lxv. 1.
[6] Ps. lxxxii. 6.
[7] Rom. viii. 15.
[8] Ex. iii. 14.
[9] Ex. iii. 8.
[10] Isa. xliii. 10.

5. And the Apostle Paul also, saying, "For though ye have served them which are no gods; ye now know God, or rather, are known of God,"[1] has made a separation between those that were not [gods] and Him who is God. And again, speaking of Antichrist, he says, "who opposeth and exalteth himself above all that is called God, or that is worshipped."[2] He points out here those who are called gods, by such as know not God, that is, idols. For the Father of all is called God, and is so; and Antichrist shall be lifted up, not above Him, but above those which are indeed called gods, but are not. And Paul himself says that this is true: "We know that an idol is nothing, and that there is none other God but one. For though there be that are called gods, whether in heaven or in earth; yet to us there is but one God, the Father, of whom are all things, and we through Him; and one Lord Jesus Christ, by whom are all things, and we by Him."[3] For he has made a distinction, and separated those which are indeed called gods, but which are none, from the one God the Father, from whom are all things, and, he has confessed in the most decided manner in his own person, one Lord Jesus Christ. But in this [clause], "whether in heaven or in earth," he does not speak of the formers of the world, as these [teachers] expound it; but his meaning is similar to that of Moses, when it is said, "Thou shalt not make to thyself any image for God, of whatsoever things are in heaven above, whatsoever in the earth beneath, and whatsoever in the waters under the earth."[4] And he does thus explain what are meant by the things in heaven: "Lest when," he says, "looking towards heaven, and observing the sun, and the moon, and the stars, and all the ornament of heaven, falling into error, thou shouldest adore and serve them."[5] And Moses himself, being a man of God, was indeed given as a god before Pharaoh;[6] but he is not properly termed Lord, nor is called God by the prophets, but is spoken of by the Spirit as "Moses, the faithful minister and servant of God,"[7] which also he was.

CHAP. VII. — REPLY TO AN OBJECTION FOUNDED ON THE WORDS OF ST. PAUL (2 COR. IV. 5). ST. PAUL OCCASIONALLY USES WORDS NOT IN THEIR GRAMMATICAL SEQUENCE.

1. As to their affirming that Paul said plainly in the Second [Epistle] to the Corinthians, "In whom the god of this world hath blinded the minds of them that believe not,"[8] and maintaining that there is indeed one god of this world, but another who is beyond all principality, and beginning, and power, we are not to blame if they, who give out that they do themselves know mysteries beyond God, know not how to read Paul. For if any one read the passage thus — according to Paul's custom, as I show elsewhere, and by many examples, that he uses transposition of words — "In whom God," then pointing it off, and making a slight interval, and at the same time read also the rest [of the sentence] in one [clause], "hath blinded the minds of them of this world that believe not," he shall find out the true [sense]; that it is contained in the expression, "God hath blinded the minds of the unbelievers of this world." And this is shown by means of the little interval [between the clause]. For Paul does not say, "the God of this world," as if recognising any other beyond Him; but he confessed God as indeed God. And he says, "the unbelievers of this world," because they shall not inherit the future age of incorruption. I shall show from Paul himself, how it is that God has blinded the minds of them that believe not, in the course of this work, that we may not just at present distract our mind from the matter in hand, [by wandering] at large.

2. From many other instances also, we may discover that the apostle frequently uses a transposed order in his sentences, due to the rapidity of his discourses, and the impetus of the Spirit which is in him. An example occurs in the [Epistle] to the Galatians, where he expresses himself as follows: "Wherefore then the law of works?[9] It was added, until the seed should come to whom the promise was made; [and it was] ordained by angels in the hand of a Mediator."[10] For the order of the words runs thus: "Wherefore then the law of works? Ordained by angels in the hand of a Mediator, it was added until the seed should come to whom the promise was made," — man thus asking the question, and the Spirit making answer. And again, in the Second to the Thessalonians, speaking of Antichrist, he says, "And then shall that wicked be revealed, whom the Lord Jesus Christ[11] shall slay with the Spirit of His mouth, and shall destroy him[11] with the presence of his coming; [even him] whose coming is after the working of Satan, with all power, and signs, and lying wonders."[12] Now in these [sentences] the order of the words is this: "And then shall be revealed that wicked, whose coming is after the working of Satan, with all power, and signs, and lying wonders, whom

---

1 Gal. iv. 8, 9.
2 2 Thess. ii. 4.
3 1 Cor. viii. 4, etc.
4 Deut. v. 8.
5 Deut. iv. 19.
6 Ex. vii. 1.
7 Heb. iii. 5; Num. xii. 7.
8 2 Cor. iv. 4.

9 This is according to the reading of the old Italic version, for it is not so read in any of our existing manuscripts of the Greek New Testament.
10 Gal. iii. 19.
11 This word is not found in the second quotation of this passage immediately following.
12 2 Thess. ii. 8.

the Lord Jesus shall slay with the Spirit of His mouth, and shall destroy with the presence of His coming." For he does not mean that the coming of the Lord is after the working of Satan; but the coming of the wicked one, whom we also call Antichrist. If, then, one does not attend to the [proper] reading [of the passage], and if he do not exhibit the intervals of breathing as they occur, there shall be not only incongruities, but also, when reading, he will utter blasphemy, as if the advent of the Lord could take place according to the working of Satan. So therefore, in such passages, the *hyperbaton* must be exhibited by the reading, and the apostle's meaning following on, preserved; and thus we do not read in that passage, "the god of this world," but, "God," whom we do truly call God; and we hear [it declared of] the unbelieving and the blinded of this world, that they shall not inherit the world of life which is to come.

CHAP. VIII. — ANSWER TO AN OBJECTION, ARISING FROM THE WORDS OF CHRIST (MATT. VI. 24). GOD ALONE IS TO BE REALLY CALLED GOD AND LORD, FOR HE IS WITHOUT BEGINNING AND END.

1. This calumny, then, of these men, having been quashed, it is clearly proved that neither the prophets nor the apostles did ever name another God, or call [him] Lord, except the true and only God. Much more [would this be the case with regard to] the Lord Himself, who did also direct us to "render unto Cæsar the things that are Cæsar's, and to God the things that are God's;"[1] naming indeed Cæsar as Cæsar, but confessing God as God. In like manner also, that [text] which says, "Ye cannot serve two masters,"[2] He does Himself interpret, saying, "Ye cannot serve God and mammon;" acknowledging God indeed as God, but mentioning mammon, a thing having also an existence. He does not call mammon Lord when He says, "Ye cannot serve two masters;" but He teaches His disciples who serve God, not to be subject to mammon, nor to be ruled by it. For He says, "He that committeth sin is the slave of sin."[3] Inasmuch, then, as He terms those "the slaves of sin" who serve sin, but does not certainly call sin itself God, thus also He terms those who serve mammon "the slaves of mammon," not calling mammon God. For mammon is, according to the Jewish language, which the Samaritans do also use, a *covetous* man, and one who wishes to have more than he ought to have. But according to the Hebrew, it is by the addition of a syllable (*adjunctive*)

called Mamuel,[4] and signifies *gulosum*, that is, one whose gullet is insatiable. Therefore, according to both these things which are indicated, we cannot serve God and mammon.

2. But also, when He spoke of the devil as strong, not absolutely so, but as in comparison with us, the Lord showed Himself under every aspect and truly to be the strong man, saying that one can in no other way "spoil the goods of a strong man, if he do not first bind the strong man himself, and then he will spoil his house."[5] Now we were the vessels and the house of this [strong man] when we were in a state of apostasy; for he put us to whatever use he pleased, and the unclean spirit dwelt within us. For he was not strong, as opposed to Him who bound him, and spoiled his house; but as against those persons who were his tools, inasmuch as he caused their thought to wander away from God: these did the Lord snatch from his grasp. As also Jeremiah declares, "The LORD hath redeemed Jacob, and has snatched him from the hand of him that was stronger than he."[6] If, then, he had not pointed out Him who binds and spoils his goods, but had merely spoken of him as being strong, the strong man should have been unconquered. But he also subjoined Him who obtains and retains possession; for *he* holds who binds, but *he is* held who is bound. And this he did without any comparison, so that, apostate slave as he was, he might not be compared to the Lord: for not he alone, but not one of created and subject things, shall ever be compared to the Word of God, by whom all things were made, who is our Lord Jesus Christ.

3. For that all things, whether Angels, or Archangels, or Thrones, or Dominions, were both established and created by Him who is God over all, through His Word, John has thus pointed out. For when he had spoken of the Word of God as having been in the Father, he added, "All things were made by Him, and without Him was not anything made."[7] David also, when he had enumerated [His] praises, subjoins by name all things whatsoever I have mentioned, both the heavens and all the powers therein: "For He commanded, and they were created; He spake, and they were made." Whom, therefore, did He command? The Word, no doubt, "by whom," he says, "the heavens were established, and all their power by the breath of His mouth."[8] But that He did Him-

---

[4] A word of which many explanations have been proposed, but none are quite satisfactory. Harvey seems inclined to suspect the reading to be corrupt, through the ignorance and carelessness of the copyist. [Irenæus undoubtedly relied for Hebrew criticisms on some incompetent retailer of rabbinical refinements.]
[5] Matt. xii. 29.
[6] Jer. xxxi. 11.
[7] John i. 3.
[8] Ps. xxxiii. 6.

[1] Matt. xxii. 21.
[2] Matt. vi. 24.
[3] John viii. 34.

self make all things freely, and as He pleased, again David says, "But our God is in the heavens above, and in the earth; He hath made all things whatsoever He pleased." [1] But the things established are distinct from Him who has established them, and what have been made from Him who has made them. For He is Himself uncreated, both without beginning and end, and lacking nothing. He is Himself sufficient for Himself; and still further, He grants to all others this very thing, existence; but the things which have been made by Him have received a beginning. But whatever things had a beginning, and are liable to dissolution, and are subject to and stand in need of Him who made them, must necessarily in all respects have a different term [applied to them], even by those who have but a moderate capacity for discerning such things; so that He indeed who made all things can alone, together with His Word, properly be termed God and Lord: but the things which have been made cannot have this term applied to them, neither should they justly assume that appellation which belongs to the Creator.

CHAP. IX. — ONE AND THE SAME GOD, THE CREATOR OF HEAVEN AND EARTH, IS HE WHOM THE PROPHETS FORETOLD, AND WHO WAS DECLARED BY THE GOSPEL. PROOF OF THIS, AT THE OUTSET, FROM ST. MATTHEW'S GOSPEL.

1. This, therefore, having been clearly demonstrated here (and it shall yet be so still more clearly), that neither the prophets, nor the apostles, nor the Lord Christ in His own person, did acknowledge any other Lord or God, but the God and Lord supreme: the prophets and the apostles confessing the Father and the Son; but naming no other as God, and confessing no other as Lord: and the Lord Himself handing down to His disciples, that He, the Father, is the only God and Lord, who alone is God and ruler of all; — it is incumbent on us to follow, if we are their disciples indeed, their testimonies to this effect. For Matthew the apostle — knowing, as one and the same God, Him who had given promise to Abraham, that He would make his seed as the stars of heaven, [2] and Him who, by His Son Christ Jesus, has called us to the knowledge of Himself, from the worship of stones, so that those who were not a people were made a people, and she beloved who was not beloved [3] — declares that John, when preparing the way for Christ, said to those who were boasting of their relationship [to Abraham] according to the flesh, but who had their mind tinged and stuffed with all manner of evil, preaching that repentance which should call them back from their evil

doings, said, "O generation of vipers, who hath shown you to flee from the wrath to come? Bring forth therefore fruit meet for repentance. And think not to say within yourselves, We have Abraham [to our] father: for I say unto you, that God is able of these stones to raise up children unto Abraham." [4] He preached to them, therefore, the repentance from wickedness, but he did not declare to them another God, besides Him who made the promise to Abraham; he, the forerunner of Christ, of whom Matthew again says, and Luke likewise, "For this is he that was spoken of from the Lord by the prophet, The voice of one crying in the wilderness, Prepare ye the way of the Lord, make straight the paths of our God. Every valley shall be filled, and every mountain and hill brought low; and the crooked shall be made straight, and the rough into smooth ways; and all flesh shall see the salvation of God." [5] There is therefore one and the same God, the Father of our Lord, who also promised, through the prophets, that He would send His forerunner; and His salvation — that is, His Word — He caused to be made visible to all flesh, [the Word] Himself being made incarnate, that in all things their King might become manifest. For it is necessary that those [beings] which are judged do see the judge, and know Him from whom they receive judgment; and it is also proper, that those which follow on to glory should know Him who bestows upon them the gift of glory.

2. Then again Matthew, when speaking of the angel, says, "The angel of the Lord appeared to Joseph in sleep." [6] Of what Lord he does himself interpret: "That it may be fulfilled which was spoken of the Lord by the prophet, Out of Egypt have I called my son." [7] "Behold, a virgin shall conceive, and shall bring forth a son, and they shall call his name Emmanuel; which is, being interpreted, God with us." [8] David likewise speaks of Him who, from the virgin, is Emmanuel: "Turn not away the face of Thine anointed. The LORD hath sworn a truth to David, and will not turn from him. Of the fruit of thy body will I set upon thy seat." [9] And again: "In Judea is God known; His place has been made in peace, and His dwelling in Zion." [10] Therefore there is one and the same God, who was proclaimed by the prophets and announced by the Gospel; and His Son, who was of the fruit of David's body, that is, of the virgin of [the house of] David, and Emmanuel; whose star also Balaam thus prophesied: "There shall come a star out of Jacob, and a

---

[1] Ps. cxv. 3.
[2] Gen. xv. 5.
[3] Rom. ix. 25.

[4] Matt. iii. 7.
[5] Matt. iii. 3.
[6] Matt. i. 20.
[7] Matt. ii. 15.
[8] Matt. i. 23.
[9] Ps. cxxxii. 11.
[10] Ps. lxxvi. 1.

leader shall rise in Israel." [1] But Matthew says, that the Magi, coming from the east, exclaimed, " For we have seen His star in the east, and are come to worship Him ; " [2] and that, having been led by the star into the house of Jacob to Emmanuel, they showed, by these gifts which they offered, who it was that was worshipped ; *myrrh*, because it was He who should die and be buried for the mortal human race ; *gold*, because He was a King, " of whose kingdom is no end ; " [3] and *frankincense*, because He was God, who also " was made known in Judea," [4] and was " declared to those who sought Him not." [5]

3. And then, [speaking of His] baptism, Matthew says, " The heavens were opened, and He saw the Spirit of God, as a dove, coming upon Him : and lo a voice from heaven, saying, This is my beloved Son, in whom I am well pleased." [6] For Christ did not at that time descend upon Jesus, neither was Christ one and Jesus another : but the Word of God—who is the Saviour of all, and the ruler of heaven and earth, who is Jesus, as I have already pointed out, who did also take upon Him flesh, and was anointed by the Spirit from the Father—was made Jesus Christ, as Esaias also says, " There shall come forth a rod from the root of Jesse, and a flower shall rise from his root ; and the Spirit of God shall rest upon Him : the spirit of wisdom and understanding, the spirit of counsel and might, the spirit of knowledge and piety, and the spirit of the fear of God, shall fill Him. He shall not judge according to glory,[7] nor reprove after the manner of speech ; but He shall dispense judgment to the humble man, and reprove the haughty ones of the earth." [8] And again Esaias, pointing out beforehand His unction, and the reason why he was anointed, does himself say, " The Spirit of God is upon Me, because He hath anointed Me : He hath sent Me to preach the Gospel to the lowly, to heal the broken up in heart, to proclaim liberty to the captives, and sight to the blind ; to announce the acceptable year of the Lord, and the day of vengeance ; to comfort all that mourn." [9] For inasmuch as the Word of God was man from the root of Jesse, and son of Abraham, in this respect did the Spirit of God rest upon Him, and anoint Him to preach the Gospel to the lowly. But inasmuch as He was God, He did not judge according to

glory, nor reprove after the manner of speech. For " He needed not that any should testify to Him of man,[10] for He Himself knew what was in man." [11] For He called all men that mourn ; and granting forgiveness to those who had been led into captivity by their sins, He loosed them from their chains, of whom Solomon says, " Every one shall be holden with the cords of his own sins." [12] Therefore did the Spirit of God descend upon Him, [the Spirit] of Him who had promised by the prophets that He would anoint Him, so that we, receiving from the abundance of His unction, might be saved. Such, then, [is the witness] of Matthew.

CHAP. X. — PROOFS OF THE FOREGOING, DRAWN FROM THE GOSPELS OF MARK AND LUKE.

1. Luke also, the follower and disciple of the apostles, referring to Zacharias and Elisabeth, from whom, according to promise, John was born, says : " And they were both righteous before God, walking in all the commandments and ordinances of the Lord blameless." [13] And again, speaking of Zacharias : " And it came to pass, that while he executed the priest's office before God in the order of his course, according to the custom of the priest's office, his lot was to burn incense ; " [14] and he came to sacrifice, " entering into the temple of the Lord." [15] Whose angel Gabriel, also, who stands prominently in the presence of the Lord, simply, absolutely, and decidedly confessed in his own person as God and Lord, Him who had chosen Jerusalem, and had instituted the sacerdotal office. For he knew of none other above Him ; since, if he had been in possession of the knowledge of any other more perfect God and Lord besides Him, he surely would never — as I have already shown — have confessed Him, whom he knew to be the fruit of a defect, as absolutely and altogether God and Lord. And then, speaking of John, he thus says : " For he shall be great in the sight of the Lord, and many of the children of Israel shall he turn to the Lord their God. And he shall go before Him in the spirit and power of Elias, to make ready a people prepared for the Lord." [16] For whom, then, did he prepare the people, and in the sight of what Lord was he made great? Truly of Him who said that John had something even " more than a prophet," [17] and that " among those born of women none is greater than John the Baptist ; " who did also make the people ready for the Lord's advent, warning his fellow-servants, and preaching to them repentance, that

---

[1] Num xxiv. 17.
[2] Matt. ii. 2.
[3] Luke i. 33.
[4] Ps. lxxvi. 1.
[5] Isa. lxv. 1. [A beautiful idea for poets and orators, but not to be pressed dogmatically.]
[6] Matt. iii. 16.
[7] This is after the version of the Septuagint, οὐ κατὰ τὴν δόξαν : but the word δόξα may have the meaning *opinio* as well as *gloria*. If this be admitted here, the passage would bear much the same sense as it does in the authorized version, " He shall not judge after the sight of His eyes."
[8] Isa. xi. 1, etc.
[9] Isa. lxi. 1.

[10] This is according to the Syriac Peschito version.
[11] John ii. 25.
[12] Prov. v. 22.
[13] Luke i. 6.
[14] Literally, " that he should place the incense." The next clause is most likely an interpolation for the sake of explanation.
[15] Luke i. 8, etc.
[16] Luke i. 15, etc.
[17] Matt. xi. 9, 11.

they might receive remission from the Lord when He should be present, having been converted to Him, from whom they had been alienated because of sins and transgressions. As also David says, "The alienated are sinners from the womb: they go astray as soon as they are born."[1] And it was on account of this that he, turning them to their Lord, prepared, in the spirit and power of Elias, a perfect people for the Lord.

2. And again, speaking in reference to the angel, he says: "But at that time the angel Gabriel was sent from God, who did also say to the virgin, Fear not, Mary; for thou hast found favour with God."[2] And he says concerning the Lord: "He shall be great, and shall be called the Son of the Highest: and the Lord God shall give unto Him the throne of His father David: and He shall reign over the house of Jacob for ever; and of His kingdom there shall be no end."[3] For who else is there who can reign uninterruptedly over the house of Jacob for ever, except Jesus Christ our Lord, the Son of the Most High God, who promised by the law and the prophets that He would make His salvation visible to all flesh; so that He would become the Son of man for this purpose, that man also might become the son of God? And Mary, exulting because of this, cried out, prophesying on behalf of the Church, "My soul doth magnify the Lord, and my spirit hath rejoiced in God my Saviour. For He hath taken up His child Israel, in remembrance of His mercy, as He spake to our fathers, Abraham, and his seed for ever."[4] By these and such like [passages] the Gospel points out that it was God who spake to the fathers; that it was He who, by Moses, instituted the legal dispensation, by which giving of the law we know that He spake to the fathers. This same God, after His great goodness, poured His compassion upon us, through which compassion "the Dayspring from on high hath looked upon us, and appeared to those who sat in darkness and the shadow of death, and has guided our feet into the way of peace;"[5] as Zacharias also, recovering from the state of dumbness which he had suffered on account of unbelief, having been filled with a new spirit, did bless God in a new manner. For all things had entered upon a new phase, the Word arranging after a new manner the advent in the flesh, that He might win back[6] to God that human nature (hominem) which had departed from God; and therefore men were taught to worship God after a new fashion, but not another god, because in truth there is but "one God, who justifieth the circumcision by

faith, and the uncircumcision through faith."[7] But Zacharias prophesying, exclaimed, "Blessed be the Lord God of Israel; for He hath visited and redeemed His people, and hath raised up an horn of salvation for us in the house of His servant David; as He spake by the mouth of His holy prophets, which have been since the world begun; salvation from our enemies, and from the hand of all that hate us; to perform the mercy [promised] to our fathers, and to remember His holy covenant, the oath which He sware to our father Abraham, that He would grant unto us, that we, being delivered out of the hand of our enemies, might serve Him without fear, in holiness and righteousness before Him, all our days."[8] Then he says to John: "And thou, child, shalt be called the prophet of the Highest: for thou shalt go before the face of the Lord to prepare His ways; to give knowledge of salvation to His people, for the remission of their sins."[9] For this is the knowledge of salvation which was wanting to them, that of the Son of God, which John made known, saying, "Behold the Lamb of God, who taketh away the sin of the world. This is He of whom I said, After me cometh a man who was made before me;[10] because He was prior to me: and of His fulness have all we received."[11] This, therefore, was the knowledge of salvation; but [it did not consist in] another God, nor another Father, nor Bythus, nor the Pleroma of thirty Æons, nor the Mother of the (lower) Ogdoad: but the knowledge of salvation was the knowledge of the Son of God, who is both called and actually is, salvation, and Saviour, and salutary. Salvation, indeed, as follows: "I have waited for Thy salvation, O Lord."[12] And then again, Saviour: "Behold my God, my Saviour, I will put my trust in Him."[13] But as bringing salvation, thus: "God hath made known His salvation (salutare) in the sight of the heathen."[14] For He is indeed Saviour, as being the Son and Word of God; but salutary, since [He is] Spirit; for he says: "The Spirit of our countenance, Christ the Lord."[15] But salvation, as being flesh: for "the Word was made flesh, and dwelt among us."[16] This knowledge of salvation, therefore, John did impart to those repenting, and believing in the Lamb of God, who taketh away the sin of the world.

3. And the angel of the Lord, he says,

---

[1] Ps. lviii. 3.
[2] Luke i. 26, etc.
[3] Luke i. 32.
[4] Luke i. 46.
[5] Luke i. 78.
[6] "Ascriberet Deo"—make the property of God.

[7] Rom. iii. 30.
[8] Luke i. 68, etc.
[9] Luke i. 76.
[10] Harvey observes that the Syriac, agreeing with the Latin here, expresses priority in point of time; but our translation, without reason, makes it the precedence of honour, viz., *was preferred before me.* The Greek is, πρῶτός μου.
[11] John i. 29, 15, 16.
[12] Gen. xlix. 18.
[13] Isa. xii. 2.
[14] Ps. xcviii. 2.
[15] Lam. iv. 20, after **LXX.**
[16] John i. 14.

appeared to the shepherds, proclaiming joy to them: "For [1] there is born in the house of David, a Saviour, which is Christ the Lord. Then [appeared] a multitude of the heavenly host, praising God, and saying, Glory in the highest to God, and on earth peace, to men of good will." [2] The falsely-called Gnostics say that these angels came from the Ogdoad, and made manifest the descent of the superior Christ. But they are again in error, when saying that the Christ and Saviour from above was not born, but that also, after the baptism of the dispensational Jesus, he, [the Christ of the Pleroma,] descended upon him as a dove. Therefore, according to these men, the angels of the Ogdoad lied, when they said, "For unto you is born this day a Saviour, who is Christ the Lord, in the city of David." For neither was Christ nor the Saviour born at that time, by their account; but it was he, the dispensational Jesus, who is of the framer of the world, the [Demiurge], and upon whom, after his baptism, that is, after [the lapse of] thirty years, they maintain the Saviour from above descended. But why did [the angels] add, "in the city of David," if they did not proclaim the glad tidings of the fulfilment of God's promise made to David, that from the fruit of his body there should be an eternal King? For the Framer [Demiurge] of the entire universe made promise to David, as David himself declares: "My help is from God, who made heaven and earth;" [3] and again: "In His hand are the ends of the earth, and the heights of the mountains are His. For the sea is His, and He did Himself make it; and His hands founded the dry land. Come ye, let us worship and fall down before Him, and weep in the presence of the Lord who made us; for He is the Lord our God." [4] The Holy Spirit evidently thus declares by David to those hearing him, that there shall be those who despise Him who formed us, and who is God alone. Wherefore he also uttered the foregoing words, meaning to say: See that ye do not err; besides or above Him there is no other God, to whom ye should rather stretch out [your hands], thus rendering us pious and grateful towards Him who made, established, and [still] nourishes us. What, then, shall happen to those who have been the authors of so much blasphemy against their Creator? This identical truth was also what the

angels [proclaimed]. For when they exclaim, "Glory to God in the highest, and in earth peace," they have glorified with these· words Him who is the Creator of the highest, that is, of super-celestial things, and the Founder of everything on earth: who has sent to His own handiwork, that is, to men, the blessing of His salvation from heaven. Wherefore he adds: "The shepherds returned, glorifying God for all which they had heard and seen, as it was told unto them." [5] For the Israelitish shepherds did not glorify another god, but Him who had been announced by the law and the prophets, the Maker of all things, whom also the angels glorified. But if the angels who were from the Ogdoad were accustomed to glorify any other, different from Him whom the shepherds [adored], these angels from the Ogdoad brought to them error and not truth.

4. And still further does Luke say in reference to the Lord: "When the days of purification were accomplished, they brought Him up to Jerusalem, to present Him before the Lord, as it is written in the law of the Lord, That every male opening the womb shall be called holy to the Lord; and that they should offer a sacrifice, as it is said in the law of the Lord, a pair of turtle-doves, or two young pigeons:" [6] in his own person most clearly calling Him Lord, who appointed the legal dispensation. But "Simeon," he also says, "blessed God, and said, Lord, now lettest Thou Thy servant depart in peace; for mine eyes have seen Thy salvation, which Thou hast prepared before the face of all people; a light for the revelation of the Gentiles, and the glory of Thy people Israel." [7] And "Anna" [8] also, "the prophetess," he says, in like manner glorified God when she saw Christ, "and spake of Him to all them who were looking for the redemption of Jerusalem." [9] Now by all these one God is shown forth, revealing to men the new dispensation of liberty, the covenant, through the new advent of His Son.

5. Wherefore also Mark, the interpreter and follower of Peter, does thus commence his Gospel narrative: "The beginning of the Gospel of Jesus Christ, the Son of God; as it is written in the prophets, Behold, I send My messenger before Thy face, which shall prepare Thy way.[10] The voice of one crying in the wilderness, Prepare ye the way of the Lord, make the paths

---

[1] Luke ii. 11, etc.
[2] Thus found also in the Vulgate. Harvey supposes that the original of Irenæus read according to our *textus receptus*, and that the Vulgate rendering was adopted in this passage by the transcribers of the Latin version of our author. [No doubt a just remark.] There can be no doubt, however, that the reading εὐδοκίας is supported by many and weighty ancient authorities. [But on this point see the facts as given by Burgon, in his refutation of the rendering adopted by late revisers, *Revision Revised*, p. 41. London, Murray, 1883.]
[3] Ps. cxxiv. 8.
[4] Ps. xcv. 4.

[5] Luke ii. 20.
[6] Luke ii. 22.
[7] Luke ii. 29, etc.
[8] Luke ii. 38.
[9] The text seems to be corrupt in the old Latin translation. The rendering here follows Harvey's conjectural restoration of the original Greek of the passage.
[10] The Greek of this passage in St. Mark [i. 2] reads, τὰς τρίβους αὐτοῦ, i.e., *His paths*, which varies from the Hebrew original, to which the text of Irenæus seems to revert, unless indeed his copy of the Gospels contained the reading of the Codex Bezæ. [See book iii. cap. xii. 3, 14, below; also, xiv. 2 and xxiii. 3. On this Codex, see Burgon, *Revision Revised*, p. 12, etc., and references.]

straight before our God." Plainly does the commencement of the Gospel quote the words of the. holy prophets, and point out Him at once, whom they confessed as God and Lord; Him, the Father of our Lord Jesus Christ, who had also made promise to Him, that He would send His messenger before His face, who was John, crying in the wilderness, in "the spirit and power of Elias,"[1] "Prepare ye the way of the Lord, make straight paths before our God." For the prophets did not announce one and another God, but one and the same; under various aspects, however, and many titles. For varied and rich in attribute is the Father, as I have already shown in the book preceding[2] this; and I shall show [the same truth] from the prophets themselves in the further course of this work. Also, towards the conclusion of his Gospel, Mark says: "So then, after the Lord Jesus had spoken to them, He was received up into heaven, and sitteth on the right hand of God;"[3] confirming what had been spoken by the prophet: "The LORD said to my Lord, Sit Thou on My right hand, until I make Thy foes Thy footstool."[4] Thus God and the Father are truly one and the same; He who was announced by the prophets, and handed down by the true Gospel; whom we Christians worship and love with the whole heart, as the Maker of heaven and earth, and of all things therein.

CHAP. XI. — PROOFS IN CONTINUATION, EXTRACTED FROM ST. JOHN'S GOSPEL. THE GOSPELS ARE FOUR IN NUMBER, NEITHER MORE NOR LESS. MYSTIC REASONS FOR THIS.

1. John, the disciple of the Lord, preaches this faith, and seeks, by the proclamation of the Gospel, to remove that error which by Cerinthus had been disseminated among men, and a long time previously by those termed Nicolaitans, who are an offset of that "knowledge" falsely so called, that he might confound them, and persuade them that there is but one God, who made all things by His Word; and not, as they allege, that the Creator was one, but the Father of the Lord another; and that the Son of the Creator was, forsooth, one, but the Christ from above another, who also continued impassible, descending upon Jesus, the Son of the Creator, and flew back again into His Pleroma; and that Monogenes was the beginning, but Logos was the true son of Monogenes; and that this creation to which we belong was not made by the primary God, but by some power lying far below Him, and shut off from communion with the things invisible and ineffable. The disciple of the Lord

therefore desiring to put an end to all such doctrines, and to establish the rule of truth in the Church, that there is one Almighty God, who made all things by His Word, both visible and invisible; showing at the same time, that by the Word, through whom God made the creation, He also bestowed salvation on the men included in the creation; thus commenced His teaching in the Gospel: "In the beginning was the Word, and the Word was with God, and the Word was God. The same was in the beginning with God. All things were made by Him, and without Him was nothing made.[5] What was made was life in Him, and the life was the light of men. And the light shineth in darkness, and the darkness comprehended it not."[6] "All things," he says, "were made by Him;" therefore in "all things" this creation of ours is [included], for we cannot concede to these men that [the words] "all things" are spoken in reference to those within their Pleroma. For if their Pleroma do indeed contain these, this creation, as being such, is not outside, as I have demonstrated in the preceding book;[7] but if they are outside the Pleroma, which indeed appeared impossible, it follows, in that case, that their Pleroma cannot be "all things:" therefore this vast creation is not outside [the Pleroma].

2. John, however, does himself put this matter beyond all controversy on our part, when he says, "He was in this world, and the world was made by Him, and the world knew Him not. He came unto His own [things], and His own [people] received Him not."[8] But according to Marcion, and those like him, neither was the world made by Him; nor did He come to His own things, but to those of another. And, according to certain of the Gnostics, this world was made by angels, and not by the Word of God. But according to the followers of Valentinus, the world was not made by Him, but by the Demiurge. For he (Soter) caused such similitudes to be made, after the pattern of things above, as they allege; but the Demiurge accomplished the work of creation. For they say that he, the Lord and Creator of the plan of creation, by whom they hold that this world was made, was produced from the Mother; while the Gospel affirms plainly, that by the Word, which was in the beginning with God, all things were made, which Word, he says, "was made flesh, and dwelt among us."[9]

3. But, according to these men, neither was the Word made flesh, nor Christ, nor the Saviour (Soter), who was produced from [the joint con-

---

[5] Irenæus frequently quotes this text, and always uses the punctuation here adopted. Tertullian and many others of the Fathers follow his example.
[6] John i. 1, etc.
[7] See ii. 1, etc.
[8] John i. 10, 11.
[9] John i. 14.

---

[1] Luke i. 17.
[2] See ii. 35, 3.
[3] Mark xvi. 19
[4] Ps. cx. 1.

tributions of] all [the Æons]. For they will have it, that the Word and Christ never came into this world; that the Saviour, too, never became incarnate, nor suffered, but that He descended like a dove upon the dispensational Jesus; and that, as soon as He had declared the unknown Father, He did again ascend into the Pleroma. Some, however, make the assertion, that this dispensational Jesus did become incarnate, and suffered, whom they represent as having passed through Mary just as water through a tube; but others allege him to be the Son of the Demiurge, upon whom the dispensational Jesus descended; while others, again, say that Jesus was born from Joseph and Mary, and that the Christ from above descended upon him, being without flesh, and impassible. But according to the opinion of no one of the heretics was the Word of God made flesh. For if any one carefully examines the systems of them all, he will find that the Word of God is brought in by all of them as not having become incarnate (*sine carne*) and impassible, as is also the Christ from above. Others consider Him to have been manifested as a transfigured man; but they maintain Him to have been neither born nor to have become incarnate; whilst others [hold] that He did not assume a human form at all, but that, as a dove, He did descend upon that Jesus who was born from Mary. Therefore the Lord's disciple, pointing them all out as false witnesses, says, "And the Word was made flesh, and dwelt among us." [1]

4. And that we may not have to ask, Of what God was the Word made flesh? he does himself previously teach us, saying, "There was a man sent from God, whose name was John. The same came as a witness, that he might bear witness of that Light. He was not that Light, but [came] that he might testify of the Light." [2] By what God, then, was John, the forerunner, who testifies of the Light, sent [into the world]? Truly it was by Him, of whom Gabriel is the angel, who also announced the glad tidings of his birth: [that God] who also had promised by the prophets that He would send His messenger before the face of His Son, [3] who should prepare His way, that is, that he should bear witness of that Light in the spirit and power of Elias. [4] But, again, of what God was Elias the servant and the prophet? Of Him who made heaven and earth, [5] as he does himself confess. John, therefore, having been sent by the founder and maker of this world, how could he testify of that Light, which came down from things unspeakable

and invisible? For all the heretics have decided that the Demiurge was ignorant of that Power above him, whose witness and herald John is found to be. Wherefore the Lord said that He deemed him "more than a prophet." [6] For all the other prophets preached the advent of the paternal Light, and desired to be worthy of seeing Him whom they preached; but John did both announce [the advent] beforehand, in a like manner as did the others, and actually saw Him when He came, and pointed Him out, and persuaded many to believe on Him, so that he did himself hold the place of both prophet and apostle. For this is to be more than a prophet, because, "first apostles, secondarily prophets;" [7] but all things from one and the same God Himself.

5. That wine,[8] which was produced by God in a vineyard, and which was first consumed, was good. None [9] of those who drank of it found fault with it; and the Lord partook of it also. But that wine was better which the Word made from water, on the moment, and simply for the use of those who had been called to the marriage. For although the Lord had the power to supply wine to those feasting, independently of any created substance, and to fill with food those who were hungry, He did not adopt this course; but, taking the loaves which the earth had produced, and giving thanks,[10] and on the other occasion making water wine, He satisfied those who were reclining [at table], and gave drink to those who had been invited to the marriage; showing that the God who made the earth, and commanded it to bring forth fruit, who established the waters, and brought forth the fountains, was He who in these last times bestowed upon mankind, by His Son, the blessing of food and the favour of drink: the Incomprehensible [acting thus] by means of the comprehensible, and the Invisible by the visible; since there is none beyond Him, but He exists in the bosom of the Father.

6. For "no man," he says, "hath seen God at any time," unless "the only-begotten Son of God, which is in the bosom of the Father, He hath declared [Him]." [11] For He, the Son who is in His bosom, declares to all the Father who is invisible. Wherefore *they* know Him to whom the Son reveals Him; and again, the Father, by means of the Son, gives knowledge of His Son to those who love Him. By whom also Nathanael, being taught, recognised [Him], he to whom also the Lord bare witness, that he was "an Israelite indeed, in whom was no guile." [12] The

---

[1] John i. 14.
[2] John i. 6.
[3] Mal. iii. 1.
[4] Luke i. 17.
[5] This evidently refers to 1 Kings xviii. 36, where Elijah invokes God as the God of Abraham, Isaac, and Jacob, etc.

[6] Matt. xi. 9; Luke vii. 26.
[7] 1. Cor. xii. 28.
[8] The transition here is so abrupt, that some critics suspect the loss of part of the text before these words.
[9] John ii. 3.
[10] John vi. 11.
[11] John i. 18.
[12] John i. 47.

Israelite recognised his King, therefore did he cry out to Him, "Rabbi, Thou art the Son of God, Thou art the King of Israel." By whom also Peter, having been taught, recognised Christ as the Son of the living God, when [God] said, "Behold My dearly beloved Son, in whom I am well pleased: I will put my Spirit upon Him, and He shall show judgment to the Gentiles. He shall not strive, nor cry; neither shall any man hear His voice in the streets. A bruised reed shall He not break, and smoking flax shall He not quench, until He send forth judgment into contention;[1] and in His name shall the Gentiles trust."[2]

7. Such, then, are the first principles of the Gospel: that there is one God, the Maker of this universe; He who was also announced by the prophets, and who by Moses set forth the dispensation of the law, — [principles] which proclaim the Father of our Lord Jesus Christ, and ignore any other God or Father except Him. So firm is the ground upon which these Gospels rest, that the very heretics themselves bear witness to them, and, starting from these [documents], each one of them endeavours to establish his own peculiar doctrine. For the Ebionites, who use Matthew's Gospel[3] only, are confuted out of this very same, making false suppositions with regard to the Lord. But Marcion, mutilating that according to Luke, is proved to be a blasphemer of the only existing God, from those [passages] which he still retains. Those, again, who separate Jesus from Christ, alleging that Christ remained impassible, but that it was Jesus who suffered, preferring the Gospel by Mark, if they read it with a love of truth, may have their errors rectified. Those, moreover, who follow Valentinus, making copious use of that according to John, to illustrate their conjunctions, shall be proved to be totally in error by means of this very Gospel, as I have shown in the first book. Since, then, our opponents do bear testimony to us, and make use of these [documents], our proof derived from them is firm and true.

8. It is not possible that the Gospels can be either more or fewer in number than they are. For, since there are four zones of the world in which we live, and four principal winds,[4] while the Church is scattered throughout all the world, and the "pillar and ground"[5] of the Church is the Gospel and the spirit of life; it is fitting that she should have four pillars, breathing out im-

mortality on every side, and vivifying men afresh. From which fact, it is evident that the Word, the Artificer of all, He that sitteth upon the cherubim, and contains all things, He who was manifested to men, has given us the Gospel under four aspects, but bound together by one Spirit. As also David says, when entreating His manifestation, "Thou that sittest between the cherubim, shine forth."[6] For the cherubim, too, were four-faced, and their faces were images of the dispensation of the Son of God. For, [as the Scripture] says, "The first living creature was like a lion,"[7] symbolizing His effectual working, His leadership, and royal power; the second [living creature] was like a calf, signifying [His] sacrificial and sacerdotal order; but "the third had, as it were, the face as of a man,"—an evident description of His advent as a human being; "the fourth was like a flying eagle," pointing out the gift of the Spirit hovering with His wings over the Church. And therefore the Gospels are in accord with these things, among which Christ Jesus is seated. For that according to John relates His original, effectual, and glorious generation from the Father, thus declaring, "In the beginning was the Word, and the Word was with God, and the Word was God."[8] Also, "all things were made by Him, and without Him was nothing made." For this reason, too, is that Gospel full of all confidence, for such is His person.[9] But that according to Luke, taking up [His] priestly character, commenced with Zacharias the priest offering sacrifice to God. For now was made ready the fatted calf, about to be immolated for[10] the finding again of the younger son. Matthew, again, relates His generation as a man, saying, "The book of the generation of Jesus Christ, the son of David, the son of Abraham;"[11] and also, "The birth of Jesus Christ was on this wise." This, then, is the Gospel of His humanity;[12] for which reason it is, too, that [the character of] a humble and meek man is kept up through the whole Gospel. Mark, on the other hand, commences with [a reference to] the prophetical spirit coming down from on high to men, saying, "The beginning of the Gospel of Jesus Christ, as it is written in Esaias the prophet," — pointing to the winged aspect of the Gospel; and on this account he made a compendious and cursory narrative, for such is the prophetical character. And the Word of God Himself used to converse with the ante-Mosaic patriarchs, in accordance with His di-

---

[1] The reading νεῖκος having been followed instead of νῖκος, victory.
[2] John i. 49, vi. 69; Matt. xii. 18
[3] Harvey thinks that this is the Hebrew Gospel of which Irenæus speaks in the opening of this book; but comp. Dr. Roberts's *Discussions on the Gospels*, part ii. chap. iv.
[4] Literally, "four catholic spirits:" Greek, τέσσαρα καθολικὰ πνεύματα: Latin, "quatuor principales spiritus."
[5] 1 Tim. iii. 15.

[6] Ps. lxxx. 1.
[7] Rev. iv. 7.
[8] John i. 1.
[9] The above is the literal rendering of this very obscure sentence; it is not at all represented in the Greek here preserved.
[10] The Greek is ὑπέρ: the Latin, "pro."
[11] Matt. i. 1, 18.
[12] The Greek text of this clause, literally rendered is, "This Gospel, then, is anthropomorphic."

vinity and glory; but for those under the law he instituted a sacerdotal and liturgical service.[1] Afterwards, being made man for us, He sent the gift of the celestial Spirit over all the earth, protecting us with His wings. Such, then, as was the course followed by the Son of God, so was also the form of the living creatures; and such as was the form of the living creatures, so was also the character of the Gospel.[2] For the living creatures are quadriform, and the Gospel is quadriform, as is also the course followed by the Lord. For this reason were four principal (καθολικαί) covenants given to the human race:[3] one, prior to the deluge, under Adam; the second, that after the deluge, under Noah; the third, the giving of the law, under Moses; the fourth, that which renovates man, and sums up all things in itself by means of the Gospel, raising and bearing men upon its wings into the heavenly kingdom.

9. These things being so, all who destroy the form of the Gospel are vain, unlearned, and also audacious; those, [I mean,] who represent the aspects of the Gospel as being either more in number than as aforesaid, or, on the other hand, fewer. The former class [do so], that they may seem to have discovered more than is of the truth; the latter, that they may set the dispensations of God aside. For Marcion, rejecting the entire Gospel, yea rather, cutting himself off from the Gospel, boasts that he has part in the [blessings of] the Gospel.[4] Others, again (the Montanists), that they may set at nought the gift of the Spirit, which in the latter times has been, by the good pleasure of the Father, poured out upon the human race, do not admit that *aspect* [of the evangelical dispensation] presented by John's Gospel, in which the Lord promised that He would send the Paraclete;[5] but set aside at once both the Gospel and the prophetic Spirit. Wretched men indeed! who wish to be pseudo-prophets, forsooth, but who set aside the gift of prophecy

from the Church; acting like those (the Encratitæ)[6] who, on account of such as come in hypocrisy, hold themselves aloof from the communion of the brethren. We must conclude, moreover, that these men (the Montanists) cannot admit the Apostle Paul either. For, in his Epistle to the Corinthians,[7] he speaks expressly of prophetical gifts, and recognises men and women prophesying in the Church. Sinning, therefore, in all these particulars, against the Spirit of God,[8] they fall into the irremissible sin. But those who are from Valentinus, being, on the other hand, altogether reckless, while they put forth their own compositions, boast that they possess more Gospels than there really are. Indeed, they have arrived at such a pitch of audacity, as to entitle their comparatively recent writing "the Gospel of Truth," though it agrees in nothing with the Gospels of the Apostles, so that they have really no Gospel which is not full of blasphemy. For if what they have published is the Gospel of truth, and yet is totally unlike those which have been handed down to us from the apostles, any who please may learn, as is shown from the Scriptures themselves, that that which has been handed down from the apostles can no longer be reckoned the Gospel of truth. But that these Gospels alone are true and reliable, and admit neither an increase nor diminution of the aforesaid number, I have proved by so many and such [arguments]. For, since God made all things in due proportion and adaptation, it was fit also that the outward aspect of the Gospel should be well arranged and harmonized. The opinion of those men, therefore, who handed the Gospel down to us, having been investigated, from their very fountainheads, let us proceed also to the remaining apostles, and inquire into their doctrine with regard to God; then, in due course we shall listen to the very words of the Lord.

CHAP. XII. — THE DOCTRINE OF THE REST OF THE APOSTLES.

1. The Apostle Peter, therefore, after the resurrection of the Lord, and His assumption into the heavens, being desirous of filling up the number of the twelve apostles, and in electing into the place of Judas any substitute who should be chosen by God, thus addressed those who were present: "Men [and] brethren, this Scripture must needs have been fulfilled, which the Holy Ghost, by the mouth of David, spake before concerning Judas, which was made guide to them that took Jesus. For he was numbered with us:[9] . . . Let his habitation be desolate,

---

[1] Or, "a sacerdotal and liturgical order," following the fragment of the Greek text recovered here. Harvey thinks that the old Latin "actum" indicates the true reading of the original πρᾶξιν, and that τάξιν is an error. The earlier editors, however, are of a contrary opinion.

[2] That is, the appearance of the Gospel taken as a whole; it being presented under a fourfold aspect.

[3] A portion of the Greek has been preserved here, but it differs materially from the old Latin version, which seems to represent the original with greater exactness, and has therefore been followed. The Greek represents the first covenant as having been given to Noah, at the deluge, under the sign of the rainbow; the second as that given to Abraham, under the sign of circumcision; the third, as being the giving of the law, under Moses; and the fourth, as that of the Gospel, through our Lord Jesus Christ. [Paradise with the *tree of life*, Adam with the *Shechinah* (Gen. iii. 24, iv. 16), Noah with the *rainbow*, Abraham with *circumcision*, Moses with *the ark*, Messiah with *the sacraments*, and heaven with the *river of life*, seem the complete system.]

[4] The old Latin reads, "partem gloriatur se habere Evangelii." Massuet changed *partem* into *pariter*, thinking that *partem* gave a sense inconsistent with the Marcionite curtailment of St. Luke. Harvey, however, observes: "But the *Gospel* here means the *blessings of the Gospel*, in which Marcion certainly claimed a share."

[5] John xiv. 16, etc.

[6] Slighting, as did some later heretics, the Pauline Epistles.

[7] 1 Cor. xi. 4, 5.

[8] Matt. xii. 31.

[9] Acts i. 16, etc.

and let no man dwell therein ; [1] and, His bishop-rick let another take ; "[2] — thus leading to the completion of the apostles, according to the words spoken by David. Again, when the Holy Ghost had descended upon the disciples, that they all might prophesy and speak with tongues, and some mocked them, as if drunken with new wine, Peter said that they were not drunken, for it was the third hour of the day ; but that this was what had been spoken by the prophet : " It shall come to pass in the last days, saith God, I will pour out of my Spirit upon all flesh, and they shall prophesy."[3] The God, therefore, who did promise by the prophet, that He would send His Spirit upon the whole human race, was He who did send ; and God Himself is announced by Peter as having fulfilled His own promise.

2. For Peter said, " Ye men of Israel, hear my words ; Jesus of Nazareth, a man approved by God among you by powers, and wonders, and signs, which God did by Him in the midst of you, as ye yourselves also know : Him, being delivered by the determined counsel and fore-knowledge of God, by the hands of wicked men ye have slain, affixing [to the cross] : whom God hath raised up, having loosed the pains of death ; because it was not possible that he should be holden of them. For David speak-eth concerning Him,[4] I foresaw the Lord always before my face ; for He is on my right hand, lest I should be moved : therefore did my heart rejoice, and my tongue was glad ; moreover also, my flesh shall rest in hope : because Thou wilt not leave my soul in hell, neither wilt Thou give Thy Holy One to see corruption."[5] Then he proceeds to speak confidently to them concern-ing the patriarch David, that he was dead and buried, and that his sepulchre is with them to this day. He said, " But since he was a prophet, and knew that God had sworn with an oath to him, that of the fruit of his body one should sit in his throne ; foreseeing this, he spake of the resurrection of Christ, that He was not left in hell, neither did His flesh see corruption. This Jesus," he said, " hath God raised up, of which we all are witnesses : who, being exalted by the right hand of God, receiving from the Father the promise of the Holy Ghost, hath shed forth this gift [6] which ye now see and hear. For David has not ascended into the heavens ; but he saith himself, The LORD said unto my Lord, Sit Thou on My right hand, until I make Thy foes Thy footstool. Therefore let all the house of Israel know assuredly, that God hath made

that same Jesus, whom ye have crucified, both Lord and Christ."[7] And when the multitudes exclaimed, " What shall we do then ? " Peter says to them, " Repent, and be baptized every one of you in the name of Jesus for the remis-sion of sins, and ye shall receive the gift of the Holy Ghost."[8] Thus the apostles did not preach another God, or another Fulness ; nor, that the Christ who suffered and rose again was one, while he who flew off on high was another, and remained impassible ; but that there was one and the same God the Father, and Christ Jesus who rose from the dead ; and they preached faith in Him, to those who did not believe on the Son of God, and exhorted them out of the prophets, that the Christ whom God promised to send, He sent in Jesus, whom they crucified and God raised up.

3. Again, when Peter, accompanied by John, had looked upon the man lame from his birth, before that gate of the temple which is called Beautiful, sitting and seeking alms, he said to him, " Silver and gold I have none ; but such as I have give I thee : In the name of Jesus Christ of Nazareth, rise up and walk. And immedi-ately his legs and his feet received strength ; and he walked, and entered with them into the tem-ple, walking, and leaping, and praising God."[9] Then, when a multitude had gathered around them from all quarters because of this unex-pected deed, Peter addressed them : " Ye men of Israel, why marvel ye at this ; or why look ye so earnestly on us, as though by our own power we had made this man to walk ? The God of Abraham, the God of Isaac, and the God of Jacob, the God of our fathers, hath glorified His Son, whom ye delivered up for judgment,[10] and denied in the presence of Pilate, when he wished to let Him go. But ye were bitterly set against [10] the Holy One and the Just, and de-sired a murderer to be granted unto you ; but ye killed the Prince of life, whom God hath raised from the dead, whereof we are witnesses. And in the faith of His name, him, whom ye see and know, hath His name made strong ; yea, the faith which is by Him, hath given him this perfect soundness in the presence of you all. And now, brethren, I wot that through ignorance ye did this wickedness.[10] . . . But those things which God before had showed by the mouth of all the prophets, that His Christ should suffer, He hath so fulfilled. Repent ye therefore, and be converted, that your sins may be blotted out, and that [11] the times of refresh-

---

[1] Ps. lxix. 25.
[2] Ps. cix. 8.
[3] Joel ii. 28.
[4] Ps. xv. 8.
[5] Acts ii. 22-27.
[6] The word δῶρον or δώρημα is supposed by some to have ex-isted in the earliest Greek texts, although not found in any extant now. It is thus quoted by others besides Irenæus.

[7] Acts ii. 30-37.
[8] Acts ii. 37, 38.
[9] Acts iii. 6, etc.
[10] These interpolations are also found in the Codex Bezæ.
[11] " Et veniant " in Latin text : ὅπως ἂν ἔλθωσιν in Greek. The translation of these Greek words by " when . . . come," is one of the most glaring errors in the authorized English version.

ing may come to you from the presence of the Lord ; and He shall send Jesus Christ, prepared for you beforehand,[1] whom the heaven must indeed receive until the times of the arrangement[2] of all things, of which God hath spoken by His holy prophets. For Moses truly said unto our fathers, Your Lord God shall raise up to you a Prophet from your brethren, like unto me ; Him shall ye hear in all things whatsoever He shall say unto you. And it shall come to pass, that every soul, whosoever will not hear that Prophet, shall be destroyed from among the people. And all [the prophets] from Samuel, and henceforth, as many as have spoken, have likewise foretold of these days. Ye are the children of the prophets, and of the covenant which God made with our fathers, saying unto Abraham, And in thy seed shall all the kindreds of the earth be blessed. Unto you first, God, having raised up His Son, sent Him blessing you, that each may turn himself from his iniquities."[3] Peter, together with John, preached to them this plain message of glad tidings, that the promise which God made to the fathers had been fulfilled by Jesus ; not certainly proclaiming another god, but the Son of God, who also was made man, and suffered ; thus leading Israel into knowledge, and through Jesus preaching the resurrection of the dead,[4] and showing, that whatever the prophets had proclaimed as to the suffering of Christ, these had God fulfilled.

4. For this reason, too, when the chief priests were assembled, Peter, full of boldness, said to them, "Ye rulers of the people, and elders of Israel, if we this day be examined by you of the good deed done to the impotent man, by what means he has been made whole ; be it known to you all, and to all the people of Israel, that by the name of Jesus Christ of Nazareth, whom ye crucified, whom God raised from the dead, even by Him doth this man stand here before you whole. This is the stone which was set at nought of you builders, which is become the head-stone of the corner. [Neither is there salvation in any other : for] there is none other name under heaven, which is given to men, whereby we must be saved."[5] Thus the apostles did not change God, but preached to the people that Christ was Jesus the crucified One, whom the same God that had sent the prophets, being God Himself, raised up, and gave in Him salvation to men.

5. They were confounded, therefore, both by this instance of healing ("for the man was above forty years old on whom this miracle of healing

took place "[6]), and by the doctrine of the apostles, and by the exposition of the prophets, when the chief priests had sent away Peter and John. [These latter] returned to the rest of their fellow-apostles and disciples of the Lord, that is, to the Church, and related what had occurred, and how courageously they had acted in the name of Jesus. The whole Church, it is then said, "when they had heard that, lifted up the voice to God with one accord, and said, Lord, Thou art God, which hast made heaven, and earth, and the sea, and all that in them is ; who, through the Holy Ghost,[7] by the mouth of our father David, Thy servant, hast said, Why did the heathen rage, and the people imagine vain things? The kings of the earth stood up, and the rulers were gathered together against the Lord, and against His Christ. For of a truth, in this city,[8] against Thy holy Son Jesus, whom Thou hast anointed, both Herod and Pontius Pilate, with the Gentiles, and the people of Israel, were gathered together, to do whatsoever Thy hand and Thy counsel determined before to be done."[9] These [are the] voices of the Church from which every Church had its origin ; these are the voices of the metropolis of the citizens of the new covenant ; these are the voices of the apostles ; these are voices of the disciples of the Lord, the truly perfect, who, after the assumption of the Lord, were perfected by the Spirit, and called upon the God who made heaven, and earth, and the sea, — who was announced by the prophets, — and Jesus Christ His Son, whom God anointed, and who knew no other [God]. For at that time and place there was neither Valentinus, nor Marcion, nor the rest of these subverters [of the truth], and their adherents. Wherefore God, the Maker of all things, heard them. For it is said, "The place was shaken where they were assembled together ; and they were all filled with the Holy Ghost, and they spake the word of God with boldness "[10] to every one that was willing to believe.[11] "And with great power," it is added, "gave the apostles witness of the resurrection of the Lord Jesus,"[12] saying to them, "The God of our fathers raised up Jesus, whom ye seized and slew, hanging [Him] upon a beam of wood : Him hath God raised up by His right hand [13] to be a Prince and Saviour, to give repentance to Israel, and

---

[1] Irenæus, like the majority of the early authorities, manifestly read προκεχειρισμένον instead of προκεκηρυγμένον, as in *textus receptus*.
[2] Dispositionis.
[3] Acts iii. 12, etc.
[4] Acts iv. 2.
[5] Acts iv. 8, etc.

[6] Acts iv. 22.
[7] These words, though not in *textus receptus*, are found in some ancient MSS. and versions; but not the words "our father," which follow.
[8] "In hac civitate" are words not represented in the *textus receptus*, but have a place in all modern critical editions of the New Testament.
[9] Acts iv. 24, etc.
[10] Acts iv. 31.
[11] The Latin is, "ut convertat se unusquisque."
[12] Acts iv. 33.
[13] This is following Grabe's emendation of the text. The old Latin reads "gloria sua," the translator having evidently mistaken δεξιᾷ for δόξῃ.

forgiveness of sins. And we are in this witnesses of these words ; as also is the Holy Ghost, whom God hath given to them that believe in Him." [1] "And daily," it is said, "in the temple, and from house to house, they ceased not to teach and preach Christ Jesus," [2] the Son of God. For this was the knowledge of salvation, which renders those who acknowledge His Son's advent perfect towards God.

6. But as some of these men impudently assert that the apostles, when preaching among the Jews, could not declare to them another god besides Him in whom they (their hearers [3]) believed, we say to them, that if the apostles used to speak to people in accordance with the opinion instilled into them of old, no one learned the truth from them, nor, at a much earlier date, from the Lord ; for they say that He did Himself speak after the same fashion. Wherefore neither do these men themselves know the truth ; but since such was their opinion regarding God, they had just received doctrine as they were able to hear it. According to this manner of speaking, therefore, the rule of truth can be with nobody ; but all learners will ascribe this practice to all [teachers], that just as every person thought, and as far as his capability extended, so was also the language addressed to him. But the advent of the Lord will appear superfluous and useless, if He did indeed come intending to tolerate and to preserve each man's idea regarding God rooted in him from of old. Besides this, also, it was a much heavier task, that He whom the Jews had seen as a man, and had fastened to the cross, should be preached as Christ the Son of God, their eternal King. Since this, however, was so, they certainly did not speak to them in accordance with their old belief. For they, who told them to their face that they were the slayers of the Lord, would themselves also much more boldly preach that Father who is above the Demiurge, and not what each individual bid himself believe [respecting God] ; and the sin was much less, if indeed they had not fastened to the cross the superior Saviour (to whom it behoved them to ascend), since He was impassible. For, as they did not speak to the Gentiles in compliance with their notions, but told them with boldness that their gods were no gods, but the idols of demons ; so would they in like manner have preached to the Jews, if they had known another greater or more perfect Father, not nourishing nor strengthening the untrue opinion of these men regarding God. Moreover, while destroying the error of the Gentiles, and bearing them away from their gods, they did not certainly induce another error upon them ; but, removing

those which were no gods, they pointed out Him who alone was God and the true Father.

7. From the words of Peter, therefore, which he addressed in Cæsarea to Cornelius the centurion, and those Gentiles with him, to whom the word of God was first preached, we can understand what the apostles used to preach, the nature of their preaching, and their idea with regard to God. For this Cornelius was, it is said, "a devout man, and one who feared God with all his house, giving much alms to the people, and praying to God always. He saw therefore, about the ninth hour of the day, an angel of God coming in to him, and saying, Thine alms are come up for a memorial before God. Wherefore send to Simon, who is called Peter." [4] But when Peter saw the vision, in which the voice from heaven said to him, "What God hath cleansed, that call not thou common," [5] this happened [to teach him] that the God who had, through the law, distinguished between clean and unclean, was He who had purified the Gentiles through the blood of His Son — He whom also Cornelius worshipped ; to whom Peter, coming in, said, "Of a truth I perceive that God is no respecter of persons : but in every nation, he that feareth Him, and worketh righteousness, is acceptable to Him." [6] He thus clearly indicates, that He whom Cornelius had previously feared as God, of whom he had heard through the law and the prophets, for whose sake also he used to give alms, is, in truth, the knowledge of the Son was, however, wanting to him ; therefore did [Peter] add, "The word, ye know, which was published throughout all Judea, beginning from Galilee, after the baptism which John preached, Jesus of Nazareth, how God anointed Him with the Holy Ghost, and with power ; who went about doing good, and healing all that were oppressed of the devil ; for God was with Him. And we are witnesses of all those things which He did both in the land of the Jews and in Jerusalem ; whom they slew, hanging Him on a beam of wood : Him God raised up the third day, and showed Him openly ; not to all the people, but unto us, witnesses chosen before of God, who did eat and drink with Him after the resurrection from the dead. And He commanded us to preach unto the people, and to testify that it is He which was ordained of God to be the Judge of quick and dead. To Him give all the prophets witness, that, through His name, every one that believeth in Him does receive remission of sins." [7] The apostles, therefore, did preach the Son of God, of whom men were ignorant ; and His advent, to those

---

1 Acts v. 30.
2 Acts v. 42.
3 These words have apparently been omitted through inadvertence.

4 Acts x. 1–5.
5 Acts x. 15.
6 Acts x. 34, 35.
7 Acts x. 37–44.

who had been already instructed as to God; but they did not bring in another god. For if Peter had known any such thing, he would have preached freely to the Gentiles, that the God of the Jews was indeed one, but the God of the Christians another; and all of them, doubtless, being awe-struck because of the vision of the angel, would have believed whatever he told them. But it is evident from Peter's words that he did indeed still retain the God who was already known to them; but he also bare witness to them that Jesus Christ was the Son of God, the Judge of quick and dead, into whom he did also command them to be baptized for the remission of sins; and not this alone, but he witnessed that Jesus was Himself the Son of God, who also, having been anointed with the Holy Spirit, is called Jesus Christ. And He is the same being that was born of Mary, as the testimony of Peter implies. Can it really be, that Peter was not at that time as yet in possession of the perfect knowledge which these men discovered afterwards? According to them, therefore, Peter was imperfect, and the rest of the apostles were imperfect; and so it would be fitting that they, coming to life again, should become disciples of these men, in order that they too might be made perfect. But this is truly ridiculous. These men, in fact, are proved to be not disciples of the apostles, but of their own wicked notions. To this cause also are due the various opinions which exist among them, inasmuch as each one adopted error just as he was capable [1] [of embracing it]. But the Church throughout all the world, having its origin firm from the apostles, perseveres in one and the same opinion with regard to God and His Son.

8. But again: Whom did Philip preach to the eunuch of the queen of the Ethiopians, returning from Jerusalem, and reading Esaias the prophet, when he and this man were alone together? Was it not He of whom the prophet spoke: "He was led as a sheep to the slaughter, and as a lamb dumb before the shearer, so He opened not the mouth?" "But who shall declare His nativity? for His life shall be taken away from the earth." [2] [Philip declared] that this was Jesus, and that the Scripture was fulfilled in Him; as did also the believing eunuch himself: and, immediately requesting to be baptized, he said, "I believe Jesus Christ to be the Son of God." [3] This man was also sent into the regions of Ethiopia, to preach what he had himself believed, that there was one God preached by the prophets, but that the Son of this [God] had

already made [His] appearance in human nature (*secundum hominem*), and had been led as a sheep to the slaughter; and all the other statements which the prophets made regarding Him.

9. Paul himself also — after that the Lord spoke to him out of heaven, and showed him that, in persecuting His disciples, he persecuted his own Lord, and sent Ananias to him that he might recover his sight, and be baptized — "preached," it is said, "Jesus in the synagogues at Damascus, with all freedom of speech, that this is the Son of God, the Christ." [4] This is the mystery which he says was made known to him by revelation, that He who suffered under Pontius Pilate, the same is Lord of all, and King, and God, and Judge, receiving power from Him who is the God of all, because He became "obedient unto death, even the death of the cross." [5] And inasmuch as this is true, when preaching to the Athenians on the Areopagus — where, no Jews being present, he had it in his power to preach God with freedom of speech — he said to them: "God, who made the world, and all things therein, He, being Lord of heaven and earth, dwelleth not in temples made with hands; neither is He touched [6] by men's hands, as though He needed anything, seeing He giveth to all life, and breath, and all things; who hath made from one blood the whole race of men to dwell upon the face of the whole earth, [7] predetermining the times according to the boundary of their habitation, to seek the Deity, if by any means they might be able to track Him out, or find Him, although He be not far from each of us. For in Him we live, and move, and have our being, as certain men of your own have said, For we are also His offspring. Inasmuch, then, as we are the offspring of God, we ought not to think that the Deity is like unto gold or silver, or stone graven by art or man's device. Therefore God, winking at the times of ignorance, does now command all men everywhere to turn to Him with repentance; because He hath appointed a day, on which the world shall be judged in righteousness by the man Jesus; whereof He hath given assurance by raising Him from the dead." [8] Now in this passage he does not only declare to them God as the Creator of the world, no Jews being present, but that He did also make one race of men to dwell upon all the earth; as also Moses declared: "When the Most High divided the nations, as He scattered the sons of Adam, He set the bounds of the nations after the number of the angels of God;" [9] but

---

[1] *Quemadmodum capiebat;* perhaps, "just as it presented itself to him."
[2] Acts viii. 32; Isa. liii. 7, 8.
[3] Acts viii. 37.

[4] Acts ix. 20.
[5] Phil. ii. 8.
[6] Latin translation, *tractatur;* which Harvey thinks affords a conclusive proof that Irenæus occasionally quotes Scripture by retranslating from the Syriac.
[7] It will be observed that Scripture is here very loosely quoted.
[8] Acts xvii. 24, etc.
[9] Deut. xxxii. 8 [LXX.].

that people which believes in God is not now under the power of angels, but under the Lord's [rule]. "For His people Jacob was made the portion of the Lord, Israel the cord of His inheritance."[1] And again, at Lystra of Lycia (Lycaonia), when Paul was with Barnabas, and in the name of our Lord Jesus Christ had made a man to walk who had been lame from his birth, and when the crowd wished to honour them as gods because of the astonishing deed, he said to them : "We are men like unto you, preaching to you God, that ye may be turned away from these vain idols to [serve] the living God, who made heaven, and earth, and the sea, and all things that are therein ; who in times past suffered all nations to walk in their own ways, although He left not Himself without witness, performing acts of goodness, giving you rain from heaven, and fruitful seasons, filling your hearts with food and gladness."[2] But that all his Epistles are consonant to these declarations, I shall, when expounding the apostle, show from the Epistles themselves, in the right place. But while I bring out by these proofs the truths of Scripture, and set forth briefly and compendiously things which are stated in various ways, do thou also attend to them with patience, and not deem them prolix ; taking this into account, that proofs [of the things which are] contained in the Scriptures cannot be shown except from the Scriptures themselves.

10. And still further, Stephen, who was chosen the first deacon by the apostles, and who, of all men, was the first to follow the footsteps of the martyrdom of the Lord, being the first that was slain for confessing Christ, speaking boldly among the people, and teaching them, says : "'The God of glory appeared to our father Abraham, . . . and said to him, Get thee out of thy country, and from thy kindred, and come into the land which I shall show thee ; . . . and He removed him into this land, wherein ye now dwell. And He gave him none inheritance in it, no, not so much as to set his foot on ; yet He promised that He would give it to him for a possession, and to his seed after him. . . . And God spake on this wise, That his seed should sojourn in a strange land, and should be brought into bondage, and should be evil-entreated four hundred years ; and the nation whom they shall serve will I judge, says the Lord. And after that shall they come forth, and serve me in this place. And He gave him the covenant of circumcision : and so [Abraham] begat Isaac."[3] And the rest of his words announce the same God, who was with Joseph and with the patriarchs, and who spake with Moses.

11. And that the whole range of the doctrine of the apostles proclaimed one and the same God, who removed Abraham, who made to him the promise of inheritance, who in due season gave to him the covenant of circumcision, who called his descendants out of Egypt, preserved outwardly by circumcision — for he gave it as a sign, that they might not be like the Egyptians — that He was the Maker of all things, that He was the Father of our Lord Jesus Christ, that He was the God of glory, — they who wish may learn from the very words and acts of the apostles, and may contemplate the fact that this God is one, above whom is no other. But even if there were another god above Him, we should say, upon [instituting] a comparison of the quantity [of the work done by each], that the latter is superior to the former. For by deeds the better man appears, as I have already remarked ;[4] and, inasmuch as these men have no works of their father to adduce, the latter is shown to be God alone. But if any one, "doting about questions,"[5] do imagine that what the apostles have declared about God should be allegorized, let him consider my previous statements, in which I set forth one God as the Founder and Maker of all things, and destroyed and laid bare their allegations ; and he shall find them agreeable to the doctrine of the apostles, and so to maintain what they used to teach, and were persuaded of, that there is one God, the Maker of all things. And when he shall have divested his mind of such error, and of that blasphemy against God which it implies, he will of himself find reason to acknowledge that both the Mosaic law and the grace of the new covenant, as both fitted for the times [at which they were given], were bestowed by one and the same God for the benefit of the human race.

12. For all those who are of a perverse mind, having been set against the Mosaic legislation, judging it to be dissimilar and contrary to the doctrine of the Gospel, have not applied themselves to investigate the causes of the difference of each covenant. Since, therefore, they have been deserted by the paternal love, and puffed up by Satan, being brought over to the doctrine of Simon Magus, they have apostatized in their opinions from Him who is God, and imagined that they have themselves discovered more than the apostles, by finding out another god ; and [maintained] that the apostles preached the Gospel still somewhat under the influence of Jewish opinions, but that they themselves are purer [in doctrine], and more intelligent, than the apostles. Wherefore also Marcion and his followers have betaken themselves to mutilating the Scriptures, not acknowledging some books

---

[1] Deut. xxxii. 9.
[2] Acts xiv. 15-17.
[3] Acts vii. 2-8.

[4] Book ii. ch. xxx. 2.
[5] 1 Tim. vi. 4.

at all; and, curtailing the Gospel according to Luke and the Epistles of Paul, they assert that these are alone authentic, which they have themselves thus shortened. In another work,[1] however, I shall, God granting [me strength], refute them out of these which they still retain. But all the rest, inflated with the false name of "knowledge," do certainly recognise the Scriptures; but they pervert the interpretations, as I have shown in the first book. And, indeed, the followers of Marcion do directly blaspheme the Creator, alleging him to be the creator of evils, [but] holding a more tolerable[2] theory as to his origin, [and] maintaining that there are two beings, gods by nature, differing from each other, —the one being good, but the other evil. Those from Valentinus, however, while they employ names of a more honourable kind, and set forth that He who is Creator is both Father, and Lord, and God, do [nevertheless] render their theory or sect more plasphemous, by maintaining that He was not produced from any one of those Æons within the Pleroma, but from that defect which had been expelled beyond the Pleroma. Ignorance of the Scriptures and of the dispensation of God has brought all these things upon them. And in the course of this work I shall touch upon the cause of the difference of the covenants on the one hand, and, on the other hand, of their unity and harmony.

13. But that both the apostles and their disciples thus taught as the Church preaches, and thus teaching were perfected, wherefore also they were called away to that which is perfect— Stephen, teaching these truths, when he was yet on earth, saw the glory of God, and Jesus on His right hand, and exclaimed, "Behold, I see the heavens opened, and the Son of man standing on the right hand of God."[3] These words he said, and was stoned; and thus did he fulfil the perfect doctrine, copying in every respect the Leader of martyrdom, and praying for those who were slaying him, in these words: "Lord, lay not this sin to their charge." Thus were they perfected who knew one and the same God, who from beginning to end was present with mankind in the various dispensations; as the prophet Hosea declares: "I have filled up visions, and used similitudes by the hands of the prophets."[4] Those, therefore, who delivered up their souls to death for Christ's Gospel—how could they have spoken to men in accordance with old-established opinion? If this had been the course adopted by them, they should not have suffered; but inasmuch as they did preach things contrary to those persons who did not assent to the truth, for that reason they suffered. It is evident, therefore, that they did not relinquish the truth, but with all boldness preached to the Jews and Greeks. To the Jews, indeed, [they proclaimed] that the Jesus who was crucified by them was the Son of God, the Judge of quick and dead, and that He has received from His Father an eternal kingdom in Israel, as I have pointed out; but to the Greeks they preached one God, who made all things, and Jesus Christ His Son.

14. This is shown in a still clearer light from the letter of the apostles, which they forwarded neither to the Jews nor to the Greeks, but to those who from the Gentiles believed in Christ, confirming their faith. For when certain men had come down from Judea to Antioch—where also, first of all, the Lord's disciples were called Christians, because of their faith in Christ—and sought to persuade those who had believed on the Lord to be circumcised, and to perform other things after the observance of the law; and when Paul and Barnabas had gone up to Jerusalem to the apostles on account of this question, and the whole Church had convened together, Peter thus addressed them: "Men, brethren, ye know how that from the days of old God made choice among you, that the Gentiles by my mouth should hear the word of the Gospel, and believe. And God, the Searcher of the heart, bare them witness, giving them the Holy Ghost, even as to us; and put no difference between us and them, purifying their hearts by faith. Now therefore why tempt ye God, to impose a yoke upon the neck of the disciples, which neither our fathers nor we were able to bear? But we believe that, through the grace of our Lord Jesus Christ, we are to be saved, even as they."[5] After him James spoke as follows: "Men, brethren, Simon hath declared how God did purpose to take from among the Gentiles a people for His name. And thus[6] do the words of the prophets agree, as it is written, After this I will return, and will build again the tabernacle of David, which is fallen down; and I will build the ruins thereof, and I will set it up: that the residue of men may seek after the Lord, and all the Gentiles, among whom my name has been invoked, saith the Lord, doing these things.[7] Known from eternity is His work to God. Wherefore I for my part give judgment, that we trouble not them who from among the Gentiles are turned to God: but that it be enjoined them, that they

---

[1] No reference is made to this promised work in the writings of his successors. Probably it never was undertaken.
[2] Most of the mss. read "intolerabiliorem," but one reads as above, and is followed by all the editors.
[3] Acts vii. 56.
[4] Hos. xii. 10.

[5] Acts xv. 15, etc.
[6] Irenæus manifestly read οὕτως for τούτῳ, and in this he agrees with Codex Bezæ. We may remark, once for all, that in the variations from the received text of the New Testament which occur in our author, his quotations are very often in accordance with the readings of the Cambridge ms.
[7] Amos ix. 11, 12.

do abstain from the vanities of idols, and from fornication, and from blood ; and whatsoever [1] they wish not to be done to themselves, let them not do to others." [2] And when these things had been said, and all had given their consent, they wrote to them after this manner : " The apostles, and the presbyters, [and] the brethren, unto those brethren from among the Gentiles who are in Antioch, and Syria, and Cilicia, greeting : Forasmuch as we have heard that certain persons going out from us have troubled you with words, subverting your souls, saying, Ye must be circumcised, and keep the law ; to whom we gave no such commandment : it seemed good unto us, being assembled with one accord, to send chosen men unto you with our beloved Barnabas and Paul ; men who have delivered up their soul for the name of our Lord Jesus Christ. We have sent therefore Judas and Silas, that they may declare our opinion by word of mouth. For it seemed good to the Holy Ghost, and to us, to lay upon you no greater burden than these necessary things ; that ye abstain from meats offered to idols, and from blood, and from fornication ; and whatsoever ye do not wish to be done to you, do not ye to others : from which preserving yourselves, ye shall do well, walking [3] in the Holy Spirit." From all these passages, then, it is evident that they did not teach the existence of another Father, but gave the new covenant of liberty to those who had lately believed in God by the Holy Spirit. But they clearly indicated, from the nature of the point debated by them, as to whether or not it were still necessary to circumcise the disciples, that they had no idea of another god.

15. Neither [in that case] would they have had such a terror with regard to the first covenant, as not even to have been willing to eat with the Gentiles. For even Peter, although he had been sent to instruct them, and had been constrained by a vision to that effect, spake nevertheless with not a little hesitation, saying to them : "Ye know how it is an unlawful thing for a man that is a Jew to keep company with, or to come unto, one of another nation ; but God hath shown me that I should not call any man common or unclean. Therefore came I without gainsaying ; " [4] indicating by these words, that he would not have come to them unless he had been commanded. Neither, for a like reason, would he have given them baptism so readily, had he not heard them prophesying when the Holy Ghost rested upon them. And therefore did he exclaim, " Can any man forbid water, that these should not be baptized, who have received the Holy Ghost as well as we ? " [5] He persuaded, at the same time, those that were with him, and pointed out that, unless the Holy Ghost had rested upon them, there might have been some one who would have raised objections to their baptism. And the apostles who were with James allowed the Gentiles to act freely, yielding us up to the Spirit of God. But they themselves, while knowing the same God, continued in the ancient observances ; so that even Peter, fearing also lest he might incur their reproof, although formerly eating with the Gentiles, because of the vision, and of the Spirit who had rested upon them, yet, when certain persons came from James, withdrew himself, and did not eat with them. And Paul said that Barnabas likewise did the same thing.[6] Thus did the apostles, whom the Lord made witnesses of every action and of every doctrine — for upon all occasions do we find Peter, and James, and John present with Him — scrupulously act according to the dispensation of the Mosaic law, showing that it was from one and the same God ; which they certainly never would have done, as I have already said, if they had learned from the Lord [that there existed] another Father besides Him who appointed the dispensation of the law.

CHAP. XIII — REFUTATION OF THE OPINION, THAT PAUL WAS THE ONLY APOSTLE WHO HAD KNOWLEDGE OF THE TRUTH.

1. With regard to those (the Marcionites) who allege that Paul alone knew the truth, and that to him the mystery was manifested by revelation, let Paul himself convict them, when he says, that one and the same God wrought in Peter for the apostolate of the circumcision, and in himself for the Gentiles.[7] Peter, therefore, was an apostle of that very God whose was also Paul ; and Him whom Peter preached as God among those of the circumcision, and likewise the Son of God, did Paul [declare] also among the Gentiles. For our Lord never came to save Paul alone, nor is God so limited in means, that He should have but one apostle who knew the dispensation of His Son. And again, when Paul says, " How beautiful are the feet of those bringing glad tidings of good things, and preaching the Gospel of peace," [8] he shows clearly that it was not merely one, but there were many who used to preach the truth. And again, in the Epistle to the Corinthians, when he had recounted all those who had seen God [9] after the resurrection, he

---

[1] This addition is also found in Codex Bezæ, and in Cyprian and others.
[2] Acts xv. 14, etc.
[3] Another addition, also found in the Codex Bezæ, and in Tertullian.
[4] Acts x. 28, 29.

[5] Acts x. 47.
[6] Gal. ii. 12, 13.
[7] Gal. ii. 8.
[8] Rom. x. 15; Isa. lii. 7.
[9] All the previous editors accept the reading Deum without remark, but Harvey argues that it must be regarded as a mistake for Dominum. He scarcely seems, however, to give sufficient weight to the quotation which immediately follows.

says in continuation, "But whether it were I or they, so we preach, and so ye believed,"[1] acknowledging as one and the same, the preaching of all those who saw God[2] after the resurrection from the dead.

2. And again, the Lord replied to Philip, who wished to behold the Father, "Have I been so long a time with you, and yet thou hast not known Me, Philip? He that sees Me, sees also the Father; and how sayest thou then, Show us the Father? For I am in the Father, and the Father in Me; and henceforth ye know Him, and have seen Him."[3] To these men, therefore, did the Lord bear witness, that in Himself they had both known and seen the Father (and the Father is truth). To allege, then, that these men did not know the truth, is to act the part of false witnesses, and of those who have been alienated from the doctrine of Christ. For why did the Lord send the twelve apostles to the lost sheep of the house of Israel,[4] if these men did not know the truth? How also did the seventy preach, unless they had themselves previously known the truth of what was preached? Or how could Peter have been in ignorance, to whom the Lord gave testimony, that flesh and blood had not revealed to him, but the Father, who is in heaven?[5] Just, then, as "Paul [was] an apostle, not of men, neither by man, but by Jesus Christ, and God the Father,"[6] [so with the rest;][7] the Son indeed leading them to the Father, but the Father revealing to them the Son.

3. But that Paul acceded to [the request of] those who summoned him to the apostles, on account of the question [which had been raised], and went up to them, with Barnabas, to Jerusalem, not without reason, but that the liberty of the Gentiles might be confirmed by them, he does himself say, in the Epistle to the Galatians: "Then, fourteen years after, I went up again to Jerusalem with Barnabas, taking also Titus. But I went up by revelation, and communicated to them that Gospel which I preached among the Gentiles."[8] And again he says, "For an hour we did give place to subjection,[9] that the truth of the gospel might continue with you." If, then, any one shall, from the Acts of the Apostles, carefully scrutinize the time concerning which it is written that he went up to Jerusalem on account of the forementioned question, he will find those years mentioned by Paul coinciding with it. Thus the statement of Paul harmonizes with, and is, as it were, identical with, the testimony of Luke regarding the apostles.

CHAP. XIV. — IF PAUL HAD KNOWN ANY MYSTERIES UNREVEALED TO THE OTHER APOSTLES, LUKE, HIS CONSTANT COMPANION AND FELLOW-TRAVELLER, COULD NOT HAVE BEEN IGNORANT OF THEM; NEITHER COULD THE TRUTH HAVE POSSIBLY LAIN HID FROM HIM, THROUGH WHOM ALONE WE LEARN MANY AND MOST IMPORTANT PARTICULARS OF THE GOSPEL HISTORY.

1. But that this Luke was inseparable from Paul, and his fellow-labourer in the Gospel, he himself clearly evinces, not as a matter of boasting, but as bound to do so by the truth itself. For he says that when Barnabas, and John who was called Mark, had parted company from Paul, and sailed to Cyprus, "we came to Troas;"[10] and when Paul had beheld in a dream a man of Macedonia, saying, "Come into Macedonia, Paul, and help us," "immediately," he says, "we endeavoured to go into Macedonia, understanding that the Lord had called us to preach the Gospel unto them. Therefore, sailing from Troas, we directed our ship's course towards Samothracia." And then he carefully indicates all the rest of their journey as far as Philippi, and how they delivered their first address: "for, sitting down," he says, "we spake unto the women who had assembled;"[11] and certain believed, even a great many. And again does he say, "But we sailed from Philippi after the days of unleavened bread, and came to Troas, where we abode seven days."[12] And all the remaining [details] of his course with Paul he recounts, indicating with all diligence both places, and cities, and number of days, until they went up to Jerusalem; and what befell Paul there,[13] how he was sent to Rome in bonds; the name of the centurion who took him in charge;[14] and the signs of the ships, and how they made shipwreck;[15] and the island upon which they escaped, and how they received kindness there, Paul healing the chief man of that island; and how they sailed from thence to Puteoli, and from that arrived at Rome; and for what period they sojourned at Rome. As Luke was present at all these occurrences, he carefully noted them down in writing, so that he cannot be convicted of falsehood or boastfulness, because all these [particulars] proved both that he was senior to all those who now teach otherwise, and that he was not ignorant of the truth. That he

---

[1] 1 Cor. xv. 11.
[2] See note 9, p. 436.
[3] John xiv. 7, 9, 10.
[4] Matt. x. 6.
[5] Matt. xvi. 17.
[6] Gal. i. 1.
[7] Some such supplement seems necessary, as Grabe suggests, though Harvey contends that no apodosis is requisite.
[8] Gal. ii. 1, 2.
[9] Latin, "Ad horam cessimus subjectioni" (Gal. ii. 5). Irenæus gives it an altogether different meaning from that which it has in the received text. Jerome says that there was as much variation in the copies of Scripture in his day with regard to the passage, — some retaining, others rejecting the negative. Tertullian argues for the removal of the negative (Adv. Marc. v. 3).

[10] Acts xvi. 8, etc.
[11] Acts xvi. 13.
[12] Acts xx. 5, 6.
[13] Acts xxi.
[14] Acts xxvii.
[15] Acts xxviii. 11.

was not merely a follower, but also a fellow-labourer of the apostles, but especially of Paul, Paul has himself declared also in the Epistles, saying: "Demas hath forsaken me, . . . and is departed unto Thessalonica; Crescens to Galatia, Titus to Dalmatia. Only Luke is with me."[1] From this he shows that he was always attached to and inseparable from him. And again he says, in the Epistle to the Colossians: "Luke, the beloved physician, greets you."[2] But surely if Luke, who always preached in company with Paul, and is called by him "the beloved," and with him performed the work of an evangelist, and was entrusted to hand down to us a Gospel, learned nothing different from him (Paul), as has been pointed out from his words, how can these men, who were never attached to Paul, boast that they have learned hidden and unspeakable mysteries?

2. But that Paul taught with simplicity what he knew, not only to those who were [employed] with him, but to those that heard him, he does himself make manifest. For when the bishops and presbyters who came from Ephesus and the other cities adjoining had assembled in Miletus, since he was himself hastening to Jerusalem to observe Pentecost, after testifying many things to them, and declaring what must happen to him at Jerusalem, he added: "I know that ye shall see my face no more. Therefore I take you to record this day, that I am pure from the blood of all. For I have not shunned to declare unto you all the counsel of God. Take heed, therefore, both to yourselves, and to all the flock over which the Holy Ghost has placed you as bishops, to rule the Church of the Lord,[3] which He has acquired for Himself through His own blood."[4] Then, referring to the evil teachers who should arise, he said: "I know that after my departure shall grievous wolves come to you, not sparing the flock. Also of your own selves shall men arise, speaking perverse things, to draw away disciples after them." "I have not shunned," he says, "to declare unto you all the counsel of God." Thus did the apostles simply, and without respect of persons, deliver to all what they had themselves learned from the Lord. Thus also does Luke, without respect of persons, deliver to us what he had learned from them, as he has himself testified, saying, "Even as they delivered them unto us, who from the beginning were eye-witnesses and ministers of the Word."[5]

3. Now if any man set Luke aside, as one who did not know the truth, he will, [by so acting,]

manifestly reject that Gospel of which he claims to be a disciple. For through him we have become acquainted with very many and important parts of the Gospel; for instance, the generation of John, the history of Zacharias, the coming of the angel to Mary, the exclamation of Elisabeth, the descent of the angels to the shepherds, the words spoken by them, the testimony of Anna and of Simeon with regard to Christ, and that at twelve years of age He was left behind at Jerusalem; also the baptism of John, the number of the Lord's years when He was baptized, and that this occurred in the fifteenth year of Tiberius Cæsar. And in His office of teacher this is what He has said to the rich: "Woe unto you that are rich, for ye have received your consolation;"[6] and, "Woe unto you that are full, for ye shall hunger; and ye who laugh now, for ye shall weep;" and, "Woe unto you when all men shall speak well of you: for so did your fathers to the false prophets." All things of the following kind we have known through Luke alone (and numerous actions of the Lord we have learned through him, which also all [the Evangelists] notice): the multitude of fishes which Peter's companions enclosed, when at the Lord's command they cast the nets;[7] the woman who had suffered for eighteen years, and was healed on the Sabbath-day;[8] the man who had the dropsy, whom the Lord made whole on the Sabbath, and how He did defend Himself for having performed an act of healing on that day; how He taught His disciples not to aspire to the uppermost rooms; how we should invite the poor and feeble, who cannot recompense us; the man who knocked during the night to obtain loaves, and did obtain them, because of the urgency of his importunity;[9] how, when [our Lord] was sitting at meat with a Pharisee, a woman that was a sinner kissed His feet, and anointed them with ointment, with what the Lord said to Simon on her behalf concerning the two debtors;[10] also about the parable of that rich man who stored up the goods which had accrued to him, to whom it was also said, "In this night they shall demand thy soul from thee; whose then shall those things bew hich thou hast prepared?"[11] and similar to this, that of the rich man, who was clothed in purple and who fared sumptuously, and the indigent Lazarus;[12] also the answer which He gave to His disciples when they said, "Increase our faith;"[13] also His conversation with Zaccheus the publican;[14] also about

---

[1] 2 Tim. iv. 10, 11.
[2] Col. iv. 14.
[3] In this very important passage of Scripture, Irenæus manifestly read Κυρίου instead of Θεοῦ, which is found in *text. rec.* The Codex Bezæ has the same reading; but all the other most ancient MSS. agree with the received text.
[4] Acts xx. 25, etc.
[5] Luke i. 2.

[6] Luke vi. 24, etc.
[7] Luke v.
[8] Luke xiii.
[9] Luke xi.
[10] Luke vii.
[11] Luke xii. 20.
[12] Luke xvi.
[13] Luke xvii. 5.
[14] Luke xix.

the Pharisee and the publican, who were praying in the temple at the same time;[1] also the ten lepers, whom He cleansed in the way simultaneously;[2] also how He ordered the lame and the blind to be gathered to the wedding from the lanes and streets;[3] also the parable of the judge who feared not God, whom the widow's importunity led to avenge her cause;[4] and about the fig-tree in the vineyard which produced no fruit. There are also many other particulars to be found mentioned by Luke alone, which are made use of by both Marcion and Valentinus. And besides all these, [he records] what [Christ] said to His disciples in the way, after* the resurrection, and how they recognised Him in the breaking of bread.[5]

4. It follows then, as of course, that these men must either receive the rest of his narrative, or else reject these parts also. For no persons of common sense can permit them to receive some things recounted by Luke as being true, and to set others aside, as if he had not known the truth. And if indeed Marcion's followers reject these, they will then possess no Gospel; for, curtailing that according to Luke, as I have said already, they boast in having the Gospel [in what remains]. But the followers of Valentinus must give up their utterly vain talk; for they have taken from that [Gospel] many occasions for their own speculations, to put an evil interpretation upon what he has well said. If, on the other hand, they feel compelled to receive the remaining portions also, then, by studying the perfect Gospel, and the doctrine of the apostles, they will find it necessary to repent, that they may be saved from the danger [to which they are exposed].

CHAP. XV.—REFUTATION OF THE EBIONITES, WHO DISPARAGED THE AUTHORITY OF ST. PAUL, FROM THE WRITINGS OF ST. LUKE, WHICH MUST BE RECEIVED AS A WHOLE. EXPOSURE OF THE HYPOCRISY, DECEIT, AND PRIDE OF THE GNOSTICS. THE APOSTLES AND THEIR DISCIPLES KNEW AND PREACHED ONE GOD, THE CREATOR OF THE WORLD.

1. But again, we allege the same against those who do not recognise Paul as an apostle: that they should either reject the other words of the Gospel which we have come to know through Luke alone, and not make use of them; or else, if they do receive all these, they must necessarily admit also that testimony concerning Paul, when he (Luke) tells us that the Lord spoke at first to him from heaven: "Saul, Saul, why persecutest thou Me? I am Jesus Christ, whom thou per-secutest;"[6] and then to Ananias, saying regarding him: "Go thy way; for he is a chosen vessel unto Me, to bear My name among the Gentiles, and kings, and the children of Israel. For I will show him, from this time, how great things he must suffer for My name's sake."[7] Those, therefore, who do not accept of him [as a teacher], who was chosen by God for this purpose, that he might boldly bear His name, as being sent to the forementioned nations, do despise the election of God, and separate themselves from the company of the apostles. For neither can they contend that Paul was no apostle, when he was chosen for this purpose; nor can they prove Luke guilty of falsehood, when he proclaims the truth to us with all diligence. It may be, indeed, that it was with this view that God set forth very many Gospel truths, through Luke's instrumentality, which all should esteem it necessary to use, in order that all persons, following his subsequent testimony, which treats upon the acts and the doctrine of the apostles, and holding the unadulterated rule of truth, may be saved. His testimony, therefore, is true, and the doctrine of the apostles is open and stedfast, holding nothing in reserve; nor did they teach one set of doctrines in private, and another in public.

2. For this is the subterfuge of false persons, evil seducers, and hypocrites, as they act who are from Valentinus. These men discourse to the multitude about those who belong to the Church, whom they do themselves term "vulgar," and "ecclesiastic."[8] By these words they entrap the more simple, and entice them, imitating our phraseology, that these [dupes] may listen to them the oftener; and then these are asked[9] regarding us, how it is, that when they hold doctrines similar to ours, we, without cause, keep ourselves aloof from their company; and [how it is, that] when they say the same things, and hold the same doctrine, we call them heretics? When they have thus, by means of questions, overthrown the faith of any, and rendered them uncontradicting hearers of their own, they describe to them in private the unspeakable mystery of their Pleroma. But they are altogether deceived, who imagine that they may learn from the Scriptural texts adduced by heretics, that [doctrine] which their words plausibly teach.[10] For error is plausible, and bears a re-

---

[6] Acts xxii. 8, xxvi. 15.
[7] Acts ix. 15, 16.
[8] Latin, "communes et ecclesiasticos:" καθολικούς is translated here "communes," as for some time after the word *catholicus* had not been added to the Latin language in its ecclesiastical sense. [The Roman Creed was remarkable for its omission of the word *Catholic*. See Bingham, *Antiquities*, book x. cap. iv. sect. 11.]
[9] We here follow the text of Harvey, who prints, without remark, *quæruntur*, instead of *queruntur*, as in Migne's edition.
[10] Such is the sense educed by Harvey from the old Latin version, which thus runs: "Decipiuntur autem omnes, qui quod est in verbis verisimile, se putant posse discere a veritate." For "omnes" he would read "omnino," and he discards the emendation proposed by the former editors, viz., "discernere" for "discere."

---

[1] Luke xviii.
[2] Luke xvii.
[3] Luke xviii.
[4] Luke xiii.
[5] Luke xxiv.

semblance to the truth, but requires to be disguised; while truth is without disguise, and therefore has been entrusted to children. And if any one of their auditors do indeed demand explanations, or start objections to them, they affirm that he is one not capable of receiving the truth, and not having from above the seed [derived] from their Mother; and thus really give him no reply, but simply declare that he is of the intermediate regions, that is, belongs to animal natures. But if any one do yield himself up to them like a little sheep, and follows out their practice, and their "redemption," such an one is puffed up to such an extent, that he thinks he is neither in heaven nor on earth, but that he has passed within the Pleroma; and having already embraced his angel, he walks with a strutting gait and a supercilious countenance, possessing all the pompous air of a cock. There are those among them who assert that that man who comes from above ought to follow a good course of conduct; wherefore they do also pretend a gravity [of demeanour] with a certain superciliousness. The majority, however, having become scoffers also, as if already perfect, and living without regard [to appearances], yea, in contempt [of that which is good], call themselves "the spiritual," and allege that they have already become acquainted with that place of refreshing which is within their Pleroma.

3. But let us revert to the same line of argument [hitherto pursued]. For when it has been manifestly declared, that they who were the preachers of the truth and the apostles of liberty termed no one else God, or named him Lord, except the only true God the Father, and His Word, who has the pre-eminence in all things; it shall then be clearly proved, that they (the apostles) confessed as the Lord God Him who was the Creator of heaven and earth, who also spoke with Moses, gave to him the dispensation of the law, and who called the fathers; and that they knew no other. The opinion of the apostles, therefore, and of those (Mark and Luke) who learned from their words, concerning God, has been made manifest.

CHAP. XVI. — PROOFS FROM THE APOSTOLIC WRITINGS, THAT JESUS CHRIST WAS ONE AND THE SAME, THE ONLY BEGOTTEN SON OF GOD, PERFECT GOD AND PERFECT MAN.

1. But [1] there are some who say that Jesus was merely a receptacle of Christ, upon whom the Christ, as a dove, descended from above, and that when He had declared the unnameable Father He entered into the Pleroma in an incomprehensible and invisible manner: for that He was not comprehended, not only by men, but not even by those powers and virtues which are in heaven, and that Jesus was the Son, but that [2] Christ was the Father, and the Father of Christ, God; while others say that He merely suffered in outward appearance, being naturally impassible. The Valentinians, again, maintain that the dispensational Jesus was the same who passed through Mary, upon whom that Saviour from the more exalted [region] descended, who was also termed *Pan*,[3] because He possessed the names (*vocabula*) of all those who had produced Him; but that [this latter] shared with Him, the dispensational one, His power and His name; so that by His means death was abolished, but the Father was made known by that Saviour who had descended from above, whom they do also allege to be Himself the receptacle of Christ and of the entire Pleroma; confessing, indeed, in tongue one Christ Jesus, but being divided in [actual] opinion: for, as I have already observed, it is the practice of these men to say that there was one Christ, who was produced by Monogenes, for the confirmation of the Pleroma; but that another, the Saviour, was sent [forth] for the glorification of the Father; and yet another, the dispensational one, and whom they represent as having suffered, who also bore [in himself] Christ, that Saviour who returned into the Pleroma. I judge it necessary therefore to take into account the entire mind of the apostles regarding our Lord Jesus Christ, and to show that not only did they never hold any such opinions regarding Him; but, still further, that they announced through the Holy Spirit, that those who should teach such doctrines were agents of Satan, sent forth for the purpose of overturning the faith of some, and drawing them away from life.

2. That John knew the one and the same Word of God, and that He was the only begotten, and that He became incarnate for our salvation, Jesus Christ our Lord, I have sufficiently proved from the word of John himself. And Matthew, too, recognising one and the same Jesus Christ, exhibiting his generation as a man from the Virgin,[4] even as God did promise David that He would raise up from the fruit of his body an eternal King, having made the same promise to Abraham a long time previously, says: "The book of the generation of Jesus Christ, the son of David, the son of Abraham."[5] Then, that he might free our mind from suspicion regarding Joseph, he says: "But the birth of Christ[6] was on this

---

[2] See book i. 12, 4.
[3] The Latin text has "Christum," which is supposed to be an erroneous reading. See also book ii. c. xii. s. 6.
[4] Ps. cxxxii. 11.
[5] Matt. i. 1.
[6] Matt. i. 18. It is to be observed that Irenæus here reads *Christ* instead of *Jesus Christ*, as in *text. rec.*, thus agreeing with the reading of the Vulgate in the passage.

[1] We here omit *since*, and insert *therefore* afterwards, to avoid the extreme length of the sentence as it stands in the Latin version. The apodosis does not occur till the words, "I judge it necessary," are reached.

wise. When His mother was espoused to Joseph, before they came together, she was found with child of the Holy Ghost." Then, when Joseph had it in contemplation to put Mary away, since she proved with child, [Matthew tells us of] the angel of God standing by him, and saying: "Fear not to take unto thee Mary thy wife: for that which is conceived in her is of the Holy Ghost. And she shall bring forth a son, and thou shalt call His name Jesus; for He shall save His people from their sins. Now this was done, that it might be fulfilled which was spoken of the Lord by the prophet: Behold, a virgin shall conceive, and bring forth a son, and they shall call His name Emmanuel, which is, God with us;" clearly signifying that both the promise made to the fathers had been accomplished, that the Son of God was born of a virgin, and that He Himself was Christ the Saviour whom the prophets had foretold; not, as these men assert, that Jesus was He who was born of Mary, but that Christ was He who descended from above. Matthew might certainly have said, "Now the birth of *Jesus* was on this wise;" but the Holy Ghost, foreseeing the corrupters [of the truth], and guarding by anticipation against their deceit, says by Matthew, "But the birth of *Christ* was on this wise;" and that He is Emmanuel, lest perchance we might consider Him as a mere man: for "not by the will of the flesh, nor by the will of man, but by the will of God, was the Word made flesh;"[1] and that we should not imagine that Jesus was one, and Christ another, but should know them to be one and the same.

3. Paul, when writing to the Romans, has explained this very point: "Paul, an apostle of Jesus Christ, predestinated unto the Gospel of God, which He had promised by His prophets in the holy Scriptures, concerning His Son, who was made to Him of the seed of David according to the flesh, who was predestinated the Son of God with power through the Spirit of holiness, by the resurrection from the dead of our Lord Jesus Christ."[2] And again, writing to the Romans about Israel, he says: "Whose are the fathers, and from whom is Christ according to the flesh, who is God over all, blessed for ever."[3] And again, in his Epistle to the Galatians, he says: "But when the fulness of time had come, God sent forth His Son, made of a woman, made under the law, to redeem them that were under the law, that we might receive the adoption;"[4] plainly indicating one God, who did by

the prophets make promise of the Son, and one Jesus Christ our Lord, who was of the seed of David according to His birth from Mary; and that Jesus Christ was appointed the Son of God with power, according to the Spirit of holiness, by the resurrection from the dead, as being the first begotten in all the creation;[5] the Son of God being made the Son of man, that through Him we may receive the adoption, — humanity[6] sustaining, and receiving, and embracing the Son of God. Wherefore Mark also says: "The beginning of the Gospel of Jesus Christ, the Son of God; as it is written in the prophets."[7] Knowing one and the same Son of God, Jesus Christ, who was announced by the prophets, who from the fruit of David's body was Emmanuel, "the messenger of great counsel of the Father;"[8] through whom God caused the day-spring and the Just One to arise to the house of David, and raised up for him an horn of salvation, "and established a testimony in Jacob;"[9] as David says when discoursing on the causes of His birth: "And He appointed a law in Israel, that another generation might know [Him,] the children which should be born from these, and they arising shall themselves declare to their children, so that they might set their hope in God, and seek after His commandments."[10] And again, the angel said, when bringing good tidings to Mary: "He shall be great, and shall be called the Son of the Highest; and the Lord shall give unto Him the throne of His father David;"[11] acknowledging that He who is the Son of the Highest, the same is Himself also the Son of David. And David, knowing by the Spirit the dispensation of the advent of this Person, by which He is supreme over all the living and dead, confessed Him as Lord, sitting on the right hand of the Most High Father.[12]

4. But Simeon also — he who had received an intimation from the Holy Ghost that he should not see death, until first he had beheld Christ Jesus — taking Him, the first-begotten of the Virgin, into his hands, blessed God, and said, "Lord, now lettest Thou Thy servant depart in peace, according to Thy word: because mine eyes have seen Thy salvation, which Thou hast prepared before the face of all people; a light to lighten the Gentiles, and the glory of Thy people Israel;"[13] confessing thus, that the infant whom he was holding in his hands, Jesus, born of Mary, was Christ Himself, the Son of God, the light of all, the glory of Israel itself,

---

[1] John i. 13, 14. From this, and also a quotation of the same passage in chap. xix. of this book, it appears that Irenæus must have read ὃς . . . ἐγεννήθη here, and not οἳ . . . ἐγεννήθησαν. Tertullian quotes the verse to the same effect (*Lib. de Carne Christi*, cap. 19 and 24).
[2] Rom. i. 1–4.
[3] Rom. ix. 5.
[4] Gal. iv. 4, 5.

[5] Col. i. 14, 15.
[6] "Homine."
[7] Mark i. 1.
[8] Isa. ix. 6 (LXX.).
[9] Luke ix. 69.
[10] Ps. lxxviii. 5.
[11] Luke i. 32.
[12] Ps. cx. 1.
[13] Luke ii. 29.

and the peace and refreshing of those who had fallen asleep. For He was already despoiling men, by removing their ignorance, conferring upon them His own knowledge, and scattering abroad those who recognised Him, as Esaias says: "Call His name, Quickly spoil, Rapidly divide." [1] Now these are the works of Christ. He therefore was Himself Christ, whom Simeon carrying [in his arms] blessed the Most High; on beholding whom the shepherds glorified God; whom John, while yet in his mother's womb, and He (Christ) in that of Mary, recognising as the Lord, saluted with leaping; whom the Magi, when they had seen, adored, and offered their gifts [to Him], as I have already stated, and prostrated themselves to the eternal King, departed by another way, not now returning by the way of the Assyrians. "For before the child shall have knowledge to cry, Father or mother, He shall receive the power of Damascus, and the spoils of Samaria, against the king of the Assyrians;" [2] declaring, in a mysterious manner indeed, but emphatically, that the Lord did fight with a hidden hand against Amalek. [3] For this cause, too, He suddenly removed those children belonging to the house of David, whose happy lot it was to have been born at that time, that He might send them on before into His kingdom; He, since He was Himself an infant, so arranging it that human infants should be martyrs, slain, according to the Scriptures, for the sake of Christ, who was born in Bethlehem of Judah, in the city of David. [4]

5. Therefore did the Lord also say to His disciples after the resurrection, "O thoughtless ones, and slow of heart to believe all that the prophets have spoken! Ought not Christ to have suffered these things, and to enter into His glory?" [5] And again does He say to them: "These are the words which I spake unto you while I was yet with you, that all things must be fulfilled which were written in the law of Moses, and in the prophets, and in the Psalms, concerning Me. Then opened He their understanding, that they should understand the Scriptures, and said unto them, Thus it is written, and thus it behoved Christ to suffer, and to rise again from the dead, and that repentance for the remission of sins be preached in His name among all nations." [6] Now this is He who was born of Mary; for He says: "The Son of man must suffer many things, and be rejected, and crucified, and on the third day rise again." [7] The Gospel, therefore, knew no other son of man but Him who was of Mary, who also suf-

fered; and no Christ who flew away from Jesus before the passion; but Him who was born it knew as Jesus Christ the Son of God, and that this same suffered and rose again, as John, the disciple of the Lord, verifies, saying: "But these are written, that ye might believe that Jesus is the Christ, the Son of God, and that believing ye might have eternal life in His name," [8] — foreseeing these blasphemous systems which divide the Lord, as far as lies in their power, saying that He was formed of two different substances. For this reason also he has thus testified to us in his Epistle: "Little children, it is the last time; and as ye have heard that Antichrist doth come, now have many antichrists appeared; whereby we know that it is the last time. They went out from us, but they were not of us; for if they had been of us, they would have continued with us: but [they departed], that they might be made manifest that they are not of us. Know ye therefore, that every lie is from without, and is not of the truth. Who is a liar, but he that denieth that Jesus is the Christ? This is Antichrist." [9]

6. But inasmuch as all those before mentioned, although they certainly do with their tongue confess one Jesus Christ, make fools of themselves, thinking one thing and saying another; [10] for their hypotheses vary, as I have already shown, alleging, [as they do,] that one Being suffered and was born, and that this was Jesus; but that there was another who descended upon Him, and that this was Christ, who also ascended again; and they argue, that he who proceeded from the Demiurge, or he who was dispensational, or he who sprang from Joseph, was the Being subject to suffering; but upon the latter there descended from the invisible and ineffable [places] the former, whom they assert to be incomprehensible, invisible, and impassible: they thus wander from the truth, because their doctrine departs from Him who is truly God, being ignorant that His only-begotten Word, who is always present with the human race, united to and mingled with His own creation, according to the Father's pleasure, and who became flesh, is Himself Jesus Christ our Lord, who did also suffer for us, and rose again on our behalf, and who will come again in the glory of His Father, to raise up all flesh, and for the manifestation of salvation, and to apply the rule of just judgment to all who were made by Him. There is therefore, as I have pointed out, one God the Father, and one Christ Jesus, who came by means of the whole dispensational arrangements [connected with Him], and gath-

---

[1] Isa. viii. 3.
[2] Isa. viii. 4.
[3] Ex. xvii. 16 (LXX.).
[4] Matt. ii. 16.
[5] Luke xxiv. 25.
[6] Luke xxiv. 44, etc.
[7] Mark viii. 31 and Luke ix. 22.

[8] John xx. 31.
[9] 1 John ii. 18, etc., loosely quoted.
[10] The text here followed is that of two Syriac MSS., which prove the loss of several consecutive words in the old Latin version, and clear up the meaning of a confused sentence, showing that the word "autem" is here, as it probably is elsewhere, merely a contraction for "aut eum."

ered together all things in Himself.[1] But in every respect, too, He is man, the formation of God; and thus He took up man into Himself, the invisible becoming visible, the incomprehen-.sible being made comprehensible, the impassible becoming capable of suffering, and the Word being made man, thus summing up all things in Himself: so that as in super-celestial, spiritual, and invisible things, the Word of God is supreme, so also in things visible and corporeal He might possess the supremacy, and, taking to Himself the pre-eminence, as well as constituting Himself Head of the Church, He might draw all things to Himself at the proper time.

7. With Him is nothing incomplete or out of due season, just as with the Father there is nothing incongruous. For all these things were foreknown by the Father; but the Son works them out at the proper time in perfect order and sequence. This was the reason why, when Mary was urging [Him] on to [perform] the wonderful miracle of the wine, and was desirous before the time to partake[2] of the cup of emblematic significance, the Lord, checking her untimely haste, said, "Woman, what have I to do with thee? mine hour is not yet come "[3] — waiting for that hour which was foreknown by the Father. This is also the reason why, when men were often desirous to take Him, it is said, "No man laid hands upon Him, for the hour of His being taken was not yet come; "[4] nor the time of His passion, which had been foreknown by the Father; as also says the prophet Habakkuk, " By this Thou shalt be known when the years have drawn nigh; Thou shalt be set forth when the time comes; because my soul is disturbed by anger, Thou shalt remember Thy mercy."[5] Paul also says: " But when the fulness of time came, God sent forth His Son."[6] By which is made manifest, that all things which had been foreknown of the Father, our Lord did accomplish in their order, season, and hour, foreknown and fitting, being indeed one and the same, but rich and great. For He fulfils the bountiful and comprehensive will of His Father, inasmuch as He is Himself the Saviour of those who are saved, and the Lord of those who are under authority, and the God of all those things which have been formed, the only-begotten of the Father, Christ who was announced, and the Word of God, who became incarnate when the fulness of time had come, at which the Son of God had to become the Son of man.

8. All, therefore, are outside of the [Christian] dispensation, who, under pretext of knowledge, understand that Jesus was one, and Christ another, and the Only-begotten another, from whom again is the Word, and that the Saviour is another, whom these disciples of error allege to be a production of those who were made Æons in a state of degeneracy. Such men are to outward appearance sheep; for they appear to be like us, by what they say in public, repeating the same words as we do; but inwardly they are wolves. Their doctrine is homicidal, conjuring up, as it does, a number of gods, and simulating many Fathers, but lowering and dividing the Son of God in many ways. These are they against whom the Lord has cautioned us beforehand; and His disciple, in his Epistle already mentioned, commands us to avoid them, when he says: " For many deceivers are entered into the world, who confess not that Jesus Christ is come in the flesh. This is a deceiver and an antichrist. Take heed to them, that ye lose not what ye have wrought."[7] And again does he say in the Epistle: " Many false prophets are gone out into the world. Hereby know ye the Spirit of God: Every spirit that confesseth that Jesus Christ is come in the flesh is of God; and every spirit which separates Jesus Christ is not of God, but is antichrist."[8] These words agree with what was said in the Gospel, that " the Word was made flesh, and dwelt among us." Wherefore he again exclaims in his Epistle, " Every one that believeth that Jesus is the Christ, has been born of God; "[9] knowing Jesus Christ to be one and the same, to whom the gates of heaven were opened, because of His taking upon Him flesh: who shall also come in the same flesh in which He suffered, revealing the glory of the Father.

9. Concurring with these statements, Paul, speaking to the Romans, declares: " Much more they who receive abundance of grace and righteousness for [eternal] life, shall reign by one, Christ Jesus."[10] It follows from this, that he knew nothing of that Christ who flew away from Jesus; nor did he of the Saviour above, whom they hold to be impassible. For if, in

---

[1] Eph. i. 10.
[2] " Participare compendii poculo," i e., the cup which *recapitulates* the suffering of Christ, and which, as Harvey thinks, refers to the symbolical character of the cup of the Eucharist, as setting forth the passion of Christ.
[3] John ii. 4.
[4] John vii. 30.
[5] Hab. iii. 2.
[6] Gal. iv. 4.

[7] 2 John, 7, 8. Irenæus seems to have read αὐτούς instead of ἑαυτούς, as in the received text.
[8] 1 John iv. 1, 2. This is a material difference from the received text of the passage: " Every spirit that confesseth not that Jesus Christ is come in the flesh." The Vulgate translation and Origen agree with Irenæus, and Tertullian seems to recognise both readings (*Adv. Marc.*, v. 16). Socrates tells us (vii. 32, p. 381) that the passage had been corrupted by those who wished to separate the humanity of Christ from His divinity, and that the old copies read, πᾶν πνεῦμα ὃ λύει τὸν Ἰησοῦν ἀπὸ τοῦ Θεοῦ οὐκ ἔστι, which exactly agrees with Origen's quotation, and very nearly with that of Irenæus, now before us. Polycarp (*Ep.*, c. vii.) seems to allude to the passage as we have it now, and so does Ignatius (*Ep. Smyr.*, c. v.) See the question discussed by Burton, in his *Ante-Nicene Testimonies* [*to the Div. of Christ.* Another work of Burton has a similar name. See British Critic, vol. ii. (of 1827), p. 265].
[9] 1 John v. 1.
[10] Rom. v. 17.

truth, the one suffered, and the other remained incapable of suffering, and the one was born, but the other descended upon him who was born, and left him again, it is not one, but two, that are shown forth. But that the apostle did know Him as one, both who was born and who suffered, namely Christ Jesus, he again says in the same Epistle : " Know ye not, that so many of us as were baptized in Christ Jesus were baptized in His death? that like as Christ rose from the dead, so should we also walk in newness of life." [1] But again, showing that Christ did suffer, and was Himself the Son of God, who died for us, and redeemed us with His blood at the time appointed beforehand, he says : " For how is it, that Christ, when we were yet without strength, in due time died for the ungodly? But God commendeth His love towards us, in that, while we were yet sinners, Christ died for us. Much more, then, being now justified by His blood, we shall be saved from wrath through Him. For if, when we were enemies, we were reconciled to God by the death of His Son ; much more, being reconciled, we shall be saved by His life." [2] He declares in the plainest manner, that the same Being who was laid hold of, and underwent suffering, and shed His blood for us, was both Christ and the Son of God, who did also rise again, and was taken up into heaven, as he himself [Paul] says : " But at the same time, [it is] Christ [that] died, yea rather, that is risen again, who is even at the right hand of God." [3] And again, " Knowing that Christ, rising from the dead, dieth no more : " [4] for, as himself foreseeing, through the Spirit, the subdivisions of evil teachers [with regard to the Lord's person], and being desirous of cutting away from them all occasion of cavil, he says what has been already stated, [and also declares :] " But if the Spirit of Him that raised up Jesus from the dead dwell in you, He that raised up Christ from the dead shall also quicken your mortal bodies." [5] This he does not utter to those alone who wish to hear : Do not err, [he says to all :] Jesus Christ, the Son of God, is one and the same, who did by suffering reconcile us to God, and rose from the dead ; who is at the right hand of the Father, and perfect in all things ; " who, when He was buffeted, struck not in return ; who, when He suffered, threatened not ; " [6] and when He underwent tyranny, He prayed His Father that He would forgive those who had crucified Him. For He did Himself truly bring in salvation : since He is Himself the Word of God,

Himself the Only-begotten of the Father, Christ Jesus our Lord.

CHAP. XVII. — THE APOSTLES TEACH THAT IT WAS NEITHER CHRIST NOR THE SAVIOUR, BUT THE HOLY SPIRIT, WHO DID DESCEND UPON JESUS. THE REASON FOR THIS DESCENT.

1. It certainly was in the power of the apostles to declare that Christ descended upon Jesus, or that the so-called superior Saviour [came down] upon the dispensational one, or he who is from the invisible places upon him from the Demiurge ; but they neither knew nor said anything of the kind : for, had they known it, they would have also certainly stated it. But what really was the case, that did they record, [namely,] that the Spirit of God as a dove descended upon Him ; this Spirit, of whom it was declared by Isaiah, " And the Spirit of God shall rest upon Him," [7] as I have already said. And again : " The Spirit of the Lord is upon Me, because He hath anointed Me." [8] That is the Spirit of whom the Lord declares, " For it is not ye that speak, but the Spirit of your Father which speaketh in you." [9] And again, giving to the disciples 'the power of regeneration into God, [10] He said to them, " Go and teach all nations, baptizing them in the name of the Father, and of the Son, and of the Holy Ghost." [11] For [God] promised, that in the last times He would pour Him [the Spirit] upon [His] servants and handmaids, that they might prophesy ; wherefore He did also descend upon the Son of God, made the Son of man, becoming accustomed in fellowship with Him to dwell in the human race, to rest with human beings, and to dwell in the workmanship of God, working the will of the Father in them, and renewing them from their old habits into the newness of Christ.

2. This Spirit did David ask for the human race, saying, " And stablish me with Thine all-governing Spirit ; " [12] who also, as Luke says, descended at the day of Pentecost upon the disciples after the Lord's ascension, having power to admit all nations to the entrance of life, and to the opening of the new covenant ; from whence also, with one accord in all languages, they uttered praise to God, the Spirit bringing distant tribes to unity, and offering to the Father the first-fruits of all nations. Wherefore also the Lord promised to send the Comforter, [13] who should join us to God. For as a compacted lump of dough cannot be formed of dry wheat

---

[1] Rom. vi. 3, 4.
[2] Rom. v. 6-10. Irenæus appears to have read, as does the Vulgate, εἰς τί γάρ, for ἔτι γάρ in text. rec.
[3] Rom. viii. 34.
[4] Rom. vi. 9.
[5] Rom. viii. 11.
[6] 1 Pet. ii. 23.

[7] Isa. xi 2.
[8] Isa. lxi. 1.
[9] Matt. x. 20.
[10] Harvey remarks on this: " The sacrament of baptism is therefore ἡ δύναμις τῆς ἀναγεννήσεως εἰς Θεόν." [Comp. book i. cap. xxi.]
[11] Matt. xxviii. 19.
[12] Ps. li. 12.
[13] John xvi. 7.

without fluid matter, nor can a loaf possess unity, so, in like manner, neither could we, being many, be made one in Christ Jesus without the water from heaven. And as dry earth does not bring forth unless it receive moisture, in like manner we also, being originally a dry tree, could never have brought forth fruit unto life without the voluntary rain from above. For our bodies have received unity among themselves by means of that laver which leads to incorruption; but our souls, by means of the Spirit. Wherefore both are necessary, since both contribute towards the life of God, our Lord compassionating that erring Samaritan woman [1] — who did not remain with one husband, but committed fornication by [contracting] many marriages — by pointing out, and promising to her living water, so that she should thirst no more, nor occupy herself in acquiring the refreshing water obtained by labour, having in herself water springing up to eternal life. The Lord, receiving this as a gift from His Father, does Himself also confer it upon those who are partakers of Himself, sending the Holy Spirit upon all the earth.

3. Gideon,[2] that Israelite whom God chose, that he might save the people of Israel from the power of foreigners, foreseeing this gracious gift, changed his request, and prophesied that there would be dryness upon the fleece of wool (a type of the people), on which alone at first there had been dew; thus indicating that they should no longer have the Holy Spirit from God, as saith Esaias, " I will also command the clouds, that they rain no rain upon it," [3] but that the dew, which is the Spirit of God, who descended upon the Lord, should be diffused throughout all the earth, " the spirit of wisdom and understanding, the spirit of counsel and might, the spirit of knowledge and piety, the spirit of the fear of God." [4] This Spirit, again, He did confer upon the Church, sending throughout all the world the Comforter from heaven, from whence also the Lord tells us that the devil, like lightning, was cast down.[5] Wherefore we have need of the dew of God, that we be not consumed by fire, nor be rendered unfruitful, and that where we have an accuser there we may have also an Advocate,[6] the Lord commending to the Holy Spirit His own man,[7] who had fallen among thieves,[8] whom He Himself compassionated, and bound up his wounds, giving two royal *denaria;* so that we, receiving by the Spirit the image and superscription of the Father and the Son, might cause the *denarium* entrusted to us to be fruitful, counting out the increase [thereof] to the Lord.[9]

4. The Spirit, therefore, descending under the predestined dispensation, and the Son of God, the Only-begotten, who is also the Word of the Father, coming in the fulness of time, having become incarnate in man for the sake of man, and fulfilling all the conditions of human nature, our Lord Jesus Christ being one and the same, as He Himself the Lord doth testify, as the apostles confess, and as the prophets announce, — all the doctrines of these men who have invented putative Ogdoads and Tetrads, and imagined subdivisions [of the Lord's person], have been proved falsehoods. These [10] men do, in fact, set the Spirit aside altogether; they understand that Christ was one and Jesus another; and they teach that there was not one Christ, but many. And if they speak of them as united, they do again separate them: for they show that one did indeed undergo sufferings, but that the other remained impassible; that the one truly did ascend to the Pleroma, but the other remained in the intermediate place; that the one does truly feast and revel in places invisible and above all name, but that the other is seated with the Demiurge, emptying him of power. It will therefore be incumbent upon thee, and all others who give their attention to this writing, and are anxious about their own salvation, not readily to express acquiescence when they hear abroad the speeches of these men: for, speaking things resembling the [doctrine of the] faithful, as I have already observed, not only do they hold opinions which are different, but absolutely contrary, and in all points full of blasphemies, by which they destroy those persons who, by reason of the resemblance of the words, imbibe a poison which disagrees with their constitution, just as if one, giving lime mixed with water for milk, should mislead by the similitude of the colour; as a man [11] superior to me has said, concerning all that in any way corrupt the things of God and adulterate the truth, " Lime is wickedly mixed with the milk of God."

CHAP. XVIII. — CONTINUATION OF THE FOREGOING ARGUMENT. PROOFS FROM THE WRITINGS OF ST. PAUL, AND FROM THE WORDS OF OUR LORD, THAT CHRIST AND JESUS CANNOT BE CONSIDERED AS DISTINCT BEINGS; NEITHER CAN IT BE ALLEGED THAT THE SON OF GOD BECAME MAN MERELY IN APPEARANCE, BUT THAT HE DID SO TRULY AND ACTUALLY.

1.[12] As it has been clearly demonstrated that

---

[1] Irenæus refers to this woman as a type of the heathen world: for, among the Jews, Samaritan and Idolater were convertible terms.
[2] Judg. vi. 37, etc.
[3] Isa. v. 6.
[4] Isa. xi. 2.
[5] Luke x. 18.
[6] 1 John ii.1.
[7] " Suum hominem," i.e., the human race.
[8] Luke x. 35.

[9] Matt. xxv. 14.
[10] The following period is translated from a Syriac fragment (see Harvey's *Irenæus*, vol. ii. p. 439), as it supplies some words inconveniently omitted in the old Latin version.
[11] Comp. book i. pref. note 2.
[12] Again a Syriac fragment supplies some important words. See Harvey, vol. ii. p. 440.

the Word, who existed in the beginning with God, by whom all things were made, who was also always present with mankind, was in these last days, according to the time appointed by the Father, united to His own workmanship, inasmuch as He became a man liable to suffering, [it follows] that every objection is set aside of those who say, "If our Lord was born at that time, Christ had therefore no previous existence." For I have shown that the Son of God did not then begin to exist, being with the Father from the beginning; but when He became incarnate, and was made man, He commenced afresh [1] the long line of human beings, and furnished us, in a brief, comprehensive manner, with salvation; so that what we had lost in Adam — namely, to be according to the image and likeness of God — that we might recover in Christ Jesus.

2. For as it was not possible that the man who had once for all been conquered, and who had been destroyed through disobedience, could reform himself, and obtain the prize of victory; and as it was also impossible that he could attain to salvation who had fallen under the power of sin, — the Son effected both these things, being the Word of God, descending from the Father, becoming incarnate, stooping low, even to death, and consummating the arranged plan of our salvation, upon whom [Paul], exhorting us unhesitatingly to believe, again says, "Who shall ascend into heaven? that is, to bring down Christ; or who shall descend into the deep? that is, to liberate Christ again from the dead." [2] Then he continues, "If thou shalt confess with thy mouth the Lord Jesus, and shalt believe in thine heart that God hath raised Him from the dead, thou shalt be saved." [3] And he renders the reason why the Son of God did these things, saying, "For to this end Christ both lived, and died, and revived, that He might rule over the living and the dead." [4] And again, writing to the Corinthians, he declares, "But we preach Christ Jesus crucified;" [5] and adds, "The cup of blessing which we bless, is it not the communion of the blood of Christ?" [6]

3. But who is it that has had fellowship with us in the matter of food? Whether is it he who is conceived of by them as the Christ above, who extended himself through Horos, and imparted a form to their mother; or is it He who is from the Virgin, Emmanuel, who did eat butter and honey, [7] of whom the prophet declared, "He is also a man, and who shall know him?" [8]

He was likewise preached by Paul: "For I delivered," he says, "unto you first of all, that Christ died for our sins, according to the Scriptures; and that He was buried, and rose again the third day, according to the Scriptures." [9] It is plain, then, that Paul knew no other Christ besides Him alone, who both suffered, and was buried, and rose again, who was also born, and whom he speaks of as man. For after remarking, "But if Christ be preached, that He rose from the dead," [10] he continues, rendering the reason of His incarnation, "For since by man came death, by man [came] also the resurrection of the dead." And everywhere, when [referring to] the passion of our Lord, and to His human nature, and His subjection to death, he employs the name of Christ, as in that passage: "Destroy not him with thy meat for whom Christ died." [11] And again: "But now, in Christ, ye who sometimes were far off are made nigh by the blood of Christ." [12] And again: "Christ has redeemed us from the curse of the law, being made a curse for us: for it is written, Cursed is every one that hangeth upon a tree." [13] And again: "And through thy knowledge shall the weak brother perish, for whom Christ died;" [14] indicating that the impassible Christ did not descend upon Jesus, but that He Himself, because He was Jesus Christ, suffered for us; He, who lay in the tomb, and rose again, who descended and ascended, — the Son of God having been made the Son of man, as the very name itself doth declare. For in the name of Christ is implied, He that anoints, He that is anointed, and the unction itself with which He is anointed. And it is the Father who anoints, but the Son who is anointed by the Spirit, who is the unction, as the Word declares by Isaiah, "The Spirit of the Lord is upon me, because He hath anointed me," [15] — pointing out both the anointing Father, the anointed Son, and the unction, which is the Spirit.

4. The Lord Himself, too, makes it evident who it was that suffered; for when He asked the disciples, "Who do men say that I, the Son of man, am?" [16] and when Peter had replied, "Thou art the Christ, the Son of the living God;" and when he had been commended by Him [in these words], "That flesh and blood had not revealed it to him, but the Father who is in heaven," He made it clear that He, the Son of man, is Christ the Son of the living God. "For from that time forth," it is said, "He began to show to His disciples, how that He must go unto Jerusalem,

---

[1] So the Syriac. The Latin has, "in seipso recapitulavit," *He summed up in Himself.* [As the Second Adam, 1 Cor. xv. 47.]
[2] Rom. x. 6, 7.
[3] Rom. x. 9.
[4] Rom. xiv. 9.
[5] 1 Cor. i. 23.
[6] 1 Cor. x. 16.
[7] Isa. viii. 14.
[8] Jer. xvii. 9.

[9] 1 Cor. xv. 3, 4.
[10] 1 Cor. xv. 12.
[11] Rom. xiv. 15.
[12] Eph. ii. 13.
[13] Gal. iii. 13; Deut. xxi. 23.
[14] 1 Cor. viii. 11.
[15] Isa. lxi. 1.
[16] Matt. xvi. 13.

and suffer many things of the priests, and be rejected, and crucified, and rise again the third day." [1] He who was acknowledged by Peter as Christ, who pronounced him blessed because the Father had revealed the Son of the living God to him, said that He must Himself suffer many things, and be crucified; and then He rebuked Peter, who imagined that He was the Christ as the generality of men supposed [2] [that the Christ should be], and was averse to the idea of His suffering, [and] said to the disciples, "If any man will come after Me, let him deny himself, and take up his cross, and follow Me. For whosoever will save his life, shall lose it; and whosoever will lose it for My sake shall save it." [3] For these things Christ spoke openly, He being Himself the Saviour of those who should be delivered over to death for their confession of Him, and lose their lives.

5. If, however, He was Himself not to suffer, but should fly away from Jesus, why did He exhort His disciples to take up the cross and follow Him, — that cross which these men represent Him as not having taken up, but [speak of Him] as having relinquished the dispensation of suffering? For that He did not say this with reference to the acknowledging of the *Stauros* (cross) above, as some among them venture to expound, but with respect to the suffering which He should Himself undergo, and that His disciples should endure, He implies when He says, "For whosoever will save his life, shall lose it; and whosoever will lose, shall find it. And that His disciples must suffer for His sake, He [implied when He] said to the Jews, "Behold, I send you prophets, and wise men, and scribes: and some of them ye shall kill and crucify." [4] And to the disciples He was wont to say, "And ye shall stand before governors and kings for My sake; and they shall scourge some of you, and slay you, and persecute you from city to city." [5] He knew, therefore, both those who should suffer persecution, and He knew those who should have to be scourged and slain because of Him; and He did not speak of any other cross, but of the suffering which He should Himself undergo first, and His disciples afterwards. For this purpose did He give them this exhortation: "Fear not them which kill the body, but are not able to kill the soul; but rather fear Him who is able to send both soul and body into hell;" [6] [thus exhorting them] to hold fast those professions of faith which they had made in reference to Him. For He promised to confess before His Father those who should confess His name before men; but declared that He

would deny those who should deny Him, and would be ashamed of those who should be ashamed to confess Him. And although these things are so, some of these men have proceeded to such a degree of temerity, that they even pour contempt upon the martyrs, and vituperate those who are slain on account of the confession of the Lord, and who suffer all things predicted by the Lord, and who in this respect strive to follow the footprints of the Lord's passion, having become martyrs of the suffering One; these we do also enrol with the martyrs themselves. For, when inquisition shall be made for their blood, [7] and they shall attain to glory, then all shall be confounded by Christ, who have cast a slur upon their martyrdom. And from this fact, that He exclaimed upon the cross, "Father, forgive them, for they know not what they do," [8] the long-suffering, patience, compassion, and goodness of Christ are exhibited, since He both suffered, and did Himself exculpate those who had maltreated Him. For the Word of God, who said to us, "Love your enemies, and pray for those that hate you," [9] Himself did this very thing upon the cross; loving the human race to such a degree, that He even prayed for those putting Him to death. If, however, any one, going upon the supposition that there are two[Christs], forms a judgment in regard to them, that [Christ] shall be found much the better one, and more patient, and the truly good one, who, in the midst of His own wounds and stripes, and the other [cruelties] inflicted upon Him, was beneficent, and unmindful of the wrongs perpetrated upon Him, than he who flew away, and sustained neither injury nor insult.

6. This also does likewise meet [the case] of those who maintain that He suffered only in appearance. For if He did not truly suffer, no thanks to Him, since there was no suffering at all; and when we shall actually begin to suffer, He will seem as leading us astray, exhorting us to endure buffeting, and to turn the other [10] cheek, if He did not Himself before us in reality suffer the same; and as He misled them by seeming to them what He was not, so does He also mislead us, by exhorting us to endure what He did not endure Himself. [In that case] we shall be even above the Master, because we suffer and sustain what our Master never bore or endured. But as our Lord is alone truly Master, so the Son of God is truly good and patient, the Word of God the Father having been made the Son of man. For He fought and conquered; for He was man contending for the fathers, [11] and

[1] Matt. xvi. 21.
[2] Literally, "supposing Him to be Christ according to the idea of men."
[3] Matt. xvi. 24, 25.
[4] Matt. xxiii. 24.
[5] Matt. x. 17, 18.
[6] Matt. x. 28.

[7] Ps. ix. 12.
[8] Luke xxiii. 34.
[9] Matt. v. 44.
[10] Matt. v. 39.
[11] "*Pro patribus,* ἀντὶ τῶν πατρῶν. The reader will here observe the clear statement of the doctrine of the atonement, whereby alone sin is done away." — HARVEY.

through obedience doing away with disobedience completely : for He bound the strong man,[1] and set free the weak, and endowed His own handiwork with salvation, by destroying sin. For He is a most holy and merciful Lord, and loves the human race.

7. Therefore, as I have already said, He caused man (human nature) to cleave to and to become one with God. For unless man had overcome the enemy of man, the enemy would not have been legitimately vanquished. And again : unless it had been God who had freely given salvation, we could never have possessed it securely. And unless man had been joined to God, he could never have become a partaker of incorruptibility. For it was incumbent upon the Mediator between God and men, by His relationship to both, to bring both to friendship and concord, and present man to God, while He revealed God to man.[2] For, in what way could we be partakers of the adoption of sons, unless we had received from Him through the Son that fellowship which refers to Himself, unless His Word, having been made flesh, had entered into communion with us? Wherefore also He passed through every stage of life, restoring to all communion with God. Those, therefore, who assert that He appeared putatively, and was neither born in the flesh nor truly made man, are as yet under the old condemnation, holding out patronage to sin ; for, by their showing, death has not been vanquished, which "reigned from Adam to Moses, even over them that had not sinned after the similitude of Adam's transgression."[3] But the law coming, which was given by Moses, and testifying of sin that it is a sinner, did truly take away his (death's) kingdom, showing that he was no king, but a robber ; and it revealed him as a murderer. It laid, however, a weighty burden upon man, who had sin in himself, showing that he was liable to death. For as the law was spiritual, it merely made sin to stand out in relief, but did not destroy it. For sin had no dominion over the spirit, but over man. For it behoved Him who was to destroy sin, and redeem man under the power of death, that He should Himself be made that very same thing which he was, that is, man ; who had been drawn by sin into bondage, but was held by death, so that sin should be destroyed by man, and man should go forth from death. For as by the disobedience of the one man who was originally moulded from virgin soil, the many were made sinners,[4] and forfeited life ; so was it necessary that, by the obedience of one man,

who was originally born from a virgin, many should be justified and receive salvation. Thus, then, was the Word of God made man, as also Moses says : "God, true are His works."[5] But if, not having been made flesh, He did appear as if flesh, His work was not a true one. But what He did appear, that He also was : God recapitulated in Himself the ancient formation of man, that He might kill sin, deprive death of its power, and vivify man ; and therefore His works are true.

CHAP. XIX. — JESUS CHRIST WAS NOT A MERE MAN, BEGOTTEN FROM JOSEPH IN THE ORDINARY COURSE OF NATURE, BUT WAS VERY GOD, BEGOTTEN OF THE FATHER MOST HIGH, AND VERY MAN, BORN OF THE VIRGIN.

1. But again, those who assert that He was simply a mere man, begotten by Joseph, remaining in the bondage of the old disobedience, are in a state of death ; having been not as yet joined to the Word of God the Father, nor receiving liberty through the Son, as He does Himself declare : "If the Son shall make you free, ye shall be free indeed."[6] But, being ignorant of Him who from the Virgin is Emmanuel, they are deprived of His gift, which is eternal life ;[7] and not receiving the incorruptible Word, they remain in mortal flesh, and are debtors to death, not obtaining the antidote of life. To whom the Word says, mentioning His own gift of grace : "I said, Ye are all the sons of the Highest, and gods ; but ye shall die like men."[8] He speaks undoubtedly these words to those who have not received the gift of adoption, but who despise the incarnation of the pure generation of the Word of God,[9] defraud human nature of promotion into God, and prove themselves ungrateful to the Word of God, who became flesh for them. For it was for this end that the Word of God was made man, and He who was the Son of God became the Son of man, that man, having been taken into the Word, and receiving the adoption, might become the son of God. For by no other means could we have attained to incorruptibility and immortality, unless we had been united to incorruptibility and immortality. But how could we be joined to incorruptibility and immortality, unless, first, incorruptibility and immortality had

---

[1] Matt. xii. 29.
[2] The Latin text, "et facere, ut et Deus assumeret hominem, et homo se dederet Deo," here differs widely from the Greek preserved by Theodoret. We have followed the latter, which is preferred by all the editors.
[3] Rom. v. 14.
[4] Rom. v. 19.

[5] Deut. xxxii. 4.
[6] John viii. 36.
[7] Rom. vi. 23.
[8] Ps. lxxxii. 6, 7.
[9] The original Greek is preserved here by Theodoret, differing in some respects from the old Latin version: καὶ ἀποστεροῦντας τὸν ἄνθρωπον τῆς εἰς Θεὸν ἀνόδου καὶ ἀχαριστοῦντας τῷ ὑπὲρ αὐτῶν σαρκωθέντι λόγῳ τοῦ Θεοῦ. Εἰς τοῦτο γὰρ ὁ λόγος ἄνθρωπος . . . ἵνα ὁ ἄνθρωπος τὸν λόγον χωρήσας, καὶ τὴν υἱοθεσίαν λαβών, υἱὸς γένηται Θεοῦ. The old Latin runs thus: " fraudantes hominem ab ea ascensione quæ est ad Dominum, et ingrate exsistentes Verbo Dei, qui incarnatus est propter ipsos. Propter hoc enim Verbum Dei homo, et qui Filius Dei est, Filius Hominis factus est . . . commixtus Verbo Dei, et adoptionem percipiens fiat filius Dei." [A specimen of the liberties taken by the Latin translators with the original of Irenæus. Others are much less innocent.]

become that which we also are, so that the corruptible might be swallowed up by incorruptibility, and the mortal by immortality, that we might receive the adoption of sons?

2. For this reason [it is said], "Who shall declare His generation?"[1] since "He is a man, and who shall recognise Him?"[2] But he to whom the Father which is in heaven has revealed Him,[3] knows Him, so that he understands that He who "was not born either by the will of the flesh, or by the will of man,"[4] is the Son of man, this is Christ, the Son of the living God. For I have shown from the Scriptures,[5] that no one of the sons of Adam is as to everything, and absolutely, called God, or named Lord. But that He is Himself in His own right, beyond all men who ever lived, God, and Lord, and King Eternal, and the Incarnate Word, proclaimed by all the prophets, the apostles, and by the Spirit Himself, may be seen by all who have attained to even a small portion of the truth. Now, the Scriptures would not have testified these things of Him, if, like others, He had been a mere man. But that He had, beyond all others, in Himself that pre-eminent birth which is from the Most High Father, and also experienced that pre-eminent generation which is from the Virgin,[6] the divine Scriptures do in both respects testify of Him: also, that He was a man without comeliness, and liable to suffering;[7] that He sat upon the foal of an ass;[8] that He received for drink, vinegar and gall;[9] that He was despised among the people, and humbled Himself even to death; and that He is the holy Lord, the Wonderful, the Counsellor, the Beautiful in appearance, and the Mighty God,[10] coming on the clouds as the Judge of all men;[11] — all these things did the Scriptures prophesy of Him.

3. For as He became man in order to undergo temptation, so also was He the Word that He might be glorified; the Word remaining quiescent, that He might be capable of being tempted, dishonoured, crucified, and of suffering death, but the human nature being swallowed up in it (the divine), when it conquered, and endured [without yielding], and performed acts of kindness, and rose again, and was received up [into heaven]. He therefore, the Son of God, our Lord, being the Word of the Father, and the Son of man, since He had a generation as to His human nature from Mary — who was descended from mankind, and who was herself a

human being — was made the Son of man.[12] Wherefore also the Lord Himself gave us a sign, in the depth below, and in the height above, which man did not ask for, because he never expected that a virgin could conceive, or that it was possible that one remaining a virgin could bring forth a son, and that what was thus born should be "*God with us*," and descend to those things which are of the earth beneath, seeking the sheep which had perished, which was indeed His own peculiar handiwork, and ascend to the height above, offering and commending to His Father that human nature (*hominem*) which had been found, making in His own person the first-fruits of the resurrection of man; that, as the Head rose from the dead, so also the remaining part of the body — [namely, the body] of every man who is found in life — when the time is fulfilled of that condemnation which existed by reason of disobedience, may arise, blended together and strengthened through means of joints and bands[13] by the increase of God, each of the members having its own proper and fit position in the body. For there are many mansions in the Father's house,[14] inasmuch as there are also many members in the body.

CHAP. XX. — GOD SHOWED HIMSELF, BY THE FALL OF MAN, AS PATIENT, BENIGN, MERCIFUL, MIGHTY TO SAVE. MAN IS THEREFORE MOST UNGRATEFUL, IF, UNMINDFUL OF HIS OWN LOT, AND OF THE BENEFITS HELD OUT TO HIM, HE DO NOT ACKNOWLEDGE DIVINE GRACE.

1. Long-suffering therefore was God, when man became a defaulter, as foreseeing that victory which should be granted to him through the Word. For, when strength was made perfect in weakness,[15] it showed the kindness and transcendent power of God. For as He patiently suffered Jonah to be swallowed by the whale, not that he should be swallowed up and perish altogether, but that, having been cast out again, he might be the more subject to God, and might glorify Him the more who had conferred upon him such an unhoped-for deliverance, and might bring the Ninevites to a lasting repentance, so that they should be converted to the Lord, who would deliver them from death, having been struck with awe by that portent which had been wrought in Jonah's case, as the Scripture says of them, "And they returned each from his evil way, and the unrighteousness which was in their hands, saying, Who knoweth if God will repent, and turn away His anger from us, and we shall not perish?"[16] — so also, from the beginning, did God permit man to be

---

1 Isa. liii. 8.
2 Jer. xvii. 9.
3 Matt. xvi. 16.
4 John i. 13.
5 See above, iii. 6.
6 Isa. vii. 14.
7 Isa liii. 2.
8 Zech. ix. 9.
9 Ps. lxix. 21.
10 Isa. ix. 6.
11 Dan. vii. 13.

12 Isa. vii. 13
13 Eph. iv. 16.
14 John xiv. 2.
15 2 Cor. xii. 9.
16 Jonah iii. 8, 9.

swallowed up by the great whale, who was the author of transgression, not that he should perish altogether when so engulphed; but, arranging and preparing the plan of salvation, which was accomplished by the Word, through the sign of Jonah, for those who held the same opinion as Jonah regarding the Lord, and who confessed, and said, "I am a servant of the Lord, and I worship the Lord God of heaven, who hath made the sea and the dry land." [1] [This was done] that man, receiving an unhoped-for salvation from God, might rise from the dead, and glorify God, and repeat that word which was uttered in prophecy by Jonah: "I cried by reason of mine affliction to the Lord my God, and He heard me out of the belly of hell;" [2] and that he might always continue glorifying God, and giving thanks without ceasing, for that salvation which he has derived from Him, "that no flesh should glory in the Lord's presence;" [3] and that man should never adopt an opposite opinion with regard to God, supposing that the incorruptibility which belongs to him is his own naturally, and by thus not holding the truth, should boast with empty superciliousness, as if he were naturally like to God. For he (Satan) thus rendered him (man) more ungrateful towards his Creator, obscured the love which God had towards man, and blinded his mind not to perceive what is worthy of God, comparing himself with, and judging himself equal to, God.

2. This, therefore, was the [object of the] long-suffering of God, that man, passing through all things, and acquiring the knowledge of moral discipline, then attaining to the resurrection from the dead, and learning by experience what is the source of his deliverance, may always live in a state of gratitude to the Lord, having obtained from Him the gift of incorruptibility, that he might love Him the more; for "he to whom more is forgiven, loveth more:" [4] and that he may know himself, how mortal and weak he is; while he also understands respecting God, that He is immortal and powerful to such a degree as to confer immortality upon what is mortal, and eternity upon what is temporal; and may understand also the other attributes of God displayed towards himself, by means of which being instructed he may think of God in accordance with the divine greatness. For the glory of man [is] God, but [His] works [are the glory] of God; and the receptacle of all His wisdom and power [is] man. Just as the physician is proved by his patients, so is God also revealed through men. And therefore Paul declares, "For God hath concluded all in unbelief,

that He may have mercy upon all;" [5] not saying this in reference to spiritual Æons, but to man, who had been disobedient to God, and being cast off from immortality, then obtained mercy, receiving through the Son of God that adoption which is [accomplished] by Himself. For he who holds, without pride and boasting, the true glory (opinion) regarding created things and the Creator, who is the Almighty God of all, and who has granted existence to all; [such an one,] continuing in His love [6] and subjection, and giving of thanks, shall also receive from Him the greater glory of promotion, [7] looking forward to the time when he shall become like Him who died for him, for He, too, "was made in the likeness of sinful flesh," [8] to condemn sin, and to cast it, as now a condemned thing, away beyond the flesh, but that He might call man forth into His own likeness, assigning him as [His own] imitator to God, and imposing on him His Father's law, in order that he may see God, and granting him power to receive the Father; [being] [9] the Word of God who dwelt in man, and became the Son of man, that He might accustom man to receive God, and God to dwell in man, according to the good pleasure of the Father.

3. On this account, therefore, the Lord Himself, [10] who is Emmanuel from the Virgin, [11] is the sign of our salvation, since it was the Lord Himself who saved them, because they could not be saved by their own instrumentality; and, therefore, when Paul sets forth human infirmity, he says: "For I know that there dwelleth in my flesh no good thing," [12] showing that the "good thing" of our salvation is not from us, but from God. And again: "Wretched man that I am, who shall deliver me from the body of this death?" [13] Then he introduces the Deliverer, [saying,] "The grace of Jesus Christ our Lord." And Isaiah declares this also, [when he says:] "Be ye strengthened, ye hands that hang down, and ye feeble knees; be ye encouraged, ye feeble-minded; be comforted, fear not: behold, our God has given judgment with retribution, and shall recompense: He will come Himself, and will save us." [14] Here we see, that not by ourselves, but by the help of God, we must be saved.

4. Again, that it should not be a mere man who should save us, nor [one] without flesh — for the angels are without flesh — [the same

---

[1] Jonah i. 9.
[2] Jonah ii. 2.
[3] 1 Cor. i. 29.
[4] Luke vii. 43.

[5] Rom. xi. 32.
[6] John xv. 9.
[7] "Provectus." This word has not a little perplexed the editors. Grabe regards it as being the *participle*, Massuet the *accusative plural* of the noun, and Harvey the *genitive singular*. We have doubtfully followed the latter.
[8] Rom. viii. 3.
[9] The punctuation and exact meaning are very uncertain.
[10] The construction and sense of this passage are disputed. Grabe, Massuet, and Harvey take different views of it. We have followed the rendering proposed by Massuet.
[11] Isa. vii. 4.
[12] Rom. vii. 18.
[13] Rom. vii. 24.
[14] Isa. xxv. 3.

prophet] announced, saying: "Neither an elder,[1] nor angel, but the Lord Himself will save them, because He loves them, and will spare them: He will Himself set them free."[2] And that He should Himself become very man, visible, when He should be the Word giving salvation, Isaiah again says: "Behold, city of Zion: thine eyes shall see our salvation."[3] And that it was not a mere man who died for us, Isaiah says: "And the holy Lord remembered His dead Israel, who had slept in the land of sepulture; and He came down to preach His salvation to them, that He might save them."[4] And Amos (Micah) the prophet declares the same: "He will turn again, and will have compassion upon us: He will destroy our iniquities, and will cast our sins into the depths of the sea."[5] And again, specifying the place of His advent, he says: "The Lord hath spoken from Zion, and He has uttered His voice from Jerusalem."[6] And that it is from that region which is towards the south of the inheritance of Judah that the Son of God shall come, who is God, and who was from Bethlehem, where the Lord was born, [and] will send out His praise through all the earth, thus[7] says the prophet Habakkuk: "God shall come from the south, and the Holy One from Mount Effrem. His power covered the heavens over, and the earth is full of His praise. Before His face shall go forth the Word, and His feet shall advance in the plains."[8] Thus he indicates in clear terms that He is God, and that His advent was [to take place] in Bethlehem, and from Mount Effrem, which is towards the south of the inheritance, and that [He is] man. For he says, "His feet shall advance in the plains:" and this is an indication proper to man.[9]

CHAP. XXI. — A VINDICATION OF THE PROPHECY IN ISAIAH (VII. 14) AGAINST THE MISINTERPRETATIONS OF THEODOTION, AQUILA, THE EBIONITES, AND THE JEWS. AUTHORITY OF THE SEPTUAGINT VERSION. ARGUMENTS IN PROOF THAT CHRIST WAS BORN OF A VIRGIN.

1. God, then, was made man, and the Lord did Himself save us, giving us the token of the

Virgin. But not as some allege, among those now presuming to expound the Scripture, [thus:] "Behold, a young woman shall conceive, and bring forth a son,"[10] as Theodotion the Ephesian has interpreted, and Aquila of Pontus,[11] both Jewish proselytes. The Ebionites, following these, assert that He was begotten by Joseph; thus destroying, as far as in them lies, such a marvellous dispensation of God, and setting aside the testimony of the prophets which proceeded from God. For truly this prediction was uttered before the removal of the people to Babylon; that is, anterior to the supremacy acquired by the Medes and Persians. But it was interpreted into Greek by the Jews themselves, much before the period of our Lord's advent, that there might remain no suspicion that perchance the Jews, complying with our humour, did put this interpretation upon these words. They indeed, had they been cognizant of our future existence, and that we should use these proofs from the Scriptures, would themselves never have hesitated to burn their own Scriptures, which do declare that all other nations partake of [eternal] life, and show that they who boast themselves as being the house of Jacob and the people of Israel, are disinherited from the grace of God.

2. For before the Romans possessed their kingdom,[12] while as yet the Macedonians held Asia, Ptolemy the son of Lagus, being anxious to adorn the library which he had founded in Alexandria, with a collection of the writings of all men, which were [works] of merit, made request to the people of Jerusalem, that they should have their Scriptures translated into the Greek language. And they — for at that time they were still subject to the Macedonians — sent to Ptolemy seventy of their elders, who were thoroughly skilled in the Scriptures and in both the languages, to carry out what he had desired.[13] But he, wishing to test them individually, and fearing lest they might perchance, by taking counsel together, conceal the truth in the Scriptures, by their interpretation, separated them from each other, and commanded them all to write the same translation. He did this with respect to all the books. But when they came together in the same place before Ptolemy, and

---

[1] Grabe remarks that the word πρέσβυς, here translated "senior," seems rather to denote a *mediator* or *messenger*.

[2] Isa. lxiii. 9.

[3] Isa. xxxiii. 20.

[4] Irenæus quotes this as from Isaiah on the present occasion; but in book iv. 22, 1, we find him referring the same passage to Jeremiah. It is somewhat remarkable that it is to be found in neither prophet, although Justin Martyr, in his dialogue with Trypho, [chap. lxxii. and notes, Dial. with Trypho, in this volume,] brings it forward as an argument against him, and directly accuses the Jews of having fraudulently removed it from the sacred text. It is, however, to be found in no ancient version or Jewish Targum, which fact may be regarded as a decisive proof of its spuriousness.

[5] Mic. vii. 9.

[6] Joel iii. 16; Amos i. 2.

[7] As Massuet observes, we must either expunge "sicut" altogether, or read "sic" as above.

[8] Hab. iii. 3, 5.

[9] This quotation from Habakkuk, here commented on by Irenæus, differs both from the Hebrew and the LXX., and comes nearest to the old Italic version of the passage.

[10] Isa. vii. 14.

[11] Epiphanius, in his *De Mensuris*, gives an account of these two men. The former published his version of the Old Testament in the year 181. The latter put forth his translation half a century earlier, about 129 A.D. This reference to the version of Theodotion furnishes a note of date as to the time when Irenæus published his work: it must have been subsequently to A.D. 181.

[12] The Greek text here is, κρατῦναι τὴν ἀρχὴν αὐτῶν, translated into Latin by "possiderent regnum suum,"—words which are somewhat ambiguous in both languages. Massuet remarks, that "regnum *eorum*" would have been a better rendering, referring the words to the *Jews*.

[13] The Greek text of this narrative has been preserved by Eusebius (*Hist. Eccl.*, v. 8). Grabe considers it to be faulty in this passage; so the Latin translation has been adopted here. Eusebius has ποιήσαντος τοῦ Θεοῦ ὅπερ ἐβούλετο — *God having accomplished what He intended.*

each of them compared his own interpretation with that of every other, God was indeed glorified, and the Scriptures were acknowledged as truly divine. For all of them read out the common translation [which they had prepared] in the very same words and the very same names, from beginning to end, so that even the Gentiles present perceived that the Scriptures had been interpreted by the inspiration of God.[1] And there was nothing astonishing in God having done this, — He who, when, during the captivity of the people under Nebuchadnezzar, the Scriptures had been corrupted, and when, after seventy years, the Jews had returned to their own land, then, in the times of Artaxerxes king of the Persians, inspired Esdras the priest, of the tribe of Levi, to recast[2] all the words of the former prophets, and to re-establish with the people the Mosaic legislation.

3. Since, therefore, the Scriptures have been interpreted with such fidelity, and by the grace of God, and since from these God has prepared and formed again our faith towards His Son, and has preserved to us the unadulterated Scriptures in Egypt, where the house of Jacob flourished, fleeing from the famine in Canaan ; where also our Lord was preserved when He fled from the persecution set on foot by Herod ; and [since] this interpretation of these Scriptures was made prior to our Lord's descent [to earth], and came into being before the Christians appeared — for our Lord was born about the forty-first year of the reign of Augustus ; but Ptolemy was much earlier, under whom the Scriptures were interpreted ; — [since these things are so, I say,] truly these men are proved to be impudent and presumptuous, who would now show a desire to make different translations, when we refute them out of these Scriptures, and shut them up to a belief in the advent of the Son of God. But *our* faith is stedfast, unfeigned, and the only true one, having clear proof from these Scriptures, which were interpreted in the way I have related ; and the preaching of the Church is without interpolation. For the apostles, since they are of more ancient date than all these [heretics], agree with this aforesaid translation ; and the translation harmonizes with the tradition of the apostles. For Peter, and John, and Matthew, and Paul, and the rest successively, as well as their followers, did set forth all prophetical [announcements], just as[3] the interpretation of the elders contains them.

4. For the one and the same Spirit of God, who proclaimed by the prophets what and of what sort the advent of the Lord should be, did by these elders give a just interpretation of what had been truly prophesied ; and He did Himself, by the apostles, announce that the fulness of the times of the adoption had arrived, that the kingdom of heaven had drawn nigh, and that *He* was dwelling within those that believe on Him who was born Emmanuel of the Virgin. To this effect they testify, [saying,] that before Joseph had come together with Mary, while she therefore remained in virginity, "she was found with child of the Holy Ghost ; "[4] and that the angel Gabriel said unto her, "The Holy Ghost shall come upon thee, and the power of the Highest shall overshadow thee ; therefore also that holy thing which shall be born of thee shall be called the Son of God ; "[5] andt hat the angel said to Joseph in a dream, " Now this was done, that it might be fulfilled which was spoken by Isaiah the prophet, Behold, a virgin shall be with child."[6] But the elders have thus interpreted what Esaias said : "And the Lord, moreover, said unto Ahaz, Ask for thyself a sign from the Lord thy God out of the depth below, or from the height above. And Ahaz said, I will not ask, and I will not tempt the Lord. And he said, It is not a small thing[7] for you to weary men ; and how does the Lord weary them? Therefore the Lord himself shall give you a sign ; Behold, a virgin shall conceive, and bear a son ; and ye shall call His name Emmanuel. Butter and honey shall He eat : before He knows or chooses out things that are evil, He shall exchange them for what is good ; for before the child knows good or evil, He shall not consent to evil, that He may choose that which is good."[8] Carefully, then, has the Holy Ghost pointed out, by what has been said, His birth from a virgin, and His essence, that He is God (for the name Emmanuel indicates this). And He shows that He is a man, when He says, " Butter and honey shall He eat ; " and in that He terms Him a child also, [in saying,] "before He knows good and evil ; " for these are all the tokens of a human infant. But that He " will not consent to evil, that He may choose that which is good," — this is proper to God ; that by the fact, that He shall eat butter and honey, we should not understand that He is a mere man only, nor, on the other hand, from the name Emmanuel, should suspect Him to be God without flesh.

5. And when He says, "Hear, O house of David,"[9] He performed the part of one indi-

[1] [See Justin Martyr, *To the Greeks*, cap. xiii. The testimony of Justin naturalized this Jewish legend among Christians.]

[2] The Greek term is ἀνατάξασθαι, which the Latin renders " re memorare," but Massuet prefers " digerere."

[3] This is a very interesting passage, as bearing on the question, From what source are the quotations made by the writers of the New Testament derived ? Massuet, indeed, argues that it is of little or no weight in the controversy; but the passage speaks for itself. Comp. Dr. Roberts's *Discussions on the Gospels*, part i. ch. iv. and vii.

[4] Matt. i. 18.
[5] Luke i. 35.
[6] Matt. i. 23.
[7] We here read " non pusillum " for " num pusillum," as in some texts Cyprian and Tertullian confirm the former reading.
[8] Isa. vii. 10-17.
[9] Isa. vii. 13.

cating that He whom God promised David that He would raise up from the fruit of his belly (*ventris*) an eternal King, is the same who was born of the Virgin, herself of the lineage of David. For on this account also, He promised that the King should be "of the fruit of his *belly*," which was the appropriate [term to use with respect] to a virgin conceiving, and not "of the fruit of his *loins*," nor "of the fruit of his *reins*," which expression is appropriate to a generating man, and a woman conceiving by a man. In this promise, therefore, the Scripture excluded all virile influence; yet it certainly is not mentioned that He who was born was not from the will of man. But it has fixed and established "the fruit of the *belly*," that it might declare the generation of Him who should be [born] from the Virgin, as Elisabeth testified when filled with the Holy Ghost, saying to Mary, "Blessed art thou among women, and blessed is the fruit of thy belly;"[1] the Holy Ghost pointing out to those willing to hear, that the promise which God had made, of raising up a King from the fruit of [David's] belly, was fulfilled in the birth from the Virgin, that is, from Mary. Let those, therefore, who alter the passage of Isaiah thus, "Behold, a young woman shall conceive," and who will have Him to be Joseph's son, also alter the form of the promise which was given to David, when God promised him to raise up, from the fruit of his belly, the horn of Christ the King. But they did not understand, otherwise they would have presumed to alter even this passage also.

6. But what Isaiah said, "From the height above, or from the depth beneath,"[2] was meant to indicate, that "He who descended was the same also who ascended."[3] But in this that he said, "The Lord Himself shall give you a sign," he declared an unlooked-for thing with regard to His generation, which could have been accomplished in no other way than by God the Lord of all, God Himself giving a sign in the house of David. For what great thing or what sign should have been in this, that a young woman conceiving by a man should bring forth, — a thing which happens to all women that produce offspring? But since an unlooked-for salvation was to be provided for men through the help of God, so also was the unlooked-for birth from a virgin accomplished; God giving this sign, but man not working it out.

7. On this account also, Daniel,[4] foreseeing His advent, said that a stone, cut out without hands, came into this world. For this is what "without hands" means, that His coming into this world was not by the operation of human hands, that is, of those men who are accustomed to stone-cutting; that is, Joseph taking no part with regard to it, but Mary alone co-operating with the pre-arranged plan. For this stone from the earth derives existence from both the power and the wisdom of God. Wherefore also Isaiah says: "Thus saith the Lord, Behold, I deposit in the foundations of Zion a stone, precious, elect, the chief, the corner-one, to be had in honour."[5] So, then, we understand that His advent in human nature was not by the will of a man, but by the will of God.

8. Wherefore also Moses giving a type, cast his rod upon the earth,[6] in order that it, by becoming flesh, might expose and swallow up all the opposition of the Egyptians, which was lifting itself up against the pre-arranged plan of God;[7] that the Egyptians themselves might testify that it is the finger of God which works salvation for the people, and not the son of Joseph. For if He were the son of Joseph, how could He be greater than Solomon, or greater than Jonah,[8] or greater than David,[9] when He was generated from the same seed, and was a descendant of these men? And how was it that He also pronounced Peter blessed, because he acknowledged Him to be the Son of the living God?[10]

9. But besides, if indeed He had been the son of Joseph, He could not, according to Jeremiah, be either king or heir. For Joseph is shown to be the son of Joachim and Jechoniah, as also Matthew sets forth in his pedigree.[11] But Jechoniah, and all his posterity, were disinherited from the kingdom; Jeremiah thus declaring, "As I live, saith the Lord, if Jechoniah the son of Joachim king of Judah had been made the signet of my right hand, I would pluck him thence, and deliver him into the hand of those seeking thy life."[12] And again: "Jechoniah is dishonoured as a useless vessel, for he has been cast into a land which he knew not. Earth, hear the word of the Lord: Write this man a disinherited person; for none of his seed, sitting on the throne of David, shall prosper, or be a prince in Judah."[13] And again, God speaks of Joachim his father: "Therefore thus saith the Lord concerning Joachim his father, king of Judea, There shall be from him none sitting upon the throne of David: and his dead body shall be cast out in the heat of day, and in the frost of night. And I will look upon him, and upon

---

[1] Luke i. 42.
[2] Isa. vii. 11.
[3] Eph. iv. 10.
[4] Dan. ii. 34.
[5] Isa. xxviii. 16.
[6] Ex. vii. 9.
[7] Ex. viii.19.
[8] Matt. xii. 41, 42.
[9] Matt. xxii. 43.
[10] Matt. xvi. 17.
[11] Matt. i. 12-16.
[12] Jer. xxii. 24, 25.
[13] Jer. xxii. 28, etc.

his sons, and will bring upon them, and upon the inhabitants of Jerusalem, upon the land of Judah, all the evils that I have pronounced against them."[1] Those, therefore, who say that He was begotten of Joseph, and that they have hope in Him, do cause themselves to be disinherited from the kingdom, falling under the curse and rebuke directed against Jechoniah and his seed. Because for this reason have these things been spoken concerning Jechoniah, the [Holy] Spirit foreknowing the doctrines of the evil teachers; that they may learn that from his seed — that is, from Joseph — He was not to be born, but that, according to the promise of God, from David's belly the King eternal is raised up, who sums up all things in Himself, and has gathered into Himself the ancient formation [of man].[2]

10. For as by one man's disobedience sin entered, and death obtained [a place] through sin; so also by the obedience of one man, righteousness having been introduced, shall cause life to fructify in those persons who in times past were dead.[3] And as the protoplast himself, Adam, had his substance from untilled and as yet virgin soil ("for God had not yet sent rain, and man had not tilled the ground"[4]), and was formed by the hand of God, that is, by the Word of God, for "all things were made by Him,"[5] and the Lord took dust from the earth and formed man; so did He who is the Word, recapitulating Adam in Himself, rightly receive a birth, enabling Him to gather up Adam [into Himself], from Mary, who was as yet a virgin. If, then, the first Adam had a man for his father, and was born of human seed, it were reasonable to say that the second Adam was begotten of Joseph. But if the former was taken from the dust, and God was his Maker, it was incumbent that the latter also, making a recapitulation in Himself, should be formed as man by God, to have an analogy with the former as respects His origin. Why, then, did not God again take dust, but wrought so that the formation should be made of Mary? It was that there might not be another formation called into being, nor any other which should [require to] be saved, but that the very same formation should be summed up [in Christ as had existed in Adam], the analogy having been preserved.

CHAP. XXII. — CHRIST ASSUMED ACTUAL FLESH, CONCEIVED AND BORN OF THE VIRGIN.

1. Those, therefore, who allege that He took nothing from the Virgin do greatly err, [since,] in order that they may cast away the inheritance of the flesh, they also reject the analogy [be-

tween Him and Adam]. For if the one [who sprang] from the earth had indeed formation and substance from both the hand and workmanship of God, but the other not from the hand and workmanship of God, then He who was made after the image and likeness of the former did not, in that case, preserve the analogy of man, and He must seem an inconsistent piece of work, not having wherewith He may show His wisdom. But this is to say, that He also appeared putatively as man when He was not man, and that He was made man while taking nothing from man. For if He did not receive the substance of flesh from a human being, He neither was made man nor the Son of man; and if He was not made what we were, He did no great thing in what He suffered and endured. But every one will allow that we are [composed of] a body taken from the earth, and a soul receiving spirit from God. This, therefore, the Word of God was made, recapitulating in Himself His own handiwork; and on this account does He confess Himself the Son of man, and blesses "the meek, because they shall inherit the earth."[6] The Apostle Paul, moreover, in the Epistle to the Galatians, declares plainly, "God sent His Son, made of a woman."[7] And again, in that to the Romans, he says, "Concerning His Son, who was made of the seed of David according to the flesh, who was predestinated as the Son of God with power, according to the spirit of holiness, by the resurrection from the dead, Jesus Christ our Lord."[8]

2.[9] Superfluous, too, in that case is His descent into Mary; for why did He come down into her if He were to take nothing of her? Still further, if He had taken nothing of Mary, He would never have availed Himself of those kinds of food which are derived from the earth, by which that body which has been taken from the earth is nourished; nor would He have hungered, fasting those forty days, like Moses and Elias, unless His body was craving after its own proper nourishment; nor, again, would John His disciple have said, when writing of Him, "But Jesus, being wearied with the journey, was sitting [to rest];"[10] nor would David have proclaimed of Him beforehand, "They have added to the grief of my wounds;"[11] nor would He have wept over Lazarus, nor have sweated great drops of blood; nor have declared, "My soul is exceeding sorrowful;"[12] nor, when His side was pierced, would there

---

[1] Jer. xxxvi. 30, 31.
[2] Harvey prefixes this last clause to the following section.
[3] Rom. v. 19.
[4] Gen. ii. 5.
[5] John i. 3.

[6] Matt. v. 5.
[7] Gal. iv. 4.
[8] Rom. i. 3, 4.
[9] In addition to the Greek text preserved by Theodoret in this place, we have for some way a *Syriac* translation, differing slightly from both Greek and Latin. It seems, however, to run smoother than either, and has therefore been followed by us.
[10] John iv. 6.
[11] Ps. lxix. 27.
[12] Matt. xxvi. 38.

have come forth blood and water. For all these are tokens of the flesh which had been derived from the earth, which He had recapitulated in Himself, bearing salvation to His own handiwork.

3. Wherefore Luke points out that the pedigree which traces the generation of our Lord back to Adam contains seventy-two generations, connecting the end with the beginning, and implying that it is He who has summed up in Himself all nations dispersed from Adam downwards, and all languages and generations of men, together with Adam himself. Hence also was Adam himself termed by Paul "the figure of Him that was to come," [1] because the Word, the Maker of all things, had formed beforehand for Himself the future dispensation of the human race, connected with the Son of God; God having predestined that the first man should be of an animal nature, with this view, that he might be saved by the spiritual One. For inasmuch as He had a pre-existence as a saving Being, it was necessary that what might be saved should also be called into existence, in order that the Being who saves should not exist in vain.

4. In accordance with this design, Mary the Virgin is found obedient, saying, "Behold the handmaid of the Lord; be it unto me according to thy word." [2] But Eve was disobedient; for she did not obey when as yet she was a virgin. And even as she, having indeed a husband, Adam, but being nevertheless as yet à virgin (for in Paradise "they were both naked, and were not ashamed," [3] inasmuch as they, having been created a short time previously, had no understanding of the procreation of children: for it was necessary that they should first come to adult age, [4] and then multiply from that time onward), having become disobedient, was made the cause of death, both to herself and to the entire human race; so also did Mary, having a man betrothed [to her], and being nevertheless a virgin, by yielding obedience, become the cause of salvation, both to herself and the whole human race. And on this account does the law term a woman betrothed to a man, the wife of him who had betrothed her, although she was as yet a virgin; thus indicating the back-reference from Mary to Eve, because what is joined together could not otherwise be put asunder than by inversion of the process by which these bonds of union had arisen; [5] so that the former ties be cancelled by the latter, that the latter may set the former again at liberty. And it has, in fact, happened that the first compact looses from the second tie, but that the second tie takes the position of the first which has been cancelled. [6] For this reason did the Lord declare that the first should in truth be last, and the last first. [7] And the prophet, too, indicates the same, saying, "Instead of fathers, children have been born unto thee." [8] For the Lord, having been born "the First-begotten of the dead," [9] and receiving into His bosom the ancient fathers, has regenerated them into the life of God, He having been made Himself the beginning of those that live, as Adam became the beginning of those who die. [10] Wherefore also Luke, commencing the genealogy with the Lord, carried it back to Adam, indicating that it was He who regenerated them into the Gospel of life, and not they Him. And thus also it was that the knot of Eve's disobedience was loosed by the obedience of Mary. For what the virgin Eve had bound fast through unbelief, this did the virgin Mary set free through faith.

CHAP. XXIII. — ARGUMENTS IN OPPOSITION TO TATIAN, SHOWING THAT IT WAS CONSONANT TO DIVINE JUSTICE AND MERCY THAT THE FIRST ADAM SHOULD FIRST PARTAKE IN THAT SALVATION OFFERED TO ALL BY CHRIST.

1. It was necessary, therefore, that the Lord, coming to the lost sheep, and making recapitulation of so comprehensive a dispensation, and seeking after His own handiwork, should save that very man who had been created after His image and likeness, that is, Adam, filling up the times of His condemnation, which had been incurred through disobedience, — [times] "which the Father had placed in His own power." [11] [This was necessary,] too, inasmuch as the whole economy of salvation regarding man came to pass according to the good pleasure of the Father, in order that God might not be conquered, nor His wisdom lessened, [in the estimation of His creatures.] For if man, who had been created by God that he might live, after losing life, through being injured by the serpent that had corrupted him, should not any more return to life, but should be utterly [and for ever] abandoned to death, God would [in that case] have been conquered, and the wickedness of the serpent would have prevailed over the will of God. But inasmuch as God is invincible and long-suffering, He did indeed show Himself to be long-suffering in the matter of the correction of man and the probation of all, as I have already

---

[1] Rom. v. 14.
[2] Luke i. 38.
[3] Gen. ii. 25.
[4] This seems quite a peculiar opinion of Irenæus, that our first parents, when created, were not of the age of maturity.
[5] Literally, "unless these bonds of union be turned backwards."

[6] It is very difficult to follow the reasoning of Irenæus in this passage. Massuet has a long note upon it, in which he sets forth the various points of comparison and contrast here indicated between Eve and Mary: but he ends with the remark, "hæc certe et quæ sequuntur, paulo subtiliora."
[7] Matt. xix. 30, xx. 16.
[8] Ps. xlv. 17.
[9] Rev. i. 5.
[10] Comp. 1 Cor. xv. 20–22.
[11] Acts i. 7.

observed ; and by means of the second man did He bind the strong man, and spoiled his goods,[1] and abolished death, vivifying that man who had been in a state of death. For at the first Adam became a vessel in his (Satan's) possession, whom he did also hold under his power, that is, by bringing sin on him iniquitously, and under colour of immortality entailing death upon him. For, while promising that they should be as gods, which was in no way possible for him to be, he wrought death in them : wherefore he who had led man captive, was justly captured in his turn by God ; but man, who had been led captive, was loosed from the bonds of condemnation.

2. But this is Adam, if the truth should be told, the first formed man, of whom the Scripture says that the Lord spake, " Let Us make man after Our own image and likeness ; "[2] and we are all from him : and as we are from him, therefore have we all inherited his title. But inasmuch as man is saved, it is fitting that he who was created the original man should be saved. For it is too absurd to maintain, that he who was so deeply injured by the enemy, and was the first to suffer captivity, was not rescued by Him who conquered the enemy, but that his children were, — those whom he had begotten in the same captivity. Neither would the enemy appear to be as yet conquered, if the old spoils remained with him. To give an illustration : If a hostile force had overcome certain [enemies], had bound them, and led them away captive, and held them for a long time in servitude, so that they begat children among them ; and somebody, compassionating those who had been made slaves, should overcome this same hostile force ; he certainly would not act equitably, were he to liberate the children of those who had been led captive, from the sway of those who had enslaved their fathers, but should leave these latter, who had suffered the act of capture, subject to their enemies, — those, too, on whose very account he had proceeded to this retaliation, — the children succeeding to liberty through the avenging of their fathers' cause, but not[3] so that their fathers, who suffered the act of capture itself, should be left [in bondage]. For God is neither devoid of power nor of justice, who has afforded help to man, and restored him to His own liberty.

3. It was for this reason, too, that immediately after Adam had transgressed, as the Scripture relates, He pronounced no curse against Adam personally, but against the ground, in reference to his works, as a certain person among the ancients has observed : " God did indeed transfer the curse to the earth, that it might not remain in man."[4] But man received, as the punishment of his transgression, the toilsome task of tilling the earth, and to eat bread in the sweat of his face, and to return to the dust from whence he was taken. Similarly also did the woman [receive] toil, and labour, and groans, and the pangs of parturition, and a state of subjection, that is, that she should serve her husband ; so that they should neither perish altogether when cursed by God, nor, by remaining unreprimanded, should be led to despise God. But the curse in all its fulness fell upon the serpent, which had beguiled them. " And God," it is declared, " said to the serpent : Because thou hast done this, cursed art thou above all cattle, and above all the beasts of the earth."[5] And this same thing does the Lord also say in the Gospel, to those who are found upon the left hand : " Depart from me, ye cursed, into everlasting fire, which my Father hath prepared for the devil and his angels ; "[6] indicating that eternal fire was not originally prepared for man, but for him who beguiled man, and caused him to offend — for him, I say, who is chief of the apostasy, and for those angels who became apostates along with him ; which [fire], indeed, they too shall justly feel, who, like him, persevere in works of wickedness, without repentance, and without retracing their steps.

4. [These act][7] as Cain [did, who], when he was counselled by God to keep quiet, because he had not made an equitable division of that share to which his brother was entitled, but with envy and malice thought that he could domineer over him, not only did not acquiesce, but even added sin to sin, indicating his state of mind by his action. For what he had planned, that did he also put in practice : he tyrannized over and slew him ; God subjecting the just to the unjust, that the former might be proved as the just one by the things which he suffered, and the latter detected as the unjust by those which he perpetrated. And he was not softened even by this, nor did he stop short with that evil deed ; but being asked where his brother was, he said, " I know not ; am I my brother's keeper ? " extending and aggravating [his] wickedness by his answer. For if it is wicked to slay a brother, much worse is it thus insolently and irreverently to reply to the omniscient God as if he could baffle Him. And for this he did himself bear a curse about with him, because he gratuitously brought

---

1 Matt. xii. 29.
2 Gen. i. 26.
3 The old Latin translation is: " Sed non relictis ipsis patribus." Grabe would cancel *non*, while Massuet pleads for retaining it. Harvey conjectures that the translator perhaps mistook οὐκ ἀνειλημμένων for οὐκ ἀναλελειμένων. We have followed Massuet, though we should prefer deleting *non*, were it not found in all the MSS.

4 Gen. iii. 16, etc.
5 Gen. iii. 14.
6 Matt. xxv. 41. This reading of Irenæus agrees with that of the Codex Bezæ, at Cambridge.
7 Gen. iv. 7, after LXX. version.

an offering of sin, having had no reverence for God, nor being put to confusion by the act of fratricide.[1]

5. The case of Adam, however, had no analogy with this, but was altogether different. For, having been beguiled by another under the pretext of immortality, he is immediately seized with terror, and hides himself; not as if he were able to escape from God; but, in a state of confusion at having transgressed His command, he feels unworthy to appear before and to hold converse with God. Now, " the fear of the Lord is the beginning of wisdom;"[2] the sense of sin leads to repentance, and God bestows His compassion upon those who are penitent. For [Adam] showed his repentance by his conduct, through means of the girdle [which he used], covering himself with fig-leaves, while there were many other leaves, which would have irritated his body in a less degree. He, however, adopted a dress conformable to his disobedience, being awed by the fear of God; and resisting the erring, the lustful propensity of his flesh (since he had lost his natural disposition and child-like mind, and had come to the knowledge of evil things), he girded a bridle of continence upon himself and his wife, fearing God, and waiting for His coming, and indicating, as it were, some such thing [as follows]: Inasmuch as, he says, I have by disobedience lost that robe of sanctity which I had from the Spirit, I do now also acknowledge that I am deserving of a covering of this nature, which affords no gratification, but which gnaws and frets the body. And he would no doubt have retained this clothing for ever, thus humbling himself, if God, who is merciful, had not clothed them with tunics of skins instead of fig-leaves. For this purpose, too, He interrogates them, that the blame might light upon the woman; and again, He interrogates her, that she might convey the blame to the serpent. For she related what had occurred. " The serpent," says she, " beguiled me, and I did eat."[3] But He put no question to the serpent; for He knew that he had been the prime mover in the guilty deed; but He pronounced the curse upon him in the first instance, that it might fall upon man with a mitigated rebuke. For God detested him who had led man astray, but by degrees, and little by little, He showed compassion to him who had been beguiled.

6. Wherefore also He drove him out of Paradise, and removed him far from the tree of life, not because He envied him the tree of life, as some venture to assert, but because He pitied him, [and did not desire] that he should continue a sinner for ever, nor that the sin which surrounded him should be immortal, and evil interminable and irremediable. But He set a bound to his [state of] sin, by interposing death, and thus causing sin to cease,[4] putting an end to it by the dissolution of the flesh, which should take place in the earth, so that man, ceasing at length to live to sin, and dying to it, might begin to live to God.

7. For this end did He put enmity between the serpent and the woman and her seed, they keeping it up mutually: He, the sole of whose foot should be bitten, having power also to tread upon the enemy's head; but the other biting, killing, and impeding the steps of man, until the seed did come appointed to tread down his head, — which was born of Mary, of whom the prophet speaks: " Thou shalt tread upon the asp and the basilisk; thou shalt trample down the lion and the dragon;"[5] — indicating that sin, which was set up and spread out against man, and which rendered him subject to death, should be deprived of its power, along with death, which rules [over men]; and that the lion, that is, antichrist, rampant against mankind in the latter days, should be trampled down by Him; and that He should bind " the dragon, that old serpent,"[6] and subject him to the power of man, who had been conquered,[7] so that all his might should be trodden down. Now Adam had been conquered, all life having been taken away from him: wherefore, when the foe was conquered in his turn, Adam received new life; and the last enemy, death, is destroyed,[8] which at the first had taken possession of man. Therefore, when man has been liberated, " what is written shall come to pass, Death is swallowed up in victory. O death, where is thy victory? O death, where is thy sting?"[9] This could not be said with justice, if that man, over whom death did first obtain dominion, were not set free. For his salvation is death's destruction. When therefore the Lord vivifies man, that is, Adam, death is at the same time destroyed.

8. All therefore speak falsely who disallow his (Adam's) salvation, shutting themselves out from life for ever, in that they do not believe that the sheep which had perished has been found.[10] For if it has not been found, the whole human race is still held in a state of perdition. False, therefore, is that man who first started this idea, or rather, this ignorance and blindness — Tatian.[11]

---

[1] The old Latin reads " parricidio." The crime of parricide was alone known to the Roman law; but it was a *generic* term, including the murder of all near relations. All the editors have supposed that the original word was ἀδελφοκτονία, which has here been adopted.
[2] Prov. i. 7, ix. 10.
[3] Gen. iii. 13.
[4] Rom. vi. 7.
[5] Ps. xci. 13.
[6] Rev. xx. 2.
[7] Luke x. 19.
[8] 1 Cor. xv. 26.
[9] 1 Cor. xv. 54, 55.
[10] Luke xv. 4.
[11] An account of Tatian will be given in a future volume with his only extant work.

As I have already indicated, this man entangled himself with all the heretics.[1] This dogma, however, has been invented by himself, in order that, by introducing something new, independently of the rest, and by speaking vanity, he might acquire for himself hearers void of faith, affecting to be esteemed a teacher, and endeavouring from time to time to employ sayings of this kind often [made use of] by Paul : " In Adam we all die ; "[2] ignorant, however, that "where sin abounded, grace did much more abound."[3] Since this, then, has been clearly shown, let all his disciples be put to shame, and let them wrangle[4] about Adam, as if some great gain were to accrue to them if he be not saved ; when they profit nothing more [by that], even as the serpent also did not profit when persuading man [to sin], except to this effect, that he proved him a transgressor, obtaining man as the first-fruits of his own apostasy.[5] But he did not know God's power.[6] Thus also do those who disallow Adam's salvation gain nothing, except this, that they render themselves heretics and apostates from the truth, and show themselves patrons of the serpent and of death.

CHAP. XXIV. — RECAPITULATION OF THE VARIOUS ARGUMENTS ADDUCED AGAINST GNOSTIC IMPIETY UNDER ALL ITS ASPECTS. THE HERETICS, TOSSED ABOUT BY EVERY BLAST OF DOCTRINE, ARE OPPOSED BY THE UNIFORM TEACHING OF THE CHURCH, WHICH REMAINS SO ALWAYS, AND IS CONSISTENT WITH ITSELF.

1. Thus, then, have all these men been exposed, who bring in impious doctrines regarding our Maker and Framer, who also formed this world, and above whom there is no other God ; and those have been overthrown by their own arguments who teach falsehoods regarding the substance of our Lord, and the dispensation which He fulfilled for the sake of His own creature man. But [it has, on the other hand, been shown], that the preaching of the Church is everywhere consistent, and continues in an even course, and receives testimony from the prophets, the apostles, and all the disciples — as I have proved — through [those in] the beginning, the middle, and the end,[7] and through the entire dispensation of God, and that well-grounded system which tends[8] to man's salva-

tion, namely, our faith ; which, having been received from the Church, we do preserve, and which always, by the Spirit of God, renewing its youth, as if it were some precious deposit in an excellent vessel, causes the vessel itself containing it to renew its youth also. For this gift of God has been entrusted to the Church, as breath was to the first created man,[9] for this purpose, that all the members receiving it may be vivified ; and the [means of] communion with Christ has been distributed throughout it, that is, the Holy Spirit, the earnest of incorruption, the means of confirming our faith, and the ladder of ascent to God. "For in the Church," it is said, "God hath set apostles, prophets, teachers,"[10] and all the other means through which the Spirit works ; of which all those are not partakers who do not join themselves to the Church, but defraud themselves of life through their perverse opinions and infamous behaviour. For where the Church is, there is the Spirit of God ; and where the Spirit of God is, there is the Church, and every kind of grace ; but the Spirit is truth. Those, therefore, who do not partake of Him, are neither nourished into life from the mother's breasts, nor do they enjoy that most limpid fountain which issues from the body of Christ ; but they dig for themselves broken cisterns[11] out of earthly trenches, and drink putrid water out of the mire, fleeing from the faith of the Church lest they be convicted ; and rejecting the Spirit, that they may not be instructed.

2. Alienated thus from the truth, they do deservedly wallow in all error, tossed to and fro by it, thinking differently in regard to the same things at different times, and never attaining to a well-grounded knowledge, being more anxious to be sophists of words than disciples of the truth. For they have not been founded upon the one rock, but upon the sand, which has in itself a multitude of stones. Wherefore they also imagine many gods, and they always have the excuse of searching [after truth] (for they are blind), but never succeed in finding it. For they blaspheme the Creator, Him who is truly God, who also furnishes power to find [the truth] ; imagining that they have discovered another god beyond God, or another Pleroma, or another dispensation. Wherefore also the light which is from God does not illumine them, because they have dishonoured and despised God, holding Him of small account, because, through His love and infinite benignity, He has come within reach of human knowledge (knowledge, however, not with regard to His greatness, or with regard to His essence — for that has no

---

[1] His heresy being just a mixture of the opinions of the various Gnostic sects.
[2] 1 Cor. xv. 22.
[3] Rom. v. 20.
[4] Though unnoticed by the editors, there seems a difficulty in the different moods of the two verbs, *erubescant* and *concertant*.
[5] "Initium et materiam apostasiæ suæ habens hominem:" the meaning is very obscure, and the editors throw no light upon it.
[6] Literally, "but he did not *see* God." The translator is supposed to have read οἶδεν, *knew*, for εἶδεν, *saw*.
[7] Literally, "through the beginnings, the means, and the end." These three terms refer to the Prophets, the Apostles, and the Church Catholic.
[8] The Latin is "solidam operationem," which we know not how to translate, in accordance with the context, except as above.

[9] This seems to be the meaning conveyed by the old Latin, "quemadmodum aspiratio plasmationi."
[10] 1 Cor. xii. 28.
[11] Jer. ii. 13.

man measured or handled — but after this sort: that we should know that He who made, and formed, and breathed in them the breath of life, and nourishes us by means of the creation, establishing all things by His Word, and binding them together by His Wisdom [1] — this is He who is the only true God) ; but they dream of a non-existent being above Him, that they may be regarded as having found out the great God, whom nobody, [they hold,] can recognise as holding communication with the human race, or as directing mundane matters : that is to say, they find out the god of Epicurus, who does nothing either for himself or others ; that is, he exercises no providence at all.

CHAP. XXV. — THIS WORLD IS RULED BY THE PROVIDENCE OF ONE GOD, WHO IS BOTH ENDOWED WITH INFINITE JUSTICE TO PUNISH THE WICKED, AND WITH INFINITE GOODNESS TO BLESS THE PIOUS, AND IMPART TO THEM SALVATION.

1. God does, however, exercise a providence over all things, and therefore He also gives counsel ; and when giving counsel, He is present with those who attend to moral discipline.[2] It follows then of course, that the things which are watched over and governed should be acquainted with their ruler ; which things are not irrational or vain, but they have understanding derived from the providence of God. And, for this reason, certain of the Gentiles, who were less addicted to [sensual] allurements and voluptuousness, and were not led away to such a degree of superstition with regard to idols, being moved, though but slightly, by His providence, were nevertheless convinced that they should call the Maker of this universe the Father, who exercises a providence over all things, and arranges the affairs of our world.

2. Again, that they might remove the rebuking and judicial power from the Father, reckoning that as unworthy of God, and thinking that they had found out a God both without anger and [merely] good, they have alleged that one [God] judges, but that another saves, unconsciously taking away the intelligence and justice of both deities. For if the judicial one is not also good, to bestow favours upon the deserving, and to direct reproofs against those requiring them, he will appear neither a just nor a wise judge. On the other hand, the good God, if he is merely good, and not one who tests those upon whom he shall send his goodness, will be out of the range of justice and goodness ; and his goodness will seem imperfect, as not saving all ; [for it should do so,] if it be not accompanied with judgment.

3. Marcion, therefore, himself, by dividing God into two, maintaining one to be good and the other judicial, does in fact, on both sides, put an end to deity. For he that is the judicial one, if he be not good, is not God, because he from whom goodness is absent is no God at all ; and again, he who is good, if he has no judicial power, suffers the same [loss] as the former, by being deprived of his character of deity. And how can they call the Father of all wise, if they do not assign to Him a judicial faculty ? For if He is wise, He is also one who tests [others] ; but the judicial power belongs to him who tests, and justice follows the judicial faculty, that it may reach a just conclusion ; justice calls forth judgment, and judgment, when it is executed with justice, will pass on to wisdom. Therefore the Father will excel in wisdom all human and angelic wisdom, because He is Lord, and Judge, and the Just One, and Ruler over all. For He is good, and merciful, and patient, and saves whom He ought : nor does goodness desert Him in the exercise of justice,[3] nor is His wisdom lessened ; for He saves those whom He should save, and judges those worthy of judgment. Neither does He show Himself unmercifully just ; for His goodness, no doubt, goes on before, and takes precedence.

4. The God, therefore, who does benevolently cause His sun to rise upon all,[4] and sends rain upon the just and unjust, shall judge those who, enjoying His equally distributed kindness, have led lives not corresponding to the dignity of His bounty ; but who have spent their days in wantonness and luxury, in opposition to His benevolence, and have, moreover, even blasphemed Him who has conferred so great benefits upon them.

5. Plato is proved to be more religious than these men, for he allowed that the same God was both just and good, having power over all things, and Himself executing judgment, expressing himself thus, " And God indeed, as He is also the ancient Word, possessing the beginning, the end, and the mean of all existing things, does everything rightly, moving round about them according to their nature ; but retributive justice always follows Him against those who depart from the divine law." [5] Then, again, he points out that the Maker and Framer of the universe is good. " And to the good," he says, " no envy ever springs up with regard to anything ; " [6] thus establishing the goodness of God, as the beginning and the cause of the creation of the world, but not ignorance, nor an erring Æon, nor the

---

[3] The text is here very uncertain, but the above seems the probable meaning.
[4] Matt. v. 45.
[5] Plato, *de Leg.*, iv. and p. 715, 16.
[6] In *Timæo*, vi. p. 29.

consequence of a defect, nor the Mother weeping and lamenting, nor another God or Father.

6. Well may their Mother bewail them, as capable of conceiving and inventing such things; for they have worthily uttered this falsehood against themselves, that their Mother is beyond the Pleroma, that is, beyond the knowledge of God, and that their entire multitude became [1] a shapeless and crude abortion: for it apprehends nothing of the truth; it falls into void and darkness: for their wisdom (*Sophia*) was void, and wrapped up in darkness; and Horos did not permit her to enter the Pleroma: for the Spirit (Achamoth) did not receive them into the place of refreshment. For their father, by begetting ignorance, wrought in them the sufferings of death. We do not misrepresent [their opinions on] these points; but they do themselves confirm, they do themselves teach, they do glory in them, they imagine a lofty [mystery] about their Mother, whom they represent as having been begotten without a father, that is, without God, a female from a female,[2] that is, corruption from error.

7. We do indeed pray that these men may not remain in the pit which they themselves have dug, but separate themselves from a Mother of this nature, and depart from Bythus, and stand away from the void, and relinquish the shadow; and that they, being converted to the Church of God, may be lawfully begotten, and that Christ may be formed in them, and that they may know the Framer and Maker of this universe, the only true God and Lord of all. We pray for these things on their behalf, loving them better than they seem to love themselves. For our love, inasmuch as it is true, is salutary to them, if they will but receive it. It may be compared to a severe remedy, extirpating the proud and sloughing flesh of a wound; for it puts an end to their pride and haughtiness. Wherefore it shall not weary us, to endeavour with all our might to stretch out the hand unto them. Over and above what has been already stated, I have deferred to the following book, to adduce the words of the Lord; if, by convincing some among them, through means of the very instruction of Christ, I may succeed in persuading them to abandon such error, and to cease from blaspheming their Creator, who is both God alone, and the Father of our Lord Jesus Christ. Amen.

[1] The Latin is "collectio eorum;" but what *collectio* here means, it is not easy to determine. Grabe, with much probability, deems it the representative of σύστασις. Harvey prefers ἐνθύμημα: but it is difficult to perceive the relevancy of his references to the rhetorical syllogism.

[2] See book i. cap. xvi. note.

ELUCIDATION

THE editor of this American Series confines himself in general to such occasional and *very* brief annotations as may suggest to students and others the practical views which are requisite to a clear comprehension of authors who wrote for past ages; for a sort and condition of men no longer existing, whose extinction as a class is, indeed, largely due to these writings. But he reserved to himself the privilege of correcting palpable mistakes, especially in points which bear upon questions of our own times.

That our learned translators have unaccountably admitted a very inaccurate translation of the crucial paragraph in book iii. cap. iii. sect. 2, I have shown in the footnote at that place. It is evident, (1) because they themselves are not satisfied with it, and (2) because I have set it side by side with the more literal rendering of a writer who would have preferred their reading if it could have borne the test of criticism.

Now, the authors of the Latin translation [1] may have designed the ambiguity which gives the Ultramontane party an apparent advantage; but it is an advantage which disappears as soon as it is examined, and hence I am content to take it as it stands. Various conjectures have been made as to the original Greek of Irenæus; but the Latin answers every purpose of the author's argument, and is fatal to the claims of the Papacy. Let me recur to the translation given, *in loco*, from a Roman Catholic, and this will be seen at once.

For he thus renders it: —

1. In this Church, "ever, *by those who are on every side*, has been preserved that tradition

---

[1] One of the Antiochian Canons probably reflects the current language of an earlier antiquity thus: διὰ τὸ ἐν τῇ μητροπόλει πανταχόθεν συντρέχειν πάντας τοὺς τὰ πράγματα ἔχοντας; and, if so, this συντρέχειν gives the meaning of *convenire*.

which is from apostles." How would such a proposition have sounded to Pius IX. in the Vatican Council? The faith is preserved *by those who come to Rome*, not by the Bishop who presides there.

2. "For to this Church, on account of more potent principality,[1] it is necessary that *every Church* (that is, those who are, on every side, faithful) resort." The greatness of Rome, that is, as the capital of the Empire, imparts to the local Church a superior dignity, even as compared with Lyons, or any other metropolitical Church. Everybody visits Rome : hence you find there faithful witnesses from every side (from all the Churches) ; and *their united testimony* it is which preserves in Rome the pure apostolic traditions.

The Latin, thus translated by a candid Roman Catholic, reverses the whole system of the Papacy. Pius IX. informed his Bishops, at the late Council, that they were not called to bear their testimony, but to hear his infallible decree ; "reducing us," said the Archbishop of Paris, "to a council of sacristans."

Sustaining these views by a few footnotes, I add (1) a literal rendering of my own, and then (2) a metaphrase of the same, bringing out the argument from the crabbed obstructions of the Latin text. This, then, is what Irenæus says : (a) "For it is necessary for every Church (that is to say, the faithful from all parts) to meet in this Church, on account of the superior magistracy ; in which Church, by those who are from all places, the tradition of the apostles has been preserved." Or, more freely rendered : (b) "On account of the chief magistracy[2] [of the empire], the faithful from all parts, representing every Church, are obliged to resort to Rome, and there to come together ; so that [it is the distinction of this Church that], in it, the tradition of the apostles has been preserved by Christians gathered together out of all the Churches." Taking the entire argument of our author with the context, then, it amounts to this : "We must ask, not for local, but universal, testimony. Now, in every Church founded by the apostles has been handed down their traditions ; but, as it would be a tedious thing to collect them all, let this suffice. Take that Church (nearest at hand, and which is the only Apostolic Church of the West), the great and glorious Church at Rome, which was there founded by the two apostles Peter and Paul. In her have been preserved the traditions *of all the Churches*, because everybody is forced to go to the seat of empire : and therefore, by these representatives of the whole Catholic Church, the apostolic traditions have been all collected in Rome :[3] and you have a synoptical view of all Churches in what is there preserved." Had the views of the modern Papacy ever entered the head of Irenæus, what an absurdity would be this whole argument. He would have said, "It is no matter what may be gathered elsewhere ; for the Bishop of Rome is the infallible oracle of all Catholic truth, and you will always find it by his mouth." It should be noted that Orthodoxy was indeed preserved there, just so long as Rome permitted other Churches to contribute their testimony on the principle of Irenæus, and thus to make her the depository of all Catholic tradition, as witnessed "by *all, everywhere*, and from the beginning." But all this is turned upside down by modern Romanism. No other Church is to be heard or considered ; but Rome takes all into her own power, and may dictate to all Churches what they are to believe, however novel, or contrary to the torrent of antiquity in the teachings of their own founders and great doctors in all past time.

---

[1] "*Its* more potent," etc., is not a strict rendering: "*the* more potent," rather; which leaves the *principalitas* to the city, not the Church.

[2] Bishop Wordsworth inclines to the idea that the original Greek was ἱκανωτέραν ἀρχαιότητα, thus conceding that Irenæus was speaking of the *greater antiquity* of Rome as compared with other (Western) Churches. Even so, he shows that the argument of Irenæus is fatal to Roman pretensions, which admit of no such ideas as he advances, and no such freedom as that of his dealings with Rome.

[3] Nobody has more forcibly stated the argument of Irenæus than the Abbé Guettée, in his exhaustive work on the Papacy. I published a translation of this valuable historical epitome in New York (Carleton), 1867; but it is out of print. The original may be had in Paris (Fischbacher), No. 33 Rue de Seine.

IRENÆUS AGAINST HERESIES

BOOK IV.

PREFACE.

1. By transmitting to thee, my very dear friend, this fourth book of the work which is [entitled] *The Detection and Refutation of False Knowledge*, I shall, as I have promised, add weight, by means of the words of the Lord, to what I have already advanced; so that thou also, as thou hast requested, mayest obtain from me the means of confuting all the heretics everywhere, and not permit them, beaten back at all points, to launch out further into the deep of error, nor to be drowned in the sea of ignorance; but that thou, turning them into the haven of the truth, mayest cause them to attain their salvation.

2. The man, however, who would undertake their conversion, must possess an accurate knowledge of their systems or schemes of doctrine. For it is impossible for any one to heal the sick, if he has no knowledge of the disease of the patients. This was the reason that my predecessors — much superior men to myself, too — were unable, notwithstanding, to refute the Valentinians satisfactorily, because they were ignorant of these men's system;[1] which I have with all care delivered to thee in the first book, in which I have also shown that their doctrine is a recapitulation of all the heretics. For which reason also, in the second, we have had, as in a mirror, a sight of their entire discomfiture. For they who oppose these men (the Valentinians) by the right method, do [thereby] oppose all who are of an evil mind; and they who overthrow them, do in fact overthrow every kind of heresy.

3. For their system is blasphemous above all [others], since they represent that the Maker and Framer, who is one God, as I have shown, was produced from a defect or apostasy. They utter blasphemy, also, against our Lord, by cutting off and dividing Jesus from Christ, and

Christ from the Saviour, and again the Saviour from the Word, and the Word from the Only-begotten. And since they allege that the Creator originated from a defect or apostasy, so have they also taught that Christ and the Holy Spirit were emitted on account of this defect, and that the Saviour was a product of those Æons who were produced from a defect; so that there is nothing but blasphemy to be found among them. In the preceding book, then, the ideas of the apostles as to all these points have been set forth, [to the effect] that not only did they, "who from the beginning were eye-witnesses and ministers of the word"[2] of truth, hold no such opinions, but that they did also preach to us to shun these doctrines,[3] foreseeing by the Spirit those weak-minded persons who should be led astray.[4]

4. For as the serpent beguiled Eve, by promising her what he had not himself,[5] so also do these men, by pretending [to possess] superior knowledge, and [to be acquainted with] ineffable mysteries; and, by promising that admittance which they speak of as taking place within the Pleroma, plunge those that believe them into death, rendering them apostates from Him who made them. And at that time, indeed, the apostate angel, having effected the disobedience of mankind by means of the serpent, imagined that he escaped the notice of the Lord; wherefore God assigned him the form[6] and name [of a serpent]. But now, since the last times are [come upon us], evil is spread abroad among men, which not only renders them apostates, but by many machinations does [the devil] raise up blasphemers against the

---

1 [The reader who marvels at the tedious recitals must note this (1) as proof of the author's practical wisdom, and (2) as evidence of his fidelity in what he exhibits.]

2 Luke i. 2.
3 2 Tim. ii. 23.
4 [The solemnity of the apostolic testimonies against the crop of tares that was to spring up receives great illustration from Irenæus. 1 John ii. 18.]
5 [2 Pet. ii. 19.]
6 [Rev. xii. 9. A little essay, *Messias and Anti-Messias*, by the Rev. C. I. Black, London (Masters, 1847), is commended to those who need light on this very mysterious subject.]

Creator, namely, by means of all the heretics already mentioned. For all these, although they issue forth from diverse regions, and promulgate different [opinions], do nevertheless concur in the same blasphemous design, wounding [men] unto death, by teaching blasphemy against God our Maker and Supporter, and derogating from the salvation of man. Now man is a mixed organization of soul and flesh, who was formed after the likeness of God, and moulded by His hands, that is, by the Son and Holy Spirit, to whom also He said, "Let Us make man."[1] This, then, is the aim of him who envies our life, to render men disbelievers in their own salvation, and blasphemous against God the Creator. For whatsoever all the heretics may have advanced with the utmost solemnity, they come to this at last, that they blaspheme the Creator, and disallow the salvation of God's workmanship, which the flesh truly is ; on behalf of which I have proved, in a variety of ways, that the Son of God accomplished the whole dispensation [of mercy], and have shown that there is none other called God by the Scriptures except the Father of all, and the Son, and those who possess the adoption.

CHAP. I. — THE LORD ACKNOWLEDGED BUT ONE GOD AND FATHER.

1. Since, therefore, this is sure and stedfast, that no other God or Lord was announced by the Spirit, except Him who, as God, rules over all, together with His Word, and those who receive the Spirit of adoption,[2] that is, those who believe in the one and true God, and in Jesus Christ the Son of God ; and likewise that the apostles did of themselves term no one else as God, or name [no other] as Lord ; and, what is much more important, [since it is true] that our Lord [acted likewise], who did also command us to confess no one as Father, except Him who is in the heavens, who is the one God and the one Father ; — those things are clearly shown to be false which these deceivers and most perverse sophists advance, maintaining that the being whom they have themselves invented is by nature both God and Father ; but that the Demiurge is naturally neither God nor Father, but is so termed merely by courtesy (*verbo tenus*), because of his ruling the creation, as these perverse mythologists state, setting their thoughts against God ; and, putting aside the doctrine of Christ, and of themselves divining falsehoods, they dispute against the entire dispensation of God. For they maintain that their Æons, and gods, and fathers, and lords, are also still further termed heavens, together with their Mother, whom they do also call " the Earth,"

and " Jerusalem," while they also style her many other names.

2. Now to whom is it not clear, that if the Lord had known many fathers and gods, He would not have taught His disciples to know [only] one God,[3] and to call Him alone Father? But He did the rather distinguish those who by word merely (*verbo tenus*) are termed gods, from Him who is truly God, that they should not err as to His doctrine, nor understand one [in mistake] for another. And if He did indeed teach us to call one Being Father and God, while He does from time to time Himself confess other fathers and gods in the same sense, then He will appear to enjoin a different course upon His disciples from what He follows Himself. Such conduct, however, does not bespeak the good teacher, but a misleading and invidious one. The apostles, too, according to these men's showing, are proved to be transgressors of the commandment, since they confess the Creator as God, and Lord, and Father, as I have shown — if He is not alone God and Father. Jesus, therefore, will be to them the author and teacher of such transgression, inasmuch as He commanded that one Being should be called Father,[4] thus imposing upon them the necessity of confessing the Creator as their Father, as has been pointed out.

CHAP. II. — PROOFS FROM THE PLAIN TESTIMONY OF MOSES, AND OF THE OTHER PROPHETS, WHOSE WORDS ARE THE WORDS OF CHRIST, THAT THERE IS BUT ONE GOD, THE FOUNDER OF THE WORLD, WHOM OUR LORD PREACHED, AND WHOM HE CALLED HIS FATHER.

1. Moses, therefore, making a recapitulation of the whole law, which he had received from the Creator (Demiurge), thus speaks in Deuteronomy : " Give ear, O ye heavens ; and I will speak ; and hear, O earth, the words of my mouth."[5] Again, David saying that his help came from the Lord, asserts : " My help is from the LORD, who made heaven and earth."[6] And Esaias confesses that words were uttered by God, who made heaven and earth, and governs them. He says : " Hear, O heavens ; and give ear, O earth : for the LORD hath spoken."[7] And again : " Thus saith the LORD God, who made the heaven, and stretched it out ; who established the earth, and the things in it ; and who giveth breath to the people upon it, and spirit to them who walk therein."[8]

2. Again, our Lord Jesus Christ confesses this same Being as His Father, where He says : " I

[1] Gen. i. 26.
[2] See iii. 6, 1.

[3] [St. John xvii. 3.]
[4] Matt. xxiii. 9.
[5] Deut. xxxii. 1.
[6] Ps. cxxiv. 8.
[7] Isa. i. 2.
[8] Isa. xlii. 5.

confess to thee, O Father, Lord of heaven and earth." [1] What Father will those men have us to understand [by these words], those who are most perverse sophists of Pandora? Whether shall it be Bythus, whom they have fabled of themselves; or their Mother; or the Only-begotten? Or shall it be he whom the Marcionites or the others have invented as god (whom I indeed have amply demonstrated to be no god at all) ; or shall it be (what is really the case) the Maker of heaven and earth, whom also the prophets proclaimed, — whom Christ, too, confesses as His Father, — whom also the law announces, saying: "Hear, O Israel; The Lord thy God is one God?" [2]

3. But since the writings (*literæ*) of Moses are the words of Christ, He does Himself declare to the Jews, as John has recorded in the Gospel: "If ye had believed Moses, ye would have believed Me : for he wrote of Me. But if ye believe not his writings, neither will ye believe My words." [3] He thus indicates in the clearest manner that the writings of Moses are His words. If, then, [this be the case with regard] to Moses, so also, beyond a doubt, the words of the other prophets are His [words], as I have pointed out. And again, the Lord Himself exhibits Abraham as having said to the rich man, with reference to all those who were still alive : "If they do not obey Moses and the prophets, neither, if any one were to rise from the dead and go to them, will they believe him." [4]

4. Now, He has not merely related to us a story respecting a poor man and a rich one ; but He has taught us, in the first place, that no one should lead a luxurious life, nor, living in worldly pleasures and perpetual feastings, should be the slave of his lusts, and forget God. " For there was," He says, " a rich man, who was clothed in purple and fine linen, and delighted himself with splendid feasts." [5]

Of such persons, too, the Spirit has spoken by Esaias : "They drink wine with [the accompaniment of] harps, and tablets, and psalteries, and flutes ; but they regard not the works of God, neither do they consider the work of His hands." [6] Lest, therefore, we should incur the same punishment as these men, the Lord reveals [to us] their end ; showing at the same time, that if they obeyed Moses and the prophets, they would believe in Him whom these had preached, the Son of God, who rose from the dead, and bestows life upon us ; and He shows that all are from one essence, that is, Abraham, and Moses, and the prophets, and also the Lord Himself, who

rose from the dead, in whom many believe who are of the circumcision, who do also hear Moses and the prophets announcing the coming of the Son of God. But those who scoff [at the truth] assert that these men were from another essence, and they do not know the first-begotten from the dead ; understanding Christ as a distinct being, who continued as if He were impassible, and Jesus, who suffered, as being altogether separate [from Him].

5. For they do not receive from the Father the knowledge of the Son ; neither do they learn who the Father is from the Son, who teaches clearly and without parables Him who truly is God. He says : "Swear not at all ; neither by heaven, for it is God's throne ; nor by the earth, for it is His footstool ; neither by Jerusalem, for it is the city of the great King." [7] For these words are evidently spoken with reference to the Creator, as also Esaias says : "Heaven is my throne, the earth is my footstool." [8] And besides this Being there is no other God ; otherwise He would not be termed by the Lord either " God " or " the great King ; " for a Being who can be so described admits neither of any other being compared with nor set above Him. For he who has any superior over him, and is under the power of another, this being never can be called either " God " or " the great King."

6. But neither will these men be able to maintain that such words were uttered in an ironical manner, since it is proved to them by the words themselves that they were in earnest. For He who uttered them was Truth, and did truly vindicate His own house, by driving out of it the changers of money, who were buying and selling, saying unto them : " It is written, My house shall be called the house of prayer ; but ye have made it a den of thieves." [9] And what reason had He for thus doing and saying, and vindicating His house, if He did preach another God? But [He did so], that He might point out the transgressors of His Father's law ; for neither did He bring any accusation against the house, nor did He blame the law, which He had come to fulfil ; but He reproved those who were putting His house to an improper use, and those who were transgressing the law. And therefore the scribes and Pharisees, too, who from the times of the law had begun to despise God, did not receive His Word, that is, they did not believe on Christ. Of these Esaias says : " Thy princes are rebellious, companions of thieves, loving gifts, following after rewards, not judging the fatherless, and negligent of the cause of the widows." [10] And Jeremiah, in like manner :

---

[1] Matt. xi. 25; Luke x. 21.
[2] Deut. vi. 4.
[3] John v. 46, 47.
[4] Luke xvi. 31.
[5] Luke xvi. 19.
[6] Isa. v. 12.

[7] Matt. v. 34.
[8] Isa. lxvi. 1.
[9] Matt. xxi. 13.
[10] Isa. i. 23.

"They," he says, "who rule my people did not know me; they are senseless and imprudent children; they are wise to do evil, but to do well they have no knowledge." [1]

7. But as many as feared God, and were anxious about His law, these ran to Christ, and were all saved. For He said to His disciples: "Go ye to the sheep of the house of Israel,[2] which have perished." And many more Samaritans, it is said, when the Lord had tarried among them two days, "believed because of His words, and said to the woman, Now we believe, not because of thy saying, for we ourselves have heard [Him], and know that this man is truly the Saviour of the world." [3] And Paul likewise declares, "And so all Israel shall be saved;" [4] but he has also said, that the law was our pedagogue [to bring us] to Christ Jesus.[5] Let them not therefore ascribe to the law the unbelief of certain [among them]. For the law never hindered them from believing in the Son of God; nay, but it even exhorted them [6] so to do, saying [7] that men can be saved in no other way from the old wound of the serpent than by believing in Him who, in the likeness of sinful flesh, is lifted up from the earth upon the tree of martyrdom, and draws all things to Himself,[8] and vivifies the dead.

CHAP. III. — ANSWER TO THE CAVILS OF THE GNOSTICS. WE ARE NOT TO SUPPOSE THAT THE TRUE GOD CAN BE CHANGED, OR COME TO AN END, BECAUSE THE HEAVENS, WHICH ARE HIS THRONE, AND THE EARTH, HIS FOOTSTOOL, SHALL PASS AWAY.

1. Again, as to their malignantly asserting that if heaven is indeed the throne of God, and earth His footstool, and if it is declared that the heaven and earth shall pass away, then when these pass away the God who sitteth above must also pass away, and therefore He cannot be the God who is over all; in the first place, they are ignorant what the expression means, that heaven is [His] throne and earth [His] footstool. For they do not know what God is, but they imagine that He sits after the fashion of a man, and is contained within bounds, but does not contain. And they are also unacquainted with [the meaning of] the passing away of the heaven and earth; but Paul was not ignorant of it when he declared, "For the figure of this world passeth away." [9] In the next place, David explains their question, for he says that when the fashion of this world passes away, not only shall God re-main, but His servants also, expressing himself thus in the 101st Psalm: "In the beginning, Thou, O Lord, hast founded the earth, and the heavens are the works of Thy hands. They shall perish, but Thou shalt endure, and all shall wax old as a garment; and as a vesture Thou shalt change them, and they shall be changed: but Thou art the same, and Thy years shall not fail. The children of Thy servants shall continue, and their seed shall be established for ever;" [10] pointing out plainly what things they are that pass away, and who it is that doth endure for ever — God, together with His servants. And in like manner Esaias says: "Lift up your eyes to the heavens, and look upon the earth beneath; for the heaven has been set together as smoke, and the earth shall wax old like a garment, and they who dwell therein shall die in like manner. But my salvation shall be for ever, and my righteousness shall not pass away." [11]

CHAP. IV. — ANSWER TO ANOTHER OBJECTION, SHOWING THAT THE DESTRUCTION OF JERUSALEM, WHICH WAS THE CITY OF THE GREAT KING, DIMINISHED NOTHING FROM THE SUPREME MAJESTY AND POWER OF GOD, FOR THAT THIS DESTRUCTION WAS PUT IN EXECUTION BY THE MOST WISE COUNSEL OF THE SAME GOD.

1. Further, also, concerning Jerusalem and the Lord, they venture to assert that, if it had been "the city of the great King," [12] it would not have been deserted.[13] This is just as if any one should say, that if straw were a creation of God, it would never part company with the wheat; and that the vine twigs, if made by God, never would be lopped away and deprived of the clusters. But as these [vine twigs] have not been originally made for their own sake, but for that of the fruit growing upon them, which being come to maturity and taken away, they are left behind, and those which do not conduce to fructification are lopped off altogether; so also [was it with] Jerusalem, which had in herself borne the yoke of bondage (under which man was reduced, who in former times was not subject to God when death was reigning, and being subdued, became a fit subject for liberty), when the fruit of liberty had come, and reached maturity, and been reaped and stored in the barn, and when those which had the power to produce fruit had been carried away from her [i.e., from Jerusalem], and scattered throughout all the world. Even as Esaias saith, "The children of

---

[1] Jer. iv. 22.
[2] Matt. x. 6.
[3] John iv. 41.
[4] Rom. xi. 26.
[5] Gal. iii. 24.
[6] Num. xxi. 8.
[7] This passage is quoted by Augustine, in his treatise on original sin, written to oppose Pelagius (lib. i. c. ii.), about 400 A.D.
[8] John xii. 32, iii. 14.
[9] 1 Cor. vii. 31.

[10] Ps. cii. 25–28. The cause of the difference in the numbering of the Psalms is that the Septuagint embraces in one psalm — the ninth — the two which form the ninth and tenth in the Hebrew text.
[11] Isa. li. 6.
[12] Matt. v. 35.
[13] [Jer. vii. 4. One of the most powerful arguments in all Scripture is contained in the first twelve verses of this chapter, and it rebukes an inveterate superstition of the human heart. Comp. Rev. ii. 5, and the message to Rome, Rom. xi. 21.]

Jacob shall strike root, and Israel shall flourish, and the whole world shall be filled with his fruit." [1] The fruit, therefore, having been sown throughout all the world, she (Jerusalem) was deservedly forsaken, and those things which had formerly brought forth fruit abundantly were taken away; for from these, according to the flesh, were Christ and the apostles enabled to bring forth fruit. But now these are no longer useful for bringing forth fruit. For all things which have a beginning in time must of course have an end in time also.

2. Since, then, the law originated with Moses, it terminated with John as a necessary consequence. Christ had come to fulfil it: wherefore "the law and the prophets were" with them "until John." [2] And therefore Jerusalem, taking its commencement from David,[3] and fulfilling its own times, must have an end of legislation [4] when the new covenant was revealed. For God does all things by measure and in order; nothing is unmeasured with Him, because nothing is out of order. Well spake he, who said that the unmeasurable Father was Himself subjected to measure in the Son; for the Son is the measure of the Father, since He also comprehends Him. But that the administration of them (the Jews) was temporary, Esaias says: "And the daughter of Zion shall be left as a cottage in a vineyard, and as a lodge in a garden of cucumbers." [5] And when shall these things be left behind? Is it not when the fruit shall be taken away, and the leaves alone shall be left, which now have no power of producing fruit?

3. But why do we speak of Jerusalem, since, indeed, the fashion of the whole world must also pass away, when the time of its disappearance has come, in order that the fruit indeed may be gathered into the garner, but the chaff, left behind, may be consumed by fire? "For the day of the Lord cometh as a burning furnace, and all sinners shall be stubble, they who do evil things, and the day shall burn them up." [6] Now, who this Lord is that brings such a day about, John the Baptist points out, when he says of Christ, "He shall baptize you with the Holy Ghost and with fire, having His fan in His hand to cleanse His floor; and He will gather His fruit into the garner, but the chaff He will burn up with unquenchable fire." [7] For He who makes the chaff and He who makes the wheat are not different persons, but one and the same, who judges them,

that is, separates them. But the wheat and the chaff, being inanimate and irrational, have been made such by nature. But man, being endowed with reason, and in this respect like to God, having been made free in his will, and with power over himself, is himself the cause to himself, that sometimes he becomes wheat, and sometimes chaff. Wherefore also he shall be justly condemned, because, having been created a rational being, he lost the true rationality, and living irrationally, opposed the righteousness of God, giving himself over to every earthly spirit, and serving all lusts; as says the prophet, "Man, being in honour, did not understand: he was assimilated to senseless beasts, and made like to them." [8]

CHAP. V. — THE AUTHOR RETURNS TO HIS FORMER ARGUMENT, AND SHOWS THAT THERE WAS BUT ONE GOD ANNOUNCED BY THE LAW AND PROPHETS, WHOM CHRIST CONFESSES AS HIS FATHER, AND WHO, THROUGH HIS WORD, ONE LIVING GOD WITH HIM, MADE HIMSELF KNOWN TO MEN IN BOTH COVENANTS.

1. God, therefore, is one and the same, who rolls up the heaven as a book, and renews the face of the earth; who made the things of time for man, so that coming to maturity in them, he may produce the fruit of immortality; and who, through His kindness, also bestows [upon him] eternal things, "that in the ages to come He may show the exceeding riches of His grace;" [9] who was announced by the law and the prophets, whom Christ confessed as His Father. Now He is the Creator, and He it is who is God over all, as Esaias says, "I am witness, saith the LORD God, and my servant whom I have chosen, that ye may know, and believe, and understand that I AM. Before me there was no other God, neither shall be after me. I am God, and besides me there is no Saviour. I have proclaimed, and I have saved." [10] And again: "I myself am the first God, and I am above things to come." [11] For neither in an ambiguous, nor arrogant, nor boastful manner, does He say these things; but since it was impossible, without God, to come to a knowledge of God, He teaches men, through His Word, to know God. To those, therefore, who are ignorant of these matters, and on this account imagine that they have discovered another Father, justly does one say, "Ye do err, not knowing the Scriptures, nor the power of God." [12]

2. For our Lord and Master, in the answer which He gave to the Sadducees, who say that there is no resurrection, and who do therefore

---

[1] Isa. xxvii. 6.
[2] Luke xvi. 16.
[3] 2 Sam. v. 7, where David is described as taking the stronghold of Zion from the Jebusites.
[4] The text fluctuates between "legis dationem" and "legis dationis." We have followed the latter.
[5] Isa. i. 8.
[6] Mal. iv. 1.
[7] Matt. iii. 11, etc.

[8] Ps. xlix. 12.
[9] Eph. ii. 7.
[10] Isa. xliii. 10, etc.
[11] Isa. xii. 4.
[12] Matt. xxii. 29.

dishonour God, and lower the credit of the law, did both indicate a resurrection, and reveal God, saying to them, "Ye do err, not knowing the Scriptures, nor the power of God." "For, touching the resurrection of the dead," He says, "have ye not read that which was spoken by God, saying, I am the God of Abraham, the God of Isaac, and the God of Jacob?"[1] And He added, "He is not the God of the dead, but of the living; for all live to Him." By these arguments He unquestionably made it clear, that He who spake to Moses out of the bush, and declared Himself to be the God of the fathers, He is the God of the living. For who is the God of the living unless He who is God, and above whom there is no other God? Whom also Daniel the prophet, when Cyrus king of the Persians said to him, "Why dost thou not worship Bel?"[2] did proclaim, saying, "Because I do not worship idols made with hands, but the living God, who established the heaven and the earth, and has dominion over all flesh." Again did he say, "I will adore the Lord my God, because He is the living God." He, then, who was adored by the prophets as the living God, He is the God of the living; and His Word is He who also spake to Moses, who also put the Sadducees to silence, who also bestowed the gift of resurrection, thus revealing [both] truths to those who are blind, that is, the resurrection and God [in His true character]. For if He be not the God of the dead, but of the living, yet was called the God of the fathers who were sleeping, they do indubitably live to God, and have not passed out of existence, since they are children of the resurrection. But our Lord is Himself the resurrection, as He does Himself declare, "I am the resurrection and the life."[3] But the fathers are His children; for it is said by the prophet: "Instead of thy fathers, thy children have been made to thee."[4] Christ Himself, therefore, together with the Father, is the God of the living, who spake to Moses, and who was also manifested to the fathers.

3. And teaching this very thing, He said to the Jews: "Your father Abraham rejoiced that he should see my day; and he saw it, and was glad."[5] What is intended? "Abraham believed God, and it was imputed unto him for righteousness."[6] In the first place, [he believed] that He was the maker of heaven and earth, the only God; and in the next place, that He would make his seed as the stars of heaven.

This is what is meant by Paul, [when he says,] "as lights in the world."[7] Righteously, therefore, having left his earthly kindred, he followed the Word of God, walking as a pilgrim with the Word, that he might [afterwards] have his abode with the Word.

4. Righteously also the apostles, being of the race of Abraham, left the ship and their father, and followed the Word. Righteously also do we, possessing the same faith as Abraham, and taking up the cross as Isaac did the wood,[8] follow Him. For in Abraham man had learned beforehand, and had been accustomed to follow the Word of God. For Abraham, according to his faith, followed the command of the Word of God, and with a ready mind delivered up, as a sacrifice to God, his only-begotten and beloved son, in order that God also might be pleased to offer up for all his seed His own beloved and only-begotten Son, as a sacrifice for our redemption.

5. Since, therefore, Abraham was a prophet and saw in the Spirit the day of the Lord's coming, and the dispensation of His suffering, through whom both he himself and all who, following the example of his faith, trust in God, should be saved, he rejoiced exceedingly. The Lord, therefore, was not unknown to Abraham, whose day he desired to see;[9] nor, again, was the Lord's Father, for he had learned from the Word of the Lord, and believed Him; wherefore it was accounted to him by the Lord for righteousness. For faith towards God justifies a man; and therefore he said, "I will stretch forth my hand to the most high God, who made the heaven and the earth."[10] All these truths, however, do those holding perverse opinions endeavour to overthrow, because of one passage, which they certainly do not understand correctly.

CHAP. VI. — EXPLANATION OF THE WORDS OF CHRIST, "NO MAN KNOWETH THE FATHER, BUT THE SON," ETC.; WHICH WORDS THE HERETICS MISINTERPRET. PROOF THAT, BY THE FATHER REVEALING THE SON, AND BY THE SON BEING REVEALED, THE FATHER WAS NEVER UNKNOWN.

1. For the Lord, revealing Himself to His disciples, that He Himself is the Word, who imparts knowledge of the Father, and reproving the Jews, who imagined that they had [the knowledge of] God, while they nevertheless rejected His Word, through whom God is made known, declared, "No man knoweth the Son, but the Father; neither knoweth any man the Father, save the Son, and he to whom the Son has willed to reveal [Him]."[11] Thus hath Matthew set it

---

[1] Matt. xxii. 29, etc.; Ex. iii. 6.
[2] In the Septuagint and Vulgate versions, this story constitutes the fourteenth chapter of the book of Daniel. It is not extant in Hebrew, and has therefore been removed to the Apocrypha, in the Anglican canon [the Greek and St. Jerome's] of Scripture, under the title of " Bel and the Dragon."
[3] John xi. 25.
[4] Ps. xlv. 17.
[5] John viii. 56.
[6] Rom. iv. 3.
[7] Phil. ii. 15.
[8] Gen. xxii. 6.
[9] John viii. 56.
[10] Gen. xiv. 22.
[11] Matt. xi. 27; Luke x. 22.

down, and Luke in like manner, and Mark [1] the very same; for John omits this passage. They, however, who would be wiser than the apostles, write [the verse] in the following manner: "No man *knew* the Father, but the Son; nor the Son, but the Father, and he to whom the Son has willed to reveal [Him] ;" and they explain it as if the true God were known to none prior to our Lord's advent; and that God who was announced by the prophets, they allege not to be the Father of Christ.

2. But if Christ did then [only] begin to have existence when He came [into the world] as man, and [if] the Father did remember [only] in the times of Tiberius Cæsar to provide for [the wants of] men, and His Word was shown to have not always coexisted with His creatures; [it may be remarked that] neither then was it necessary that another God should be proclaimed, but [rather] that the reasons for so great carelessness and neglect on His part should be made the subject of investigation. For it is fitting that no such question should arise, and gather such strength, that it would indeed both change God, and destroy our faith in that Creator who supports us by means of His creation. For as we do direct our faith towards the Son, so also should we possess a firm and immoveable love towards the Father. In his book against Marcion, Justin [2] does well say: "I would not have believed the Lord Himself, if He had announced any other than He who is our framer, maker, and nourisher. But because the only-begotten Son came to us from the one God, who both made this world and formed us, and contains and administers all things, summing up His own handiwork in Himself, my faith towards Him is stedfast, and my love to the Father immoveable, God bestowing both upon us."

3. For no one can know the Father, unless through the Word of God, that is, unless by the Son revealing [Him] ; neither can he have knowledge of the Son, unless through the good pleasure of the Father. But the Son performs the good pleasure of the Father; for the Father sends, and the Son is sent, and comes. And His Word knows that His Father is, as far as regards us, invisible and infinite; and since He cannot be declared [by any one else], He does Himself declare Him to us; and, on the other hand, it is the Father alone who knows His own Word. And both these truths has our Lord declared. Wherefore the Son reveals the knowledge of the Father through His own manifesta-

tion. For the manifestation of the Son is the knowledge of the Father; for all things are manifested through the Word. In order, therefore, that we might know that the Son who came is He who imparts to those believing on Him a knowledge of the Father, He said to His disciples: [3] "No man knoweth the Son but the Father, nor the Father but the Son, and those to whomsoever the Son shall reveal Him ;" thus setting Himself forth and the Father as He [really] is, that we may not receive any other Father, except Him who is revealed by the Son.

4. But this [Father] is the Maker of heaven and earth, as is shown from His words; and not he, the false father, who has been invented by Marcion, or by Valentinus, or by Basilides, or by Carpocrates, or by Simon, or by the rest of the " Gnostics," falsely so called. For none of these was the Son of God; but Christ Jesus our Lord [was], against whom they set their teaching in opposition, and have the daring to preach an unknown God. But they ought to hear [this] against themselves: How is it that He is unknown, who is known by them? for, whatever is known even by a few, is not unknown. But the Lord did not say that both the Father and the Son could not be known at all (*in totum*), for in that case His advent would have been superfluous. For why did He come hither? Was it that He should say to us, "Never mind seeking after God; for He is unknown, and ye shall not find Him ;" as also the disciples of Valentinus falsely declare that Christ said to their Æons? But this is indeed vain. For the Lord taught us that no man is capable of knowing God, unless he be taught of God; that is, that God cannot be known without God: but that this is the express will of the Father, that God should be known. For they shall know [4] Him to whomsoever the Son has revealed Him.

5. And for this purpose did the Father reveal the Son, that through His instrumentality He might be manifested to all, and might receive those righteous ones who believe in Him into incorruption and everlasting enjoyment (now, to believe in Him is to do His will) ; but He shall righteously shut out into the darkness which they have chosen for themselves, those who do not believe, and who do consequently avoid His light. The Father therefore has revealed Himself to all, by making His Word visible to all; and, conversely, the Word has declared to all the Father and the Son, since He has become visible to all. And therefore the righteous judgment of God [shall fall] upon all who, like

---

[1] Not now to be found in Mark's Gospel.

[2] Photius, 125, makes mention of Justin Martyr's work, λόγοι κατὰ Μαρκίωνος. See also Eusebius's *Ecclesiastical History*, book iv. c. 18, where this passage of Irenæus is quoted. [The vast importance of Justin's startling remark is that it hinges on the words of Christ Himself, concerning His antecedents and notes as set forth in the Scriptures, St. John v. 30–39.]

[3] [A most emphatic and pregnant text which Irenæus here expounds with great beauty. The reference (St. Matt. xi. 27) seems to have been inadvertently omitted in this place where the repetition is desirable.]

[4] The ordinary text reads *cognoscunt*, i.e., do know; but Harvey thinks it should be the future — *cognoscent*.

others, have seen, but have not, like others, believed.

6. For by means of the creation itself, the Word reveals God the Creator; and by means of the world [does He declare] the Lord the Maker of the world; and by means of the formation [of man] the Artificer who formed him; and by the Son that Father who begat the Son: and these things do indeed address all men in the same manner, but all do not in the same way believe them. But by the law and the prophets did the Word preach both Himself and the Father alike [to all]; and all the people heard Him alike, but all did not alike believe. And through the Word Himself who had been made visible and palpable, was the Father shown forth, although all did not equally believe in Him; but all saw the Father in the Son: for the Father is the invisible of the Son, but the Son the visible of the Father. And for this reason all spake with Christ when He was present [upon earth], and they named Him God. Yea, even the demons exclaimed, on beholding the Son: "We know Thee who Thou art, the Holy One of God." [1] And the devil looking at Him, and tempting Him, said: "If Thou art the Son of God;" [2] — all thus indeed seeing and speaking of the Son and the Father, but all not believing [in them].

7. For it was fitting that the truth should receive testimony from all, and should become [a means of] judgment for the salvation indeed of those who believe, but for the condemnation of those who believe not; that all should be fairly judged, and that the faith in the Father and Son should be approved by all, that is, that it should be established by all [as the one means of salvation], receiving testimony from all, both from those belonging to it, since they are its friends, and by those having no connection with it, though they are its enemies. For that evidence is true, and cannot be gainsaid, which elicits even from its adversaries striking [3] testimonies in its behalf; they being convinced with respect to the matter in hand by their own plain contemplation of it, and bearing testimony to it, as well as declaring it. [4] But after a while they break forth into enmity, and become accusers [of what they had approved], and are desirous that their own testimony should not be [regarded as] true. He, therefore, who was known, was not a different being from Him who declared, "No man knoweth the Father," but one and the same, the Father making all things subject to Him; while He received testimony from all

that He was very man, and that He was very God, from the Father, from the Spirit, from angels, from the creation itself, from men, from apostate spirits and demons, from the enemy, and last of all, from death itself. But the Son, administering all things for the Father, works from the beginning even to the end, and without Him no man can attain the knowledge of God. For the Son is the knowledge of the Father; but the knowledge of the Son is in the Father, and has been revealed through the Son; and this was the reason why the Lord declared: "No man knoweth the Son, but the Father; nor the Father, save the Son, and those to whomsoever the Son shall reveal [Him]." [5] For "shall reveal" was said not with reference to the future alone, as if then [only] the Word had begun to manifest the Father when He was born of Mary, but it applies indifferently throughout all time. For the Son, being present with His own handiwork from the beginning, reveals the Father to all; to whom He wills, and when He wills, and as the Father wills. Wherefore, then, in all things, and through all things, there is one God, the Father, and one Word, and one Son, and one Spirit, and one salvation to all who believe in Him.

CHAP. VII. — RECAPITULATION OF THE FOREGOING ARGUMENT, SHOWING THAT ABRAHAM, THROUGH THE REVELATION OF THE WORD, KNEW THE FATHER, AND THE COMING OF THE SON OF GOD. FOR THIS CAUSE, HE REJOICED TO SEE THE DAY OF CHRIST, WHEN THE PROMISES MADE TO HIM SHOULD BE FULFILLED. THE FRUIT OF THIS REJOICING HAS FLOWED TO POSTERITY, VIZ., TO THOSE WHO ARE PARTAKERS IN THE FAITH OF ABRAHAM, BUT NOT TO THE JEWS WHO REJECT THE WORD OF GOD.

1. Therefore Abraham also, knowing the Father through the Word, who made heaven and earth, confessed Him to be God; and having learned, by an announcement [made to him], that the Son of God would be a man among men, by whose advent his seed should be as the stars of heaven, he desired to see that day, so that he might himself also embrace Christ; and, seeing it through the spirit of prophecy, he rejoiced. [6] Wherefore Simeon also, one of his descendants, carried fully out the rejoicing of the patriarch, and said: "Lord, now lettest Thou Thy servant depart in peace. For mine eyes have seen Thy salvation, which Thou hast pre-

---

[1] Mark i. 24.
[2] Matt. iv. 3; Luke iv. 3.
[3] *Singula*, which with Massuet we here understand in the sense of *singularia*.
[4] Some, instead of *significantibus*, read *signantibus*, "stamping it as true."

[5] Matt. xi. 27; Luke x. 22. Harvey observes here, that "it is remarkable that this text, having been correctly quoted a short time previously in accordance with the received Greek text, ᾦ ἐὰν βουλη-ται ὁ υἱὸς ἀποκαλύψαι, the translator now not only uses the single verb *revelaverit*, but says pointedly that it was so written by the venerable author. It is probable, therefore, that the previous passage has been made to harmonize with the received text by a later hand; with which, however, the Syriac form agrees."
[6] Gen. xvii. 17.

pared before the face of all people : a light for the revelation of the Gentiles,[1] and the glory of the people Israel."[2] And the angels, in like manner, announced tidings of great joy to the shepherds who were keeping watch by night.[3] Moreover, Mary said, " My soul doth magnify the Lord, and my spirit hath rejoiced in God my salvation ; "[4] — the rejoicing of Abraham descending upon those who sprang from him, — those, namely, who were watching, and who beheld Christ, and believed in Him ; while, on the other hand, there was a reciprocal rejoicing which passed backwards from the children to Abraham, who did also desire to see the day of Christ's coming. Rightly, then, did our Lord bear witness to him, saying, " Your father Abraham rejoiced to see my day ; and he saw it, and was glad."

2. For not alone upon Abraham's account did He say these things, but also that He might point out how all who have known God from the beginning, and have foretold the advent of Christ, have received the revelation from the Son Himself; who also in the last times was made visible and passable, and spake with the human race, that He might from the stones raise up children unto Abraham, and fulfil the promise which God had given him, and that He might make his seed as the stars of heaven,[5] as John the Baptist says : " For God is able from these stones to raise up children unto Abraham."[6] Now, this Jesus did by drawing us off from the religion of stones, and bringing us over from hard and fruitless cogitations, and establishing in us a faith like to Abraham. As Paul does also testify, saying that we are children of Abraham because of the similarity of our faith, and the promise of inheritance.[7]

3. He is therefore one and the same God, who called Abraham and gave him the promise. But He is the Creator, who does also through Christ prepare lights in the world, [namely] those who believe from among the Gentiles. And He says, " Ye are the light of the world ; "[8] that is, as the stars of heaven. Him, therefore, I have rightly shown to be known by no man, unless by the Son, and to whomsoever the Son shall reveal Him. But the Son reveals the Father to all to whom He wills that He should be known ; and neither without the goodwill of the Father, nor without the agency of the Son, can any man know God. Wherefore did the Lord say to His disciples, " I am the way, the truth, and the life : and no man cometh unto the Father but by Me. If ye had known Me, ye would have known My

Father also : and from henceforth ye have both known Him, and have seen Him."[9] From these words it is evident, that He is known by the Son, that is, by the Word.

4. Therefore have the Jews departed from God, in not receiving His Word, but imagining that they could know the Father [apart] by Himself, without the Word, that is, without the Son ; they being ignorant of that God who spake in human shape to Abraham,[10] and again to Moses, saying, " I have surely seen the affliction of My people in Egypt, and I have come down to deliver them."[11] For the Son, who is the Word of God, arranged these things beforehand from the beginning, the Father being in no want of angels, in order that He might call the creation into being, and form man, for whom also the creation was made ; nor, again, standing in need of any instrumentality for the framing of created things, or for the ordering of those things which had reference to man ; while, [at the same time,] He has a vast and unspeakable number of servants. For His *offspring* and His *similitude*[12] do minister to Him in every respect ; that is, the Son and the Holy Spirit, the Word and Wisdom ; whom all the angels serve, and to whom they are subject. Vain, therefore, are those who, because of that declaration, " No man knoweth the Father, but the Son,"[13] do introduce another unknown Father.

CHAP. VIII. — VAIN ATTEMPTS OF MARCION AND HIS FOLLOWERS, WHO EXCLUDE ABRAHAM FROM THE SALVATION BESTOWED BY CHRIST, WHO LIBERATED NOT ONLY ABRAHAM, BUT THE SEED OF ABRAHAM, BY FULFILLING AND NOT DESTROYING THE LAW WHEN HE HEALED ON THE SABBATH-DAY.

1. Vain, too, is [the effort of] Marcion and his followers when they [seek to] exclude Abraham from the inheritance, to whom the Spirit through many men, and now by Paul, bears witness, that " he believed God, and it was imputed unto him for righteousness."[14] And the Lord [also bears witness to him,] in the first place, indeed, by raising up children to him from the stones, and making his seed as the stars of heaven, saying, " They shall come from the east and from the west, from the north and from the south, and shall recline with Abraham, and Isaac, and Jacob in the kingdom of heaven ; "[15] and then again by saying to the Jews, " When ye shall see Abraham, and Isaac, and Jacob, and all the prophets in the kingdom of heaven, but you

---

1 The text has *oculorum*, probably by mistake for *populorum*.
2 Luke ii. 29, etc.
3 Luke ii. 8.
4 Luke i. 46.
5 Gen. xv. 5.
6 Matt. iii. 9.
7 Rom. iv. 12 ; Gal. iv. 28.
8 Matt. v. 14.

9 John xiv. 6, 7.
10 Gen. xviii. 1.
11 Ex. iii. 7, 8.
12 Massuet here observes, that the fathers called the Holy Spirit the similitude of the Son.
13 Matt. xi. 27 ; Luke x. 22.
14 Rom. iv. 3.
15 Matt. viii. 11.

yourselves cast out." [1] This, then, is a clear point, that those who disallow his salvation, and frame the idea of another God besides Him who made the promise to Abraham, are outside the kingdom of God, and are disinherited from [the gift of] incorruption, setting at naught and blaspheming God, who introduces, through Jesus Christ, Abraham to the kingdom of heaven, and his seed, that is, the Church, upon which also is conferred the adoption and the inheritance promised to Abraham.

2. For the Lord vindicated Abraham's posterity by loosing them from bondage and calling them to salvation, as He did in the case of the woman whom He healed, saying openly to those who had not faith like Abraham, " Ye hypocrites,[2] doth not each one of you on the Sabbath-days loose his ox or his ass, and lead him away to watering? And ought not this woman, being a daughter of Abraham, whom Satan hath bound these eighteen years, be loosed from this bond on the Sabbath-days?" [3] It is clear, therefore, that He loosed and vivified those who believe in Him as Abraham did, doing nothing contrary to the law when He healed upon the Sabbath-day. For the law did not prohibit men from being healed upon the Sabbaths; [on the contrary,] it even circumcised them upon that day, and gave command that the offices should be performed by the priests for the people; yea, it did not disallow the healing even of dumb animals. Both at Siloam and on frequent subsequent [4] occasions, did He perform cures upon the Sabbath; and for this reason many used to resort to Him on the Sabbath-days. For the law commanded them to abstain from every servile work, that is, from all grasping after wealth which is procured by trading and by other worldly business; but it exhorted them to attend to the exercises of the soul, which consist in reflection, and to addresses of a beneficial kind for their neighbours' benefit. And therefore the Lord reproved those who unjustly blamed Him for having healed upon the Sabbath-days. For He did not make void, but fulfilled the law, by performing the offices of the high priest, propitiating God for men, and cleansing the lepers, healing the sick, and Himself suffering death, that exiled man might go forth from condemnation, and might return without fear to his own inheritance.

3. And again, the law did not forbid those who were hungry on the Sabbath-days to take food lying ready at hand: it did, however, forbid them to reap and to gather into the barn. And therefore did the Lord say to those who were blaming His disciples because they plucked and ate the ears of corn, rubbing them in their hands, " Have ye not read this, what David did, when himself was an hungered; how he went into the house of God, and ate the shew-bread, and gave to those who were with him; which it is not lawful to eat, but for the priests alone?" [5] justifying His disciples by the words of the law, and pointing out that it was lawful for the priests to act freely. For David had been appointed a priest by God, although Saul persecuted him. For all the righteous possess the sacerdotal rank.[6] And all the apostles of the Lord are priests, who do inherit here neither lands nor houses, but serve God and the altar continually. Of whom Moses also says in Deuteronomy, when blessing Levi, " Who said unto his father and to his mother, I have not known thee; neither did he acknowledge his brethren, and he disinherited his own sons: he kept Thy commandments, and observed Thy covenant." [7] But who are they that have left father and mother, and have said adieu to all their neighbours, on account of the word of God and His covenant, unless the disciples of the Lord? Of whom again Moses says, " They shall have no inheritance, for the Lord Himself is their inheritance." [8] And again, "The priests the Levites shall have no part in the whole tribe of Levi, nor substance with Israel; their substance is the offerings (*fructifications*) of the Lord: these shall they eat." [9] Wherefore also Paul says, " I do not seek after a gift, but I seek after fruit." [10] To His disciples He said, who had a priesthood of the Lord,[11] to whom it was lawful when hungry to eat the ears of corn,[12] " For the workman is worthy of his meat." [13] And the priests in the temple profaned the Sabbath, and were blameless. Wherefore, then, were they blameless? Because when in the temple they were not engaged in secular affairs, but in the service of the Lord, fulfilling the law, but not going beyond it, as that man did, who of his own accord carried dry wood into the camp of God, and was justly stoned to death.[14] " For every tree that bringeth not forth good fruit shall be hewn down, and cast into the fire;" [15] and "whosoever shall defile the temple of God, him shall God defile." [16]

---

[1] Luke xiii. 28.
[2] Harvey prefers the singular — " *hypocrite.*"
[3] Luke xiii. 15, 16.
[4] The text here is rather uncertain. Harvey's conjectural reading of *et jam* for *etiam* has been followed.

[5] Luke vi. 3, 4.
[6] This clause is differently quoted by Antonius Melissa and John Damascenus, thus: Πᾶς βασιλεὺς δίκαιος ἱερατικὴν ἔχει τάξιν, i.e., *Every righteous king possesses a priestly order.* Comp. 1 Pet. ii. 5, 9. [And with St. Peter's testimony to the priesthood of the laity, compare the same under the law. Ex. xix. 6. The Western Church has recognised the " Episcopate *ab extra*" of sovereigns; while, in the East, it has grown into *Cæsaropapism.*]
[7] Deut. xxxiii. 9.
[8] Num. xviii. 20.
[9] Deut. xviii. 1.
[10] Phil. iv. 17.
[11] Literally, " the Lord's Levitical substance" — *Domini Leviticam substantiam.*
[12] Literally, " to take food from seeds."
[13] Matt. x. 10.
[14] Num. xv. 32, etc.
[15] Matt. iii. 10.
[16] 1 Cor. iii. 17.

CHAP. IX.—THERE IS BUT ONE AUTHOR, AND ONE END TO BOTH COVENANTS.

1. All things therefore are of one and the same substance, that is, from one and the same God; as also the Lord says to the disciples: "Therefore every scribe, which is instructed unto the kingdom of heaven, is like unto a man that is an householder, which bringeth forth out of his treasure things new and old." [1] He did not teach that he who brought forth the old was one, and he that brought forth the new, another; but that they were one and the same. For the Lord is the good man of the house, who rules the entire house of His Father; and who delivers a law suited both for slaves and those who are as yet undisciplined; and gives fitting precepts to those that are free, and have been justified by faith, as well as throws His own inheritance open to those that are sons. And He called His disciples "scribes" and "teachers of the kingdom of heaven;" of whom also He elsewhere says to the Jews: "Behold, I send unto you wise men, and scribes, and teachers; and some of them ye shall kill, and persecute from city to city." [2] Now, without contradiction, He means by those things which are brought forth from the treasure new and old, the two covenants; the old, that giving of the law which took place formerly; and He points out as the new, that manner of life required by the Gospel, of which David says, "Sing unto the LORD a new song;" [3] and Esaias, "Sing unto the LORD a new hymn. His beginning (*initium*), His name is glorified from the height of the earth: they declare His powers in the isles." [4] And Jeremiah says: "Behold, I will make a new covenant, not as I made with your fathers" [5] in Mount Horeb. But one and the same householder produced both covenants, the Word of God, our Lord Jesus Christ, who spake with both Abraham and Moses, and who has restored us anew to liberty, and has multiplied that grace which is from Himself.

2. He declares: "For in this place is One greater than the temple." [6] But [the words] *greater* and *less* are not applied to those things which have nothing in common between themselves, and are of an opposite nature, and mutually repugnant; but are used in the case of those of the same substance, and which possess properties in common, but merely differ in number and size; such as water from water, and light from light, and grace from grace. Greater, therefore, is that legislation which has been given in order to liberty than that given in order to bondage; and

therefore it has also been diffused, not throughout one nation [only], but over the whole world. For one and the same Lord, who is greater than the temple, greater than Solomon, and greater than Jonah, confers gifts upon men, that is, His own presence, and the resurrection from the dead; but He does not change God, nor proclaim another Father, but that very same one, who always has more to measure out to those of His household. And as their love towards God increases, He bestows more and greater [gifts]; as also the Lord said to His disciples: "Ye shall see greater things than these." [7] And Paul declares: "Not that I have already attained, or that I am justified, or already have been made perfect. For we know in part, and we prophesy in part; but when that which is perfect has come, the things which are in part shall be done away." [8] As, therefore, when that which is perfect is come, we shall not see another Father, but Him whom we now desire to see (for "blessed are the pure in heart: for they shall see God" [9]); neither shall we look for another Christ and Son of God, but Him who [was born] of the Virgin Mary, who also suffered, in whom too we trust, and whom we love; as Esaias says: "And they shall say in that day, Behold our LORD God, in whom we have trusted, and we have rejoiced in our salvation;" [10] and Peter says in his Epistle: "Whom, not seeing, ye love; in whom, though now ye see Him not, ye have believed, ye shall rejoice with joy unspeakable;" [11] neither do we receive another Holy Spirit, besides Him who is with us, and who cries, "Abba, Father;" [12] and we shall make increase in the very same things [as now], and shall make progress, so that no longer through a glass, or by means of enigmas, but face to face, we shall enjoy the gifts of God;—so also now, receiving more than the temple, and more than Solomon, that is, the advent of the Son of God, we have not been taught another God besides the Framer and the Maker of all, who has been pointed out to us from the beginning; nor another Christ, the Son of God, besides Him who was foretold by the prophets.

3. For the new covenant having been known and preached by the prophets, He who was to carry it out according to the good pleasure of the Father was also preached, having been revealed to men as God pleased; that they might always make progress through believing in Him, and by means of the [successive] covenants,

---

[1] Matt. xiii. 52.
[2] Matt. xxiii. 34.
[3] Ps. xcvi. 1.
[4] Isa. xlii. 10, quoted from memory.
[5] Jer. xxxi. 31.
[6] Matt. xii. 6.
[7] John i. 50.
[8] These words of Scripture are quoted by memory from Phil. iii. 12, 1 Cor. iv. 4, and xiii. 9, 10. It is remarkable that the second is incorporated with the preceding in a similar way, in the ancient Italic version known as the St. Germain copy.
[9] Matt. v. 8.
[10] Isa. xxv. 9.
[11] 1 Pet. i. 8.
[12] Rom. viii. 15.

should gradually attain to perfect salvation.[1] For there is one salvation and one God; but the precepts which form the man are numerous, and the steps which lead man to God are not a few. It is allowable for an earthly and temporal king, though he is [but] a man, to grant to his subjects greater advantages at times: shall not this then be lawful for God, since He is [ever] the same, and is always willing to confer a greater [degree of] grace upon the human race, and to honour continually with many gifts those who please Him? But if this be to make progress, [namely,] to find out another Father besides Him who was preached from the beginning; and again, besides him who is imagined to have been discovered in the second place, to find out a third other, — then the progress of this man will consist in his also proceeding from a third to a fourth; and from this, again, to another and another: and thus he who thinks that he is always making progress of such a kind, will never rest in one God. For, being driven away from Him who truly is [God], and being turned backwards, he shall be for ever seeking, yet shall never find out God;[2] but shall continually swim in an abyss without limits, unless, being converted by repentance, he return to the place from which he had been cast out, confessing one God, the Father, the Creator, and believing [in Him] who was declared by the law and the prophets, who was borne witness to by Christ, as He did Himself declare to those who were accusing His disciples of not observing the tradition of the elders: "Why do ye make void the law of God by reason of your tradition? For God said, Honour thy father and mother; and, Whosoever curseth father or mother, let him die the death."[3] And again, He says to them a second time: "And ye have made void the word of God[4] by reason of your tradition;" Christ confessing in the plainest manner Him to be Father and God, who said in the law, "Honour thy father and mother; that it may be well with thee."[5] For the true God did confess the commandment of the law as the word of God, and called no one else God besides His own Father.

CHAP. X. — THE OLD TESTAMENT SCRIPTURES, AND THOSE WRITTEN BY MOSES IN PARTICULAR, DO EVERYWHERE MAKE MENTION OF THE SON OF GOD, AND FORETELL HIS ADVENT AND PASSION.

FROM THIS FACT IT FOLLOWS THAT THEY WERE INSPIRED BY ONE AND THE SAME GOD.

1. Wherefore also John does appropriately relate that the Lord said to the Jews: "Ye search the Scriptures, in which ye think ye have eternal life; these are they which testify of me. And ye are not willing to come unto Me, that ye may have life."[6] How therefore did the Scriptures testify of Him, unless they were from one and the same Father, instructing men beforehand as to the advent of His Son, and foretelling the salvation brought in by Him? "For if ye had believed Moses, ye would also have believed Me; for he wrote of Me;"[7] [saying this,] no doubt, because the Son of God is implanted everywhere throughout his writings: at one time, indeed, speaking with Abraham, when about to eat with him; at another time with Noah, giving to him the dimensions [of the ark]; at another, inquiring after Adam; at another, bringing down judgment upon the Sodomites; and again, when He becomes visible,[8] and directs Jacob on his journey, and speaks with Moses from the bush.[9] And it would be endless to recount [the occasions] upon which the Son of God is shown forth by Moses. Of the day of His passion, too, he was not ignorant; but foretold Him, after a figurative manner, by the name given to the passover;[10] and at that very festival, which had been proclaimed such a long time previously by Moses, did our Lord suffer, thus fulfilling the passover. And he did not describe the day only, but the place also, and the time of day at which the sufferings ceased,[11] and the sign of the setting of the sun, saying: "Thou mayest not sacrifice the passover within any other of thy cities which the LORD God gives thee; but in the place which the LORD thy God shall choose that His name be called on there, thou shalt sacrifice the passover at even, towards the setting of the sun."[12]

2. And already he had also declared His advent, saying, "There shall not fail a chief in Judah, nor a leader from his loins, until He come for whom it is laid up, and He is the hope of the nations; binding His foal to the vine, and His ass's colt to the creeping ivy. He shall wash His stole in wine, and His upper garment

---

[1] This is in accordance with Harvey's text — "Maturescere profectum salutis." Grabe, however, reads, "Maturescere prefectum salutis;" making this equivalent to "ad prefectam salutem." In most MSS "profectum" and "prefectum" would be written alike. The same word ("profectus") occurs again almost immediately, with an evident reference to and comparison with this clause.

[2] 2 Tim. iii. 7.

[3] Matt. xv. 3, 4.

[4] Another variation from the *textus receptus* borne out by the Codex Bezæ, and some ancient versions.

[5] Ex. xx. 12, LXX.

[6] John v. 39, 40.

[7] John v. 46.

[8] See Gen. xviii. 13 and xxxi. 11, etc. There is an allusion here to a favourite notion among the Fathers, derived from Philo the Jew, that the name *Israel* was compounded from the three Hebrew words אֵל רָאָה אִישׁ, i.e., "the man seeing God."

[9] Ex. iii. 4, etc.

[10] Feuardent infers with great probability from this passage, that Irenæus, like Tertullian and others of the Fathers, connected the word *Pascha* with πάσχειν, *to suffer*. [The LXX. constantly giving colour to early Christian ideas in this manner, they concluded, perhaps, that such coincidences were designed. The LXX. were credited with a sort of inspiration, as we learn from our author.]

[11] Latin, "et extremitatem temporum."

[12] Deut. xvi. 5, 6.

in the blood of the grape; His eyes shall be more joyous than wine,[1] and His teeth whiter than milk."[2] For, let those who have the reputation of investigating everything, inquire at what time a prince and leader failed out of Judah, and who is the hope of the nations, who also is the vine, what was the ass's colt [referred to as] His, what the clothing, and what the eyes, what the teeth, and what the wine, and thus let them investigate every one of the points mentioned; and they shall find that there was none other announced than our Lord, Christ Jesus. Wherefore Moses, when chiding the ingratitude of the people, said, "Ye infatuated people, and unwise, do ye thus requite the LORD?"[3] And again, he indicates that He who from the beginning founded and created them, the Word, who also redeems and vivifies us in the last times, is shown as hanging on the tree, and they will not believe on Him. For he says, "And thy life shall be hanging before thine eyes, and thou wilt not believe thy life."[4] And again, "Has not this same one thy Father owned thee, and made thee, and created thee?"[5]

CHAP. XI. — THE OLD PROPHETS AND RIGHTEOUS MEN KNEW BEFOREHAND OF THE ADVENT OF CHRIST, AND EARNESTLY DESIRED TO SEE AND HEAR HIM, HE REVEALING HIMSELF IN THE SCRIPTURES BY THE HOLY GHOST, AND WITHOUT ANY CHANGE IN HIMSELF, ENRICHING MEN DAY BY DAY WITH BENEFITS, BUT CONFERRING THEM IN GREATER ABUNDANCE ON LATER THAN ON FORMER GENERATIONS.

1. But that it was not only the prophets and many righteous men, who, foreseeing through the Holy Spirit His advent, prayed that they might attain to that period in which they should see their Lord face to face, and hear His words, the Lord has made manifest, when He says to His disciples, "Many prophets and righteous men have desired to see those things which ye see, and have not seen them; and to hear those things which ye hear, and have not heard them."[6] In what way, then, did they desire both to hear and to see, unless they had foreknowledge of His future advent? But how could they have foreknown it, unless they had previously received foreknowledge from Himself? And how do the Scriptures testify of Him, unless all things had ever been revealed and shown to believers by one and the same God through the Word; He at one time

conferring with His creature, and at another propounding His law; at one time, again, reproving, at another exhorting, and then setting free His servant, and adopting him as a son (in filium); and, at the proper time, bestowing an incorruptible inheritance, for the purpose of bringing man to perfection? For He formed him for growth and increase, as the Scripture says: "Increase and multiply."[7]

2. And in this respect God differs from man, that God indeed makes, but man is made; and truly, He who makes is always the same; but that which is made must receive both beginning, and middle, and addition, and increase. And God does indeed create after a skilful manner, while, [as regards] man, he is created skilfully. God also is truly perfect in all things, Himself equal and similar to Himself, as He is all light, and all mind, and all substance, and the fount of all good; but man receives advancement and increase towards God. For as God is always the same, so also man, when found in God, shall always go on towards God. For neither does God at any time cease to confer benefits upon, or to enrich man; nor does man ever cease from receiving the benefits, and being enriched by God. For the receptacle of His goodness, and the instrument of His glorification, is the man who is grateful to Him that made him; and again, the receptacle of His just judgment is the ungrateful man, who both despises his Maker and is not subject to His Word; who has promised that He will give very much to those always bringing forth fruit, and more [and more] to those who have the Lord's money. "Well done," He says, "good and faithful servant: because thou hast been faithful in little, I will appoint thee over many things; enter thou into the joy of thy Lord."[8] The Lord Himself thus promises very much.

3. As, therefore, He has promised to give very much to those who do now bring forth fruit, according to the gift of His grace, but not according to the changeableness of "knowledge;" for the Lord remains the same, and the same Father is revealed; thus, therefore, has the one and the same Lord granted, by means of His advent, a greater gift of grace to those of a later period, than what He had granted to those under the Old Testament dispensation. For they indeed used to hear, by means of [His] servants, that the King would come, and they rejoiced to a certain extent, inasmuch as they hoped for His coming; but those who have beheld Him actually present, and have obtained liberty, and been made partakers of His gifts, do possess a greater amount of grace, and a higher degree of exultation, rejoicing because of the King's arrival: as

---

[1] The Latin is, "lætifici oculi ejus a vino," the Hebrew method of indicating comparison being evidently imitated.
[2] Gen. xlix. 10-12, LXX.
[3] Deut. xxxii. 6.
[4] Deut. xxviii. 66. Tertullian, Cyprian, and other early Fathers, agree with Irenæus in his exposition of this text.
[5] Deut. xxxii. 6. "Owned thee," i.e., following the meaning of the Hebrew, "owned thee by generation."
[6] Matt. xiii. 17.
[7] Gen. i. 28.
[8] Matt. xxv. 21, etc.

also David says, "My soul shall rejoice in the Lord ; it shall be glad in His salvation." [1] And for this cause, upon His entrance into Jerusalem, all those who were in the way [2] recognised David their king in His sorrow of soul, and spread their garments for Him, and ornamented the way with green boughs, crying out with great joy and gladness, "Hosanna to the Son of David ; blessed is He that cometh in the name of the Lord : hosanna in the highest." [3] But to the envious wicked stewards, who circumvented those under them, and ruled over those that had no great intelligence, [4] and for this reason were unwilling that the king should come, and who said to Him, "Hearest thou what these say?" did the Lord reply, "Have ye never read, Out of the mouths of babes and sucklings hast Thou perfected praise?" [5] — thus pointing out that what had been declared by David concerning the Son of God, was accomplished in His own person ; and indicating that they were indeed ignorant of the meaning of the Scripture and the dispensation of God ; but declaring that it was Himself who was announced by the prophets as Christ, whose name is praised in all the earth, and who perfects praise to His Father from the mouth of babes and sucklings ; wherefore also His glory has been raised above the heavens.

4. If, therefore, the self-same person is present who was announced by the prophets, our Lord Jesus Christ, and if His advent has brought in a fuller [measure of] grace and greater gifts to those who have received Him, it is plain that the Father also is Himself the same who was proclaimed by the prophets, and that the Son, on His coming, did not spread the knowledge of another Father, but of the same who was preached from the beginning ; from whom also He has brought down liberty to those who, in a lawful manner, and with a willing mind, and with all the heart, do Him service ; whereas to scoffers, and to those not subject to God, but who follow outward purifications for the praise of men (which observances had been given as a type of future things, — the law typifying, as it were, certain things in a shadow, and delineating eternal things by temporal, celestial by terrestrial), and to those who pretend that they do themselves observe more than what has been prescribed, as if preferring their own zeal to God Himself, while within they are full of hypocrisy, and covetousness, and all wickedness, — [to such] has He assigned everlasting perdition by cutting them off from life.

CHAP. XII. — IT CLEARLY APPEARS THAT THERE WAS BUT ONE AUTHOR OF BOTH THE OLD AND THE NEW LAW, FROM THE FACT THAT CHRIST CONDEMNED TRADITIONS AND CUSTOMS REPUGNANT TO THE FORMER, WHILE HE CONFIRMED ITS MOST IMPORTANT PRECEPTS, AND TAUGHT THAT HE WAS HIMSELF THE END OF THE MOSAIC LAW.

1. For the tradition of the elders themselves, which they pretended to observe from the law, was contrary to the law given by Moses. Wherefore also Esaias declares : "Thy dealers mix the wine with water," [6] showing that the elders were in the habit of mingling a watered tradition with the simple command of God ; that is, they set up a spurious law, and one contrary to the [true] law ; as also the Lord made plain, when He said to them, "Why do ye transgress the commandment of God, for the sake of your tradition?" [7] For not only by actual transgression did they set the law of God at nought, mingling the wine with water ; but they also set up their own law in opposition to it, which is termed, even to the present day, the pharisaical. In this [law] they suppress certain things, add others, and interpret others, again, as they think proper, which their teachers use, each one in particular ; and desiring to uphold these traditions, they were unwilling to be subject to the law of God, which prepares them for the coming of Christ. But they did even blame the Lord for healing on the Sabbath-days, which, as I have already observed, the law did not prohibit. For they did themselves, in one sense, perform acts of healing upon the Sabbath-day, when they circumcised a man [on that day] ; but they did not blame themselves for transgressing the command of God through tradition and the aforesaid pharisaical law, and for not keeping the commandment of the law, which is the love of God.

2. But that this is the first and greatest commandment, and that the next [has respect to love] towards our neighbour, the Lord has taught, when He says that the entire law and the prophets hang upon these two commandments. Moreover, He did not Himself bring down [from heaven] any other commandment greater than this one, but renewed this very same one to His disciples, when He enjoined them to love God with all their heart, and others as themselves. But if He had descended from another Father, He never would have made use of the first and greatest commandment of the law ; but He would undoubtedly have endeavoured by all means to bring down a greater one than this from the perfect Father, so as not to make use of that which had been given by the

---

[1] Ps. xxxv. 9.
[2] Or, "all those who were in the *way of David*" — *omnes qui erant in via David, in dolore animæ cognoverunt suum regem.*
[3] Matt. xxi. 8.
[4] The Latin text is ambiguous: "dominabantur eorum, quibus ratio non constabat." The rendering may be, "and ruled over those things with respect to which it was not right that they should do so."
[5] Matt. xxi. 16; Ps. viii. 3.

[6] Isa. i. 22.
[7] Matt. xv. 3.

God of the law. And Paul in like manner declares, "Love is the fulfilling of the law : "[1] and [he declares] that when all other things have been destroyed, there shall remain "faith, hope, and love ; but the greatest of all is love ; "[2] and that apart from the love of God, neither knowledge avails anything,[3] nor the understanding of mysteries, nor faith, nor prophecy, but that without love all are hollow and vain ; moreover, that love makes man perfect ; and that he who loves God is perfect, both in this world and in that which is to come. For we do never cease from loving God ; but in proportion as we continue to contemplate Him, so much the more do we love Him.

3. As in the law, therefore, and in the Gospel [likewise], the first and greatest commandment is, to love the Lord God with the whole heart, and then there follows a commandment like to it, to love one's neighbour as one's self; the author of the law and the Gospel is shown to be one and the same. For the precepts of an absolutely perfect life, since they are the same in each Testament, have pointed out [to us] the same God, who certainly has promulgated particular laws adapted for each ; but the more prominent and the greatest [commandments], without which salvation cannot [be attained], He has exhorted [us to observe] the same in both.

4. The Lord, too, does not do away with this [God], when He shows that the law was not derived from another God, expressing Himself as follows to those who were being instructed by Him, to the multitude and to His disciples : "The scribes and Pharisees sit in Moses' seat. All, therefore, whatsoever they bid you observe, that observe and do ; but do not ye after their works : for they say, and do not. For they bind heavy burdens, and lay them upon men's shoulders ; but they themselves will not so much as move them with a finger."[4] He therefore did not throw blame upon that law which was given by Moses, when He exhorted it to be observed, Jerusalem being as yet in safety ; but He *did* throw blame upon those persons, because they repeated indeed the words of the law, yet were without love. And for this reason were they held as being unrighteous as respects God, and as respects their neighbours. As also Isaiah says : "This people honoureth Me with their lips, but their heart is far from Me : howbeit in vain do they worship Me, teaching the doctrines and the commandments of men."[5] He does not call the law given by Moses commandments of men, but the traditions of the elders themselves which they had invented, and in upholding which they made the law of God of none effect, and were on this account also not subject to His Word. For this is what Paul says concerning these men : "For they, being ignorant of God's righteousness, and going about to establish their own righteousness, have not submitted themselves to the righteousness of God. For Christ is the end of the law for righteousness to every one that believeth."[6] And how is Christ the end of the law, if He be not also the final cause of it? For He who has brought in the end has Himself also wrought the beginning ; and it is He who does Himself say to Moses, "I have surely seen the affliction of my people which is in Egypt, and I have come down to deliver them ; "[7] it being customary from the beginning with the Word of God to ascend and descend for the purpose of saving those who were in affliction.

5. Now, that the law did beforehand teach mankind the necessity of following Christ, He does Himself make manifest, when He replied as follows to him who asked Him what he should do that he might inherit eternal life : "If thou wilt enter into life, keep the commandments."[8] But upon the other asking "Which ? " again the Lord replies : "Do not commit adultery, do not kill, do not steal, do not bear false witness, honour father and mother, and thou shalt love thy neighbour as thyself," — setting as an ascending series (*velut gradus*) before those who wished to follow Him, the precepts of the law, as the entrance into life ; and what He then said to one He said to all. But when the former said, "All these have I done" (and most likely he had not kept them, for in that case the Lord would not have said to him, "Keep the commandments"), the Lord, exposing his covetousness, said to him, "If thou wilt be perfect, go, sell all that thou hast, and distribute to the poor ; and come, follow me ; " promising to those who would act thus, the portion belonging to the apostles (*apostolorum partem*). And He did not preach to His followers another God the Father, besides Him who was proclaimed by the law from the beginning ; nor another Son ; nor the Mother, the enthymesis of the Æon, who existed in suffering and apostasy ; nor the Pleroma of the thirty Æons, which has been proved vain, and incapable of being believed in ; nor that fable invented by the other heretics. But He taught that they should obey the commandments which God enjoined from the beginning, and do away with their former covetousness by good works,[9] and follow after Christ. But that

---

[1] Rom. xiii. 10.
[2] 1 Cor. xiii. 13.
[3] 1 Cor. xiii. 2.
[4] Matt. xxiii. 2-4.
[5] Isa. xxix. 13.

[6] Rom. x. 3, 4.
[7] Ex. iii. 7, 8.
[8] Matt. xix. 17, 18, etc.
[9] Harvey here remarks : " In a theological point of view, it should be observed, that no saving merit is ascribed to almsgiving : it is spoken of here as the negation of the vice of covetousness, which is wholly inconsistent with the state of salvation to which we are called."

possessions distributed to the poor do annul former covetousness, Zaccheus made evident, when he said, " Behold, the half of my goods I give to the poor ; and if I have defrauded any one, I restore fourfold." [1]

CHAP. XIII. — CHRIST DID NOT ABROGATE THE NATURAL PRECEPTS OF THE LAW, BUT RATHER FULFILLED AND EXTENDED THEM. HE REMOVED THE YOKE AND BONDAGE OF THE OLD LAW, SO THAT MANKIND, BEING NOW SET FREE, MIGHT SERVE GOD WITH THAT TRUSTFUL PIETY WHICH BECOMETH SONS.

1. And that the Lord did not abrogate the natural [precepts] of the law, by which man [2] is justified, which also those who were justified by faith, and who pleased God, did observe previous to the giving of the law, but that He extended and fulfilled them, is shown from His words. " For," He remarks, " it has been said to them of old time, Do not commit adultery. But I say unto you, That every one who hath looked upon a woman to lust after her, hath committed adultery with her already in his heart." [3] And again : " It has been said, Thou shalt not kill. But I say unto you, Every one who is angry with his brother without a cause, shall be in danger of the judgment." [4] And, " It hath been said, Thou shalt not forswear thyself. But I say unto you, Swear not at all ; but let your conversation be, Yea, yea, and Nay, nay." [5] And other statements of a like nature. For all these do not contain or imply an opposition to and an overturning of the [precepts] of the past, as Marcion's followers do strenuously maintain ; but [they exhibit] a fulfilling and an extension of them, as He does Himself declare : " Unless your righteousness shall exceed that of the scribes and Pharisees, ye shall not enter into the kingdom of heaven." [6] For what meant the excess referred to? In the first place, [we must] believe not only in the Father, but also in His Son now revealed ; for He it is who leads man into fellowship and unity with God. In the next place, [we must] not only say, but we must do ; for they said, but did not. And [we must] not only abstain from evil deeds, but even from the desires after them. Now He did not teach us these things as being opposed to the law, but as fulfilling the law, and implanting in us the varied righteousness of the law. That would have been contrary to the law, if He had commanded His disciples to do anything which the law had prohibited. But this which He did command — namely, not only to abstain from things forbidden by the law, but even from longing after them — is not contrary to [the law], as I have remarked, neither is it the utterance of one destroying the law, but of one fulfilling, extending, and affording greater scope to it.

2. For the law, since it was laid down for those in bondage, used to instruct the soul by means of those corporeal objects which were of an external nature, drawing it, as by a bond, to obey its commandments, that man might learn to serve God. But the Word set free the soul, and taught that through it the body should be willingly purified. Which having been accomplished, it followed as of course, that the bonds of slavery should be removed, to which man had now become accustomed, and that he should follow God without fetters : moreover, that the laws of liberty should be extended, and subjection to the king increased, so that no one who is converted should appear unworthy to Him who set him free, but that the piety and obedience due to the Master of the household should be equally rendered both by servants and children ; while the children possess greater confidence [than the servants], inasmuch as the working of liberty is greater and more glorious than that obedience which is rendered in [a state of] slavery.

3. And for this reason did the Lord, instead of that [commandment], "Thou shalt not commit adultery," forbid even concupiscence ; and instead of that which runs thus, "Thou shalt not kill," He prohibited anger ; and instead of the law enjoining the giving of tithes, [He told us] to share [7] all our possessions with the poor ; and not to love our neighbours only, but even our enemies ; and not merely to be liberal givers and bestowers, but even that we should present a gratuitous gift to those who take away our goods. For "to him that taketh away thy coat," He says, "give to him thy cloak also ; and from him that taketh away thy goods, ask them not again ; and as ye would that men should do unto you, do ye unto them : " [8] so that we may not grieve as those who are unwilling to be defrauded, but may rejoice as those who have given willingly, and as rather conferring a favour upon our neighbours than yielding to necessity. "And if any one," He says, "shall compel thee [to go] a mile, go with him twain ; " [9] so that thou mayest not follow him as a slave, but may as a free man go before him, showing thyself in all things kindly disposed and useful to thy neighbour, not regarding their evil intentions, but performing thy kind offices, assimilating thyself to the Father, "who maketh His sun to rise upon the evil and the good, and sendeth

---

[1] Luke xix. 8.
[2] That is, as Harvey observes, *the natural man*, as described in Rom. ii. 27.
[3] Matt. v. 27, 28.
[4] Matt. v. 21, 22.
[5] Matt. v. 33, etc.
[6] Matt. v. 20.
[7] Matt. xix. 21.
[8] Luke vi. 29–31.
[9] Matt. v. 41.

rain upon the just and unjust."[1] Now all these [precepts], as I have already observed, were not [the injunctions] of one doing away with the law, but of one fulfilling, extending, and widening it among us; just as if one should say, that the more extensive operation of liberty implies that a more complete subjection and affection towards our Liberator had been implanted within us. For He did not set us free for this purpose, that we should depart from Him (no one, indeed, while placed out of reach of the Lord's benefits, has power to procure for himself the means of salvation), but that the more we receive His grace, the more we should love Him. Now the more we have loved Him, the more glory shall we receive from Him, when we are continually in the presence of the Father.

4. Inasmuch, then, as all natural precepts are common to us and to them (the Jews), they had in them indeed the beginning and origin; but in us they have received growth and completion. For to yield assent to God, and to follow His Word, and to love Him above all, and one's neighbour as one's self (now man is neighbour to man), and to abstain from every evil deed, and all other things of a like nature which are common to both [covenants], do reveal one and the same God. But this is our Lord, the Word of God, who in the first instance certainly drew slaves to God, but afterwards He set those free who were subject to Him, as He does Himself declare to His disciples : " I will not now call you servants, for the servant knoweth not what his lord doeth ; but I have called you friends, for all things which I have heard from My Father I have made known."[2] For in that which He says, " I will not now call you servants," He indicates in the most marked manner that it was Himself who did originally appoint for men that bondage with respect to God through the law, and then afterwards conferred upon them freedom. And in that He says, " For the servant knoweth not what his lord doeth," He points out, by means of His own advent, the ignorance of a people in a servile condition. But when He terms His disciples " the friends of God," He plainly declares Himself to be the Word of God, whom Abraham also followed voluntarily and under no compulsion (*sine vinculis*), because of the noble nature of his faith, and so became " the friend of God."[3] But the Word of God did not accept of the friendship of Abraham, as though He stood in need of it, for He was perfect from the beginning (" Before Abraham was," He says, " I am "[4]), but that He in His goodness might bestow eternal life upon Abraham himself, inasmuch as the friendship of God imparts immortality to those who embrace it.

CHAP. XIV. — IF GOD DEMANDS OBEDIENCE FROM MAN, IF HE FORMED MAN, CALLED HIM AND PLACED HIM UNDER LAWS, IT WAS MERELY FOR MAN'S WELFARE ; NOT THAT GOD STOOD IN NEED OF MAN, BUT THAT HE GRACIOUSLY CONFERRED UPON MAN HIS FAVOURS IN EVERY POSSIBLE MANNER.

1. In the beginning, therefore, did God form Adam, not as if He stood in need of man, but that He might have [some one] upon whom to confer His benefits. For not alone antecedently to Adam, but also before all creation, the Word glorified His Father, remaining in Him ; and was Himself glorified by the Father, as He did Himself declare, " Father, glorify Thou Me with the glory which I had with Thee before the world was."[5] Nor did He stand in need of our service when He ordered us to follow Him ; but He thus bestowed salvation upon ourselves. For to follow the Saviour is to be a partaker of salvation, and to follow light is to receive light. But those who are in light do not themselves illumine the light, but are illumined and revealed by it : they do certainly contribute nothing to it, but, receiving the benefit, they are illumined by the light. Thus, also, service [rendered] to God does indeed profit God nothing, nor has God need of human obedience ; but He grants to those who follow and serve Him life and incorruption and eternal glory, bestowing benefit upon those who serve [Him], because they do serve Him, and on His followers, because they do follow Him ; but does not receive any benefit from them : for He is rich, perfect, and in need of nothing. But for this reason does God demand service from men, in order that, since He is good and merciful, He may benefit those who continue in His service. For, as much as God is in want of nothing, so much does man stand in need of fellowship with God. For this is the glory of man, to continue and remain permanently in God's service. Wherefore also did the Lord say to His disciples, " Ye have not chosen Me, but I have chosen you ; "[6] indicating that they did not glorify Him when they followed Him ; but that, in following the Son of God, they were glorified by Him. And again, " I will, that where I am, there they also may be, that they may behold My glory ; "[7] not vainly boasting because of this, but desiring that His disciples should share in His glory : of whom Esaias also says, " I will bring thy seed from the east, and will gather thee from the

[1] Matt. v. 45.
[2] John xv. 15.
[3] Jas. ii. 23.
[4] John viii. 58.

[5] John xvii. 5.
[6] John xv. 16.
[7] John xvii. 24.

west; and I will say to the north, Give up; and to the south, Keep not back: bring My sons from far, and My daughters from the ends of the earth; all, as many as have been called in My name: for in My glory I have prepared, and formed, and made him." [1] Inasmuch as, then, "wheresoever the carcase is, there shall also the eagles be gathered together," [2] we do participate in the glory of the Lord, who has both formed us, and prepared us for this, that, when we are with Him, we may partake of His glory.

2. Thus it was, too, that God formed man at the first, because of His munificence; but chose the patriarchs for the sake of their salvation; and prepared a people beforehand, teaching the headstrong to follow God; and raised up prophets upon earth, accustoming man to bear His Spirit [within him], and to hold communion with God: He Himself, indeed, having need of nothing, but granting communion with Himself to those who stood in need of it, and sketching out, like an architect, the plan of salvation to those that pleased Him. And He did Himself furnish guidance to those who beheld Him not in Egypt, while to those who became unruly in the desert He promulgated a law very suitable [to their condition]. Then, on the people who entered into the good land He bestowed a noble inheritance; and He killed the fatted calf for those converted to the Father, and presented them with the finest robe. [3] Thus, in a variety of ways, He adjusted the human race to an agreement with salvation. On this account also does John declare in the Apocalypse, "And His voice as the sound of many waters." [4] For the Spirit [of God] is truly [like] many waters, since the Father is both rich and great. And the Word, passing through all those [men], did liberally confer benefits upon His subjects, by drawing up in writing a law adapted and applicable to every class [among them].

3. Thus, too, He imposed upon the [Jewish] people the construction of the tabernacle, the building of the temple, the election of the Levites, sacrifices also, and oblations, legal monitions, and all the other service of the law. He does Himself truly want none of these things, for He is always full of all good, and had in Himself all the odour of kindness, and every perfume of sweet-smelling savours, even before Moses existed. Moreover, He instructed the people, who were prone to turn to idols, instructing them by repeated appeals to persevere and to serve God, calling them to the things of primary importance by means of those which were

secondary; that is, to things that are real, by means of those that are typical; and by things temporal, to eternal; and by the carnal to the spiritual; and by the earthly to the heavenly; as was also said to Moses, "Thou shalt make all things after the pattern of those things which thou sawest in the mount." [5] For during forty days He was learning to keep [in his memory] the words of God, and the celestial patterns, and the spiritual images, and the types of things to come; as also Paul says: "For they drank of the rock which followed them: and the rock was Christ." [6] And again, having first mentioned what are contained in the law, he goes on to say: "Now all these things happened to them in a figure; but they were written for our admonition, upon whom the end of the ages is come." For by means of types they learned to fear God, and to continue devoted to His service.

CHAP. XV. — AT FIRST GOD DEEMED IT SUFFICIENT TO INSCRIBE THE NATURAL LAW, OR THE DECALOGUE, UPON THE HEARTS OF MEN; BUT AFTERWARDS HE FOUND IT NECESSARY TO BRIDLE, WITH THE YOKE OF THE MOSAIC LAW, THE DESIRES OF THE JEWS, WHO WERE ABUSING THEIR LIBERTY; AND EVEN TO ADD SOME SPECIAL COMMANDS, BECAUSE OF THE HARDNESS OF THEIR HEARTS.

1. They (the Jews) had therefore a law, a course of discipline, and a prophecy of future things. For God at the first, indeed, warning them by means of natural precepts, which from the beginning He had implanted in mankind, that is, by means of the Decalogue (which, if any one does not observe, he has no salvation), did then demand nothing more of them. As Moses says in Deuteronomy, "These are all the words which the Lord spake to the whole assembly of the sons of Israel on the mount, and He added no more; and He wrote them on two tables of stone, and gave them to me." [7] For this reason [He did so], that they who are willing to follow Him might keep these commandments. But when they turned themselves to make a calf, and had gone back in their minds to Egypt, desiring to be slaves instead of freemen, they were placed for the future in a state of servitude suited to their wish, — [a slavery] which did not indeed cut them off from God, but subjected them to the yoke of bondage; as Ezekiel the prophet, when stating the reasons for the giving of such a law, declares: "And their eyes were after the desire of their heart; and I gave them statutes that were not good, and judgments in which they shall not live." [8]

---

1 Isa. xliii. 5.
2 Matt. xxiv. 28.
3 Luke xv. 22, 23.
4 Rev. i. 15.

5 Ex. xxv. 40.
6 1 Cor. x. 11.
7 Deut. v. 22.
8 Ezek. xx. 24.

Luke also has recorded that Stephen, who was the first elected into the diaconate by the apostles,[1] and who was the first slain for the testimony of Christ, spoke regarding Moses as follows: "This man did indeed receive the commandments of the living God to give to us, whom your fathers would not obey, but thrust [Him from them], and in their hearts turned back again into Egypt, saying unto Aaron, Make us gods to go before us; for we do not know what has happened to [this] Moses, who led us from the land of Egypt. And they made a calf in those days, and offered sacrifices to the idol, and were rejoicing in the works of their own hands. But God turned, and gave them up to worship the hosts of heaven; as it is written in the book of the prophets:[2] O ye house of Israel, have ye offered to Me sacrifices and oblations for forty years in the wilderness? And ye took up the tabernacle of Moloch, and the star of the god Remphan,[3] figures which ye made to worship them;"[4] pointing out plainly, that the law being such, was not given to them by another God, but that, adapted to their condition of servitude, [it originated] from the very same [God as we worship]. Wherefore also He says to Moses in Exodus: "I will send forth My angel before thee; for I will not go up with thee, because thou art a stiff-necked people."[5]

2. And not only so, but the Lord also showed that certain precepts were enacted for them by Moses, on account of their hardness [of heart], and because of their unwillingness to be obedient, when, on their saying to Him, "Why then did Moses command to give a writing of divorcement, and to send away a wife?" He said to them, "Because of the hardness of your hearts he permitted these things to you; but from the beginning it was not so;"[6] thus exculpating Moses as a faithful servant, but acknowledging one God, who from the beginning made male and female, and reproving them as hard-hearted and disobedient. And therefore it was that they received from Moses this law of divorcement, adapted to their hard nature. But why say I these things concerning the Old Testament? For in the New also are the apostles found doing this very thing, on the ground which has been mentioned, Paul plainly declaring, But these things I say, not the Lord."[7] And again: "But this I speak by permission, not by commandment."[8] And again: "Now, as concerning virgins, I have no commandment

from the Lord; yet I give my judgment, as one that hath obtained mercy of the Lord to be faithful."[9] But further, in another place he says: "That Satan tempt you not for your incontinence."[10] If, therefore, even in the New Testament, the apostles are found granting certain precepts in consideration of human infirmity, because of the incontinence of some, lest such persons, having grown obdurate, and despairing altogether of their salvation, should become apostates from God, — it ought not to be wondered at, if also in the Old Testament the same God permitted similar indulgences for the benefit of His people, drawing them on by means of the ordinances already mentioned, so that they might obtain the gift of salvation through them, while they obeyed the Decalogue, and being restrained by Him, should not revert to idolatry, nor apostatize from God, but learn to love Him with the whole heart. And if certain persons, because of the disobedient and ruined Israelites, do assert that the giver (*doctor*) of the law was limited in power, they will find in our dispensation, that "many are called, but few chosen;"[11] and that there are those who inwardly are wolves, yet wear sheep's clothing in the eyes of the world (*foris*); and that God has always preserved freedom, and the power of self-government in man,[12] while at the same time He issued His own exhortations, in order that those who do not obey Him should be righteously judged (condemned) because they have not obeyed Him; and that those who have obeyed and believed on Him should be honoured with immortality.

CHAP. XVI. — PERFECT RIGHTEOUSNESS WAS CONFERRED NEITHER BY CIRCUMCISION NOR BY ANY OTHER LEGAL CEREMONIES. THE DECALOGUE, HOWEVER, WAS NOT CANCELLED BY CHRIST, BUT IS ALWAYS IN FORCE: MEN WERE NEVER RELEASED FROM ITS COMMANDMENTS.

1. Moreover, we learn from the Scripture itself, that God gave circumcision, not as the completer of righteousness, but as a sign, that the race of Abraham might continue recognisable. For it declares: "God said unto Abraham, Every male among you shall be circumcised; and ye shall circumcise the flesh of your foreskins, as a token of the covenant between Me and you."[13] This same does Ezekiel the prophet say with regard to the Sabbaths: "Also I gave them My Sabbaths, to be a sign between Me and them, that they might know that I am the Lord, that sanctify them."[14] And in Exodus, God says to

---

[1] [Acts vi. 3-7. It is evident that the laity *elected*, and the apostles ordained.]
[2] Amos v 25, 26.
[3] In accordance with the Codex Bezæ.
[4] Acts vii 38, etc.
[5] Ex. xxxiii. 2, 3.
[6] Matt. xix. 7, 8.
[7] 1 Cor. vii. 12.
[8] 1 Cor. vii. 6.

[9] 1 Cor. vii. 25.
[10] 1 Cor. vii. 5.
[11] Matt. xx. 16.
[12] [Note this stout assertion of the freedom of human actions.]
[13] Gen. xvii. 9-11.
[14] Ezek. xx. 12.

Moses: "And ye shall observe My Sabbaths; for it shall be a sign between Me and you for your generations." [1] These things, then, were given for a sign; but the signs were not unsymbolical, that is, neither unmeaning nor to no purpose, inasmuch as they were given by a wise Artist; but the circumcision after the flesh typified that after the Spirit. For "we," says the apostle, "have been circumcised with the circumcision made without hands." [2] And the prophet declares, "Circumcise the hardness of your heart." [3] But the Sabbaths taught that we should continue day by day in God's service. [4] "For we have been counted," says the Apostle Paul, "all the day long as sheep for the slaughter;" [5] that is, consecrated [to God], and ministering continually to our faith, and persevering in it, and abstaining from all avarice, and not acquiring or possessing treasures upon earth. [6] Moreover, the Sabbath of God (requietio Dei), that is, the kingdom, was, as it were, indicated by created things; in which [kingdom], the man who shall have persevered in serving God (Deo assistere) shall, in a state of rest, partake of God's table.

2. And that man was not justified by these things, but that they were given as a sign to the people, this fact shows, — that Abraham himself, without circumcision and without observance of Sabbaths, "believed God, and it was imputed unto him for righteousness; and he was called the friend of God." [7] Then, again, Lot, without circumcision, was brought out from Sodom, receiving salvation from God. So also did Noah, pleasing God, although he was uncircumcised, receive the dimensions [of the ark], of the world of the second race [of men]. Enoch, too, pleasing God, without circumcision, discharged the office of God's legate to the angels although he was a man, and was translated, and is preserved until now as a witness of the just judgment of God, because the angels when they had transgressed fell to the earth for judgment, but the man who pleased [God] was translated for salvation. [8] Moreover, all the rest of the multitude of those righteous men who lived before Abraham, and of those patriarchs who preceded Moses, were justified independently of the things above

mentioned, and without the law of Moses. As also Moses himself says to the people in Deuteronomy: "The LORD thy God formed a covenant in Horeb. The LORD formed not this covenant with your fathers, but for you." [9]

3. Why, then, did the Lord not form the covenant for the fathers? Because "the law was not established for righteous men." [10] But the righteous fathers had the meaning of the Decalogue written in their hearts and souls, [11] that is, they loved the God who made them, and did no injury to their neighbour. There was therefore no occasion that they should be cautioned by prohibitory mandates (correptoriis literis), [12] because they had the righteousness of the law in themselves. But when this righteousness and love to God had passed into oblivion, and became extinct in Egypt, God did necessarily, because of His great goodwill to men, reveal Himself by a voice, and led the people with power out of Egypt, in order that man might again become the disciple and follower of God; and He afflicted those who were disobedient, that they should not contemn their Creator; and He fed them with manna, that they might receive food for their souls (uti rationalem acciperent escam); as also Moses says in Deuteronomy: "And fed thee with manna, which thy fathers did not know, that thou mightest know that man doth not live by bread alone; but by every word of God proceeding out of His mouth doth man live." [13] And it enjoined love to God, and taught just dealing towards our neighbour, that we should neither be unjust nor unworthy of God, who prepares man for His friendship through the medium of the Decalogue, and likewise for agreement with his neighbour, — matters which did certainly profit man himself; God, however, standing in no need of anything from man.

4. And therefore does the Scripture say, "These words the Lord spake to all the assembly of the children of Israel in the mount, and He added no more;" [14] for, as I have already observed, He stood in need of nothing from them. And again Moses says: "And now Israel, what doth the LORD thy God require of thee, but to fear the LORD thy God, to walk in all His ways, and to love Him, and to serve the LORD thy God with all thy heart, and with all thy soul?" [15] Now these things did indeed make man glorious, by supplying what was wanting to him, namely, the friendship of God; but they profited God nothing, for God did not at all

---

1 Ex. xxi. 13.
2 Col. ii. 11.
3 Deut. x. 16, LXX. version.
4 The Latin text here is: "Sabbata autem perseverantiam totius diei erga Deum deservitionis edocebant:" which might be rendered, "The Sabbaths taught that we should continue the whole day in the service of God;" but Harvey conceives the original Greek to have been, τὴν καθημερινὴν διαμονὴν τῆς περὶ τὸν Θεὸν λατρείας.
5 Rom. viii. 36.
6 Matt. vi. 19.
7 Jas. ii. 23.
8 Massuet remarks here that Irenæus makes a reference to the apocryphal book of Enoch, in which this history is contained. It was the belief of the later Jews, followed by the Christian fathers, that "the sons of God" (Gen. vi. 2) who took wives of the daughters of men, were the apostate angels. The LXX. translation of that passage accords with this view. See the articles "Enoch," "Enoch, Book of," in Smith's Dictionary of the Bible. [See Paradise Lost, b. i. 323-431.]

9 Deut. v. 2.
10 1 Tim. i. 9.
11 [Hearts and souls: i.e., moral and mental natures. For a correct view of the patristic conceptions of the Gentiles before the law, this is valuable.]
12 i.e., the letters of the Decalogue on the two tables of stone.
13 Deut. viii. 3.
14 Deut. v. 22.
15 Deut. x. 12.

stand in need of man's love. For the glory of God was wanting to man, which he could obtain in no other way than by serving God. And therefore Moses says to them again: "Choose life, that thou mayest live, and thy seed, to love the LORD thy God, to hear His voice, to cleave unto Him; for this is thy life, and the length of thy days."[1] Preparing man for this life, the Lord Himself did speak in His own person to all alike the words of the Decalogue; and therefore, in like manner, do they remain permanently with us,[2] receiving by means of His advent in the flesh, extension and increase, but not abrogation.

5. The laws of bondage, however, were one by one promulgated to the people by Moses, suited for their instruction or for their punishment, as Moses himself declared: "And the LORD commanded me at that time to teach you statutes and judgments."[3] These things, therefore, which were given for bondage, and for a sign to them, He cancelled by the new covenant of liberty. But He has increased and widened those laws which are natural, and noble, and common to all, granting to men largely and without grudging, by means of adoption, to know God the Father, and to love Him with the whole heart, and to follow His word unswervingly, while they abstain not only from evil deeds, but even from the desire after them. But He has also increased the feeling of reverence; for sons should have more veneration than slaves, and greater love for their father. And therefore the Lord says, "As to every idle word that men have spoken, they shall render an account for it in the day of judgment."[4] And, "he who has looked upon a woman to lust after her, hath committed adultery with her already in his heart;"[5] and, "he that is angry with his brother without a cause, shall be in danger of the judgment."[6] [All this is declared,] that we may know that we shall give account to God not of deeds only, as slaves, but even of words and thoughts, as those who have truly received the power of liberty, in which [condition] a man is more severely tested, whether he will reverence, and fear, and love the Lord. And for this reason Peter says "that we have not liberty as a cloak of maliciousness,"[7] but as the means of testing and evidencing faith.

CHAP. XVII.—PROOF THAT GOD DID NOT APPOINT THE LEVITICAL DISPENSATION FOR HIS OWN SAKE, OR AS REQUIRING SUCH SERVICE; FOR HE DOES, IN FACT, NEED NOTHING FROM MEN.

1. Moreover, the prophets indicate in the fullest manner that God stood in no need of their slavish obedience, but that it was upon their own account that He enjoined certain observances in the law. And again, that God needed not their oblation, but [merely demanded it], on account of man himself who offers it, the Lord taught distinctly, as I have pointed out. For when He perceived them neglecting righteousness, and abstaining from the love of God, and imagining that God was to be propitiated by sacrifices and the other typical observances, Samuel did even thus speak to them: "God does not desire whole burnt-offerings and sacrifices, but He will have His voice to be hearkened to. Behold, a ready obedience is better than sacrifice, and to hearken than the fat of rams."[8] David also says: "Sacrifice and oblation Thou didst not desire, but mine ears hast Thou perfected;[9] burnt-offerings also for sin Thou hast not required."[10] He thus teaches them that God desires obedience, which renders them secure, rather than sacrifices and holocausts, which avail them nothing towards righteousness; and [by this declaration] he prophesies the new covenant at the same time. Still clearer, too, does he speak of these things in the fiftieth Psalm: "For if Thou hadst desired sacrifice, then would I have given it: Thou wilt not delight in burnt-offerings. The sacrifice of God is a broken spirit; a broken and contrite heart the Lord will not despise."[11] Because, therefore, God stands in need of nothing, He declares in the preceding Psalm: "I will take no calves out of thine house, nor he-goats out of thy fold. For Mine are all the beasts of the earth, the herds and the oxen on the mountains: I know all the fowls of heaven, and the various tribes[12] of the field are Mine. If I were hungry, I would not tell thee: for the world is Mine, and the fulness thereof. Shall I eat the flesh of bulls, or drink the blood of goats?"[13] Then, lest it might be supposed that He refused these things in His anger, He continues, giving him (man) counsel: "Offer unto God the sacrifice of praise, and pay thy vows to the Most High; and call upon Me in the day of thy trouble, and I will deliver thee, and thou shalt glorify Me;"[14] rejecting, indeed, those things by which sinners imagined they could propitiate God, and showing that He does Himself stand in need of nothing; but He exhorts and advises them to those

---

[1] Deut. xxx. 19, 20.
[2] [Most noteworthy among primitive testimonies to the catholic reception of the Decalogue.]
[3] Deut. iv. 14.
[4] Matt. xii. 36.
[5] Matt. v. 28.
[6] Matt. v. 22.
[7] 1 Pet. ii. 16.

[8] 1 Sam. xv. 22.
[9] Latin, "aures autem perfecisti mihi;" a reading agreeable to neither the Hebrew nor Septuagint version, as quoted by St. Paul in Heb. x. 9. Harvey, however, is of opinion that the text of the old Latin translation was originally "perforasti;" indicating thus an entire concurrence with the Hebrew, as now read in this passage. [Both readings illustrated by their apparent reference to Ex. xxi. 6, compared with Heb. v. 7, 8, 9.]
[10] Ps. xl. 6.
[11] Ps. li. 17.
[12] Or, "the beauty," *species*.
[13] Ps. l. 9.
[14] Ps. l. 14, 15.

things by which man is justified and draws nigh to God. This same declaration does Esaias make: "To what purpose is the multitude of your sacrifices unto Me? saith the Lord. I am full." [1] And when He had repudiated holocausts, and sacrifices, and oblations, as likewise the new moons, and the sabbaths, and the festivals, and all the rest of the services accompanying these, He continues, exhorting them to what pertained to salvation: "Wash you, make you clean, take away wickedness from your hearts from before mine eyes: cease from your evil ways, learn to do well, seek judgment, relieve the oppressed, judge the fatherless, plead for the widow; and come, let us reason together, saith the LORD."

2. For it was not because He was angry, like a man, as many venture to say, that He rejected their sacrifices; but out of compassion to their blindness, and with the view of suggesting to them the true sacrifice, by offering which they shall appease God, that they may receive life from Him. As He elsewhere declares: "The sacrifice to God is an afflicted heart: a sweet savour to God is a heart glorifying Him who formed it." [2] For if, when angry, He had repudiated these sacrifices of theirs, as if they were persons unworthy to obtain His compassion, He would not certainly have urged these same things upon them as those by which they might be saved. But inasmuch as God is merciful, He did not cut them off from good counsel. For after He had said by Jeremiah, "To what purpose bring ye Me incense from Saba, and cinnamon from a far country? Your whole burnt-offerings and sacrifices are not acceptable to Me;" [3] He proceeds: "Hear the word of the Lord, all Judah. These things saith the LORD, the God of Israel, Make straight your ways and your doings, and I will establish you in this place. Put not your trust in lying words, for they will not at all profit you, saying, The temple of the LORD, The temple of the LORD, it is [here]." [4]

3. And again, when He points out that it was not for this that He led them out of Egypt, that they might offer sacrifice to Him, but that, forgetting the idolatry of the Egyptians, they should be able to hear the voice of the Lord, which was to them salvation and glory, He declares by this same Jeremiah: "Thus saith the LORD; Collect together your burnt-offerings with your sacrifices, and eat flesh. For I spake not unto your fathers, nor commanded them in the day that I brought them out of Egypt, concerning burnt-offerings

or sacrifices: but this word I commanded them, saying, Hear My voice, and I will be your God, and ye shall be My people; and walk in all My ways whatsoever I have commanded you, that it may be well with you. But they obeyed not, nor hearkened; but walked in the imaginations of their own evil heart, and went backwards, and not forwards." [5] And again, when He declares by the same man, "But let him that glorieth, glory in this, to understand and know that I am the LORD, who doth exercise loving-kindness, and righteousness, and judgment in the earth;" [6] He adds, "For in these things I delight, says the LORD," but not in sacrifices, nor in holocausts, nor in oblations. For the people did not receive these precepts as of primary importance (*principaliter*), but as secondary, and for the reason already alleged, as Isaiah again says: "Thou hast not [brought to] Me the sheep of thy holocaust, nor in thy sacrifices hast thou glorified Me: thou hast not served Me in sacrifices, nor in [the matter of] frankincense hast thou done anything laboriously; neither hast thou bought for Me incense with money, nor have I desired the fat of thy sacrifices; but thou hast stood before Me in thy sins and in thine iniquities." [7] He says, therefore, "Upon this man will I look, even upon him that is humble, and meek, and who trembles at My words." [8] "For the fat and the fat flesh shall not take away from thee thine unrighteousness." [9] "This is the fast which I have chosen, saith the LORD. Loose every band of wickedness, dissolve the connections of violent agreements, give rest to those that are shaken, and cancel every unjust document. Deal thy bread to the hungry willingly, and lead into thy house the roofless stranger. If thou hast seen the naked, cover him, and thou shalt not despise those of thine own flesh and blood (*domesticos seminis tui*). Then shall thy morning light break forth, and thy health shall spring forth more speedily; and righteousness shall go before thee, and the glory of the LORD shall surround thee: and whilst thou art yet speaking, I will say, Behold, here I am." [10] And Zechariah also, among the twelve prophets, pointing out to the people the will of God, says: "These things does the LORD Omnipotent declare: Execute true judgment, and show mercy and compassion each one to his brother. And oppress not the widow, and the orphan, and the proselyte, and the poor; and let none imagine evil against your brother in his heart." [11] And again, he says: "These are the words which ye

---

[1] Isa. i. 11.
[2] This passage is not now found in holy Scripture. Harvey conjectures that it may have been taken from the apocryphal Gospel according to the Egyptians. It is remarkable that we find the same words quoted also by Clement of Alexandria. [But he (possibly with this place in view) merely quotes it as a *saying*, in close connection with Ps. li. 19, which is here partially cited. See Clement, *Pædagogue*, b. iii. cap. xii.]
[3] Jer. vi. 20.
[4] Jer. vii. 2, 3.

[5] Jer. vii. 21.
[6] Jer. ix 24.
[7] Isa. xliii. 23, 24.
[8] Isa. xlvi. 2.
[9] Jer. xi. 15.
[10] Isa. lviii. 6, etc.
[11] Zech. vii. 9, 10.

shall utter. Speak ye the truth every man to his neighbour, and execute peaceful judgment in your gates, and let none of you imagine evil in his heart against his brother, and ye shall not love false swearing: for all these things I hate, saith the LORD Almighty."[1] Moreover, David also says in like manner: "What man is there who desireth life, and would fain see good days? Keep thy tongue from evil, and thy lips that they speak no guile. Shun evil, and do good: seek peace, and pursue it."[2]

4. From all these it is evident that God did not seek sacrifices and holocausts from them, but faith, and obedience, and righteousness, because of their salvation. As God, when teaching them His will in Hosea the prophet, said, "I desire mercy rather than sacrifice, and the knowledge of God more than burnt-offerings."[3] Besides, our Lord also exhorted them to the same effect, when He said, "But if ye had known what [this] meaneth, I will have mercy, and not sacrifice, ye would not have condemned the guiltless."[4] Thus does He bear witness to the prophets, that they preached the truth; but accuses these men (His hearers) of being foolish through their own fault.

5. Again, giving directions to His disciples to offer to God the first-fruits[5] of His own created things — not as if He stood in need of them, but that they might be themselves neither unfruitful nor ungrateful — He took that created thing, bread, and gave thanks, and said, "This is My body."[6] And the cup likewise, which is part of that creation to which we belong, He confessed to be His blood, and taught the new oblation of the new covenant; which the Church receiving from the apostles, offers to God throughout all the world, to Him who gives us as the means of subsistence the first-fruits of His own gifts in the New Testament, concerning which Malachi, among the twelve prophets, thus spoke beforehand: "I have no pleasure in you, saith the LORD Omnipotent, and I will not accept sacrifice at your hands. For from the rising of the sun, unto the going down [of the same], My name is glorified among the Gentiles, and in every place incense is offered to My name, and a pure sacrifice; for great is My name among the Gentiles, saith the LORD Omnipotent;"[7] — indicating in the plainest manner, by these words, that the former people [the Jews] shall indeed cease to make offerings to God, but that in every place

sacrifice shall be offered to Him, and that a pure one; and His name is glorified among the Gentiles.[8]

6. But what other name is there which is glorified among the Gentiles than that of our Lord, by whom the Father is glorified, and man also? And because it is [the name] of His own Son, who was made man by Him, He calls it His own. Just as a king, if he himself paints a likeness of his son, is right in calling this likeness his own, for both these reasons, because it is [the likeness] of his son, and because it is his own production; so also does the Father confess the name of Jesus Christ, which is throughout all the world glorified in the Church, to be His own, both because it is that of His Son, and because He who thus describes it gave Him for the salvation of men. Since, therefore, the name of the Son belongs to the Father, and since in the omnipotent God the Church makes offerings through Jesus Christ, He says well on both these grounds, "And in every place incense is offered to My name, and a pure sacrifice." Now John, in the Apocalypse, declares that the "incense" is "the prayers of the saints."[9]

CHAP. XVIII. — CONCERNING SACRIFICES AND OBLATIONS, AND THOSE WHO TRULY OFFER THEM.

1. The oblation of the Church, therefore, which the Lord gave instructions to be offered throughout all the world, is accounted with God a pure sacrifice, and is acceptable to Him; not that He stands in need of a sacrifice from us, but that he who offers is himself glorified in what he does offer, if his gift be accepted. For by the gift both honour and affection are shown forth towards the King; and the Lord, wishing us to offer it in all simplicity and innocence, did express Himself thus: "Therefore, when thou offerest thy gift upon the altar, and shalt remember that thy brother hath ought against thee, leave thy gift before the altar, and go thy way; first be reconciled to thy brother, and then return and offer thy gift."[10] We are bound, therefore, to offer to God the first-fruits of His creation, as Moses also says, "Thou shalt not appear in the presence of the Lord thy God empty;"[11] so that man, being accounted as grateful, by those things in which he has shown his gratitude, may receive that honour which flows from Him.[12]

2. And the class of oblations in general has not been set aside; for there were both oblations

---

[1] Zech. viii. 16, 17.
[2] Ps. xxxiv. 13, 14.
[3] Hos. vi. 6.
[4] Matt. xii. 7.
[5] Grabe has a long and important note on this passage and what follows, which may be seen in Harvey, *in loc.* See, on the other side, and in connection with the whole of the following chapter, Massuet's third dissertation on the doctrine of Irenæus, art. vii., reprinted in Migne's edition.
[6] Matt. xxvi. 26, etc.
[7] Mal. i. 10, 11.

[8] [One marvels that there should be any critical difficulty here as to our author's teaching. Creatures of bread and wine are the body and blood; materially one thing, mystically another. See cap. xviii. 5 below.]
[9] Rev. v. 8. [Material incense seems to be always disclaimed by the primitive writers.]
[10] Matt. v. 23, 24.
[11] Deut. xvi. 16.
[12] The text of this passage is doubtful in some words.

there [among the Jews], and there are oblations here [among the Christians]. Sacrifices there were among the people ; sacrifices there are, too, in the Church : but the species alone has been changed, inasmuch as the offering is now made, not by slaves, but by freemen. For the Lord is [ever] one and the same ; but the character of a servile oblation is peculiar [to itself], as is also that of freemen, in order that, by the very oblations, the indication of liberty may be set forth. For with Him there is nothing purposeless, nor without signification, nor without design. And for this reason they (the Jews) had indeed the tithes of their goods consecrated to Him, but those who have received liberty set aside all their possessions for the Lord's purposes, bestowing joyfully and freely not the less valuable portions of their property, since they have the hope of better things [hereafter] ; as that poor widow acted who cast all her living into the treasury of God.[1]

3. For at the beginning God had respect to the gifts of Abel, because he offered with single-mindedness and righteousness ; but He had no respect unto the offering of Cain, because his heart was divided with envy and malice, which he cherished against his brother, as God says when reproving his hidden [thoughts], " Though thou offerest rightly, yet, if thou dost not divide rightly, hast thou not sinned ? Be at rest ; "[2] since God is not appeased by sacrifice. For if any one shall endeavour to offer a sacrifice merely to outward appearance, unexceptionably, in due order, and according to appointment, while in his soul he does not assign to his neighbour that fellowship with him which is right and proper, nor is under the fear of God ; — he who thus cherishes secret sin does not deceive God by that sacrifice which is offered correctly as to outward appearance ; nor will such an oblation profit him anything, but [only] the giving up of that evil which has been conceived within him, so that sin may not the more, by means of the hypocritical action, render him the destroyer of himself.[3] Wherefore did the Lord also declare : " Woe unto you, scribes and Pharisees, hypocrites, for ye are like whited sepulchres. For the sepulchre appears beautiful outside, but within it is full of dead men's bones, and all uncleanness ; even so ye also outwardly appear righteous unto men, but within ye are full of wickedness and hypocrisy."[4] For while they were thought to offer correctly so far as outward appearance went, they had in themselves jealousy like to Cain ; therefore they slew the Just One, slighting the counsel of the Word, as did also Cain. For [God] said to him, " Be at rest ; " but he did not assent. Now what else is it to " be at rest " than to forego purposed violence ? And saying similar things to these men, He declares : " Thou blind Pharisee, cleanse that which is within the cup, that the outside may be clean also."[5] And they did not listen to Him. For Jeremiah says, " Behold, neither thine eyes nor thy heart are good ; but [they are turned] to thy covetousness, and to shed innocent blood, and for injustice, and for man-slaying, that thou mayest do it."[6] And again Isaiah saith, " Ye have taken counsel, but not of Me ; and made covenants, [but] not by My Spirit."[7] In order, therefore, that their inner wish and thought, being brought to light, may show that God is without blame, and worketh no evil — that God who reveals what is hidden [in the heart], but who worketh not evil — when Cain was by no means at rest, He saith to him : " To thee shall be his desire, and thou shalt rule over him."[8] Thus did He in like manner speak to Pilate : " Thou shouldest have no power at all against Me, unless it were given thee from above ; "[9] God always giving up the righteous one [in this life to suffering], that he, having been tested by what he suffered and endured, may [at last] be accepted ; but that the evil-doer, being judged by the actions he has performed, may be rejected. Sacrifices, therefore, do not sanctify a man, for God stands in no need of sacrifice ; but it is the conscience of the offerer that sanctifies the sacrifice when it is pure, and thus moves God to accept [the offering] as from a friend. " But the sinner," says He, " who kills a calf [in sacrifice] to Me, is as if he slew a dog."[10]

4. Inasmuch, then, as the Church offers with single-mindedness, her gift is justly reckoned a pure sacrifice with God. As Paul also says to the Philippians, " I am full, having received from Epaphroditus the things that were sent from you, the odour of a sweet smell, a sacrifice acceptable, pleasing to God."[11] For it behoves us to make an oblation to God, and in all things to be found grateful to God our Maker, in a pure mind, and in faith without hypocrisy, in well-grounded hope, in fervent love, offering the first-fruits of His own created things. And the Church alone offers this pure oblation to the Creator, offering to Him, with giving of thanks, [the things taken] from His creation. But the Jews do not offer thus : for their hands are full of blood ; for they have not received the Word,

---

[1] Luke xxi. 4. [The law of tithes abrogated ; the law of Acts ii. 44, 45, morally binding. This seems to be our author's view.]
[2] Gen. iv. 7, LXX.
[3] The Latin text is : " ne per assimulatam operationem, magis autem peccatum, ipsum sibi homicidam faciat hominem."
[4] Matt. xxiii. 27, 28.

[5] Matt. xxiii. 26.
[6] Jer. xxii. 17.
[7] Isa. xxx. 1.
[8] Gen. iv. 7.
[9] John xix. 11.
[10] Isa. lxvi. 3.
[11] Phil. iv. 18.

through whom it is offered to God.[1]　Nor, again, do any of the conventicles (*synagogæ*) of the heretics [offer this].　For some, by maintaining that the Father is different from the Creator, do, when they offer to Him what belongs to this creation of ours, set Him forth as being covetous of another's property, and desirous of what is not His own.　Those, again, who maintain that the things around us originated from apostasy, ignorance, and passion, do, while offering unto Him the fruits of ignorance, passion, and apostasy, sin against their Father, rather subjecting Him to insult than giving Him thanks.　But how can they be consistent with themselves, [when they say] that the bread over which thanks have been given is the body of their Lord,[2] and the cup His blood, if they do not call Himself the Son of the Creator of the world, that is, His Word, through whom the wood fructifies, and the fountains gush forth, and the earth gives " first the blade, then the ear, then the full corn in the ear." [3]

5.　Then, again, how can they say that the flesh, which is nourished with the body of the Lord and with His blood, goes to corruption, and does not partake of life?　Let them, therefore, either alter their opinion, or cease from offering the things just mentioned.[4]　But our opinion is in accordance with the Eucharist, and the Eucharist in turn establishes our opinion. For we offer to Him His own, announcing consistently the fellowship and union of the flesh and Spirit.[5]　For as the bread, which is produced from the earth, when it receives the invocation of God, is no longer common bread,[6] but the Eucharist, consisting of two realities, earthly and heavenly ; so also our bodies, when they receive the Eucharist, are no longer corruptible, having the hope of the resurrection to eternity.

6.　Now we make offering to Him, not as though He stood in need of it, but rendering

thanks for His gift,[7] and thus sanctifying what has been created.　For even as God does not need our possessions, so do we need to offer something to God ; as Solomon says : " He that hath pity upon the poor, lendeth unto the Lord." [8] For God, who stands in need of nothing, takes our good works to Himself for this purpose, that He may grant us a recompense of His own good things, as our Lord says : " Come, ye blessed of My Father, receive the kingdom prepared for you.　For I was an hungered, and ye gave Me to eat : I was thirsty, and ye gave Me drink : I was a stranger, and ye took Me in : naked, and ye clothed Me ; sick, and ye visited Me ; in prison, and ye came to Me." [9]　As, therefore, He does not stand in need of these [services], yet does desire that we should render them for our own benefit, lest we be unfruitful ; so did the Word give to the people that very precept as to the making of oblations, although He stood in no need of them, that they might learn to serve God : thus is it, therefore, also His will that we, too, should offer a gift at the altar, frequently and without intermission.　The altar, then, is in heaven [10] (for towards that place are our prayers and oblations directed) ; the temple likewise [is there], as John says in the Apocalypse, " And the temple of God was opened : " [11] the tabernacle also : " For, behold, " He says, " the tabernacle of God, in which He will dwell with men."

CHAP. XIX. — EARTHLY THINGS MAY BE THE TYPE OF HEAVENLY, BUT THE LATTER CANNOT BE THE TYPES OF OTHERS STILL SUPERIOR AND UNKNOWN ; NOR CAN WE, WITHOUT ABSOLUTE MADNESS, MAINTAIN THAT GOD IS KNOWN TO US ONLY AS THE TYPE OF A STILL UNKNOWN AND SUPERIOR BEING.

1.　Now the gifts, oblations, and all the sacrifices, did the people receive in a figure, as was shown to Moses in the mount, from one and the same God, whose name is now glorified in the Church among all nations.　But it is congruous that those earthly things, indeed, which are spread all around us, should be types of the celestial, being [both], however, created by the same God.　For in no other way could He assimilate an image of spiritual things [to suit our comprehension].　But to allege that those things which are super-celestial and spiritual, and, as far as we are concerned, invisible and ineffable, are in their turn the types of celestial

---

[1] The text here fluctuates between *quod offertur Deo*, and *per quod offertur Deo*.　Massuet adopts the former, and Harvey the latter.　If the first reading be chosen, the translation will be, " the Word who is offered to God," implying, according to Massuet, that the body of Christ is really offered as a sacrifice in the Eucharist; if the second reading be followed, the translation will be as above. [Massuet's idea is no more to be found, even in his text, than Luther's or Calvin's.　The crucial point is, *how* offered ?　One may answer " figuratively," " corporally," " mystically," or otherwise.　Irenæus gives no answer in this place.　But see below.]

[2] Comp. Massuet and Harvey respectively for the meaning to be attached to these words.

[3] Mark iv. 28.

[4] " Either let them acknowledge that *the earth is the Lord's, and the fulness thereof*, or let them cease to offer to God those elements that they deny to be vouchsafed by Him." — HARVEY.

[5] That is, according to Harvey, " while we offer to Him His own creatures of bread and wine, we tell forth the fellowship of flesh with spirit ; i.e., that the flesh of every child of man is receptive of the Spirit." The words, καὶ ὁμολογοῦντες . . . ἔγερσιν, which here occur in the Greek text, are rejected as an interpolation by Grabe and Harvey, but defended as genuine by Massuet.

[6] See Harvey's long note on this passage, and what immediately follows. [But, note, we are only asking what Irenæus teaches.　Could words be plainer, — " *two* realities," — (i.) bread, (ii.) spiritual food ? Bread — but not " common bread; " matter and grace, flesh and Spirit. In the Eucharist, an earthly and a heavenly part.]

[7] The text fluctuates between *dominationi* and *donationi*.

[8] Prov. xix. 17.

[9] Matt. xxv. 34, etc.

[10] [The *Sursum Corda* seems here in mind.　The object of Eucharistic adoration is the Creator, our " great High Priest, passed into the heavens," and in bodily substance there enthroned, according to our author.]

[11] Rev. xi. 19.

things and of another Pleroma, and [to say] that God is the image of another Father, is to play the part both of wanderers from the truth, and of absolutely foolish and stupid persons. For, as I have repeatedly shown, such persons will find it necessary to be continually finding out types of types, and images of images, and will never [be able to] fix their minds on one and the true God. For their imaginations range beyond God, they having in their hearts surpassed the Master Himself, being indeed in idea elated and exalted above [Him], but in reality turning away from the true God.

2. To these persons one may with justice say (as Scripture itself suggests), To what distance above God do ye lift up your imaginations, O ye rashly elated men? Ye have heard "that the heavens are meted out in the palm of [His] hand:"[1] tell me the measure, and recount the endless multitude of cubits, explain to me the fulness, the breadth, the length, the height, the beginning and end of the measurement, — things which the heart of man understands not, neither does it comprehend them. For the heavenly treasuries are indeed great : God cannot be measured in the heart, and incomprehensible is He in the mind ; He who holds the earth in the hollow of His hand. Who perceives the measure of His right hand? Who knoweth His finger? Or who doth understand His hand, — that hand which measures immensity ; that hand which, by its own measure, spreads out the measure of the heavens, and which comprises in its hollow the earth with the abysses ; which contains in itself the breadth, and length, and the deep below, and the height above of the whole creation ; which is seen, which is heard and understood, and which is invisible? And for this reason God is " above all principality, and power, and dominion, and every name that is named,"[2] of all things which have been created and established. He it is who fills the heavens, and views the abysses, who is also present with every one of us. For he says, " Am I a God at hand, and not a God afar off? If any man is hid in secret places, shall I not see him?"[3] For His hand lays hold of all things, and that it is which illumines the heavens, and lightens also the things which are under the heavens, and trieth the reins and the hearts, is also present in hidden things, and in our secret [thoughts], and does openly nourish and preserve us.

3. But if man comprehends not the fulness and the greatness of His hand, how shall any one be able to understand or know in his heart so great a God? Yet, as if they had now measured and thoroughly investigated Him, and

explored Him on every side,[4] they feign that beyond Him there exists another Pleroma of Æons, and another Father ; certainly not looking up to celestial things, but truly descending into a profound abyss (Bythus) of madness ; maintaining that their Father extends only to the border of those things which are beyond the Pleroma, but that, on the other hand, the Demiurge does not reach so far as the Pleroma ; and thus they represent neither of them as being perfect and comprehending all things. For the former will be defective in regard to the whole world formed outside of the Pleroma, and the latter in respect of that [ideal] world which was formed within the Pleroma ; and [therefore] neither of these can be the God of all. But that no one can fully declare the goodness of God from the things made by Him, is a point evident to all. And that His greatness is not defective, but contains all things, and extends even to us, and is with us, every one will confess who entertains worthy conceptions of God.

CHAP. XX. — THAT ONE GOD FORMED ALL THINGS IN THE WORLD, BY MEANS OF THE WORD AND THE HOLY SPIRIT : AND THAT ALTHOUGH HE IS TO US IN THIS LIFE INVISIBLE AND INCOMPREHENSIBLE, NEVERTHELESS HE IS NOT UNKNOWN ; INASMUCH AS HIS WORKS DO DECLARE HIM, AND HIS WORD HAS SHOWN THAT IN MANY MODES HE MAY BE SEEN AND KNOWN.

1. As regards His greatness, therefore, it is not possible to know God, for it is impossible that the Father can be measured ; but as regards His love (for this it is which leads us to God by His Word), when we obey Him, we do always learn that there is so great a God, and that it is He who by Himself has established, and selected, and adorned, and contains all things ; and among the all things, both ourselves and this our world. We also then were made, along with those things which are contained by Him. And this is He of whom the Scripture says, " And God formed man, taking clay of the earth, and breathed into his face the breath of life."[5] It was not angels, therefore, who made us, nor who formed us, neither had angels power to make an image of God, nor any one else, except the Word of the Lord, nor any Power remotely distant from the Father of all things. For God did not stand in need of these [beings], in order to the accomplishing of what He had Himself determined with Himself beforehand should be done, as if He did not possess His own hands. For with Him were always present the Word and Wisdom, the Son and the Spirit, by whom and in whom,

---

[1] Isa. xl. 12.
[2] Eph. i. 21.
[3] Jer. xxiii. 23.

[4] The Latin is, " et universum eum decurrerint." Harvey imagines that this last word corresponds to καταρρέχωσι, but it is difficult to fit such a meaning into the context.
[5] Gen. ii. 7.

freely and spontaneously, He made all things, to whom also He speaks, saying, " Let Us make man after Our image and likeness ; "[1] He taking from Himself the substance of the creatures [formed], and the pattern of things made, and the type of all the adornments in the world.

2. Truly, then, the Scripture declared, which says, " First[2] of all believe that there is one God, who has established all things, and completed them, and having caused that from what had no being, all things should come into existence : " He who contains all things, and is Himself contained by no one. Rightly also has Malachi said among the prophets : " Is it not one God who hath established us? Have we not all one Father? "[3] In accordance with this, too, does the apostle say, " There is one God, the Father, who is above all, and in us all."[4] Likewise does the Lord also say : " All things are delivered to Me by My Father ; "[5] manifestly by Him who made all things ; for He did not deliver to Him the things of another, but His own. But in *all things* [it is implied that] nothing has been kept back [from Him], and for this reason the same person is the Judge of the living and the dead ; " having the key of David : He shall open, and no man shall shut : He shall shut, and no man shall open."[6] For no one was able, either in heaven or in earth, or under the earth, to open the book of the Father, or to behold Him, with the exception of the Lamb who was slain, and who redeemed us with His own blood, receiving power over all things from the same God who made all things by the Word, and adorned them by [His] Wisdom, when " the Word was made flesh ; " that even as the Word of God had the sovereignty in the heavens, so also might He have the sovereignty in earth, inasmuch as [He was] a righteous man, " who did no sin, neither was there found guile in His mouth ; "[7] and that He might have the pre-eminence over those things which are under the earth, He Himself being made " the first-begotten of the dead ; "[8] and that all things, as I have already said, might behold their King ; and that the paternal light might meet with and rest upon the flesh of our Lord, and come to us from His resplendent flesh, and that thus man might attain to immortality, having been invested with the paternal light.

3. I have also largely demonstrated, that the Word, namely the Son, was always with the Father ; and that Wisdom also, which is the Spirit, was present with Him, anterior to all creation, He declares by Solomon : " God by Wisdom founded the earth, and by understanding hath He established the heaven. By His knowledge the depths burst forth, and the clouds dropped down the dew."[9] And again : " The Lord created me the beginning of His ways in His work : He set me up from everlasting, in the beginning, before He made the earth, before He established the depths, and before the fountains of waters gushed forth ; before the mountains were made strong, and before all the hills, He brought me forth."[10] And again : " When He prepared the heaven, I was with Him, and when He established the fountains of the deep ; when He made the foundations of the earth strong, I was with Him preparing [them]. I was He in whom He rejoiced, and throughout all time I was daily glad before His face, when He rejoiced at the completion of the world, and was delighted in the sons of men."[11]

4. There is therefore one God, who by the Word and Wisdom created and arranged all things ; but this is the Creator (Demiurge) who has granted this world to the human race, and who, as regards His greatness, is indeed unknown to all who have been made by Him (for no man has searched out His height, either among the ancients who have gone to their rest, or any of those who are now alive) ; but as regards His love, He is always known through Him by whose means He ordained all things. Now this is His Word, our Lord Jesus Christ, who in the last times was made a man among men, that He might join the end to the beginning, that is, man to God. Wherefore the prophets, receiving the prophetic gift from the same Word, announced His advent according to the flesh, by which the blending and communion of God and man took place according to the good pleasure of the Father, the Word of God foretelling from the beginning that God should be seen by men, and hold converse with them upon earth, should confer with them, and should be present with His own creation, saving it, and becoming capable of being perceived by it, and freeing us from the hands of all that hate us, that is, from every spirit of wickedness ; and causing us to serve Him in holiness and righteousness all our days,[12] in order that man, having embraced the Spirit of God, might pass into the glory of the Father.

5. These things did the prophets set forth in a prophetical manner ; but they did not, as some allege, [proclaim] that He who was seen by the prophets was a different [God], the Father of

---

[1] Gen. i. 26.
[2] This quotation is taken from the *Shepherd of Hermas*, book ii. sim. 1.
[3] Mal. ii. 10.
[4] Eph. iv. 6.
[5] Matt. xi. 27.
[6] Rev. iii. 7.
[7] 1 Pet. ii. 23.
[8] Col. i. 18.

[9] Prov. iii. 19, 20.
[10] Prov. viii. 22–25. [This is one of the favourite Messianic quotations of the Fathers, and is considered as the base of the first chapter of St. John's Gospel.]
[11] Prov. viii. 27–31.
[12] Luke i. 71, 75.

all being invisible. Yet this is what those [heretics] declare, who are altogether ignorant of the nature of prophecy. For prophecy is a prediction of things future, that is, a setting forth beforehand of those things which shall be afterwards. The prophets, then, indicated beforehand that God should be seen by men; as the Lord also says, "Blessed are the pure in heart, for they shall see God." [1] But in respect to His greatness, and His wonderful glory, "no man shall see God and live," [2] for the Father is incomprehensible; but in regard to His love, and kindness, and as to His infinite power, even this He grants to those who love Him, that is, to see God, which thing the prophets did also predict. "For those things that are impossible with men, are possible with God." [3] For man does not see God by his own powers; but when He pleases He is seen by men, by whom He wills, and when He wills, and as He wills. For God is powerful in all things, having been seen at that time indeed, prophetically through the Spirit, and seen, too, adoptively through the Son; and He shall also be seen paternally in the kingdom of heaven, the Spirit truly preparing man in the Son [4] of God, and the Son leading him to the Father, while the Father, too, confers [upon him] incorruption for eternal life, which comes to every one from the fact of his seeing God. For as those who see the light are within the light, and partake of its brilliancy; even so, those who see God are in God, and receive of His splendour. But [His] splendour vivifies them; those, therefore, who see God, do receive life. And for this reason, He, [although] beyond comprehension, and boundless and invisible, rendered Himself visible, and comprehensible, and within the capacity of those who believe, that He might vivify those who receive and behold Him through faith. [5] For as His greatness is past finding out, so also His goodness is beyond expression; by which having been seen, He bestows life upon those who see Him. It is not possible to live apart from life, and the means of life is found in fellowship with God; but fellowship with God is to know God, and to enjoy His goodness.

6. Men therefore shall see God, that they may live, being made immortal by that sight, and attaining even unto God; which, as I have already said, was declared figuratively by the prophets, that God should be seen by men who bear His Spirit [in them], and do always wait patiently for His coming. As also Moses says in Deuteronomy, "We shall see in that day that God will talk to man, and he shall live." [6] For certain of these men used to see the prophetic Spirit and His active influences poured forth for all kinds of gifts; others, again, [beheld] the advent of the Lord, and that dispensation which obtained from the beginning, by which He accomplished the will of the Father with regard to things both celestial and terrestrial; and others [beheld] paternal glories adapted to the times, and to those who saw and who heard them then, and to all who were subsequently to hear them. Thus, therefore, was God revealed; for God the Father is shown forth through all these [operations], the Spirit indeed working, and the Son ministering, while the Father was approving, and man's salvation being accomplished. As He also declares through Hosea the prophet: "I," He says, "have multiplied visions, and have used similitudes by the ministry (*in manibus*) of the prophets." [7] But the apostle expounded this very passage, when he said, "Now there are diversities of gifts, but the same Spirit; and there are differences of ministrations, but the same Lord; and there are diversities of operations, but it is the same God which worketh all in all. But the manifestation of the Spirit is given to every man to profit withal." [8] But as He who worketh all things in all is God, [as to the points] of what nature and how great He is, [God] is invisible and indescribable to all things which have been made by Him, but He is by no means unknown: for all things learn through His Word that there is one God the Father, who contains all things, and who grants existence to all, as is written in the Gospel: "No man hath seen God at any time, except the only-begotten Son, who is in the bosom of the Father; He has declared [Him.]" [9]

7. Therefore the Son of the Father declares [Him] from the beginning, inasmuch as He was with the Father from the beginning, who did also show to the human race prophetic visions, and diversities of gifts, and His own ministrations, and the glory of the Father, in regular order and connection, at the fitting time for the benefit [of mankind]. For where there is a regular succession, there is also fixedness; and where fixedness, there suitability to the period; and where suitability, there also utility. And for this reason did the Word become the dispenser of the paternal grace for the benefit of men, for whom He made such great dispensations, revealing God indeed to men, but presenting man to God, and preserving at the same time the invisibility of the Father, lest man should at any time become a despiser of God, and that he should

---

[1] Matt. v. 8.
[2] Ex. xxxiii. 20.
[3] Luke xviii. 27.
[4] Some read "in filium" instead of "in filio," as above.
[5] A part of the original Greek text is preserved here, and has been followed, as it makes the better sense.
[6] Deut. v. 24.
[7] Hos. xii. 10.
[8] 1 Cor. xii. 4–7.
[9] John i. 18.

always possess something towards which he might advance; but, on the other hand, revealing God to men through many dispensations, lest man, falling away from God altogether, should cease to exist. For the glory of God is a living man; and the life of man consists in beholding God. For if the manifestation of God which is made by means of the creation, affords life to all living in the earth, much more does that revelation of the Father which comes through the Word, give life to those who see God.

8. Inasmuch, then, as the Spirit of God pointed out by the prophets things to come, forming and adapting us beforehand for the purpose of our being made subject to God, but it was still a future thing that man, through the good pleasure of the Holy Spirit, should see [God], it necessarily behoved those through whose instrumentality future things were announced, to see God, whom they intimated as to be seen by men; in order that God, and the Son of God, and the Son, and the Father, should not only be prophetically announced, but that He should also be seen by all His members who are sanctified and instructed in the things of God, that man might be disciplined beforehand and previously exercised for a reception into that glory which shall afterwards be revealed in those who love God. For the prophets used not to prophesy in word alone, but in visions also, and in their mode of life, and in the actions which they performed, according to the suggestions of the Spirit. After this invisible manner, therefore, did they see God, as also Esaias says, "I have seen with mine eyes the King, the LORD of hosts,"[1] pointing out that man should behold God with his eyes, and hear His voice. In this manner, therefore, did they also see the Son of God as a man conversant with men, while they prophesied what was to happen, saying that He who was not come as yet was present; proclaiming also the impassible as subject to suffering, and declaring that He who was then in heaven had descended into the dust of death.[2] Moreover, [with regard to] the other arrangements concerning the summing up that He should make, some of these they beheld through visions, others they proclaimed by word, while others they indicated typically by means of [outward] action, seeing visibly those things which were to be seen; heralding by word of mouth those which should be heard; and performing by actual operation what should take place by action; but [at the same time] announcing all prophetically. Wherefore also Moses declared that God was indeed a consuming fire[3] (*igneum*) to the people that transgressed the law, and

threatened that God would bring upon them a day of fire; but to those who had the fear of God he said, "The LORD God is merciful and gracious, and long-suffering, and of great commiseration, and true, and keeps justice and mercy for thousands, forgiving unrighteousness, and transgressions, and sins."[4]

9. And the Word spake to Moses, appearing before him, "just as any one might speak to his friend."[5] But Moses desired to see Him openly who was speaking with him, and was thus addressed: "Stand in the deep place of the rock, and with My hand I will cover thee. But when My splendour shall pass by, then thou shalt see My back parts, but My face thou shalt not see: for no man sees My face, and shall live."[6] Two facts are thus signified: that it is impossible for man to see God; and that, through the wisdom of God, man shall see Him in the last times, in the depth of a rock, that is, in His coming as a man. And for this reason did He [the Lord] confer with him face to face on the top of a mountain, Elias being also present, as the Gospel relates,[7] He thus making good in the end the ancient promise.

10. The prophets, therefore, did not openly behold the actual face of God, but [they saw] the dispensations and the mysteries through which man should afterwards see God. As was also said to Elias: "Thou shalt go forth to-morrow, and stand in the presence of the LORD; and, behold, a wind great and strong, which shall rend the mountains, and break the rocks in pieces before the LORD. And the LORD [was] not in the wind; and after the wind an earthquake, but the LORD [was] not in the earthquake; and after the earthquake a fire, but the Lord [was] not in the fire; and after the fire a scarcely audible voice" (*vox auræ tenuis*).[8] For by such means was the prophet — very indignant, because of the transgression of the people and the slaughter of the prophets — both taught to act in a more gentle manner; and the Lord's advent as a man was pointed out, that it should be subsequent to that law which was given by Moses, mild and tranquil, in which He would neither break the bruised reed, nor quench the smoking flax.[9] The mild and peaceful repose of His kingdom was indicated likewise. For, after the wind which rends the mountains, and after the earthquake, and after the fire, come the tranquil and peaceful times of His kingdom, in which the Spirit of God does, in the most gentle manner, vivify and increase mankind. This, too, was made still clearer by Ezekiel, that the proph-

---

[1] Isa. vi. 5.
[2] Ps. xxii. 15.
[3] Deut. iv. 24.

[4] Ex. xxxiv. 6, 7.
[5] Num. xii. 8.
[6] Ex. xxxiii. 20–22.
[7] Matt. xvii. 3, etc.
[8] 1 Kings xix. 11, 12.
[9] Isa. xlii. 3.

ets saw the dispensations of God in part, but not actually God Himself. For when this man had seen the vision [1] of God, and the cherubim, and their wheels, and when he had recounted the mystery of the whole of that progression, and had beheld the likeness of a throne above them, and upon the throne a likeness as of the figure of a man, and the things which were upon his loins as the figure of amber, and what was below like the sight of fire, and when he set forth all the rest of the vision of the thrones, lest any one might happen to think that in those [visions] he had actually seen God, he added : "This was the appearance of the likeness of the glory of God." [2]

11. If, then, neither Moses, nor Elias, nor Ezekiel, who had all many celestial visions, did see God ; but if what they did see were similitudes of the splendour of the Lord, and prophecies of things to come ; it is manifest that the Father is indeed invisible, of whom also the Lord said, "No man hath seen God at any time." [3] But His Word, as He Himself willed it, and for the benefit of those who beheld, did show the Father's brightness, and explained His purposes (as also the Lord said : "The only-begotten God, [4] which is in the bosom of the Father, He hath declared [Him] ; " and He does Himself also interpret the Word of the Father as being rich and great) ; not, in one figure, nor in one character, did He appear to those seeing Him, but according to the reasons and effects aimed at in His dispensations, as it is written in Daniel. For at one time He was seen with those who were around Ananias, Azarias, Misael, as present with them in the furnace of fire, in the burning, and preserving them from [the effects of] fire : "And the appearance of the fourth," it is said, "was like to the Son of God." [5] At another time [He is represented as] "a stone cut out of the mountain without hands," [6] and as smiting all temporal kingdoms, and as blowing them away (*ventilans ea*), and as Himself filling all the earth. Then, too, is this same individual beheld as the Son of man coming in the clouds of heaven, and drawing near to the Ancient of Days, and receiving from Him all power and glory, and a kingdom. "His dominion," it is said, "is an everlasting dominion, and His kingdom shall not perish." [7] John also, the Lord's disciple, when beholding the sacerdotal and glorious advent of His kingdom, says in the Apocalypse : "I turned to see the voice that spake with me. And, being turned, I saw seven golden candlesticks ; and in the midst of the candlesticks One like unto the Son of man, clothed with a garment reaching to the feet, and girt about the paps with a golden girdle ; and His head and His hairs were white, as white as wool, and as snow ; and His eyes were as a flame of fire ; and His feet like unto fine brass, as if He burned in a furnace. And His voice [was] as the voice of waters ; and He had in His right hand seven stars ; and out of His mouth went a sharp two-edged sword ; and His countenance was as the sun shining in his strength." [8] For in these words He sets forth something of the glory [which He has received] from His Father, as [where He makes mention of] the head ; something in reference to the priestly office also, as in the case of the long garment reaching to the feet. And this was the reason why Moses vested the high priest after this fashion. Something also alludes to the end [of all things], as [where He speaks of] the fine brass burning in the fire, which denotes the power of faith, and the continuing instant in prayer, because of the consuming fire which is to come at the end of time. But when John could not endure the sight (for he says, "I fell at his feet as dead ; " [9] that what was written might come to pass : "No man sees God, and shall live " [10]), and the Word reviving him, and reminding him that it was He upon whose bosom he had leaned at supper, when he put the question as to who should betray Him, declared : "I am the first and the last, and He who liveth, and was dead, and behold I am alive for evermore, and have the keys of death and of hell." And after these things, seeing the same Lord in a second vision, he says : "For I saw in the midst of the throne, and of the four living creatures, and in the midst of the elders, a Lamb standing as it had been slain, having seven horns, and seven eyes, which are the seven spirits of God, sent forth into all the earth." [11] And again, he says, speaking of this very same Lamb : "And behold a white horse ; and He that sat upon him was called Faithful and True ; and in righteousness doth He judge and make war. And His eyes were as a flame of fire, and on His head were many crowns ; having a name written, that no man knoweth but Himself : and He was girded around with a vesture sprinkled with blood : and His name is called The Word of God. And the armies of heaven followed Him upon white horses, clothed in pure white linen. And out of His mouth goeth a sharp sword, that with it He may smite the nations ; and He shall

---

[1] Ezek. i. 1.
[2] Ezek. ii. 1.
[3] John i. 18.
[4] " This text, as quoted a short time ago, indicated ' the only-begotten Son ; ' but the agreement of the Syriac version induces the belief that the present reading was that expressed by Irenæus, and that the previous quotation has been corrected to suit the Vulgate. The former reading, however, occurs in book iii. c. xi. 5." — HARVEY.
[5] Dan. iii. 26.
[6] Dan. vii. 13, 14.
[7] Dan. vii. 4.

[8] Rev. i. 12.
[9] Rev. i. 17.
[10] Ex. xxxiii. 20.
[11] Rev. v. 6.

rule (*pascet*) them with a rod of iron: and He treadeth the wine-press of the fierceness of the wrath of God Almighty. And He hath upon His vesture and upon His thigh a name written, KING OF KINGS AND LORD OF LORDS."[1] Thus does the Word of God always preserve the outlines, as it were, of things to come, and points out to men the various forms (*species*), as it were, of the dispensations of the Father, teaching us the things pertaining to God.

12. However, it was not by means of visions alone which were seen, and words which were proclaimed, but also in actual works, that He was beheld by the prophets, in order that through them He might prefigure and show forth future events beforehand. For this reason did Hosea the prophet take "a wife of whoredoms," prophesying by means of the action, "that in committing fornication the earth should fornicate from the LORD,"[2] that is, the men who are upon the earth; and from men of this stamp it will be God's good pleasure to take out[3] a Church which shall be sanctified by fellowship with His Son, just as that woman was sanctified by intercourse with the prophet. And for this reason, Paul declares that the "unbelieving wife is sanctified by the believing husband."[4] Then again, the prophet names his children, "Not having obtained mercy," and "Not a people,"[5] in order that, as says the apostle, "what was not a people may become a people; and she who did not obtain mercy may obtain mercy. And it shall come to pass, that in the place where it was said, This is not a people, there shall they be called the children of the living God."[6] That which had been done typically through his actions by the prophet, the apostle proves to have been done truly by Christ in the Church. Thus, too, did Moses also take to wife an Ethiopian woman, whom he thus made an Israelitish one, showing by anticipation that the wild olive tree is grafted into the cultivated olive, and made to partake of its fatness. For as He who was born Christ according to the flesh, had indeed to be sought after by the people in order to be slain, but was to be set free in Egypt, that is, among the Gentiles, to sanctify those who were there in a state of infancy, from whom also He perfected His Church in that place (for Egypt was Gentile from the beginning, as was Ethiopia also); for this reason, by means of the marriage of Moses, was shown forth the marriage of the Word;[7]

and by means of the Ethiopian bride, the Church taken from among the Gentiles was made manifest; and those who do detract from, accuse, and deride it, shall not be pure. For they shall be full of leprosy, and expelled from the camp of the righteous. Thus also did Rahab the harlot, while condemning herself, inasmuch as she was a Gentile, guilty of all sins, nevertheless receive the three spies,[8] who were spying out all the land, and hid them at her home; [which three were] doubtless [a type of] the Father and the Son, together with the Holy Spirit. And when the entire city in which she lived fell to ruins at the sounding of the seven trumpets, Rahab the harlot was preserved, when all was over [*in ultimis*], together with all her house, through faith of the scarlet sign; as the Lord also declared to those who did not receive His advent, — the Pharisees, no doubt, nullify the sign of the scarlet thread, which meant the passover, and the redemption and exodus of the people from Egypt, — when He said, "The publicans and the harlots go into the kingdom of heaven before you."[9]

CHAP. XXI. — ABRAHAM'S FAITH WAS IDENTICAL WITH OURS; THIS FAITH WAS PREFIGURED BY THE WORDS AND ACTIONS OF THE OLD PATRIARCHS.

1. But that our faith was also prefigured in Abraham, and that he was the patriarch of our faith, and, as it were, the prophet of it, the apostle has very fully taught, when he says in the Epistle to the Galatians: "He therefore that ministereth to you the Spirit, and worketh miracles among you, [doeth he it] by the works of the law, or by the hearing of faith? Even as Abraham believed God, and it was accounted unto him for righteousness. Know ye therefore, that they which are of faith, the same are the children of Abraham. But the Scripture, foreseeing that God would justify the heathen through faith, announced beforehand unto Abraham, that in him all nations should be blessed. So then they which be of faith shall be blessed with faithful Abraham."[10] For which [reasons the apostle] declared that this man was not only the prophet of faith, but also the father of those who from among the Gentiles believe in Jesus Christ, because his faith and ours are one and the same: for he believed in things future, as if they were already accomplished, because of the promise of God; and in like manner do we also, because of the promise of God, behold through faith that inheritance [laid up for us] in the [future] kingdom.

2. The history of Isaac, too, is not without a

---

[1] Rev. xix. 11–17.
[2] Hos. i. 2, 3.
[3] Acts xv. 14.
[4] 1 Cor. vii. 14. [But Hosea himself says (xii. 10), "I have used similitudes;" and this history may be fairly referred to prophetic vision. Dr. Pusey, in his *Minor Prophets, in loc.*, argues against this view, however; and his reasons deserve consideration.]
[5] Hos. i. 6–9.
[6] Rom. ix. 25, 26.
[7] The text is here uncertain; and while the general meaning of the sentence is plain, its syntax is confused and obscure.

[8] Irenæus seems here to have written "three" for "two" from a lapse of memory.
[9] Matt. xxi. 31.
[10] Gal. iii. 5–9; Gen. xii. 3.

symbolical character. For in the Epistle to the Romans, the apostle declares : " Moreover, when Rebecca had conceived by one, even by our father Isaac," she received answer [1] from the Word, " that the purpose of God according to election might stand, not of works, but of Him that calleth, it was said unto her, Two nations are in thy womb, and two manner of people are in thy body ; and the one people shall overcome the other, and the elder shall serve the younger." [2] From which it is evident, that not only [were there] prophecies of the patriarchs, but also that the children brought forth by Rebecca were a prediction of the two nations ; and that the one should be indeed the greater, but the other the less ; that the one also should be under bondage, but the other free ; but [that both should be] of one and the same father. Our God, one and the same, is also their God, who knows hidden things, who knoweth all things before they can come to pass ; and for this reason has He said, " Jacob have I loved, but Esau have I hated." [3]

3. If any one, again, will look into Jacob's actions, he shall find them not destitute of meaning, but full of import with regard to the dispensations. Thus, in the first place, at his birth, since he laid hold on his brother's heel,[4] he was called Jacob, that is, *the supplanter* — one who holds, but is not held ; binding the feet, but not being bound ; striving and conquering ; grasping in his hand his adversary's heel, that is, victory. For to this end was the Lord born, the type of whose birth he set forth beforehand, of whom also John says in the Apocalypse : " He went forth conquering, that He should conquer." [5] In the next place, [Jacob] received the rights of the first-born, when his brother looked on them with contempt ; even as also the younger nation received Him, Christ, the first-begotten, when the elder nation rejected Him, saying, " We have no king but Cæsar." [6] But in Christ every blessing [is summed up], and therefore the latter people has snatched away the blessings of the former from the Father, just as Jacob took away the blessing of this Esau. For which cause his brother suffered the plots and persecutions of a brother, just as the Church suffers this self-same thing from the Jews. In a foreign country were the twelve tribes born, the race of Israel, inasmuch as Christ was also, in a strange country, to generate the twelve-pillared foundation of the Church. Various coloured sheep were allotted to this Jacob as his wages ; and the wages of Christ are human beings, who from various and diverse

nations come together into one cohort of faith, as the Father promised Him, saying, " Ask of Me, and I will give Thee the heathen for Thine inheritance, the uttermost parts of the earth for Thy possession." [7] And as from the multitude of his sons the prophets of the Lord [afterwards] arose, there was every necessity that Jacob should beget sons from the two sisters, even as Christ did from the two laws of one and the same Father ; and in like manner also from the handmaids, indicating that Christ should raise up sons of God, both from freemen and from slaves after the flesh, bestowing upon all, in the same manner, the gift of the Spirit, who vivifies us.[8] But he (Jacob) did all things for the sake of the younger, she who had the handsome eyes,[9] Rachel, who prefigured the Church, for which Christ endured patiently ; who at that time, indeed, by means of His patriarchs and prophets, was prefiguring and declaring beforehand future things, fulfilling His part·by anticipation in the dispensations of God, and accustoming His inheritance to obey God, and to pass through the world as in a state of pilgrimage, to follow His word, and to indicate beforehand things to come. For with God there is nothing without purpose or due signification.

CHAP. XXII. — CHRIST DID NOT COME FOR THE SAKE OF THE MEN OF ONE AGE ONLY, BUT FOR ALL WHO, LIVING RIGHTEOUSLY AND PIOUSLY, HAD BELIEVED UPON HIM ; AND FOR THOSE, TOO, WHO SHALL BELIEVE.

1. Now in the last days, when the fulness of the time of liberty had arrived, the Word Himself did by Himself " wash away the filth of the daughters of Zion," [10] when He washed the disciples' feet with His own hands.[11] For this is the end of the human race inheriting God ; that as in the beginning, by means of our first [parents], we were all brought into bondage, by being made subject to death ; so at last, by means of the New Man, all who from the beginning [were His] disciples, having been cleansed and washed from things pertaining to death, should come to the life of God. For He who washed the feet of the disciples sanctified the entire body, and rendered it clean. For this reason, too, He administered food to them in a recumbent posture, indicating that those who were lying in the earth were they to whom He came to impart life. As Jeremiah declares, " The holy Lord remembered His dead Israel, who slept in the land of sepulture ; and He descended to them to make known to them His

---

[1] Massuet would cancel these words.
[2] Rom. ix. 10-13; Gen. xxv. 23.
[3] Rom. ix. 13; Mal. i. 2.
[4] Gen. xxv. 26.
[5] Rev. vi. 2.
[6] John xix. 15.

[7] Ps. ii. 8.
[8] The text of this sentence is in great confusion, and we can give only a doubtful translation.
[9] [Leah's eyes were *weak*, according to the LXX.; and Irenæus infers that Rachel's were " beautiful exceedingly." Canticles, i. 15.]
[10] Isa. iv. 4.
[11] John xiii. 5.

salvation, that they might be saved." [1] For this reason also were the eyes of the disciples weighed down when Christ's passion was approaching; and when, in the first instance, the Lord found them sleeping, He let it pass, — thus indicating the patience of God in regard to the state of slumber in which men lay; but coming the second time, He aroused them, and made them stand up, in token that His passion is the arousing of His sleeping disciples, on whose account "He also descended into the lower parts of the earth," [2] to behold with His eyes the state of those who were resting from their labours, [3] in reference to whom He did also declare to the disciples: "Many prophets and righteous men have desired to see and hear what ye do see and hear." [4]

2. For it was not merely for those who believed on Him in the time of Tiberius Cæsar that Christ came, nor did the Father exercise His providence for the men only who are now alive, but for all men altogether, who from the beginning, according to their capacity, in their generation have both feared and loved God, and practised justice and piety towards their neighbours, and have earnestly desired to see Christ, and to hear His voice. Wherefore He shall, at His second coming, first rouse from their sleep all persons of this description, and shall raise them up, as well as the rest who shall be judged, and give them a place in His kingdom. For it is truly "one God who" directed the patriarchs towards His dispensations, and "has justified the circumcision by faith, and the uncircumcision through faith." [5] For as in the first we were prefigured, so, on the other hand, are they represented in us, that is, in the Church, and receive the recompense for those things which they accomplished.

CHAP. XXIII. — THE PATRIARCHS AND PROPHETS, BY POINTING OUT THE ADVENT OF CHRIST, FORTIFIED THEREBY, AS IT WERE, THE WAY OF POSTERITY TO THE FAITH OF CHRIST; AND SO THE LABOURS OF THE APOSTLES WERE LESSENED, INASMUCH AS THEY GATHERED IN THE FRUITS OF THE LABOURS OF OTHERS.

1. For which reason the Lord declared to the disciples: "Behold, I say unto you, Lift up your eyes, and look upon the districts (*regiones*), for they are white [already] to harvest. For the harvest-man receiveth wages, and gathereth fruit unto life eternal, that both he that soweth and he that reapeth may rejoice together. For in this is the saying true, that one soweth and another reapeth. For I have sent you forward to reap that whereon ye bestowed no labour; other men have laboured, and ye have entered into their labours." [6] Who, then, are they that have laboured, and have helped forward the dispensations of God? It is clear that they are the patriarchs and prophets, who even prefigured our faith, and disseminated through the earth the advent of the Son of God, who and what He should be: so that posterity, possessing the fear of God, might easily accept the advent of Christ, having been instructed by the prophets. And for this reason it was, that when Joseph became aware that Mary was with child, and was minded to put her away privily, the angel said to him in sleep: "Fear not to take to thee Mary thy wife; for that which is conceived in her is of the Holy Ghost. For she shall bring forth a son, and thou shalt call His name Jesus; for He shall save His people from their sins." [7] And exhorting him [to this], he added: "Now all this has been done, that it might be fulfilled which was spoken from the Lord by the prophet, saying, Behold, a virgin shall be with child, and shall bring forth a son, and His name shall be called Emmanuel;" thus influencing him by the words of the prophet, and warding off blame from Mary, pointing out that it was she who was the virgin mentioned by Isaiah beforehand, who should give birth to Emmanuel. Wherefore, when Joseph was convinced beyond all doubt, he both did take Mary, and joyfully yielded obedience in regard to all the rest of the education of Christ, undertaking a journey into Egypt and back again, and then a removal to Nazareth. [For this reason,] those who knew not the Scriptures nor the promise of God, nor the dispensation of Christ, at last called him the father of the child. For this reason, too, did the Lord Himself read at Capernaum the prophecies of Isaiah: [8] "The Spirit of the Lord is upon Me, because He hath anointed Me; to preach the Gospel to the poor hath He sent Me, to heal the broken-hearted, to preach deliverance to the captives, and sight to the blind." [9] At the same time, showing that it was He Himself who had been foretold by Esaias the prophet, He said to them: "This day is this Scripture fulfilled in your ears."

2. For this reason, also, Philip, when he had discovered the eunuch of the Ethiopians' queen reading these words which had been written: "He was led as a sheep to the slaughter; and as a lamb is dumb before the shearer, so He opened not His mouth: in His humiliation His judgment was taken away;" [10] and all the rest which the prophet proceeded to relate in regard

---

[1] This spurious quotation has been introduced before. See book iii. 20, 4.
[2] Eph. iv. 9.
[3] So Harvey understands the obscure Latin text, "id quod erat inoperatum conditionis."
[4] Matt. xiii. 17.
[5] Rom. iii. 30.

[6] John iv. 35, etc.
[7] Matt. i. 20, etc.
[8] Luke iv. 18.
[9] Isa. lxi. 1.
[10] Acts viii. 27; Isa. liii. 7.

to His passion and His coming in the flesh, and how He was dishonoured by those who did not believe Him; easily persuaded him to believe on Him, that He was Christ Jesus, who was crucified under Pontius Pilate, and suffered whatsoever the prophet had predicted, and that He was the Son of God, who gives eternal life to men. And immediately when [Philip] had baptized him, he departed from him. For nothing else [but baptism] was wanting to him who had been already instructed by the prophets: he was not ignorant of God the Father, nor of the rules as to the [proper] manner of life, but was merely ignorant of the advent of the Son of God, which, when he had become acquainted with, in a short space of time, he went on his way rejoicing, to be the herald in Ethiopia of Christ's advent. Therefore Philip had no great labour to go through with regard to this man, because he was already prepared in the fear of God by the prophets. For this reason, too, did the apostles, collecting the sheep which had perished of the house of Israel, and discoursing to them from the Scriptures, prove that this crucified Jesus was the Christ, the Son of the living God; and they persuaded a great multitude, who, however, [already] possessed the fear of God. And there were, in one day, baptized three, and four, and five thousand men.[1]

CHAP. XXIV. — THE CONVERSION OF THE GENTILES WAS MORE DIFFICULT THAN THAT OF THE JEWS; THE LABOURS OF THOSE APOSTLES, THEREFORE, WHO ENGAGED IN THE FORMER TASK, WERE GREATER THAN THOSE WHO UNDERTOOK THE LATTER.

1. Wherefore also Paul, since he was the apostle of the Gentiles, says, " I laboured more than they all." [2] For the instruction of the former, [viz., the Jews,] was an easy task, because they could allege proofs from the Scriptures, and because they, who were in the habit of hearing Moses and the prophets, did also readily receive the First-begotten of the dead, and the Prince of the life of God, — Him who, by the spreading forth of hands, did destroy Amalek, and vivify man from the wound of the serpent, by means of faith which was [exercised] towards Him. As I have pointed out in the preceding book, the apostle did, in the first place, instruct the Gentiles to depart from the superstition of idols, and to worship one God, the Creator of heaven and earth, and the Framer of the whole creation; and that His Son was His Word, by whom He founded all things; and that He, in the last times, was made a man among men; that He re-formed the human race, but destroyed and conquered the enemy of man, and gave to His handiwork

victory against the adversary. But although they who were of the circumcision still did not obey the words of God, for they were despisers, yet they were previously instructed not to commit adultery, nor fornication, nor theft, nor fraud; and that whatsoever things are done to our neighbours' prejudice, were evil, and detested by God. Wherefore also they did readily agree to abstain from these things, because they had been thus instructed.

2. But they were bound to teach the Gentiles also this very thing, that works of such a nature were wicked, prejudicial, and useless, and destructive to those who engaged in them. Wherefore he who had received the apostolate to the Gentiles,[3] did labour more than those who preached the Son of God among them of the circumcision. For they were assisted by the Scriptures, which the Lord confirmed and fulfilled, in coming such as He had been announced; but here, [in the case of the Gentiles,] there was a certain foreign erudition, and a new doctrine [to be received, namely], that the gods of the nations not only were no gods at all, but even the idols of demons; and that there is one God, who is "above all principality, and dominion, and power, and every name which is named;"[4] and that His Word, invisible by nature, was made palpable and visible among men, and did descend "to death, even the death of the cross;"[5] also, that they who believe in Him shall be incorruptible and not subject to suffering, and shall receive the kingdom of heaven. These things, too, were preached to the Gentiles by word, without [the aid of] the Scriptures: wherefore, also, they who preached among the Gentiles underwent greater labour. But, on the other hand, the faith of the Gentiles is proved to be of a more noble description, since they followed the word of God without the instruction [derived] from the [sacred] writings (sine instructione literarum).

CHAP. XXV. — BOTH COVENANTS WERE PREFIGURED IN ABRAHAM, AND IN THE LABOUR OF TAMAR; THERE WAS, HOWEVER, BUT ONE AND THE SAME GOD TO EACH COVENANT.

1. For thus it had behoved the sons of Abraham [to be], whom God has raised up to him from the stones,[6] and caused to take a place beside him who was made the chief and the forerunner of our faith (who did also receive the covenant of circumcision, after that justification by faith which had pertained to him, when he was yet in uncircumcision, so that in him both covenants might be prefigured, that he might be

---

[1] Acts ii. 41, iv. 4.
[2] 1 Cor. xv. 10.

[3] [A clear note of recognition on the part of our author, that St. Paul's mission was world-wide, while St. Peter's was limited.]
[4] Eph. i. 21.
[5] Phil. ii. 8.
[6] Matt. iii. 9.

the father of all who follow the Word of God, and who sustain a life of pilgrimage in this world, that is, of those who from among the circumcision and of those from among the uncircumcision are faithful, even as also "Christ [1] is the chief corner-stone," sustaining all things) ; and He gathered into the one faith of Abraham those who, from either covenant, are eligible for God's building. But this faith which is in uncircumcision, as connecting the end with the beginning, has been made [both] the first and the last. For, as I have shown, it existed in Abraham antecedently to circumcision, as it also did in the rest of the righteous who pleased God : and in these last times, it again sprang up among mankind through the coming of the Lord. But circumcision and the law of works occupied the intervening period.[2]

2. This fact is indeed set forth by many other [occurrences], but typically by [the history of] Thamar, Judah's daughter-in-law.[3] For when she had conceived twins, one of them put forth his hand first ; and as the midwife supposed that he was the first-born, she bound a scarlet token on his hand. But after this had been done, and he had drawn back his hand, his brother Phares came forth the first ; then, after him, Zara, upon whom was the scarlet line, [was born] the second : the Scripture clearly pointing out that people which possessed the scarlet sign, that is, faith in a state of circumcision, which was shown beforehand, indeed, in the patriarchs first ; but after that withdrawn, that his brother might be born ; and also, in like manner, him who was the elder, as being born in the second place, [him] who was distinguished by the scarlet token, which was [fastened] on him, that is, the passion of the Just One, which was prefigured from the beginning in Abel, and described by the prophets, but perfected in the last times in the Son of God.

3. For it was requisite that certain facts should be announced beforehand by the fathers in a paternal manner, and others prefigured by the prophets in a legal one, but others, described after the form of Christ, by those who have received the adoption ; while in one God are all things shown forth. For although Abraham was one, he did in himself prefigure the two covenants, in which some indeed have sown, while others have reaped ; for it is said, " In this is the saying true, that it is one ' people ' who sows, but another who shall reap ; " [4] but it is one God

who bestows things suitable upon both — seed to the sower, but bread for the reaper to eat. Just as it is one that planteth, and another who watereth, but one God who giveth the increase.[5] For the patriarchs and prophets sowed the word [concerning] Christ, but the Church reaped, that is, received the fruit. For this reason, too, do these very men (the prophets) also pray to have a dwelling-place in it, as Jeremiah says, " Who will give me in the desert the last dwelling-place ? " [6] in order that both the sower and the reaper may rejoice together in the kingdom of Christ, who is present with all those who were from the beginning approved by God, who granted them His Word to be present with them.[7]

CHAP. XXVI. — THE TREASURE HID IN THE SCRIPTURES IS CHRIST ; THE TRUE EXPOSITION OF THE SCRIPTURES IS TO BE FOUND IN THE CHURCH ALONE.

1. If any one, therefore, reads the Scriptures with attention, he will find in them an account of Christ, and a foreshadowing of the new calling (vocationis). For Christ is the treasure which was hid in the field,[8] that is, in this world (for " the field is the world " [9]) ; but the treasure hid in the Scriptures is Christ, since He was pointed out by means of types and parables. Hence His human nature could not [10] be understood, prior to the consummation of those things which had been predicted, that is, the advent of Christ. And therefore it was said to Daniel the prophet : " Shut up the words, and seal the book even to the time of consummation, until many learn, and knowledge be completed. For at that time, when the dispersion shall be accomplished, they shall know all these things." [11] But Jeremiah also says, " In the last days they shall understand these things." [12] For every prophecy, before its fulfilment, is to men [full of] enigmas and ambiguities. But when the time has arrived, and the prediction has come to pass, then the prophecies have a clear and certain exposition. And for this reason, indeed, when at this present time the law is read to the Jews, it is like a fable ; for they do not possess the explanation of all things pertaining to the advent of the Son of God, which took place in human nature ; but when it is read by the Christians, it is a treasure, hid indeed in a field, but brought to light by the cross of Christ, and

---

[1] Eph. ii. 20.
[2] [Note, the Gentile Church was the old religion and was Catholic ; in Christ it became Catholic again : the Mosaic system was a parenthetical thing of fifteen hundred years only. Such is the luminous and clarifying scheme of Irenæus, expounding St. Paul (Gal. iii. 14-20). Inferences : (1) They who speak as if the Mosaic system covered the whole Old Testament darken the divine counsels. (2) The God of Scripture was never the God of the Jews only.]
[3] Gen. xxxviii. 28, etc.
[4] John iv. 37.

[5] 1 Cor. iii. 7.
[6] Jer. ix. 2. [A " remote dwelling-place " rather (σταθμὸν ἐσχατον according to LXX.) to square with the argument.]
[7] [The touching words which conclude the former paragraph are illustrated by the noble sentence which begins this paragraph. The childlike spirit of these Fathers recognises Christ everywhere, in the Old Testament, prefigured by countless images and tokens in paternal and legal (ceremonial) forms.]
[8] Matt. xiii. 44.
[9] Matt. xiii. 38.
[10] Harvey cancels " non," and reads the sentence interrogatively.
[11] Dan. xii. 4, 7.
[12] Jer. xxiii. 20.

explained, both enriching the understanding of men, and showing forth the wisdom of God, and declaring His dispensations with regard to man, and forming the kingdom of Christ beforehand, and preaching by anticipation the inheritance of the holy Jerusalem, and proclaiming beforehand that the man who loves God shall arrive at such excellency as even to see God, and hear His word, and from the hearing of His discourse be glorified to such an extent, that others cannot behold the glory of his countenance, as was said by Daniel : " Those who do understand, shall shine as the brightness of the firmament, and many of the righteous [1] as the stars for ever and ever." [2] Thus, then, I have shown it to be,[3] if any one read the Scriptures. For thus it was that the Lord discoursed with the disciples after His resurrection from the dead, proving to them from the Scriptures themselves " that Christ must suffer, and enter into His glory, and that remission of sins should be preached in His name throughout all the world." [4] And the disciple will be perfected, and [rendered] like the householder, " who bringeth forth from his treasure things new and old." [5]

2. Wherefore it is incumbent to obey the presbyters who are in the Church, — those who, as I have shown, possess the succession from the apostles ; those who, together with the succession of the episcopate, have received the certain gift of truth, according to the good pleasure of the Father. But [it is also incumbent] to hold in suspicion others who depart from the primitive succession, and assemble themselves together in any place whatsoever, [looking upon them] either as heretics of perverse minds, or as schismatics puffed up and self-pleasing, or again as hypocrites, acting thus for the sake of lucre and vainglory. For all these have fallen from the truth. And the heretics, indeed, who bring strange fire to the altar of God — namely, strange doctrines — shall be burned up by the fire from heaven, as were Nadab and Abiud.[6] But such as rise up in opposition to the truth, and exhort others against the Church of God, [shall] remain among those in hell (apud inferos), being swallowed up by an earthquake, even as those who were with Chore, Dathan, and Abiron.[7]

But those who cleave asunder, and separate the unity of the Church, [shall] receive from God the same punishment as Jeroboam did.[8]

3. Those, however, who are believed to be presbyters by many, but serve their own lusts, and, do not place the fear of God supreme in their hearts, but conduct themselves with contempt towards others, and are puffed up with the pride of holding the chief seat, and work evil deeds in secret, saying, " No man sees us," shall be convicted by the Word, who does not judge after outward appearance (secundum gloriam), nor looks upon the countenance, but the heart ; and they shall hear those words, to be found in Daniel the prophet : " O thou seed of Canaan, and not of Judah, beauty hath deceived thee, and lust perverted thy heart.[9] Thou that art waxen old in wicked days, now thy sins which thou hast committed aforetime are come to light ; for thou hast pronounced false judgments, and hast been accustomed to condemn the innocent, and to let the guilty go free, albeit the Lord saith, The innocent and the righteous shalt thou not slay." [10] Of whom also did the Lord say : " But if the evil servant shall say in his heart, My lord delayeth his coming, and shall begin to smite the man-servants and maidens, and to eat and drink and be drunken ; the lord of that servant shall come in a day that he looketh not for him, and in an hour that he is not aware of, and shall cut him asunder, and appoint him his portion with the unbelievers." [11]

4. From all such persons, therefore, it behoves us to keep aloof, but to adhere to those who, as I have already observed, do hold the doctrine of the apostles, and who, together with the order of priesthood (presbyterii ordine), display sound speech and blameless conduct for the confirmation and correction of others.[12] In this way, Moses, to whom such a leadership was entrusted, relying on a good conscience, cleared himself before God, saying, " I have not in covetousness taken anything belonging to one of these men, nor have I done evil to one of them." [13] In this way, too, Samuel, who judged the people so many years, and bore rule over Israel without any pride, in the end cleared himself, saying, " I have walked before you from my childhood even unto this day : answer me in the sight of God, and before His anointed (Christi ejus) ; whose ox or whose ass of yours have I taken, or over whom have I tyrannized, or whom have I oppressed ? or if I have received from the hand of any a bribe or [so much as] a shoe, speak out

---

[1] The Latin is "a multis justis," corresponding to the Greek version of the Hebrew text. If the translation be supposed as corresponding to the Hebrew comparative, the English equivalent will be, "and above (more than) many righteous."
[2] Dan. xii. 3.
[3] The text and punctuation are here in great uncertainty, and very different views of both are taken by the editors.
[4] Luke xxiv. 26, 47. [The walk to Emmaus is the fountain-head of Scriptural exposition, and the forty days (Acts i. 3) is the river that came forth like that which went out of Eden. Ecclesiasticus iv. 31.]
[5] Matt. xiii. 52. [I must express my delight in the great principle of exposition here unfolded. The Old Scriptures are a night-bound wilderness, till Christ rises and illuminates them, glorifying alike hill and dale, and, as this author supposes, every shrub and flower, also, making the smallest leaf with its dewdrops glitter like the rainbow.]
[6] Lev. x. 1, 2.
[7] Num. xvi. 33.

[8] 1 Kings xiv. 10.
[9] Hist. Sus. ver. 56.
[10] Ibid. ver. 52, etc.; Ex. xxiii. 7.
[11] Matt. xxiv. 48, etc.; Luke xii. 45.
[12] [Contrast this spirit of a primitive Father, with the state of things which Wiclif rose up to purify, five hundred years ago.]
[13] Num. xvi. 15.

against me, and I will restore it to you." [1] And when the people had said to him, "Thou hast not tyrannized, neither hast thou oppressed us, neither hast thou taken ought of any man's hand," he called the Lord to witness, saying, "The LORD is witness, and His Anointed is witness this day, that ye have not found ought in my hand. And they said to him, He is witness." In this strain also the Apostle Paul, inasmuch as he had a good conscience, said to the Corinthians : " For we are not as many, who corrupt the Word of God : but as of sincerity, but as of God, in the sight of God speak we in Christ ; " [2] " We have injured no man, corrupted no man, circumvented no man." [3]

5. Such presbyters does the Church nourish, of whom also the prophet says : " I will give thy rulers in peace, and thy bishops in righteousness." [4] Of whom also did the Lord declare, "Who then shall be a faithful steward (actor), good and wise, whom the Lord sets over His household, to give them their meat in due season? Blessed is that servant whom his Lord, when He cometh, shall find so doing." [5] Paul then, teaching us where one may find such, says, " God hath placed in the Church, first, apostles ; secondly, prophets ; thirdly, teachers." [6] Where, therefore, the gifts of the Lord have been placed, there it behoves us to learn the truth, [namely,] from those who possess that succession of the Church which is from the apostles, [7] and among whom exists that which is sound and blameless in conduct, as well as that which is unadulterated and incorrupt in speech. For these also preserve this faith of ours in one God who created all things ; and they increase that love [which we have] for the Son of God, who accomplished such marvellous dispensations for our sake : and they expound the Scriptures to us without danger, neither blaspheming God, nor dishonouring the patriarchs, nor despising the prophets.

CHAP. XXVII. — THE SINS OF THE MEN OF OLD TIME, WHICH INCURRED THE DISPLEASURE OF GOD, WERE, BY HIS PROVIDENCE, COMMITTED TO WRITING, THAT WE MIGHT DERIVE INSTRUCTION THEREBY, AND NOT BE FILLED WITH PRIDE. WE MUST NOT, THEREFORE, INFER THAT THERE WAS ANOTHER GOD THAN HE WHOM CHRIST PREACHED ; WE SHOULD RATHER FEAR, LEST THE ONE AND THE SAME GOD WHO INFLICTED PUNISHMENT ON THE ANCIENTS, SHOULD BRING DOWN HEAVIER UPON US.

1. As I have heard from a certain presby-

ter, [8] who had heard it from those who had seen the apostles, and from those who had been their disciples, the punishment [declared] in Scripture was sufficient for the ancients in regard to what they did without the Spirit's guidance. For as God is no respecter of persons, He inflicted a proper punishment on deeds displeasing to Him. As in the case of David, [9] when he suffered persecution from Saul for righteousness' sake, and fled from King Saul, and would not avenge himself of his enemy, he both sung the advent of Christ, and instructed the nations in wisdom, and did everything after the Spirit's guidance, and pleased God. But when his lust prompted him to take Bathsheba, the wife of Uriah, the Scripture said concerning him, "Now, the thing (sermo) which David had done appeared wicked in the eyes of the LORD ; " [10] and Nathan the prophet is sent to him, pointing out to him his crime, in order that he, passing sentence upon and condemning himself, might obtain mercy and forgiveness from Christ : "And [Nathan] said to him, There were two men in one city ; the one rich, and the other poor. The rich man had exceeding many flocks and herds ; but the poor man had nothing, save one little ewe-lamb, which he possessed, and nourished up ; and it had been with him and with his children together : it did eat of his own bread, and drank of his cup, and was to him as a daughter. And there came a guest unto the rich man ; and he spared to take of the flock of his own ewe-lambs, and from the herds of his own oxen, to entertain the guest ; but he took the ewe-lamb of the poor man, and set it before the man that had come unto him. And David's anger was greatly kindled against the man ; and he said to Nathan, As the LORD liveth, the man that hath done this thing shall surely die (filius mortis est) : and he shall restore the lamb fourfold, because he hath done this thing, and because he had no pity for the poor man. And Nathan said unto him, Thou art the man who hast done this." [11] And then he proceeds with the rest [of the narrative], upbraiding him, and recounting God's benefits towards him, and [showing him] how much his conduct had displeased the Lord. For [he declared] that works of this nature were not pleasing to God, but that great wrath was suspended over his house. David, however, was struck with remorse on hearing this, and exclaimed, " I have sinned against the LORD ; " and he sung a penitential psalm, waiting for the coming of the Lord, who washes and makes clean the man who had

---

[1] 1 Sam. xii. 3.
[2] 2 Cor. ii. 17.
[3] 2 Cor. vii. 2.
[4] Isa. lx. 17.
[5] Matt. xxiv. 45, 46.
[6] 1 Cor. xii. 28.
[7] [Note the limitation: not the succession only, but with it (1) pure morality and holiness and (2) unadulterated testimony. No catholicity apart from these.]

[8] Polycarp, Papias, Pothinus, and others, have been suggested as probably here referred to, but the point is involved in utter uncertainty. [Surely this testimony is a precious intimation of the apostle's meaning (Rom. ii. 12-16), and the whole chapter is radiant with the purity of the Gospel.]
[9] 1 Sam. xviii.
[10] 2 Sam. xi. 27.
[11] 2 Sam. xii. 1, etc

been fast bound with [the chain of] sin. In like manner it was with regard to Solomon, while he continued to judge uprightly, and to declare the wisdom of God, and built the temple as the type of truth, and set forth the glories of God, and announced the peace about to come upon the nations, and prefigured the kingdom of Christ, and spake three thousand parables about the Lord's advent, and five thousand songs, singing praise to God, and expounded the wisdom of God in creation, [discoursing] as to the nature of every tree, every herb, and of all fowls, quadrupeds, and fishes; and he said, "Will God, whom the heavens cannot contain, really dwell with men upon the earth?" [1] And he pleased God, and was the admiration of all; and all kings of the earth sought an interview with him (*quærebant faciem ejus*) that they might hear the wisdom which God had conferred upon him.[2] The queen of the south, too, came to him from the ends of the earth, to ascertain the wisdom that was in him: [3] she whom the Lord also referred to as one who should rise up in the judgment with the nations of those men who do hear His words, and do not believe in Him, and should condemn them, inasmuch as she submitted herself to the wisdom announced by the servant of God, while these men despised that wisdom which proceeded directly from the Son of God. For Solomon was a servant, but Christ is indeed the Son of God, and the Lord of Solomon. While, therefore, he served God without blame, and ministered to His dispensations, then was he glorified: but when he took wives from all nations, and permitted them to set up idols in Israel, the Scripture spake thus concerning him: "And King Solomon was a lover of women, and he took to himself foreign women; and it came to pass, when Solomon was old, his heart was not perfect with the LORD his God. And the foreign women turned away his heart after strange gods. And Solomon did evil in the sight of the LORD: he did not walk after the LORD, as did David his father. And the LORD was angry with Solomon; for his heart was not perfect with the LORD, as was the heart of David his father." [4] The Scripture has thus sufficiently reproved him, as the presbyter remarked, in order that no flesh may glory in the sight of the Lord.

2. It was for this reason, too, that the Lord descended into the regions beneath the earth, preaching His advent there also, and [declaring] the remission of sins received by those who believe in Him.[5] Now all those believed in Him who had hope towards Him, that is, those who proclaimed His advent, and submitted to His dispensations, the righteous men, the prophets, and the patriarchs, to whom He remitted sins in the same way as He did to us, which sins we should not lay to their charge, if we would not despise the grace of God. For as these men did not impute unto us (the Gentiles) our transgressions, which we wrought before Christ was manifested among us, so also it is not right that *we* should lay blame upon those who sinned before Christ's coming. For "all men come short of the glory of God," [6] and are not justified of themselves, but by the advent of the Lord,—they who earnestly direct their eyes towards His light. And it is for our instruction that their actions have been committed to writing, that we might know, in the first place, that our God and theirs is one, and that sins do not please Him although committed by men of renown; and in the second place, that we should keep from wickedness. For if these men of old time, who preceded us in the gifts [bestowed upon them], and for whom the Son of God had not yet suffered, when they committed any sin and served fleshly lusts, were rendered objects of such disgrace, what shall the men of the present day suffer, who have despised the Lord's coming, and become the slaves of their own lusts? And truly the death of the Lord became [the means of] healing and remission of sins to the former, but Christ shall not die again in behalf of those who now commit sin, for death shall no more have dominion over Him; but the Son shall come in the glory of the Father, requiring from His stewards and dispensers the money which He had entrusted to them, with usury; and from those to whom He had given most shall He demand most. We ought not, therefore, as that presbyter remarks, to be puffed up, nor be severe upon those of old time, but ought ourselves to fear, lest perchance, after [we have come to] the knowledge of Christ, if we do things displeasing to God, we obtain no further forgiveness of sins, but be shut out from His kingdom.[6] And therefore it was that Paul said, "For if [God] spared not the natural branches, [take heed] lest He also spare not thee, who, when thou wert a wild olive tree, wert grafted into the fatness of the olive tree, and wert made a partaker of its fatness." [7]

3. Thou wilt notice, too, that the transgressions of the common people have been described in like manner, not for the sake of those who did then transgress, but as a means of instruction unto us, and that we should understand that it is one and the same God against whom these

1 1 Kings viii. 27.
2 1 Kings iv. 34.
3 1 Kings x. 1.
4 1 Kings xi. 1.
5 [1 Pet. iii. 19, 20.]

6 Rom. iii. 23. [Another testimony to the mercy of God in the judgment of the unevangelized. There must have been some reason for the secrecy with which "that presbyter's" name is guarded. Irenæus may have scrupled to draw the wrath of the Gnostics upon any name but his own.]
7 Rom. xi. 21, 17.

men sinned, and against whom certain persons do now transgress from among those who profess to have believed in Him. But this also, [as the presbyter states,] has Paul declared most plainly in the Epistle to the Corinthians, when he says, " Brethren, I would not that ye should be ignorant, how that all our fathers were under the cloud, and were all baptized unto Moses in the sea, and did all eat the same spiritual meat, and did all drink the same spiritual drink : for they drank of that spiritual rock that followed them ; and the rock was Christ. But with many of them God was not well pleased, for they were overthrown in the wilderness. These things were for our example (*in figuram nostri*), to the intent that we should not lust after evil things, as they also lusted ; neither be ye idolaters, as were some of them, as it is written : [1] The people sat down to eat and drink, and rose up to play. Neither let us commit fornication, as some of them also did, and fell in one day three and twenty thousand. Neither let us tempt Christ, as some of them also tempted, and were destroyed of serpents. Neither murmur ye, as some of them murmured, and were destroyed of the destroyer. But all these things happened to them in a figure, and were written for our admonition, upon whom the end of the world (*sæculorum*) is come. Wherefore let him that thinketh he standeth, take heed lest he fall." [2]

4. Since therefore, beyond all doubt and contradiction, the apostle shows that there is one and the same God, who did both enter into judgment with these former things, and who does inquire into those of the present time, and points out why these things have been committed to writing ; all these men are found to be unlearned and presumptuous, nay, even destitute of common sense, who, because of the transgressions of them of old time, and because of the disobedience of a vast number of them, do allege that there was indeed one God of these men, and that He was the maker of the world, and existed in a state of degeneracy ; but that there was another Father declared by Christ, and that this Being is He who has been conceived by the mind of each of them ; not understanding that as, in the former case, God showed Himself not well pleased in many instances towards those who sinned, so also in the latter, " many are called, but few are chosen." [3] As then the unrighteous, the idolaters, and fornicators perished, so also is it now : for both the Lord declares, that such persons are sent into eternal fire ; [4] and the apostle says, " Know ye not that the unrighteous shall not inherit the kingdom of God ? Be not deceived : neither fornicators, nor idolaters, nor adulterers, nor effeminate, nor abusers of themselves with mankind, nor thieves, nor covetous, nor drunkards, nor revilers, nor extortioners, shall inherit the kingdom of God." [5] And as it was not to those who are without that he said these things, but to us, lest we should be cast forth from the kingdom of God, by doing any such thing, he proceeds to say, " And such indeed were ye ; but ye are washed, but ye are sanctified in the name of the Lord Jesus Christ, and by the Spirit of our God." And just as then, those who led vicious lives, and put other people astray, were condemned and cast out, so also even now the offending eye is plucked out, and the foot and the hand, lest the rest of the body perish in like manner.[6] And we have the precept : " If any man that is called a brother be a fornicator, or covetous, or an idolater, or a railer, or a drunkard, or an extortioner, with such an one no not to eat." [7] And again does the apostle say, " Let no man deceive you with vain words ; for because of these things cometh the wrath of God upon the sons of mistrust. Be not ye therefore partakers with them." [8] And as then the condemnation of sinners extended to others who approved of them, and joined in their society ; so also is it the case at present, that " a little leaven leaveneth the whole lump." [9] And as the wrath of God did then descend upon the unrighteous, here also does the apostle likewise say : " For the wrath of God shall be revealed from heaven against all ungodliness and unrighteousness of those men who hold back the truth in unrighteousness." [10] And as, in those times, vengeance came from God upon the Egyptians who were subjecting Israel to unjust punishment, so is it now, the Lord truly declaring, " And shall not God avenge His own elect, which cry day and night unto Him ? I tell you, that He will avenge them speedily." [11] So says the apostle, in like manner, in the Epistle to the Thessalonians : " Seeing it is a righteous thing with God to recompense tribulation to them that trouble you ; and to you who are troubled rest with us, at the revealing of our Lord Jesus Christ from heaven with His mighty angels, and in a flame of fire, to take vengeance upon those who know not God, and upon those that obey not the Gospel of our Lord Jesus Christ : who shall also be punished with everlasting destruction from the presence of the Lord, and from the glory of His power ; when He shall come to be glorified in

---

[1] Ex. xxxii. 6.
[2] 1 Cor. x. 1, etc.
[3] Matt. xx. 16.
[4] Matt. xxv. 41.
[5] 1 Cor. vi. 9, 10.
[6] Matt. xviii. 8, 9.
[7] 1 Cor. v. 11.
[8] Eph. v. 6, 7.
[9] 1 Cor. v. 6.
[10] Rom. i. 18.
[11] Luke xviii. 7, 8.

His saints, and to be admired in all them who have believed in Him." [1]

CHAP. XXVIII. — THOSE PERSONS PROVE THEM-
SELVES SENSELESS WHO EXAGGERATE THE MERCY
OF CHRIST, BUT ARE SILENT AS TO THE JUDG-
MENT, AND LOOK ONLY AT THE MORE ABUN-
DANT GRACE OF THE NEW TESTAMENT ; BUT,
FORGETFUL OF THE GREATER DEGREE OF PER-
FECTION WHICH IT DEMANDS FROM US, THEY
ENDEAVOUR TO SHOW THAT THERE IS ANOTHER
GOD BEYOND HIM WHO CREATED THE WORLD.

1. Inasmuch, then, as in both Testaments there is the same righteousness of God [displayed] when God takes vengeance, in the one case indeed typically, temporarily, and more moderately ; but in the other, really, enduringly, and more rigidly : for the fire is eternal, and the wrath of God which shall be revealed from heaven from the face of our Lord (as David also says, " But the face of the Lord is against them that do evil, to cut off the remembrance of them from the earth " [2]), entails a heavier punishment on those who incur it, — the elders pointed out that those men are devoid of sense, who, [arguing] from what happened to those who formerly did not obey God, do endeavour to bring in another Father, setting over against [these punishments] what great things the Lord had done at His coming to save those who received Him, taking compassion upon them ; while they keep silence with regard to His judgment, and all those things which shall come upon such as have heard His words, but done them not, and that it were better for them if they had not been born,[3] and that it shall be more tolerable for Sodom and Gomorrha in the judgment than for that city which did not receive the word of His disciples.[4]

2. For as, in the New Testament, that faith of men [to be placed] in God has been increased, receiving in addition [to what was already revealed] the Son of God, that man too might be a partaker of God ; so is also our walk in life required to be more circumspect, when we are directed not merely to abstain from evil actions, but even from evil thoughts, and from idle words, and empty talk, and scurrilous language : [5] thus also the punishment of those who do not believe the Word of God, and despise His advent, and are turned away backwards, is increased ; being not merely temporal, but rendered also eternal. For to whomsoever

the Lord shall say, " Depart from me, ye cursed, into everlasting fire," [6] these shall be damned for ever ; and to whomsoever He shall say, " Come, ye blessed of my Father, inherit the kingdom prepared for you for eternity," [7] these do receive the kingdom for ever, and make constant advance in it ; since there is one and the same God the Father, and His Word, who has been always present with the human race, by means indeed of various dispensations, and has wrought out many things, and saved from the beginning those who are saved, (for these are they who love God, and follow the Word of God according to the class to which they belong,) and has judged those who are judged, that is, those who forget God, and are blasphemous, and transgressors of His word.

3. For the sesame heretics already mentioned by us have fallen away from themselves, by accusing the Lord, in whom they say that they believe. For those points to which they call attention with regard to the God who then awarded temporal punishments to the unbelieving, and smote the Egyptians, while He saved those that were obedient ; these same [facts, I say,] shall nevertheless repeat themselves in the Lord, who judges for eternity those whom He doth judge, and lets go free for eternity those whom He does let go free : and He shall [thus] be discovered, according to the language used by these men, as having been the cause of their most heinous sin to those who laid hands upon Him, and pierced Him. For if He had not so come, it follows that these men could not have become the slayers of their Lord ; and if He had not sent prophets to them, they certainly could not have killed them, nor the apostles either. To those, therefore, who assail us, and say, If the Egyptians had not been afflicted with plagues, and, when pursuing after Israel, been choked in the sea, God could not have saved His people, this answer may be given ; — Unless, then, the Jews had become the slayers of the Lord (which did, indeed, take eternal life away from them), and, by killing the apostles and persecuting the Church, had fallen into an abyss of wrath, we could not have been saved. For as they were saved by means of the blindness of the Egyptians, so are we, too, by that of the Jews ; if, indeed, the death of the Lord is the condemnation of those who fastened Him to the cross, and who did not believe His advent, but the salvation of those who believe in Him. For the apostle does also say in the Second [Epistle] to the Corinthians : " For we are unto God a sweet savour of Christ, in them which are saved, and in them which perish : to the one indeed the savour of death unto death,

---

[1] 2 Thess. i. 6-10.
[2] Ps. xxxiv. 16.
[3] Matt. xxvi. 24.
[4] Matt. x. 15.
[5] [Eph. v. 4. Even from the ἐυτραπελία which might signify a bon-mot, literally, and which certainly is not " scurrility," unless the apostle was ironical, reflecting on jokes which heathen considered " good."]

[6] Matt. xxv. 41.
[7] Matt. xxv. 34.

but to the other the savour of life unto life." [1] To whom, then, is there the savour of death unto death, unless to those who believe not, neither are subject to the Word of God? And who are they that did even then give themselves over to death? Those men, doubtless, who do not believe, nor submit themselves to God. And again, who are they that have been saved, and received the inheritance? Those, doubtless, who do believe God, and who have continued in His love; as did Caleb [the son] of Jephunneh and Joshua [the son] of Nun,[2] and innocent children,[3] who have had no sense of evil. But who are they that are saved now, and receive life eternal? Is it not those who love God, and who believe His promises, and who " in malice have become as little children?" [4]

CHAP. XXIX. — REFUTATION OF THE ARGUMENTS OF THE MARCIONITES, WHO ATTEMPTED TO SHOW THAT GOD WAS THE AUTHOR OF SIN, BECAUSE HE BLINDED PHARAOH AND HIS SERVANTS.

1. " But," say they, " God hardened the heart of Pharaoh and of his servants." [5] Those, then, who allege such difficulties, do not read in the Gospel that passage where the Lord replied to the disciples, when they asked Him, " Why speakest Thou unto them in parables?" — " Because it is given unto you to know the mystery of the kingdom of heaven; but to them I speak in parables, that seeing they may not see, and hearing they may not hear, understanding they may not understand; in order that the prophecy of Isaiah regarding them may be fulfilled, saying, Make the heart of this people gross, and make their ears dull, and blind their eyes. But blessed are your eyes, which see the things that ye see; and your ears, which hear what ye do hear." [6] For one and the same God [that blesses others] inflicts blindness upon those who do not believe, but who set Him at naught; just as the sun, which is a creature of His, [acts with regard] to those who, by reason of any weakness of the eyes, cannot behold his light; but to those who believe in Him and follow Him, He grants a fuller and greater illumination of mind. In accordance with this word, therefore, does the apostle say, in the Second [Epistle] to the Corinthians: " In whom the god of this world hath blinded the minds of them that believe not, lest the light of the glorious Gospel of Christ should shine [unto them]." [7] And again, in that to the Romans: " And as they did not think fit to have God in their knowl-

edge, God gave them up to a reprobate mind, to do those things that are not convenient." [8] Speaking of antichrist, too, he says clearly in the Second to the Thessalonians: " And for this cause God shall send them the working of error, that they should believe a lie; that they all might be judged who believed not the truth, but consented to iniquity." [9]

2. If, therefore, in the present time also, God, knowing the number of those who will not believe, since He foreknows all things, has given them over to unbelief, and turned away His face from men of this stamp, leaving them in the darkness which they have themselves chosen for themselves, what is there wonderful if He did also at that time give over to their unbelief, Pharaoh, who never would have believed, along with those who were with him? As the Word spake to Moses from the bush: " And I am sure that the king of Egypt will not let you go, unless by a mighty hand." [10] And for the reason that the Lord spake in parables, and brought blindness upon Israel, that seeing they might not see, since He knew the [spirit of] unbelief in them, for the same reason did He harden Pharaoh's heart; in order that, while seeing that it was the finger of God which led forth the people, he might not believe, but be precipitated into a sea of unbelief, resting in the notion that the exit of these [Israelites] was accomplished by magical power, and that it was not by the operation of God that the Red Sea afforded a passage to the people, but that this occurred by merely natural causes (sed naturaliter sic se habere).

CHAP. XXX. — REFUTATION OF ANOTHER ARGUMENT ADDUCED BY THE MARCIONITES, THAT GOD DIRECTED THE HEBREWS TO SPOIL THE EGYPTIANS.

1. Those, again, who cavil and find fault because the people did, by God's command, upon the eve of their departure, take vessels of all kinds and raiment from the Egyptians,[11] and so went away, from which [spoils], too, the tabernacle was constructed in the wilderness, prove themselves ignorant of the righteous dealings of God, and of His dispensations; as also the presbyter remarked: For if God had not accorded this in the typical exodus, no one could now be saved in our true exodus; that is, in the faith in which we have been established, and by which we have been brought forth from among the number of the Gentiles. For in some cases there follows us a small, and in others a large

---

[1] 2 Cor. ii. 15, 16.
[2] Num. xiv. 30.
[3] [Jonah iv. 11. The tenderness of our author constantly asserts itself, as in this reference to children.]
[4] 1 Cor. xiv. 20.
[5] Ex. ix. 35.
[6] Matt. xiii. 11–16; Isa. vi. 10.
[7] 2 Cor. iv. 4.

[8] Rom. i. 28.
[9] 2 Thess. ii. 11.
[10] Ex. iii. 19.
[11] Ex. iii. 22, xi. 2. [Our English translation "borrow" is a gratuitous injury to the text. As "King of kings" the Lord enjoins a just tax, which any earthly sovereign might have imposed uprightly. Our author argues well.]

amount of property, which we have acquired from the mammon of unrighteousness. For from what source do we derive the houses in which we dwell, the garments in which we are clothed, the vessels which we use, and everything else ministering to our every-day life, unless it be from those things which, when we were Gentiles, we acquired by avarice, or received them from our heathen parents, relations, or friends who unrighteously obtained them? — not to mention that even now we acquire such things when we are in the faith. For who is there that sells, and does not wish to make a profit from him who buys? Or who purchases anything, and does not wish to obtain good value from the seller? Or who is there that carries on a trade, and does not do so that he may obtain a livelihood thereby? And as to those believing ones who are in the royal palace, do they not derive the utensils they employ from the property which belongs to Cæsar; and to those who have not, does not each one of these [Christians] give according to his ability? The Egyptians were debtors to the [Jewish] people, not alone as to property, but as to their very lives, because of the kindness of the patriarch Joseph in former times; but in what way are the heathen debtors to us, from whom we receive both gain and profit? Whatsoever they amass with labour, these things do we make use of without labour, although we are in the faith.

2. Up to that time the people served the Egyptians in the most abject slavery, as saith the Scripture: "And the Egyptians exercised their power rigorously upon the children of Israel; and they made life bitter to them by severe labours, in mortar and in brick, and in all manner of service in the field which they did, by all the works in which they oppressed them with rigour."[1] And with immense labour they built for them fenced cities, increasing the substance of these men throughout a long course of years, and by means of every species of slavery; while these [masters] were not only ungrateful towards them, but had in contemplation their utter annihilation. In what way, then, did [the Israelites] act unjustly, if out of many things they took a few, they who might have possessed much property had they not served them, and might have gone forth wealthy, while, in fact, by receiving only a very insignificant recompense for their heavy servitude, they went away poor? It is just as if any free man, being forcibly carried away by another, and serving him for many years, and increasing his substance, should be thought, when he ultimately obtains some support, to possess some small portion of his [master's] property, but should in reality depart,

having obtained only a little as the result of his own great labours, and out of vast possessions which have been acquired, and this should be made by any one a subject of accusation against him, as if he had not acted properly.[2] He (the accuser) will rather appear as an unjust judge against him who had been forcibly carried away into slavery. Of this kind, then, are these men also, who charge the people with blame, because they appropriated a few things out of many, but who bring no charge against those who did not render them the recompense due to their fathers' services; nay, but even reducing them to the most irksome slavery, obtained the highest profit from them. And [these objectors] allege that [the Israelites] acted dishonestly, because, forsooth, they took away for the recompense of their labours, as I have observed, unstamped gold and silver in a few vessels; while they say that they themselves (for let truth be spoken, although to some it may seem ridiculous) do act honestly, when they carry away in their girdles from the labours of others, coined gold, and silver, and brass, with Cæsar's inscription and image upon it.

3. If, however, a comparison be instituted between us and them, [I would ask] which party shall seem to have received [their worldly goods] in the fairer manner? Will it be the [Jewish] people, [who took] from the Egyptians, who were at all points their debtors; or we, [who receive property] from the Romans and other nations, who are under no similar obligation to us? Yea, moreover, through their instrumentality the world is at peace, and we walk on the highways without fear, and sail where we will.[3] Therefore, against men of this kind (namely, the heretics) the word of the Lord applies, which says: "Thou hypocrite, first cast the beam out of thine eye, and then shalt thou see clearly to pull out the mote out of thy brother's eye."[4] For if he who lays these things to thy charge, and glories in his own wisdom, has been separated from the company of the Gentiles, and possesses nothing [derived from] other people's goods, but is literally naked, and barefoot, and dwells homeless among the mountains, as any of those animals do which feed on grass, he will stand excused [in using such language], as being ignorant of the necessities of our mode of life. But if he do partake of what, in the opinion of men, is the property of others, and if [at the same time] he runs down their type,[5] he proves him-

---

[1] Ex. i. 13, 14.

[2] This perplexed sentence is pointed by Harvey interrogatively, but we prefer the above.
[3] [A touching tribute to the imperial law, at a moment when Christians were "dying daily" and "as sheep for the slaughter." So powerfully worked the divine command, Luke vi. 29.]
[4] Matt. vii. 5.
[5] This is, if he inveighs against the Israelites for spoiling the Egyptians; the former being a type of the Christian Church in relation to the Gentiles.

self most unjust, turning this kind of accusation against himself. For he will be found carrying about property not belonging to him, and coveting goods which are not his. And therefore has the Lord said : " Judge not, that ye be not judged : for with what judgment ye shall judge, ye shall be judged." [1] [The meaning is] not certainly that we should not find fault with sinners, nor that we should consent to those who act wickedly ; but that we should not pronounce an unfair judgment on the dispensations of God, inasmuch as He has Himself made provision that all things shall turn out for good, in a way consistent with justice. For, because He knew that we would make a good use of our substance, which we should possess by receiving it from another, He says, " He that hath two coats, let him impart to him that hath none ; and he that hath meat, let him do likewise." [2] And, " For I was an hungered, and ye gave Me meat ; I was thirsty, and ye gave Me drink ; I was naked, and ye clothed Me." [3] And, " When thou doest thine alms, let not thy left hand know what thy right hand doeth." [4] And we are proved to be righteous by whatsoever else we do well, redeeming, as it were, our property from strange hands. But thus do I say, " from strange hands," not as if the world were not God's possession, but that we have gifts of this sort, and receive them from others, in the same way as these men had them from the Egyptians who knew not God ; and by means of these same do we erect in ourselves the tabernacle of God : for God dwells in those who act uprightly, as the Lord says : " Make to yourselves friends of the mammon of unrighteousness, that they, when ye shall be put to flight," [5] may receive you into eternal tabernacles." [6] For whatsoever we acquired from unrighteousness when we were heathen, we are proved righteous, when we have become believers, by applying it to the Lord's advantage.

4. As a matter of course, therefore, these things were done beforehand in a type, and from them was the tabernacle of God constructed ; those persons justly receiving them, as I have shown, while we were pointed out beforehand in them, — [we] who should afterwards serve God by the things of others. For the whole exodus of the people out of Egypt, which took place under divine guidance,[7] was a type and image of the exodus of the Church which should take

place from among the Gentiles ; [8] and for this cause He leads it out at last from this world into His own inheritance, which Moses the servant of God did not [bestow], but which Jesus the Son of God shall give for an inheritance. And if any one will devote a close attention to those things which are stated by the prophets with regard to the [time of the] end, and those which John the disciple of the Lord saw in the Apocalypse,[9] he will find that the nations [are to] receive the same plagues universally, as Egypt then did particularly.

CHAP. XXXI. — WE SHOULD NOT HASTILY IMPUTE AS CRIMES TO THE MEN OF OLD TIME THOSE ACTIONS WHICH THE SCRIPTURE HAS NOT CONDEMNED, BUT SHOULD RATHER SEEK IN THEM TYPES OF THINGS TO COME : AN EXAMPLE OF THIS IN THE INCEST COMMITTED BY LOT.

1. WHEN recounting certain matters of this kind respecting them of old time, the presbyter [before mentioned] was in the habit of instructing us, and saying : " With respect to those misdeeds for which the Scriptures themselves blame the patriarchs and prophets, we ought not to inveigh against them, nor become like Ham, who ridiculed the shame of his father, and so fell under a curse ; but we should [rather] give thanks to God in their behalf, inasmuch as their sins have been forgiven them through the advent of our Lord ; for He said that they gave thanks [for us], and gloried in our salvation.[10] With respect to those actions, again, on which the Scriptures pass no censure, but which are simply set down [as having occurred], we ought not to become the accusers [of those who committed them], for we are not more exact than God, nor can we be superior to our Master ; but we should search for a type [in them]. For not one of those things which have been set down in Scripture without being condemned is without significance." An example is found in the case of Lot, who led forth his daughters from Sodom, and these then conceived by their own father ; and who left behind him within the confines [of the land] his wife, [who remains] a pillar of salt unto this day. For Lot, not acting under the impulse of his own will, nor at the prompting of carnal concupiscence, nor having any knowledge or thought of anything of the kind, did [in fact] work out a type [of future events]. As says the Scripture : " And that night the elder went in

---

[1] Matt. vii. 1, 2.
[2] Luke iii. 11.
[3] Matt. xxv. 35, 36.
[4] Matt. vi. 3.
[5] As Harvey remarks, this is " a strange translation for ἐκλίπητε " of the *text. rec.*, and he adds that " possibly the translator read ἐκτράπητε."
[6] Luke xvi. 9.
[7] We here follow the punctuation of Massuet in preference to that of Harvey.

[8] [The Fathers regarded the whole Mosaic system, and the history of the faithful under it, as one great allegory. In everything they saw " similitudes," as we do in the *Faery Queen* of Spenser, or the *Pilgrim's Progress*. The ancients may have carried this principle too far, but as a principle it receives countenance from our Lord Himself and His apostles. To us there is often a barren bush, where the Fathers saw a bush that burned with fire.]
[9] See Rev. xv., xvi.
[10] [Thus far we have a most edifying instruction. The reader will be less edified with what follows, but it is a very striking example of what is written: " to the pure all things are pure." Tit. i. 15.]

and lay with her father; and Lot knew not when she lay down, nor when she arose."[1] And the same thing took place in the case of the younger: "And he knew not," it is said, "when she slept with him, nor when she arose."[2] Since, therefore, Lot knew not [what he did], nor was a slave to lust [in his actions], the arrangement [designed by God] was carried out, by which the two daughters (that is, the two churches[3]), who gave birth to children begotten of one and the same father, were pointed out, apart from [the influence of] the lust of the flesh. For there was no other person, [as they supposed], who could impart to them quickening seed, and the means of their giving birth to children, as it is written : " And the elder said unto the younger, And there is not a man on the earth to enter in unto us after the manner of all the earth : come, let us make our father drunk with wine, and let us lie with him, and raise up seed from our father."[4]

2. Thus, after their simplicity and innocence, did these daughters [of Lot] so speak, imagining that all mankind had perished, even as the Sodomites had done, and that the anger of God had come down upon the whole earth. Wherefore also they are to be held excusable, since they supposed that they only, along with their father, were left for the preservation of the human race; and for this reason it was that they deceived their father. Moreover, by the words they used this fact was pointed out — that there is no other one who can confer upon the elder and younger church the [power of] giving birth to children, besides our Father. Now the father of the human race is the Word of God, as Moses points out when he says, " Is not He thy father who hath obtained thee [by generation], and formed thee, and created thee?"[5] At what time, then, did He pour out upon the human race the life-giving seed — that is, the Spirit of the remission of sins, through means of whom we are quickened? Was it not then, when He was eating with men, and drinking wine upon the earth? For it is said, "The Son of man came eating and drinking;"[6] and when He had lain down, He fell asleep, and took repose. As He does Himself say in David, "I slept, and took repose."[7] And because He used thus to act while He dwelt and lived among us, He says again, " And my sleep became sweet unto me."[8]

Now this whole matter was indicated through Lot, that the seed of the Father of all — that is, of the Spirit of God, by whom all things were made — was commingled and united with flesh — that is, with His own workmanship; by which commixture and unity the two synagogues — that is, the two churches — produced from their own father living sons to the living God.

3. And while these things were taking place, his wife remained in [the territory of] Sodom, no longer corruptible flesh, but a pillar of salt which endures for ever;[9] and by those natural processes[10] which appertain to the human race, indicating that the Church also, which is the salt of the earth,[11] has been left behind within the confines of the earth, and subject to human sufferings; and while entire members are often taken away from it, the pillar of salt still endures,[12] thus typifying the foundation of the faith which maketh strong, and sends forward, children to their Father.

CHAP. XXXII. — THAT ONE GOD WAS THE AUTHOR OF BOTH TESTAMENTS, IS CONFIRMED BY THE AUTHORITY OF A PRESBYTER WHO HAD BEEN TAUGHT BY THE APOSTLES.

1. After this fashion also did a presbyter,[13] a disciple of the apostles, reason with respect to the two testaments, proving that both were truly from one and the same God. For [he maintained] that there was no other God besides Him who made and fashioned us, and that the discourse of those men has no foundation who affirm that this world of ours was made either by angels, or by any other power whatsoever, or by another God. For if a man be once moved away from the Creator of all things, and if he grant that this creation to which we belong was formed by any other or through any other [than the one God], he must of necessity fall into much inconsistency, and many contradictions of this sort; to which he will [be able to] furnish

---

[1] Gen. xix. 33.
[2] Gen. xix. 35.
[3] " Id est duæ synagogæ," referring to the Jews and Gentiles. Some regard the words as a marginal gloss which has crept into the text.
[4] Gen. xix. 31, 32.
[5] Deut. xxxii. 6, LXX. [Let us reflect that this effort to spiritualize this awful passage in the history of Lot is an innocent but unsuccessful attempt to imitate St. Paul's allegory, Gal. iv. 24.]
[6] Matt. xi. 19.
[7] Ps. iii. 6.
[8] Jer. xxxi. 26.

[9] Comp. Clem. Rom., chap. xi. Josephus (Antiq., i. 11, 4) testifies that he had himself seen this pillar.
[10] The Latin is " per naturalia," which words, according to Harvey, correspond to δὶ ἐμμηνορροίας. There is a poem entitled Sodoma preserved among the works of Tertullian and Cyprian which contains the following lines: —

" Dicitur et vivens, alio jam corpore, sexus
Munificos solito dispungere sanguine menses."

[11] Matt. v. 13.
[12] The poem just referred to also says in reference to this pillar: →

" Ipsaque imago sibi formam sine corpore servans
Durat adhuc, et enim nuda statione sub æthram
Nec pluviis dilapsa situ, nec diruta ventis.
Quin etiam si quis mutilaverit advena formam,
Protinus ex sese suggestu vulnera complet."

[That a pillar of salt is still to be seen in this vicinity, is now confirmed by many modern travellers (report of Lieut. Lynch, United States Navy), which accounts for the natural inference of Josephus and others on whom our author relied. The coincidence is noteworthy.]

[13] Harvey remarks here, that this can hardly be the same presbyter mentioned before, "who was only a hearer of those who had heard the apostles. Irenæus may here mean the venerable martyr Polycarp, bishop of Smyrna."

no explanations which can be regarded as either probable or true. And, for this reason, those who introduce other doctrines conceal from us the opinion which they themselves hold respecting God, because they are aware of the untenable [1] and absurd nature of their doctrine, and are afraid lest, should they be vanquished, they should have some difficulty in making good their escape. But if any one believes in [only] one God, who also made all things by the Word, as Moses likewise says, "God said, Let there be light : and there was light ; " [2] and as we read in the Gospel, "All things were made by Him ; and without Him was nothing made ; " [3] and the Apostle Paul [says] in like manner, "There is one Lord, one faith, one baptism, one God and Father, who is above all, and through all, and in us all " [4] — this man will first of all "hold the head, from which the whole body is compacted and bound together, and, through means of every joint according to the measure of the ministration of each several part, maketh increase of the body to the edification of itself in love." [5] And then shall every word also seem consistent to him, [6] if he for his part diligently read the Scriptures in company with those who are presbyters in the Church, among whom is the apostolic doctrine, as I have pointed out.

2. For all the apostles taught that there were indeed two testaments among the two peoples ; but that it was one and the same God who appointed both for the advantage of those men (for whose [7] sakes the testaments were given) who were to believe in God, I have proved in the third book from the very teaching of the apostles ; and that the first testament was not given without reason, or to no purpose, or in an accidental sort of manner ; but that it subdued [8] those to whom it was given to the service of God, for their benefit (for God needs no service from men), and exhibited a type of heavenly things, inasmuch as man was not yet able to see the things of God through means of immediate vision ; [9] and foreshadowed the images of those things which [now actually] exist in the Church, in order that our faith might be firmly established ; [10] and contained a prophecy of things to come, in order that man might learn that God has foreknowledge of all things.

CHAP. XXXIII. — WHOSOEVER CONFESSES THAT ONE GOD IS THE AUTHOR OF BOTH TESTAMENTS, AND DILIGENTLY READS THE SCRIPTURES IN COMPANY WITH THE PRESBYTERS OF THE CHURCH, IS A TRUE SPIRITUAL DISCIPLE ; AND HE WILL RIGHTLY UNDERSTAND AND INTERPRET ALL THAT THE PROPHETS HAVE DECLARED RESPECTING CHRIST AND THE LIBERTY OF THE NEW TESTAMENT.

1. A spiritual disciple of this sort truly receiving the Spirit of God, who was from the beginning, in all the dispensations of God, present with mankind, and announced things future, revealed things present, and narrated things past — [such a man] does indeed "judge all men, but is himself judged by no man." [11] For he judges the Gentiles, "who serve the creature more than the Creator," [12] and with a reprobate mind spend all their labour on vanity. And he also judges the Jews, who do not accept of the word of liberty, nor are willing to go forth free, although they have a Deliverer present [with them] ; but they pretend, at a time unsuitable [for such conduct], to serve, [with observances] beyond [those required by] the law, God who stands in need of nothing, and do not recognise the advent of Christ, which He accomplished for the salvation of men, nor are willing to understand that all the prophets announced His two advents : the one, indeed, in which He became a man subject to stripes, and knowing what it is to bear infirmity, [13] and sat upon the foal of an ass, [14] and was a stone rejected by the builders, [15] and was led as a sheep to the slaughter, [16] and by the stretching forth of His hands destroyed Amalek ; [17] while He gathered from the ends of the earth into His Father's fold the children who were scattered abroad, [18] and remembered His own dead ones who had formerly fallen asleep, [19] and came down to them that He might deliver them : but the second in which He will come on the clouds, [20] bringing on the day which burns as a furnace, [21] and smiting the earth with the word of His mouth, [22] and slaying the impious with the breath of His lips, and having a fan in His hands, and cleansing His floor, and gathering the wheat indeed into His barn, but burning the chaff with unquenchable fire. [23]

2. Moreover, he shall also examine the doc-

---

1 "Quassum et futile." The text varies much in the MSS.
2 Gen. i. 3.
3 John i. 3.
4 Eph. iv. 5, 6.
5 Eph iv. 16; Col. ii. 19.
6 "Constabit ei."
7 We here read "secundum quos" with Massuet, instead of the usual "secundum quod."
8 "Concurvans," corresponding to συγκάμπτων, which, says Harvey, "would be expressive of those who were brought under the law, as the neck of the steer is bent to the yoke."
9 The Latin is, "per proprium visum."
10 [If this and the former chapter seem to us superfluous, we must reflect that such testimony, from the beginning, has established the unity of Holy Scripture, and preserved to us — THE BIBLE.]

11 1 Cor. ii. 15. [The argument of this chapter hinges on Ps. xxv. 14, and expounds a difficult text of St. Paul. A man who has the mind of God's Spirit is the only judge of spiritual things. Worldly men are incompetent critics of Scripture and of Christian exposition.]
12 Rom. i. 21.
13 Isa. liii. 3.
14 Zech. ix. 9.
15 Ps. cxviii. 22.
16 Isa. liii. 7.
17 Ex. xvii. 11.
18 Isa. xi. 12.
19 Comp. book iii. 20, 4.
20 Dan. vii. 13.
21 Mal. iv. 1.
22 Isa. xi. 4.
23 Matt. iii. 12; Luke iii. 17.

trine of Marcion, [inquiring] how he holds that there are two gods, separated from each other by an infinite distance.[1] Or how can *he* be good who draws away men that do not belong to him from him who made them, and calls them into his own kingdom? And why is his goodness, which does not save all [thus], defective? Also, why does he, indeed, seem to be good as respects men, but most unjust with regard to him who made men, inasmuch as he deprives him of his possessions? Moreover, how could the Lord, with any justice, if He belonged to another father, have acknowledged the bread to be His body, while He took it from that creation to which we belong, and affirmed the mixed cup to be His blood?[2] And why did He acknowledge Himself to be the Son of man, if He had not gone through that birth which belongs to a human being? How, too, could He forgive us those sins for which we are answerable to our Maker and God? And how, again, supposing that He was not flesh, but was a man merely in appearance, could He have been crucified, and could blood and water have issued from His pierced side?[3] What body, moreover, was it that those who buried Him consigned to the tomb? And what was that which rose again from the dead?

3. [This spiritual man] shall also judge all the followers of Valentinus, because they do indeed confess with the tongue one God the Father, and that all things derive their existence from Him, but do at the same time maintain that He who formed all things is the fruit of an apostasy or defect. [He shall judge them, too, because] they do in like manner confess with the tongue one Lord Jesus Christ, the Son of God, but assign in their [system of] doctrine a production of his own to the Only-begotten, one of his own also to the Word, another to Christ, and yet another to the Saviour; so that, according to them, all these beings are indeed said [in Scripture to be], as it were, one; [while they maintain], notwithstanding, that each one of them should be understood [to exist] separately [from the rest], and to have [had] his own special origin, according to his peculiar conjunction. [It appears], then,[4] that their tongues alone, forsooth, have conceded the unity [of God], while their [real] opinion and their understanding (by their habit of investigating profundities) have fallen away from [this doctrine of] unity, and taken up the notion of manifold deities, — [this, I

say, must appear] when they shall be examined by Christ as to the points [of doctrine] which they have invented. Him, too, they affirm to have been born at a later period than the Pleroma of the Æons, and that His production took place after [the occurrence of] a degeneracy or apostasy; and they maintain that, on account of the passion which was experienced by Sophia, they themselves were brought to the birth. But their own special prophet Homer, listening to whom they have invented such doctrines, shall himself reprove them, when he expresses himself as follows: —

"Hateful to me that man as Hades' gates,
Who one thing thinks, while he another states."[5]

[This spiritual man] shall also judge the vain speeches of the perverse Gnostics, by showing that they are the disciples of Simon Magus.

4. He will judge also the Ebionites; [for] how can they be saved unless it was God who wrought out their salvation upon earth? Or how shall man pass into God, unless God has [first] passed into man? And how shall he (man) escape from the generation subject to death, if not by means[6] of a new generation, given in a wonderful and unexpected manner (but as a sign of salvation) by God — [I mean] that regeneration which flows from the virgin through faith?[7] Or how shall they receive adoption from God if they remain in this [kind of] generation, which is naturally possessed by man in this world? And how could He (Christ) have been greater than Solomon,[8] or greater than Jonah, or have been the Lord of David,[9] who was of the same substance as they were? How, too, could He have subdued[10] him who was stronger than men,[11] who had not only overcome man, but also retained him under his power, and conquered him who had conquered, while he set free mankind who had been conquered, unless He had been greater than man who had thus been vanquished? But who else is superior to, and more eminent than, that man who was formed after the likeness of God, except the Son of God, after whose image man was created? And for this reason He did in these last days[12] exhibit the similitude; [for] the Son of God was made man, assuming the ancient production [of His hands] into His own nature,[13] as I have shown in the immediately preceding book.

---

[1] Harvey points this sentence interrogatively.
[2] "Temperamentum calicis:" on which Harvey remarks that "the mixture of water with the wine in the holy Eucharist was the universal practice of antiquity . . . the wine signifying the mystical Head of the Church, the water the body." [Whatever the significance, it harmonizes with the Paschal chalice, and with 1 John v. 6, and St John's Gospel, xix. 34, 35.]
[3] John xix. 34.
[4] This sentence is very obscure in the Latin text.

[5] *Iliad*, ix. 312, 313.
[6] The text is obscure, and the construction doubtful.
[7] The Latin here is, "quæ est ex virgine per fidem regenerationem." According to Massuet, "virgine" here refers not to Mary, but to the Church. Grabe suspects that some words have been lost.
[8] Matt. xii. 41, 42.
[9] Matt. xxii. 43.
[10] Matt. xxii. 29; Luke xi. 21, 22.
[11] Literally, "who was strong against men."
[12] In fine; lit. "in the end."
[13] In semetipsum: lit. "unto Himself."

5. He shall also judge those who describe Christ as [having become man] only in [human] opinion. For how can they imagine that they do themselves carry on a real discussion, when their Master was a mere imaginary being? Or how can they receive anything stedfast from Him, if He was a merely imagined being, and not a verity? And how can these men really be partakers of salvation, if He in whom they profess to believe, manifested Himself as a merely imaginary being? Everything, therefore, connected with these men is unreal, and nothing [possessed of the character of] truth; and, in these circumstances, it may be made a question whether (since, perchance, they themselves in like manner are not men, but mere dumb animals) they do not present,[1] in most cases, simply a shadow of humanity.

6. He shall also judge false prophets, who, without having received the gift of prophecy from God, and not possessed of the fear of God, but either for the sake of vainglory, or with a view to some personal advantage, or acting in some other way under the influence of a wicked spirit, pretend to utter prophecies, while all the time they lie against God.

7. He shall also judge those who give rise to schisms, who are destitute of the love of God, and who look to their own special advantage rather than to the unity of the Church; and who for trifling reasons, or any kind of reason which occurs to them, cut in pieces and divide the great and glorious body of Christ, and so far as in them lies, [positively] destroy it, — men who prate of peace while they give rise to war, and do in truth strain out a gnat, but swallow a camel.[2] For no reformation of so great importance can be effected by them, as will compensate for the mischief arising from their schism. He shall also judge all those who are beyond the pale of the truth, that is, who are outside the Church; but he himself shall be judged by no one. For to him all things are consistent: he has a full faith in one God Almighty, of whom are all things; and in the Son of God, Jesus Christ our Lord, by whom are all things, and in the dispensations connected with Him, by means of which the Son of God became man; and a firm belief in the Spirit of God, who furnishes us with a knowledge of the truth, and has set forth the dispensations of the Father and the Son, in virtue of which He dwells with every generation of men,[3] according to the will of the Father.

8. True knowledge[4] is [that which consists in] the doctrine of the apostles, and the ancient constitution[5] of the Church throughout all the world, and the distinctive manifestation of the body[6] of Christ according to the successions of the bishops, by which they have handed down that Church which exists in every place, and has come even unto us, being guarded and preserved,[7] without any forging of Scriptures, by a very complete system[8] of doctrine, and neither receiving addition nor [suffering] curtailment [in the truths which she believes]; and [it consists in] reading [the word of God] without falsification, and a lawful and diligent exposition in harmony with the Scriptures, both without danger and without blasphemy; and [above all, it consists in] the pre-eminent gift of love,[9] which is more precious than knowledge, more glorious than prophecy, and which excels all the other gifts [of God].

9. Wherefore the Church does in every place, because of that love which she cherishes towards God, send forward, throughout all time, a multitude of martyrs to the Father; while all others[10] not only have nothing of this kind to point to among themselves, but even maintain that such witness-bearing is not at all necessary, for that their system of doctrines is the true witness [for Christ], with the exception, perhaps, that one or two among them, during the whole time which has elapsed since the Lord appeared on earth, have occasionally, along with our martyrs, borne the reproach of the name (as if he too [the heretic] had obtained mercy), and have been led forth with them [to death], being, as it were, a sort of retinue granted unto them. For the Church alone sustains with purity the reproach of those who suffer persecution for righteousness' sake, and endure all sorts of punishments, and are put to death because of the love which they bear to God, and their confession of His Son; often weakened indeed, yet immediately increasing her members, and becoming whole again, after the same manner as her type,[11] Lot's wife, who became a pillar of salt. Thus, too, [she passes through an experience] similar to that of the ancient prophets, as the Lord declares, "For so persecuted they

---

[1] We here follow the reading "proferant:" the passage is difficult and obscure, but the meaning is as above.
[2] Matt. xxiii. 24.
[3] The Greek text here is σκηνοβατοῦν (lit. "to tabernacle:" comp. ἐσκήνωσεν, John i. 14) καθ' ἑκάστην γενεὰν ἐν τοῖς ἀνθρώποις: the Latin is, "Secundum quas (dispositiones) aderat generi humano." We have endeavoured to express the meaning of both.

[4] The following section is an important one, but very difficult to translate with undoubted accuracy. The editors differ considerably both as to the construction and the interpretation. We have done our best to represent the meaning in English, but may not have been altogether successful.
[5] The Greek is σύστημα: the Latin text has "status."
[6] The Latin is, "character corporis."
[7] The text here is, "custodita sine fictione scripturarum;" some prefer joining "scripturarum" to the following words.
[8] We follow Harvey's text, "tractatione;" others read "tractatio." According to Harvey, the creed of the Church is denoted by "tractatione;" but Massuet renders the clause thus: ["True knowledge consists in] a very complete *tractatio* of the Scriptures, which has come down to us by being preserved ('custoditione' being read instead of 'custodita') without falsification."
[9] Comp. 2 Cor. viii. 1; 1 Cor. xiii.
[10] i.e., the heretics.
[11] Comp. above, xxxi. 2.

the prophets who were before you;"[1] inasmuch as she does indeed, in a new fashion, suffer persecution from those who do not receive the word of God, while the self-same spirit rests upon her[2] [as upon these ancient prophets].

10. And indeed the prophets, along with other things which they predicted, also foretold this, that all those on whom the Spirit of God should rest, and who would obey the word of the Father, and serve Him according to their ability, should suffer persecution, and be stoned and slain. For the prophets prefigured in themselves all these things, because of their love to God, and on account of His word. For since they themselves were members of Christ, each one of them in his place as a member did, in accordance with this, set forth the prophecy [assigned him]; all of them, although many, prefiguring only one, and proclaiming the things which pertain to one. For just as the working of the whole body is exhibited through means of our members, while the figure of a complete man is not displayed by one member, but through means of all taken together, so also did all the prophets prefigure the one [Christ]; while every one of them, in his special place as a member, did, in accordance with this, fill up the [established] dispensation, and shadowed forth beforehand that particular working of Christ which was connected with that member.

11. For some of them, beholding Him in glory, saw His glorious life (*conversationem*) at the Father's right hand;[3] others beheld Him coming on the clouds as the Son of man;[4] and those who declared regarding Him, "They shall look on Him whom they have pierced,"[5] indicated His [second] advent, concerning which He Himself says, "Thinkest thou that when the Son of man cometh, He shall find faith on the earth?"[6] Paul also refers to this event when he says, "If, however, it is a righteous thing with God to recompense tribulation to them that trouble you, and to you that are troubled rest with us, at the revelation of the Lord Jesus from heaven, with His mighty angels, and in a flame of fire."[7] Others again, speaking of Him as a judge, and [referring], as if it were a burning furnace, [to] the day of the Lord, who "gathers the wheat into His barn, but will burn up the chaff with unquenchable fire,"[8] were accustomed to threaten those who were unbelieving, concerning whom also the Lord Himself declares, "Depart from me, ye cursed, into everlasting fire,

which my Father has prepared for the devil and his angels."[9] And the apostle in like manner says [of them], "Who shall be punished with everlasting death from the face of the Lord, and from the glory of His power, when He shall come to be glorified in His saints, and to be admired in those who believe in Him."[10] There are also some [of them] who declare, "Thou art fairer than the children of men;"[11] and, "God, Thy God, hath anointed Thee with the oil of gladness above Thy fellows;"[12] and, "Gird Thy sword upon Thy thigh, O Most Mighty, with Thy beauty and Thy fairness, and go forward and proceed prosperously; and rule Thou because of truth, and meekness, and righteousness."[13] And whatever other things of a like nature are spoken regarding Him, these indicated that beauty and splendour which exist in His kingdom, along with the transcendent and preeminent exaltation [belonging] to all who are under His sway, that those who hear might desire to be found there, doing such things as are pleasing to God. Again, there are those who say, "He is a man, and who shall know him?"[14] and, "I came unto the prophetess, and she bare a son, and His name is called Wonderful, Counsellor, the Mighty God;"[15] and those [of them] who proclaimed Him as Immanuel, [born] of the Virgin, exhibited the union of the Word of God with His own workmanship, [declaring] that the Word should become flesh, and the Son of God the Son of man (the pure One opening purely that pure womb which regenerates men unto God, and which He Himself made pure); and having become this which we also are, He [nevertheless] is the Mighty God, and possesses a generation which cannot be declared. And there are also some of them who say, "The Lord hath spoken in Zion, and uttered His voice from Jerusalem;"[16] and, "In Judah is God known;"[17] — these indicated His advent which took place in Judea. Those, again, who declare that "God comes from the south, and from a mountain thick with foliage,"[18] announced His advent at Bethlehem, as I have pointed out in the preceding book.[19] From that place, also, He who rules, and who feeds the people of His Father, has come. Those, again, who declare that at His coming "the lame man shall leap as an hart, and the tongue of the dumb shall

---

1 Matt. v. 12.
2 Comp. 1 Pet. iv. 14.
3 Isa. vi. 1; Ps. cx. 1.
4 Dan. vii. 13.
5 Zech. xii. 10.
6 Luke xviii. 8. There is nothing to correspond with " putas " in the received text.
7 2 Thess. i. 6–8.
8 Matt. iii. 12.

9 Matt. xxv. 41.
10 2 Thess. i. 9, 10.
11 Ps. xlv. 2.
12 Ps. xlv. 7.
13 Ps. xlv. 3, 4.
14 Jer. xvii. 9 (Sept.). Harvey here remarks: "The LXX. read אֱנוֹשׁ instead of אֱנשׁ. Thus, from a text that teaches us that *the heart is deceitful above all things*, the Fathers extract a proof of the manhood of Christ."
15 Isa. viii. 3, ix. 6, vii. 14. [A confusion of texts.]
16 Joel iii. 16.
17 Ps. lxxvi. 1.
18 Hab. iii. 3.
19 See III. xx. 4.

[speak] plainly, and the eyes of the blind shall be opened, and the ears of the deaf shall hear," [1] and that " the hands which hang down, and the feeble knees, shall be strengthened," [2] and that " the dead which are in the grave shall arise," [3] and that He Himself " shall take [upon Him] our weaknesses, and bear our sorrows," [4] — [all these] proclaimed those works of healing which were accomplished by Him.

12. Some of them, moreover — [when they predicted that] as a weak and inglorious man, and as one who knew what it was to bear infirmity, [5] and sitting upon the foal of an ass, [6] He should come to Jerusalem ; and that He should give His back to stripes, [7] and His cheeks to palms [which struck Him] ; and that He should be led as a sheep to the slaughter ; [8] and that He should have vinegar and gall given Him to drink ; [9] and that He should be forsaken by His friends and those nearest to Him ; [10] and that He should stretch forth His hands the whole day long ; [11] and that He should be mocked and maligned by those who looked upon Him ; [12] and that His garments should be parted, and lots cast upon His raiment ; [13] and that He should be brought down to the dust of death, [14] with all [the other] things of a like nature — prophesied His coming in the character of a man as He entered Jerusalem, in which by His passion and crucifixion He endured all the things which have been mentioned. Others, again, when they said, " The holy Lord remembered His own dead ones who slept in the dust, and came down to them to raise them up, that He might save them," [15] furnished us with the reason on account of which He suffered all these things. Those, moreover, who said, " In that day, saith the Lord, the sun shall go down at noon, and there shall be darkness over the earth in the clear day ; and I will turn your feast days into mourning, and all your songs into lamentation," [16] plainly announced that obscuration of the sun which at the time of His crucifixion took place from the sixth hour onwards, and that after this event, those days which were their festivals according to the law, and their songs, should be changed into grief and lamentation when they were handed over to the Gentiles. Jeremiah, too, makes this point still clearer, when he thus speaks concerning Jerusalem : " She that hath born [seven] languisheth ; her soul hath become weary ; her sun hath gone down while it was yet noon ; she hath been confounded, and suffered reproach : the remainder of them will I give to the sword in the sight of their enemies." [17]

13. Those of them, again, who spoke of His having slumbered and taken sleep, and of His having risen again because the Lord sustained Him, [18] and who enjoined the principalities of heaven to set open the everlasting doors, that the King of glory might go in, [19] proclaimed beforehand His resurrection from the dead through the Father's power, and His reception into heaven. And when they expressed themselves thus, " His going forth is from the height of heaven, and His returning even to the highest heaven ; and there is no one who can hide himself from His heat," [20] they announced that very truth of His being taken up again to the place from which He came down, and that there is no one who can escape His righteous judgment. And those who said, " The LORD hath reigned ; let the people be enraged : [even] He who sitteth upon the cherubim ; let the earth be moved," [21] were thus predicting partly that wrath from all nations which after His ascension came upon those who believed in Him, with the movement of the whole earth against the Church ; and partly the fact that, when He comes from heaven with His mighty angels, the whole earth shall be shaken, as He Himself declares, " There shall be a great earthquake, such as has not been from the beginning." [22] And again, when one says, " Whosoever is judged, let him stand opposite ; and whosoever is justified, let him draw near to the servant [23] of God ; " [24] and, " Woe unto you, for ye shall wax old as doth a garment, and the moth shall eat you up ; " and, " All flesh shall be humbled, and the LORD alone shall be exalted in the highest," [25] — it is thus indicated that, after His passion and ascension, God shall cast down under His feet all who were opposed to Him, and He shall be exalted above all, and there shall be no one who can be justified or compared to Him.

14. And those of them who declare that God would make a new covenant [26] with men, not such as that which He made with the fathers at Mount Horeb, and would give to men a new heart and a new spirit ; [27] and again, " And remember ye not the things of old : behold, I

---

[1] Isa. xxxv. 5, 6.
[2] Isa. xxxv. 3.
[3] Isa. xxvi. 19.
[4] Isa. liii. 4.
[5] Isa. liii. 3.
[6] Zech. ix. 9.
[7] Isa. l. 6.
[8] Isa. liii. 7.
[9] Ps. lxix. 21.
[10] Ps. xxxviii. 11.
[11] Isa. lxv. 2.
[12] Ps. xxii. 7.
[13] Ps. xxii. 18.
[14] Ps. xxii. 15.
[15] Comp. book iii. cap. xx. 4 and book iv. cap. xxii. 1.
[16] Amos viii. 9, 10.

[17] Jer. xv. 9.
[18] Ps. iii. 5.
[19] Ps. xxiv. 7.
[20] Ps. xix. 6.
[21] Ps. xcix. 1.
[22] Matt. xxiv. 21.
[23] Or " son."
[24] Isa. l. 8, 9 (loosely quoted).
[25] Isa. ii. 17.
[26] Jer. xxxi. 31, 32.
[27] Ezek. xxxvi. 26.

make new things which shall now arise, and ye shall know it; and I will make a way in the desert, and rivers in a dry land, to give drink to my chòsen people, my people whom I have acquired, that they may show forth my praise," [1] — plainly announced that liberty which distinguishes the new covenant, and the new wine which is put into new bottles,[2] [that is], the faith which is in Christ, by which He has proclaimed the way of righteousness sprung up in the desert, and the streams of the Holy Spirit in a dry land, to give water to the elect people of God, whom He has acquired, that they might show forth His praise, but not that they might blaspheme Him who made these things, that is, God.

15. And all those other points which I have shown the prophets to have uttered by means of so long a series of Scriptures, he who is truly spiritual will interpret by pointing out, in regard to every one of the things which have been spoken, to what special point in the dispensation of the Lord is referred, and [by thus exhibiting] the entire system of the work of the Son of God, knowing always the same God; and always acknowledging the same Word of God, although He has [but] now been manifested to us; acknowledging also at all times the same Spirit of God, although He has been poured out upon us after a new fashion in these last times, [knowing that He descends] even from the creation of the world to its end upon the human race simply as such, from whom those who believe God and follow His word receive that salvation which flows from Him. Those, on the other hand, who depart from Him, and despise His precepts, and by their deeds bring dishonour on Him who made them, and by their opinions blaspheme Him who nourishes them, heap up against themselves most righteous judgment.[3] He therefore (i.e., the spiritual man) sifts and tries them all, but he himself is tried by no man:[4] he neither blasphemes his Father, nor sets aside His dispensations, nor inveighs against the fathers, nor dishonours the prophets, by maintaining that they were [sent] from another God [than he worships], or again, that their prophecies were derived from different sources.[5]

CHAP. XXXIV. — PROOF AGAINST THE MARCIONITES, THAT THE PROPHETS REFERRED IN ALL THEIR PREDICTIONS TO OUR CHRIST.

1. Now I shall simply say, in opposition to all the heretics, and principally against the followers of Marcion, and against those who are like to these, in maintaining that the prophets were from another God [than He who is announced in the Gospel], read with earnest care that Gospel which has been conveyed to us by the apostles, and read with earnest care the prophets, and you will find that the whole conduct, and all the doctrine, and all the sufferings of our Lord, were predicted through them. But if a thought of this kind should then suggest itself to you, to say, What then did the Lord bring to us by His advent? — know ye that He brought all [possible] novelty, by bringing Himself who had been announced. For this very thing was proclaimed beforehand, that a novelty should come to renew and quicken mankind. For the advent of the King is previously announced by those servants who are sent [before Him], in order to the preparation and equipment of those men who are to entertain their Lord. But when the King has actually come, and those who are His subjects have been filled with that joy which was proclaimed beforehand, and have attained to that liberty which He bestows, and share in the sight of Him, and have listened to His words, and have enjoyed the gifts which He confers, the question will not then be asked by any that are possessed of sense what new thing the King has brought beyond [that proclaimed by] those who announced His coming. For He has brought Himself, and has bestowed on men those good things which were announced beforehand, which things the angels desired to look into.[6]

2. But the servants would then have been proved false, and not sent by the Lord, if Christ on His advent, by being found exactly such as He was previously announced, had not fulfilled their words. Wherefore He said, "Think not that I have come to destroy the law or the prophets; I came not to destroy, but to fulfil. For verily I say unto you, Until heaven and earth pass away, one jot or one tittle shall not pass from the law and the prophets till all come to pass."[7] For by His advent He Himself fulfilled all things, and does still fulfil in the Church the new covenant foretold by the law, onwards to the consummation [of all things]. To this effect also Paul, His apostle, says in the Epistle to the Romans, "But now,[8] without the law, has the righteousness of God been manifested, being witnessed by the law and the prophets; for the just shall live by faith."[9] But this fact, that the just shall live by faith, had been previously announced[10] by the prophets.

3. But whence could the prophets have had power to predict the advent of the King, and to preach beforehand that liberty which was be-

---

[1] Isa. xliii. 19-21.
[2] Matt. ix. 17.
[3] Rom. ii. 5.
[4] 1 Cor. ii 15.
[5] "Ex alia et alia substantia fuisse prophetias."

[6] 1 Pet. i. 12.
[7] Rom. iii. 21.
[8] Matt. v. 17, 18.
[9] Rom. i. 17.
[10] Hab. ii. 4.

stowed by Him, and previously to announce all things which were done by Christ, His words, His works, and His sufferings, and to predict the new covenant, if they had received prophetical inspiration from another God [than He who is revealed in the Gospel], they being ignorant, as ye allege, of the ineffable Father, of His kingdom, and His dispensations, which the Son of God fulfilled when He came upon earth in these last times? Neither are ye in a position to say that these things came to pass by a certain kind of chance, as if they were spoken by the prophets in regard to some other person, while like events happened to the Lord. For all the prophets prophesied these same things, but they never came to pass in the case of any one of the ancients. For if these things had happened to any man among them of old time, those [prophets] who lived subsequently would certainly not have prophesied that these events should come to pass in the last times. Moreover, there is in fact none among the fathers, nor the prophets, nor the ancient kings, in whose case any one of these things properly and specifically took place. For all indeed prophesied as to the sufferings of Christ, but they themselves were far from enduring sufferings similar to what was predicted. And the points connected with the passion of the Lord, which were foretold, were realized in no other case. For neither did it happen at the death of any man among the ancients that the sun set at mid-day, nor was the veil of the temple rent, nor did the earth quake, nor were the rocks rent, nor did the dead rise up, nor was any one of these men [of old] raised up on the third day, nor received into heaven, nor at his assumption were the heavens opened, nor did the nations believe in the name of any other; nor did any from among them, having been dead and rising again, lay open the new covenant of liberty. Therefore the prophets spake not of any one else but of the Lord, in whom all these aforesaid tokens concurred.

4. If any one, however, advocating the cause of the Jews, do maintain that this new covenant consisted in the rearing of that temple which was built under Zerubbabel after the emigration to Babylon, and in the departure of the people from thence after the lapse of seventy years, let him know that the temple constructed of stones was indeed then rebuilt (for as yet that law was observed which had been made upon tables of stone), yet no new covenant was given, but they used the Mosaic law until the coming of the Lord; but from the Lord's advent, the new covenant which brings back peace, and the law which gives life, has gone forth over the whole earth, as the prophets said: "For out of Zion shall go forth the law, and the word of the Lord from Jerusalem; and He shall rebuke many people; and they shall break down their swords into ploughshares, and their spears into pruning-hooks, and they shall no longer learn to fight."[1] If therefore another law and word, going forth from Jerusalem, brought in such a [reign of] peace among the Gentiles which received it (the word), and convinced, through them, many a nation of its folly, then [only] it appears that the prophets spake of some other person. But if the law of liberty, that is, the word of God, preached by the apostles (who went forth from Jerusalem) throughout all the earth, caused such a change in the state of things, that these [nations] did form the swords and war-lances into ploughshares, and changed them into pruning-hooks for reaping the corn, [that is], into instruments used for peaceful purposes, and that they are now unaccustomed to fighting, but when smitten, offer also the other cheek,[2] then the prophets have not spoken these things of any other person, but of Him who effected them. This person is our Lord, and in Him is that declaration borne out; since it is He Himself who has made the plough, and introduced the pruning-hook, that is, the first semination of man, which was the creation exhibited in Adam,[3] and the gathering in of the produce in the last times by the Word; and, for this reason, since He joined the beginning to the end, and is the Lord of both, He has finally displayed the plough, in that the wood has been joined on to the iron, and has thus cleansed His land; because the Word, having been firmly united to flesh, and in its mechanism fixed with pins,[4] has reclaimed the savage earth. In the beginning, He figured forth the pruning-hook by means of Abel, pointing out that there should be a gathering in of a righteous race of men. He says, "For behold how the just man perishes, and no man considers it; and righteous men are taken away, and no man layeth it to heart."[5] These things were acted beforehand in Abel, were also previously declared by the prophets, but were accomplished in the Lord's person; and the same [is still true] with regard to us, the body following the example of the Head.

5. Such are the arguments proper[6] [to be used] in opposition to those who maintain that the prophets [were inspired] by a different God, and that our Lord [came] from another Father, if perchance [these heretics] may at length de-

---

[1] Isa. ii. 3, 4; Mic. iv. 2, 3.
[2] Matt. v. 39.
[3] Book i. p. 327, this volume.
[4] This is following Harvey's conjectural emendation of the text, viz., "taleis" for "talis." He considers the *pius* here as symbolical of the *nails* by which our Lord was fastened to the cross. The whole passage is almost hopelessly obscure, though the general meaning maybe guessed.
[5] Isa. lvii. 1.
[6] [If it be remembered that we know Irenæus here, only through a most obscure Latin rendering, we shall be slow to censure this conclusion.]

sist from such extreme folly. This is my earnest object in adducing these Scriptural proofs, that confuting them, as far as in me lies, by these very passages, I may restrain them from such great blasphemy, and from insanely fabricating a multitude of gods.

CHAP. XXXV. — A REFUTATION OF THOSE WHO ALLEGE THAT THE PROPHETS UTTERED SOME PREDICTIONS UNDER THE INSPIRATION OF THE HIGHEST, OTHERS FROM THE DEMIURGE. DISAGREEMENTS OF THE VALENTINIANS AMONG THEMSELVES WITH REGARD TO THESE SAME PREDICTIONS.

1. Then again, in opposition to the Valentinians, and the other Gnostics, falsely so called, who maintain that some parts of Scripture were spoken at one time from the Pleroma (*a summitate*) through means of the seed [derived] from that place, but at another time from the intermediate abode through means of the audacious mother Prunica, but that many are due to the Creator of the world, from whom also the prophets had their mission, we say that it is altogether irrational to bring down the Father of the universe to such straits, as that He should not be possessed of His own proper instruments, by which the things in the Pleroma might be perfectly proclaimed. For of whom was He afraid, so that He should not reveal His will after His own way and independently, freely, and without being involved with that spirit which came into being in a state of degeneracy and ignorance? Was it that He feared that very many would be saved, when more should have listened to the unadulterated truth? Or, on the other hand, was He incapable of preparing for Himself those who should announce the Saviour's advent?

2. But if, when the Saviour came to this earth, He sent His apostles into the world to proclaim with accuracy His advent, and to teach the Father's will, having nothing in common with the doctrine of the Gentiles or of the Jews, much more, while yet existing in the Pleroma, would He have appointed His own heralds to proclaim His future advent into this world, and having nothing in common with those prophecies originating from the Demiurge. But if, when within the Pleroma, He availed Himself of those prophets who were under the law, and declared His own matters through their instrumentality; much more would He, upon His arrival hither, have made use of these same teachers, and have preached the Gospel to us by their means. Therefore let them not any longer assert that Peter and Paul and the other apostles proclaimed the truth, but that it was the scribes and Pharisees, and the others, through whom the law was propounded. But if, at His advent, He sent forth His own apostles in the spirit of truth, and

not in that of error, He did the very same also in the case of the prophets; for the Word of God was always the self-same: and if the Spirit from the Pleroma was, according to these men's system, the Spirit of light, the Spirit of truth, the Spirit of perfection, and the Spirit of knowledge, while that from the Demiurge was the spirit of ignorance, degeneracy, and error, and the offspring of obscurity; how can it be, that in one and the same being there exists perfection and defect, knowledge and ignorance, error and truth, light and darkness? But if it was impossible that such should happen in the case of the prophets, for they preached the word of the Lord from one God, and proclaimed the advent of His Son, much more would the Lord Himself never have uttered words, on one occasion from above, but on another from degeneracy below, thus becoming the teacher at once of knowledge and of ignorance; nor would He have ever glorified as Father at one time the Founder of the world, and at another Him who is above this one, as He does Himself declare: " No man putteth a piece of a new garment upon an old one, nor do they put new wine into old bottles." [1] Let these men, therefore, either have nothing whatever to do with the prophets, as with those that are ancients, and allege no longer that these men, being sent beforehand by the Demiurge, spake certain things under that new influence which pertains to the Pleroma ; or, on the other hand, let them be convinced by our Lord, when He declares that new wine cannot be put into old bottles.

3. But from what source could the offspring of their mother derive his knowledge of the mysteries within the Pleroma, and power to discourse regarding them? Suppose that the mother, while beyond the Pleroma, did bring forth this very offspring ; but what is beyond the Pleroma they represent as being beyond the pale of knowledge, that is, ignorance. How, then, could that seed, which was conceived in ignorance, possess the power of declaring knowledge? Or how did the mother herself, a shapeless and undefined being, one cast out of doors as an abortion, obtain knowledge of the mysteries within the Pleroma, she who was organized outside it and given a form there, and prohibited by Horos from entering within, and who remains outside the Pleroma till the consummation [of all things], that is, beyond the pale of knowledge? Then, again, when they say that the Lord's passion is a type of the extension of the Christ above, which he effected through Horos, and so imparted a form to their mother, they are refuted in the other particulars [of the Lord's passion], for they have no semblance of a type to show with regard

---

[1] Luke v. 36, 37.

to them. For when did the Christ above have vinegar and gall given him to drink? Or when was his raiment parted? Or when was he pierced, and blood and water came forth? Or when did he sweat great drops of blood? And [the same may be demanded] as to the other particulars which happened to the Lord, of which the prophets have spoken. From whence, then, did the mother or her offspring divine the things which had not yet taken place, but which should occur afterwards?

4. They affirm that certain things still, besides these, were spoken from the Pleroma, but are confuted by those which are referred to in the Scriptures as bearing on the advent of Christ. But what these are [that are spoken from the Pleroma] they are not agreed, but give different answers regarding them. For if any one, wishing to test them, do question one by one with regard to any passage those who are their leading men, he shall find one of them referring the passage in question to the Propator — that is, to Bythus; another attributing it to Arche — that is, to the Only-begotten; another to the Father of all — that is, to the Word; while another, again, will say that it was spoken of that one Æon who was [formed from the joint contributions] of the Æons in the Pleroma;[1] others [will regard the passage] as referring to Christ, while another [will refer it] to the Saviour. One, again, more skilled than these,[2] after a long protracted silence, declares that it was spoken of Horos; another that it signifies the Sophia which is within the Pleroma; another that it announces the mother outside the Pleroma; while another will mention the God who made the world (the Demiurge). Such are the variations existing among them with regard to one [passage], holding discordant opinions as to the same Scriptures; and when the same identical passage is read out, they all begin to purse up their eyebrows, and to shake their heads, and they say that they might indeed utter a discourse transcendently lofty, but that all cannot comprehend the greatness of that thought which is implied in it; and that, therefore, among the wise the chief thing is silence. For that Sige (*silence*) which is above must be typified by that silence which they preserve. Thus do they, as many as they are, all depart [from each other], holding so many opinions as to one thing, and bearing about their clever notions in secret within themselves. When, therefore, they shall have agreed among themselves as to the things predicted in the Scriptures, then also shall they be confuted by us. For, though holding wrong opinions, they do in the meanwhile, however, convict themselves, since they are not of one mind with

regard to the same words. But as we follow for our teacher the one and only true God, and possess His words as the rule of truth, we do all speak alike with regard to the same things, knowing but one God, the Creator of this universe, who sent the prophets, who led forth the people from the land of Egypt, who in these last times manifested His own Son, that He might put the unbelievers to confusion, and search out the fruit of righteousness.

CHAP. XXXVI. — THE PROPHETS WERE SENT FROM ONE AND THE SAME FATHER FROM WHOM THE SON WAS SENT.

1. Which [God] the Lord does not reject, nor does He say that the prophets [spake] from another god than His Father; nor from any other essence, but from one and the same Father; nor that any other being made the things in the world, except His own Father, when He speaks as follows in His teaching: "There was a certain householder, and he planted a vineyard, and hedged it round about, and digged in it a winepress, and built a tower, and let it out to husbandmen, and went into a far country: And when the time of the fruit drew near, he sent his servants unto the husbandmen, that they might receive the fruits of it. And the husbandmen took his servants: they cut one to pieces, stoned another, and killed another. Again he sent other servants more than the first: and they did unto them likewise. But last of all he sent unto them his only son, saying, Perchance they will reverence my son. But when the husbandmen saw the son, they said among themselves, This is the heir; come, let us kill him, and we shall possess his inheritance. And they caught him, and cast him out of the vineyard, and slew him. When, therefore, the lord of the vineyard shall come, what will he do unto these husbandmen? They say unto him, He will miserably destroy these wicked men, and will let out his vineyard to other husbandmen, who shall render him the fruits in their season."[3] Again does the Lord say: "Have ye never read, The stone which the builders rejected, the same is become the head of the corner: this is the Lord's doing, and it is marvellous in our eyes? Therefore I say unto you, that the kingdom of God shall be taken from you, and given to a nation bringing forth the fruits thereof."[4] By these words He clearly points out to His disciples one and the same Householder — that is, one God the Father, who made all things by Himself; while [He shows] that there are various husbandmen, some obstinate, and proud, and worthless, and slayers of the Lord, but others who render Him, with all obedience, the fruits

---

[1] Book i. p. 334, this volume.
[2] Illorum; following the Greek form of the comparative degree.

[3] Matt. xxi. 33–41.
[4] Matt. xxi. 42–44.

in their seasons; and that it is the same House-holder who sends at one time His servants, at another His Son. From that Father, therefore, from whom the Son was sent to those husband-men who slew Him, from Him also were the servants [sent]. But the Son, as coming from the Father with supreme authority (*principali auctoritate*), used to express Himself thus: "But I say unto you."[1] The servants, again, [who came] as from their Lord, spake after the man-ner of servants, [delivering a message]; and they therefore used to say, "Thus saith the Lord."

2. Whom these men did therefore preach to the unbelievers as Lord, Him did Christ teach to those who obey Him; and the God who had called those of the former dispensation, is the same as He who has received those of the latter. In other words, He who at first used that law which entails bondage, is also He who did in after times [call His people] by means of adop-tion. For God planted the vineyard of the human race when at the first He formed Adam and chose the fathers; then He let it out to hus-bandmen when He established the Mosaic dis-pensation: He hedged it round about, that is, He gave particular instructions with regard to their worship: He built a tower, [that is], He chose Jerusalem: He digged a winepress, that is, He prepared a receptacle of the prophetic Spirit. And thus did He send prophets prior to the transmigration to Babylon, and after that event others again in greater number than the former, to seek the fruits, saying thus to them (the Jews): "Thus saith the Lord, Cleanse your ways and your doings, execute just judg-ment, and look each one with pity and compas-sion on his brother: oppress not the widow nor the orphan, the proselyte nor the poor, and let none of you treasure up evil against his brother in your hearts, and love not false swearing. Wash you, make you clean, put away evil from your hearts, learn to do well, seek judgment, protect the oppressed, judge the fatherless (*pupillo*), plead for the widow; and come, let us reason together, saith the Lord."[2] And again: "Keep thy tongue from evil, and thy lips that they speak no guile; depart from evil, and do good; seek peace, and pursue it."[3] In preaching these things, the prophets sought the fruits of right-eousness. But last of all He sent to those un-believers His own Son, our Lord Jesus Christ, whom the wicked husbandmen cast out of the vineyard when they had slain Him. Wherefore the Lord God did even give it up (no longer hedged around, but thrown open throughout all the world) to other husbandmen, who render the

fruits in their seasons, — the beautiful elect tower being also raised everywhere. For the illustrious Church is [now] everywhere, and everywhere is the winepress digged: because those who do re-ceive the Spirit are everywhere. For inasmuch as the former have rejected the Son of God, and cast Him out of the vineyard when they slew Him, God has justly rejected them, and given to the Gentiles outside the vineyard the fruits of its cultivation. This is in accordance with what Jeremiah says, "The Lord hath rejected and cast off the nation which does these things; for the children of Judah have done evil in my sight, saith the Lord."[4] And again in like man-ner does Jeremiah speak: "I set watchmen over you; hearken to the sound of the trumpet; and they said, We will not hearken. Therefore have the Gentiles heard, and they who feed the flocks in them."[5] It is therefore one and the same Father who planted the vineyard, who led forth the people, who sent the prophets, who sent His own Son, and who gave the vineyard to those other husbandmen that render the fruits in their season.

3. And therefore did the Lord say to His dis-ciples, to make us become good workmen: "Take heed to yourselves, and watch continually upon every occasion, lest at any time your hearts be overcharged with surfeiting and drunkenness, and cares of this life, and, that day shall come upon you unawares; for as a snare shall it come upon all dwelling upon the face of the earth."[6] "Let your loins, therefore, be girded about, and your lights burning, and ye like to men who wait for their lord, when he shall return from the wedding."[7] "For as it was in the days of Noe, they did eat and drink, they bought and sold, they married and were given in marriage, and they knew not, until Noe entered into the ark, and the flood came and destroyed them all; as also it was in the days of Lot, they did eat and drink, they bought and sold, they planted and builded, until the time that Lot went out of Sodom; it rained fire from heaven, and de-stroyed them all: so shall it also be at the com-ing of the Son of man."[8] "Watch ye therefore, for ye know not in what day your Lord shall come."[9] [In these passages] He declares one and the same Lord, who in the times of Noah brought the deluge because of men's disobedi-ence, and who also in the days of Lot rained fire from heaven because of the multitude of sinners among the Sodomites, and who, on account of this same disobedience and similar sins, will bring on the day of judgment at the end of

---

[1] Matt. v. 22.
[2] Jer. vii. 3; Zech. vii. 9, 10, viii. 17; Isa. i. 17-19.
[3] Ps. xxxiv. 13, 14.

[4] Jer. vii. 29, 30.
[5] Jer. vi. 17, 18.
[6] Luke xxi. 34, 35.
[7] Luke xii. 35, 36.
[8] Luke xvii. 26, etc.
[9] Matt. xxiv. 42.

time (*in novissimo*) ; on which day He declares that it shall be more tolerable for Sodom and Gomorrah than for that city and house which shall not receive the word of His apostles. "And thou, Capernaum," He said, "is it that thou shalt be exalted to heaven?[1] Thou shalt go down to hell. For if the mighty works which have been done in thee had been done in Sodom, it would have remained unto this day. Verily I say unto you, that it shall be more tolerable for Sodom in the day of judgment than for you."[2]

4. Since the Son of God is always one and the same, He gives to those who believe on Him a well of water[3] [springing up] to eternal life, but He causes the unfruitful fig-tree immediately to dry up ; and in the days of Noah He justly brought on the deluge for the purpose of extinguishing that most infamous race of men then existent, who could not bring forth fruit to God, since the angels that sinned had commingled with them, and [acted as He did] in order that He might put a check upon the sins of these men, but [that at the same time] He might preserve the archetype,[4] the formation of Adam. And it was He who rained fire and brimstone from heaven, in the days of Lot, upon Sodom and Gomorrah, "an example of the righteous judgment of God,"[5] that all may know, "that every tree that bringeth not forth good fruit shall be cut down, and cast into the fire."[6] And it is He who uses [the words], that it will be more tolerable for Sodom in the general judgment than for those who beheld His wonders, and did not believe on Him, nor receive His doctrine.[7] For as He gave by His advent a greater privilege to those who believed on Him, and who do His will, so also did He point out that those who did not believe on Him should have a more severe punishment in the judgment; thus extending equal justice to all, and being to exact more from those to whom He gives the more ; the more, however, not because He reveals the knowledge of another Father, as I have shown so fully and so repeatedly, but because He has, by means of His advent, poured upon the human race the greater gift of paternal grace.

5. If, however, what I have stated be insuffi-cient to convince any one that the prophets were sent from one and the same Father, from whom also our Lord was sent, let such a one, opening the mouth of his heart, and calling upon the Master, Christ Jesus the Lord, listen to Him when He says, "The kingdom of heaven is like unto a king who made a marriage for his son, and he sent forth his servants to call them who were bidden to the marriage." And when they would not obey, He goes on to say, "Again he sent other servants, saying, Tell them that are bidden, Come ye, I have prepared my dinner; my oxen and all the fatlings are killed, and every-thing is ready ; come unto the wedding. But they made light of it, and went their way, some to their farm, and others to their merchandize ; but the remnant took his servants, and some they treated despitefully, while others they slew. But when the king heard this, he was wroth, and sent his armies and destroyed these murderers, and burned up their city, and said to his servants, The wedding is indeed ready, but they which were bidden were not worthy. Go out therefore into the highways, and as many as ye shall find, gather in to the marriage. So the servants went out, and collected together as many as they found, bad and good, and the wedding was furnished with guests. But when the king came in to see the guests, he saw there a man not having on a wedding garment ; and he said unto him, Friend, how camest thou hither, not having on a wedding garment? But he was speechless. Then said the king to his servants, Take him away, hand and foot, and cast him into outer darkness : there shall be weeping and gnashing of teeth. For many are called, but few are chosen."[8] Now, by these words of His, does the Lord clearly show all [these points, viz.,] that there is one King and Lord, the Father of all, of whom He had previously said, "Neither shalt thou swear by Jerusalem, for it is the city of the great King ; "[9] and that He had from the beginning prepared the marriage for His Son, and used, with the utmost kindness, to call, by the instru-mentality of His servants, the men of the former dispensation to the wedding feast ; and when they would not obey, He still invited them by sending out other servants, yet that even then they did not obey Him, but even stoned and slew those who brought them the message of in-vitation. He accordingly sent forth His armies and destroyed them, and burned down their city ; but He called together from all the highways, that is, from all nations, [guests] to the marriage feast of His Son, as also He says by Jeremiah : "I have sent also unto you my servants the prophets to say, Return ye now, every man, from

---

[1] No other of the Greek Fathers quotes this text as above; from which fact Grabe infers that the old Latin translator, or his transcrib-ers, altered the words of Irenæus [N.B. — From one example infer the rest] to suit the Latin versions.

[2] Matt. xi. 23, 24.

[3] John iv. 14.

[4] This is Massuet's conjectural emendation of the text, viz., *archetypum* for *arcætypum*. Grabe would insert *per* before *arcæ*, and he thinks the passage to have a reference to 1 Pet. iii. 20. Ire-næus, in common with the other ancient Fathers, believed that the fallen angels were the " sons of God " who commingled with " the daughters of men," and thus produced a race of spurious men. [Gen. vi. 1, 2, 3, and Josephus.]

[5] Jude 7. [And note " strange flesh " (Gr. σαρκὸς ἑτέρας) as to the angels. Gen. xix. 4, 5.]

[6] Matt. iii. 10.

[7] Matt. xi. 24; Luke x. 12.

[8] Matt. xxii. 1, etc.

[9] Matt. v. 35. Instead of placing a period here, as the editors do, it seems to us preferable to carry on the construction.

his very evil way, and amend your doings." [1] And again He says by the same prophet: "I have also sent unto you my servants the prophets throughout the day and before the light; yet they did not obey me, nor incline their ears unto me. And thou shalt speak this word to them: This is a people that obeyeth not the voice of the Lord, nor receiveth correction; faith has perished from their mouth." [2] The Lord, therefore, who has called us everywhere by the apostles, is He who called those of old by the prophets, as appears by the words of the Lord; and although they preached to various nations, the prophets were not from one God, and the apostles from another; but, [proceeding] from one and the same, some of them announced the Lord, others preached the Father, and others again foretold the advent of the Son of God, while yet others declared Him as already present to those who then were afar off.

6. Still further did He also make it manifest, that we ought, after our calling, to be also adorned with works of righteousness, so that the Spirit of God may rest upon us; for this is the wedding garment, of which also the apostle speaks, "Not for that we would be unclothed, but clothed upon, that mortality might be swallowed up by immortality." [3] But those who have indeed been called to God's supper, yet have not received the Holy Spirit, because of their wicked conduct "shall be," He declares, "cast into outer darkness." [4] He thus clearly shows that the very same King who gathered from all quarters the faithful to the marriage of His Son, and who grants them the incorruptible banquet, [also] orders that man to be cast into outer darkness who has not on a wedding garment, that is, one who despises it. For as in the former covenant, "with many of them was He not well pleased;" [5] so also is it the case here, that "many are called, but few chosen." [6] It is not, then, one God who judges, and another Father who calls us together to salvation; nor one, forsooth, who confers eternal light, but another who orders those who have not on the wedding garment to be sent into outer darkness. But it is one and the same God, the Father of our Lord, from whom also the prophets had their mission, who does indeed, through His infinite kindness, call the unworthy; but He examines those who are called, [to ascertain] if they have on the garment fit and proper for the marriage of His Son, because nothing unbecoming or evil pleases Him. This is in accordance with what the Lord said to the man who had been healed: "Behold, thou art made whole; sin no more, lest a worse thing come unto thee." [7] For he who is good, and righteous, and pure, and spotless, will endure nothing evil, nor unjust, nor detestable in His wedding chamber. This is the Father of our Lord, by whose providence all things consist, and all are administered by His command; and He confers His free gifts upon those who should [receive them]; but the most righteous Retributor metes out [punishment] according to their deserts, most deservedly, to the ungrateful and to those that are insensible of His kindness; and therefore does He say, "He sent His armies, and destroyed those murderers, and burned up their city." [8] He says here, "His armies," because all men are the property of God. For "the earth is the Lord's, and the fulness thereof; the world, and all that dwell therein." [9] Wherefore also the Apostle Paul says in the Epistle to the Romans, "For there is no power but of God; the powers that be are ordained of God. Whosoever resisteth the power, resisteth the ordinance of God; and they that resist shall receive unto themselves condemnation. For rulers are not for a terror to a good work, but to an evil. Wilt thou then not be afraid of the power? Do that which is good, and thou shalt have praise of the same; for he is the minister of God to thee for good. But if thou do that which is evil, be afraid; for he beareth not the sword in vain: for he is the minister of God, the avenger for wrath upon him that doeth evil. Wherefore ye must needs be subject, not only for wrath, but also for conscience sake. For this cause pay ye tribute also; for they are God's ministers, attending continually upon this very thing." [10] Both the Lord, then, and the apostles announce as the one only God the Father, Him who gave the law, who sent the prophets, who made all things; and therefore does He say, "He sent His armies," because every man, inasmuch as he is a man, is His workmanship, although he may be ignorant of his God. For He gives existence to all; He, "who maketh His sun to rise upon the evil and the good, and sendeth rain upon the just and unjust." [11]

7. And not alone by what has been stated, but also by the parable of the two sons, the younger of whom consumed his substance by living luxuriously with harlots, did the Lord teach one and the same Father, who did not even allow a kid to his elder son; but for him who had been lost, [namely] his younger son, he ordered the fatted calf to be killed, and he gave him the best robe. [12]

---

1 Jer. xxxv. 15.
2 Jer. vii. 25, etc.
3 2 Cor. v. 4.
4 Matt. xxii. 13.
5 1 Cor. x. 5.
6 Matt. xxii. 14.

7 John v. 14.
8 Matt. xxii. 7.
9 Ps. xxiv. 1.
10 Rom. xiii. 1-7.
11 Matt. v. 45.
12 Luke xv. 11.

Also by the parable of the workmen who were sent into the vineyard at different periods of the day, one and the same God is declared [1] as having called some in the beginning, when the world was first created; but others afterwards, and others during the intermediate period, others after a long lapse of time, and others again in the end of time; so that there are many workmen in their generations, but only one householder who calls them together. For there is but one vineyard, since there is also but one righteousness, and one dispensator, for there is one Spirit of God who arranges all things; and in like manner is there one hire, for they all received a penny each man, having [stamped upon it] the royal image and superscription, the knowledge of the Son of God, which is immortality. And therefore He began by giving the hire to those [who were engaged] last, because in the last times, when the Lord was revealed, He presented Himself to all [as their reward].

8. Then, in the case of the publican, who excelled the Pharisee in prayer, [we find] that it was not because he worshipped another Father that he received testimony from the Lord that he was justified rather [than the other]; but because with great humility, apart from all boasting and pride, he made confession to the same God.[2] The parable of the two sons also: those who are sent into the vineyard, of whom one indeed opposed his father, but afterwards repented, when repentance profited him nothing; the other, however, promised to go, at once assuring his father, but he did not go (for "every man is a liar;"[3] "to will is present with him, but he finds not means to perform"[4]), — [this parable, I say], points out one and the same Father. Then, again, this truth was clearly shown forth by the parable of the fig-tree, of which the Lord says, "Behold, now these three years 'I come seeking fruit on this fig-tree, but I find none"[5] (pointing onwards, by the prophets, to His advent, by whom He came from time to time, seeking the fruit of righteousness from them, which he did not find), and also by the circumstance that, for the reason already mentioned, the fig-tree should be hewn down. And, without using a parable, the Lord said to Jerusalem, 'O Jerusalem, Jerusalem, thou that killest the prophets, and stonest those that are sent unto thee; how often would I have gathered thy children together, as a hen gathereth her chickens under her wings, and ye would not! Behold, your house shall be left unto you desolate."[6] For that which had been said in the parable, "Behold,

for three years I come seeking fruit," and in clear terms, again, [where He says], "How often would I have gathered thy children together," shall be [found] a falsehood, if we do not understand His advent, which is [announced] by the prophets — if, in fact, He came to them but once, and then for the first time. But since He who chose the patriarchs and those [who lived under the first covenant], is the same Word of God who did both visit them through the prophetic Spirit, and us also who have been called together from all quarters by His advent; in addition to what has been already said, He truly declared, "Many shall come from the east and from the west, and shall recline with Abraham, and Isaac, and Jacob, in the kingdom of heaven. But the children of the kingdom shall go into outer darkness; there shall be weeping and gnashing of teeth."[7] If, then, those who do believe in Him through the preaching of His apostles throughout the east and west shall recline with Abraham, Isaac, and Jacob, in the kingdom of heaven, partaking with them of the [heavenly] banquet, one and the same God is set forth as He who did indeed choose the patriarchs, visited also the people, and called the Gentiles.

CHAP. XXXVII. — MEN ARE POSSESSED OF FREE WILL, AND ENDOWED WITH THE FACULTY OF MAKING A CHOICE. IT IS NOT TRUE, THEREFORE, THAT SOME ARE BY NATURE GOOD, AND OTHERS BAD.

1. This expression [of our Lord], "How often would I have gathered thy children together, and thou wouldest not,"[8] set forth the ancient law of human liberty, because God made man a free [agent] from the beginning, possessing his own power, even as he does his own soul, to obey the behests (ad utendum sententia) of God voluntarily, and not by compulsion of God. For there is no coercion with God, but a good will [towards us] is present with Him continually. And therefore does He give good counsel to all. And in man, as well as in angels, He has placed the power of choice (for angels are rational beings), so that those who had yielded obedience might justly possess what is good, given indeed by God, but preserved by themselves. On the other hand, they who have not obeyed shall, with justice, be not found in possession of the good, and shall receive condign punishment: for God did kindly bestow on them what was good; but they themselves did not diligently keep it, nor deem it something precious, but poured contempt upon His super-eminent goodness. Rejecting therefore the good, and as it were spuing it out, they shall all deservedly incur

---

[1] Matt. xx. 1, etc.
[2] Luke xviii. 10.
[3] Ps. cxvi. 2.
[4] Rom. vii. 18.
[5] Luke xiii. 6.
[6] Luke xiii. 34; Matt. xxiii. 37.

[7] Matt. viii. 11, 12.
[8] Matt. xxiii. 37.

the just judgment of God, which also the Apostle Paul testifies in his Epistle to the Romans, where he says, " But dost thou despise the riches of His goodness, and patience, and long-suffering, being ignorant that the goodness of God leadeth thee to repentance? But according to thy hardness and impenitent heart, thou treasurest to thyself wrath against the day of wrath, and the revelation of the righteous judgment of God." " But glory and honour," he says, " to every one that doeth good." [1] God therefore has given that which is good, as the apostle tells us in this Epistle, and they who work it shall receive glory and honour, because they have done that which is good when they had it in their power not to do it ; but those who do it not shall receive the just judgment of God, because they did not work good when they had it in their power so to do.

2. But if some had been made by nature bad, and others good, these latter would not be deserving of praise for being good, for such were they created ; nor would the former be reprehensible, for thus they were made [originally]. But since all men are of the same nature, able both to hold fast and to do what is good ; and, on the other hand, having also the power to cast it from them and not to do it, — some do justly receive praise even among men who are under the control of good laws (and much more from God), and obtain deserved testimony of their choice of good in general, and of persevering therein ; but the others are blamed, and receive a just condemnation, because of their rejection of what is fair and good. And therefore the prophets used to exhort men to what was good, to act justly and to work righteousness, as I have so largely demonstrated, because it is in our power so to do, and because by excessive negligence we might become forgetful, and thus stand in need of that good counsel which the good God has given us to know by means of the prophets.

3. For this reason the Lord also said, " Let your light so shine before men, that they may see your good deeds, and glorify your Father who is in heaven." [2] And, " Take heed to yourselves, lest perchance your hearts be overcharged with surfeiting, and drunkenness, and worldly cares." [3] And, " Let your loins be girded about, and your lamps burning, and ye like unto men that wait for their Lord, when He returns from the wedding, that when He cometh and knocketh, they may open to Him. Blessed is that servant whom his Lord, when He cometh, shall find so doing." [4] And again, " The servant who

knows his Lord's will, and does it not, shall be beaten with many stripes." [5] And, " Why call ye me, Lord, Lord, and do not the things which I say ? " [6] And again, " But if the servant say in his heart, The Lord delayeth, and begin to beat his fellow-servants, and to eat, and drink, and to be drunken, his Lord will come in a day on which he does not expect Him, and shall cut him in sunder, and appoint his portion with the hypocrites." [7] All such passages demonstrate the independent will [8] of man, and at the same time the counsel which God conveys to him, by which He exhorts us to submit ourselves to Him, and seeks to turn us away from [the sin of] unbelief against Him, without, however, in any way coercing us.

4. No doubt, if any one is unwilling to follow the Gospel itself, it is in his power [to reject it], but it is not expedient. For it is in man's power to disobey God, and to forfeit what is good ; but [such conduct] brings no small amount of injury and mischief. And on this account Paul says, " All things are lawful to me, but all things are not expedient ; " [9] referring both to the liberty of man, in which respect " all things are lawful," God exercising no compulsion in regard to him ; and [by the expression] " not expedient " pointing out that we " should not use our liberty as a cloak of maliciousness," [10] for this is not expedient. And again he says, " Speak ye every man truth with his neighbour." [11] And, " Let no corrupt communication proceed out of your mouth, neither filthiness, nor foolish talking, nor scurrility, which are not convenient, but rather giving of thanks." [12] And, " For ye were sometimes darkness, but now are ye light in the Lord ; walk honestly as children of the light, not in rioting and drunkenness, not in chambering and wantonness, not in anger and jealousy. And such were some of you ; but ye have been washed, but ye have been sanctified in the name of our Lord." [13] If then it were not in our power to do or not to do these things, what reason had the apostle, and much more the Lord Himself, to give us counsel to do some things, and to abstain from others ? But because man is possessed of free will from the beginning, and God is possessed of free will, in whose likeness man was created, advice is always given to him to keep fast the good, which thing is done by means of obedience to God.

5. And not merely in works, but also in faith, has God preserved the will of man free and under his own control, saying, " According to thy faith

---

[1] Rom. ii. 4, 5, 7.
[2] Matt. v. 16.
[3] Luke xxi. 34.
[4] Luke xii. 35, 36.

[5] Luke xii. 47.
[6] Luke vi. 46.
[7] Luke xii. 45 46; Matt. xxiv. 48 51.
[8] τὸ αὐτεξούσιον.
[9] 1 Cor. vi. 12.
[10] 1 Pet. ii. 16.
[11] Eph. iv. 25.
[12] Eph. iv. 29.
[13] 1 Cor. vi. 11.

be it unto thee ; "[1] thus showing that there is a faith specially belonging to man, since he has an opinion specially his own. And again, "All things are possible to him that believeth ; "[2] and, "Go thy way ; and as thou hast believed, so be it done unto thee."[3] Now all such expressions demonstrate that man is in his own power with respect to faith. And for this reason, "he that believeth in Him has eternal life ; while he who believeth not the Son hath not eternal life, but the wrath of God shall remain upon him."[4] In the same manner therefore the Lord, both showing His own goodness, and indicating that man is in his own free will and his own power, said to Jerusalem, "How often have I wished to gather thy children together, as a hen [gathereth] her chickens under her wings, and ye would not ! Wherefore your house shall be left unto you desolate."[5]

6. Those, again, who maintain the opposite to these [conclusions], do themselves present the Lord as destitute of power, as if, forsooth, He were unable to accomplish what He willed ; or, on the other hand, as being ignorant that they were by nature "material," as these men express it, and such as cannot receive His immortality. "But He should not," say they, "have created angels of such a nature that they were capable of transgression, nor men who immediately proved ungrateful towards Him ; for they were made rational beings, endowed with the power of examining and judging, and were not [formed] as things irrational or of a [merely] animal nature, which can do nothing of their own will, but are drawn by necessity and compulsion to what is good, in which things there is one mind and one usage, working mechanically in one groove (*inflexibiles et sine judicio*), who are incapable of being anything else except just what they had been created." But upon this supposition, neither would what is good be grateful to them, nor communion with God be precious, nor would the good be very much to be sought after, which would present itself without their own proper endeavour, care, or study, but would be implanted of its own accord and without their concern. Thus it would come to pass, that their being good would be of no consequence, because they were so by nature rather than by will, and are possessors of good spontaneously, not by choice ; and for this reason they would not understand this fact, that good is a comely thing, nor would they take pleasure in it. For how can those who are ignorant of good enjoy it ? Or what credit is it to those who have not aimed at it ? And what crown is it to those who have not followed in pursuit of it, like those victorious in the contest?

7. On this account, too, did the Lord assert that the kingdom of heaven was the portion of "the violent ; " and He says, "The violent take it by force ; "[6] that is, those who by strength and earnest striving are on the watch to snatch it away on the moment. On this account also Paul the Apostle says to the Corinthians, "Know ye not, that they who run in a racecourse, do all indeed run, but one receiveth the prize ? So run, that ye may obtain. Every one also who engages in the contest is temperate in all things : now these men [do it] that they may obtain a corruptible crown, but we an incorruptible. But I so run, not as uncertainty ; I fight, not as one beating the air ; but I make my body livid, and bring it into subjection, lest by any means, when preaching to others, I may myself be rendered a castaway."[7] This able wrestler, therefore, exhorts us to the struggle for immortality, that we may be crowned, and may deem the crown precious, namely, that which is acquired by our struggle, but which does not encircle us of its own accord (*sed non ultro coalitam*). And the harder we strive, so much is it the more valuable ; while so much the more valuable it is, so much the more should we esteem it. And indeed those things are not esteemed so highly which come spontaneously, as those which are reached by much anxious care. Since, then, this power has been conferred upon us, both the Lord has taught and the apostle has enjoined us the more to love God, that we may reach this [prize] for ourselves by striving after it. For otherwise, no doubt, this our good would be [virtually] irrational, because not the result of trial. Moreover, the faculty of seeing would not appear to be so desirable, unless we had known what a loss it were to be devoid of sight ; and health, too, is rendered all the more estimable by an acquaintance with disease ; light, also, by contrasting it with darkness ; and life with death. Just in the same way is the heavenly kingdom honourable to those who have known the earthly one. But in proportion as it is more honourable, so much the more do we prize it ; and if we have prized it more, we shall be the more glorious in the presence of God. The Lord has therefore endured all these things on our behalf, in order that we, having been instructed by means of them all, may be in all respects circumspect for the time to come, and that, having been rationally taught to love God, we may continue in His perfect love : for God has displayed long-suffering in the case of man's apostasy ; while man has been instructed by means of it, as also the prophet says, "Thine own apostasy shall heal thee ; "[8] God thus determining all things beforehand for the

---

[1] Matt. ix. 29.
[2] Mark ix. 23.
[3] Matt. viii. 13.
[4] John iii. 36.
[5] Matt. xxiii. 37, 38.

[6] Matt. xi. 12.
[7] 1 Cor. ix. 24-27.
[8] Jer. ii. 19.

bringing of man to perfection, for his edification, and for the revelation of His dispensations, that goodness may both be made apparent, and righteousness perfected, and that the Church may be fashioned after the image of His Son, and that man may finally be brought to maturity at some future time, becoming ripe through such privileges to see and comprehend God.[1]

CHAP. XXXVIII. — WHY MAN WAS NOT MADE PERFECT FROM THE BEGINNING.

1. If, however, any one say, "What then? Could not God have exhibited man as perfect from the beginning?" let him know that, inasmuch as God is indeed always the same and unbegotten as respects Himself, all things are possible to Him. But created things must be inferior to Him who created them, from the very fact of their later origin; for it was not possible for things recently created to have been uncreated. But inasmuch as they are not uncreated, for this very reason do they come short of the perfect. Because, as these things are of later date, so are they infantile; so are they unaccustomed to, and unexercised in, perfect discipline. For as it certainly is in the power of a mother to give strong food to her infant, [but she does not do so], as the child is not yet able to receive more substantial nourishment; so also it was possible for God Himself to have made man perfect from the first, but man could not receive this [perfection], being as yet an infant. And for this cause our Lord, in these last times, when He had summed up all things into Himself, came to us, not as He might have come, but as we were capable of beholding Him. He might easily have come to us in His immortal glory, but in that case we could never have endured the greatness of the glory; and therefore it was that He, who was the perfect bread of the Father, offered Himself to us as milk, [because we were] as infants. He did this when He appeared as a man, that we, being nourished, as it were, from the breast of His flesh, and having, by such a course of milk-nourishment, become accustomed to eat and drink the Word of God, may be able also to contain in ourselves the Bread of immortality, which is the Spirit of the Father.

2. And on this account does Paul declare to the Corinthians, "I have fed you with milk, not with meat, for hitherto ye were not able to bear it."[2] That is, ye have indeed learned the advent of our Lord as a man; nevertheless, because of your infirmity, the Spirit of the Father has not as yet rested upon you. "For when envying and strife," he says, "and dissensions are among you, are ye not carnal, and walk as men?"[3] That is, that the Spirit of the Father was not yet with them, on account of their imperfection and shortcomings of their walk in life. As, therefore, the apostle had the power to give them strong meat — for those upon whom the apostles laid hands received the Holy Spirit, who is the food of life [eternal] — but they were not capable of receiving it, because they had the sentient faculties of the soul still feeble and undisciplined in the practice of things pertaining to God; so, in like manner, God had power at the beginning to grant perfection to man; but as the latter was only recently created, he could not possibly have received it, or even if he had received it, could he have contained it, or containing it, could he have retained it. It was for this reason that the Son of God, although He was perfect, passed through the state of infancy in common with the rest of mankind, partaking of it thus not for His own benefit, but for that of the infantile stage of man's existence, in order that man might be able to receive Him. There was nothing, therefore, impossible to and deficient in God, [implied in the fact] that man was not an uncreated being; but this merely applied to him who was lately created, [namely] man.

3. With God there are simultaneously exhibited power, wisdom, and goodness. His power and goodness [appear] in this, that of His own will He called into being and fashioned things having no previous existence; His wisdom [is shown] in His having made created things parts of one harmonious and consistent whole; and those things which, through His super-eminent kindness, receive growth and a long period of existence, do reflect the glory of the uncreated One, of that God who bestows what is good ungrudgingly. For from the very fact of these things having been created, [it follows] that they are not uncreated; but by their continuing in being throughout a long course of ages, they shall receive a faculty of the Uncreated, through the gratuitous bestowal of eternal existence upon them by God. And thus in all things God has the pre-eminence, who alone is uncreated, the first of all things, and the primary cause of the existence of all, while all other things remain under God's subjection. But being in subjection to God is continuance in immortality, and immortality is the glory of the uncreated One. By this arrangement, therefore, and these harmonies, and a sequence of this nature, man, a created and organized being, is rendered after the image and likeness of the uncreated God, — the Father planning everything well and giving His commands, the Son carrying these into exe-

---

[1] [If we but had the original, this would doubtless be found in all respects a noble specimen of primitive theology.]
[2] 1 Cor. iii. 2.
[3] 1 Cor. iii. 3.

cution and performing the work of creating, and the Spirit nourishing and increasing [what is made], but man making progress day by day, and ascending towards the perfect, that is, approximating to the uncreated One. For the Uncreated is perfect, that is, God. Now it was necessary that man should in the first instance be created; and having been created, should receive growth; and having received growth, should be strengthened; and having been strengthened, should abound; and having abounded, should recover [from the disease of sin]; and having recovered, should be glorified; and being glorified, should see his Lord. For God is He who is yet to be seen, and the beholding of God is productive of immortality, but immortality renders one nigh unto God.

4. Irrational, therefore, in every respect, are they who await not the time of increase, but ascribe to God the infirmity of their nature. Such persons know neither God nor themselves, being insatiable and ungrateful, unwilling to be at the outset what they have also been created — men subject to passions; but go beyond the law of the human race, and before that they become men, they wish to be even now like God their Creator, and they who are more destitute of reason than dumb animals [insist] that there is no distinction between the uncreated God and man, a creature of to-day. For these, [the dumb animals], bring no charge against God for not having made them men; but each one, just as he has been created, gives thanks that he has been created. For we cast blame upon Him, because we have not been made gods from the beginning, but at first merely men, then at length gods; although God has adopted this course out of His pure benevolence, that no one may impute to Him invidiousness or grudgingness. He declares, "I have said, Ye are gods; and ye are all sons of the Highest." [1] But since we could not sustain the power of divinity, He adds, "But ye shall die like men," setting forth both truths — the kindness of His free gift, and our weakness, and also that we were possessed of power over ourselves. For after His great kindness He graciously conferred good [upon us], and made men like to Himself, [that is] in their own power; while at the same time by His prescience He knew the infirmity of human beings, and the consequences which would flow from it; but through [His] love and [His] power, He shall overcome the substance of created nature. [2] For it was necessary, at first, that nature should be exhibited; then, after that, that what was mortal should be conquered and swallowed up by

immortality, and the corruptible by incorruptibility, and that man should be made after the image and likeness of God, having received the knowledge of good and evil.

CHAP. XXXIX. — MAN IS ENDOWED WITH THE FACULTY OF DISTINGUISHING GOOD AND EVIL; SO THAT, WITHOUT COMPULSION, HE HAS THE POWER, BY HIS OWN WILL AND CHOICE, TO PERFORM GOD'S COMMANDMENTS, BY DOING WHICH HE AVOIDS THE EVILS PREPARED FOR THE REBELLIOUS.

1. Man has received the knowledge of good and evil. It is good to obey God, and to believe in Him, and to keep His commandment, and this is the life of man; as not to obey God is evil, and this is his death. Since God, therefore, gave [to man] such mental power (*magnanimitatem*) man knew both the good of obedience and the evil of disobedience, that the eye of the mind, receiving experience of both, may with judgment make choice of the better things; and that he may never become indolent or neglectful of God's command; and learning by experience that it is an evil thing which deprives him of life, that is, disobedience to God, may never attempt it at all, but that, knowing that what preserves his life, namely, obedience to God, is good, he may diligently keep it with all earnestness. Wherefore he has also had a twofold experience, possessing knowledge of both kinds, that with dicipline he may make choice of the better things. But how, if he had no knowledge of the contrary, could he have had instruction in that which is good? For there is thus a surer and an undoubted comprehension of matters submitted to us than the mere surmise arising from an opinion regarding them. For just as the tongue receives experience of sweet and bitter by means of tasting, and the eye discriminates between black and white by means of vision, and the ear recognises the distinctions of sounds by hearing; so also does the mind, receiving through the experience of both the knowledge of what is good, become more tenacious of its preservation, by acting in obedience to God: in the first place, casting away, by means of repentance, disobedience, as being something disagreeable and nauseous; and afterwards coming to understand what it really is, that it is contrary to goodness and sweetness, so that the mind may never even attempt to taste disobedience to God. But if any one do shun the knowledge of both these kinds of things, and the twofold perception of knowledge, he unawares divests himself of the character of a human being.

2. How, then, shall he be a God, who has not as yet been made a man? Or how can he be perfect who was but lately created? How, again, can he be immortal, who in his mortal nature

---

[1] Ps. lxxxii. 6, 7.
[2] That is, that man's human nature should not prevent him from becoming a partaker of the divine.

did not obey his Maker? For it must be that thou, at the outset, shouldest hold the rank of a man, and then afterwards partake of the glory of God. For thou dost not make God, but God thee. If, then, thou art God's workmanship, await the hand of thy Maker which creates everything in due time; in due time as far as thou art concerned, whose creation is being carried out.[1] Offer to Him thy heart in a soft and tractable state, and preserve the form in which the Creator has fashioned thee, having moisture in thyself, lest, by becoming hardened, thou lose the impressions of His fingers. But by preserving the framework thou shalt ascend to that which is perfect, for the moist clay which is in thee is hidden [there] by the workmanship of God. His hand fashioned thy substance; He will cover thee over [too] within and without with pure gold and silver, and He will adorn thee to such a degree, that even "the King Himself shall have pleasure in thy beauty."[2] But if thou, being obstinately hardened, dost reject the operation of His skill, and show thyself ungrateful towards Him, because thou wert created a [mere] man, by becoming thus ungrateful to God, thou hast at once lost both His workmanship and life. For creation is an attribute of the goodness of God; but to be created is that of human nature. If, then, thou shalt deliver up to Him what is thine, that is, faith towards Him and subjection, thou shalt receive His handiwork, and shalt be a perfect work of God.

3. If, however, thou wilt not believe in Him, and wilt flee from His hands, the cause of imperfection shall be in thee who didst not obey, but not in Him who called [thee]. For He commissioned [messengers] to call people to the marriage, but they who did not obey Him deprived themselves of the royal supper.[3] The skill of God, therefore, is not defective, for He has power of the stones to raise up children to Abraham;[4] but the man who does not obtain it, is the cause to himself of his own imperfection. Nor, [in like manner], does the light fail because of those who have blinded themselves; but while it remains the same as ever, those who are [thus] blinded are involved in darkness through their own fault. The light does never enslave any one by necessity; nor, again, does God exercise compulsion upon any one unwilling to accept the exercise of His skill. Those persons, therefore, who have apostatized from the light given by the Father, and transgressed the law of liberty, have done so through their own fault, since they have been created free agents, and possessed of power over themselves.

4. But God, foreknowing all things, prepared fit habitations for both, kindly conferring that light which they desire on those who seek after the light of incorruption, and resort to it; but for the despisers and mockers who avoid and turn themselves away from this light, and who do, as it were, blind themselves, He has prepared darkness suitable to persons who oppose the light, and He has inflicted an appropriate punishment upon those who try to avoid being subject to Him. Submission to God is eternal rest, so that they who shun the light have a place worthy of their flight; and those who fly from eternal rest, have a habitation in accordance with their fleeing. Now, since all good things are with God, they who by their own determination fly from God, do defraud themselves of all good things; and having been [thus] defrauded of all good things with respect to God, they shall consequently fall under the just judgment of God. For those persons who shun rest shall justly incur punishment, and those who avoid the light shall justly dwell in darkness. For as in the case of this temporal light, those who shun it do deliver themselves over to darkness, so that they do themselves become the cause to themselves that they are destitute of light, and do inhabit darkness; and, as I have already observed, the light is not the cause of such an [unhappy] condition of existence to them; so those who fly from the eternal light of God, which contains in itself all good things, are themselves the cause to themselves of their inhabiting eternal darkness, destitute of all good things, having become to themselves the cause of [their consignment to] an abode of that nature.

CHAP. XL. — ONE AND THE SAME GOD THE FATHER INFLICTS PUNISHMENT ON THE REPROBATE, AND BESTOWS REWARDS ON THE ELECT.

1. It is therefore one and the same God the Father who has prepared good things with Himself for those who desire His fellowship, and who remain in subjection to Him; and who has prepared the eternal fire for the ringleader of the apostasy, the devil, and those who revolted with him, into which [fire] the Lord[5] has declared those men shall be sent who have been set apart by themselves on His left hand. And this is what has been spoken by the prophet, "I am a jealous God, making peace, and creating evil things;"[6] thus making peace and friendship with those who repent and turn to Him, and bringing [them to] unity, but preparing for the impenitent, those who shun the light, eternal fire and outer darkness, which are evils indeed to those persons who fall into them.

---

[1] Efficeris.
[2] Ps. xlv. 11.
[3] Matt. xxii. 3, etc.
[4] Matt. iii. 9.
[5] Matt. xxv. 41.
[6] Isa. xlv. 7.

2. If, however, it were truly one Father who confers rest, and another God who has prepared the fire, their sons would have been equally different [one from the other]; one, indeed, sending [men] into the Father's kingdom, but the other into eternal fire. But inasmuch as one and the same Lord has pointed out that the whole human race shall be divided at the judgment, "as a shepherd divideth the sheep from the goats," [1] and that to some He will say, "Come, ye blessed of My Father, receive the kingdom which has been prepared for you," [2] but to others, "Depart from me, ye cursed, into everlasting fire, which My Father has prepared for the devil and his angels," [3] one and the same Father is manifestly declared [in this passage], "making peace and creating evil things," preparing fit things for both; as also there is one Judge sending both into a fit place, as the Lord sets forth in the parable of the tares and the wheat, where He says, "As therefore the tares are gathered together, and burned in the fire, so shall it be at the end of the world. The Son of man shall send His angels, and they shall gather from His kingdom everything that offendeth, and those who work iniquity, and shall send them into a furnace of fire: there shall be weeping and gnashing of teeth. Then shall the just shine forth as the sun in the kingdom of their Father." [4] The Father, therefore, who has prepared the kingdom for the righteous, into which the Son has received those worthy of it, is He who has also prepared the furnace of fire, into which these angels commissioned by the Son of man shall send those persons who deserve it, according to God's command.

3. The Lord, indeed, sowed good seed in His own field; [5] and He says, "The field is the world." But while men slept, the enemy came, and "sowed tares in the midst of the wheat, and went his way." [6] Hence we learn that this was the apostate angel and the enemy, because he was envious of God's workmanship, and took in hand to render this [workmanship] an enmity with God. For this cause also God has banished from His presence him who did of his own accord stealthily sow the tares, that is, him who brought about the transgression; [7] but He took compassion upon man, who, through want of care no doubt, but still wickedly [on the part of another], became involved in disobedience; and He turned the enmity by which [the devil]

had designed to make [man] the enemy of God, against the author of it, by removing His own anger from man, turning it in another direction, and sending it instead upon the serpent. As also the Scripture tells us that God said to the serpent, "And I will place enmity between thee and the woman, and between thy seed and her seed. He [8] shall bruise thy head, and thou shalt bruise his heel." [9] And the Lord summed up in Himself this enmity, when He was made man from a woman, and trod upon his [the serpent's] head, as I have pointed out in the preceding book.

CHAP. XLI. — THOSE PERSONS WHO DO NOT BELIEVE IN GOD, BUT WHO ARE DISOBEDIENT, ARE ANGELS AND SONS OF THE DEVIL, NOT INDEED BY NATURE, BUT BY IMITATION. CLOSE OF THIS BOOK, AND SCOPE OF THE SUCCEEDING ONE.

1. Inasmuch as the Lord has said that there are certain angels, [viz., those] of the devil, for whom eternal fire is prepared; and as, again, He declares with regard to the tares, "The tares are the children of the wicked one," [10] it must be affirmed that He has ascribed all who are of the apostasy to him who is the ringleader of this transgression. But He made neither angels nor men so by nature. For we do not find that the devil created anything whatsoever, since indeed he is himself a creature of God, like the other angels. For God made all things, as also David says with regard to all things of the kind: "For He spake the word, and they were made; He commanded, and they were created." [11]

2. Since, therefore, all things were made by God, and since the devil has become the cause of apostasy to himself and others, justly does the Scripture always term those who remain in a state of apostasy "sons of the devil" and "angels of the wicked one" (maligni). For [the word] "son," as one before me has observed, has a twofold meaning: one [is a son] in the order of nature, because he was born a son; the other, in that he was made so, is reputed a son, although there be a difference between being born so and being made so. For the first is indeed born from the person referred to; but the second is made so by him, whether as respects his creation or by the teaching of his doctrine. For when any person has been taught from the mouth of another, he is termed the son of him who instructs him, and the latter [is called] his father. According to nature, then — that is, according to creation, so to speak — we are all sons of God, because we have all been created by God. But with respect to obedience

---

[1] Matt. xxv. 32.
[2] Matt. xxv. 34.
[3] Matt. xxv. 41.
[4] Matt. xiii. 40–43.
[5] Matt. xiii. 34. [Applicable to the origin of heresies.]
[6] Matt. xiii. 28.
[7] The old Latin translator varies from this (the Greek of which was recovered by Grabe from two ancient *Catenæ Patrum*), making the clause run thus, *that is, the transgression which he had himself introduced*, making the explanatory words to refer to the *tares*, and not, as in the Greek, to the *sower of the tares*.

[8] Following the reading of the LXX., αὐτός σου τηρήσει κεφαλήν.
[9] Gen. iii. 15.
[10] Matt. xiii. 38.
[11] Ps. cxlix. 5.

and doctrine we are not all the sons of God : those only are so who believe in Him and do His will. And those who do not believe, and do not obey His will, are sons and angels of the devil, because they do the works of the devil. And that such is the case He has declared in Isaiah : "I have begotten and brought up children, but they have rebelled against Me."[1] And again, where He says that these children are aliens : "Strange children have lied unto Me."[2] According to nature, then, they are [His] children, because they have been so created ; but with regard to their works, they are not His children.

3. For as, among men, those sons who disobey their fathers, being disinherited, are still their sons in the course of nature, but by law are disinherited, for they do not become the heirs of their natural parents ; so in the same way is it with God, — those who do not obey Him being disinherited by Him, have ceased to be His sons. Wherefore they cannot receive His inheritance : as David says, "Sinners are alienated from the womb ; their anger is after the likeness of a serpent."[3] And therefore did the Lord term those whom He knew to be the offspring of men "a generation of vipers ; "[4] because after the manner of these animals they go about in subtilty, and injure others. For He said, " Beware of the leaven of the Pharisees and of the Sadducees."[5] Speaking of Herod, too, He says, " Go ye and tell that fox,"[6] aiming at his wicked cunning and deceit. Wherefore the prophet David says, " Man, being placed in honour, is made like unto cattle."[7] And again Jeremiah says, "They are become like horses, furious about females ; each one neighed after his neighbour's wife."[8] And Isaiah, when preaching in Judea, and reasoning with Israel, termed them "rulers of Sodom " and "people of Gomorrah ; "[9] intimating that they were like the Sodomites in wickedness, and that the same description of sins was rife among them, calling them by the same name, because of the similarity of their conduct. And inasmuch as they were not by nature so created by God, but had power also to act rightly, the same person said to them, giving them good counsel, "Wash ye, make you clean ; take away iniquity from your souls before mine eyes ; cease from your iniquities."[10] Thus, no doubt, since they had trans-

gressed and sinned in the same manner, so did they receive the same reproof as did the Sodomites. But when they should be converted and come to repentance, and cease from evil, they should have power to become the sons of God, and to receive the inheritance of immortality which is given by Him. For this reason, therefore, He has termed those " angels of the devil," and "children of the wicked one,"[11] who give heed to the devil, and do his works. But these are, at the same time, all created by the one and the same God. When, however, they believe and are subject to God, and go on and keep His doctrine, they are the sons of God ; but when they have apostatized and fallen into transgression, they are ascribed to their chief, the devil — to him who first became the cause of apostasy to himself, and afterwards to others.

4. Inasmuch as the words of the Lord are numerous, while they all proclaim one and the same Father, the Creator of this world, it was incumbent also upon me, for their own sake, to refute by many [arguments] those who are involved in many errors, if by any means, when they are confuted by many [proofs], they may be converted to the truth and saved. But it is necessary to subjoin to this composition, in what follows, also the doctrine of Paul after the words of the Lord, to examine the opinion of this man, and expound the apostle, and to explain whatsoever [passages] have received other interpretations from the heretics, who have altogether misunderstood what Paul has spoken, and to point out the folly of their mad opinions ; and to demonstrate from that same Paul, from whose [writings] they press questions upon us, that they are indeed utterers of falsehood, but that the apostle was a preacher of the truth, and that he taught all things agreeable to the preaching of the truth ; [to the effect that] it was one God the Father who spake with Abraham, who gave the law, who sent the prophets beforehand, who in the last times sent His Son, and conferred salvation upon His own handiwork — that is, the substance of flesh. Arranging, then, in another book, the rest of the words of the Lord, which He taught concerning the Father not by parables, but by expressions taken in their obvious meaning (*sed simpliciter ipsis dictionibus*), and the exposition of the Epistles of the blessed apostle, I shall, with God's aid, furnish thee with the complete work of the exposure and refutation of knowledge, falsely so called ; thus practising myself and thee in [these] five books for presenting opposition to all heretics.

---

[1] Isa. i. 2.
[2] Ps. xviii. 45.
[3] Ps. lviii. 3, 4.
[4] Matt. xxiii. 33.
[5] Matt. xvi. 6.
[6] Luke xiii. 32.
[7] Ps. xlix. 21.
[8] Jer. v. 8.
[9] Isa. i. 10.
[10] Isa. i. 16.

[11] Matt. xxv. 41, xiii. 38.

IRENÆUS AGAINST HERESIES

BOOK V.

PREFACE.

In the four preceding books, my very dear friend, which I put forth to thee, all the heretics have been exposed, and their doctrines brought to light, and these men refuted who have devised irreligious opinions. [I have accomplished this by adducing] something from the doctrine peculiar to each of these men, which they have left in their writings, as well as by using arguments of a more general nature, and applicable to them all.[1] Then I have pointed out the truth, and shown the preaching of the Church, which the prophets proclaimed (as I have already demonstrated), but which Christ brought to perfection, and the apostles have handed down, from whom the Church, receiving [these truths], and throughout all the world alone preserving them in their integrity (*bene*), has transmitted them to her sons. Then also — having disposed of all questions which the heretics propose to us, and having explained the doctrine of the apostles, and clearly set forth many of those things which were said and done by the Lord in parables — I shall endeavour, in this the fifth book of the entire work which treats of the exposure and refutation of knowledge falsely so called, to exhibit proofs from the rest of the Lord's doctrine and the apostolical epistles: [thus] complying with thy demand, as thou didst request of me (since indeed I have been assigned a place in the ministry of the word); and, labouring by every means in my power to furnish thee with large assistance against the contradictions of the heretics, as also to reclaim the wanderers and convert them to the Church of God, to confirm at the same time the minds of the neophytes, that they may preserve stedfast the faith which they have received, guarded by the Church in its integrity, in order that they be in no way perverted by those who endeavour to teach them false doctrines, and lead them away from the truth. It will be incumbent upon thee, however, and all who may happen to read this writing, to peruse with great attention what I have already said, that thou mayest obtain a knowledge of the subjects against which I am contending. For it is thus that thou wilt both controvert them in a legitimate manner, and wilt be prepared to receive the proofs brought forward against them, casting away their doctrines as filth by means of the celestial faith; but following the only true and stedfast Teacher, the Word of God, our Lord Jesus Christ, who did, through His transcendent love, become what we are, that He might bring us to be even what He is Himself.

CHAP. I. — CHRIST ALONE IS ABLE TO TEACH DIVINE THINGS, AND TO REDEEM US: HE, THE SAME, TOOK FLESH OF THE VIRGIN MARY, NOT MERELY IN APPEARANCE, BUT ACTUALLY, BY THE OPERATION OF THE HOLY SPIRIT, IN ORDER TO RENOVATE US. STRICTURES ON THE CONCEITS OF VALENTINUS AND EBION.

1. For in no other way could we have learned the things of God, unless our Master, existing as the Word, had become man. For no other being had the power of revealing to us the things of the Father, except His own proper Word. For what other person "knew the mind of the Lord," or who else "has become His counsellor?"[2] Again, we could have learned in no other way than by seeing our Teacher, and hearing His voice with our own ears, that, having become imitators of His works as well as doers of His words, we may have communion with Him, receiving increase from the perfect One, and from Him who is prior to all creation. We — who were but lately created by the only best and good Being, by Him also who has the gift of immortality, having been formed after

---

[1] Ex ratione universis ostensionibus procedente. The words are very obscure.

[2] Rom. xi. 34.

His likeness (predestinated, according to the prescience of the Father, that we, who had as yet no existence, might come into being), and made the first-fruits of creation [1] — have received, in the times known beforehand, [the blessings of salvation] according to the ministration of the Word, who is perfect in all things, as the mighty Word, and very man, who, redeeming us by His own blood in a manner consonant to reason, gave Himself as a redemption for those who had been led into captivity. And since the apostasy tyrannized over us unjustly, and, though we were by nature the property of the omnipotent God, alienated us contrary to nature, rendering us its own disciples, the Word of God, powerful in all things, and not defective with regard to His own justice, did righteously turn against that apostasy, and redeem from it His own property, not by violent means, as the [apostasy] had obtained dominion over us at the beginning, when it insatiably snatched away what was not its own, but by means of persuasion, as became a God of counsel, who does not use violent means to obtain what He desires; so that neither should justice be infringed upon, nor the ancient handiwork of God go to destruction. Since the Lord thus has redeemed us through His own blood, giving His soul for our souls, and His flesh for our flesh,[2] and has also poured out the Spirit of the Father for the union and communion of God and man, imparting indeed God to men by means of the Spirit, and, on the other hand, attaching man to God by His own incarnation, and bestowing upon us at His coming immortality durably and truly, by means of communion with God, — all the doctrines of the heretics fall to ruin.

2. Vain indeed are those who allege that He appeared in mere seeming. For these things were not done in appearance only, but in actual reality. But if He did appear as a man, when He was not a man, neither could the Holy Spirit have rested upon Him, — an occurrence which did actually take place — as the Spirit is invisible; nor, [in that case], was there any degree of truth in Him, for He was not that which He seemed to be. But I have already remarked that Abraham and the other prophets beheld Him after a prophetical manner, foretelling in vision what should come to pass. If, then, such a being has now appeared in outward semblance different from what he was in reality, there has been a certain prophetical vision made to men; and another advent of His must be looked forward to, in which He shall be such as He has now been seen in a prophetic manner. And I have proved already, that it is the same thing to say that He appeared merely to outward seeming,

and [to affirm] that He received nothing from Mary. For He would not have been one truly possessing flesh and blood, by which He redeemed us, unless He had summed up in Himself the ancient formation of Adam. Vain therefore are the disciples of Valentinus who put forth this opinion, in order that they may exclude the flesh from salvation, and cast aside what God has fashioned.

3. Vain also are the Ebionites, who do not receive by faith into their soul the union of God and man, but who remain in the old leaven of [the natural] birth, and who do not choose to understand that the Holy Ghost came upon Mary, and the power of the Most High did overshadow her:[3] wherefore also what was generated is a holy thing, and the Son of the Most High God the Father of all, who effected the incarnation of this being, and showed forth a new [kind of] generation; that as by the former generation we inherited death, so by this new generation we might inherit life. Therefore do these men reject the commixture of the heavenly wine,[4] and wish it to be water of the world only, not receiving God so as to have union with Him, but they remain in that Adam who had been conquered and was expelled from Paradise: not considering that as, at the beginning of our formation in Adam, that breath of life which proceeded from God, having been united to what had been fashioned, animated the man, and manifested him as a being endowed with reason; so also, in [the times of] the end, the Word of the Father and the Spirit of God, having become united with the ancient substance of Adam's formation, rendered man living and perfect, receptive of the perfect Father, in order that as in the natural [Adam] we all were dead, so in the spiritual we may all be made alive.[5] For never at any time did Adam escape the *hands* [6] of God, to whom the Father speaking, said, "Let Us make man in Our image, after Our likeness." And for this reason in the last times (*fine*), not by the will of the flesh, nor by the will of man, but by the good pleasure of the Father,[7] His hands formed a living man, in order that Adam might be created [again] after the image and likeness of God.

CHAP. II. — WHEN CHRIST VISITED US IN HIS GRACE, HE DID NOT COME TO WHAT DID NOT BELONG TO HIM : ALSO, BY SHEDDING HIS TRUE BLOOD FOR US, AND EXHIBITING TO US HIS TRUE FLESH IN THE EUCHARIST, HE CONFERRED UPON OUR FLESH THE CAPACITY OF SALVATION.

1. And vain likewise are those who say that

---

[1] " Initium facturæ," which Grabe thinks should be thus translated with reference to Jas. i. 18.
[2] [Compare Clement, cap. 49, p.18, this volume.]
[3] Luke i. 35.
[4] In allusion to the mixture of water in the eucharistic cup, as practised in these primitive times. The Ebionites and others used to consecrate the element of water alone.
[5] 1 Cor. xv. 22.
[6] Viz., the Son and the Spirit.
[7] John i. 13.

God came to those things which did not belong to Him, as if covetous of another's property ; in order that He might deliver up that man who had been created by another, to that God who had neither made nor formed anything, but who also was deprived from the beginning of His own proper formation of men. The advent, therefore, of Him whom these men represent as coming to the things of others, was not righteous ; nor did He truly redeem us by His own blood, if He did not really become man, restoring to His own handiwork what was said [of it] in the beginning, that man was made after the image and likeness of God ; not snatching away by stratagem the property of another, but taking possession of His own in a righteous and gracious manner. As far as concerned the apostasy, indeed, He redeems us righteously from it by His own blood ; but as regards us who have been redeemed, [He does this] graciously. For we have given nothing to Him previously, nor does He desire anything from us, as if He stood in need of it ; but we do stand in need of fellowship with Him. And for this reason it was that He graciously poured Himself out, that He might gather us into the bosom of the Father.

2. But vain in every respect are they who despise the entire dispensation of God, and disallow the salvation of the flesh, and treat with contempt its regeneration, maintaining that it is not capable of incorruption. But if this indeed do not attain salvation, then neither did the Lord redeem us with His blood, nor is the cup of the Eucharist the communion of His blood, nor the bread which we break the communion of His body.[1] For blood can only come from veins and flesh, and whatsoever else makes up the substance of man, such as the Word of God was actually made. By His own blood he redeemed us, as also His apostle declares, " In whom we have redemption through His blood, even the remission of sins." [2] And as we are His members, we are also nourished by means of the creation (and He Himself grants the creation to us, for He causes His sun to rise, and sends rain when He wills [3]). He has acknowledged the cup (which is a part of the creation) as His own blood, from which He bedews our blood ; and the bread (also a part of the creation) He has established as His own body, from which He gives increase to our bodies.[4]

3. When, therefore, the mingled cup and the manufactured bread receives the Word of God, and the Eucharist of the blood and the body of Christ is made,[5] from which things the substance of our flesh is increased and supported, how can they affirm that the flesh is incapable of receiving the gift of God, which is life eternal, which [flesh] is nourished from the body and blood of the Lord, and is a member of Him? — even as the blessed Paul declares in his Epistle to the Ephesians, that " we are members of His body, of His flesh, and of His bones." [6] He does not speak these words of some spiritual and invisible man, for a spirit has not bones nor flesh ; [7] but [he refers to] that dispensation [by which the Lord became] an actual man, consisting of flesh, and nerves, and bones, — that [flesh] which is nourished by the cup which is His blood, and receives increase from the bread which is His body. And just as a cutting from the vine planted in the ground fructifies in its season, or as a corn of wheat falling into the earth and becoming decomposed, rises with manifold increase by the Spirit of God, who contains all things, and then, through the wisdom of God, serves for the use of men, and having received the Word of God, becomes the Eucharist, which is the body and blood of Christ ; so also our bodies, being nourished by it, and deposited in the earth, and suffering decomposition there, shall rise at their appointed time, the Word of God granting them resurrection to the glory of God, even the Father, who freely gives to this mortal immortality, and to this corruptible incorruption,[8] because the strength of God is made perfect in weakness,[9] in order that we may never become puffed up, as if we had life from ourselves, and exalted against God, our minds becoming ungrateful ; but learning by experience that we possess eternal duration from the excelling power of this Being, not from our own nature, we may neither undervalue that glory which surrounds God as He is, nor be ignorant of our own nature, but that we may know what God can effect, and what benefits man receives, and thus never wander from the true comprehension of things as they are, that is, both with regard to God and with regard to man. And might it not be the case, perhaps, as I have already observed, that for this purpose God permitted our resolution into the common dust of mortality,[10] that we, being instructed by every mode, may be accurate in all things for the future, being ignorant neither of God nor of ourselves?

---

[1] 1 Cor. x. 16.
[2] Col i. 14.
[3] Matt. v. 45.
[4] [Again, he carefully asserts that the *bread* is the *body*, and the *wine* (cup) is the *blood*. The elements are sanctified, not changed materially.]

[5] The Greek text, of which a considerable portion remains here, would give, " and the Eucharist becomes the body of Christ."
[6] Eph. v. 30.
[7] Luke xxiv. 39.
[8] 1 Cor. xv. 53.
[9] 2 Cor. xii. 3.
[10] This is Harvey's free rendering of the passage, which is in the Greek (as preserved in the Catena of John of Damascus): καὶ διὰ τοῦτο ἠνέσχετο ὁ Θεὸς τὴν εἰς τὴν γῆν ἡμῶν ἀνάλυσιν. In the Latin: Propter hoc passus est Deus fieri in nobis resolutionem. See Book iii. cap. xx. 2.

CHAP. III. — THE POWER AND GLORY OF GOD SHINE FORTH IN THE WEAKNESS OF HUMAN FLESH, AS HE WILL RENDER OUR BODY A PARTICIPATOR OF THE RESURRECTION AND OF IMMORTALITY, ALTHOUGH HE HAS FORMED IT FROM THE DUST OF THE EARTH; HE WILL ALSO BESTOW UPON IT THE ENJOYMENT OF IMMORTALITY, JUST AS HE GRANTS IT THIS SHORT LIFE IN COMMON WITH THE SOUL.

1. The Apostle Paul has, moreover, in the most lucid manner, pointed out that man has been delivered over to his own infirmity, lest, being uplifted, he might fall away from the truth. Thus he says in the second [Epistle] to the Corinthians : " And lest I should be lifted up by the sublimity of the revelations, there was given unto me a thorn in the flesh, the messenger of Satan to buffet me. And upon this I besought the Lord three times, that it might depart from me. But he said unto me, My grace is sufficient for thee ; for strength is made perfect in weakness. Gladly therefore shall I rather glory in infirmities, that the power of Christ may dwell in me." [1] What, therefore? (as some may exclaim :) did the Lord wish, in that case, that His apostles should thus undergo buffeting, and that he should endure such infirmity? Even so it was ; the word says it. For strength is made perfect in weakness, rendering him a better man who by means of his infirmity becomes acquainted with the power of God. For how could a man have learned that he is himself an infirm being, and mortal by nature, but that God is immortal and powerful, unless he had learned by experience what is in both? For there is nothing evil in learning one's infirmities by endurance ; yea, rather, it has even the beneficial effect of preventing him from forming an undue opinion of his own nature (*non aberrare in natura sua*). But the being lifted up against God, and taking His glory to one's self, rendering man ungrateful, has brought much evil upon him. [And thus, I say, man must learn both things by experience], that he may not be destitute of truth and love either towards himself or his Creator. [2] But the experience of both confers upon him the true knowledge as to God and man, and increases his love towards God. Now, where there exists an increase of love, there a greater glory is wrought out by the power of God for those who love Him.

2. Those men, therefore, set aside the power of God, and do not consider what the word declares, when they dwell upon the infirmity of the flesh, but do not take into consideration the power of Him who raises it up from the dead. For if He does not vivify what is mortal, and does not bring back the corruptible to incorruption, He is not a God of power. But that He is powerful in all these respects, we ought to perceive from our origin, inasmuch as God, taking dust from the earth, formed man. And surely it is much more difficult and incredible, from non-existent bones, and nerves, and veins, and the rest of man's organization, to bring it about that all this should be, and to make man an animated and rational creature, than to re-integrate again that which had been created and then afterwards decomposed into earth (for the reasons already mentioned), having thus passed into those [elements] from which man, who had no previous existence, was formed. For He who in the beginning caused him to have being who as yet was not, just when He pleased, shall much more reinstate again those who had a former existence, when it is His will [that they should inherit] the life granted by Him. And that flesh shall also be found fit for and capable of receiving the power of God, which at the beginning received the skilful touches of God ; so that one part became the eye for seeing ; another, the ear for hearing ; another, the hand for feeling and working ; another, the sinews stretched out everywhere, and holding the limbs together ; another, arteries and veins, passages for the blood and the air ; [3] another, the various internal organs ; another, the blood, which is the bond of union between soul and body. But why go [on in this strain]? Numbers would fail to express the multiplicity of parts in the human frame, which was made in no other way than by the great wisdom of God. But those things which partake of the skill and wisdom of God, do also partake of His power.

3. The flesh, therefore, is not destitute [of participation] in the constructive wisdom and power of God. But if the power of Him who is the bestower of life is made perfect in weakness — that is, in the flesh — let them inform us, when they maintain the incapacity of flesh to receive the life granted by God, whether they do say these things as being living men at present, and partakers of life, or acknowledge that, having no part in life whatever, they are at the present moment dead men. And if they really are dead men, how is it that they move about, and speak, and perform those other functions which are not the actions of the dead, but of the living? But if they are now alive, and if their whole body partakes of life, how can they venture the assertion that the flesh is not quali-

---

[1] 2 Cor. xii. 7-9.
[2] We have adopted here the explanation of Massuet, who considers the preceding period as merely parenthetical. Both Grabe and Harvey, however, would make conjectural emendations in the text, which seem to us to be inadmissible.

[3] The ancients erroneously supposed that the arteries were *air-vessels*, from the fact that these organs, after death, appear quite empty, from all the blood stagnating in the veins when death supervenes.

fied to be a partaker of life, when they do confess that they have life at the present moment? It is just as if anybody were to take up a sponge full of water, or a torch on fire, and to declare that the sponge could not possibly partake of the water, or the torch of the fire. In this very manner do those men, by alleging that they are alive and bear life about in their members, contradict themselves afterwards, when they represent these members as not being capable of [receiving] life. But if the present temporal life, which is of such an inferior nature to eternal life, can nevertheless effect so much as to quicken our mortal members, why should not eternal life, being much more powerful than this, vivify the flesh, which has already held converse with, and been accustomed to sustain, life? For that the flesh can really partake of life, is shown from the fact of its being alive; for it lives on, as long as it is God's purpose that it should do so. It is manifest, too, that God has the power to confer life upon it, inasmuch as He grants life to us who are in existence. And, therefore, since the Lord has power to infuse life into what He has fashioned, and since the flesh is capable of being quickened, what remains to prevent its participating in incorruption, which is a blissful and never-ending life granted by God?

CHAP. IV. — THOSE PERSONS ARE DECEIVED WHO FEIGN ANOTHER GOD THE FATHER BESIDES THE CREATOR OF THE WORLD ; FOR HE MUST HAVE BEEN FEEBLE AND USELESS, OR ELSE MALIGNANT AND FULL OF ENVY, IF HE BE EITHER UNABLE OR UNWILLING TO EXTEND EXTERNAL LIFE TO OUR BODIES.

1. Those persons who feign the existence of another Father beyond the Creator, and who term him the good God, do deceive themselves ; for they introduce him as a feeble, worthless, and negligent being, not to say malign and full of envy, inasmuch as they affirm that our bodies are not quickened by him. For when they say of things which it is manifest to all do remain immortal, such as the spirit and the soul, and such other things, that they are quickened by the Father, but that another thing [viz. the body] which is quickened in no different manner than by God granting [life] to it, is abandoned by life, — [they must either confess] that this proves their Father to be weak and powerless, or else envious and malignant. For since the Creator does even here quicken our mortal bodies, and promises them resurrection by the prophets, as I have pointed out ; who [in that case] is shown to be more powerful, stronger, or truly good? Whether is it the Creator who vivifies the whole man, or is it their Father, falsely so called? He feigns to be the quickener of those things which are immortal by nature, to which things life is always present by their very nature ; but he does not benevolently quicken those things which required his assistance, that they might live, but leaves them carelessly to fall under the power of death. Whether is it the case, then, that their Father does not bestow life upon them when he has the power of so doing, or is it that he does not possess the power? If, on the one hand, it is because he cannot, he is, upon that supposition, not a powerful being, nor is he more perfect than the Creator ; for the Creator grants, as we must perceive, what *He* is unable to afford. But if, on the other hand, [it be that he does not grant this] when he has the power of so doing, then he is proved to be not a good, but an envious and malignant Father.

2. If, again, they refer to any cause on account of which their Father does not impart life to bodies, then that cause must necessarily appear superior to the Father, since it restrains Him from the exercise of His benevolence ; and His benevolence will thus be proved weak, on account of that cause which they bring forward. Now every one must perceive that bodies are capable of receiving life. For they live to the extent that God pleases that they should live ; and that being so, the [heretics] cannot maintain that [these bodies] are utterly incapable of receiving life. If, therefore, on account of necessity and any other cause, those [bodies] which are capable of participating in life are not vivified, their Father shall be the slave of necessity and that cause, and not therefore a free agent, having His will under His own control.

CHAP. V. — THE PROLONGED LIFE OF THE ANCIENTS, THE TRANSLATION OF ELIJAH AND OF ENOCH IN THEIR OWN BODIES, AS WELL AS THE PRESERVATION OF JONAH, OF SHADRACH, MESHACH, AND ABEDNEGO, IN THE MIDST OF EXTREME PERIL, ARE CLEAR DEMONSTRATIONS THAT GOD CAN RAISE UP OUR BODIES TO LIFE ETERNAL.

1. [In order to learn] that bodies did continue in existence for a lengthened period, as long as it was God's good pleasure that they should flourish, let [these heretics] read the Scriptures, and they will find that our predecessors advanced beyond seven hundred, eight hundred, and nine hundred years of age ; and that their bodies kept pace with the protracted length of their days, and participated in life as long as God willed that they should live. But why do I refer to these men? For Enoch, when he pleased God, was translated in the same body in which he did please Him, thus pointing out by anticipation the translation of the just. Elijah, too, was caught up [when he was yet] in the substance of the [natural] form ; thus exhibiting in prophecy the

assumption of those who are spiritual, and that nothing stood in the way of their body being translated and caught up. For by means of the very same hands through which they were moulded at the beginning, did they receive this translation and assumption. For in Adam the hands of God had become accustomed to set in order, to rule, and to sustain His own workmanship, and to bring it and place it where they pleased. Where, then, was the first man placed? In paradise certainly, as the Scripture declares: "And God planted a garden [*paradisum*] eastward in Eden, and there He placed the man whom He had formed." [1] And then afterwards, when [man] proved disobedient, he was cast out thence into this world. Wherefore also the elders who were disciples of the apostles tell us that those who were translated were transferred to that place (for paradise has been prepared for righteous men, such as have the Spirit; in which place also Paul the apostle, when he was caught up, heard words which are unspeakable as regards us in our present condition [2]), and that there shall they who have been translated remain until the consummation [of all things], as a prelude to immortality.

2. If, however, any one imagine it impossible that men should survive for such a length of time, and that Elias was not caught up in the flesh, but that his flesh was consumed in the fiery chariot, let him consider that Jonah, when he had been cast into the deep, and swallowed down into the whale's belly, was by the command of God again thrown out safe upon the land. [3] And then, again, when Ananias, Azarias, and Misaël were cast into the furnace of fire sevenfold heated, they sustained no harm whatever, neither was the smell of fire perceived upon them. As, therefore, the hand of God was present with them, working out marvellous things in their case — [things] impossible [to be accomplished] by man's nature — what wonder was it, if also in the case of those who were translated it performed something wonderful, working in obedience to the will of God, even the Father? Now this is the Son of God, as the Scripture represents Nebuchadnezzar the king as having said, "Did not we cast three men bound into the furnace? and, lo, I do see four walking in the midst of the fire, and the fourth is like the Son of God." [4] Neither the nature of any created thing, therefore, nor the weakness of the flesh, can prevail against the will of God. For God is not subject to created things, but created things to God; and all things yield obedience to His will. Wherefore also the Lord declares,

"The things which are impossible with men, are possible with God." [5] As, therefore, it might seem to the men of the present day, who are ignorant of God's appointment, to be a thing incredible and impossible that any man could live for such a number of years, yet those who were before us did live [to such an age], and those who were translated do live as an earnest of the future length of days; and [as it might also appear impossible] that from the whale's belly and from the fiery furnace men issued forth unhurt, yet they nevertheless did so, led forth as it were by the hand of God, for the purpose of declaring His power: so also now, although some, not knowing the power and promise of God, may oppose their own salvation, deeming it impossible for God, who raises up the dead, to have power to confer upon them eternal duration, yet the scepticism of men of this stamp shall not render the faithfulness of God of none effect.

CHAP. VI. — GOD WILL BESTOW SALVATION UPON THE WHOLE NATURE OF MAN, CONSISTING OF BODY AND SOUL IN CLOSE UNION, SINCE THE WORD TOOK IT UPON HIM, AND ADORNED IT WITH THE GIFTS OF THE HOLY SPIRIT, OF WHOM OUR BODIES ARE, AND ARE TERMED, THE TEMPLES.

1. Now God shall be glorified in His handiwork, fitting it so as to be conformable to, and modelled after, His own Son. For by the hands of the Father, that is, by the Son and the Holy Spirit, man, and not [merely] a part of man, was made in the likeness of God. Now the soul and the spirit are certainly a *part* of the man, but certainly not *the* man; for the perfect man consists in the commingling and the union of the soul receiving the spirit of the Father, and the admixture of that fleshly nature which was moulded after the image of God. For this reason does the apostle declare, "We speak wisdom among them that are perfect," [6] terming those persons "perfect" who have received the Spirit of God, and who through the Spirit of God do speak in all languages, as he used Himself also to speak. In like manner we do also hear [7] many brethren in the Church, who possess prophetic gifts, and who through the Spirit speak all kinds of languages, and bring to light for the general benefit the hidden things of men, and declare the mysteries of God, whom also the apostle terms "spiritual," they being spiritual because they partake of the Spirit, and not because their flesh has been stripped off and taken away, and because they have become purely spiritual. For if any one take away the sub-

---

[1] Gen. ii 8.
[2] 2 Cor. xii. 4.
[3] Jon. ii. 11.
[4] Dan. iii. 19-25.

[5] Luke xviii. 27.
[6] 1 Cor. ii. 6.
[7] The old Latin has "audivimus," *have heard*.

stance of flesh, that is, of the handiwork [of God], and understand that which is purely spiritual, such then would not be a spiritual man, but would be the spirit of a man, or the Spirit of God. But when the spirit here blended with the soul is united to [God's] handiwork, the man is rendered spiritual and perfect because of the outpouring of the Spirit, and this is he who was made in the image and likeness of God. But if the Spirit be wanting to the soul, he who is such is indeed of an animal nature, and being left carnal, shall be an imperfect being, possessing indeed the image [of God] in his formation (*in plasmate*), but not receiving the similitude through the Spirit; and thus is this being imperfect. Thus also, if any one take away the image and set aside the handiwork, he cannot then understand this as being a man, but as either some part of a man, as I have already said, or as something else than a man. For that flesh which has been moulded is not a perfect man in itself, but the body of a man, and part of a man. Neither is the soul itself, considered apart by itself, the man; but it is the soul of a man, and part of a man. Neither is the spirit a man, for it is called the spirit, and not a man; but the commingling and union of all these constitutes the perfect man. And for this cause does the apostle, explaining himself, make it clear that the saved man is a complete man as well as a spiritual man; saying thus in the first Epistle to the Thessalonians, "Now the God of peace sanctify you perfect (*perfectos*); and may your spirit, and soul, and body be preserved whole without complaint to the coming of the Lord Jesus Christ." [1] Now what was his object in praying that these three — that is, soul, body, and spirit — might be preserved to the coming of the Lord, unless he was aware of the [future] reintegration and union of the three, and [that they should be heirs of] one and the same salvation? For this cause also he declares that those are "the perfect" who present unto the Lord the three [component parts] without offence. Those, then, are the perfect who have had the Spirit of God remaining in them, and have preserved their souls and bodies blameless, holding fast the faith of God, that is, that faith which is [directed] towards God, and maintaining righteous dealings with respect to their neighbours.

2. Whence also he says, that this handiwork is "the temple of God," thus declaring: "Know ye not that ye are the temple of God, and that the Spirit of God dwelleth in you? If any man, therefore, will defile the temple of God, him will God destroy: for the temple of God is holy,

which [temple] ye are." [2] Here he manifestly declares the body to be the temple in which the Spirit dwells. As also the Lord speaks in reference to Himself, "Destroy this temple, and in three days I will raise it up. He spake this, however," it is said, "of the temple of His body." [3] And not only does he (the apostle) acknowledge our bodies to be a temple, but even the temple of Christ, saying thus to the Corinthians, "Know ye not that your bodies are members of Christ? Shall I then take the members of Christ, and make them the members of an harlot?" [4] He speaks these things, not in reference to some other spiritual man; for a being of such a nature could have nothing to do with an harlot: but he declares "our body," that is, the flesh which continues in sanctity and purity, to be "the members of Christ;" but that when it becomes one with an harlot, it becomes the members of an harlot. And for this reason he said, "If any man defile the temple of God, him will God destroy." How then is it not the utmost blasphemy to allege, that the temple of God, in which the Spirit of the Father dwells, and the members of Christ, do not partake of salvation, but are reduced to perdition? Also, that our bodies are raised not from their own substance, but by the power of God, he says to the Corinthians, "Now the body is not for fornication, but for the Lord, and the Lord for the body. But God hath both raised up the Lord, and shall raise us up by His own power." [5]

CHAP. VII. — INASMUCH AS CHRIST DID RISE IN OUR FLESH, IT FOLLOWS THAT WE SHALL BE ALSO RAISED IN THE SAME; SINCE THE RESURRECTION PROMISED TO US SHOULD NOT BE REFERRED TO SPIRITS NATURALLY IMMORTAL, BUT TO BODIES IN THEMSELVES MORTAL.

1. In the same manner, therefore, as Christ did rise in the substance of flesh, and pointed out to His disciples the mark of the nails and the opening in His side [6] (now these are the tokens of that flesh which rose from the dead), so "shall He also," it is said, "raise us up by His own power." [7] And again to the Romans. he says, "But if the Spirit of Him that raised up Jesus from the dead dwell in you, He that raised up Christ from the dead shall also quicken your mortal bodies." [8] What, then, are mortal bodies? Can they be souls? Nay, for souls are incorporeal when put in comparison with mortal bodies; for God "breathed into the face of man the breath of life, and man became a living soul." Now the breath of life is an incorporeal

[1] 1 Thess. v. 23. [I have before referred the student to the "Biblical Psychology" of Prof. Delitzsch (translation), T. & T. Clark, Edinburgh, 1868.]

[2] 1 Cor. iii. 16.
[3] John ii. 19-21.
[4] 1 Cor. iii. 17.
[5] 1 Cor. vi. 13, 14.
[6] John xx. 20, 25, 27.
[7] 1 Cor. vi. 14.
[8] Rom. viii. 11.

thing. And certainly they cannot maintain that the very breath of life is mortal. Therefore David says, "My soul also shall live to Him,"[1] just as if its substance were immortal. Neither, on the other hand, can they say that the spirit is the mortal body. What therefore is there left to which we may apply the term "mortal body," unless it be the thing that was moulded, that is, the flesh, of which it is also said that God will vivify it? For this it is which dies and is decomposed, but not the soul or the spirit. For to die is to lose vital power, and to become henceforth breathless, inanimate, and devoid of motion, and to melt away into those [component parts] from which also it derived the commencement of [its] substance. But this event happens neither to the soul, for it is the breath of life; nor to the spirit, for the spirit is simple and not composite, so that it cannot be decomposed, and is itself the life of those who receive it. We must therefore conclude that it is in reference to the flesh that death is mentioned; which [flesh], after the soul's departure, becomes breathless and inanimate, and is decomposed gradually into the earth from which it was taken. This, then, is what is mortal. And it is this of which he also says, "He shall also quicken your mortal bodies." And therefore in reference to it he says, in the first [Epistle] to the Corinthians: "So also is the resurrection of the dead: it is sown in corruption, it rises in incorruption."[2] For he declares, "That which thou sowest cannot be quickened, unless first it die."[3]

2. But what is that which, like a grain of wheat, is sown in the earth and decays, unless it be the bodies which are laid in the earth, into which seeds are also cast? And for this reason he said, "It is sown in dishonour, it rises in glory."[4] For what is more ignoble than dead flesh? Or, on the other hand, what is more glorious than the same when it arises and partakes of incorruption? "It is sown in weakness, it is raised in power:"[5] in its own weakness certainly, because since it is earth it goes to earth; but [it is quickened] by the power of God, who raises it from the dead. "It is sown an animal body, it rises a spiritual body."[6] He has taught, beyond all doubt, that such language was not used by him, either with reference to the soul or to the spirit, but to bodies that have become corpses. For these are animal bodies, that is, [bodies] which partake of life, which when they have lost, they succumb to death; then, rising through the Spirit's instrumentality, they become spiritual bodies, so that by the Spirit they pos-

sess a perpetual life. "For now," he says, "we know in part, and we prophesy in part, but then face to face."[7] And this it is which has been said also by Peter: "Whom having not seen, ye love; in whom now also, not seeing, ye believe; and believing, ye shall rejoice with joy unspeakable."[8] For our face shall see the face of the Lord,[9] and shall rejoice with joy unspeakable, — that is to say, when it shall behold its own Delight.

CHAP. VIII. — THE GIFTS OF THE HOLY SPIRIT WHICH WE RECEIVE PREPARE US FOR INCORRUPTION, RENDER US SPIRITUAL, AND SEPARATE US FROM CARNAL MEN. THESE TWO CLASSES ARE SIGNIFIED BY THE CLEAN AND UNCLEAN ANIMALS IN THE LEGAL DISPENSATION.

1. But we do now receive a certain portion of His Spirit, tending towards perfection, and preparing us for incorruption, being little by little accustomed to receive and bear God; which also the apostle terms "an earnest," that is, a part of the honour which has been promised us by God, where he says in the Epistle to the Ephesians, "In which ye also, having heard the word of truth, the Gospel of your salvation, believing in which ye have been sealed with the Holy Spirit of promise, which is the earnest of our inheritance."[10] This earnest, therefore, thus dwelling in us, renders us spiritual even now, and the mortal is swallowed up by immortality.[11] "For ye," he declares, "are not in the flesh, but in the Spirit, if so be that the Spirit of God dwell in you."[12] This, however, does not take place by a casting away of the flesh, but by the impartation of the Spirit. For those to whom he was writing were not without flesh, but they were those who had received the Spirit of God, "by which we cry, Abba, Father."[13] If therefore, at the present time, having the earnest, we do cry, "Abba, Father," what shall it be when, on rising again, we behold Him face to face; when all the members shall burst out into a continuous hymn of triumph, glorifying Him who raised them from the dead, and gave the gift of eternal life? For if the earnest, gathering man into itself, does even now cause him to cry, "Abba, Father," what shall the complete grace of the Spirit effect, which shall be given to men by God? It will render us like unto Him, and accomplish the will[14] of the Father; for it shall make man after the image and likeness of God.

1 Ps. xxii. 31, LXX.
2 1 Cor. xv. 42.
3 1 Cor. xv. 36.
4 1 Cor. xv. 43.
5 1 Cor. xv. 43.
6 1 Cor. xv. 44.

7 1 Cor. xiii. 9, 12.
8 1 Pet. i. 8.
9 Grabe, Massuet, and Stieren prefer to read, "the face of the living God;" while Harvey adopts the above, reading merely "Domini," and not "Dei vivi."
10 Eph. i. 13, etc.
11 2 Cor. v. 4.
12 Rom. viii. 9.
13 Rom. viii. 15.
14 This is adopting Harvey's emendation of "voluntatem" for "voluntate."

2. Those persons, then, who possess the earnest of the Spirit, and who are not enslaved by the lusts of the flesh, but are subject to the Spirit, and who in all things walk according to the light of reason, does the apostle properly term "spiritual," because the Spirit of God dwells in them. Now, spiritual men shall not be incorporeal spirits; but our substance, that is, the union of flesh and spirit, receiving the Spirit of God, makes up the spiritual man. But those who do indeed reject the Spirit's counsel, and are the slaves of fleshly lusts, and lead lives contrary to reason, and who, without restraint, plunge headlong into their own desires, having no longing after the Divine Spirit, do live after the manner of swine and of dogs; these men, [I say], does the apostle very properly term "carnal," because they have no thought of anything else except carnal things.

3. For the same reason, too, do the prophets compare them to irrational animals, on account of the irrationality of their conduct, saying, "They have become as horses raging for the females; each one of them neighing after his neighbour's wife."[1] And again, "Man, when he was in honour, was made like unto cattle."[2] This denotes that, for his own fault, he is likened to cattle, by rivalling their irrational life. And we also, as the custom is, do designate men of this stamp as cattle and irrational beasts.

4. Now the law has figuratively predicted all these, delineating man by the [various] animals:[3] whatsoever of these, says [the Scripture], have a double hoof and ruminate, it proclaims as clean; but whatsoever of them do not possess one or other of these [properties], it sets aside by themselves as unclean. Who then are the clean? Those who make their way by faith steadily towards the Father and the Son; for this is denoted by the steadiness of those which divide the hoof; and they meditate day and night upon the words of God,[4] that they may be adorned with good works: for this is the meaning of the ruminants. The unclean, however, are those which do neither divide the hoof nor ruminate; that is, those persons who have neither faith in God, nor do meditate on His words: and such is the abomination of the Gentiles. But as to those animals which do indeed chew the cud, but have not the double hoof, and are themselves unclean, we have in them a figurative description of the Jews, who certainly have the words of God in their mouth, but who do not fix their rooted stedfastness in the Father and in the Son; wherefore they are an unstable generation. For those animals which have the hoof all in one piece easily slip; but those which have it divided are more sure-footed, their cleft hoofs succeeding each other as they advance, and the one hoof supporting the other. In like manner, too, those are unclean which have the double hoof but do not ruminate: this is plainly an indication of all heretics, and of those who do not meditate on the words of God, neither are adorned with works of righteousness; to whom also the Lord says, "Why call ye Me Lord, Lord, and do not the things which I say to you?"[5] For men of this stamp do indeed say that they believe in the Father and the Son, but they never meditate as they should upon the things of God, neither are they adorned with works of righteousness; but, as I have already observed, they have adopted the lives of swine and of dogs, giving themselves over to filthiness, to gluttony, and recklessness of all sorts. Justly, therefore, did the apostle call all such "carnal" and "animal,"[6] — [all those, namely], who through their own unbelief and luxury do not receive the Divine Spirit, and in their various phases cast out from themselves the life-giving Word, and walk stupidly after their own lusts: the prophets, too, spake of them as beasts of burden and wild beasts; custom likewise has viewed them in the light of cattle and irrational creatures; and the law has pronounced them unclean.

CHAP. IX. — SHOWING HOW THAT PASSAGE OF THE APOSTLE WHICH THE HERETICS PERVERT, SHOULD BE UNDERSTOOD; VIZ., "FLESH AND BLOOD SHALL NOT POSSESS THE KINGDOM OF GOD."

1. Among the other [truths] proclaimed by the apostle, there is also this one, "That flesh and blood cannot inherit the kingdom of God."[7] This is [the passage] which is adduced by all the heretics in support of their folly, with an attempt to annoy us, and to point out that the handiwork of God is not saved. They do not take this fact into consideration, that there are three things out of which, as I have shown, the complete man is composed — flesh, soul, and spirit. One of these does indeed preserve and fashion [the man] — this is the spirit; while as to another it is united and formed — that is the flesh; then [comes] that which is between these two — that is the soul, which sometimes indeed, when it follows the spirit, is raised up by it, but sometimes it sympathizes with the flesh, and falls into carnal lusts. Those then, as many as they be, who have not that which saves and forms [us] into life [eternal], shall be, and shall be called, [mere] flesh and blood; for these are they

---

[1] Jer. v. 3.
[2] Ps. xlix. 20.
[3] Lev. xi. 2; Deut. xiv. 3, etc.
[4] Ps. i. 2.

[5] Luke vi. 46.
[6] 1 Cor. ii. 14, iii. 1, etc.
[7] 1 Cor. xv. 50.

who have not the Spirit of God in themselves. Wherefore men of this stamp are spoken of by the Lord as "dead;" for, says He, "Let the dead bury their dead," [1] because they have not the Spirit which quickens man.

2. On the other hand, as many as fear God and trust in His Son's advent, and who through faith do establish the Spirit of God in their hearts, — such men as these shall be properly called both "pure," and "spiritual," and "those living to God," because they possess the Spirit of the Father, who purifies man, and raises him up to the life of God. For as the Lord has testified that "the flesh is weak," so [does He also say] that "the spirit is willing." [2] For this latter is capable of working out its own suggestions. If, therefore, any one admix the ready inclination of the Spirit to be, as it were, a stimulus to the infirmity of the flesh, it inevitably follows that what is strong will prevail over the weak, so that the weakness of the flesh will be absorbed by the strength of the Spirit; and that the man in whom this takes place cannot in that case be carnal, but spiritual, because of the fellowship of the Spirit. Thus it is, therefore, that the martyrs bear their witness, and despise death, not after the infirmity of the flesh, but because of the readiness of the Spirit. For when the infirmity of the flesh is absorbed, it exhibits the Spirit as powerful; and again, when the Spirit absorbs the weakness [of the flesh], it possesses the flesh as an inheritance in itself, and from both of these is formed a living man, — living, indeed, because he partakes of the Spirit, but man, because of the substance of flesh.

3. The flesh, therefore, when destitute of the Spirit of God, is dead, not having life, and cannot possess the kingdom of God: [it is as] irrational blood, like water poured out upon the ground. And therefore he says, "As is the earthy, such are they that are earthy." [3] But where the Spirit of the Father is, there is a living man; [there is] the rational blood preserved by God for the avenging [of those that shed it]; [there is] the flesh possessed by the Spirit, forgetful indeed of what belongs to it, and adopting the quality of the Spirit, being made conformable to the Word of God. And on this account he (the apostle) declares, "As we have borne the image of him who is of the earth, we shall also bear the image of Him who is from heaven." [4] What, therefore, is the earthly? That which was fashioned. And what is the heavenly? The Spirit. As therefore he says, when we were destitute of the celestial Spirit, we walked in

former times in the oldness of the flesh, not obeying God; so now let us, receiving the Spirit, walk in newness of life, obeying God. Inasmuch, therefore, as without the Spirit of God we cannot be saved, the apostle exhorts us through faith and chaste conversation to preserve the Spirit of God, lest, having become non-participators of the Divine Spirit, we lose the kingdom of heaven; and he exclaims, that flesh in itself, and blood, cannot possess the kingdom of God.

4. If, however, we must speak strictly, [we would say that] the flesh *does not* inherit, but *is* inherited; as also the Lord declares, "Blessed are the meek, for they shall possess the earth by inheritance;" [5] as if in the [future] kingdom, the earth, from whence exists the substance of our flesh, is to be possessed by inheritance. This is the reason for His wishing the temple (i.e., the flesh) to be clean, that the Spirit of God may take delight therein, as a bridegroom with a bride. As, therefore, the bride cannot [be said] to wed, but to be wedded, when the bridegroom comes and takes her, so also the flesh cannot by itself possess the kingdom of God by inheritance; but it can be taken *for* an inheritance into the kingdom of God. For a living person inherits the goods of the deceased; and it is one thing to inherit, another to be inherited. The former rules, and exercises power over, and orders the things inherited at his will; but the latter things are in a state of subjection, are under order, and are ruled over by him who has obtained the inheritance. What, therefore, is it that lives? The Spirit of God, doubtless. What, again, are the possessions of the deceased? The various parts of the man, surely, which rot in the earth. But these are inherited by the Spirit when they are translated into the kingdom of heaven. For this cause, too, did Christ die, that the Gospel covenant being manifested and known to the whole world, might in the first place set free His slaves; and then afterwards, as I have already shown, might constitute them heirs of His property, when the Spirit possesses them by inheritance. For he who lives inherits, but the flesh is inherited. In order that we may not lose life by losing that Spirit which possesses us, the apostle, exhorting us to the communion of the Spirit, has said, according to reason, in those words already quoted, "That flesh and blood cannot inherit the kingdom of God." Just as if he were to say, "Do not err; for unless the Word of God dwell with, and the Spirit of the Father be in you, and if ye shall live frivolously and carelessly as if ye were this only, viz., mere flesh and blood, ye cannot inherit the kingdom of God."

Luke x. 60.
[2] Matt. xxvi. 41.
[3] 1 Cor. xv. 48.
[4] 1 Cor. xv. 49.

---

[5] Matt. v. 5.

CHAP. X. — BY A COMPARISON DRAWN FROM THE WILD OLIVE-TREE, WHOSE QUALITY BUT NOT WHOSE NATURE IS CHANGED BY GRAFTING, HE PROVES MORE IMPORTANT THINGS ; HE POINTS OUT ALSO THAT MAN WITHOUT THE SPIRIT IS NOT CAPABLE OF BRINGING FORTH FRUIT, OR OF INHERITING THE KINGDOM OF GOD.

1. This truth, therefore, [he declares], in order that we may not reject the engrafting of the Spirit while pampering the flesh. "But thou, being a wild olive-tree," he says, "hast been grafted into the good olive-tree, and been made a partaker of the fatness of the olive-tree." [1] As, therefore, when the wild olive has been engrafted, if it remain in its former condition, viz., a wild olive, it is "cut off, and cast into the fire ; " [2] but if it takes kindly to the graft, and is changed into the good olive-tree, it becomes a fruit-bearing olive, planted, as it were, in a king's park (paradiso) : so likewise men, if they do truly progress by faith towards better things, and receive the Spirit of God, and bring forth the fruit thereof, shall be spiritual, as being planted in the paradise of God. But if they cast out the Spirit, and remain in their former condition, desirous of being of the flesh rather than of the Spirit, then it is very justly said with regard to men of this stamp, "That flesh and blood shall not inherit the kingdom of God ; " [3] just as if any one were to say that the wild olive is not received into the paradise of God. Admirably therefore does the apostle exhibit our nature, and God's universal appointment, in his discourse about flesh and blood and the wild olive. For as the good olive, if neglected for a certain time, if left to grow wild and to run to wood, does itself become a wild olive ; or again, if the wild olive be carefully tended and grafted, it naturally reverts to its former fruit-bearing condition : so men also, when they become careless, and bring forth for fruit the lusts of the flesh like woody produce, are rendered, by their own fault, unfruitful in righteousness. For when men sleep, the enemy sows the material of tares ; [4] and for this cause did the Lord command His disciples to be on the watch. [5] And again, those persons who are not bringing forth the fruits of righteousness, and are, as it were, covered over and lost among brambles, if they use diligence, and receive the word of God as a graft, [6] arrive at the pristine nature of man — that which was created after the image and likeness of God.

2. But as the engrafted wild olive does not certainly lose the substance of its wood, but changes the quality of its fruit, and receives another name, being now not a wild olive, but a fruit-bearing olive, and is called so ; so also, when man is grafted in by faith and receives the Spirit of God, he certainly does not lose the substance of flesh, but changes the quality of the fruit [brought forth, i.e.,] of his works, and receives another name, [7] showing that he has become changed for the better, being now not [mere] flesh and blood, but a spiritual man, and is called such. Then, again, as the wild olive, if it be not grafted in, remains useless to its lord because of its woody quality, and is cut down as a tree bearing no fruit, and cast into the fire ; so also man, if he does not receive through faith the engrafting of the Spirit, remains in his old condition, and being [mere] flesh and blood, he cannot inherit the kingdom of God. Rightly therefore does the apostle declare, "Flesh and blood cannot inherit the kingdom of God ; " [8] and, "Those who are in the flesh cannot please God : " [9] not repudiating [by these words] the substance of flesh, but showing that into it the Spirit must be infused. [10] And for this reason, he says, "This mortal must put on immortality, and this corruptible must put on incorruption." [11] And again he declares, "But ye are not in the flesh, but in the Spirit, if so be that the Spirit of God dwell in you." [12] He sets this forth still more plainly, where he says, "The body indeed is dead, because of sin ; but the Spirit is life, because of righteousness. But if the Spirit of Him who raised up Jesus from the dead dwell in you, He that raised up Christ from the dead shall also quicken your mortal bodies, because of His Spirit dwelling in you." [13] And again he says, in the Epistle to the Romans, "For if ye live after the flesh, ye shall die." [14] [Now by these words] he does not prohibit them from living their lives in the flesh, for he was himself in the flesh when he wrote to them ; but he cuts away the lusts of the flesh, those which bring death upon a man. And for this reason he says in continuation, "But if ye through the Spirit do mortify the works of the flesh, ye shall live. For whosoever are led by the Spirit of God, these are the sons of God."

CHAP. XI. — TREATS UPON THE ACTIONS OF CARNAL AND OF SPIRITUAL PERSONS ; ALSO, THAT THE SPIRITUAL CLEANSING IS NOT TO BE REFERRED TO THE SUBSTANCE OF OUR BODIES, BUT TO THE MANNER OF OUR FORMER LIFE.

1. [The apostle], foreseeing the wicked speeches of unbelievers, has particularized the

---

1 Rom. xi. 17.
2 Matt. vii. 19.
3 1 Cor. xv. 50.
4 Matt. xiii. 25.
5 Matt. xxiv. 42, xxv. 13; Mark xiii. 33.
6 Jas. i. 21.

7 Rev. ii. 17.
8 1 Cor. xv. 50.
9 Rom. viii. 8.
10 The Latin has, "sed infusionem Spiritus attrahens."
11 1 Cor. xv. 53.
12 Rom. viii. 9.
13 Rom. viii. 10, etc.
14 Rom. viii. 13.

works which he terms carnal; and he explains himself, lest any room for doubt be left to those who do dishonestly pervert his meaning, thus saying in the Epistle to the Galatians : "Now the works of the flesh are manifest, which are : adulteries, fornications, uncleanness, luxuriousness, idolatries, witchcrafts,[1] hatreds, contentions, jealousies, wraths, emulations, animosities, irritable speeches, dissensions, heresies, envyings, drunkenness, carousings, and such like ; of which I warn you, as also I have warned you, that they who do such things shall not inherit the kingdom of God."[2] Thus does he point out to his hearers in a more explicit manner what it is [he means when he declares], "Flesh and blood shall not inherit the kingdom of God." For they who do these things, since they do indeed walk after the flesh, have not the power of living unto God. And then, again, he proceeds to tell us the spiritual actions which vivify a man, that is, the engrafting of the Spirit ; thus saying, "But the fruit of the Spirit is love, joy, peace, long-suffering, goodness, benignity, faith, meekness, continence, chastity : against these there is no law."[3] As, therefore, he who has gone forward to the better things, and has brought forth the fruit of the Spirit, is saved altogether because of the communion of the Spirit ; so also he who has continued in the aforesaid works of the flesh, being truly reckoned as carnal, because he did not receive the Spirit of God, shall not have power to inherit the kingdom of heaven. As, again, the same apostle testifies, saying to the Corinthians, "Know ye not that the unrighteous shall not inherit the kingdom of God? Do not err," he says : "neither fornicators, nor idolaters, nor adulterers, nor effeminate, nor abusers of themselves with mankind, nor thieves, nor covetous, nor revilers, nor rapacious persons, shall inherit the kingdom of God. And these ye indeed have been ; but ye have been washed, but ye have been sanctified, but ye have been justified in the name of the Lord Jesus Christ, and in the Spirit of our God."[4] He shows in the clearest manner through what things it is that man goes to destruction, if he has continued to live after the flesh ; and then, on the other hand, [he points out] through what things he is saved. Now he says that the things which save are the name of our Lord Jesus Christ, and the Spirit of our God.

2. Since, therefore, in that passage he recounts those works of the flesh which are without the Spirit, which bring death [upon their doers], he exclaimed at the end of his Epistle, in accordance with what he had already declared,

"And as we have borne the image of him who is of the earth, we shall also bear the image of Him who is from heaven. For this I say, brethren, that flesh and blood cannot inherit the kingdom of God."[5] Now this which he says, "as we have borne the image of him who is of the earth," is analogous to what has been declared, "And such indeed ye were ; but ye have been washed, but ye have been sanctified, but ye have been justified in the name of our Lord Jesus Christ, and in the Spirit of our God." When, therefore, did we bear the image of him who is of the earth? Doubtless it was when those actions spoken of as "works of the flesh" used to be wrought in us. And then, again, when [do we bear] the image of the heavenly? Doubtless when he says, "Ye have been washed," believing in the name of the Lord, and receiving His Spirit. Now we have washed away, not the substance of our body, nor the image of our [primary] formation, but the former vain conversation. In these members, therefore, in which we were going to destruction by working the works of corruption, in these very members are we made alive by working the works of the Spirit.

CHAP. XII. — OF THE DIFFERENCE BETWEEN LIFE AND DEATH ; OF THE BREATH OF LIFE AND THE VIVIFYING SPIRIT : ALSO HOW IT IS THAT THE SUBSTANCE OF FLESH REVIVES WHICH ONCE WAS DEAD.

1. For as the flesh is capable of corruption, so is it also of incorruption ; and as it is of death, so is it also of life. These two do mutually give way to each other ; and both cannot remain in the same place, but one is driven out by the other, and the presence of the one destroys that of the other. If, then, when death takes possession of a man, it drives life away from him, and proves him to be dead, much more does life, when it has obtained power over the man, drive out death, and restore him as living unto God. For if death brings mortality, why should not life, when it comes, vivify man? Just as Esaias the prophet says, "Death devoured when it had prevailed."[6] And again, "God has wiped away every tear from every face." Thus that former life is expelled, because it was not given by the Spirit, but by the breath.

2. For the breath of life, which also rendered man an animated being, is one thing, and the vivifying Spirit another, which also caused him to become spiritual. And for this reason Isaiah said, "Thus saith the LORD, who made heaven and established it, who founded the earth and the things therein, and gave breath to the people

---

[1] Or, "poisonings."
[2] Gal. v. 19, etc.
[3] Gal. v. 22.
[4] 1 Cor. vi. 9-11.

[5] 1 Cor. xv. 49, etc.
[6] Isa. xxv. 8, LXX.

upon it, and Spirit to those walking upon it ; " [1] thus telling us that breath is indeed given in common to all people upon earth, but that the Spirit is theirs alone who tread down earthly desires. And therefore Isaiah himself, distinguishing the things already mentioned, again exclaims, " For the Spirit shall go forth from Me, and I have made every breath." [2] Thus does he attribute the Spirit as peculiar to God, which in the last times He pours forth upon the human race by the adoption of sons ; but [he shows] that breath was common throughout the creation, and points it out as something created. Now what has been made is a different thing from him who makes it. The breath, then, is temporal, but the Spirit eternal. The breath, too, increases [in strength] for a short period, and continues for a certain time ; after that it takes its departure, leaving its former abode destitute of breath. But when the Spirit pervades the man within and without, inasmuch as it continues there, it never leaves him. " But that is not first which is spiritual," says the apostle, speaking this as if with reference to us human beings ; " but that is first which is animal, afterwards that which is spiritual," [3] in accordance with reason. For there had been a necessity that, in the first place, a human being should be fashioned, and that what was fashioned should receive the soul ; afterwards that it should thus receive the communion of the Spirit. Wherefore also " the first Adam was made " by the Lord " a living soul, the second Adam a quickening spirit." [4] As, then, he who was made a living soul forfeited life when he turned aside to what was evil, so, on the other hand, the same individual, when he reverts to what is good, and receives the quickening Spirit, shall find life.

3. For it is not one thing which dies and another which is quickened, as neither is it one thing which is lost and another which is found, but the Lord came seeking for that same sheep which had been lost. What was it, then, which was dead ? Undoubtedly it was the substance of the flesh ; the same, too, which had lost the breath of life, and had become breathless and dead. This same, therefore, was what the Lord came to quicken, that as in Adam we do all die, as being of an animal nature, in Christ we may all live, as being spiritual, not laying aside God's handiwork, but the lusts of the flesh, and receiving the Holy Spirit ; as the apostle says in the Epistle to the Colossians : " Mortify, therefore, your members which are upon the earth." And what these are he himself explains : " Fornica-

tion, uncleanness, inordinate affection, evil concupiscence, and covetousness, which is idolatry." [5] The laying aside of these is what the apostle preaches ; and he declares that those who do such things, as being merely flesh and blood, cannot inherit the kingdom of heaven. For their soul, tending towards what is worse, and descending to earthly lusts, has become a partaker in the same designation which belongs to these [lusts, viz., " earthly "], which, when the apostle commands us to lay aside, he says in the same Epistle, " Cast ye off the old man with his deeds." [6] But when he said this, he does not remove away the ancient formation [of man] ; for in that case it would be incumbent on us to rid ourselves of its company by committing suicide.

4. But the apostle himself also, being one who had been formed in a womb, and had issued thence, wrote to us, and confessed in his Epistle to the Philippians that " to live in the flesh was the fruit of [his] work ; " [7] thus expressing himself. Now the final result of the work of the Spirit is the salvation of the flesh. [8] For what other visible fruit is there of the invisible Spirit, than the rendering of the flesh mature and capable of incorruption ? If then [he says], " To live in the flesh, this is the result of labour to me," he did not surely contemn the substance of flesh in that passage where he said, " Put ye off the old man with his works ; " [9] but he points out that we should lay aside our former conversation, that which waxes old and becomes corrupt ; and for this reason he goes on to say, " And put ye on the new man, that which is renewed in knowledge, after the image of Him who created him." In this, therefore, that he says, " which is renewed in knowledge," he demonstrates that he, the selfsame man who was in ignorance in times past, that is, in ignorance of God, is renewed by that knowledge which has respect to Him. For the knowledge of God renews man. And when he says, " after the image of the Creator," he sets forth the recapitulation of the same man, who was at the beginning made after the likeness of God.

5. And that he, the apostle, was the very same person who had been born from the womb, that is, of the ancient substance of flesh, he does himself declare in the Epistle to the Galatians : " But when it pleased God, who separated me from my mother's womb, and called me by His grace, to reveal His Son in me, that I might preach Him among the Gentiles," [10] it was not, as I have already observed, one person who had

---

[1] Isa. xlii. 5.
[2] Isa. lvii. 16.
[3] 1 Cor. xv. 46.
[4] 1 Cor. xv. 45.

[5] Col. iii. 5.
[6] Col. iii. 9.
[7] 1 Phil. i. 22.
[8] Following Harvey's explanation of a somewhat obscure passage.
[9] Col. iii. 10.
[10] Gal. i. 15, 16.

been born from the womb, and another who preached the Gospel of the Son of God; but that same individual who formerly was ignorant, and used to persecute the Church, when the revelation was made to him from heaven, and the Lord conferred with him, as I have pointed out in the third book,[1] preached the Gospel of Jesus Christ the Son of God, who was crucified under Pontius Pilate, his former ignorance being driven out by his subsequent knowledge: just as the blind men whom the Lord healed did certainly lose their blindness, but received the substance of their eyes perfect, and obtained the power of vision in the very same eyes with which they formerly did not see; the darkness being merely driven away by the power of vision, while the substance of the eyes was retained, in order that, by means of those eyes through which they had not seen, exercising again the visual power, they might give thanks to Him who had restored them again to sight. And thus, also, he whose withered hand was healed, and all who were healed generally, did not change those parts of their bodies which had at their birth come forth from the womb, but simply obtained these anew in a healthy condition.

6. For the Maker of all things, the Word of God, who did also from the beginning form man, when He found His handiwork impaired by wickedness, performed upon it all kinds of healing. At one time [He did so], as regards each separate member, as it is found in His own handiwork; and at another time He did once for all restore man sound and whole in all points, preparing him perfect for Himself unto the resurrection. For what was His object in healing [different] portions of the flesh, and restoring them to their original condition, if those parts which had been healed by Him were not in a position to obtain salvation? For if it was [merely] a temporary benefit which He conferred, He granted nothing of importance to those who were the subjects of His healing. Or how can they maintain that the flesh is incapable of receiving the life which flows from Him, when it received healing from Him? For life is brought about through healing, and incorruption through life. He, therefore, who confers healing, the same does also confer life; and He [who gives] life, also surrounds His own handiwork with incorruption.

CHAP. XIII. — IN THE DEAD WHO WERE RAISED BY CHRIST WE POSSESS THE HIGHEST PROOF OF THE RESURRECTION; AND OUR HEARTS ARE SHOWN TO BE CAPABLE OF LIFE ETERNAL, BECAUSE THEY CAN NOW RECEIVE THE SPIRIT OF GOD.

1. Let our opponents — that is, they who speak against their own salvation — inform us [as to this point]: The deceased daughter of the high priest;[2] the widow's dead son, who was being carried out [to burial] near the gate [of the city];[3] and Lazarus, who had lain four days in the tomb,[4] — in what bodies did they rise again? In those same, no doubt, in which they had also died. For if it were not in the very same, then certainly those same individuals who had died did not rise again. For [the Scripture] says, "The Lord took the hand of the dead man, and said to him, Young man, I say unto thee, Arise. And the dead man sat up, and He commanded that something should be given him to eat; and He delivered him to his mother."[5] Again, He called Lazarus "with a loud voice, saying, Lazarus, come forth; and he that was dead came forth bound with bandages, feet and hands." This was symbolical of that man who had been bound in sins. And therefore the Lord said, "Loose him, and let him depart." As, therefore, those who were healed were made whole in those members which had in times past been afflicted; and the dead rose in the identical bodies, their limbs and bodies receiving health, and that life which was granted by the Lord, who prefigures eternal things by temporal, and shows that it is He who is Himself able to extend both healing and life to His handiwork, that His words concerning its [future] resurrection may also be believed; so also at the end, when the Lord utters His voice "by the last trumpet,"[6] the dead shall be raised, as He Himself declares: "The hour shall come, in which all the dead which are in the tombs shall hear the voice of the Son of man, and shall come forth; those that have done good to the resurrection of life, and those that have done evil to the resurrection of judgment."[7]

2. Vain, therefore, and truly miserable, are those who do not choose to see what is so manifest and clear, but shun the light of truth, blinding themselves like the tragic Œdipus. And as those who are not practised in wrestling, when they contend with others, laying hold with a determined grasp of some part of [their opponent's] body, really fall by means of that which they grasp, yet when they fall, imagine that they are gaining the victory, because they have obstinately kept their hold upon that part which they seized at the outset, and besides falling, become

---

[1] Vol. i. pp. 306, 321.

[2] Mark v. 22. Irenæus confounds the ruler of the synagogue with the high priest. [Let not those who possess printed Bibles and concordances and commentaries, and all manner of helps to memory, blame the Fathers for such mistakes, until they at least equal them in their marvellous and minute familiarity with the inspired writers.]
[3] Luke vii. 12.
[4] John ix. 30.
[5] The two miracles of raising the widow's son and the rabbi's daughter are here amalgamated.
[6] 1 Cor. xv. 52.
[7] John v. 28.

subjects of ridicule ; so is it with respect to that [favourite] expression of the heretics : " Flesh and blood cannot inherit the kingdom of God ; " while taking two expressions of Paul's, without having perceived the apostle's meaning, or examined critically the force of the terms, but keeping fast hold of the mere expressions by themselves, they die in consequence of their influence (περὶ αὐτάς), overturning as far as in them lies the entire dispensation of God.

3. For thus they will allege that this passage refers to the flesh strictly so called, and not to fleshly works, as I have pointed out, so representing the apostle as contradicting himself. For immediately following, in the same Epistle, he says conclusively, speaking thus in reference to the flesh : " For this corruptible must put on incorruption, and this mortal must put on immortality. So, when this mortal shall have put on immortality, then shall be brought to pass the saying which is written, Death is swallowed up in victory. O death, where is thy sting ? O death, where is thy victory ? " [1] Now these words shall be appropriately said at the time when this mortal and corruptible flesh, which is subject to death, which also is pressed down by a certain dominion of death, rising up into life, shall put on incorruption and immortality. For then, indeed, shall death be truly vanquished, when that flesh which is held down by it shall go forth from under its dominion. And again, to the Philippians he says : " But our conversation is in heaven, from whence also we look for the Saviour, the Lord Jesus, who shall transfigure the body of our humiliation conformable to the body of His glory, even as He is able (ita ut possit) according to the working of His own power." [2] What, then, is this "body of humiliation" which the Lord shall transfigure, [so as to be] conformed to "the body of His glory ? " Plainly it is this body composed of flesh, which is indeed humbled when it falls into the earth. Now its transformation [takes place thus], that while it is mortal and corruptible, it becomes immortal and incorruptible, not after its own proper substance, but after the mighty working of the Lord, who is able to invest the mortal with immortality, and the corruptible with incorruption. And therefore he says,[3] "that mortality may be swallowed up of life. He who has perfected us for this very thing is God, who also has given unto us the earnest of the Spirit." [4] He uses these words most manifestly in reference to the flesh ; for the soul is

not mortal, neither is the spirit. Now, what is mortal shall be swallowed up of life, when the flesh is dead no longer, but remains living and incorruptible, hymning the praises of God, who has perfected us for this very thing. In order, therefore, that we may be perfected for this, aptly does he say to the Corinthians, "Glorify God in your body." [5] Now God is He who gives rise to immortality.

4. That he uses these words with respect to the body of flesh, and to none other, he declares to the Corinthians manifestly, indubitably, and free from all ambiguity : " Always bearing about in our body the dying of Jesus,[6] that also the life of Jesus Christ might be manifested in our body. For if we who live are delivered unto death for Jesus' sake, it is that the life of Jesus may also be manifested in our mortal flesh." [7] And that the Spirit lays hold on the flesh, he says in the same Epistle, " That ye are the epistle of Christ, ministered by us, inscribed not with ink, but with the Spirit of the living God, not in tables of stone, but in the fleshly tables of the heart." [8] If, therefore, in the present time, fleshly hearts are made partakers of the Spirit, what is there astonishing if, in the resurrection, they receive that life which is granted by the Spirit ? Of which resurrection the apostle speaks in the Epistle to the Philippians : " Having been made conformable to His death, if by any means I might attain to the resurrection which is from the dead." [9] In what other mortal flesh, therefore, can life be understood as being manifested, unless in that substance which is also put to death on account of that confession which is made of God ?— as he has himself declared, " If, as a man, I have fought with beasts [10] at Ephesus, what advantageth it me if the dead rise not ? For if the dead rise not, neither has Christ risen. Now, if Christ has not risen, our preaching is vain, and your faith is vain. In that case, too, we are found false witnesses for God, since we have testified that He raised up Christ, whom [upon that supposition] He did not raise up.[11] For if the dead rise not, neither has Christ risen. But if Christ be not risen, your faith is vain, since ye are yet in your sins. Therefore those who have fallen asleep in Christ have perished. If in this life only we have hope in Christ, we are more miserable than all men. But now Christ has

---

[1] 1 Cor. xv. 53.
[2] Phil. iii. 29, etc.
[3] The original Greek text is preserved here, as above ; the Latin translator inserts, " in secunda ad Corinthios." Harvey observes : " The interpolation of the Scriptural reference by the translator suggests the suspicion that the greater number of such references have come in from the margin."
[4] 2 Cor. v. 4.

[5] 1 Cor. vi. 20.
[6] Agreeing with the Syriac version in omitting " the Lord " before the word " Jesus," and in reading ἀεὶ as εἰ, which Harvey considers the true text.
[7] 2 Cor. iv. 10, etc.
[8] 2 Cor. iii. 3.
[9] Phil. iii. 11.
[10] The Syriac translation seems to take a literal meaning out of this passage : " If, as one of the sons of men, I have been cast forth to the wild beasts at Ephesus."
[11] This is in accordance with the Syriac, which omits the clause, εἴπερ ἄρα νεκροὶ οὐκ ἐγείρονται.

risen from the dead, the first-fruits of those that sleep ; for as by man [came] death, by man also [came] the resurrection of the dead." [1]

5. In all these passages, therefore, as I have already said, these men must either allege that the apostle expresses opinions contradicting himself, with respect to that statement, " Flesh and blood cannot inherit the kingdom of God ; " or, on the other hand, they will be forced to make perverse and crooked interpretations of all the passages, so as to overturn and alter the sense of the words. For what sensible thing can they say, if they endeavour to interpret otherwise this which he writes : " For this corruptible must put on incorruption, and this mortal put on immortality ; " [2] and, "That the life of Jesus may be made manifest in our mortal flesh ; " [3] and all the other passages in which the apostle does manifestly and clearly declare the resurrection and incorruption of the flesh? And thus shall they be compelled to put a false interpretation upon passages such as these, they who do not choose to understand one correctly.

CHAP. XIV. — UNLESS THE FLESH WERE TO BE SAVED, THE WORD WOULD NOT HAVE TAKEN UPON HIM FLESH OF THE SAME SUBSTANCE AS OURS : FROM THIS IT WOULD FOLLOW THAT NEITHER SHOULD WE HAVE BEEN RECONCILED BY HIM.

1. And inasmuch as the apostle has not pronounced against the very substance of flesh and blood, that it cannot inherit the kingdom of God, the same apostle has everywhere adopted the term " flesh and blood " with regard to the Lord Jesus Christ, partly indeed to establish His human nature (for He did Himself speak of Himself as the Son of man), and partly that He might confirm the salvation of our flesh. For if the flesh were not in a position to be saved, the Word of God would in no wise have become flesh. And if the blood of the righteous were not to be inquired after, the Lord would certainly not have had blood [in His composition]. But inasmuch as blood cries out (*vocalis est*) from the beginning [of the world], God said to Cain, when he had slain his brother, " The voice of thy brother's blood crieth to Me." [4] And as their blood will be inquired after, He said to those with Noah, " For your blood of your souls will I require, [even] from the hand of all beasts ; " [5] and again, " Whosoever will shed man's blood,[6] it shall be shed for his blood." In like manner, too, did the Lord say to those who should afterwards shed His blood, " All

righteous blood shall be required which is shed upon the earth, from the blood of righteous Abel to the blood of Zacharias the son of Barachias, whom ye slew between the temple and the altar. Verily I say unto you, All these things shall come upon this generation." [7] He thus points out the recapitulation that should take place in his own person of the effusion of blood from the beginning, of all the righteous men and of the prophets, and that by means of Himself there should be a requisition of their blood. Now this [blood] could not be required unless it also had the capability of being saved ; nor would the Lord have summed up these things in Himself, unless He had Himself been made flesh and blood after the way of the original formation [of man], saving in his own person at the end that which had in the beginning perished in Adam.

2. But if the Lord became incarnate for any other order of things, and took flesh of any other substance, He has not then summed up human nature in His own person, nor in that case can He be termed flesh. For flesh has been truly made [to consist in] a transmission of that thing moulded originally from the dust. But if it had been necessary for Him to draw the material [of His body] from another substance, the Father would at the beginning have moulded the material [of flesh] from a different substance [than from what He actually did]. But now the case stands thus, that the Word has saved that which really was [created, viz.,] humanity which had perished, effecting by means of Himself that communion which should be held with it, and seeking out its salvation. But the thing which had perished possessed flesh and blood. For the Lord, taking dust from the earth, moulded man ; and it was upon his behalf that all the dispensation of the Lord's advent took place. He had Himself, therefore, flesh and blood, recapitulating in Himself not a certain other, but that original handiwork of the Father, seeking out that thing which had perished. And for this cause the apostle, in the Epistle to the Colossians, says, " And though ye were formerly alienated, and enemies to His knowledge by evil works, yet now ye have been reconciled in the body of His flesh, through His death, to present yourselves holy and chaste, and without fault in His sight." [8] He says, " Ye have been reconciled in the body of His flesh," because the righteous flesh has reconciled that flesh which was being kept under bondage in sin, and brought it into friendship with God.

3. If, then, any one allege that in this respect the flesh of the Lord was different from ours, because it indeed did not commit sin, neither

---

[1] 1 Cor. xv. 13, etc.
[2] 1 Cor. xv. 53.
[3] 2 Cor. iv. 11.
[4] Gen. iv. 10.
[5] Gen. ix. 5, 6, LXX.
[6] One of the MSS. reads here: Sanguis pro sanguine ejus effundetur.

[7] Matt. xxiii. 35, etc.; Luke xi. 50.
[8] Col. i. 21, etc.

was deceit found in His soul, while we, on the other hand, are sinners, he says what is the fact. But if he pretends that the Lord possessed another substance of flesh, the sayings respecting reconciliation will not agree with that man. For that thing is reconciled which had formerly been in enmity. Now, if the Lord had taken flesh from another substance, He would not, by so doing, have reconciled that one to God which had become inimical through transgression. But now, by means of communion with Himself, the Lord has reconciled man to God the Father, in reconciling us to Himself by the body of His own flesh, and redeeming us by His own blood, as the apostle says to the Ephesians, " In whom we have redemption through His blood, the remission of sins ; "[1] and again to the same he says, "Ye who formerly were far off have been brought near in the blood of Christ ; "[2] and again, "Abolishing in His flesh the enmities, [even] the law of commandments [contained] in ordinances."[3] And in every Epistle the apostle plainly testifies, that through the flesh of our Lord, and through His blood, we have been saved.

4. If, therefore, flesh and blood are the things which procure for us life, it has not been declared of flesh and blood, in the literal meaning (*proprie*) of the terms, that they cannot inherit the kingdom of God ; but [these words apply] to those carnal deeds already mentioned, which, perverting man to sin, deprive him of life. And for this reason he says, in the Epistle to the Romans : " Let not sin, therefore, reign in your mortal body, to be under its control : neither yield ye your members instruments of unrighteousness unto sin ; but yield yourselves to God, as being alive from the dead, and your members as instruments of righteousness unto God."[4] In these same members, therefore, in which we used to serve sin, and bring forth fruit unto death, does He wish us to [be obedient] unto righteousness, that we may bring forth fruit unto life. Remember, therefore, my beloved friend, that thou hast been redeemed by the flesh of our Lord, re-established[5] by His blood ; and " holding the Head, from which the whole body of the Church, having been fitted together, takes increase "[6] — that is, acknowledging the advent in the flesh of the Son of God, and [His] divinity (*deum*), and looking forward with constancy to His human nature[7] (*hominem*), availing thy-

self also of these proofs drawn from Scripture — thou dost easily overthrow, as I have pointed out, all those notions of the heretics which were concocted afterwards.

CHAP. XV. — PROOFS OF THE RESURRECTION FROM ISAIAH AND EZEKIEL ; THE SAME GOD WHO CREATED US WILL ALSO RAISE US UP.

1. Now, that He who at the beginning created man, did promise him a second birth after his dissolution into earth, Esaias thus declares : " The dead shall rise again, and they who are in the tombs shall arise, and they who are in the earth shall rejoice. For the dew which is from Thee is health to them."[8] And again : " I will comfort you, and ye shall be comforted in Jerusalem : and ye shall see, and your heart shall rejoice, and your bones shall flourish as the grass ; and the hand of the Lord shall be known to those who worship Him."[9] And Ezekiel speaks as follows : " And the hand of the LORD came upon me, and the LORD led me forth in the Spirit, and set me down in the midst of the plain, and this place was full of bones. And He caused me to pass by them round about : and, behold, there were many upon the surface of the plain very dry. And He said unto me, Son of man, can these bones live ? And I said, Lord, Thou who hast made them dost know. And He said unto me, Prophesy upon these bones, and thou shalt say to them, Ye dry bones, hear the word of the LORD. Thus saith the LORD to these bones, Behold, I will cause the spirit of life to come upon you, and I will lay sinews upon you, and bring up flesh again upon you, and I will stretch skin upon you, and will put my Spirit into you, and ye shall live ; and ye shall know that I am the LORD. And I prophesied as the Lord had commanded me. And it came to pass, when I was prophesying, that, behold, an earthquake, and the bones were drawn together, each one to its own articulation : and I beheld, and, lo, the sinews and flesh were produced upon them, and the skins rose upon them round about, but there was no breath in them. And He said unto me, Prophesy to the breath, son of man, and say to the breath, These things saith the LORD, Come from the four winds (*spiritibus*), and breathe upon these dead, that they may live. So I prophesied as the Lord had commanded me, and the breath entered into them ; and they did live, and stood upon their feet, an exceeding great gathering."[10] And again he says, "Thus saith the LORD, Behold, I will set your graves open, and cause you to come out of your graves, and bring you into the land of Israel ; and ye shall know that I am the LORD,

---

[1] Eph. i. 7.
[2] Eph. ii. 13.
[3] Eph. ii. 15.
[4] Rom. vi. 12, etc.
[5] " Et sanguine ejus redhibitus," corresponding to the Greek term ἀποκατασταθείς. " Redhibere " is properly a *forensic* term, meaning to cause any article to be restored to the vendor.
[6] Col. ii. 19.
[7] Harvey restores the Greek thus, καὶ τὸν αὐτοῦ ἄνθρωπον βεβαίως ἐκδεχόμενος, which he thinks has a reference to the patient waiting for " Christ's second advent to judge the world." The phrase might also be translated, and " receiving stedfastly His human nature."

[8] Isa. xxvi. 19.
[9] Isa. lxvi. 13.
[10] Ezek. xxxvii. 1, etc.

when I shall open your sepulchres, that I may bring my people again out of the sepulchres: and I will put my Spirit into you, and ye shall live; and I will place you in your land, and ye shall know that I am the LORD. I have said, and I will do, saith the LORD." [1] As we at once perceive that the Creator (*Demiurgo*) is in this passage represented as vivifying our dead bodies, and promising resurrection to them, and resuscitation from their sepulchres and tombs, conferring upon them immortality also (He says, "For as the tree of life, so shall their days be" [2]), He is shown to be the only God who accomplishes these things, and as Himself the good Father, benevolently conferring life upon those who have not life from themselves.

2. And for this reason did the Lord most plainly manifest Himself and the Father to His disciples, lest, forsooth, they might seek after another God besides Him who formed man, and who gave him the breath of life; and that men might not rise to such a pitch of madness as to feign another Father above the Creator. And thus also He healed by a word all the others who were in a weakly condition because of sin; to whom also He said, "Behold, thou art made whole, sin no more, lest a worse thing come upon thee:" [3] pointing out by this, that, because of the sin of disobedience, infirmities have come upon men. To that man, however, who had been blind from his birth, He gave sight, nôt by means of a word, but by an outward action; doing this not without a purpose, or because it so happened, but that He might show forth the hand of God, that which at the beginning had moulded man. And therefore, when His disciples asked Him for what cause the man had been born blind, whether for his own or his parents' fault, He replied, "Neither hath this man sinned, nor his parents, but that the works of God should be made manifest in him." [4] Now the work of God is the fashioning of man. For, as the Scripture says, He made [man] by a kind of process: "And the Lord took clay from the earth, and formed man." [5] Wherefore also the Lord spat on the ground and made clay, and smeared it upon the eyes, pointing out the original fashioning [of man], how it was effected, and manifesting the hand of God to those who can understand by what [hand] man was formed out of the dust. For that which the artificer, the Word, had omitted to form in the womb, [viz., the blind man's eyes], He then supplied in public, that the works of God might be manifested in him, in order that we might not be seeking out another hand by which man was fashioned, nor

another Father; knowing that this hand of God which formed us at the beginning, and which does form us in the womb, has in the last times sought us out who were lost, winning back His own, and taking up the lost sheep upon His shoulders, and with joy restoring it to the fold of life.

3. Now, that the Word of God forms us in the womb, He says to Jeremiah, "Before I formed thee in the womb, I knew thee; and before thou wentest forth from the belly, I sanctified thee, and appointed thee a prophet among the nations." [6] And Paul, too, says in like manner, "But when it pleased God, who separated me from my mother's womb, that I might declare Him among the nations." [7] As, therefore, we are by the Word formed in the womb, this very same Word formed the visual power in him who had been blind from his birth; showing openly who it is that fashions us in secret, since the Word Himself had been made manifest to men: and declaring the original formation of Adam, and the manner in which he was created, and by what hand he was fashioned, indicating the whole from a part. For the Lord who formed the visual powers is He who made the whole man, carrying out the will of the Father. And inasmuch as man, with respect to that formation which was after Adam, having fallen into transgression, needed the laver of regeneration, [the Lord] said to him [upon whom He had conferred sight], after He had smeared his eyes with the clay, "Go to Siloam, and wash;" [8] thus restoring to him both [his perfect] confirmation, and that regeneration which takes place by means of the laver. And for this reason when he was washed he came seeing, that he might both know Him who had fashioned him, and that man might learn [to know] Him who has conferred upon him life.

4. All the followers of Valentinus, therefore, lose their case, when they say that man was not fashioned out of this earth, but from a fluid and diffused substance. For, from the earth out of which the Lord formed eyes for that man, from the same earth it is evident that man was also fashioned at the beginning. For it were incompatible that the eyes should indeed be formed from one source and the rest of the body from another; as neither would it be compatible that one [being] fashioned the body, and another the eyes. But He, the very same who formed Adam at the beginning, with whom also the Father spake, [saying], "Let Us make man after Our image and likeness," [9] revealing Himself in these last times to men, formed visual organs (*visionem*) for him who had been blind [in

1 Ezek. xxxvii. 12, etc.
2 Isa. lxv. 22.
3 John v. 14.
4 John ix. 3.
5 Gen. ii. 7.

6 Jer. i. 5.
7 Gal. i 15.
8 John ix. 7.
9 Gen. i. 25.

that body which he had derived] from Adam. Wherefore also the Scripture, pointing out what should come to pass, says, that when Adam had hid himself because of his disobedience, the Lord came to him at eventide, called him forth, and said, "Where art thou?"[1] That means that in the last times the very same Word of God came to call man, reminding him of his doings, living in which he had been hidden from the Lord. For just as at that time God spake to Adam at eventide, searching him out; so in the last times, by means of the same voice, searching out his posterity, He has visited them.

CHAP. XVI. — SINCE OUR BODIES RETURN TO THE EARTH, IT FOLLOWS THAT THEY HAVE THEIR SUBSTANCE FROM IT; ALSO, BY THE ADVENT OF THE WORD, THE IMAGE OF GOD IN US APPEARED IN A CLEARER LIGHT.

1. And since Adam was moulded from this earth to which we belong, the Scripture tells us that God said to him, "In the sweat of thy face shalt thou eat thy bread, until thou turnest again to the dust from whence thou wert taken."[2] If then, after death, our bodies return to any other substance, it follows that from it also they have their substance. But if it be into this very [earth], it is manifest that it was also from it that man's frame was created; as also the Lord clearly showed, when from this very substance He formed eyes for the man [to whom He gave sight]. And thus was the hand of God plainly shown forth, by which Adam was fashioned, and we too have been formed; and since there is one and the same Father, whose voice from the beginning even to the end is present with His handiwork, and the substance from which we were formed is plainly declared through the Gospel, we should therefore not seek after another Father besides Him, nor [look for] another substance from which we have been formed, besides what was mentioned beforehand, and shown forth by the Lord; nor another hand of God besides that which, from the beginning even to the end, forms us and prepares us for life, and is present with His handiwork, and perfects it after the image and likeness of God.

2. And then, again, this Word was manifested when the Word of God was made man, assimilating Himself to man, and man to Himself, so that by means of his resemblance to the Son, man might become precious to the Father. For in times long past, it was *said* that man was created after the image of God, but it was not [actually] *shown;* for the Word was as yet invisible, after whose image man was created. Wherefore also he did easily lose the similitude. When, however, the Word of God became flesh, He

confirmed both these: for He both showed forth the image truly, since He became Himself what was His image; and He re-established the similitude after a sure manner, by assimilating man to the invisible Father through means of the visible Word.

3. And not by the aforesaid things alone has the Lord manifested Himself, but [He has done this] also by means of His passion. For doing away with [the effects of] that disobedience of man which had taken place at the beginning by the occasion of a tree, "He became obedient unto death, even the death of the cross;"[3] rectifying that disobedience which had occurred by reason of a tree, through that obedience which was [wrought out] upon the tree [of the cross]. Now He would not have come to do away, by means of that same [image], the disobedience which had been incurred towards our Maker if He proclaimed another Father. But inasmuch as it was by these things that we disobeyed God, and did not give credit to His word, so was it also by these same that He brought in obedience and consent as respects His Word; by which things He clearly shows forth God Himself, whom indeed we had offended in the first Adam, when he did not perform His commandment. In the second Adam, however, we are reconciled, being made obedient even unto death. For we were debtors to none other but to Him whose commandment we had transgressed at the beginning.

CHAP. XVII. — THERE IS BUT ONE LORD AND ONE GOD, THE FATHER AND CREATOR OF ALL THINGS, WHO HAS LOVED US IN CHRIST, GIVEN US COMMANDMENTS, AND REMITTED OUR SINS; WHOSE SON AND WORD CHRIST PROVED HIMSELF TO BE, WHEN HE FORGAVE OUR SINS.

1. Now this being is the Creator (*Demiurgus*), who is, in respect of His love, the Father; but in respect of His power, He is Lord; and in respect of His wisdom, our Maker and Fashioner; by transgressing whose commandment we became His enemies. And therefore in the last times the Lord has restored us into friendship through His incarnation, having become "the Mediator between God and men;"[4] propitiating indeed for us the Father against whom we had sinned, and cancelling (*consolatus*) our disobedience by His own obedience; conferring also upon us the gift of communion with, and subjection to, our Maker. For this reason also He has taught us to say in prayer, "And forgive us our debts;"[5] since indeed He is our Father, whose debtors we were, having transgressed His commandments. But who is this Being? Is He some unknown one, and a Father who gives no com-

---

[1] Gen. iii. 9.
[2] Gen. iii. 19.

[3] Phil. ii. 8.
[4] 1 Tim. ii. 5.
[5] Matt. vi. 12.

mandment to any one? Or is He the God who is proclaimed in the Scriptures, to whom we were debtors, having transgressed His commandment? Now the commandment was given to man by the Word. For Adam, it is said, "heard the voice of the LORD God." [1] Rightly then does His Word say to man, "Thy sins are forgiven thee;" [2] He, the same against whom we had sinned in the beginning, grants forgiveness of sins in the end. But if indeed we had disobeyed the command of any other, while it was a different being who said, "Thy sins are forgiven thee;" [2] such an one is neither good, nor true, nor just. For how can he be good, who does not give from what belongs to himself? Or how can he be just, who snatches away the goods of another? And in what way can sins be truly remitted, unless that He against whom we have sinned has Himself granted remission "through the bowels of mercy of our God," in which "He has visited us" [3] through His Son?

2. And therefore, when He had healed the man sick of the palsy, [the evangelist] says: "The people upon seeing it glorified God, who gave such power unto men." [4] What God, then, did the bystanders glorify? Was it indeed that unknown Father invented by the heretics? And how could they glorify him who was altogether unknown to them? It is evident, therefore, that the Israelites glorified Him who has been proclaimed as God by the law and the prophets, who is also the Father of our Lord; and therefore He taught men, by the evidence of their senses through those signs which He accomplished, to give glory to God. If, however, He Himself had come from another Father, and men glorified a different Father when they beheld His miracles, He [in that case] rendered the mungrateful to that Father who had sent the gift of healing. But as the only-begotten Son had come for man's salvation from Him who is God, He did both stir up the incredulous by the miracles which He was in the habit of working, to give glory to the Father; and to the Pharisees, who did not admit the advent of His Son, and who consequently did not believe in the remission [of sins] which was conferred by Him, He said, "That ye may know that the Son of man hath power to forgive sins." [5] And when He had said this, He commanded the paralytic man to take up the pallet upon which he was lying, and go into his house. By this work of His He confounded the unbelievers, and showed that He is Himself the voice of God, by which man received commandments, which he broke, and became a sinner; for the paralysis followed as a consequence of sins.

3. Therefore, by remitting sins, He did indeed heal man, while He also manifested Himself who He was. For if no one can forgive sins but God alone, while the Lord remitted them and healed men, it is plain that He was Himself the Word of God made the Son of man, receiving from the Father the power of remission of sins; since He was man, and since He was God, in order that since as man He suffered for us, so as God He might have compassion on us, and forgive us our debts, in which we were made debtors to God our Creator. And therefore David said beforehand, "Blessed are they whose iniquities are forgiven, and whose sins are covered. Blessed is the man to whom the LORD has not imputed sin;" [6] pointing out thus that remission of sins which follows upon His advent, by which "He has destroyed the handwriting" of our debt, and "fastened it to the cross;" [7] so that as by means of a tree we were made debtors to God, [so also] by means of a tree we may obtain the remission of our debt.

3. This fact has been strikingly set forth by many others, and especially through means of Elisha the prophet. For when his fellow-prophets were hewing wood for the construction of a tabernacle, and when the iron [head], shaken loose from the axe, had fallen into the Jordan and could not be found by them, upon Elisha's coming to the place, and learning what had happened, he threw some wood into the water. Then, when he had done this, the iron part of the axe floated up, and they took up from the surface of the water what they had previously lost. [8] By this action the prophet pointed out that the sure word of God, which we had negligently lost by means of a tree, and were not in the way of finding again, we should receive anew by the dispensation of a tree, [viz., the cross of Christ]. For that the word of God is likened to an axe, John the Baptist declares [when he says] in reference to it, "But now also is the axe laid to the root of the trees." [9] Jeremiah also says to the same purport: "The word of God cleaveth the rock as an axe." [10] This word, then, what was hidden from us, did the dispensation of the tree make manifest, as I have already remarked. For as we lost it by means of a tree, by means of a tree again was it made manifest to all, showing the height, the length, the breadth, the depth in itself; and, as a certain man among our predecessors observed, "Through the extension of the hands of a divine person," gathering together the two peoples to one God."

---

[1] Gen. iii. 8.
[2] Matt. ix. 2: Luke v. 20.
[3] Luke i. 78.
[4] Matt. ix. 8.
[5] Matt. ix. 6.

[6] Ps. xxxii. 1, 2.
[7] Col. ii. 14.
[8] 2 Kings vi. 6.
[9] Matt. iii. 10.
[10] Jer. xxiii. 29.
[11] The Greek is preserved here, and reads, διὰ τῆς θείας ἐκτάσεως τῶν χειρῶν — literally, "through the divine extension of hands." The old Latin merely reads, "per extensionem manuum."

For these were two hands, because there were two peoples scattered to the ends of the earth ; but there was one head in the middle, as there is but one God, who is above all, and through all, and in us all.

CHAP. XVIII. — GOD THE FATHER AND HIS WORD HAVE FORMED ALL CREATED THINGS (WHICH THEY USE) BY THEIR OWN POWER AND WISDOM, NOT OUT OF DEFECT OR IGNORANCE. THE SON OF GOD, WHO RECEIVED ALL POWER FROM THE FATHER, WOULD OTHERWISE NEVER HAVE TAKEN FLESH UPON HIM.

1. And such or so important a dispensation He did not bring about by means of the creations of others, but by His own ; neither by those things which were created out of ignorance and defect, but by those which had their substance from the wisdom and power of His Father. For He was neither unrighteous, so that He should covet the property of another ; nor needy, that He could not by His own means impart life to His own, and make use of His own creation for the salvation of man. For indeed the creation could not have sustained Him [on the cross], if He had sent forth [simply by commission] what was the fruit of ignorance and defect. Now we have repeatedly shown that the incarnate Word of God was suspended upon a tree, and even the very heretics do acknowledge that He was crucified. How, then, could the fruit of ignorance and defect sustain Him who contains the knowledge of all things, and is true and perfect ? Or how could that creation which was concealed from the Father, and far removed from Him, have sustained His Word ? And if this world were made by the angels (it matters not whether we suppose their ignorance or their cognizance of the Supreme God), when the Lord declared, "For I am in the Father, and the Father in Me," [1] how could this workmanship of the angels have borne to be burdened at once with the Father and the Son ? How, again, could that creation which is beyond the Pleroma have contained Him who contains the entire Pleroma ? Inasmuch, then, as all these things are impossible and incapable of proof, that preaching of the Church is alone true [which proclaims] that His own creation bare Him, which subsists by the power, the skill, and the wisdom of God ; which is sustained, indeed, after an invisible manner by the Father, but, on the contrary, after a visible manner it bore His Word : and this is the true [Word].

2. For the Father bears the creation and His own Word simultaneously, and the Word borne by the Father grants the Spirit to all as the Father wills.[2] To some He gives after the manner of creation what is made ; [3] but to others [He gives] after the manner of adoption, that is, what is from God, namely generation. And thus one God the Father is declared, who is above all, and through all, and in all. The Father is indeed above all, and He is the Head of Christ ; but the Word is through all things, and is Himself the Head of the Church ; while the Spirit is in us all, and He is the living water,[4] which the Lord grants to those who rightly believe in Him, and love Him, and who know that "there is one Father, who is above all, and through all, and in us all." [5] And to these things does John also, the disciple of the Lord, bear witness, when he speaks thus in the Gospel : "In the beginning was the Word, and the Word was with God, and the Word was God. This was in the beginning with God. All things were made by Him, and without Him was nothing made." [6] And then he said of the Word Himself : "He was in the world, and the world was made by Him, and the world knew Him not. To His own things He came, and His own people received Him not. However, as many as did receive Him, to these gave He power to become the sons of God, to those that believe in His name." [7] And again, showing the dispensation with regard to His human nature, John said : "And the Word was made flesh, and dwelt among us." [8] And in continuation he says, "And we beheld His glory, the glory as of the Only-begotten by the Father, full of grace and truth." He thus plainly points out to those willing to hear, that is, to those having ears, that there is one God, the Father over all, and one Word of God, who is through all, by whom all things have been made ; and that this world belongs to Him, and was made by Him, according to the Father's will, and not by angels ; nor by apostasy, defect, and ignorance ; nor by any power of Prunicus, whom certain of them also call " the Mother ; " nor by any other maker of the world ignorant of the Father.

3. For the Creator of the world is truly the Word of God : and this is our Lord, who in the last times was made man, existing in this world, and who in an invisible manner contains all things created, and is inherent in the entire creation, since the Word of God governs and arranges all

---

[2] From this passage Harvey infers that Irenæus held the procession of the Holy Spirit from the Father and the Son, — a doctrine denied by the Oriental Church in after times. [Here is nothing about the " procession: " only the " mission " of the Spirit is here concerned. And the Easterns object to the double procession itself olny in so far as any one means thereby to deny " quod solus Pater est divinarum personarum, Principium et Fons," — ῥίζα καὶ πηγή. See Procopowicz, *De Processione*, Gothæ, 1772].

[3] Grabe and Harvey insert the words, " quod est conditionis," but on slender authority.

[4] John vii. 39.

[5] Eph. iv. 6.

[6] John i. 1, etc.

[7] John i. 10, etc.

[8] John i. 14.

[1] John xiv. 11.

things; and therefore He came to His own in a visible [1] manner, and was made flesh, and hung upon the tree, that He might sum up all things in Himself. "And His own peculiar people did not receive Him," as Moses declared this very thing among the people : "And thy life shall be hanging before thine eyes, and thou wilt not believe thy life." [2] Those therefore who did not receive Him did not receive life. "But to as many as received Him, to them gave He power to become the sons of God." [3] For it is He who has power from the Father over all things, since He is the Word of God, and very man, communicating with invisible beings after the manner of the intellect, and appointing a law observable to the outward senses, that all things should continue each in its own order; and He reigns manifestly over things visible and pertaining to men; and brings in just judgment and worthy upon all; as David also, clearly pointing to this, says, "Our God shall openly come, and will not keep silence." [4] Then he shows also the judgment which is brought in by Him, saying, "A fire shall burn in His sight, and a strong tempest shall rage round about Him. He shall call upon the heaven from above, and the earth, to judge His people."

CHAP. XIX. — A COMPARISON IS INSTITUTED BETWEEN THE DISOBEDIENT AND SINNING EVE AND THE VIRGIN MARY, HER PATRONESS. VARIOUS AND DISCORDANT HERESIES ARE MENTIONED.

1. That the Lord then was manifestly coming to His own things, and was sustaining them by means of that creation which is supported by Himself, and was making a recapitulation of that disobedience which had occurred in connection with a tree, through the obedience which was [exhibited by Himself when He hung] upon a tree, [the effects] also of that deception being done away with, by which that virgin Eve, who was already espoused to a man, was unhappily misled,—was happily announced, through means of the truth [spoken] by the angel to the Virgin Mary, who was [also espoused] to a man. [5] For just as the former was led astray by the word of an angel, so that she fled from God when she had transgressed His word; so did the latter, by an angelic communication, receive the glad tidings that she should sustain (*portaret*) God, being obedient to His word. And if the former did disobey God, yet the latter was persuaded to be obedient to God, in order that the Virgin Mary might become the patroness [6] (*advocata*)

of the virgin Eve. And thus, as the human race fell into bondage to death by means of a virgin, so is it rescued by a virgin; virginal disobedience having been balanced in the opposite scale by virginal obedience. For in the same way the sin of the first created man (*protoplasti*) receives amendment by the correction of the First-begotten, and the coming of the serpent is conquered by the harmlessness of the dove, those bonds being unloosed by which we had been fast bound to death.

2. The heretics being all unlearned and ignorant of God's arrangements, and not acquainted with that dispensation by which He took upon Him human nature (*inscii ejus quæ est secundum hominem dispensationis*), inasmuch as they blind themselves with regard to the truth, do in fact speak against their own salvation. Some of them introduce another Father besides the Creator; some, again, say that the world and its substance was made by certain angels; certain others [maintain] that it was widely separated by Horos [7] from him whom they represent as being the Father—that it sprang forth (*floruisse*) of itself, and from itself was born. Then, again, others [of them assert] that it obtained substance in those things which are contained by the Father, from defect and ignorance; others still, despise the advent of the Lord manifest [to the senses], for they do not admit His incarnation; while others, ignoring the arrangement [that He should be born] of a virgin, maintain that He was begotten by Joseph. And still further, some affirm that neither their soul nor their body can receive eternal life, but merely the inner man. Moreover, they will have it that this [inner man] is that which is the understanding (*sensum*) in them, and which they decree as being the only thing to ascend to "the perfect." Others [maintain], as I have said in the first book, that while the soul is saved, their body does not participate in the salvation which comes from God; in which [book] I have also set forward the hypotheses of all these men, and in the second have pointed out their weakness and inconsistency.

CHAP. XX. — THOSE PASTORS ARE TO BE HEARD TO WHOM THE APOSTLES COMMITTED THE CHURCHES, POSSESSING ONE AND THE SAME DOCTRINE OF SALVATION ; THE HERETICS, ON THE OTHER HAND, ARE TO BE AVOIDED. WE MUST THINK SOBERLY WITH REGARD TO THE MYSTERIES OF THE FAITH.

1. Now all these [heretics] are of much later date than the bishops to whom the apostles committed the Churches; which fact I have in the third book taken all pains to demonstrate. It follows, then, as a matter of course, that these

---

[1] The text reads "invisibiliter," which seems clearly an error.
[2] Deut. xxviii. 66.
[3] John i. 13.
[4] Ps. l. 3, 4.
[5] The text is here most uncertain and obscure.
[6] [This word *patroness* is ambiguous. The Latin may stand for Gr. ἀντίληψις, — a person called in to help, or to take hold of the other end of a burden. The argument implies that Mary was thus the counterpart or balance of Eve.]

[7] The text reads "porro," which makes no sense; so that Harvey looks upon it as a corruption of the reading "per Horum."

heretics aforementioned, since they are blind to the truth, and deviate from the [right] way, will walk in various roads; and therefore the footsteps of their doctrine are scattered here and there without agreement or connection. But the path of those belonging to the Church circumscribes the whole world, as possessing the sure tradition from the apostles, and gives unto us to see that the faith of all is one and the same, since all receive one and the same God the Father, and believe in the same dispensation regarding the incarnation of the Son of God, and are cognizant of the same gift of the Spirit, and are conversant with the same commandments, and preserve the same form of ecclesiastical constitution,[1] and expect the same advent of the Lord, and await the same salvation of the complete man, that is, of the soul and body. And undoubtedly the preaching of the Church is true and stedfast, in which one and the same way of salvation is shown throughout the whole world. For to her is entrusted the light of God; and therefore the "wisdom" of God, by means of which she saves all men, " is declared in [its] going forth; it uttereth [its voice] faithfully in the streets, is preached on the tops of the walls, and speaks continually in the gates of the city."[3] For the Church preaches the truth everywhere, and she is the seven-branched candlestick which bears the light of Christ.

2. Those, therefore, who desert the preaching of the Church, call in question the knowledge of the holy presbyters, not taking into consideration of how much greater consequence is a religious man, even in a private station, than a blasphemous and impudent sophist.[4] Now, such are all the heretics, and those who imagine that they have hit upon something more beyond the truth, so that by following those things already mentioned, proceeding on their way variously, inharmoniously, and foolishly, not keeping always to the same opinions with regard to the same things, as blind men are led by the blind, they shall deservedly fall into the ditch of ignorance lying in their path, ever seeking and never finding out the truth.[5] It behoves us, therefore, to avoid their doctrines, and to take careful heed lest we suffer any injury from them; but to flee to the Church, and be brought up in her bosom, and be nourished with the Lord's Scriptures. For the Church has been planted as a garden (*paradisus*) in this world; therefore says the Spirit of God, "Thou mayest freely eat from every tree of the

garden,"[6] that is, Eat ye from every Scripture of the Lord; but ye shall not eat with an uplifted mind, nor touch any heretical discord. For these men do profess that they have themselves the knowledge of good and evil; and they set their own impious minds above the God who made them. They therefore form opinions on what is beyond the limits of the understanding. For this cause also the apostle says, "Be not wise beyond what it is fitting to be wise, but be wise prudently,"[7] that we be not cast forth by eating of the "knowledge" of these men (that knowledge which knows more than it should do) from the paradise of life. Into this paradise the Lord has introduced those who obey His call, "summing up in Himself all things which are in heaven, and which are on earth;"[8] but the things in heaven are spiritual, while those on earth constitute the dispensation in human nature (*secundum hominem est dispositio*). These things, therefore, He recapitulated in Himself: by uniting man to the Spirit, and causing the Spirit to dwell in man, He is Himself made the head of the Spirit, and gives the Spirit to be the head of man: for through Him (the Spirit) we see, and hear, and speak.

CHAP. XXI. — CHRIST IS THE HEAD OF ALL THINGS ALREADY MENTIONED. IT WAS FITTING THAT HE SHOULD BE SENT BY THE FATHER, THE CREATOR OF ALL THINGS, TO ASSUME HUMAN NATURE, AND SHOULD BE TEMPTED BY SATAN, THAT HE MIGHT FULFIL THE PROMISES, AND CARRY OFF A GLORIOUS AND PERFECT VICTORY.

1. He has therefore, in His work of recapitulation, summed up all things, both waging war against our enemy, and crushing him who had at the beginning led us away captives in Adam, and trampled upon his head, as thou canst perceive in Genesis that God said to the serpent, " And I will put enmity between thee and the woman, and between thy seed and her seed; He shall be on the watch for (*observabit*[9]) thy head, and thou on the watch for His heel."[10] For from that time, He who should be born of a woman, [namely] from the Virgin, after the likeness of Adam, was preached as keeping watch for the head of the serpent. This is the seed of which the apostle says in the Epistle to the Galatians, " that the law of works was established until the seed should come to whom the promise was made."[11] This fact is exhibited in a still clearer light in the same Epistle, where he thus speaks: " But when the fulness of time was come, God

---

[1] " Et eandem figuram ejus quæ est erga ecclesiam ordinationis custodientibus." Grabe supposes this refers to the ordained ministry of the Church, but Harvey thinks it refers more probably to its general constitution.
[2] [He thus outlines the creed, and epitomizes " the faith once delivered to the saints," as all that is requisite to salvation.]
[3] Prov. i. 20, 21.
[4] That is, the private Christian as contrasted with the sophist of the schools.
[5] 2 Tim. iii. 7.

[6] Gen. ii. 16.
[7] Rom. xii. 3.
[8] Eph. i. 10.
[9] τηρήσει and τερέσει have probably been confounded.
[10] Gen. iii. 15.
[11] Gal. iii. 19.

sent forth His Son, made of a woman."[1] For indeed the enemy would not have been fairly vanquished, unless it had been a man [born] of a woman who conquered him. For it was by means of a woman that he got the advantage over man at first, setting himself up as man's opponent. And therefore does the Lord profess Himself to be the Son of man, comprising in Himself that original man out of whom the woman was fashioned (*ex quo ea quæ secundum mulierem est plasmatio facta est*), in order that, as our species went down to death through a vanquished man, so we may ascend to life again through a victorious one ; and as through a man death received the palm [of victory] against us, so again by a man we may receive the palm against death.

2. Now the Lord would not have recapitulated in Himself that ancient and primary enmity against the serpent, fulfilling the promise of the Creator (*Demiurgi*), and performing His command, if He had come from another Father. But as He is one and the same, who formed us at the beginning, and sent His Son at the end, the Lord did perform His command, being made of a woman, by both destroying our adversary, and perfecting man after the image and likeness of God. And for this reason He did not draw the means of confounding him from any other source than from the words of the law, and made use of the Father's commandment as a help towards the destruction and confusion of the apostate angel. Fasting forty days, like Moses and Elias, He afterwards hungered, first, in order that we may perceive that He was a real and substantial man — for it belongs to a man to suffer hunger when fasting ; and secondly, that His opponent might have an opportunity of attacking Him. For as at the beginning it was by means of food that [the enemy] persuaded man, although not suffering hunger, to transgress God's commandments, so in the end he did not succeed in persuading Him that .was an hungered to take that food which proceeded from God. For, when tempting Him, he said, "If thou be the Son of God, command that these stones be made bread."[2] But the Lord repulsed him by the commandment of the law, saying, "It is written, Man doth not live by bread alone."[3] As to those words [of His enemy,] "If thou be the Son of God," [the Lord] made no remark ; but by thus acknowledging His human nature He baffled His adversary, and exhausted the force of his first attack by means of His Father's word. The corruption of man, therefore, which occurred in paradise by both [of our first parents] eating, was done away with by [the Lord's] want of food in this world.[4] But he, being thus vanquished by the law, endeavoured again to make an assault by himself quoting a commandment of the law. For, bringing Him to the highest pinnacle of the temple, he said to Him, "If thou art the Son of God, cast thyself down. For it is written, That God shall give His angels charge concerning thee, and in their hands they shall bear thee up, lest perchance thou dash thy foot against a stone ; "[5] thus concealing a falsehood under the guise of Scripture, as is done by all the heretics. For that was indeed written, [namely], "That He hath given His angels charge concerning Him ; " but "cast thyself down from hence " no Scripture said in reference to Him : this kind of persuasion the devil produced from himself. The Lord therefore confuted him out of the law, when He said, " It is written again, Thou shalt not tempt the LORD thy God ; "[6] pointing out by the word contained in the law that which is the duty of man, that he should not tempt God ; and in regard to Himself, since He appeared in human form, [declaring] that He would not tempt the LORD his God.[7] The pride of reason, therefore, which was in the serpent, was put to nought by the humility found in the man [Christ] , and now twice was the devil conquered from Scripture, when he was detected as advising things contrary to God's commandment, and was shown to be the enemy of God by [the expression of] his thoughts. He then, having been thus signally defeated, and then, as it were, concentrating his forces, drawing up in order all his available power for falsehood, in the third place " showed Him all the kingdoms of the world, and the glory of them,"[8] saying, as Luke relates, " All these will I give thee, — for they are delivered to me ; and to whom I will, I give them, — if thou wilt fall down and worship me." The Lord then, exposing him in his true character, says, " Depart, Satan ; for it is written, Thou shalt worship the Lord thy God, and Him only shalt thou serve."[9] He both revealed him by this name, and showed [at the same time] who He Himself was. For the Hebrew word " Satan " signifies an apostate. And thus, vanquishing him for the third time, He spurned him from Him finally as being conquered out of the law ; and there was done away with that infringement of God's commandment which had occurred in Adam, by means of the precept of the law, which the Son of man ob-

---

[4] The Latin of this obscure sentence is: Quæ ergo fuit in Paradiso repletio hominis per duplicem gustationem, dissoluta est per eam, quæ fuit in hoc mundo, indigentiam. Harvey thinks that *repletio* is an error of the translation reading ἀναπλήρωσις for ἀναπήρωσις. This conjecture is adopted above.
[5] Ps. lxxxix. 11.
[6] Deut. vi. 16.
[7] This sentence is one of great obscurity.
[8] Luke iv. 6, 7.
[9] Matt. iv. 10.

---

[1] Gal. iv. 4.
[2] Matt. iv. 3.
[3] Deut. viii. 3.

served, who did not transgress the commandment of God.

3. Who, then, is this Lord God to whom Christ bears witness, whom no man shall tempt, whom all should worship, and serve Him alone? It is, beyond all manner of doubt, that God who also gave the law. For these things had been predicted in the law, and by the words (*sententiam*) of the law the Lord showed that the law does indeed declare the Word of God from the Father ; and the apostate angel of God is destroyed by its voice, being exposed in his true colours, and vanquished by the Son of man keeping the commandment of God. For as in the beginning he enticed man to transgress his Maker's law, and thereby got him into his power; yet his power consists in transgression and apostasy, and with these he bound man [to himself] ; so again, on the other hand, it was necessary that through man himself he should, when conquered, be bound with the same chains with which he had bound man, in order that man, being set free, might return to his Lord, leaving to him (Satan) those bonds by which he himself had been fettered, that is, sin. For when Satan is bound, man is set free; since "none can enter a strong man's house and spoil his goods, unless he first bind the strong man himself." [1] The Lord therefore exposes him as speaking contrary to the word of that God who made all things, and subdues him by means of the commandment. Now the law is the commandment of God. The Man proves him to be a fugitive from and a transgressor of the law, an apostate also from God. After [the Man had done this], the Word bound him securely as a fugitive from Himself, and made spoil of his goods, — namely, those men whom he held in bondage, and whom he unjustly used for his own purposes. And justly indeed is he led captive, who had led men unjustly into bondage ; while man, who had been led captive in times past, was rescued from the grasp of his possessor, according to the tender mercy of God the Father, who had compassion on His own handiwork, and gave to it salvation, restoring it by means of the Word — that is, by Christ — in order that men might learn by actual proof that he receives incorruptibility not of himself, but by the free gift of God.

CHAP. XXII. — THE TRUE LORD AND THE ONE GOD IS DECLARED BY THE LAW, AND MANIFESTED BY CHRIST HIS SON IN THE GOSPEL ; WHOM ALONE WE SHOULD ADORE, AND FROM HIM WE MUST LOOK FOR ALL GOOD THINGS, NOT FROM SATAN.

1. Thus then does the Lord plainly show that it was the true Lord and the one God who had been set forth by the law; for Him whom the law proclaimed as God, the same did Christ point out as the Father, whom also it behoves the disciples of Christ alone to serve. By means of the statements of the law, He put our adversary to utter confusion ; and the law directs us to praise God the Creator (*Demiurgum*), and to serve Him alone. Since this is the case, we must not seek for another Father besides Him, or above Him, since there is one God who justifies the circumcision by faith, and the uncircumcision through faith. [2] For if there were any other perfect Father above Him, He (Christ) would by no means have overthrown Satan by means of His words and commandments. For one ignorance cannot be done away with by means of another ignorance, any more than one defect by another defect. If, therefore, the law is due to ignorance and defect, how could the statements contained therein bring to nought the ignorance of the devil, and conquer the strong man? For a strong man can be conquered neither by an inferior nor by an equal, but by one possessed of greater power. But the Word of God is the superior above all, He who is loudly proclaimed in the law : "Hear, O Israel, the LORD thy God is one God ; " and, "Thou shalt love the LORD thy God with all thy heart ; " and, "Him shalt thou adore, and Him alone shalt thou serve." [3] Then in the Gospel, casting down the apostasy by means of these expressions, He did both overcome the strong man by His Father's voice, and He acknowledges the commandment of the law to express His own sentiments, when He says, "Thou shalt not tempt the LORD thy God." [4] For He did not confound the adversary by the saying of any other, but by that belonging to His own Father, and thus overcame the strong man.

2. He taught by His commandment that we who have been set free should, when hungry, take that food which is given by God ; and that, when placed in the exalted position of every grace [that can be received], we should not, either by trusting to works of righteousness, or when adorned with super-eminent [gifts of] ministration, by any means be lifted up with pride, nor should we tempt God, but should feel humility in all things, and have ready to hand [this saying], "Thou shalt not tempt the LORD thy God." [5] As also the apostle taught, saying, "Minding not high things, but consenting to things of low estate ; " [6] that we should neither be ensnared with riches, nor mundane glory, nor present fancy, but should know that we must "worship the LORD thy God, and serve Him alone," and

---

[1] Matt. xii. 29 and Mark iii. 27.

[2] Rom. iii. 30.
[3] Deut. vi. 4, 5, 13.
[4] Matt. iv. 7.
[5] Deut. vi. 16.
[6] Rom. xii. 16.

give no heed to him who falsely promised things not his own, when he said, " All these will I give thee, if, falling down, thou wilt worship me." For he himself confesses that to adore him, and to do his will, is to fall from the glory of God. And in what thing either pleasant or good can that man who has fallen participate? Or what else can such a person hope for or expect, except death? For death is next neighbour to him who has fallen. Hence also it follows that he will not give what he has promised. For how can he make grants to him who has fallen? Moreover, since God rules over men and him too, and without the will of our Father in heaven not even a sparrow falls to the ground,[1] it follows that his declaration, " All these things are delivered unto me, and to whomsoever I will I give them," proceeds from him when puffed up with pride. For the creation is not subjected to his power, since indeed he is himself but one among created things. Nor shall he give away the rule over men to men; but both all other things, and all human affairs, are arranged according to God the Father's disposal. Besides, the Lord declares that " the devil is a liar from the beginning, and the truth is not in him." [2] If then he be a liar, and the truth be not in him, he certainly did not speak truth, but a lie, when he said, " For all these things are delivered to me, and to whomsoever I will I give them." [3]

CHAP. XXIII. — THE DEVIL IS WELL PRACTISED IN FALSEHOOD, BY WHICH ADAM HAVING BEEN LED ASTRAY, SINNED ON THE SIXTH DAY OF THE CREATION, IN WHICH DAY ALSO HE HAS BEEN RENEWED BY CHRIST.

1. He had indeed been already accustomed to lie against God, for the purpose of leading men astray. For at the beginning, when God had given to man a variety of things for food, while He commanded him not to eat of one tree only, as the Scripture tells us that God said to Adam : " From every tree which is in the garden thou shalt eat food ; but from the tree of knowledge of good and evil, from this ye shall not eat : for in the day that ye shall eat of it, ye shall die by death ; " [4] he then, lying against the Lord, tempted man, as the Scripture says that the serpent said to the woman : " Has God indeed said this, Ye shall not eat from every tree of the garden?" [5] And when she had exposed the falsehood, and simply related the command, as He had said, " From every tree of the garden we shall eat ; but of the fruit of the tree which is in the midst of the garden, God hath said, Ye shall not eat of it, neither shall ye touch it, lest

ye die : " [6] when he had [thus] learned from the woman the command of God, having brought his cunning into play, he finally deceived her by a falsehood, saying, " Ye shall not die by death ; for God knew that in the day ye shall eat of it your eyes shall be opened, and ye shall be as gods, knowing good and evil." [7] In the first place, then, in the garden of God he disputed about God, as if God was not there, for he was ignorant of the greatness of God ; and then, in the next place, after he had learned from the woman that God had said that they should die if they tasted the aforesaid tree, opening his mouth, he uttered the third falsehood, " Ye shall not die by death." But that God was true, and the serpent a liar, was proved by the result, death having passed upon them who had eaten. For along with the fruit they did also fall under the power of death, because they did eat in disobedience ; and disobedience to God entails death. Wherefore, as they became forfeit to death, from that [moment] they were handed over to it.

2. Thus, then, in the day that they did eat, in the same did they die, and became death's debtors, since it was one day of the creation. For it is said, " There was made in the evening, and there was made in the morning, one day." Now in this same day that they did eat, in that also did they die. But according to the cycle and progress of the days, after which one is termed first, another second, and another third, if anybody seeks diligently to learn upon what day out of the seven it was that Adam died, he will find it by examining the dispensation of the Lord. For by summing up in Himself the whole human race from the beginning to the end, He has also summed up its death. From this it is clear that the Lord suffered death, in obedience to His Father, upon that day on which Adam died while he disobeyed God. Now he died on the same day in which he did eat. For God said, " In that day on which ye shall eat of it, ye shall die by death." The Lord, therefore, recapitulating in Himself this day, underwent His sufferings upon the day preceding the Sabbath, that is, the sixth day of the creation, on which day man was created ; thus granting him a second creation by means of His passion, which is that [creation] out of death. And there are some, again, who relegate the death of Adam to the thousandth year ; for since " a day of the Lord is as a thousand years," [8] he did not overstep the thousand years, but died within them, thus bearing out the sentence of his sin. Whether, therefore, with respect to disobedience, which is death ; whether

---

[1] Matt. x. 29.
[2] John viii. 44.
[3] Luke iv. 6.
[4] Gen. ii. 16, 17.
[5] Gen. iii. 1.

[6] Gen. iii. 2, 3.
[7] Gen. iii. 4.
[8] 2 Pet. iii. 8.

[we consider] that, on account of that, they were delivered over to death, and made debtors to it; whether with respect to [the fact that on] one and the same day on which they ate they also died (for it is one day of the creation); whether [we regard this point], that, with respect to this cycle of days, they died on the day in which they did also eat, that is, the day of the preparation, which is termed "the pure supper," that is, the sixth day of the feast, which the Lord also exhibited when He suffered on that day; or whether [we reflect] that he (Adam) did not overstep the thousand years, but died within their limit, — it follows that, in regard to all these significations, God is indeed true. For they died who tasted of the tree; and the serpent is proved a liar and a murderer, as the Lord said of him: "For he is a murderer from the beginning, and the truth is not in him."[1]

CHAP. XXIV. — OF THE CONSTANT FALSEHOOD OF THE DEVIL, AND OF THE POWERS AND GOVERNMENTS OF THE WORLD, WHICH WE OUGHT TO OBEY, INASMUCH AS THEY ARE APPOINTED OF GOD, NOT OF THE DEVIL.

1. As therefore the devil lied at the beginning, so did he also in the end, when he said, "All these are delivered unto me, and to whomsoever I will I give them."[2] For it is not he who has appointed the kingdoms of this world, but God; for "the heart of the king is in the hand of God."[3] And the Word also says by Solomon, "By me kings do reign, and princes administer justice. By me chiefs are raised up, and by me kings rule the earth."[4] Paul the apostle also says upon this same subject: "Be ye subject to all the higher powers; for there is no power but of God: now those which are have been ordained of God."[5] And again, in reference to them he says, "For he beareth not the sword in vain; for he is the minister of God, the avenger for wrath to him who does evil."[6] Now, that he spake these words, not in regard to angelical powers, nor of invisible rulers — as some venture to expound the passage — but of those of actual human authorities, [he shows when] he says, "For this cause pay ye tribute also: for they are God's ministers, doing service for this very thing."[7] This also the Lord confirmed, when He did not do what He was tempted to by the devil; but He gave directions that tribute should be paid to the tax-gatherers for Himself and Peter;[8] because "they are

the ministers of God, serving for this very thing."

2. For since man, by departing from God, reached such a pitch of fury as even to look upon his brother as his enemy, and engaged without fear in every kind of restless conduct, and murder, and avarice; God imposed upon mankind the fear of man, as they did not acknowledge the fear of God, in order that, being subjected to the authority of men, and kept under restraint by their laws, they might attain to some degree of justice, and exercise mutual forbearance through dread of the sword suspended full in their view, as the apostle says: "For he beareth not the sword in vain; for he is the minister of God, the avenger for wrath upon him who does evil." And for this reason too, magistrates themselves, having laws as a clothing of righteousness whenever they act in a just and legitimate manner, shall not be called in question for their conduct, nor be liable to punishment. But whatsoever they do to the subversion of justice, iniquitously, and impiously, and illegally, and tyrannically, in these things shall they also perish; for the just judgment of God comes equally upon all, and in no case is defective. Earthly rule, therefore, has been appointed by God for the benefit of nations,[9] and not by the devil, who is never at rest at all, nay, who does not love to see even nations conducting themselves after a quiet manner, so that under the fear of human rule, men may not eat each other up like fishes; but that, by means of the establishment of laws, they may keep down an excess of wickedness among the nations. And considered from this point of view, those who exact tribute from us are "God's ministers, serving for this very purpose."

3. As, then, "the powers that be are ordained of God," it is clear that the devil lied when he said, "These are delivered unto me; and to whomsoever I will, I give them." For by the law of the same Being as calls men into existence are kings also appointed, adapted for those men who are at the time placed under their government. Some of these [rulers] are given for the correction and the benefit of their subjects, and for the preservation of justice; but others, for the purposes of fear and punishment and rebuke: others, as [the subjects] deserve it, are for deception, disgrace, and pride; while the just judgment of God, as I have observed already, passes equally upon all. The devil, however, as he is the apostate angel, can only go to this length, as he did at the beginning, [namely] to deceive and lead astray the mind of man into disobeying the commandments of God, and grad-

---

[1] John viii. 44.
[2] Matt. iv. 9; Luke iv. 6.
[3] Prov. xxi. 1.
[4] Prov. viii. 15.
[5] Rom. xiii. 1.
[6] Rom. xiii. 4.
[7] Rom. xiii. 6.
[8] Matt. xvii. 27.

[9] [Well says Benjamin Franklin: "He who shall introduce into public affairs the principles of primitive Christianity will change the face of the world." See Bancroft, *Hist. U.S.*, vol. ix. p. 492.]

ually to darken the hearts of those who would endeavour to serve him, to the forgetting of the true God, but to the adoration of himself as God.

4. Just as if any one, being an apostate, and seizing in a hostile manner another man's territory, should harass the inhabitants of it, in order that he might claim for himself the glory of a king among those ignorant of his apostasy and robbery; so likewise also the devil, being one among those angels who are placed over the spirit of the air, as the Apostle Paul has declared in his Epistle to the Ephesians,[1] becoming envious of man, was rendered an apostate from the divine law: for envy is a thing foreign to God. And as his apostasy was exposed by man, and man became the [means of] searching out his thoughts (*et examinatio sententiæ ejus, homo factus est*), he has set himself to this with greater and greater determination, in opposition to man, envying his life, and wishing to involve him in his own apostate power. The Word of God, however, the Maker of all things, conquering him by means of human nature, and showing him to be an apostate, has, on the contrary, put him under the power of man. For He says, "Behold, I confer upon you the power of treading upon serpents and scorpions, and upon all the power of the enemy,"[2] in order that, as he obtained dominion over man by apostasy, so again his apostasy might be deprived of power by means of man turning back again to God.

CHAP. XXV. — THE FRAUD, PRIDE, AND TYRANNICAL KINGDOM OF ANTICHRIST, AS DESCRIBED BY DANIEL AND PAUL.

1. And not only by the particulars already mentioned, but also by means of the events which shall occur in the time of Antichrist is it shown that he, being an apostate and a robber, is anxious to be adored as God; and that, although a mere slave, he wishes himself to be proclaimed as a king. For he (Antichrist) being endued with all the power of the devil, shall come, not as a righteous king, nor as a legitimate king, [i.e., one] in subjection to God, but an impious, unjust, and lawless one; as an apostate, iniquitous and murderous; as a robber, concentrating in himself [all] satanic apostasy, and setting aside idols to persuade [men] that he himself is God, raising up himself as the only idol, having in himself the multifarious errors of the other idols. This he does, in order that they who do [now] worship the devil by means of many abominations, may serve himself by this one idol, of whom the apostle thus speaks in the second Epistle to the Thessalonians: "Unless there shall come a falling away first, and the

man of sin shall be revealed, the son of perdition, who opposeth and exalteth himself above all that is called God, or that is worshipped; so that he sitteth in the temple of God, showing himself as if he were God." The apostle therefore clearly points out his apostasy, and that he is lifted up above all that is called God, or that is worshipped — that is, above every idol — for these are indeed so called by men, but are not [really] gods; and that he will endeavour in a tyrannical manner to set himself forth as God.

2. Moreover, he (the apostle) has also pointed out this which I have shown in many ways, that the temple in Jerusalem was made by the direction of the true God. For the apostle himself, speaking in his own person, distinctly called it the temple of God. Now I have shown in the third book, that no one is termed God by the apostles when speaking for themselves, except Him who truly is God, the Father of our Lord, by whose directions the temple which is at Jerusalem was constructed for those purposes which I have already mentioned; in which [temple] the enemy shall sit, endeavouring to show himself as Christ, as the Lord also declares: "But when ye shall see the abomination of desolation, which has been spoken of by Daniel the prophet, standing in the holy place (let him that readeth understand), then let those who are in Judea flee into the mountains; and he who is upon the house-top, let him not come down to take anything out of his house: for there shall then be great hardship, such as has not been from the beginning of the world until now, nor ever shall be."[3]

3. Daniel too, looking forward to the end of the last kingdom, i.e., the ten last kings, amongst whom the kingdom of those men shall be partitioned, and upon whom the son of perdition shall come, declares that ten horns shall spring from the beast, and that another little horn shall arise in the midst of them, and that three of the former shall be rooted up before his face. He says: "And, behold, eyes were in this horn as the eyes of a man, and a mouth speaking great things, and his look was more stout than his fellows. I was looking, and this horn made war against the saints, and prevailed against them, until the Ancient of days came and gave judgment to the saints of the most high God, and the time came, and the saints obtained the kingdom."[4] Then, further on, in the interpretation of the vision, there was said to him: "The fourth beast shall be the fourth kingdom upon earth, which shall excel all other kingdoms, and devour the whole earth, and tread it down, and cut it in pieces. And its ten horns are ten kings which shall arise; and after them shall arise another, who shall surpass in evil deeds all that were be-

---

[1] Eph. ii. 2.
[2] Luke x. 19.

[3] Matt. xxiv. 15, 21.
[4] Dan. vii. 8, etc.

fore him, and shall overthrow three kings ; and he shall speak words against the most high God, and wear out the saints of the most high God, and shall purpose to change times and laws ; and [everything] shall be given into his hand until a time of times and a half time,"[1] that is, for three years and six months, during which time, when he comes, he shall reign over the earth. Of whom also the Apostle Paul again, speaking in the second [Epistle] to the Thessalonians, and at the same time proclaiming the cause of his advent, thus says : "And then shall the wicked one be revealed, whom the Lord Jesus shall slay with the spirit of His mouth, and destroy by the presence of His coming ; whose coming [i.e., the wicked one's] is after the working of Satan, in all power, and signs, and portents of lies, and with all deceivableness of wickedness for those who perish ; because they did not receive the love of the truth, that they might be saved. And therefore God will send them the working of error, that they may believe a lie ; that they all may be judged who did not believe the truth, but gave consent to iniquity."[2]

4. The Lord also spoke as follows to those who did not believe in Him : "I have come in my Father's name, and ye have not received Me : when another shall come in his own name, him ye will receive,"[3] calling Antichrist "the other," because he is alienated from the Lord. This is also the unjust judge, whom the Lord mentioned as one "who feared not God, neither regarded man,"[4] to whom the widow fled in her forgetfulness of God, — that is, the earthly Jerusalem, — to be avenged of her adversary. Which also he shall do in the time of his kingdom : he shall remove his kingdom into that [city], and shall sit in the temple of God, leading astray those who worship him, as if he were Christ. To this purpose Daniel says again : "And he shall desolate the holy place ; and sin has been given for a sacrifice,[5] and righteousness been cast away in the earth, and he has been active (fecit), and gone on prosperously."[6] And the angel Gabriel, when explaining his vision, states with regard to this person : "And towards the end of their kingdom a king of a most fierce countenance shall arise, one understanding [dark] questions, and exceedingly powerful, full of wonders ; and he shall corrupt, direct, influence (faciet), and put strong men down, the holy people likewise ; and his yoke shall be directed as a wreath [round their neck] ; deceit shall be

in his hand, and he shall be lifted up in his heart : he shall also ruin many by deceit, and lead many to perdition, bruising them in his hand like eggs."[7] And then he points out the time that his tyranny shall last, during which the saints shall be put to flight, they who offer a pure sacrifice unto God : "And in the midst of the week," he says, "the sacrifice and the libation shall be taken away, and the abomination of desolation [shall be brought] into the temple : even unto the consummation of the time shall the desolation be complete."[8] Now three years and six months constitute the half-week.

5. From all these passages are revealed to us, not merely the particulars of the apostasy, and [the doings] of him who concentrates in himself every satanic error, but also, that there is one and the same God the Father, who was declared by the prophets, but made manifest by Christ. For if what Daniel prophesied concerning the end has been confirmed by the Lord, when He said, "When ye shall see the abomination of desolation, which has been spoken of by Daniel the prophet"[9] (and the angel Gabriel gave the interpretation of the visions to Daniel, and he is the archangel of the Creator (Demiurgi), who also proclaimed to Mary the visible coming and the incarnation of Christ), then one and the same God is most manifestly pointed out, who sent the prophets, and made promise[10] of the Son, and called us into His knowledge.

CHAP. XXVI. — JOHN AND DANIEL HAVE PREDICTED THE DISSOLUTION AND DESOLATION OF THE ROMAN EMPIRE, WHICH SHALL PRECEDE THE END OF THE WORLD AND THE ETERNAL KINGDOM OF CHRIST. THE GNOSTICS ARE REFUTED, THOSE TOOLS OF SATAN, WHO INVENT ANOTHER FATHER DIFFERENT FROM THE CREATOR.

1. In a still clearer light has John, in the Apocalypse, indicated to the Lord's disciples what shall happen in the last times, and concerning the ten kings who shall then arise, among whom the empire which now rules [the earth] shall be partitioned. He teaches us what the ten horns shall be which were seen by Daniel, telling us that thus it had been said to him : "And the ten horns which thou sawest are ten kings, who have received no kingdom as yet, but shall receive power as if kings one hour with the beast. These have one mind, and give their strength and power to the beast. These shall make war with the Lamb, and the Lamb shall overcome them, because He is the Lord of lords and the King of kings."[11] It is manifest, therefore, that

---

[1] Dan. vii. 23, etc.
[2] 2 Thess. ii. 8.
[3] John v. 43.
[4] Luke xviii. 2, etc.
[5] This may refer to Antiochus Epiphanes, Antichrist's prototype, who offered swine upon the altar in the temple at Jerusalem. The LXX. version has, ἐδόθη ἐπὶ τὴν θυσίαν ἁμαρτία, i.e., sin has been given against (or, upon) the sacrifice.
[6] Dan. viii. 12.

[7] Dan. viii. 23, etc.
[8] Dan. ix. 27.
[9] Matt. xxiv. 15.
[10] The MSS. have "præmisit," but Harvey suggests "promisit," which we have adopted.
[11] Rev. xvii. 12, etc.

of these [potentates], he who is to come shall slay three, and subject the remainder to his power, and that he shall be himself the eighth among them. And they shall lay Babylon waste, and burn her with fire, and shall give their kingdom to the beast, and put the Church to flight. After that they shall be destroyed by the coming of our Lord. For that the kingdom must be divided, and thus come to ruin, the Lord [declares when He] says: "Every kingdom divided against itself is brought to desolation, and every city or house divided against itself shall not stand." [1] It must be, therefore, that the kingdom, the city, and the house be divided into ten; and for this reason He has already foreshadowed the partition and division [which shall take place]. Daniel also says particularly, that the end of the fourth kingdom consists in the toes of the image seen by Nebuchadnezzar, upon which came the stone cut out without hands; and as he does himself say: "The feet were indeed the one part iron, the other part clay, until the stone was cut out without hands, and struck the image upon the iron and clay feet, and dashed them into pieces, even to the end." [2] Then afterwards, when interpreting this, he says: "And as thou sawest the feet and the toes, partly indeed of clay, and partly of iron, the kingdom shall be divided, and there shall be in it a root of iron, as thou sawest iron mixed with baked clay. And the toes were indeed the one part iron, but the other part clay." [3] The ten toes, therefore, are these ten kings, among whom the kingdom shall be partitioned, of whom some indeed shall be strong and active, or energetic; others, again, shall be sluggish and useless, and shall not agree; as also Daniel says: "Some part of the kingdom shall be strong, and part shall be broken from it. As thou sawest the iron mixed with the baked clay, there shall be minglings among the human race, but no cohesion one with the other, just as iron cannot be welded on to pottery ware." [4] And since an end shall take place, he says: "And in the days of these kings shall the God of heaven raise up a kingdom which shall never decay, and His kingdom shall not be left to another people. It shall break in pieces and shatter all kingdoms, and shall itself be exalted for ever. As thou sawest that the stone was cut without hands from the mountain, and brake in pieces the baked clay, the iron, the brass, the silver, and the gold, God has pointed out to the king what shall come to pass after these things; and the dream is true, and the interpretation trustworthy." [5]

2. If therefore the great God showed future things by Daniel, and confirmed them by His Son; and if Christ is the stone which is cut out without hands, who shall destroy temporal kingdoms, and introduce an eternal one, which is the resurrection of the just; as he declares, "The God of heaven shall raise up a kingdom which shall never be destroyed," — let those thus confuted come to their senses, who reject the Creator (*Demiurgum*), and do not agree that the prophets were sent beforehand from the same Father from whom also the Lord came, but who assert that prophecies originated from diverse powers. For those things which have been predicted by the Creator alike through all the prophets has Christ fulfilled in the end, ministering to His Father's will, and completing His dispensations with regard to the human race. Let those persons, therefore, who blaspheme the Creator, either by openly expressed words, such as the disciples of Marcion, or by a perversion of the sense [of Scripture], as those of Valentinus and all the Gnostics falsely so called, be recognised as agents of Satan by all those who worship God; through whose agency Satan now, and not before, has been seen to speak against God, even Him who has prepared eternal fire for every kind of apostasy. For he did not venture to blaspheme his Lord openly of himself; as also in the beginning he led man astray through the instrumentality of the serpent, concealing himself as it were from God. Truly has Justin remarked: [6] That before the Lord's appearance Satan never dared to blaspheme God, inasmuch as he did not yet know his own sentence, because it was contained in parables and allegories; but that after the Lord's appearance, when he had clearly ascertained from the words of Christ and His apostles that eternal fire has been prepared for him as he apostatized from God of his own free-will, and likewise for all who unrepentant continue in the apostasy, he now blasphemes, by means of such men, the Lord who brings judgment [upon him] as being already condemned, and imputes the guilt of his apostasy to his Maker, not to his own voluntary disposition. Just as it is with those who break the laws, when punishment overtakes them: they throw the blame upon those who frame the laws, but not upon themselves. In like manner do those men, filled with a satanic spirit, bring innumerable accusations against our Creator, who has both given to us the spirit of life, and established a law adapted for all; and they will not admit that the judgment of God is just. Wherefore also they set about imagining some other Father who neither cares about nor exercises a providence

---

[1] Matt. xii. 25.
[2] Dan. ii. 33, 34.
[3] Dan. ii. 41, 42.
[4] Dan. ii. 42, 43.
[5] Dan. ii. 44, 45.

[6] The Greek text is here preserved by Eusebius, *Hist. Eccl.*, iv. 18; but we are not told from what work of Justin Martyr it is extracted. The work is now lost. An ancient catena continues the Greek for several lines further.

over our affairs, nay, one who even approves of all sins.

CHAP. XXVII. — THE FUTURE JUDGMENT BY CHRIST. COMMUNION WITH AND SEPARATION FROM THE DIVINE BEING. THE ETERNAL PUNISHMENT OF UNBELIEVERS.

1. If the Father, then, does not exercise judgment, [it follows] that judgment does not belong to Him, or that He consents to all those actions which take place; and if He does not judge, all persons will be equal, and accounted in the same condition. The advent of Christ will therefore be without an object, yea, absurd, inasmuch as [in that case] He exercises no judicial power. For " He came to divide a man against his father, and the daughter against the mother, and the daughter-in-law against the mother-in-law; "[1] and when two are in one bed, to take the one, and to leave the other; and of two women grinding at the mill, to take one and leave the other:[2] [also] at the time of the end, to order the reapers to collect first the tares together, and bind them in bundles, and burn them with unquenchable fire, but to gather up the wheat into the barn;[3] and to call the lambs into the kingdom prepared for them, but to send the goats into everlasting fire, which has been prepared by His Father for the devil and his angels.[4] And why is this? Has the Word come for the ruin and for the resurrection of many? For the ruin, certainly, of those who do not believe Him, to whom also He has threatened a greater damnation in the judgment-day than that of Sodom and Gomorrah;[5] but for the resurrection of believers, and those who do the will of His Father in heaven. If then the advent of the Son comes indeed alike to all, but is for the purpose of judging, and separating the believing from the unbelieving, since, as those who believe do His will agreeably to their own choice, and as, [also] agreeably to their own choice, the disobedient do not consent to His doctrine; it is manifest that His Father has made all in a like condition, each person having a choice of his own, and a free understanding; and that He has regard to all things, and exercises a providence over all, " making His sun to rise upon the evil and on the good, and sending rain upon the just and unjust." [6]

2. And to as many as continue in their love towards God, does He grant communion with Him. But communion with God is life and light, and the enjoyment of all the benefits which He has in store. But on as many as,

according to their own choice, depart from God. He inflicts that separation from Himself which they have chosen of their own accord. But separation from God is death, and separation from light is darkness; and separation from God consists in the loss of all the benefits which He has in store. Those, therefore, who cast away by apostasy these forementioned things, being in fact destitute of all good, do experience every kind of punishment. God, however, does not punish them immediately of Himself, but that punishment falls upon them because they are destitute of all that is good. Now, good things are eternal and without end with God, and therefore the loss of these is also eternal and never-ending. It is in this matter just as occurs in the case of a flood of light: those who have blinded themselves, or have been blinded by others, are for ever deprived of the enjoyment of light. It is not, [however], that the light has inflicted upon them the penalty of blindness, but it is that the blindness itself has brought calamity upon them: and therefore the Lord declared, " He that believeth in Me is not condemned," [7] that is, is not separated from God, for he is united to God through faith. On the other hand, He says, " He that believeth not is condemned already, because he has not believed in the name of the only-begotten Son of God; " that is, he separated himself from God of his own accord. " For this is the condemnation, that light is come into this world, and men have loved darkness rather than light. For every one who doeth evil hateth the light, and cometh. not to the light, lest his deeds should be reproved. But he that doeth truth cometh to the light, that his deeds may be made manifest, that he has wrought them in God."

CHAP. XXVIII. — THE DISTINCTION TO BE MADE BETWEEN THE RIGHTEOUS AND THE WICKED. THE FUTURE APOSTASY IN THE TIME OF ANTICHRIST, AND THE END OF THE WORLD.

1. Inasmuch, then, as in this world (αἰῶνι) some persons betake themselves to the light, and by faith unite themselves with God, but others shun the light, and separate themselves from God, the Word of God comes preparing a fit habitation for both. For those indeed who are in the light, that they may derive enjoyment from it, and from the good things contained in it; but for those in darkness, that they may partake in its calamities. And on this account He says, that those upon the right hand are called into the kingdom of heaven, but that those on the left He will send into eternal fire; for they have deprived themselves of all good.

2. And for this reason the apostle says : " Be-

---

[1] Matt. x. 25.
[2] Luke xvii. 34.
[3] Matt. xiii. 30.
[4] Matt. xxv. 33, etc.
[5] Luke x. 12.
[6] Matt. v. 45.

[7] John iii. 18, 21.

cause they received not the love of God, that they might be saved, therefore God shall also send them the operation of error, that they may believe a lie, that they all may be judged who have not believed the truth, but consented to unrighteousness."[1] For when he (Antichrist) is come, and of his own accord concentrates in his own person the apostasy, and accomplishes whatever he shall do according to his own will and choice, sitting also in the temple of God, so that his dupes may adore him as the Christ; wherefore also shall he deservedly "be cast into the lake of fire:"[2] [this will happen according to divine appointment], God by His prescience foreseeing all this, and at the proper time sending such a man, "that they may believe a lie, that they all may be judged who did not believe the truth, but consented to unrighteousness;" whose coming John has thus described in the Apocalypse: "And the beast which I had seen was like unto a leopard, and his feet as of a bear, and his mouth as the mouth of a lion; and the dragon conferred his own power upon him, and his throne, and great might. And one of his heads was as it were slain unto death; and his deadly wound was healed, and all the world wondered after the beast. And they worshipped the dragon because he gave power to the beast; and they worshipped the beast, saying, Who is like unto this beast, and who is able to make war with him? And there was given unto him a mouth speaking great things, and blasphemy and power was given to him during forty and two months. And he opened his mouth for blasphemy against God, to blaspheme His name and His tabernacle, and those who dwell in heaven. And power was given him over every tribe, and people, and tongue, and nation. And all who dwell upon the earth worshipped him, [every one] whose name was not written in the book of the Lamb slain from the foundation of the world. If any one have ears, let him hear. If any one shall lead into captivity, he shall go into captivity. If any shall slay with the sword, he must be slain with the sword. Here is the endurance and the faith of the saints."[3] After this he likewise describes his armour-bearer, whom he also terms a false prophet: "He spake as a dragon, and exercised all the power of the first beast in his sight, and caused the earth, and those that dwell therein, to adore the first beast, whose deadly wound was healed. And he shall perform great wonders, so that he can even cause fire to descend from heaven upon the earth in the sight of men, and he shall lead the inhabitants of the earth astray."[4]

Let no one imagine that he performs these wonders by divine power, but by the working of magic. And we must not be surprised if, since the demons and apostate spirits are at his service, he through their means performs wonders, by which he leads the inhabitants of the earth astray. John says further: "And he shall order an image of the beast to be made, and he shall give breath to the image, so that the image shall speak; and he shall cause those to be slain who will not adore it." He says also: "And he will cause a mark [to be put] in the forehead and in the right hand, that no one may be able to buy or sell, unless he who has the mark of the name of the beast or the number of his name; and the number is six hundred and sixty-six,"[5] that is, six times a hundred, six times ten, and six units. [He gives this] as a summing up of the whole of that apostasy which has taken place during six thousand years.

3. For in as many days as this world was made, in so many thousand years shall it be concluded. And for this reason the Scripture says: "Thus the heaven and the earth were finished, and all their adornment. And God brought to a conclusion upon the sixth day the works that He had made; and God rested upon the seventh day from all His works."[6] This is an account of the things formerly created, as also it is a prophecy of what is to come. For the day of the Lord is as a thousand years;[7] and in six days created things were completed: it is evident, therefore, that they will come to an end at the sixth thousand year.

4. And therefore throughout all time, man, having been moulded at the beginning by the hands of God, that is, of the Son and of the Spirit, is made after the image and likeness of God: the chaff, indeed, which is the apostasy, being cast away; but the wheat, that is, those who bring forth fruit to God in faith, being gathered into the barn. And for this cause tribulation is necessary for those who are saved, that having been after a manner broken up, and rendered fine, and sprinkled over by the patience of the Word of God, and set on fire [for purification], they may be fitted for the royal banquet. As a certain man of ours said, when he was condemned to the wild beasts because of his testimony with respect to God: "I am the wheat of Christ, and am ground by the teeth of the wild beasts, that I may be found the pure bread of God."[8]

---

[1] 2 Thess. ii. 10-12.
[2] Rev. xix. 20.
[3] Rev. xiii. 2, etc
[4] Rev. xiii. 11, etc.

[5] Rev. xiii. 14, etc.
[6] Gen. ii. 2.
[7] 2 Pet. iii. 8.
[8] This is quoted from the Epistle of Ignatius to the Romans, ch. iv. It is found in the two Greek recensions of his works, and also in the Syriac. See pp. 75 and 103 of this volume. The Latin translation is here followed: the Greek of Ignatius would give "the wheat of God," and omits "of God" towards the end, as quoted by Eusebius.

CHAP. XXIX. — ALL THINGS HAVE BEEN CREATED FOR THE SERVICE OF MAN. THE DECEITS, WICKEDNESS, AND APOSTATE POWER OF ANTICHRIST. THIS WAS PREFIGURED AT THE DELUGE, AS AFTERWARDS BY THE PERSECUTION OF SHADRACH, MESHACH, AND ABEDNEGO.

1. In the previous books I have set forth the causes for which God permitted these things to be made, and have pointed out that all such have been created for the benefit of that human nature which is saved, ripening for immortality that which is [possessed] of its own free will and its own power, and preparing and rendering it more adapted for eternal subjection to God. And therefore the creation is suited to [the wants of] man; for man was not made for its sake, but creation for the sake of man. Those nations, however, who did not of themselves raise up their eyes unto heaven, nor returned thanks to their Maker, nor wished to behold the light of truth, but who were like blind mice concealed in the depths of ignorance, the word justly reckons "as waste water from a sink, and as the turning-weight of a balance — in fact, as nothing;"[1] so far useful and serviceable to the just, as stubble conduces towards the growth of the wheat, and its straw, by means of combustion, serves for working gold. And therefore, when in the end the Church shall be suddenly caught up from this, it is said, "There shall be tribulation such as has not been since the beginning, neither shall be."[2] For this is the last contest of the righteous, in which, when they overcome, they are crowned with incorruption.

2. And there is therefore in this beast, when he comes, a recapitulation made of all sorts of iniquity and of every deceit, in order that all apostate power, flowing into and being shut up in him, may be sent into the furnace of fire. Fittingly, therefore, shall his name possess the number six hundred and sixty-six, since he sums up in his own person all the commixture of wickedness which took place previous to the deluge, due to the apostasy of the angels. For Noah was six hundred years old when the deluge came upon the earth, sweeping away the rebellious world, for the sake of that most infamous generation which lived in the times of Noah. And [Antichrist] also sums up every error of devised idols since the flood, together with the slaying of the prophets and the cutting off of the just. For that image which was set up by Nebuchadnezzar had indeed a height of sixty cubits, while the breadth was six cubits; on account of which Ananias, Azarias, and Misaël, when they did not worship it, were cast into a furnace of fire, pointing out prophetically, by

what happened to them, the wrath against the righteous which shall arise towards the [time of the] end. For that image, taken as a whole, was a prefiguring of this man's coming, decreeing that he should undoubtedly himself alone be worshipped by all men. Thus, then, the six hundred years of Noah, in whose time the deluge occurred because of the apostasy, and the number of the cubits of the image for which these just men were sent into the fiery furnace, do indicate the number of the name of that man in whom is concentrated the whole apostasy of six thousand years, and unrighteousness, and wickedness, and false prophecy, and deception; for which things' sake a cataclysm of fire shall also come [upon the earth].

CHAP. XXX. — ALTHOUGH CERTAIN AS TO THE NUMBER OF THE NAME OF ANTICHRIST, YET WE SHOULD COME TO NO RASH CONCLUSIONS AS TO THE NAME ITSELF, BECAUSE THIS NUMBER IS CAPABLE OF BEING FITTED TO MANY NAMES. REASONS FOR THIS POINT BEING RESERVED BY THE HOLY SPIRIT. ANTICHRIST'S REIGN AND DEATH.

1. Such, then, being the state of the case, and this number being found in all the most approved and ancient copies[3] [of the Apocalypse], and those men who saw John face to face bearing their testimony [to it]; while reason also leads us to conclude that the number of the name of the beast, [if reckoned] according to the Greek mode of calculation by the [value of] the letters contained in it, will amount to six hundred and sixty and six; that is, the number of tens shall be equal to that of the hundreds, and the number of hundreds equal to that of the units (for that number which [expresses] the digit six being adhered to throughout, indicates the recapitulations of that apostasy, taken in its full extent, which occurred at the beginning, during the intermediate periods, and which shall take place at the end), — I do not know how it is that some have erred following the ordinary mode of speech, and have vitiated the middle number in the name, deducting the amount of fifty from it, so that instead of six decads they will have it that there is but one. [I am inclined to think that this occurred through the fault of the copyists, as is wont to happen, since numbers also are expressed by letters; so that the Greek letter which expresses the number sixty was easily expanded into the letter Iota of the Greeks.][4] Others then received this read-

---

[1] Isa. xl. 15.
[2] Matt. xxiv. 21.

[3] ἐν πᾶσι τοῖς σπουδαίοις καὶ ἀρχαίοις ἀντιγράφοις. This passage is interesting, as showing how very soon the autographs of the New Testament must have perished, and various readings crept into the MSS. of the canonical books.
[4] That is, Ξ into ΕΙ, according to Harvey, who considers the whole of this clause as an evident interpolation. It does not occur in the Greek here preserved by Eusebius (Hist. Eccl., v. 8).

ing without examination; some in their simplicity, and upon their own responsibility, making use of this number expressing one decad; while some, in their inexperience, have ventured to seek out a name which should contain the erroneous and spurious numbe.. Now, as regards those who have done this in simplicity, and without evil intent, we are at liberty to assume that pardon will be granted them by God. But as for those who, for the sake of vainglory, lay it down for certain that names containing the spurious number are to be accepted, and affirm that this name, hit upon by themselves, is that of him who is to come; such persons shall not come forth without loss, because they have led into error both themselves and those who confided in them. Now, in the first place, it is loss to wander from the truth, and to imagine that as being the case which is not; then again, as there shall be no light punishment [inflicted] upon him who either adds or subtracts anything from the Scripture,[1] under that such a person must necessarily fall. Moreover, another danger, by no means trifling, shall overtake those who falsely presume that they know the name of Antichrist. For if these men assume one [number], when this [Antichrist] shall come having another, they will be easily led away by him, as supposing him not to be the expected one, who must be guarded against.

2. These men, therefore, ought to learn [what really is the state of the case], and go back to the true number of the name, that they be not reckoned among false prophets. But, knowing the sure number declared by Scripture, that is, six hundred sixty and six, let them await, in the first place, the division of the kingdom into ten; then, in the next place, when these kings are reigning, and beginning to set their affairs in order, and advance their kingdom, [let them learn] to acknowledge that he who shall come claiming the kingdom for himself, and shall terrify those men of whom we have been speaking, having a name containing the aforesaid number, is truly the abomination of desolation. This, too, the apostle affirms: "When they shall say, Peace and safety, then sudden destruction shall come upon them."[2] And Jeremiah does not merely point out his sudden coming, but he even indicates the tribe from which he shall come, where he says, "We shall hear the voice of his swift horses from Dan; the whole earth shall be moved by the voice of the neighing of his galloping horses: he shall also come and devour the earth, and the fulness thereof, the city also, and they that dwell therein."[3] This, too, is the reason that this tribe is not reckoned in the Apocalypse along with those which are saved.[4]

3. It is therefore more certain, and less hazardous, to await the fulfilment of the prophecy, than to be making surmises, and casting about for any names that may present themselves, inasmuch as many names can be found possessing the number mentioned; and the same question will, after all, remain unsolved. For if there are many names found possessing this number, it will be asked which among them shall the coming man bear. It is not through a want of names containing the number of that name that I say this, but on account of the fear of God, and zeal for the truth: for the name *Evanthas* (EYAN-ΘΑΣ) contains the required number, but I make no allegation regarding it. Then also *Lateinos* (ΛΑΤΕΙΝΟΣ) has the number six hundred and sixty-six; and it is a very probable [solution], this being the name of the last kingdom [of the four seen by Daniel]. For the Latins are they who at present bear rule:[5] I will not, however, make any boast over this [coincidence]. *Teitan* too, (ΤΕΙΤΑΝ, the first syllable being written with the two Greek vowels ε and ι), among all the names which are found among us, is rather worthy of credit. For it has in itself the predicted number, and is composed of six letters, each syllable containing three letters; and [the word itself] is ancient, and removed from ordinary use; for among our kings we find none bearing this name Titan, nor have any of the idols which are worshipped in public among the Greeks and barbarians this appellation. Among many persons, too, this name is accounted divine, so that even the sun is termed "Titan" by those who do now possess [the rule]. This word, too, contains a certain outward appearance of vengeance, and of one inflicting merited punishment because he (Antichrist) pretends that he vindicates the oppressed.[6] And besides this, it is an ancient name, one worthy of credit, of royal dignity, and still further, a name belonging to a tyrant. Inasmuch, then, as this name "Titan" has so much to recommend it, there is a strong degree of probability, that from among the many [names suggested], we infer, that perchance he who is to come shall be called "Titan." We will not, however, incur the risk of pronouncing positively as to the name of Antichrist; for if it were necessary that his name should be distinctly revealed in this present time, it would have been announced by him who beheld the apocalyptic vision. For that was seen no very long time

---

[1] Rev. xxii. 19.
[2] 1 Thess. v. 3.
[3] Jer. viii. 16.

[4] Rev. vii. 5-7. [The Danites (though not all) corrupted the Hebrew church and the Levitical priesthood, by image-worship, (Judg. xviii.), and forfeited the blessings of the old covenant.]
[5] [A very pregnant passage, as has often been noted. But let us imitate the pious reticence with which this section concludes.]
[6] Massuet here quotes Cicero and Ovid in proof of the sun being termed *Titan*. The Titans waged war against the gods, to avenge themselves upon Saturn.

since, but almost in our day, towards the end of Domitian's reign.

4. But he indicates the number of the name now, that when this man comes we may avoid him, being aware who he is: the name, however, is suppressed, because it is not worthy of being proclaimed by the Holy Spirit. For if it had been declared by Him, he (Antichrist) might perhaps continue for a long period. But now as "he was, and is not, and shall ascend out of the abyss, and goes into perdition,"[1] as one who has no existence; so neither has his name been declared, for the name of that which does not exist is not proclaimed. But when this Antichrist shall have devastated all things in this world, he will reign for three years and six months, and sit in the temple at Jerusalem; and then the Lord will come from heaven in the clouds, in the glory of the Father, sending this man and those who follow him into the lake of fire; but bringing in for the righteous the times of the kingdom, that is, the rest, the hallowed seventh day; and restoring to Abraham the promised inheritance, in which kingdom the Lord declared, that "many coming from the east and from the west should sit down with Abraham, Isaac, and Jacob."[2]

CHAP. XXXI. — THE PRESERVATION OF OUR BODIES IS CONFIRMED BY THE RESURRECTION AND ASCENSION OF CHRIST: THE SOULS OF THE SAINTS DURING THE INTERMEDIATE PERIOD ARE IN A STATE OF EXPECTATION OF THAT TIME WHEN THEY SHALL RECEIVE THEIR PERFECT AND CONSUMMATED GLORY.

1. Since, again, some who are reckoned among the orthodox go beyond the pre-arranged plan for the exaltation of the just, and are ignorant of the methods by which they are disciplined beforehand for incorruption, they thus entertain heretical opinions. For the heretics, despising the handiwork of God, and not admitting the salvation of their flesh, while they also treat the promise of God contemptuously, and pass beyond God altogether in the sentiments they form, affirm that immediately upon their death they shall pass above the heavens and the Demiurge, and go to the Mother (Achamoth) or to that Father whom they have feigned. Those persons, therefore, who disallow a resurrection affecting the whole man (*universam reprobant resurrectionem*), and as far as in them lies remove it from the midst [of the Christian scheme], how can they be wondered at, if again they know nothing as to the plan of the resurrection? For they do not choose to understand, that if these things are as they say, the Lord Himself, in whom they profess to believe, did not rise again upon the third day; but

immediately upon His expiring on the cross, undoubtedly departed on high, leaving His body to the earth. But the case was, that for three days He dwelt in the place where the dead were, as the prophet says concerning Him: "And the Lord remembered His dead saints who slept formerly in the land of sepulture; and He descended to them, to rescue and save them."[3] And the Lord Himself says, "As Jonas remained three days and three nights in the whale's belly, so shall the Son of man be in the heart of the earth."[4] Then also the apostle says, "But when He ascended, what is it but that He also descended into the lower parts of the earth?"[5] This, too, David says when prophesying of Him, "And thou hast delivered my soul from the nethermost hell;"[6] and on His rising again the third day, He said to Mary, who was the first to see and to worship Him, "Touch Me not, for I have not yet ascended to the Father; but go to the disciples, and say unto them, I ascend unto My Father, and unto your Father."[7]

2. If, then, the Lord observed the law of the dead, that He might become the first-begotten from the dead, and tarried until the third day "in the lower parts of the earth;"[8] then afterwards rising in the flesh, so that He even showed the print of the nails to His disciples,[9] He thus ascended to the Father; — [if all these things occurred, I say], how must these men not be put to confusion, who allege that "the lower parts" refer to this world of ours, but that their inner man, leaving the body here, ascends into the super-celestial place? For as the Lord "went away in the midst of the shadow of death,"[10] where the souls of the dead were, yet afterwards arose in the body, and after the resurrection was taken up [into heaven], it is manifest that the souls of His disciples also, upon whose account the Lord underwent these things, shall go away into the invisible place allotted to them by God, and there remain until the resurrection, awaiting that event; then receiving their bodies, and rising in their entirety, that is bodily, just as the Lord arose, they shall come thus into the presence of God. "For no disciple is above the Master, but every one that is perfect shall be as his Master."[11] As our Master, therefore, did not at once depart, taking flight [to heaven], but awaited the time of His resurrection prescribed by the Father, which had been also shown forth through Jonas, and rising again after three days was taken up [to heaven];

---

[1] Rev. xvii. 8.
[2] Matt. viii. 11.

[3] See the note, book iii. xx. 4.
[4] Matt. xi. 40.
[5] Eph. iv. 9.
[6] Ps. lxxxvi. 23.
[7] John xx. 17.
[8] Eph. iv. 9.
[9] John xx. 20, 27.
[10] Ps. xxiii. 4.
[11] Luke vi. 40.

so ought we also to await the time of our resurrection prescribed by God and foretold by the prophets, and so, rising, be taken up, as many as the Lord shall account worthy of this [privilege].[1]

CHAP. XXXII. — IN THAT FLESH IN WHICH THE SAINTS HAVE SUFFERED SO MANY AFFLICTIONS, THEY SHALL RECEIVE THE FRUITS OF THEIR LABOURS ; ESPECIALLY SINCE ALL CREATION WAITS FOR THIS, AND GOD PROMISES IT TO ABRAHAM AND HIS SEED.

1. Inasmuch, therefore, as the opinions of certain [orthodox persons] are derived from heretical discourses, they are both ignorant of God's dispensations, and of the mystery of the resurrection of the just, and of the [earthly] kingdom which is the commencement of incorruption, by means of which kingdom those who shall be worthy are accustomed gradually to partake of the divine nature (*capere Deum*[2]) ; and it is necessary to tell them respecting those things, that it behoves the righteous first to receive the promise of the inheritance which God promised to the fathers, and to reign in it, when they rise again to behold God in this creation which is renovated, and that the judgment should take place afterwards. For it is just that in that very creation in which they toiled or were afflicted, being proved in every way by suffering, they should receive the reward of their suffering ; and that in the creation in which they were slain because of their love to God, in that they should be revived again ; and that in the creation in which they endured servitude, in that they should reign. For God is rich in all things, and all things are His. It is fitting, therefore, that the creation itself, being restored to its primeval condition, should without restraint be under the dominion of the righteous ; and the apostle has made this plain in the Epistle to the Romans, when he thus speaks : " For the expectation of the creature waiteth for the manifestation of the sons of God. For the creature has been subjected to vanity, not willingly, but by reason of him who hath subjected the same in hope ; since the creature itself shall also be delivered from the bondage of corruption into the glorious liberty of the sons of God." [3]

2. Thus, then, the promise of God, which He gave to Abraham, remains stedfast. For thus He said : " Lift up thine eyes, and look from this place where now thou art, towards the north and south, and east and west. For all the earth which thou seest, I will give to thee and to thy seed, even for ever." [4] And again He says, " Arise, and go through the length and breadth of the land, since I will give it unto thee ; " [5] and [yet] he did not receive an inheritance in it, not even a footstep, but was always a stranger and a pilgrim therein.[6] And upon the death of Sarah his wife, when the Hittites were willing to bestow upon him a place where he might bury her, he declined it as a gift, but bought the burying-place (giving for it four hundred talents of silver) from Ephron the son of Zohar the Hittite.[7] Thus did he await patiently the promise of God, and was unwilling to appear to receive from men, what God had promised to give him, when He said again to him as follows : " I will give this land to thy seed, from the river of Egypt even unto the great river Euphrates." [8] If, then, God promised him the inheritance of the land, yet he did not receive it during all the time of his sojourn there, it must be, that together with his seed, that is, those who fear God and believe in Him, he shall receive it at the resurrection of the just. For his seed is the Church, which receives the adoption to God through the Lord, as John the Baptist said : " For God is able from the stones to raise up children to Abraham." [9] Thus also the apostle says in the Epistle to the Galatians : " But ye, brethren, as Isaac was, are the children of the promise." [10] And again, in the same Epistle, he plainly declares that they who have believed in Christ do receive Christ, the promise to Abraham thus saying, " The promises were spoken to Abraham, and to his seed. Now He does not say, And of seeds, as if [He spake] of many, but as of one, And to thy seed, which is Christ." [11] And again, confirming his former words, he says, " Even as Abraham believed God, and it was accounted to him for righteousness. Know ye therefore, that they which are of faith are the children of Abraham. But the Scripture, foreseeing that God would justify the heathen through faith, declared to Abraham beforehand, That in thee shall all nations be blessed. So then they which are of faith shall be blessed with faithful Abraham." [12] Thus, then, they who are of faith shall be blessed with faithful Abraham, and these are the children of Abraham. Now God made promise of the earth to Abraham and his seed ; yet neither Abraham nor his seed, that is, those who are justified by faith, do now receive any

---

[1] The five following chapters were omitted in the earlier editions, but added by Feuardentius. Most mss., too, did not contain them. It is probable that the scribes of the middle ages rejected them on account of their inculcating millenarian notions, which had been long extinct in the Church. Quotations from these five chapters have been collected by Harvey from Syriac and Armenian mss. lately come to light.
[2] Or, " gradually to comprehend God."
[3] Rom. viii. 19, etc.

[4] Gen. xiii. 13, 14.
[5] Gen. xiii. 17.
[6] Acts vii. 5 ; Heb. xi. 13.
[7] Gen. xxiii. 11.
[8] Gen. xv. 13.
[9] Luke iii. 8.
[10] Gal. iv. 28.
[11] Gal. iii. 16.
[12] Gal. iii. 6, etc.

inheritance in it; but they shall receive it at the resurrection of the just. For God is true and faithful; and on this account He said, "Blessed are the meek, for they shall inherit the earth."[1]

CHAP. XXXIII. — FURTHER PROOFS OF THE SAME PROPOSITION, DRAWN FROM THE PROMISES MADE BY CHRIST, WHEN HE DECLARED THAT HE WOULD DRINK OF THE FRUIT OF THE VINE WITH HIS DISCIPLES IN HIS FATHER'S KINGDOM, WHILE AT THE SAME TIME HE PROMISED TO REWARD THEM AN HUNDRED-FOLD, AND TO MAKE THEM PARTAKE OF BANQUETS. THE BLESSING PRONOUNCED BY JACOB HAD POINTED OUT THIS ALREADY, AS PAPIAS AND THE ELDERS HAVE INTERPRETED IT.

1. For this reason, when about to undergo His sufferings, that He might declare to Abraham and those with him the glad tidings of the inheritance being thrown open, [Christ], after He had given thanks while holding the cup, and had drunk of it, and given it to the disciples, said to them: "Drink ye all of it: this is My blood of the new covenant, which shall be shed for many for the remission of sins. But I say unto you, I will not drink henceforth of the fruit of this vine, until that day when I will drink it new with you in my Father's kingdom."[2] Thus, then, He will Himself renew the inheritance of the earth, and will re-organize the mystery of the glory of [His] sons; as David says, "He who hath renewed the face of the earth."[3] He promised to drink of the fruit of the vine with His disciples, thus indicating both these points: the inheritance of the earth in which the new fruit of the vine is drunk, and the resurrection of His disciples in the flesh. For the new flesh which rises again is the same which also received the new cup. And He cannot by any means be understood as drinking of the fruit of the vine when settled down with his [disciples] above in a super-celestial place; nor, again, are they who drink it devoid of flesh, for to drink of that which flows from the vine pertains to flesh, and not spirit.

2. And for this reason the Lord declared, "When thou makest a dinner or a supper, do not call thy friends, nor thy neighbours, nor thy kinsfolk, lest they ask thee in return, and so repay thee. But call the lame, the blind, and the poor, and thou shalt be blessed, since they cannot recompense thee, but a recompense shall be made thee at the resurrection of the just."[4] And again He says, "Whosoever shall have left lands, or houses, or parents, or brethren, or children because of Me, he shall receive in this world an hundred-fold, and in that to come he shall inherit eternal life."[5] For what are the hundred-fold [rewards] in this world, the entertainments given to the poor, and the suppers for which a return is made? These are [to take place] in the times of the kingdom, that is, upon the seventh day, which has been sanctified, in which God rested from all the works which He created, which is the true Sabbath of the righteous, which they shall not be engaged in any earthly occupation; but shall have a table at hand prepared for them by God, supplying them with all sorts of dishes.

3. The blessing of Isaac with which he blessed his younger son Jacob has the same meaning, when he says, "Behold, the smell of my son is as the smell of a full field which the Lord has blessed."[6] But "the field is the world."[7] And therefore he added, "God give to thee of the dew of heaven, and of the fatness of the earth, plenty of corn and wine. And let the nations serve thee, and kings bow down to thee; and be thou lord over thy brother, and thy father's sons shall bow down to thee: cursed shall be he who shall curse thee, and blessed shall be he who shall bless thee."[8] If any one, then, does not accept these things as referring to the appointed kingdom, he must fall into much contradiction and contrariety, as is the case with the Jews, who are involved in absolute perplexity. For not only did not the nations in this life serve this Jacob; but even after he had received the blessing, he himself going forth [from his home], served his uncle Laban the Syrian for twenty years;[9] and not only was he not made lord of his brother, but he did himself bow down before his brother Esau, upon his return from Mesopotamia to his father, and offered many gifts to him.[10] Moreover, in what way did he inherit much corn and wine here, he who emigrated to Egypt because of the famine which possessed the land in which he was dwelling, and became subject to Pharaoh, who was then ruling over Egypt? The predicted blessing, therefore, belongs unquestionably to the times of the kingdom, when the righteous shall bear rule upon their rising from the dead;[11] when also the creation, having been renovated and set free, shall fructify with an abundance of all kinds of food, from the dew of heaven, and from the fertility of the earth: as the elders who saw John, the disciple of the Lord, related that they had heard

---

[1] Matt. v. 5.
[2] Matt. xxvi. 27.
[3] Ps. civ. 30.
[4] Luke xiv. 12, 13.
[5] Matt. xix. 29; Luke xviii. 29, 30.
[6] Gen. xxvii. 27, etc.
[7] Matt. xiii. 38.
[8] Gen. xxvii. 28, 29.
[9] Gen. xxxi. 41.
[10] Gen. xxxiii. 3.
[11] From this to the end of the section there is an Armenian version extant, to be found in the *Spicil. Solesm.* i. p. 1, edited by M. Pitra, Paris 1852, and which was taken by him from an Armenian MS. in the Mechitarist Library at Venice, described as being of the twelfth century.

from him how the Lord used to teach in regard to these times, and say: The days will come, in which vines shall grow, each having ten thousand branches, and in each branch ten thousand twigs, and in each true [1] twig ten thousand shoots, and in each one of the shoots ten thousand clusters, and on every one of the clusters ten thousand grapes, and every grape when pressed will give five and twenty metretes of wine. And when any one of the saints shall lay hold of a cluster,[2] another shall cry out, "I am a better cluster, take me; bless the Lord through me." In like manner [the Lord declared] that a grain of wheat would produce ten thousand ears, and that every ear should have ten thousand grains, and every grain would yield ten pounds (*quinque bilibres*) of clear, pure, fine flour; and that all other fruit-bearing trees,[3] and seeds and grass, would produce in similar proportions (*secundum congruentiam iis consequentem*); and that all animals feeding [only] on the productions of the earth, should [in those days] become peaceful and harmonious among each other, and be in perfect subjection to man.

4. And these things are borne witness to in writing by Papias, the hearer of John, and a companion of Polycarp, in his fourth book; for there were five books compiled (συντεταγμένα) by him.[4] And he says in addition, "Now these things are credible to believers." And he says that, "when the traitor Judas did not give credit to them, and put the question, 'How then can things about to bring forth so abundantly be wrought by the Lord?' the Lord declared, 'They who shall come to these [times] shall see.'" When prophesying of these times, therefore, Esaias says: "The wolf also shall feed with the lamb, and the leopard shall take his rest with the kid; the calf also, and the bull, and the lion shall eat together; and a little boy shall lead them. The ox and the bear shall feed together, and their young ones shall agree together; and the lion shall eat straw as well as the ox. And the infant boy shall thrust his hand into the asp's den, into the nest also of the adder's brood; and they shall do no harm, nor have power to hurt anything in my holy mountain." And again he says, in recapitulation, "Wolves and lambs shall then browse together, and the lion shall eat straw like the ox, and the serpent earth as if it were bread; and they shall neither hurt nor annoy anything in my holy mountain, saith the Lord."[5] I am quite aware that some persons endeavour to refer these words to the case of savage men, both of different nations and various

habits, who come to believe, and when they have believed, act in harmony with the righteous. But although this is [true] now with regard to some men coming from various nations to the harmony of the faith, nevertheless in the resurrection of the just [the words shall also apply] to those animals mentioned. For God is rich in all things. And it is right that when the creation is restored, all the animals should obey and be in subjection to man, and revert to the food originally given by God (for they had been originally subjected in obedience to Adam), that is, the productions of the earth. But some other occasion, and not the present, is [to be sought] for showing that the lion shall [then] feed on straw. And this indicates the large size and rich quality of the fruits. For if that animal, the lion, feeds upon straw [at that period], of what a quality must the wheat itself be whose straw shall serve as suitable food for lions?

CHAP. XXXIV. — HE FORTIFIES HIS OPINIONS WITH REGARD TO THE TEMPORAL AND EARTHLY KINGDOM OF THE SAINTS AFTER THEIR RESURRECTION, BY THE VARIOUS TESTIMONIES OF ISAIAH, EZEKIEL, JEREMIAH, AND DANIEL; ALSO BY THE PARABLE OF THE SERVANTS WATCHING, TO WHOM THE LORD PROMISED THAT HE WOULD MINISTER.

1. Then, too, Isaiah himself has plainly declared that there shall be joy of this nature at the resurrection of the just, when he says: "The dead shall rise again; those, too, who are in the tombs shall arise, and those who are in the earth shall rejoice. For the dew from Thee is health to them."[6] And this again Ezekiel also says: "Behold, I will open your tombs, and will bring you forth out of your graves; when I will draw my people from the sepulchres, and I will put breath in you, and ye shall live; and I will place you on your own land, and ye shall know that I am the LORD."[7] And again the same speaks thus: "These things saith the LORD, I will gather Israel from all nations whither they have been driven, and I shall be sanctified in them in the sight of the sons of the nations: and they shall dwell in their own land, which I gave to my servant Jacob. And they shall dwell in it in peace; and they shall build houses, and plant vineyards, and dwell in hope, when I shall cause judgment to fall among all who have dishonoured them, among those who encircle them round about; and they shall know that I am the LORD their God, and the God of their fathers."[8] Now I have shown a short time ago that the church is the seed of Abraham; and for this reason, that we may know that He who in the New Testament "raises up from the stones children unto

---

[1] This word "true" is not found in the Armenian.
[2] Or, following Arm. vers., "But if any one shall lay hold of an holy cluster."
[3] The Arm. vers. is here followed; the old Latin reads, "Et reliqua autem poma."
[4] [See pp. 151-154, this volume.]
[5] Isa. xl. 6, etc.

[6] Isa. xxvi. 19.
[7] Ezek. xxxvii. 12, etc.
[8] Ezek. xxviii. 25, 26.

Abraham," [1] is He who will gather, according to the Old Testament, those that shall be saved from all the nations, Jeremiah says : " Behold, the days come, saith the LORD, that they shall no more say, The LORD liveth, who led the children of Israel from the north, and from every region whither they had been driven ; He will restore them to their own land which He gave to their fathers." [2]

2. That the whole creation shall, according to God's will, obtain a vast increase, that it may bring forth and sustain fruits such [as we have mentioned], Isaiah declares : " And there shall be upon every high mountain, and upon every prominent hill, water running everywhere in that day, when many shall perish, when walls shall fall. And the light of the moon shall be as the light of the sun, seven times that of the day, when He shall heal the anguish of His people, and do away with the pain of His stroke." [3] Now " the pain of the stroke " means that inflicted at the beginning upon disobedient man in Adam, that is, death ; which [stroke] the Lord will heal when He raises us from the dead, and restores the inheritance of the fathers, as Isaiah again says : " And thou shalt be confident in the LORD, and He will cause thee to pass over the whole earth, and feed thee with the inheritance of Jacob thy father." [4] This is what the Lord declared : " Happy are those servants whom the Lord when He cometh shall find watching. Verily I say unto you, that He shall gird Himself, and make them to sit down [to meat], and will come forth and serve them. And if He shall come in the evening watch, and find them so, blessed are they, because He shall make them sit down, and minister to them ; or if this be in the second, or it be in the third, blessed are they." [5] Again John also says the very same in the Apocalypse : " Blessed and holy is he who has part in the first resurrection." [6] Then, too, Isaiah has declared the time when these events shall occur ; he says : " And I said, Lord, how long ? Until the cities be wasted without inhabitant, and the houses be without men, and the earth be left a desert. And after these things the LORD shall remove us men far away (*longe nos faciet Deus homines*), and those who shall remain shall multiply upon the earth." [7] Then Daniel also says this very thing : " And the kingdom and dominion, and the greatness of those under the heaven, is given to the saints of the Most High God, whose kingdom is everlasting, and all dominions shall serve and obey

Him." [8] And lest the promise named should be understood as referring to this time, it was declared to the prophet : " And come thou, and stand in thy lot at the consummation of the days." [9]

3. Now, that the promises were not announced to the prophets and the fathers alone, but to the Churches united to these from the nations, whom also the Spirit terms " the islands " (both because they are established in the midst of turbulence, suffer the storm of blasphemies, exist as a harbour of safety to those in peril, and are the refuge of those who love the height [of heaven], and strive to avoid Bythus, that is, the depth of error), Jeremiah thus declares : " Hear the word of the LORD, ye nations, and declare it to the isles afar off ; say ye, that the LORD will scatter Israel, He will gather him, and keep him, as one feeding his flock of sheep. For the Lord hath redeemed Jacob, and rescued him from the hand of one stronger than he. And they shall come and rejoice in Mount Zion, and shall come to what is good, and into a land of wheat, and wine, and fruits, of animals and of sheep ; and their soul shall be as a tree bearing fruit, and they shall hunger no more. At that time also shall the virgins rejoice in the company of the young men : the old men, too, shall be glad, and I will turn their sorrow into joy ; and I will make them exult, and will magnify them, and satiate the souls of the priests the sons of Levi ; and my people shall be satiated with my goodness." [10] Now, in the preceding book [11] I have shown that all the disciples of the Lord are Levites and priests, they who used in the temple to profane the Sabbath, but are blameless. [12] Promises of such a nature, therefore, do indicate in the clearest manner the feasting of that creation in the kingdom of the righteous, which God promises that He will Himself serve.

4. Then again, speaking of Jerusalem, and of Him reigning there, Isaiah declares, " Thus saith the LORD, Happy is he who hath seed in Zion, and servants in Jerusalem. Behold, a righteous king shall reign, and princes shall rule with judgment." [13] And with regard to the foundation on which it shall be rebuilt, he says : " Behold, I will lay in order for thee a carbuncle stone, and sapphire for thy foundations ; and I will lay thy ramparts with jasper, and thy gates with crystal, and thy wall with choice stones : and all thy children shall be taught of God, and great shall be the peace of thy children ; and in righteousness shalt thou be built up." [14] And yet again

---

[1] Matt. iii. 9.
[2] Jer. xxiii. 7, 6.
[3] Isa. xxx. 25, 26.
[4] Isa. lviii. 14.
[5] Luke xii. 37, 38.
[6] Rev. xx. 6.
[7] Isa. vi. 11.

[8] Dan. vii. 27.
[9] Dan. xii. 13.
[10] Jer. xxxi. 10, etc.
[11] See iv. 8, 3.
[12] Matt. xii. 5.
[13] Isa. xxxi. 9, xxxii. 1.
[14] Isa. liv. 11-14.

does he say the same thing: "Behold, I make Jerusalem a rejoicing, and my people [a joy]; for the voice of weeping shall be no more heard in her, nor the voice of crying. Also there shall not be there any immature [one], nor an old man who does not fulfil his time: for the youth shall be of a hundred years; and the sinner shall die a hundred years old, yet shall be accursed. And they shall build houses, and inhabit them themselves; and shall plant vineyards, and eat the fruit of them themselves, and shall drink wine. And they shall not build, and others inhabit; neither shall they prepare the vineyard, and others eat. For as the days of the tree of life shall be the days of the people in thee; for the works of their hands shall endure." [1]

CHAP. XXXV. — HE CONTENDS THAT THESE TESTI-MONIES ALREADY ALLEGED CANNOT BE UNDER-STOOD ALLEGORICALLY OF CELESTIAL BLESSINGS, BUT THAT THEY SHALL HAVE THEIR FULFILMENT AFTER THE COMING OF ANTICHRIST, AND THE RESURRECTION, IN THE TERRESTRIAL JERUSALEM. TO THE FORMER PROPHECIES HE SUBJOINS OTHERS DRAWN FROM ISAIAH, JEREMIAH, AND THE APOC-ALYPSE OF JOHN.

1. If, however, any shall endeavour to alleg-orize [prophecies] of this kind, they shall not be found consistent with themselves in all points, and shall be confuted by the teaching of the very expressions [in question]. For example: "When the cities" of the Gentiles "shall be desolate, so that they be not inhabited, and the houses so that there shall be no men in them, and the land shall be left desolate." [2] "For, behold," says Isaiah, "the day of the LORD cometh past remedy, full of fury and wrath, to lay waste the city of the earth, and to root sin-ners out of it." [3] And again he says, "Let him be taken away, that he behold not the glory of God." [4] And when these things are done, he says, "God will remove men far away, and those that are left shall multiply in the earth." [5] "And they shall build houses, and shall inhabit them themselves: and plant vineyards, and eat of them themselves." [6] For all these and other words were unquestionably spoken in reference to the resurrection of the just, which takes place after the coming of Antichrist, and the destruc-tion of all nations under his rule; in [the times of] which [resurrection] the righteous shall reign in the earth, waxing stronger by the sight of the Lord: and through Him they shall be-come accustomed to partake in the glory of God the Father, and shall enjoy in the kingdom in-

tercourse and communion with the holy angels, and union with spiritual beings; and [with re-spect to] those whom the Lord shall find in the flesh, awaiting Him from heaven, and who have suffered tribulation, as well as escaped the hands of the Wicked one. For it is in reference to them that the prophet says: "And those that are left shall multiply upon the earth." And Jere-miah [7] the prophet has pointed out, that as many believers as God has prepared for this purpose, to multiply those left upon earth, should both be under the rule of the saints to minister to this Jerusalem, and that [His] kingdom shall be in it, saying, "Look around Jerusalem towards the east, and behold the joy which comes to thee from God Himself. Behold, thy sons shall come whom thou hast sent forth: they shall come in a band from the east even unto the west, by the word of that Holy One, rejoicing in that splen-dour which is from thy God. O Jerusalem, put off thy robe of mourning and of affliction, and put on that beauty of eternal splendour from thy God. Gird thyself with the double garment of that righteousness proceeding from thy God; place the mitre of eternal glory upon thine head. For God will show thy glory to the whole earth under heaven. For thy name shall for ever be called by God Himself, the peace of righteous-ness and glory to him that worships God. Arise, Jerusalem, stand on high, and look towards the east, and behold thy sons from the rising of the sun, even to the west, by the word of that Holy One, rejoicing in the very remembrance of God. For the footmen have gone forth from thee, while they were drawn away by the enemy. God shall bring them in to thee, being borne with glory as the throne of a kingdom. For God has decreed that every high mountain shall be brought low, and the eternal hills, and that the valleys be filled, so that the surface of the earth be rendered smooth, that Israel, the glory of God, may walk in safety. The woods, too, shall make shady places, and every sweet-smell-ing tree shall be for Israel itself by the command of God. For God shall go before with joy in the light of His splendour, with the pity and righteousness which proceeds from Him."

2. Now all these things being such as they are, cannot be understood in reference to super-celestial matters; "for God," it is said, "will show to the whole earth that is under heaven thy glory." But in the times of the kingdom, the earth has been called again by Christ [to its pristine condition], and Jerusalem rebuilt after the pattern of the Jerusalem above, of which the prophet Isaiah says, "Behold, I have depicted thy walls upon my hands, and thou art always in

---

[1] Isa. lxv. 18.
[2] Isa. vi. 11.
[3] Isa. xiii. 9.
[4] Isa. xxvi. 10.
[5] Isa. vi. 12.
[6] Isa. lxv. 21.

[7] The long quotation following is not found in Jeremiah, but in the apocryphal book of Baruch, chap. iv. 36, etc., and the whole of chap. v.

my sight." [1]   And the apostle, too, writing to the Galatians, says in like manner, " But the Jerusalem which is above is free, which is the mother of us all." [2]   He does not say this with any thought of an erratic Æon, or of any other power which departed from the Pleroma, or of Prunicus, but of the Jerusalem which has been delineated on [God's] hands.   And in the Apocalypse John saw this new [Jerusalem] descending upon the new earth.[3]   For after the times of the kingdom, he says, " I saw a great white throne, and Him who sat upon it, from whose face the earth fled away, and the heavens ; and there was no more place for them." [4]   And he sets forth, too, the things connected with the general resurrection and the judgment, mentioning " the dead, great and small."   "The sea," he says, "gave up the dead which it had in it, and death and hell delivered up the dead that they contained ; and the books were opened.   Moreover," he says, " the book of life was opened, and the dead were judged out of those things that were written in the books, according to their works ; and death and hell were sent into the lake of fire, the second death." [5]   Now this is what is called Gehenna, which the Lord styled eternal fire.[6]   " And if any one," it is said, " was not found written in the book of life, he was sent into the lake of fire." [7]   And after this, he says, " I saw a new heaven and a new earth, for the first heaven and earth have passed away ; also there was no more sea.   And I saw the holy city, new Jerusalem, coming down from heaven, as a bride adorned for her husband."   "And I heard," it is said, "a great voice from the throne, saying, Behold, the tabernacle of God is with men, and He will dwell with them ; and they shall be His people, and God Himself shall be with them as their God.   And He will wipe away every tear from their eyes ; and death shall be no more, neither sorrow, nor crying, neither shall there be any more pain, because the former things have passed away." [8]   Isaiah also declares the very same : " For there shall be a new heaven and a new earth ; and there shall be no remembrance of the former, neither shall the heart think about them, but they shall find in it joy and exultation." [9]   Now this is what has been said by the apostle : " For the fashion of this world passeth away." [10]   To the same purpose did the Lord also declare, " Heaven and earth shall pass away." [11]   When these things, therefore, pass away above the earth,

John, the Lord's disciple, says that the new Jerusalem above shall [then] descend, as a bride adorned for her husband ; and that this is the tabernacle of God, in which God will dwell with men.   Of this Jerusalem the former one is an image — that Jerusalem of the former earth in which the righteous are disciplined beforehand for incorruption and prepared for salvation.   And of this tabernacle Moses received the pattern in the mount ; [12] and nothing is capable of being allegorized, but all things are stedfast, and true, and substantial, having been made by God for righteous men's enjoyment.   For as it is God truly who raises up man, so also does man truly rise from the dead, and not allegorically, as I have shown repeatedly.   And as he rises actually, so also shall he be actually disciplined beforehand for incorruption, and shall go forwards and flourish in the times of the kingdom, in order that he may be capable of receiving the glory of the Father.   Then, when all things are made new, he shall truly dwell in the city of God.   For it is said, " He that sitteth on the throne said, Behold, I make all things new.   And the Lord says, Write all this ; for these words are faithful and true.   And He said to me, They are done." [13] And this is the truth of the matter.

CHAP. XXXVI. — MEN SHALL BE ACTUALLY RAISED : THE WORLD SHALL NOT BE ANNIHILATED ; BUT THERE SHALL BE VARIOUS MANSIONS FOR THE SAINTS, ACCORDING TO THE RANK ALLOTTED TO EACH INDIVIDUAL.   ALL THINGS SHALL BE SUBJECT TO GOD THE FATHER, AND SO SHALL HE BE ALL IN ALL.

1.   For since there are real men, so must there also be a real establishment (*plantationem*), that they vanish not away among non-existent things, but progress among those which have an actual existence.   For neither is the substance nor the essence of the creation annihilated (for faithful and true is He who has established it), but " the *fashion* of the world passeth away ; " [14] that is, those things among which transgression has occurred, since man has grown old in them.   And therefore this [present] fashion has been formed temporary, God foreknowing all things ; as I have pointed out in the preceding book,[15] and have also shown, as far as was possible, the cause of the creation of this world of temporal things.   But when this [present] fashion [of things] passes away, and man has been renewed, and flourishes in an incorruptible state, so as to preclude the possibility of becoming old, [then] there shall be the new heaven and the new earth, in which the new man shall remain [con-

1 Isa. xlix. 16.
2 Gal. iv. 26.
3 Rev. xxi. 2.
4 Rev. xx. 11.
5 Rev. xx. 12–14.
6 Matt. xxv. 41.
7 Rev. xx. 15.
8 Rev. xxi. 1–4.
9 Isa lxv. 17, 18.
10 1 Cor. vii. 31.
11 Matt. xxvi. 35.

12 Ex. xxv. 40.
13 Rev. xxi. 5, 6.
14 1 Cor. vii. 31.
15 Lib. iv. 5, 6.

tinually], always holding fresh converse with God. And since (*or*, that) these things shall ever continue without end, Isaiah declares, "For as the new heavens and the new earth which I do make, continue in my sight, saith the LORD, so shall your seed and your name remain."[1] And as the presbyters say, Then those who are deemed worthy of an abode in heaven shall go there, others shall enjoy the delights of paradise, and others shall possess the splendour of the city; for everywhere the Saviour[2] shall be seen according as they who see Him shall be worthy.

2. [They say, moreover], that there is this distinction between the habitation of those who produce an hundred-fold, and that of those who produce sixty-fold, and that of those who produce thirty-fold: for the first will be taken up into the heavens, the second will dwell in paradise, the last will inhabit the city; and that it was on this account the Lord declared, "In My Father's house are many mansions."[3] For all things belong to God, who supplies all with a suitable dwelling-place; even as His Word says, that a share is allotted to all by the Father, according as each person is or shall be worthy. And this is the couch on which the guests shall recline, having been invited to the wedding.[4] The presbyters, the disciples of the apostles, affirm that this is the gradation and arrangement of those who are saved, and that they advance through steps of this nature; also that they ascend through the Spirit to the Son, and through the Son to the Father, and that in due time the Son will yield up His work to the Father, even as it is said by the apostle, "For He must reign till He hath put all enemies under His feet. The last enemy that shall be destroyed is death."[5] For in the times of the kingdom, the righteous man who is upon the earth shall then forget to die. "But when He saith, All things shall be subdued unto Him, it is manifest that He is excepted who did put all things under Him. And when all things shall be subdued unto Him, then shall the Son also Himself be subject unto Him who put all things under Him, that God may be all in all."[6]

3. John, therefore, did distinctly foresee the first "resurrection of the just,"[7] and the inheritance in the kingdom of the earth; and what the prophets have prophesied concerning it harmonize [with his vision]. For the Lord also taught these things, when He promised that He would have the mixed cup new with His disciples in the kingdom. The apostle, too, has confessed that the creation shall be free from the bondage of corruption, [so as to pass] into the liberty of the sons of God.[8] And in all these things, and by them all, the same God the Father is manifested, who fashioned man, and gave promise of the inheritance of the earth to the fathers, who brought it (the creature) forth [from bondage] at the resurrection of the just, and fulfils the promises for the kingdom of His Son; subsequently bestowing in a paternal manner those things which neither the eye has seen, nor the ear has heard, nor has [thought concerning them] arisen within the heart of man,[9] For there is the one Son, who accomplished His Father's will; and one human race also in which the mysteries of God are wrought, "which the angels desire to look into;"[10] and they are not able to search out the wisdom of God, by means of which His handiwork, confirmed and incorporated with His Son, is brought to perfection; that His offspring, the First-begotten Word, should descend to the creature (*facturam*), that is, to what had been moulded (*plasma*), and that it should be contained by Him; and, on the other hand, the creature should contain the Word, and ascend to Him, passing beyond the angels, and be made after the image and likeness of God.[11]

---

[1] Isa. lxvi. 22.
[2] Thus in a Greek fragment; in the Old Latin, *Deus*.
[3] John xiv. 2.
[4] Matt. xxii. 10.
[5] 1 Cor. xx. 25, 26.

[6] 1 Cor. xv. 27, 28.
[7] Luke xiv. 14.
[8] Rom. viii. 21.
[9] 1 Cor. ii. 9; Isa. lxiv. 4.
[10] 1 Pet. i. 12.
[11] Grabe and others suppose that some part of the work has been lost, so that the above was not its original conclusion.

FRAGMENTS FROM THE LOST WRITINGS OF IRENÆUS

I.

I ADJURE thee, who shalt transcribe this book,[1] by our Lord Jesus Christ, and by His glorious appearing, when He comes to judge the living and the dead, that thou compare what thou hast transcribed, and be careful to set it right according to this copy from which thou hast transcribed; also, that thou in like manner copy down this adjuration, and insert it in the transcript.

II.

These[2] opinions, Florinus, that I may speak in mild terms, are not of sound doctrine; these opinions are not consonant to the Church, and involve their votaries in the utmost impiety; these opinions, even the heretics beyond the Church's pale have never ventured to broach; these opinions, those presbyters who preceded us, and who were conversant with the apostles, did not hand down to thee. For, while I was yet a boy, I saw thee in Lower Asia with Polycarp, distinguishing thyself in the royal court,[3] and endeavouring to gain his approbation. For I have a more vivid recollection of what occurred at that time than of recent events (inasmuch as the experiences of childhood, keeping pace with the growth of the soul, become incorporated with it); so that I can even describe the place where the blessed Polycarp used to sit and discourse — his going out, too, and his coming in — his general mode of life and personal appearance, together with the discourses which he delivered to the people; also how he would speak of his familiar intercourse with John, and with the rest of those who had seen the Lord; and how he would call their words to remembrance. Whatsoever things he had heard from them respecting the Lord, both with regard to His miracles and His teaching, Polycarp having thus received [information] from the eye-witnesses of the Word of life, would recount them all in harmony with the Scriptures. These things, through God's mercy which was upon me, I then listened to attentively, and treasured them up not on paper, but in my heart; and I am continually, by God's grace, revolving these things accurately in my mind. And I can bear witness before God, that if that blessed and apostolical presbyter had heard any such thing, he would have cried out, and stopped his ears, exclaiming as he was wont to do: "O good God, for what times hast Thou reserved me, that I should endure these things?" And he would have fled from the very spot where, sitting or standing, he had heard such words. This fact, too, can be made clear, from his Epistles which he despatched, whether to the neighbouring Churches to confirm them, or to certain of the brethren, admonishing and exhorting them.

III.

For[4] the controversy is not merely as regards the day, but also as regards the form itself of the fast.[5] For some consider themselves bound to fast one day, others two days, others still more, while others [do so during] forty: the diurnal and the nocturnal hours they measure out together as their [fasting] day.[6] And this variety among the observers [of the fasts] had not its origin in our time, but long before in that of our predecessors, some of whom probably, being not very accurate in their observance of it,

---

[1] This fragment is quoted by Eusebius, *Hist. Eccl.*, v. 20. It occurred at the close of the lost treatise of Irenæus entitled *De Ogdoade*.

[2] This interesting extract we also owe to Eusebius, who (*ut sup.*) took it from the work *De Ogdoade*, written after this former friend of Irenæus had lapsed to Valentinianism. Florinus had previously held that God was the author of evil, which sentiment Irenæus opposed in a treatise, now lost, called περὶ μοναρχίας.

[3] Comp. p. 32, this volume, and Phil. iv. 22.

[4] See pp. 31 and 312, of this volume. We are indebted again to Eusebius for this valuable fragment from the Epistle of Irenæus to Victor Bishop of Rome (*Hist. Eccl.*, v. 24: copied also by Nicephorus, iv. 39). It appears to have been a synodical epistle to the head of the Roman Church, the historian saying that it was written by Irenæus, "in the name of (ἐκ προσώπου) those brethren over whom he ruled throughout Gaul." Neither are these expressions to be limited to the Church at Lyons, for the same authority records (v. 23) that it was the testimony "of the dioceses throughout Gaul, which Irenæus superintended" (Harvey).

[5] According to Harvey, the early paschal controversy resolved itself into two particulars: (a) as regards the precise day on which our Lord's resurrection should be celebrated; (b) as regards the custom of the fast preceding it.

[6] Both reading and punctuation are here subjects of controversy. We have followed Massuet and Harvey.

handed down to posterity the custom as it had, through simplicity or private fancy, been [introduced among them]. And yet nevertheless all these lived in peace one with another, and we also keep peace together. Thus, in fact, the difference [in observing] the fast establishes the harmony of [our common] faith.[1] And the presbyters preceding Soter in the government of the Church which thou dost now rule — I mean, Anicetus and Pius, Hyginus and Telesphorus, and Sixtus — did neither themselves observe it [after that fashion], nor permit those with them[2] to do so. Notwithstanding this, those who did not keep [the feast in this way] were peacefully disposed towards those who came to them from other dioceses in which it was [so] observed, although such observance was [felt] in more decided contrariety [as presented] to those who did not fall in with it; and none were ever cast out [of the Church] for this matter. On the contrary, those presbyters who preceded thee, and who did not observe [this custom], sent the Eucharist to those of other dioceses who did observe it.[3] And when the blessed Polycarp was sojourning in Rome in the time of Anicetus, although a slight controversy had arisen among them as to certain other points, they were at once well inclined towards each other [with regard to the matter in hand], not willing that any quarrel should arise between them upon this head. For neither could Anicetus persuade Polycarp to forego the observance [in his own way], inasmuch as these things had been always [so] observed by John the disciple of our Lord, and by other apostles with whom he had been conversant; nor, on the other hand, could Polycarp succeed in persuading Anicetus to keep [the observance in his way], for he maintained that he was bound to adhere to the usage of the presbyters who preceded him. And in this state of affairs they held fellowship with each other; and Anicetus conceded to Polycarp in the Church the celebration of the Eucharist, by way of showing him respect; so that they parted in peace one from the other, maintaining peace with the whole Church, both those who did observe [this custom] and those who did not.[4]

IV.

As[5] long as any one has the means of doing

good to his neighbours, and does not do so, he shall be reckoned a stranger to the love of the Lord.[6]

V.

The[7] will and the energy of God is the effective and foreseeing cause of every time and place and age, and of every nature. The will is the reason (λόγος) of the intellectual soul, which [reason] is within us, inasmuch as it is the faculty belonging to it which is endowed with freedom of action. The will is the mind desiring [some object], and an appetite possessed of intelligence, yearning after that thing which is desired.

VI.

Since[8] God is vast, and the Architect of the world, and omnipotent, He created things that reach to immensity both by the Architect of the world and by an omnipotent will, and with a new effect, potently and efficaciously, in order that the entire fulness of those things which have been produced might come into being, although they had no previous existence — that is, whatever does not fall under [our] observation, and also what lies before our eyes. And so does He contain all things in particular, and leads them on to their own proper result, on account of which they were called into being and produced, in no way changed into anything else than what it (the end) had originally been by nature. For this is the property of the working of God, not merely to proceed to the infinitude of the understanding, or even to overpass [our] powers of mind, reason and speech, time and place, and every age; but also to go beyond substance, and fulness or perfection.

VII.

This[9] [custom], of not bending the knee upon Sunday, is a symbol of the resurrection, through which we have been set free, by the grace of Christ, from sins, and from death, which has been put to death under Him. Now this custom took its rise from apostolic times, as the blessed Irenæus, the martyr and bishop of Lyons, declares in his treatise *On Easter*, in which he makes mention of Pentecost also; upon which [feast] we do not bend the knee, because it is

---

[1] "The observance of *a* day, though not everywhere the same, showed unity, so far as faith in the Lord's resurrection was concerned." — HARVEY.

[2] Following the reading of Rufinus, the ordinary text has μετ' αὐτούς, i.e., after them.

[3] This practice was afterwards forbidden by the Council of Laodicea [held about A.D. 360].

[4] It was perhaps in reference to this pleasing episode in the annals of the Church, that the Council of Arles, A.D. 314, decreed that the holy Eucharist should be consecrated by any foreign bishop present at its celebration.

[5] Quoted by Maximus Bishop of Turin, A.D. 422, *Serm.* vii. *de Eleemos.*, as from the Epistle to Pope Victor. It is also found in some other ancient writers.

[6] One of the MSS. reads here τοῦ Θεοῦ, of God.

[7] Also quoted by Maximus Turinensis, *Op.* ii. 152, who refers it to Irenæus's *Sermo de Fide*, which work, not being referred to by Eusebius or Jerome, causes Massuet to doubt the authenticity of the fragment. Harvey, however, accepts it.

[8] We owe this fragment also to Maximus, who quoted it from the same work, *de Fide*, written by Irenæus to Demetrius, a deacon of Vienne. This and the last fragment were first printed by Feuardentius, who obtained them from Faber: no reference, however, being given as to the source from whence the Latin version was derived. The Greek of this Fragment vi. is not extant.

[9] Taken from a work (*Quæs. et Resp. ad Othod.*) ascribed to Justin Martyr, but certainly written after the Nicene Council. It is evident that this is not an exact quotation from Irenæus, but a summary of his words. The "Sunday" here referred to must be Easter Sunday. Massuet's emendation of the text has been adopted, ἐπ' αὐτοῦ for ἐπ' αὐτῶν.

of equal significance with the Lord's day, for the reason already alleged concerning it.

VIII.

For [1] as the ark [of the covenant] was gilded within and without with pure gold, so was also the body of Christ pure and resplendent; for it was adorned within by the Word, and shielded without by the Spirit, in order that from both [materials] the splendour of the natures might be clearly shown forth.

IX.

Ever [2], indeed, speaking well of the deserving, but never ill of the undeserving, we also shall attain to the glory and kingdom of God.

X.

It is indeed proper to God, and befitting His character, to show mercy and pity, and to bring salvation to His creatures, even though they be brought under danger of destruction. "For with Him," says the Scripture, "is propitiation." [3]

XI.

The business of the Christian is nothing else than to be ever preparing for death (μελεπᾶν ἀποθνήσκειν).

XII.

We therefore have formed the belief that [our] bodies also do rise again. For although they go to corruption, yet they do not perish; for the earth, receiving the remains, preserves them, even like fertile seed mixed with more fertile ground. Again, as a bare grain is sown, and, germinating by the command of God its Creator, rises again, clothed upon and glorious, but not before it has died and suffered decomposition, and become mingled with the earth; so [it is seen from this, that] we have not entertained a vain belief in the resurrection of the body. But although it is dissolved at the appointed time, because of the primeval disobedience, it is placed, as it were, in the crucible of the earth, to be recast again; not then as this corruptible [body], but pure, and no longer subject to decay: so that to each body its own soul shall be restored; and when it is clothed upon with this, it shall not experience sorrow, but shall rejoice, continuing permanently in a state of purity, having for its companion a just consort, not an insidious

one, possessing in every respect the things pertaining to it, it shall receive these with perfect accuracy; [4] it shall not receive bodies diverse from what they had been, nor delivered from suffering or disease, nor as [rendered] glorious, but as they departed this life, in sins or in righteous actions: and such as they were, such shall they be clothed with upon resuming life; and such as they were in unbelief, such shall they be faithfully judged.

XIII.

For [5] when the Greeks, having arrested the slaves of Christian catechumens, then used force against them, in order to learn from them some secret thing [practised] among Christians, these slaves, having nothing to say that would meet the wishes of their tormentors, except that they had heard from their masters that the divine communion was the body and blood of Christ, and imagining that it was actually flesh and blood, gave their inquisitors answer to that effect. Then these latter, assuming such to be the case with regard to the practices of Christians, gave information regarding it to other Greeks, and sought to compel the martyrs Sanctus and Blandina to confess, under the influence of torture, [that the allegation was correct]. To these men Blandina replied very admirably in these words: "How should those persons endure such [accusations], who, for the sake of the practice [of piety], did not avail themselves even of the flesh that was permitted [them to eat]?"

XVI.

How [6] is it possible to say that the serpent, created by God dumb and irrational, was endowed with reason and speech? For if it had the power of itself to speak, to discern, to understand, and to reply to what was spoken by the woman, there would have been nothing to prevent every serpent from doing this also. If, however, they say again that it was according to the divine will and dispensation that this [serpent] spake with a human voice to Eve, they render God the author of sin. Neither was it possible for the evil demon to impart speech to a speechless nature, and thus from that which is not to produce that which is; for if that were the case, he never would have ceased (with the view of leading men astray) from conferring with and deceiving them by means of serpents, and beasts, and birds. From what quarter, too, did it, being a beast, obtain information regarding the injunc-

---

1 Cited by Leontius of Byzantium, who flourished about the year A.D. 600; but he does not mention the writing of Irenæus from which it is extracted. Massuet conjectures that it is from the *De Ogdoade*, addressed to the apostate Florinus.

2 This fragment and the next three are from the *Parallela* of John of Damascus. Frag. ix. x. xii. seem to be quotations from the treatise of Irenæus on the resurrection. No. xi. is extracted from his *Miscellaneous Dissertations*, a work mentioned by Eusebius, βιβλίον τι διαλεξέων διαφόρων.

3 Ps. cxxx. 7.

4 This sentence in the original seems incomplete; we have followed the conjectural restoration of Harvey.

5 "This extract is found in Œcumenius upon 1 Pet. c. iii. p. 198: and the words used by him indicate, as Grabe has justly observed, that he only condensed a longer passage." — HARVEY.

6 From the *Contemplations* of Anastasius Sinaita, who flourished A.D. 685. Harvey doubts as to this fragment being a genuine production of Irenæus; and its whole style of reasoning confirms the suspicion.

tion of God to the man given to him alone, and in secret, not even the woman herself being aware of it? Why also did it not prefer to make its attack upon the man instead of the woman? And if thou sayest that it attacked her as being the weaker of the two, [I reply that], on the contrary, she was the stronger, since she appears to have been the helper of the man in the transgression of the commandment. For she did by herself alone resist the serpent, and it was after holding out for a while and making opposition that she ate of the tree, being circumvented by craft; whereas Adam, making no fight whatever, nor refusal, partook of the fruit handed to him by the woman, which is an indication of the utmost imbecility and effeminacy of mind. And the woman indeed, having been vanquished in the contest by a demon, is deserving of pardon; but Adam shall deserve none, for he was worsted by a woman, — he who, in his own person, had received the command from God. But the woman, having heard of the command from Adam, treated it with contempt, either because she deemed it unworthy of God to speak by means of it, or because she had her doubts, perhaps even held the opinion that the command was given to her by Adam of his own accord. The serpent found her working alone, so that he was enabled to confer with her apart. Observing her then either eating or not eating from the trees, he put before her the fruit of the [forbidden] tree. And if he saw her eating, it is manifest that she was partaker of a body subject to corruption. "For everything going in at the mouth, is cast out into the draught." [1] If then corruptible, it is obvious that she was also mortal. But if mortal, then there was certainly no curse; nor was that a [condemnatory] sentence, when the voice of God spake to the man, "For earth thou art, and unto earth shalt thou return," [2] as the true course of things proceeds [now and always]. Then again, if the serpent observed the woman not eating, how did he induce her to eat who never had eaten? And who pointed out to this accursed man-slaying serpent that the sentence of death pronounced against them by God would not take [immediate] effect, when He said, "For in the day that ye eat thereof, ye shall surely die?" And not this merely, but that along with the impunity [3] [attending their sin] the eyes of those should be opened who had not seen until then? But with the opening [of their eyes] referred to, they made entrance upon the path of death.

[1] Matt. xv. 17.
[2] Gen. iii. 19.
[3] The Greek reads the barbarous word ἀθριξία, which Massuet thinks is a corruption of ἀθανασία, immortality. We have, however, followed the conjecture of Harvey, who would substitute ἀπληξία, which seems to agree better with the context.

XV.

When, [4] in times of old, Balaam spake these things in parables, he was not acknowledged; and now, when Christ has appeared and fulfilled them, He was not believed. Wherefore [Balaam], foreseeing this, and wondering at it, exclaimed, "Alas! alas! who shall live when God brings these things to pass?" [5]

XVI.

Expounding again the law to that generation which followed those who were slain in the wilderness, he published Deuteronomy; not as giving to them a different law from that which had been appointed for their fathers, but as recapitulating this latter, in order that they, by hearing what had happened to their fathers, might fear God with their whole heart.

XVII.

By these Christ was typified, and acknowledged, and brought into the world; for He was prefigured in Joseph: then from Levi and Judah He was descended according to the flesh, as King and Priest; and He was acknowledged by Simeon in the temple: through Zebulon He was believed in among the Gentiles, as says the prophet, "the land of Zabulon;" [6] and through Benjamin [that is, Paul] He was glorified, by being preached throughout all the world. [7]

XVIII.

And this was not without meaning; but that by means of the number of the ten men, [8] he (Gideon) might appear as having Jesus for a helper, as [is indicated] by the compact entered into with them. And when he did not choose to partake with them in their idol-worship, they threw the blame upon him: for "Jerubbaal" signifies the judgment-seat of Baal.

XIX.

"Take unto thee Joshua (Ἰησοῦν) the son of Nun." [9] For it was proper that Moses should lead the people out of Egypt, but that Jesus (*Joshua*) should lead them into the inheritance. Also that Moses, as was the case with the law, should cease to be, but that Joshua (Ἰησοῦν), as the word, and no untrue type of the Word made

[4] This and the eight following fragments may be referred to the *Miscellaneous Dissertations* of our author; see note on Frag. ix. They are found in three MSS. in the Imperial Collection at Paris, on the Pentateuch, Joshua, Judges, and Ruth.
[5] Num. xxiv. 23.
[6] Isa. ix. 1.
[7] Compare the statement of Clemens Romanus (page 6 of this volume), where, speaking of St. Paul, he says: "After preaching both in the east and west . . . . having taught righteousness to the whole world, and come to the extreme limit of the west."
[8] See Judg. vi. 27. It is not very clear how Irenæus makes out this allegory, but it is thought that he refers to the initial letter in the name Ἰησοῦς, which stands for *ten* in the Greek enumeration. Compare the *Epistle of Barnabas*, cap. ix. p. 143, of this volume.
[9] Num. xxvii. 18.

flesh (ἐνυποστάτου), should be a preacher to the people. Then again, [it was fit] that Moses should give manna as food to the fathers, but Joshua wheat;[1] as the first-fruits of life, a type of the body of Christ, as also the Scripture declares that the manna of the Lord ceased when the people had eaten wheat from the land.[2]

XX.

"And[3] he laid his hands upon him."[4] The countenance of Joshua was also glorified by the imposition of the hands of Moses, but not to the same degree [as that of Moses]. Inasmuch, then, as he had obtained a certain degree of grace, [the Lord] said, "And thou shalt confer upon him of thy glory."[5] For [in this case] the thing given does not cease to belong to the giver.

XXI.

But he does not give, as Christ did, by means of breathing, because he is not the fount of the Spirit.

XXII.

"Thou shalt not go with them, neither shalt thou curse the people."[6] He does not hint at anything with regard to the people, for they all lay before his view, but [he refers] to the mystery of Christ pointed out beforehand. For as He was to be born of the fathers according to the flesh, the Spirit gives instructions to the man (Balaam) beforehand, lest, going forth in ignorance, he might pronounce a curse upon the people.[7] Not, indeed, that [his curse] could take any effect contrary to the will of God; but [this was done] as an exhibition of the providence of God which He exercised towards them on account of their forefathers.

XXIII.

"And he mounted upon his ass."[8] The ass was the type of the body of Christ, upon whom all men, resting from their labours, are borne as in a chariot. For the Saviour has taken up the burden of our sins.[9] Now the angel who appeared to Balaam was the Word Himself; and in His hand He held a sword, to indicate the power which He had from above.

XXIV.

"God is not as a man."[10] He thus shows that all men are indeed guilty of falsehood, inasmuch as they change from one thing to another (μεταφερόμενοι); but such is not the case with God, for He always continues true, perfecting whatever He wishes.

XXV.

"To inflict vengeance from the Lord on Midian."[11] For this man (Balaam), when he speaks no longer in the Spirit of God, but contrary to God's law, by setting up a different law with regard to fornication,[12] is certainly not then to be counted as a prophet, but as a soothsayer. For he who did not keep to the commandment of God, received the just recompense of his own evil devices.[13]

XXVI.

Know[14] thou that every man is either empty or full. For if he has not the Holy Spirit, he has no knowledge of the Creator; he has not received Jesus Christ the Life; he knows not the Father who is in heaven; if he does not live after the dictates of reason, after the heavenly law, he is not a sober-minded person, nor does he act uprightly: such an one is empty. If, on the other hand, he receives God, who says, "I will dwell with them, and walk in them, and I will be their God,"[15] such an one is not empty, but full.

XXVII.

The little boy, therefore, who guided Samson by the hand,[16] pre-typified John the Baptist, who showed to the people the faith in Christ. And the house in which they were assembled signifies the world, in which dwell the various heathen and unbelieving nations, offering sacrifice to their idols. Moreover, the two pillars are the two covenants. The fact, then, of Samson leaning himself upon the pillars, [indicates] this, that the people, when instructed, recognized the mystery of Christ.

XXVIII.

"And the man of God said, Where did it fall? And he showed him the place. And he cut down a tree, and cast it in there, and the iron floated."[17] This was a sign that souls should be borne aloft (ἀναγωγῆς ψυχῶν) through the instrumentality of wood, upon which He suffered who can lead those souls aloft that follow His ascension. This event was also an indication of

---

[1] Harvey conceives the reading here (which is doubtful) to have been τὸν νέον σῖτον, the new wheat; and sees an allusion to the wave-sheaf of the new corn offered in the temple on the morning of our Lord's resurrection.
[2] Josh. v. 12.
[3] Massuet seems to more than doubt the genuineness of this fragment and the next, and would ascribe them to the pen of Apollinaris, bishop of Hierapolis in Phrygia, a contemporary of Irenæus. Harvey passes over these two fragments.
[4] Num. xxvii. 23.
[5] Num. xxvii. 20.
[6] Num. xxii. 12.
[7] The conjectural emendation of Harvey has been adopted here, but the text is very corrupt and uncertain.
[8] Num. xxii. 22, 23.
[9] From one of the MSS. Stieren would insert ἐν τῷ ἰδίῳ σώματι, in His own body; see 1 Pet. ii. 24.

[10] Num. xxiii. 19.
[11] Num. xxxi. 3.
[12] Num. xxxi. 16.
[13] Num. xxxi. 8.
[14] It is not certain from what work of Irenæus this extract is derived; Harvey thinks it to be from his work περὶ ἐπιστήμης, i.e., concerning Knowledge.
[15] Lev. xxvi. 12.
[16] Judg. xvi. 26.
[17] 2 Kings vi. 6. Comp. book v. chap. xvii. 4.

the fact, that when the holy soul of Christ descended [to Hades], many souls ascended and were seen in their bodies.[1] For just as the wood, which is the lighter body, was submerged in the water; but the iron, the heavier one, floated: so, when the Word of God became one with flesh, by a physical and hypostatic union, the heavy and terrestrial [part], having been rendered immortal, was borne up into heaven, by the divine nature, after the resurrection.

XXIX.

The[2] Gospel according to Matthew was written to the Jews. For they laid particular stress upon the fact that Christ [should be] of the seed of David. Matthew also, who had a still greater desire [to establish this point], took particular pains to afford them convincing proof that Christ is of the seed of David; and therefore he commences with [an account of] His genealogy.

XXX.[3]

"The axe unto the root,"[4] he says, urging us to the knowledge of the truth, and purifying us by means of fear, as well as preparing [us] to bring forth fruit in due season.

XXXI.

Observe[5] that, by means of the grain of mustard seed in the parable, the heavenly doctrine is denoted which is sown like seed in the world, as in a field, [seed] which has an inherent force, fiery and powerful. For the Judge of the whole world is thus proclaimed, who, having been hidden in the heart of the earth in a tomb for three days, and having become a great tree, has stretched forth His branches to the ends of the earth. Sprouting out from Him, the twelve apostles, having become fair and fruitful boughs, were made a shelter for the nations as for the fowls of heaven, under which boughs, all having taken refuge, as birds flocking to a nest, have been made partakers of that wholesome and celestial food which is derived from them.

XXXII.[6]

Josephus says, that when Moses had been brought up in the royal palaces, he was chosen as general against the Ethiopians; and having proved victorious, obtained in marriage the daughter of that king, since indeed, out of her affection for him, she delivered the city up to him.[7]

Why was it, that when these two (Aaron and Miriam) had both acted with despite towards him (Moses), the latter alone was adjudged punishment?[8] First, because the woman was the more culpable, since both nature and the law place the woman in a subordinate condition to the man. Or perhaps it was that Aaron was to a certain degree excusable, in consideration of his being the elder [brother], and adorned with the dignity of high priest. Then again, inasmuch as the leper was accounted by the law unclean, while at the same time the origin and foundation of the priesthood lay in Aaron, [the Lord] did not award a similar punishment to him, lest this stigma should attach itself to the entire [sacerdotal] race; but by means of his sister's [example] He awoke his fears, and taught him the same lesson. For Miriam's punishment affected him to such an extent, that no sooner did she experience it, than he entreated [Moses], who had been injured, that he would by his intercession do away with the affliction. And he did not neglect to do so, but at once poured forth his supplication. Upon this the Lord, who loves mankind, made him understand how He had not chastened her as a judge, but as a father; for He said, "If her father had spit in her face, should she not be ashamed? Let her be shut out from the camp seven days, and after that let her come in again."[9]

XXXIII.

Inasmuch[10] as certain men, impelled by what considerations I know not, remove from God the half of His creative power, by asserting that He is merely the cause of quality resident in matter, and by maintaining that matter itself is uncreated, come now let us put the question, What is at any time ... is immutable. Matter, then, is immutable. But if matter be immutable, and the immutable suffers no change in regard to quality, it does not form the substance of the world. For which reason it seems to them superfluous, that God has annexed qualities to matter, since indeed matter admits of no possible alteration, it being in itself an uncreated thing. But further, if matter be uncreated, it has been made altogether according to a certain

[1] Matt. xxvii. 52.
[2] Edited by P. Possin, in a *Catena Patrum* on St. Matthew. See book iii. chap. xi. 8.
[3] From the same *Catena*. Compare book v. chap. xvii. 4.
[4] Matt. iii. 10.
[5] First edited in Latin by Corderius, afterwards in Greek by Grabe, and also by Dr. Cramer in his *Catena* on St. Luke.
[6] Massuet's Fragment xxxii. is here passed over; it is found in book iii. chap. xviii. 7.

[7] See Josephus' *Antiquities*, book ii. chap. x., where we read that this king's daughter was called Tharbis. Immediately upon the surrender of this city (Saba, afterwards called Meroë) Moses married her, and returned to Egypt. Whiston, in the notes to his translation of Josephus, says, "Nor, perhaps, did St. Stephen refer to anything else when he said of Moses, before he was sent by God to the Israelites, that he was not only learned in all the wisdom of the Egyptians, but was also mighty in words and in deeds" (Acts vii. 22).
[8] Num. xii. 1, etc.
[9] Num. xii. 14.
[10] Harvey considers this fragment to be a part of the work of Irenæus referred to by Photius under the title *De Universo*, or *de Substantiâ Mundi*. It is to be found in Codex 3011 of the Bodleian Library, Oxford.

quality, and this immutable, so that it cannot be receptive of more qualities, nor can it be the thing of which the world is made. But if the world be not made from it, [this theory] entirely excludes God from exercising power on the creation [of the world].

XXXIV.

"And [1] dipped himself," says [the Scripture], "seven times in Jordan." [2] It was not for nothing that Naaman of old, when suffering from leprosy, was purified upon his being baptized, but [it served] as an indication to us. For as we are lepers in sin, we are made clean, by means of the sacred water and the invocation of the Lord, from our old transgressions; being spiritually regenerated as new-born babes, even as the Lord has declared: "Except a man be born again through water and the Spirit, he shall not enter into the kingdom of heaven." [3]

XXXV.

If the corpse of Elisha raised a dead man,[4] how much more shall God, when He has quickened men's dead bodies, bring them up for judgment?

XXXVI.

True [5] knowledge, then, consists in the understanding of Christ, which Paul terms the wisdom of God hidden in a mystery, which " the natural man receiveth not," [6] the doctrine of the cross; of which if any man " taste," [7] he will not accede to the disputations and quibbles of proud and puffed-up men,[8] who go into matters of which they have no perception.[9] For the truth is unsophisticated (ἀσχημάτιστος); and " the word is nigh thee, in thy mouth and in thy heart," [10] as the same apostle declares, being easy of comprehension to those who are obedient. For it renders us like to Christ, if we experience " the power of his resurrection and the fellowship of His sufferings." [11] For this is the affinity [12] of the apostolical teaching and the most holy " faith

delivered unto us," [13] which the unlearned receive, and those of slender knowledge have taught, not " giving heed to endless genealogies," [14] but studying rather [to observe] a straightforward course of life; lest, having been deprived of the Divine Spirit, they fail to attain to the kingdom of heaven. For truly the first thing is to deny one's self and to follow Christ; and those who do this are borne onward to perfection, having fulfilled all their Teacher's will, becoming sons of God by spiritual regeneration, and heirs of the kingdom of heaven; those who seek which first shall not be forsaken.

XXXVII.

Those who have become acquainted with the secondary (i.e., under Christ) constitutions of the apostles,[15] are aware that the Lord instituted a new oblation in the new covenant, according to [the declaration of] Malachi the prophet. For, " from the rising of the sun even to the setting my name has been glorified among the Gentiles, and in every place incense is offered to my name, and a pure sacrifice;" [16] as John also declares in the Apocalypse: " The incense is the prayers of the saints." [17] Then again, Paul exhorts us " to present our bodies a living sacrifice, holy, acceptable unto God, which is your reasonable service." [18] And again, " Let us offer the sacrifice of praise, that is, the fruit of the lips." [19] Now those oblations are not according to the law, the handwriting of which the Lord took away from the midst by cancelling it; [20] but they are according to the Spirit, for we must worship God " in spirit and in truth." [21] And therefore the oblation of the Eucharist is not a carnal one, but a spiritual; and in this respect it is pure. For we make an oblation to God of the bread and the cup of blessing, giving Him thanks in that He has commanded the earth to bring forth these fruits for our nourishment. And then, when we have perfected the oblation, we invoke the Holy Spirit, that He may exhibit this sacrifice, both the bread the body of Christ, and the cup the blood of Christ, in order that the receivers of these antitypes [22] may obtain remission of sins and life eternal. Those persons, then, who perform these oblations in remem-

---

[1] This and the next fragment first appeared in the Benedictine edition reprinted at Venice, 1734. They were taken from a MS. *Catena* on the book of Kings in the Coislin Collection.
[2] 2 Kings v. 14.
[3] John iii. 5.
[4] 2 Kings xiii. 21.
[5] This extract and the next three were discovered in the year 1715 by [Christopher Matthew] Pfaff, a learned Lutheran, in the Royal Library at Turin. The MSS. from which they were taken were neither catalogued nor classified, and have now disappeared from the collection. It is impossible to say with any degree of probability from what treatises of our author these four fragments have been culled. For a full account of their history, see Stieren's edition of Irenæus, vol. ii. p. 381. [But, in all candor, let Pfaff himself be heard. His little work is full of learning. and I have long possessed it as a treasure to which I often recur. Pfaff's *Irenæi Fragmenta* was published at The Hague, 1715.]
[6] 1 Cor. ii. 14.
[7] 1 Pet. ii. 3.
[8] 1 Tim. vi. 4, 5.
[9] Col. ii. 18.
[10] Rom. x. 8; Deut. xxx. 14.
[11] Phil. iii. 10.
[12] Harvey's conjectural emendation, ἐπιπλοκὴ for ἐπιλογὴ, has been adopted here.

[13] Jude 3.
[14] 1 Tim. i. 4.
[15] ταῖς δευτέραις τῶν ἀποστόλων διατάξεσι. Harvey thinks that these words imply, " the formal constitution, which the apostles, acting under the impulse of the Spirit, though still in a secondary capacity, gave to the Church."
[16] Mal. i. 11.
[17] Rev. v. 8. The same view of the eucharistic oblation, etc., is found in book iv. chap. xvii.: as also in Justin Martyr; see *Trypho*, cap. xli. *supra* in this volume.
[18] Rom. xii. 1.
[19] Heb. xiii. 15.
[20] Col. ii. 14.
[21] John iv. 24.
[22] Harvey explains this word ἀντιτύπων as meaning an " exact counterpart." He refers to the word where it occurs in *Contra Hæreses*, lib. i. chap. xxiv. (p. 349, this vol.) as confirmatory of his view.

brance of the Lord, do not fall in with Jewish views, but, performing the service after a spiritual manner, they shall be called sons of wisdom.

XXXVIII.

The [1] apostles ordained, that " we should not judge any one in respect to meat or drink, or in regard to a feast day, or the new moons, or the sabbaths." [2] Whence then these contentions? whence these schisms? We keep the feast, but in the leaven of malice and wickedness, cutting in pieces the Church of God; and we preserve what belongs to its exterior, that we may cast away these better things, faith and love. We have heard from the prophetic words that these feasts and fasts are displeasing to the Lord.[3]

XXXIX.

Christ,[4] who was called the Son of God before the ages, was manifested in the fulness of time, in order that He might cleanse us through His blood, who were under the power of sin, presenting us as pure sons to His Father, if we yield ourselves obediently to the chastisement of the Spirit. And in the end of time He shall come to do away with all evil, and to reconcile all things, in order that there may be an end of all impurities.

XL.

"And [5] he found the jaw-bone of an ass." [6] It is to be observed that, after [Samson had committed] fornication, the holy Scripture no longer speaks of the things happily accomplished by him in connection with the formula, "The Spirit of the Lord came upon him." [7] For thus, according to the holy apostle, the sin of fornication is perpetrated against the body, as involving also sin against the temple of God.[8]

XLI.

This [9] indicates the persecution against the Church set on foot by the nations who still continue in unbelief. But he (Samson) who suffered those things, trusted that there would be a retaliation against those waging this war. But retaliation through what means? First of all, by his betaking himself to the Rock [10] not cog-

nizable to the senses; [11] secondly, by the finding of the jaw-bone of an ass. Now the type of the jaw-bone is the body of Christ.

XLII.

Speaking always well of the worthy, but never ill of the unworthy, we also shall attain to the glory and kingdom of God.

XLIII.

In [12] these things there was signified by prophecy that the people, having become transgressors, shall be bound by the chains of their own sins. But the breaking of the bonds of their own accord indicates that, upon repentance, they shall be again loosed from the shackles of sin.

XLIV.

It [13] is not an easy thing for a soul, under the influence of error, to be persuaded of the contrary opinion.

XLV.

"And [14] Balaam the son of Beor they slew with the sword." [15] For, speaking no longer by the Spirit of God, but setting up another law of fornication contrary to the law of God,[16] this man shall no longer be reckoned as a prophet, but as a soothsayer. For, as he did not continue in the commandment of God, he received the just reward of his evil devices.

XLVI.

"The [17] god of the world;" [18] that is, Satan, who was designated God to those who believe not.

XLVII.

The [19] birth of John [the Baptist] brought the dumbness of Zacharias to an end. For he did not burden his father, when the voice issued forth from silence; but as when not believed it rendered him tongue-tied, so did the voice sounding out clearly set his father free, to whom he had both been announced and born. Now the voice and the burning light [20] were a precursor of the Word and the Light.

---

[1] Taken apparently from the *Epistle to Blastus, de Schismate*. Compare a similar passage, lib. iv. chap. xxxiii. 7.
[2] Col. ii. 16.
[3] Isa. i. 14.
[4] " From the same collection at Turin. The passage seems to be of cognate matter with the treatise *De Resurrec*. Pfaff referred it either to the διαλέξεις διάφοροι or to the ἐπίδειξις ἀποστολικοῦ κηρύγματος." — HARVEY.
[5] This and the four following fragments are taken from MSS. in the Vatican Library at Rome. They are apparently quoted from the homiletical expositions of the historical books already referred to.
[6] Judg. xv. 15.
[7] Judg. xiv. 6-19.
[8] 1 Cor. iii. 16, 17.
[9] These words were evidently written during a season of persecution in Gaul; but what that persecution was, it is useless to conjecture.
[10] Judg. xv. 11.

[11] That is, when he fled to the rock Etam, he typified the true believer taking refuge in the spiritual Rock, Christ.
[12] Most probably from a homily upon the third and fourth chapters of Ezekiel. It is found repeated in Stieren's and Migne's edition as Fragment xlviii. extracted from a *Catena* on the Book of Judges.
[13] We give this brief fragment as it appears in the editions of Stieren, Migne, and Harvey, who speculate as to its origin. They seem to have overlooked the fact that it is the Greek original of the old Latin, *non facile est ab errore apprehensam resipiscere animam*, — a sentence found towards the end of book iii. chap. ii.
[14] With the exception of the initial text, this fragment is almost identical with No. xxv.
[15] Num. xxxi. 8.
[16] Rev. ii. 14.
[17] From the *Catena* on St. Paul's Epistles to the Corinthians, edited by Dr. Cramer, and reprinted by Stieren.
[18] 2 Cor. iv. 4.
[19] Extracted from a MS. of Greek theology in the Palatine Library at Vienna. The succeeding fragment in the editions of Harvey, Migne, and Stieren, is omitted, as it is merely a transcript of book iii. ch. x. 4.
[20] John v. 35.

XLVIII.

As [1] therefore seventy tongues are indicated by number, and from [2] dispersion the tongues are gathered into one by means of their interpretation; so is that ark declared a type of the body of Christ, which is both pure and immaculate. For [3] as that ark was gilded with pure gold both within and without, so also is the body of Christ pure and resplendent, being adorned within by the Word, and shielded on the outside by the Spirit, in order that from both [materials] the splendour of the natures might be exhibited together.

XLIX.

Now [4] therefore, by means of this which has been already brought forth a long time since, the Word has assigned an interpretation. We are convinced that there exist [so to speak] two men in each one of us. The one is confessedly a hidden thing, while the other stands apparent; one is corporeal, the other spiritual; although the generation of both may be compared to that of twins. For both are revealed to the world as but one, for the soul was not anterior to the body in its essence; nor, in regard to its formation, did the body precede the soul: but both these were produced at one time; and their nourishment consists in purity and sweetness.

L.

For [5] then there shall in truth be a common joy consummated to all those who believe unto life, and in each individual shall be confirmed the mystery of the Resurrection, and the hope of incorruption, and the commencement of the eternal kingdom, when God shall have destroyed death and the devil. For that human nature and flesh which has risen again from the dead shall die no more; but after it had been changed to incorruption, and made like to spirit, when the heaven was opened, [our Lord] full of glory offered it (the flesh) to the Father.

LI.

Now, [6] however, inasmuch as the books of these men may possibly have escaped your observation, but have come under our notice, I call your attention to them, that for the sake of your reputation you may expel these writings from among you, as bringing disgrace upon you, since their author boasts himself as being one of your company. For they constitute a stumbling-block to many, who simply and unreservedly receive, as coming from a presbyter, the blasphemy which they utter against God. Just [consider] the writer of these things, how by means of them he does not injure assistants [in divine service] only, who happen to be prepared in mind for blasphemies against God, but also damages those among us, since by his books he imbues their minds with false doctrines concerning God.

LII.

The [7] sacred books acknowledge with regard to Christ, that as He is the Son of man, so is the same Being not a [mere] man; and as He is flesh, so is He also spirit, and the Word of God, and God. And as He was born of Mary in the last times, so did He also proceed from God as the First-begotten of every creature; and as He hungered, so did He satisfy [others]; and as He thirsted, so did He of old cause the Jews to drink, for the "Rock was Christ" [8] Himself: thus does Jesus now give to His believing people power to drink spiritual waters, which spring up to life eternal. [9] And as He was the son of David, so was He also the Lord of David. And as He was from Abraham, so did He also exist before Abraham. [10] And as He was the servant of God, so is He the Son of God, and Lord of the universe. And as He was spit upon ignominiously, so also did He breathe the Holy Spirit into His disciples. [11] And as He was saddened, so also did He give joy to His people. And as He was capable of being handled and touched, so again did He, in a non-apprehensible form, pass through the midst of those who sought to injure Him, [12] and entered without impediment through closed doors. [13] And as He slept, so did He also rule the sea, the winds, and the storms. And as He suffered, so also is He alive, and life-giving, and healing all our infirmity. And as He died, so is He also the Resurrection of the dead. He suffered shame on earth, while He is higher than all glory and praise in heaven; who, "though He was crucified through weakness, yet He liveth by divine power;" [14] who "descended into the lower parts of the earth," and who "ascended up above the heavens;" [15] for whom a manger

---

1 This fragment commences a series derived from the Nitrian Collection of Syriac MSS. in the British Museum.
2 The Syriac text is here corrupt and obscure.
3 See No. viii., which is the same as the remainder of this fragment.
4 The Syriac MS. introduces this quotation as follows: "From the holy Irenæus Bp. of Lyons, from the first section of his interpretation of the Song of Songs."
5 This extract is introduced as follows: "For Irenæus Bishop of Lyons, who was a contemporary of the disciple of the apostle, Polycarp Bishop of Smyrna, and martyr, and for this reason is held in just estimation, wrote to an Alexandrian to the effect that it is right, with respect to the feast of the Resurrection, that we should celebrate it upon the first day of the week." This shows us that the extract must have been taken from the work *Against Schism* addressed to Blastus.
6 From the same MS. as the preceding fragment It is thus introduced: "And Irenæus Bp. of Lyons, to Victor Bp. of Rome, concerning Florinus, a presbyter, who was a partisan of the error of Valentinus, and published an abominable book, thus wrote."

7 This extract had already been printed by M. Pitra in his *Spicilegium Solesmense*, p. 6.
8 1 Cor. x. 4.
9 John iv. 14.
10 John viii. 58.
11 John xx. 22.
12 John viii. 59.
13 John xx. 26.
14 2 Cor. xiii. 4.
15 Eph. iv. 9, 10.

sufficed, yet who filled all things ; who was dead, yet who liveth for ever and ever. Amen.

LIII.

With [1] regard to Christ, the law and the prophets and the evangelists have proclaimed that He was born of a virgin, that He suffered upon a beam of wood, and that He appeared from the dead ; that He also ascended to the heavens, and was glorified by the Father, and is the Eternal King ; that He is the perfect Intelligence, the Word of God, who was begotten before the light ; that He was the Founder of the universe, along with it (light), and the Maker of man ; that He is All in all : Patriarch among the patriarchs ; Law in the laws ; Chief Priest among priests ; Ruler among kings ; the Prophet among prophets ; the Angel among angels ; the Man among men ; Son in the Father ; God in God ; King to all eternity. For it is He who sailed [in the ark] along with Noah, and who guided Abraham ; who was bound along with Isaac, and was a Wanderer with Jacob ; the Shepherd of those who are saved, and the Bridegroom of the Church ; the Chief also of the cherubim, the Prince of the angelic powers ; God of God ; Son of the Father ; Jesus Christ ; King for ever and ever. Amen.

LIV.

The [2] law and the prophets and evangelists have declared that Christ was born of a virgin, and suffered on the cross ; was raised also from the dead, and taken up to heaven ; that He was glorified, and reigns for ever. He is Himself termed the Perfect Intellect, the Word of God. He is the First-begotten,[3] after a transcendent manner, the Creator of man ; All in all ; Patriarch among the patriarchs ; Law in the law ; the Priest among priests ; among kings Prime Leader ; the Prophet among the prophets ; the Angel among angels ; the Man among men ; Son in the Father ; God in God ; King to all eternity. He was sold with Joseph, and He guided Abraham ; was bound along with Isaac, and wandered with Jacob ; with Moses He was Leader, and, respecting the people, Legislator. He preached in the prophets ; was incarnate of a virgin ; born in Bethlehem ; received by John, and baptized in Jordan ; was tempted in the desert, and proved to be the Lord. He gathered the apostles together, and preached the kingdom of heaven ; gave light to the blind, and raised the dead ; was seen in the temple,

but was not held by the people as worthy of credit ; was arrested by the priests, conducted before Herod, and condemned in the presence of Pilate ; He manifested Himself in the body, was suspended upon a beam of wood, and raised from the dead ; shown to the apostles, and, having been carried up to heaven, sitteth on the right hand of the Father, and has been glorified by Him as the Resurrection of the dead. Moreover, He is the Salvation of the lost, the Light to those dwelling in darkness, and Redemption to those who have been born ; the Shepherd of the saved, and the Bridegroom of the Church ; the Charioteer of the cherubim, the Leader of the angelic host ; God of God ; Jesus Christ our Saviour.

LV.

"Then [4] drew near unto Him the mother of Zebedee's children, with her sons, worshipping, and seeking a certain thing from Him." [5] These people are certainly not void of understanding, nor are the words set forth in that passage of no signification : being stated beforehand like a preface, they have some agreement with those points formerly expounded.

"Then drew near." Sometimes virtue excites our admiration, not merely on account of the display which is given of it, but also of the occasion when it was manifested. I may refer, for example, to the premature fruit of the grape, or of the fig, or to any fruit whatsoever, from which, during its process [of growth], no man expects maturity or full development ; yet, although any one may perceive that it is still somewhat imperfect, he does not for that reason despise as useless the immature grape when plucked, but he gathers it with pleasure as appearing early in the season ; nor does he consider whether the grape is possessed of perfect sweetness ; nay, he at once experiences satisfaction from the thought that this one has appeared before the rest. Just in the same way does God also, when He perceives the faithful possessing wisdom though still imperfect, and but a small degree of faith, overlook their defect in this respect, and therefore does not reject them ; nay, but on the contrary, He kindly welcomes and accepts them as premature fruits, and honours the mind, whatsoever it may be, which is stamped with virtue, although not yet perfect. He makes allowance for it, as being among the harbingers of the vintage,[6] and esteems it highly, inasmuch as, being of a readier disposition than the rest, it has forestalled, as it were, the blessing to itself.

---

[1] This extract from the Syriac is a shorter form of the next fragment, which seems to be interpolated in some places. The latter is from an Armenian MS. in the Mechitarist Library at Venice.

[2] This fragment is thus introduced in the Armenian copy : " From St. Irenæus, bishop, follower of the apostles, on the Lord's resurrection."

[3] The Armenian text is confused here ; we have adopted the conjectural emendation of Quatremere.

[4] From an Armenian MS. in the Library of the Mechitarist Convent at Vienna, edited by M. Pitra, who considers this fragment as of very doubtful authority. It commences with this heading : " From the second series of Homilies of Saint Irenæus, follower of the Apostles ; a Homily upon the Sons of Zebedee."

[5] Matt. xx. 20.

[6] That is, the wine which flows from the grapes before they are trodden out.

Abraham therefore, Isaac, and Jacob, our fathers, are to be esteemed before all, since they did indeed afford us such early examples of virtue. How many martyrs can be compared to Daniel? How many martyrs, I ask, can rival the three youths in Babylon, although the memory of the former has not been brought before us so conspicuously as that of the latter? These were truly first-fruits, and indications of the [succeeding] fructification. Hence God has directed their life to be recorded, as a model for those who should come after.

And that their virtue was thus accepted by God, as the first-fruits of the produce, hear what He has Himself declared: "As a grape," He says, "I have found Israel in the wilderness, and as first-ripe figs your fathers." [1] Call not therefore the faith of Abraham merely blessed because he believed. Do you wish to look upon Abraham with admiration? Then behold how that one man alone professed piety when in the world six hundred had been contaminated with error. Dost thou wish Daniel to carry thee away to amazement? Behold that [city] Babylon, haughty in the flower and pride of impiousness, and its inhabitants completely given over to sin of every description. But he, emerging from the depth, spat out the brine of sins, and rejoiced to plunge into the sweet waters of piety. And now, in like manner, with regard to that mother of Zebedee's children, do not admire merely what she said, but also the time at which she uttered these words. For when was it that she drew near to the Redeemer? Not after the resurrection, nor after the preaching of His name, nor after the establishment of His kingdom; but it was when the Lord said, "Behold, we go up to Jerusalem, and the Son of man shall be delivered to the chief priests and the scribes; and they shall kill Him, and on the third day He shall rise again." [2]

[1] Hos. ix. 10.
[2] Matt. xx. 18.

These things the Saviour told in reference to His sufferings and cross; to these persons He predicted His passion. Nor did He conceal the fact that it should be of a most ignominious kind, at the hands of the chief priests. This woman, however, had attached another meaning to the dispensation of His sufferings. The Saviour was foretelling death; and she asked for the glory of immortality. The Lord was asserting that He must stand arraigned before impious judges; but she, taking no note of that judgment, requested as of the judge: "Grant," she said, "that these my two sons may sit, one on the right hand, and the other on the left, in Thy glory." In the one case the passion is referred to, in the other the kingdom is understood. The Saviour was speaking of the cross, while she had in view the glory which admits no suffering. This woman, therefore, as I have already said, is worthy of our admiration, not merely for what she sought, but also for the occasion of her making the request.

She did indeed suffer, not merely as a pious person, but also as a woman. For, having been instructed by His words, she considered and believed that it would come to pass, that the kingdom of Christ should flourish in glory, and walk in its vastness throughout the world, and be increased by the preaching of piety. She understood, as was [in fact] the case, that He who appeared in a lowly guise had delivered and received every promise. I will inquire upon another occasion, when I come to treat upon this humility, whether the Lord rejected her petition concerning His kingdom. But she thought that the same confidence would not be possessed by her, when, at the appearance of the angels, He should be ministered to by the angels, and receive service from the entire heavenly host. Taking the Saviour, therefore, apart in a retired place, she earnestly desired of Him those things which transcend every human nature.

POSTSCRIPT.

The American editor omitted in the proper place (p. 315, note 4, after what is said by the translator) to insert this important note: viz., —

[On this matter of quotations from anonymous authors of the apostolic times, not infrequently made by Irenæus, consult the important tractate of Dr. Routh, in his *Reliquiæ Sacræ*, vol. i. pp. 45-68.]

Printed in the United States
210081BV00006BA/33/A

9 781933 993478